Saving the Jews

Franklin D. Roosevelt and the Holocaust

Robert N. Rosen

THUNDER'S MOUTH PRESS
NEW YORK

EUROPE 1942

0   100   200   300
MILES

NORWAY

Bredtveit
Grini
Oslo
SWE
Berg
Stock

North Sea

IRELAND

DENMARK   Horseroed
Copenhage

GREAT
BRITAIN

Hamburg
Neuengamme
Ravensbrück
London
Amsterdam
Flushing
NETHERLANDS
Sachsenhausen
Vught
Bergen-Belsen
Berlin

Secondary Fortifications △
The Atlantic Wall ▬
Fortresses ⬠

Dunkirk
Calais
Cherbourg   Boulogne
Brest
Le Havre
BELGIUM
Mechelen
GERMANY
Mittelbau Dora
Buchenwald
Theresienstadt

Compiegne
Paris
Fuensbrunnen
Draney
Flossenberg
Pragu
BOHEMIA
MORAVIA

Atlantic Ocean

Lorient
Saint-Nazaire
Natzweiler
Shirmeck
Dachau
Munich
Mautha
Vienna

La Pallice
FRANCE
SWITZERLAND
Bolzano
AUSTRIA

Vichy
Trieste
Zagre

PORTUGAL
Gurs
Rivesaltes
ITALY
Gosp
CRO

SPAIN
S

Lisbon
Madrid

Rome

The D-Day Invasion

London
Portsmouth

Cherbourg
Le Havre
Caen

Mediterr

SAVING THE JEWS:
Franklin D. Roosevelt and the Holocaust

Copyright © 2006 by Robert N. Rosen
Foreword © 2006 by Gerhard Weinberg
Afterword © 2006 by Alan M. Dershowitz

Published by
Thunder's Mouth Press
An Imprint of Avalon Publishing Group, Inc.
245 West 17th Street, 11th floor
New York, NY 10011

AVALON
publishing group incorporated

First printing April 2006

Library of Congress Cataloging-in-Publication Data is available.

ISBN-10: 1-56025-995-7
ISBN-13: 978-1-56025-995-4

9 8 7 6 5 4 3 2 1

Book design by Sue Canavan

Printed in the United States of America
Distributed by Publishers Group West

For two young servicemen of the millions of Americans who risked their lives to defeat the Axis, 1941–1945: my father, Morris D. Rosen, lieutenant, U.S. Coast Guard, who served on a Navy LST (Landing Ship, Tank), that indispensable workhorse of the fleet, in combat in the Pacific theater; and my father-in-law, Ernest W. Corner, first lieutenant, U.S. Army Air Forces, who flew the incredible, long-range fighter escort, the P-51 Mustang, in missions over Europe. You did your part to end the killing of innocents.

And for Susan, who fought a different kind of war.

Table of Contents

"Politics is the art of the possible"

—Otto von Bismarck

"I think the impression was that Lincoln was a pretty sad man . . . because he could not do all he wanted to do at one time, and I think you will find examples where Lincoln had to compromise to gain a little something. He had to compromise to make a few gains. Lincoln was one of those unfortunate people called a 'politician' but he was a politician who was practical enough to get a great many things for this country. He was a sad man because he couldn't get it all at once. And nobody can . . . If you ever sit here, you will learn that you cannot, just by shouting from the housetops, get what you want all the time."

—FDR to the leaders of the American Youth Congress,
June, 1940

"In war everything is simple, but the simple is very difficult."

—Karl von Clausewitz

Foreword

In the national election of November 1920 Franklin Delano Roosevelt suffered his only electoral defeat. He was the candidate for vice president of the United States on the ticket of the Democratic Party and was defeated by Calvin Coolidge, the candidate of the Republican Party. That meant that Coolidge became president when President Warren G. Harding died in August 1923. It was, therefore, President Coolidge who signed the 1924 immigration law. This law was carefully and deliberately designed both to limit the number of immigrants who could legally enter the United States in any one year and also to keep out of the country as much as possible the Catholics and Jews from Eastern and Southern Europe who had come in very large numbers in the years from 1880 to 1914. National quotas were based on the pre-1880 composition of the country as specified by the 1921 law signed by President Harding. This quota system was in effect with minor variations until 1965.

It has always seemed both curious and, in a way, reprehensible to me that Franklin Roosevelt is blamed by many scholars for adhering to and continuing to enforce a law that had been placed on the books by the one person who had succeeded in defeating him in a campaign for public office. In the context of a worldwide depression, Roosevelt knew, when he was president himself, that any congressional review of the immigration law during the 1930s was certain to lead to even further restrictions, if not a complete closure of the country. When, during World War II, he tried to utilize his power as commander in chief of the armed forces, which allowed the temporary moving into the country of prisoners of war, for the temporary bringing into the country of refugees, as he did with the Oswego experiment, there were immediate calls for impeachment. It is hardly a coincidence that the White House announcement that there would be no further such experiments and the end of impeachment talk came within days of each other.

If one asks how Roosevelt came to be blamed for the deeds of the man he had unsuccessfully opposed, the answer is to be found in the unwillingness of many to look at the Holocaust in the context of the time. Just as far too many scholars and other writers about World War II treat it as some sort of dangerous chess game with no aim or purpose, so others treat the Holocaust as an event removed from its contemporary setting. As the Germans initiated World War II to carry out a demographic revolution on the globe—with the Holocaust as a central element of that revolution—so the Holocaust and the response to it by others has to be seen in the context of a world depression and a world war. It is clear today in retrospect that German persecution of Jews after Adolf Hitler became chancellor of Germany in 1933 did not lead to the sort of restricted life for Jews of the sort with which they had coped in prior centuries. These measures were instead a prelude to systematic mass murder. However, neither most Jews themselves nor those observing the process anticipated anything of the sort during the 1930s or in the early years of World War II. And many, both Jews and non-Jews alike, found it terribly difficult to grasp the reality when the killing was actually under way in areas under German control or influence.

The merit and the importance of this book is that it bridges the conceptual divide between the Holocaust and the American reaction to it by providing the context of reality instead of the outrage of retrospective analysis blinded by the enormity of human suffering. This is critical for any understanding of those sad events. With over half a million American Jews in the uniform of their country, is it really any wonder that their families worried primarily about them as they fought, among other things, to put an end to the Holocaust? It is about time that the part that American non-Jews and Jews played in the halting and crushing of those carrying out the Holocaust be included in any review of the American reaction to what was happening in the German-controlled portions of the world. And in this whole process, President Roosevelt played a central role.

Whether withdrawing the American ambassador from Berlin in protest against the German pogrom of November 1938—as the only head of state to do so—or publicly denouncing the mass murder of Jews while it was occurring, Roosevelt never left anyone in doubt about his position on these issues. It is only in retrospect that many have ignored this record. Similarly, most have ignored the critical role that Roosevelt's actions to ensure the supply of the British army fighting in North Africa and to provide it with the equipment needed to defend the southern approach to Palestine played in enabling that army to stop the Germans. The Germans did not send the Afrika Korps into Egypt to dismantle the pyramids for shipment to Berlin but rather to make possible the killing of the Jewish inhabitants of the Palestine mandate, as Hitler promised the grand mufti of Jerusalem.

There is a curious irony in the fact that the first American president who was comfortable with individuals who openly identified themselves as Jews and who was often vehemently attacked for this should be converted posthumously to the opposite position. A major advantage of this book is that it sets the record straight on a large number of issues related to the role of President Roosevelt in connection with the systematic killing of Jews during World War II. No reader is required to agree with all the conclusions set forth here. However, those who have in recent years divorced the events of those dark years from the reality of the time will need to reexamine their own views and positions in the light of the evidence the author provides. There is no way to bring back any of the millions who were murdered, but surely the time has come to insist that responsibility for those terrible deeds remain with those who committed them rather than those who fought a war to contain and halt the slaughter. And among the latter, as this book demonstrates, President Franklin Roosevelt played a central role.

Gerhard L. Weinberg
Efland, NC, October 2005

List of Illustrations

At Fort Bragg, North Carolina, shortly before the 45th Field Hospital shipped out to England, the nurses posed in front of one of the cookie-cutter barracks. Frances Slanger is fourth from the left, both hands in pockets. – p. 311

"We Will Never Die" Pageant, March 9, 1943, Madison Square Garden. In front of a backdrop of two towering tablets inscribed in Hebrew with the Ten Commandments, a rabbi opened a performance dedicated to the murdered Jews of Europe. The event was the brainchild of members of the Committee for a Jewish Army headed by Peter Bergson and some of the most prominent Jews in show business, including scriptwriter Ben Hecht. – p. 326

American Jewish soldiers in the China-Burma-India Theater of Operations during World War II. – p. 331

Meeting of War Refugee Board: Secretary of State Cordell Hull, Secretary of the Treasury Henry Morgenthau, Jr., Secretary of War Henry Stimson, and John Pehle, Director of the War Refugee Board, Washington, D.C., March 21, 1944. – p. 351

The Normandy Invasion. Chaplain Meyer holds Jewish services on board Ancon, flagship of Force "O," in early June. – p. 373

An aerial reconnaissance photograph of Auschwitz. – p. 389

Campaign tour near Hyde Park with Henry Morgenthau, Jr., November 6, 1944. – p. 403

Franklin D. Roosevelt at Great Bitter Lake where he received King Ihn Saud of Saudia Arabia on board the USS Quincy, at 11:30 A.M. for lunch, February 14, 1945 after the Yalta Conference. – p. 403

In 1944, in occupied Germany, NBC radio, together with the American Jewish Committee, broadcast the first Jewish service since the rise of Hitler. – p. 417

Franklin D. Roosevelt, Warm Springs, GA, April 11, 1945, the day before his death. – p. 422

While touring the newly liberated Ohrdruf camp, General Dwight Eisenhower and other high-ranking U.S. Army officers view the bodies of prisoners who were killed during the evacuation of the camp, April 12, 1045. – p. 429

Chaplains at War, Kobler Field, Saipan, Marianas, 1944. – p. 489

As American troops arrived, a homemade American flag was raised by the prisoners of Dachau prison camp. As it waved in the breeze, it seemed to reflect the joy of inmates who realized freedom for the first time in many years. – p. 494

Abbreviations

AJA	American Jewish Archives, Cincinnati, Ohio
AJ Committee	American Jewish Committee
AJ Congress	American Jewish Congress
AJH	*American Jewish History*
AJHQ	*American Jewish Historical Quarterly*
AJHS	American Jewish Historical Society, New York City
CJA	Committee for a Jewish Army
ER	Eleanor Roosevelt
FDR	Franklin Delano Roosevelt
FDRL	Franklin D. Roosevelt Library
HIAS	Hebrew Immigrant Aid Society
IGCR	Intergovernmental Committee on Refugees
JAE	Jewish Agency Executive
JEC	Joint Emergency Committee on European Jewish Affairs
Joint	American Jewish Joint Distribution Committee
LC	Library of Congress
MD	Morgenthau Diaries
NA	National Archives, Washington, D.C.
PACPR	President's Advisory Committee on Political Refugees
USAAF	U.S. Army Air Forces
USO	Universal Service Organization
WJ Congress	World Jewish Congress
WRB	War Refugee Board

Preface

The Jews have three velten *["worlds" in Yiddish]:*
die velt *[this world],* yene velt *[the next world], and*
Roosevelt.[1]

      —Congressman Jonah J. Goldstein

Know ye not that there is a prince and a great man
fallen this day in Israel.
  —Rabbi G. George Fox's eulogy of Franklin Roosevelt,

            April 1945.[2]

In April 2001 I visited my daughter Ali, then a fifteen-year-old student at Phillips Academy in Andover, near Boston. We went to the Holocaust Memorial near Quincy Market in downtown Boston, and I was taken aback by a seemingly innocuous but in fact outrageous statement engraved in stone: "By late 1942, the United States and its Allies were aware of the death camps but did nothing to destroy them." I knew that in 1942 the Allies lacked the ability to destroy the Nazi death camps. Over lunch, this Jewish American father explained to his Jewish American daughter that the United States was not even a belligerent in World War II until the attack on Pearl Harbor on December 7, 1941, and that our armed forces and citizens, I believed, were woefully unprepared for war at that moment.

I told Ali that in 1942, President Roosevelt began fighting what, for Americans, appeared to be a desperate multifront war against brutal Japanese militarists in the Pacific and a triumphant Nazi Germany and Fascist Italy in Europe and North Africa. We strove mightily, I explained, to save Great Britain, the Soviet Union, and all of Europe from the German juggernaut.

"But why didn't we try to save the Jews?" Ali asked.

"FDR did the best he could," I told her.

But was I right?

It certainly did not appear so when I began my research. In fact it appeared I was badly mistaken. Annie, my oldest daughter, and Will, my son, wanted to know why it mattered, but they patiently listened or pretended to listen to my arguments and stories.

How did it happen, I wondered after reading the literature on the subject, that Franklin Delano Roosevelt, the man who detested the Nazi regime, who was key to the destruction of Nazism and Adolf Hitler, and who earned the support of more than 90 percent of American Jews when he ran for president, now stood in the dock of history, accused of the willful failure to rescue European Jewry from the Holocaust and of being antisemitic? My own generation of rabbis, journalists, and historians regularly implied or directly accused Roosevelt of being an antisemite. Even the respected historian Paul Johnson, author of *Modern Times* (1991) and *A History of the Jews* (1987), described Roosevelt as being "antisemitic, in a mild way."[3]

The verdict of history appeared to be worse than I could have imagined. Journalists, film-makers, Holocaust experts, and historians had produced a body of work that not only condemned Roosevelt, the United States government, and American Jewry for their failure to save the Jews of Europe, but also accused them of being accomplices of the Nazis in their most horrific war crimes. These critics claimed that Roosevelt "abandoned the Jews" of Europe (David Wyman); that he was a coward who was guilty of "indifference and even complicity in the Final Solution" (Henry I. Feingold); his "policies endangered European Jews" (Rafael Medoff); that he "enabled the Nazi Germans . . . to slaughter six million Jewish men, women and children" (Herbert Druks); and was an accomplice "to history's most monstrous crime" (Monty Penkower). The Allies "played a major role in the whole extermination process," according to Gerhart M. Riegner. Saul Friedman declared that a "yoke of shame" hung over the United States for its failure to rescue the Jews of Europe.[4]

To be consistent, these authors also blamed Roosevelt's loyal supporters, American Jewry, for not coming to the aid of their brethren in Europe. Rabbi Stephen S. Wise failed to convince FDR to act, they said. American Jewish congressmen and organizations all failed to save the Jews of Europe. "The American Jew," Rabbi

Haskel Lookstein opined, "could not stand up proudly . . . his natural posture was bowed and bent." American Jewish GIs who fought and died on the battlefields of France and Germany made no appearance in these works.[5]

My research in the archives and the history of the times led me to a far different conclusion. After years of study and the discovery of documentary evidence other historians had not cited, I concluded that Roosevelt did not abandon the Jews of Europe. On the contrary, he led the worldwide coalition against Nazism in a war that took fifty million lives.[6] He marshaled American opinion against antisemitism at home and Nazism abroad. He did not ignore the passengers on the SS *St. Louis*, an episode much trumpeted against him. Indeed, his close Jewish friends, including Henry Morgenthau, saved all the passengers on the *St. Louis*. He spoke out about the Holocaust. He denounced the Nazi massacres of Jews in July 1942. He warned Germans of "fearful retribution" in August of that year. On December 17, 1942, Roosevelt and Churchill issued the United Nations Declaration on Jewish Massacres, denouncing "in the strongest possible terms this bestial policy of cold-blooded extermination" of the "Jewish people in Europe."[7] The American government was correct, not indifferent, in refusing to bomb Auschwitz or the railway lines leading to it. Jewish leaders and organizations, including David Ben-Gurion, the Jewish Agency, and the World Jewish Congress, opposed the Allies' bombing "places where there are Jews." American Jews were not cowards. Five hundred and fifty thousand of them fought against the Axis, and thousands died to free Europe from the yoke of Nazi slavery.

I learned that Roosevelt's strength of character and political skills were key factors in preventing Hitler's conquest of the British Isles and the Soviet Union in addition to all of Western Europe in 1941. Had Germany conquered these nations, the Nazis would have murdered every Jew in Europe, the Soviet Union, *and* Great Britain by 1942 *and* every Jew in Palestine by 1943. The Führer's ultimate goal was a world dominated by Germany. Hitler's "ultimate objective," Roosevelt told the Senate Military Affairs Committee in January 1939, was "world domination." The extermination of every Jew on the planet, including every Jew in America, may sound preposterous today, but it was not preposterous to Adolf Hitler. "The 'Jewish Question' will be radically solved in the whole world," the Nazi editor of *Stürmer* proclaimed. As early as 1935 the Nazis were disseminating antisemitic propaganda around the world. Hitler's immediate and seemingly attainable goal in Europe was to murder eleven million Jews, not six million. That fact bears repeating. The Nazi Schutzstaffel (SS) general Reinhard Heydrich's list of Jews to be killed in January 1942 totaled eleven million, not six million. Franklin Roosevelt prevented Hitler from achieving his goal.[8]

The fact that Roosevelt, Churchill, and Stalin managed to hold the alliance of the United States, Britain, and the USSR together— by opening a second front in North Africa, then Italy, then D-Day— meant that by 1943 "about two-thirds of the world's approximately nineteen million Jews had been spared the death the Germans intended for the 'extinct race' about which they were assembling artifacts for a museum in Prague." This is the conclusion of the eminent historian Gerhard L. Weinberg, himself a Jewish refugee from Hitler's Germany. Hitler's biographer Ian Kershaw agrees. "World Jewry," including American Jews, were "on the verge of a historic downfall," in Hitler's worldview. Roosevelt's attack on Nazism saved Palestinian Jewry, saved the future State of Israel, and saved twelve million Jews worldwide.[9]

I was surprised to learn that few in the United States prior to Pearl Harbor saw the vital importance of defeating Hitler or the enormity of the task. Roosevelt's foresight, one New Dealer wrote, was superior to the country's best minds and "this foresight saved us all." Pierre van Paassen, a journalist, wrote in 1943: "President Roosevelt was one who early grasped the stupendous magnitude and significance of the plot." When Britain stood alone, Roosevelt's quiet support sustained Churchill. Joachim von Ribbentrop told Japanese foreign minister Yosuke Matsuoka in March 1940 that the British "would long since have abandoned the war if Roosevelt had not always given Churchill new hope."[10]

My purpose in writing this book is to describe the events of the 1930s and 1940s so that the reader may comprehend, as FDR's contemporaries did, the realities and limitations the president faced in his war to the death with Hitler. *Saving the Jews: Franklin D. Roosevelt and the Holocaust* is an attempt to understand the Nazi persecution of the Jews and the Holocaust from Franklin Roosevelt's and America's perspective, including that of America's Jewish leadership. As with most history, we know much more today than FDR knew at the time. How did the events of 1933 to 1945 appear to Franklin Roosevelt? What did he know? When did he know it? What did he do with his knowledge? And how do we evaluate what FDR did or what he failed to do? These are questions I have endeavored to answer.

I have written this book for the general reader as well as historians and have put the Holocaust into the context of the history of the Roosevelt administration, the Great Depression, and World War II. This, I believe, is critical to a genuine understanding of the Holocaust, because that event—as horrible as it was—did not occur in a vacuum. For example, it is important for the reader to know that the SS *St. Louis* sailed from Hamburg, Germany, in May 1939 before World War II or the Final Solution had begun and before the Auschwitz extermination camp was constructed. Surprising as it may seem to us today, Anne Frank's family was living openly in Nazi-occupied Amsterdam as late as June 1942. Much of the misunderstanding about Franklin Roosevelt's role in the Holocaust is the result of historians' descriptions of the Holocaust without reference to other crucial events taking place at the time. For example, the bombing of Auschwitz could only have been accomplished from May to November 1944, a brief time period that coincided exactly with D-Day, the Normandy invasion, and the Allies' push to Berlin.

One final note. There is an old saying that he who is able to read *tomorrow's* newspaper *today* can rule the world. A German Jewish refugee from Nazi Germany said of the Holocaust, *"Hinterher ist es leicht, weise zu erscheinan"* (In hindsight, it is easy to appear wise). A common fallacy, and one most of Roosevelt's critics are guilty of, is the "historian's fallacy." It consists in the failure of historians to keep in mind that their subjects did not know how their stories ended. "Imagine a letter written in France, on May 24, 1337," David Hackett Fischer wrote in *Historians' Fallacies* (1970) "which announced 'the Hundred Years' War began here today.'"

We will follow Hitler's rise to power and his campaign to humiliate, impoverish, and finally exterminate the Jews of Europe, as Franklin Roosevelt saw it, not knowing, unlike his critics today, how events would unfold *and* not knowing, as we do now, about the Holocaust, *and* not knowing if the battle with Hitler and his henchmen would become a Hundred Years' War, *and* most of all, not knowing that the Allied nations would win.

Robert N. Rosen
April 2006

Prologue

On March 4, 1933, a cold and cloudy day in Washington, D.C., Franklin Delano Roosevelt stood, his legs encased in iron braces as a result of crippling polio, and took the oath of office as the thirty-second President of the United States. America was in the throes of the Great Depression. Most of the nation's banks were closed, and thirteen million people were unemployed. The American people were filled with dread of the future. The strong, confident voice of their new leader gave them hope: "We face the arduous days that lie before us in the warm courage of national unity." He promised "a leadership of freshness and vigor."[1]

Across the Atlantic Ocean, on the same day as Roosevelt's inauguration, bonfires blazed and Nazis marched in eerie torchlight parades to "reawaken" Germany on the eve of a rigged national election. Adolf Hitler was the Chancellor of Germany. He had taken the oath of office in January and three months later had consolidated his dictatorial powers. He became, in John Lukacs' words, "the most popular leader in the history of the Germans," and he aspired to become the greatest German of all time. He, too, had become the hope of millions of his fellow citizens, who also were filled with dread of the future. The Depression had struck Germany with special harshness, and Germans were profoundly bitter about the treaties of Versailles, which had concluded the Great War and humiliated their nation. Sinister people throughout the world, especially Jews, had somehow "stabbed Germany in the back" and were thwarting the nation's rise to greatness.[2]

In Great Britain, Winston Spencer Churchill, a quirky member of Parliament, a short, fat man perceived by his countrymen as an alarmist warmonger, a compulsive talker, a disreputable imbiber of strong drink, and an imperialist from the nineteenth century, also was fearful about the future. He had visited the United States—his mother was American and he loved Americans—but he also had visited Germany. "All these bands of sturdy Teutonic youths," he said, "marching through the streets and roads of Germany . . . are not looking for status. They are looking for weapons." He admired Roosevelt's New Deal and inscribed a copy of his latest book, *Marlborough: His Life and Times,* to the new president with these words: "With earnest best wishes for the success of the greatest crusade of modern times."[3]

In Berlin, Rabbi Leo Baeck also worried about the future. "The thousand-year history of the German Jews," he said prophetically in 1933, "has come to an end." But German Jews did not agree with him. They believed that Hitler was a passing phenomenon. In Palestine, David Ben-Gurion, the Polish-born Zionist organizer and future first prime minister of Israel, worried specifically about the Jewish people. The world, he said, is inhabited by "beasts of prey." The German people would not be destroyed by Hitler, but the Jews "are liable to be ruined."[4] None of these men had any idea what the future actually had in store. Neither did Anne Frank, a toddler living comfortably with her sister, mother, and father in Frankfurt, nor did millions of European and Soviet Jews.

Who was Franklin Delano Roosevelt, on whose shoulders rested the hopes and dreams of the American people? His contemporaries were not sure. Born to privilege, he was drawn to liberal politics and people, as well as to his distant cousin Anna Eleanor

Franklin D. Roosevelt giving his March 4, 1933, Inaugural Address.

Courtesy of the Franklin D. Roosevelt Library

Roosevelt, who volunteered at settlement houses and worked tire-lessly to help slum dwellers. From his earliest days as a politician he was eager to seek support from Jews, Catholics, and other minorities, which surprised both his conservative mother and his liberal wife. Many believed Roosevelt was weak, vain, spoiled, a dilettante, and something of a playboy; that he was naive, igno-rant, and amateurish in foreign affairs.[5] "He is a pleasant man," the well-respected newspaper columnist Walter Lippmann opined in 1932, "who, without any important qualifications for the office, would very much like to be President." In 1933 Neville Chamber-lain, Chancellor of the Exchequer, described Roosevelt as "a med-icine man" uttering "Mumbo Jumbo . . . I look upon him as a dangerous and unreliable horse in any team."[6]

Samuel I. Rosenman, a young Jewish New York legislator, met Roosevelt in 1928. He had heard the negative stories, but Roo-sevelt's "broad jaw and upthrust chin, the piercing, flashing eyes, the firm hands" won Rosenman over. Supreme Court justice Oliver Wendell Holmes Jr. also liked the new president. "You know," Holmes said to his clerk, "his [cousin] Ted appointed me to the Court." His clerk replied, "Yes, Mr. Justice?" Holmes then rendered his famous, erroneous verdict on Roosevelt: "A second-class intellect. But a first-class temperament."[7]

Was Roosevelt's character influenced by his college experience of rejection by Porcellian, the snootiest club at Harvard? By his law practice, which took him to New York City's poor East Side? By his belief in a "strenuous Christianity" learned at Groton? By his wife, Eleanor? By his paralysis due to polio?

The new president's chief personality traits were his boundless confidence and his practicality. "His most outstanding character-istic is an air of supreme confidence," W. M. Kiplinger wrote. "The guy," Harry Hopkins once said, "*never* knows when he is licked." Rosenman, who became one of FDR's closest confidants and knew him well, felt Roosevelt was born a liberal: "It was in the heart and soul of the man, in his love of people, his own sense of social jus-tice, his hatred of greed and of the exploitation of the weak, his contempt for the bully—whether it was a Hitler or Mussolini or an owner of a sweatshop or an exploiter of child labor." Roosevelt wrote to Jan Smuts, the prime minister of South Africa, in 1942, "I dream dreams but am, at the same time, an intensely practical person." He abhorred abstractions and theories. "His mind," James McGregor Burns felt, "yearned for the detail, the particular, the specific. . . . He had a passion for the concrete." The president, Francis Biddle said, was "never theoretical about things."[8]

The reporter John Gunther once asked Eleanor Roosevelt, "Just how does the President think?" She replied, "My dear Mr. Gunther, the President never thinks. He decides."[9]

Chapter 1

The New Deal, "The Jew Deal"

The tragic, complicated story of the Holocaust embraced millions of people and myriad events. But it began and it ended with two men as different as, and indeed symbolized by, night and day: Adolf Hitler and Franklin Roosevelt. From their vastly different childhoods and families to their fundamentally different views of the world, to their personal habits and temperaments, the two men were polar opposites. Roosevelt had been raised in a wealthy, loving, and secure family with a tradition of public service; Hitler hated and feared his father, and his mother moved from place to place. FDR bravely battled a crippling disease; Hitler was a hypersensitive hypochondriac. "A world-wide distance separates Roosevelt's ideas and my ideas," the Führer told the Reichstag after Pearl Harbor. Roosevelt had quoted Hitler's statement that "There are two worlds that stand opposed to each other. . . . In other words, the Axis not only admits but *proclaims* that there can be no ultimate peace" between these two worlds.[1]

Nothing demonstrated the difference between the pathological Nazi fanatic and the practical, ebullient American politician more clearly than their attitude toward the Jewish people. Hitler's worldview was organized around the principle of racial identity and the demonization of Jews as evil incarnate, enemies of mankind generally and Germans in particular. Roosevelt was born and raised in New York and had been governor of the state with his nation's largest Jewish population. Indeed, by 1920 the largest Jewish and Yiddish community in the world was in New York City.[2]

Roosevelt could not understand Adolf Hitler and thought him insane. "The situation is alarming," FDR told the French ambassador in 1933. Hitler's "counselors, some of whom I personally know, are even madder than he is." Roosevelt had read Hitler's *Mein Kampf* in German and was aware that early English translations omitted much of the author's antisemitic diatribes. Roosevelt's earliest impressions of Hitler filled him with detestation, dread, and hostility.[3]

Roosevelt surrounded himself with Jewish political allies and advisers. He had learned from his political mentor, New York governor Alfred E. Smith, the "Irisher Mensch" who spoke passable Yiddish, the value of the Jewish vote, the pool of talented Jews available for government service, and the dedication of American Jews to his own liberal principles. Roosevelt's speechwriter, close adviser, and friend, Samuel Rosenman, came from the Smith camp and was Roosevelt's confidant from 1928 to 1945. Roosevelt had chosen Herbert H. Lehman as his running mate in 1928. Lehman served cordially and well as Governor Roosevelt's lieutenant governor. Roosevelt's early Jewish friends and advisers included his Hyde Park neighbor Henry Morgenthau Jr., who also held a post in Governor Roosevelt's administration; Supreme Court Justice Louis D. Brandeis, whom Roosevelt admired and referred to reverently as "Isaiah"; and Brandeis's protégé Felix Frankfurter, an energetic Harvard law professor.

"Dig me up fifteen or twenty youthful Abraham Lincolns from Manhattan and the Bronx," he told one aide early in his presidency. And he found them among America's Jewish citizens. Frankfurter's protégé Benjamin V. Cohen, the son of a Polish refugee and a committed Zionist, coauthored the New Deal's most important legislation with Tommy "the Cork" Corcoran. Jerome Frank, another Frankfurter protégé, became general counsel of the Agricultural Adjustment Administration. Herbert Feis was a top State Department adviser on economic affairs, and David K. Niles, special assistant to the president on political affairs, was a confidant of Harry Hopkins. Abe Fortas became counsel to the Securities and Exchange Commission. David E. Lilienthal served as director of the Tennessee Valley Authority, and Morgenthau became Secretary of the Treasury. Jesse Straus served as ambassador to France and Laurence Steinhardt as ambassador to the Soviet Union and Turkey. Other prominent Jews included Nathan R. Margold (solicitor, Interior Department); Robert Nathan (director, National Income Division, Department of Commerce); Saul K. Padover Jr. (Harold Ickes' assistant at the Interior Department); Michael W. Straus (director of the War Resource Council); Ernest Gruening (appointed governor of Alaska); Felix Cohen

(Indian Affairs); Mordecai Ezekiel (General Counsel, Department of Agriculture); Charles Wyzanski Jr. (General Counsel, Department of Labor); and Isador Lubin (FDR's "favorite economist," commissioner of labor statistics). Roosevelt offered the solicitor generalship to Frankfurter but he declined. Although Jews were 3 percent of the U.S. population, they constituted 15 percent of Roosevelt's high-level appointments.[4]

Henry Morgenthau Jr. was with Roosevelt from the beginning of his political career to the end. He came from a prominent Jewish extended family, which included the Guggenheims and the Lehmans. His father, Henry Morgenthau Sr., was a German Jew born in Mannheim, who had been a spectacularly successful real estate lawyer and investor. Henry Sr. was the founder and first president of the Free Synagogue, established to provide a pulpit for Stephen S. Wise, a widely acclaimed Reform rabbi. After a mediocre career at Phillips Exeter and Cornell, young Henry moved to Dutchess County, New York, and became a gentleman farmer. There in 1915, he and Elinor Morgenthau met and befriended Franklin and Eleanor Roosevelt. When Roosevelt was elected governor, Morgenthau served as chairman of the Agricultural Advisory Commission and as state conservation commissioner. He waited with Roosevelt as the returns were tallied in the November 1932 presidential election.[5]

These wealthy sons of wealthy fathers were good friends. Roosevelt wrote across a photograph of himself and Morgenthau, "to Henry from one of two of a kind." They often visited each other's homes, and Morgenthau was Roosevelt's straight man when the president told jokes. Because of Morgenthau's serious nature, FDR called him "Henry the Morgue." Morgenthau was often, in Eleanor's words, "Franklin's conscience." "In the President and Mrs. Roosevelt, my wife and I were favored with a unique friendship," Morgenthau wrote in his memoirs.[6] The Morgenthaus and the Roosevelts were close social friends, spending time aboard the presidential yacht and at "Shangri-La," the rustic presidential retreat in Maryland now known as Camp David. The Morgenthaus sat with the Roosevelt family at the 1933 inauguration.[7]

FDR had so many Jewish advisers, supporters, and appointees that he was regularly attacked by hate-mongers as the dupe of a Jewish conspiracy. Tales circulated that FDR was a Jew. Reverend Gerald Winrod of Kansas, founder of the Defenders of the Christian Faith, claimed that Roosevelt was descended from Rosenbergs, Rosenbaums, Roosenvelts, Rosenblums, and Rosenthals. One woman wrote the president in 1934 that "you have sold out the country to the Jews. . . . You have over two hundred Jews, they say, in the executive offices in Washington, and Jew bankers run the government." As early as 1934, Father Charles E. Coughlin, the antisemitic Catholic "Radio Priest," attacked FDR as pro-Jewish, lumping him with the "godless Capitalists, the Jews, communists, international bankers, and plutocrats."[8]

Historically, the Jews of America were part and parcel of American society. They had served in all of the nation's wars, as soldiers in the Union and Confederate armies, and in the trenches of World War I. Two Jews—Louis Brandeis and Benjamin Cardozo—sat on the United States Supreme Court. Jews had served for many decades in Congress. Many had risen to prominence in business, the arts, the media, and the professions.

But in 1933, most American Jews were either immigrants or the children of immigrants from the Pale of Settlement (western Russia and eastern Poland). European antisemitism and pogroms had spurred Jewish immigrants to leave their homelands. Beginning in Odessa in 1871 and continuing in 1881 after the murder of Tsar Alexander II, a reign of terror was visited on Russian and Ukrainian Jewry by the government forces of the left and of the right. Pogroms in Odessa and Bialystok caused the deaths of hundreds of Jews. American Jewish immigrants had vivid recollections of these antisemitic pogroms as well as the political massacres of Jews during World War I and the Russian Revolution. Poles had persecuted Jews before Hitler was born. As late as 1937, Felix Warburg, head of the American Jewish Joint Distribution Committee (the "Joint"), said that while German Jews were mistreated "in a most terrible way . . . they had some reserves" and were not starving. "In Poland, it is altogether different; there are no reserves." Indeed, the Poles were at that very moment waging an undeclared war on the Jews, complete with pogroms and boycotts. Romania, too, was a hotbed of antisemitism. The chief American Jewish rescue agency, the Joint, was founded in 1914 at Temple Emanu-El in New York City to help masses of Jews brutalized by one nation and another in Europe.[9]

Although twentieth-century Europeans had raised Jew-hatred to a fine art and made it a central tenet of their belief systems, antisemitism was not only a European phenomenon. Prejudice against

6

Jews had long been a part of American life, although the nation had historically treated its Jewish citizens well. Nevertheless, to most Americans in the 1930s there was a wall of separation between Christians and Jews. Antisemitism and racism had grown in the early twentieth century. Leo Frank, a Jew, had been lynched in Georgia in 1913, causing B'nai B'rith to found the Anti-Defamation League. The Ku Klux Klan reappeared on the American scene in the 1920s. Many white Protestants shared the Klan's hatred and suspicion of blacks, Jews, Catholics, and foreigners. The Klan, H. L. Mencken quipped, "was just what it pretended to be, an order devoted to the ideals most Americans held sacred." It influenced elections all over the country and helped deny Al Smith the presidency in 1928. Discrimination prevailed in employment, housing, and college admission. Harvard University maintained quotas. "You are Menorah boys," the president of Harvard told one Jew; "we are Crimson boys."

Many Americans believed the tide of immigrants from Bolshevik Russia after 1918 had brought millions of Jewish Communists to the United States. "Judeobolshevikism" was seen as a threat to the American way of life. Some American Jews were Communists, and Jews had been prominent in Socialist and Communist circles in Europe. Leon Trotsky and Rosa Luxemburg—even Karl Marx—were all Jews or perceived as Jews. The choice between the antisemitic Russian Tsars Alexander III and Nicholas II and the Communist Party, which stood forthrightly for the equality of Jews, was an easy choice for Russian Jews. New York Jews constituted 20 percent of the American Communist Party membership in the 1930s. While the majority of American Jews were neither Communists nor Socialists and American rabbis excoriated communism, the perception of Jews as Communists and radicals was widespread.[10]

New Dealer David E. Lilienthal of Morton, Illinois, did not suffer antisemitism as a child. "As a boy, growing up in little Midwestern towns, I recall hardly a single incident, certainly no single instance of exclusion or hindrance because of my being a Jew," he wrote in his journal. But by 1939 Lilienthal felt that "it is clear that anti-Jewish prejudice is more widespread than before—at least so it seems to me." Lilienthal attributed the rise in antisemitism to Depression-driven competition for jobs between lower-income Jews and Catholics. FDR's New Deal also played a part. "The fact that a good number of Jews are in The New Deal has," he wrote in December 1939, "I think furnished an excuse for intensifying the feeling."[11]

The deepening economic crisis of the 1930s, the rise of Protestant and Catholic demagogues, and widespread expressions of anti-Jewish attitudes by respectable leaders led to an explosion of antisemitism. Hitler's early ideas won adherents in the United States. The chief demagogues—William Dudley Pelley, founder of the Silver Shirts; Rev. Gerald Winrod of the Defenders of the Christian Faith; and Father Coughlin of the National Union for Social Justice publicly praised Adolf Hitler and his Nazi policies. Pelley said, "I feel exactly as the Nazi Party in Germany felt . . . regarding the Jews."[12]

Coughlin, a Roman Catholic priest, delivered political sermons over the radio and by the 1930s had a huge national audience for the *Golden Hour from the Shrine of the Little Flower.* He had bigger audiences than *Amos 'n' Andy* and *Burns and Allen.* An early Roosevelt supporter, the "radio priest" helped elect FDR in 1932 by viciously attacking Hoover. But by 1934 he had turned on Roosevelt. He compared "Morgenthau and his Jewish cohorts" to the gangster John Dillinger and warned against the "Kuhn-Loebs, the Rothschilds . . . the scribes and Pharisees, the Baruchs." Like Hitler, Coughlin saw a Jewish-Communist conspiracy everywhere he looked, including in the New Deal. It is no surprise that the Roosevelt administration was frequently derided as "the Jew Deal."[13]

The Roosevelt family was not isolated from these prejudices. Both Franklin and Eleanor Roosevelt* were products of their time, place, upbringing, and social class. Both were raised in a wealthy, white, Anglo-Saxon, Protestant world in which Jews, blacks, Catholics, Irish, Italians, Germans, Slavs, Poles, Japanese, and other immigrants and ethnic Americans were clearly not their social equals. Antisemitism was bred into the American ruling classes of Boston, New York City, and Philadelphia.

ER's youthful prejudice was more pronounced than Franklin's. "The Jew party [was] appalling," she wrote her mother-in-law, Sara Roosevelt, in 1918. "I never wish to hear money, jewels or sables mentioned again." Felix Frankfurter, she said, was "an interesting little man, but very Jew." When Roosevelt was elected governor, ER urged him not to retain Al Smith's advisers Robert Moses and Belle Moskowitz, whose "race" had "nerves of iron

---

* Eleanor Roosevelt will sometimes be referred to as "ER" and Franklin D. Roosevelt as "FDR."

and tentacles of steel." As a teacher she gave tacit approval to a Jewish quota at the Todhunter School for Girls because Jews were "very unlike ourselves." Sara Roosevelt, FDR's mother, once called Belle Moskowitz "that fat Jewess" and described Elinor Morgenthau to Eleanor Roosevelt as "very Jewish but [she] appeared very well." Both Roosevelt women had the same condescending view of Irish Catholics and other immigrants as they did of Jews.[14]

Roosevelt's older half brother Rosy was an outright antisemite. "The whole village reeks of Jews," Rosy once wrote from Lake Placid. From Bermuda he complained, "Mostly an awful class of Jews, most objectionable when sober, and worse when drunk." Franklin Roosevelt used expressions and made statements that meant little at the time but sound jarring today. When Franklin Jr. was born, for example, FDR suggested the name Isaac "after my grandfather and great great grandfather, but this is not met with enthusiasm, especially as the baby's nose is slightly Hebraic & the family have visions of Ikey Rosenfelt, though I insist it is very good New Amsterdam Dutch." FDR told ethnic jokes about Lower East Side Jews with his friend Henry Morgenthau Jr. laughing with him. Like most people, from time to time Roosevelt made remarks that were out of character. Over lunch with a Catholic businessman and politician, Leo T. Crowley, FDR is alleged to have said, "Leo, you know this is a Protestant country, and the Catholics and Jews are here under sufferance. It is up to you [Crowley and Morgenthau] to go along with anything that I want." It is doubtful that Roosevelt ever made this particular statement, but he did make inappropriate remarks at times. FDR's patrician (we would now say "patronizing") attitude toward Jews, like ER's, was the same as his attitude toward Irish Catholics, other minorities, and indeed all of his many social inferiors.[15]

Roosevelt was, above all, a practical man. He could look a problem in the eye and address it. He told Henry Morgenthau in 1941:

> *Some years ago a third of the entering class at Harvard were Jews and the question came up as to how it should be handled. . . . I talked it over at that time with your father [Ambassador Henry Morgenthau Sr.]. . . . it was decided that over a period of years the number of Jews should be reduced one or two percent a year until it was down to 15 percent. . . .*
>
> *I treat the Catholic situation just the same. . . . I appointed three men in Nebraska—all Catholics—and they wanted me to appoint another Catholic, and I said that I wouldn't do it. . . . You can't get a disproportionate amount of any one religion.[16]*

Despite his elitist background and the influence of his wife and mother, Franklin Roosevelt was remarkably free of prejudice against Jews. His heroes, cousin Teddy Roosevelt and Woodrow Wilson, had warm relationships with Jews. TR had appointed the first Jew to the cabinet (Oscar S. Straus, secretary of commerce, in 1906), and Wilson, the first Jew to the Supreme Court, Louis D. Brandeis. At the end of World War I, when Rosy asked him to speak to a rally on "the United War Work Campaign" at Hyde

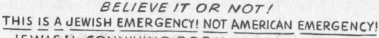

Antisemitic propaganda cartoon depicting Franklin D. Roosevelt as a part of the so-called "Jewish Conspiracy."

Courtesy of the Franklin D. Roosevelt Library. The Walter Winchell Papers.

Park, Franklin wired back, "VERY GLAD TO SPEAK . . . WILL MAKE SPECIAL APPEAL FOR JEWISH WELFARE BOARD." He had never embraced antisemitism. When he was attacked by antisemites, isolationists, and reactionaries as being Jewish, he replied that his ancestors "may have been Jewish or Catholics or Protestants. What I am more interested in is whether they were good citizens and believers in God. I hope they were both." Looking down on people, Peter Grose observed, was "not a way to make them like you," and Roosevelt wanted to be liked.[17]

Whatever Franklin and Eleanor's backgrounds, by the 1930s they had long since outgrown early tinctures of antisemitism. ER had traveled far from her upbringing. By 1940 she was honorary chairwoman of Hadassah's Youth Aleya, an organization that helped Jewish children immigrate to Palestine. "FDR did not have an anti-semitic bone in his body," according to Joseph Lash's widow, Trude, who knew Roosevelt well. His close friend Sam Rosenman agreed.

Antisemitism was only one of a broad set of social beliefs, preju-dices, class and ethnic loyalties, biases, and antagonisms that perme-ated American society. In Franklin Roosevelt's America, prejudice against Jews, blacks, Catholics, Irish, Germans, Eastern Europeans, Japanese, Italians, and American Indians was taken for granted. Roo-sevelt knew that he had been asked to nominate Al Smith in 1928 because, as Joseph Proskauer told the Happy Warrior, "you're a Bowery mick and [Roosevelt is] a Protestant patrician and he'd take some of the curse off you." He called Jim Farley's wife "real shanty Irish" and Joe Kennedy "a temperamental Irish boy." Roosevelt understood the sometimes brutal racial, religious, and ethnic reality of American politics. He told Senator Burton K. Wheeler of Montana in 1939 that Jack Garner could not run because of the black vote; that Jim Farley wanted Cordell Hull to run for president so that Farley, a Catholic, could then run for vice president and become pres-ident if Hull died. But Hull would not run because Mrs. Hull was "part Jewish and you don't have to go back through your ancestors or mine to find out if there's any Jewish blood in our veins."[18]

If Roosevelt had any deep-seated prejudice, it was against Ger-mans. His parents had summered at the stodgy Hessian spa of Bad Nauheim to treat his father's heart disease, and the young Franklin attended German schools for five summers. His family referred to Germans as "swine." Father and son enjoyed mocking German

13

speech. "Blease expectorate me on ze dwendy ninse," Franklin jokingly wrote his father in 1897. During his honeymoon with Eleanor in 1905, he wrote his mother that he sat as far away as he could from the German "pigsties." Like many Americans, Roosevelt had strong anti-German memories of World War I and the fight against "the Huns." He kept an eye on Americans of German descent, a group not well represented among his supporters.[19]

FDR's legendary Hundred Days began on Inauguration Day, March 4, 1933. "The first days of the Roosevelt Administration charged the air with the snap and the zigzag of electricity," Congressman Emanuel Celler recalled. The next day, the new president issued two proclamations, one declaring a four-day national banking holiday and the other calling for a special session of Congress. When the banks reopened on Monday, March 8, Roosevelt was the nation's savior. On March 9 Congress enacted the Emergency Banking Act. There followed a plethora of federal legislation repealing prohibition, drastic reform of the agricultural economy, and establishment of the Agricultural Adjustment Administration (AAA), the Civilian Conservation Corps (CCC), the Federal Emergency Relief Administration (FERA), the Public Works Administration (PWA), the Tennessee Valley Authority (TVA), and the National Recovery Administration (NRA). None of these actions ended the Depression on their own, but they began to restore citizens' confidence that the federal government was addressing the nation's woes.[20]

Despite his domestic initiatives, the new president was intensely interested in foreign affairs. "Aside from his cousin Theodore," Robert Dallek wrote, "Franklin D. Roosevelt was the most cosmopolitan American to enter the White House since John Quincy Adams in 1825." Young Roosevelt spoke German and French and had traveled extensively in Europe. He served Woodrow Wilson as assistant secretary of the navy. An internationalist, he had supported the League of Nations. But Roosevelt had seen Wilson win the war and lose the peace. He witnessed the failure of the treaties of Versailles, the refusal of the United States to join the League of Nations, and the dire toll it took on the president. A candidate for vice president in 1920, Roosevelt saw that his hero was a broken man. The specter of Woodrow Wilson, a once-powerful president destroyed by foreign policy failures in Europe, haunted Roosevelt from his first inauguration day to his death twelve years later.[21]

Roosevelt loved foreign policy, but he knew its pitfalls. The Foreign Service and the State Department were filled with hidebound conservatives who were difficult to control. Powerful congressmen had strong ties to career diplomats. Roosevelt distrusted the lot of them. He was well aware that many were openly hostile to his policies. The new president had no mandate to do anything about foreign affairs, and he was not about to wreck his critical domestic agenda on the shoals of foreign policy. "In the present European situation," he wrote, "I feel very much as if I were groping for a door in a blank wall."[22]

Hitler began to degrade European Jews just as Roosevelt began to bring Jews more fully into the American government. Hitler ousted Jews from political office as Roosevelt brought them in. Some German Jews were imprisoned. Jewish businesses were boycotted and Jewish protests were unavailing. By 1935 Jews were no longer German citizens. Marriage between Germans and Jews was forbidden. They were excluded from the professions and many businesses. Hitler sought to drive Jews out of Germany and stir up antisemitism around the world by dumping impoverished Jews all over the globe. Half of Germany's Jews left the country between 1933 and 1939. Hitler's Schutzstaffel (SS or Protection Squad) even helped train a few Jews to acquire skills they would need to immigrate to Palestine! The Ha'avarah ("transfer") Agreement of 1933 allowed 41,000 Jews to immigrate to Palestine so long as they left their property in Germany. The British cooperated with Jewish immigration to Palestine during much of the 1930s. But German Jews did not want to go to Palestine. The Nazis wanted the Jews to emigrate, but then began to impede their emigration by confiscating their assets. Jews could leave Germany with 35 percent of their capital in 1936, 10 percent in 1938, and by June 1938, nothing.[23]

Americans did not know what to make of the situation in Germany. Many believed Hitler a ridiculous figure. When Dorothy Thompson, a popular newspaper columnist, met him in 1932, she was struck by "the startling insignificance of this man." Others believed Hitler's antics would cease once he was firmly in power. Many isolationists believed the German people were reacting to the injustices of the Versailles treaties. Some agreed with the Germans that the Jews were to blame. Others believed Hitler represented the wave of the future, while others believed it was all hysteria and propaganda. The *New York Herald Tribune* blamed Jews for spreading "atrocity tales." Protestant newspapers blamed Jewish "commercial clannishness" and Jewish beliefs for German persecution. Walter Lippmann, the nation's most influential columnist and a self-hating Jew, minimized the activities of the Nazis and wrote that one should not judge "Protestantism by the Ku Klux Klan or Jews by their parvenus."[24]

From the beginning, the Nazis engaged in a disinformation campaign about their atrocities against Jews. H. R. Knickerbocker of the *New York Evening Post* described their policy as "first, they

"We Want America for Gentile Americans. Wake Up! Wake Up! For God's Sake—Wake Up! Your country needs you!" Antisemitic cartoon that presents President Roosevelt as a modern day Moses, welcoming millions of unwanted Jews into the United States.

Courtesy of the Urban Archives Center, California State University Library never happened; second, they will be investigated; third, they will never happen again." German officials regularly lied about events involving Jews. "Even while Hitler [denied] that such terror existed . . . the Jewish persecution [was] in full swing," the *New York Times* reported in June 1933.[25]

Unlike leaders of other nations in the 1930s, Roosevelt associated with Jews and was sensitive to their faith and strong ethnic ties. The Roosevelts socialized with Jews. As governor of New York, Roosevelt observed Jewish legislators who did not eat when invited to lunch at the mansion. When told they were Orthodox Jews and could eat only kosher food, he had them served dairy and vegetable meals, and had a set of china purchased to be used only for kosher meals. In the 1936 presidential campaign Sam Rosenman told FDR he thought it best that he and his wife not ride on the campaign train. He thought that FDR ought not to have two Jews on the train as it traveled through the Bible Belt. An angry FDR replied, "That's no way to handle antisemitism. The way to handle it is to meet it head on." The Rosenmans went.[26]

Roosevelt detested Prussian militarism and disliked Hitler from the start. Roosevelt claimed that as a teenager he was involved in an altercation with a Prussian officer on a train to Berlin when the rude soldier refused to permit Roosevelt's mother and her companion to open a window. He despised Nazi brutality against Jews and political opponents and their hatred for democracy. Indeed, he despised everything about them. Roosevelt's enmity toward Hitler so impressed the German novelist Thomas Mann in June 1935 that he later wrote, "When I left the White House . . . I knew Hitler was lost." FDR appointed a liberal scholar, Wilson's biographer William E. Dodd, as ambassador to Germany because he wanted "an American liberal in Germany as a standing example." ER also was disturbed by the Nazis and made a point of appearing at large Jewish gatherings such as the 1933 Jewish Federation luncheon at the Hotel Commodore in New York. Her appearance at Jewish affairs, like her appearance at black functions, generated controversy. She spoke out against antisemitism and race hatred. In 1934 she spoke to the Hadassah convention in Washington and praised its efforts in Palestine.[27]

By 1935 it was clear to Palestinian leader David Ben-Gurion that the formerly liberal British policy toward Jews was changing. At the end of World War I Great Britain was given a mandate to govern Palestine and help the Jews establish a national home there. Arab efforts to drive Jews out of Palestine put a strain on British resources. Anti-British demonstrations, riots, and strikes in Palestine affected British and Zionist attitudes. In March 1936 Ben-Gurion called for the establishment of a Jewish state as an "ultimate goal." He wanted a million Jews to escape from Europe to Palestine. A major Arab revolt against the British mandate occurred in April 1936. To Ben-Gurion it was clear that there would no peace with the Arabs: "We and they want the same thing. . . . We both want Palestine."[28]

Germany had withdrawn from the League of Nations in 1933. In violation of the Versailles treaties, Hitler rebuilt the German army and navy and secretly developed an air force. The British and French, enthralled by pacifism, appeasement, and bitter memories of World War I, acquiesced in Germany's rearmament. In 1935

Hitler attacked the Versailles Treaty which had "promised peace, but which brought in its wake endless bitterness and oppression." Many in Britain, France, and America agreed. In November 1936, when the Nazis and the Japanese signed the Anti-Comintern Pact, Roosevelt was reduced to moralizing to the Europeans.[29]

Hitler expanded his power by any and all means. The Reichstag, the German capitol building, was set ablaze on February 27, 1933, ostensibly by enemies of the Reich, and Hitler grasped permanent emergency powers in the aftermath. The Nazi Party and the SA (Brown Shirts) began a reign of intimidation, murder, and extortion to consolidate Hitler's hold on German society. When Churchill and Roosevelt referred to Hitler and his supporters as "criminals" and "gangsters," they meant it literally. Hitler imprisoned, tortured, and murdered his fellow Germans if they were Communists, Socialists, intellectuals, writers, clergymen, priests, or labor leaders. A well-worn quotation attributed to the German anti-Nazi pastor Martin Niemöller reflected these events:

> *First they came for the Communists, but I was not a Communist—so I said nothing. Then they came for the Social Democrats, but I was not a Social Democrat—so I did nothing. Then came the trade unionists, but I was not a trade unionist. And then they came for the Jews, but I was not a Jew—so I did little. Then when they came for me, there was no one left who could stand up for me.[30]*

The first concentration camp, Dachau, was established twelve miles from Munich on March 22, 1933, to incarcerate political dissidents, not Jews. There was no secret about Dachau. The camp was founded as a deterrent to anyone who opposed the Nazis and did its job for twelve years. Two hundred twenty-five thousand Germans were sent to concentration camps between 1933 and 1939 for political crimes. Soon all political parties except the Nazi Party were banned. The Geheime Staatspolizei, the Secret State Police or Gestapo, was created in April 1933. The Roman Catholic Church made a pact with Hitler to stay out of politics in exchange for freedom from oppression. On June 30, 1934, Hitler brazenly murdered his rivals for the leadership of the Nazi Party in "The Night of the Long Knives." When he killed Nazi Party leaders more radical than himself, he won over the army, industry, and the business community.

By early 1936 Hitler was on his way toward absolute dictatorship. Hans Frank said, "our Constitution is the Will of the Führer." The "New Germany," according to Hitler's worldview, would be a healthier body politic if all inferior and unhealthy people were exiled or killed. Eventually Nazi logic led to compulsory sterilization and the killing of mental patients, the handicapped, and homosexuals.[31]

FDR's Jewish friends and supporters lost no time in lobbying the new president to help German Jewry. Irving Lehman, Governor Herman Lehman's brother and a New York State Court of Appeals judge, visited FDR on March 14, 1933, ten days after his inauguration. He urged the president to speak out against Hitler's persecution of the Jews and to liberalize the Hoover administration's immigration guidelines. Representatives of the American Jewish Committee and B'nai B'rith lobbied Secretary of State Cordell Hull. FDR raised the issue in a cabinet meeting. Justice Frankfurter bombarded FDR with letters from England urging him to speak out against Hitler. He suggested the president broadcast in German and say "some plain things that need to be said." Frances Perkins, the new secretary of labor, responded enthusiastically to Jewish requests for help.[32]

While antisemitism was clearly a factor in American attitudes and policies toward immigration, Americans detested Hitler and Nazism and were sympathetic toward Jewish refugees fleeing Germany. Ambassador William Dodd said of Hitler, "I cannot endure his presence." Secretary of State Hull told the German ambassador after an incident in Chicago that protests would continue in the United States until Germany stopped persecuting Jews. The Boston Jewish community organized an anti-Nazi rally at Faneuil Hall, and Rabbi Stephen Wise organized a mass protest demonstration in New York City.

Twenty-two thousand people gathered at Madison Square Garden on March 27, 1933, to protest Hitler's persecution of German Jewry. Al Smith told a packed house, with 35,000 more people jamming the streets outside, that Americans should give the Nazis "the same treatment that we gave the Ku Klux Klan . . . it don't make any difference to me whether it is a brown shirt or a night shirt." Senator Robert F. Wagner of New York, Mayor John O'Brien, Rabbi Wise, and Catholic and Protestant bishops spoke to the assembly. "City Leaders of All Faiths Voice Indignation at

Antisemitism in Huge Rally," a headline read in the *New York Times*. At a mass meeting in Albany, Governor Lehman appealed to the German nation to restore equality to the Jews. Speaking as a Jew whose forebears had lived in Germany for generations, he denied any personal animosity toward the German people and insisted that most Germans opposed discrimination. On April 3 Massachusetts governor Joseph B. Ely, Boston mayor James M. Curley, and Christian religious leaders joined Jews in criticizing Hitler. Curley denounced the "oppression and tyranny directed at the Jewish people by the Hitlerites."[33]

Immediately after the rallies, the Nazis began a boycott of Jewish businesses. They claimed Jewish Americans had started a controversy with "atrocity propaganda." Leaders of the American Jewish Committee (AJ Committee) and B'nai B'rith felt vindicated. Had not these moderate Jewish leaders told their militant colleagues such as Rabbi Wise that their protest would backfire? But many American Jews continued their vociferous criticism of Nazism. Jewish Americans organized a counterboycott of German goods. The Non-Sectarian Anti-Nazi League, chaired by Samuel Untermyer, a distinguished corporate lawyer, led the boycott. Prominent Catholics and Protestants served on the board. Many Jewish department stores, such as Gimbel's, Saks, and Abraham & Straus, participated, as did a number of labor unions. Jewish New Yorkers, the Yiddish-speaking leadership, Jewish War Veterans, Zionist and labor groups, and other Jewish organizations supported the boycott. So did the Yiddish press and Justice Brandeis.[34]

New Dealers sought to help Jews who wished to emigrate from

Germany. The Department of Labor had major responsibilities in the area of immigration through its Bureau of Immigration. Labor Secretary Perkins was sympathetic to the plight of European Jewry. Her old ally Frankfurter drafted executive orders to expand and liberalize the "likely to become public charge" (LPC) provision of the law for those fleeing religious persecution. Frankfurter sent the drafts directly to the president, while Perkins went to work to ease immigration restrictions. She advocated Frankfurter's order at a cabinet meeting, but Secretary of State Hull disagreed.[35]

Even those sympathetic to German Jewry could not ignore the immigration laws, the Depression, and massive unemployment in the United States. Undersecretary of State William Phillips convinced FDR that Frankfurter's proposed executive orders were a serious mistake, that the labor unions would be irate. Perkins was furious with the State Department. She called Phillips and said she would "press for an immediate decision," and if she did not get it, would unleash upon the State Department "the most formidable instance of Jewish pressure. In fact, she quite blew our poor Under Secretary off his end of the telephone," Jay Pierrepont Moffat wrote in his diary.[36]

The Labor and State Departments heated up their long-standing competition to control immigration. Labor wanted to increase it and liberalize quotas for Jews. State wanted to restrict it for a variety of reasons, including "protecting" the nation's racial and religious makeup, fear of Communists and malcontents, a desire to follow to the letter laws enacted by a xenophobic Congress, and fear of congressional wrath if the department failed it its duties. The president's advisers were divided. Some advocated compassion for refugees, and others not to make exceptions even for persecuted foreigners at the expense of desperate, unemployed American citizens.

By late 1935 Roosevelt, moved by the plight of the German Jews, and at substantial political risk, loosened the restrictions President Hoover had imposed on immigration in 1930. The "conditions in Germany," his old friend Governor Lehman told Roosevelt, "appear to be getting worse continually." It was imperative that as many German Jews as possible be given the opportunity to immigrate. FDR replied twelve days later. The State Department, the president told Lehman, had ordered its consuls to give the refugees "the most considerate attention and the most generous and favorable treatment possible under the laws." Roosevelt wrote Lehman again in July 1936 addressing specific problems at the American consulate in Stuttgart and assuring his old friend that four new employees had been sent there to handle the increase in Jewish visa applicants. He assured Lehman that the consulate officers "are issuing considerably more immigration visas to German Jewish applicants." German Jewish immigration increased 78 percent in 1936 and 1937.[37]

Between 1933 and 1937 one-quarter (129,000) of Germany's Jews escaped the Nazis. The number of Jews entering the United States increased significantly in 1935. Yehuda Bauer estimated that 60 percent of those Jews who professed their faith escaped from Germany and Austria. William D. Rubinstein noted that 72 percent of German Jewry escaped Nazi Germany before large-scale emigration ceased in 1939. The United States took in even more Jews fleeing Nazi Germany between 1938 and 1939. Young German Jews, in particular, escaped in such numbers that 52 percent of all Jews remaining in Germany in 1939 were over fifty years old.[38]

More German Jews could have come to America, but they believed the Nazi persecution, like previous European pogroms, would blow over. Oral interviews with German Jews after the war revealed that many did not fear the Nazis before the *Kristallnacht* pogrom of November 1938. They believed, as one father told his son, "Oh come on, it's not going to last." Another remembered "we should have left in 1933 or 1934 or 1935, but we never believed that the Germans were capable of doing the things they did later. Though practically every German had a copy of *Mein Kampf*, few ever read it." Incredibly, 16,000 German Jews *returned* to Germany in 1934 after fleeing in 1933. Synagogues remained open, and the Nazis seemed agreeable to Zionism until *Kristallnacht*. German Jews fought to stay in their beloved Fatherland. Lucy Dawidowicz pointed out that every Jewish organization in Germany, from Orthodox to Reform, right to left, Zionist and non-Zionist, demanded *daseinrecht*, the right of Jews to live in Germany. German Jewish leaders told American Jews that they could hold their own against "Herr Hitler and his followers."[39]

In 1934 Rabbi Leo Baeck was preaching in Berlin to three or four services each Saturday. "My message is the same," he told his flock, "let no drop of bitterness enter your hearts no matter what comes." Max Liebermann, an eminent German artist ousted from the presidency of the Berlin Academy of Art, quipped, "German Jewry is like a man who is mortally wounded and in addition has a cold. So he calls in a doctor to stop his snuffling."[40]

The Roosevelt administration facilitated German Jewish immigration to the United States in the early years of the Reich. The number increased dramatically after *Kristallnacht* when it became clear that Jews in Germany were in real physical danger. Between July 1, 1933, and June 30, 1942, 161,051 Jews immigrated to the United States—35.5 percent of *all* immigrants to America. Jews comprised more than half of all immigrants to the United States between 1938 and 1940. There is no doubt that antisemites in the consular bureaucracy hindered the efforts of many Jews to immigrate. However, inconclusive data suggested that until *Kristallnacht*, fewer German Jews wished to enter the United States than one would assume.[41]

The State Department bureaucracy was much more conservative, xenophobic, and antisemitic than FDR's top-level appointees. Roosevelt thought the Foreign Service was made up of "wealthy young men . . . out of touch with American affairs." Indeed, Roosevelt acted as his own Secretary of State and complained about the difficulty of getting "changes in the thinking, policy, and action of the career diplomats." While the president appointed the secretary of state, his top assistants, and his ambassadors, he had little or no control over the Foreign Service and civil servants who were not political appointees. Among those staffers there was a wide variety of feelings on issues affecting Jews. Assistant Secretary of State Wilbur J. Carr, for example, had drafted the restrictive immigration laws of the 1920s and was guardian of the visa policy in the 1930s. Carr disliked Jews and most other immigrant groups. He believed that they could not assimilate into American society. The epitome of a bureaucrat, he used his position to reinforce his prejudices to strictly control immigration. He resisted special consideration for Jewish refugees because he believed his chief responsibility was to enforce the laws enacted by Congress.[42] Undersecretary of State William Phillips also disliked Jews. He was descended from a long line of patrician Boston antisemites who included the abolitionist Wendell Phillips. "Phillips's wrong action on Germany's Jews," Brandeis wrote, "will not end until he leaves the State Department." But the man was close to FDR, and he wielded great power until 1936, when he became ambassador to Italy.[43]

Career diplomat George S. Messersmith, on the other hand, sympathized with the plight of German Jews and detested Nazis. He succeeded Wilbur J. Carr as assistant secretary of state in 1937. Jewish leaders lobbied in favor of Messersmith's appointment as minister to Austria, and Roosevelt, who thought Messersmith one of the best men in the Foreign Service, readily complied. Messersmith urged the administration to boycott the 1936 Olympics because it would be a tool of Nazi propaganda. The Nazis claimed Messersmith was half Jewish. Messersmith's protégé Raymond Geist, consul at Berlin throughout the 1930s, was one of the few Americans who perceived Hitler's long-range goals. After *Kristallnacht*, Geist worked diligently to get Jews out of Germany but was criticized for granting too many visas. He persuaded the Gestapo to release Jews and even went into concentration camps to find people. At times Geist bent the rules too much and was reined in by Messersmith.[44]

American Jews were acutely aware that an influx of Jewish refugees exacerbated anti-alien sentiment. The admission of refugees was opposed by a slight majority of American Jews. Both B'nai B'rith and the National Federation of Temple Brotherhoods urged removing refugees from New York City. The American Jewish Committee (AJ Committee) and the American Jewish Congress (AJ Congress) agreed that they should not "lend our hand to helter-skelter [immigration]. We must not help [raise] a new Jewish question in other parts of the world." Indeed, they had no other option, given the nearly global support for restrictive immigration laws. When Herbert Lehman wrote his moving letter to FDR seeking some loosening of restrictions, he knew his old friend's hands were tied.[45]

Jews close to FDR were divided on how to approach the president. Some, such as Wise and Frankfurter, pressured him to do more for the Jews. Rosenman felt it was inappropriate to take advantage of his friendship to lobby for Jewish causes. Wise believed that FDR was surrounded by "timorous Jews." He was angry when Roosevelt told him that "Max Warburg wrote to me that the situation in Germany is so hopeless that nothing can be done!" Wise felt Warburg had "no right so to dispirit the president." Morgenthau and Irving Lehman met with FDR in September 1934 to complain that the State Department was dragging its feet and to discuss the boycott of German goods. But Jews within the government were careful not to get their popular president so far out on a limb that he could be damaged politically. Charles E. Wyzanski Jr. worked diligently as a lawyer in the Labor Department to loosen the State Department's visa restrictions. He employed a little-known law allowing the secretary of labor to accept bonds to avoid the LPC problem. Yet, even as Wyzanski won a small legal battle inside the administration, he knew the plan would blow up in FDR's face and arouse hostility in Congress. Other Jewish insiders had the same concern.[46]

The Roosevelt administration admitted intellectuals, scientists, and artists as refugees. According to Jean Medawar and David Pyke, the United States admitted more of these classes of refugees from the Reich than any other country. American activists led by the Rockefeller Foundation assisted hundreds of Jewish intellectuals in coming to the United States. Many found jobs in American schools, which prided themselves on taking in men whose books were being burned by Nazi hooligans. University professors and ministers, including rabbis, were admitted outside of the immigration quota. One ironic result of Nazi barbarism toward Jewish scientists was that some of them later built the atomic bomb for the Allies. Leo Szilard, a Hungarian Jew who had renounced Judaism and was a creator of the atomic bomb, escaped first to Britain and then to the United States. The father of the hydrogen bomb, Edward Teller, a Hungarian Jew who taught in Germany, fled to the United States and settled at Princeton University.[47]

The best-known of these Jewish intellectuals was Albert Einstein. By the 1930s he was thought to be the greatest scientist of the time. But he was also a leftist and a pacifist. He was called a Communist and a radical by Nazis and right-wing Americans alike. When Hitler came to power, Einstein was already teaching in the United States. Scheduled to return to Germany, Einstein instead surrendered his German citizenship. "As long as I have any choice in the matter, I shall live only in a country where civil liberty, tolerance and equality of all citizens before the law prevail," he said. "These conditions do not exist in Germany at the present time." He had many offers of refuge but settled on the new Institute for Advanced Studies at Princeton University, where his only job was to think about physics. Before and during World War II, Einstein remained a symbol to the world of contempt for Nazism and American support for decency and humanity.[48]

When Einstein applied for a visa in 1932, the Woman Patriot Corporation, an anti-women's suffrage, anti-alien group, notified the State Department that Einstein was a Communist and an undesirable. Certainly his support for human rights, pacifism, and Zionism did not endear him to the antisemitic elements in the United States. Typical of State Department personnel, an assistant consul interrogated Einstein about his political beliefs before he would issue a visa.[49]

At the suggestion of Stephen Wise, FDR invited Einstein to the White House in November 1933. The great scientist wrote to Mrs. Roosevelt, "You can hardly imagine of what great interest it would [be] for me to meet the man who is tackling with the gigantic energy the greatest and most difficult problem of our time."[50] The Einsteins later stayed at the White House in January 1934.

American Jews protested their country's participation in the 1936 Olympic Games at Berlin. In 1933, when the games were planned, Wise urged the American Olympic Committee to withdraw. Al Smith convinced the Catholic War Veterans to join the protest in 1935. But Avery Brundage, chairman of the AOC, responded bluntly, "certain Jews must now understand that they cannot use these Games as a weapon in their boycott against the Nazis." He denounced Jews as radicals. Retired brigadier general Charles H. Sherrill, a member of both the International and the American Olympic Committees, said, "Why there are not a dozen Jews in the world of Olympic calibre," and blamed German Jews for the controversy. Many Americans agreed. A proboycott resolution was defeated by a narrow margin. After the games, Brundage appeared before twenty thousand German Americans at Madison Square Garden to thank them for their support. The crowd mockingly responded with shouts of "Sieg Heil" and the Nazi salute.[51]

Despite his abhorrence of Nazism, Roosevelt shied away from anything that smacked of war, the League of Nations, internationalism, or European alliances. He was careful not to antagonize German or Italian Americans. In July 1933, Nazi Germany and the Vatican signed a concordat guaranteeing the rights of the Roman Catholic Church in Germany. As Hitler rebuilt Germany's military, FDR was helpless to stop him. The powerful currents of isolationism, appeasement and pacifism were so strong that Roosevelt could not even convince the Senate to approve American membership on the World Court at the Hague. Congress defeated a proposal allowing the president to designate the aggressor in enforcing an American embargo on munitions. The "wind everywhere blows against us," FDR wrote Elihu Root.[52]

The Roosevelts had to stay above the battle. They hoped the German love affair with Nazism would end. They were keenly aware of antisemitism in the United States and admiration of Hitler and

Mussolini in some quarters. They agreed with many of their Jewish friends that American hatred of Jews might be fanned by protests against German internal affairs. There was nothing the United States could do about Hitler's anti-Jewish policies in any event. American politics were too volatile for Eleanor even to write about Nazi atrocities. Privately and publicly, she helped individual Jewish refugees, needy Jewish families and philanthropies, and was keenly aware of prejudice against Jews and others. "And what can one do?" she said. "The will of the people is a difficult thing." But when the Colony Club blackballed her friend Elinor Morgenthau in 1937, ER resigned.[53]

As Roosevelt reluctantly signed the Neutrality Act of 1935, Mussolini's army invaded Ethiopia. FDR had no desire to pick a fight with Benito Mussolini. The Duce was a hero to many Italian Americans and other Americans, including FDR's ambassador to Italy, Breckinridge Long, were enthusiastic about his accomplishments. So was Winston Churchill. The United States was officially neutral. There was widespread agreement that America should not be the world's arms merchant.[54] The Nye Committee, chaired by the outspoken isolationist and Republican senator Gerald P. Nye of North Dakota, held hearings on the unpopular munitions industry, on how armsmakers, those "bloodsucking" "merchants of death," had bribed politicians in World War I and encouraged war for profit. "Rarely have Senate hearings fallen with such heavy impact on the stream of American opinion," James MacGregor Burns concluded. It was clear to Roosevelt that for now his role in foreign affairs would be severely limited.[55]

Despite defections, notably Al Smith, Roosevelt's coalition held firm in the 1934 congressional elections. The more the Republicans and the isolationist American Liberty League called Roosevelt a socialist and a threat to liberty, the more popular he became. Democrats gained thirteen seats in the House and nine in the Senate. "He has been all but crowned by the people," William Allan White wrote of FDR. Historian Charles A. Beard called the results "thunder on the left." FDR felt energized to fight for his liberal agenda.[56]

The Second Hundred Days in 1935, in response to growing radicalism and discontent in the country and to the Supreme Court's "horse-and-buggy decision" invalidating the National Recovery Act, produced the Wagner Labor Relations Act, the Social Security Act, and major legislation on taxes, holding companies, banking, and the TVA. FDR supported an estate tax, a gift tax, and a corporate income tax. Abandoned by big business, conservatives, and the political right, the president veered to the left with gusto. By 1935 conservatives and big business detested Roosevelt. To them he was a traitor to his class. "We have earned the hatred of entrenched greed," he said. Huey Long took credit for Roosevelt's new liberalism and strutted up and down the aisles of the Senate bragging about his role in FDR's "soak the rich" or "wealth tax" bill. William Randolph Hearst instructed his editors to substitute "Raw Deal" for "New Deal." He called Roosevelt a Communist and privately referred to him as "Stalin Delano Roosevelt." Many conservatives and moderates actually feared the Roosevelt administration.[57]

Chapter 2

Wops, Dagoes, Bulls, Hebrews, and Niggers

We have not developed a nation, but a polyglot boarding house.

—Theodore Roosevelt

The myth of the melting pot has been discredited . . . the United States is our *land.*

—Representative Albert Johnson, 1924, speaking to the Daughters of the American Revolution[1]

A flood of Chinese immigrants to California, the arrival of millions of Slavs, Jews, and Italians, labor strikes, urban violence, the trauma of World War I and the Bolshevik Revolution profoundly disturbed the majority of Americans who were of Protestant, Western European stock. They were frightened by these earth-shaking events and by the growing number of immigrants in their midst who spoke different languages, wore different clothes, followed different religious practices, at times engaged in criminal or subversive behavior, and who, it appeared, could and would never assimilate into the majority culture. Native white Protestant Americans were scared by what they saw: xenophobia ran rampant, fueled by fear of radical immigrants, revolutionaries, and the growing power of the Roman Catholic Church.

The 1886 Haymarket bombing in Chicago had involved foreign-born, bomb-throwing anarchists, and the assassination of President William McKinley in 1901 by Leon Czolgosz, a young Polish anarchist (which made FDR's cousin Teddy president), had increased Americans' fears. New England intelligentsia founded the Immigration Restriction League, propagated a pseudoscientific ideology of the division of mankind into biological types and touted the racial superiority of Anglo-Saxons and Nordic people. Led by WASP elitists such as Senator Henry Cabot Lodge of Massachusetts, the U.S. Congress began enacting restrictions on European immigration.[2]

Antisemitic propaganda such as the vitriol disseminated by Henry Ford in the *Dearborn Independent* also played a role. Populist antisemitism grew in the heartland and elitist antisemitism increased in eastern cities and Ivy League universities. The teeming, crime-ridden, poverty-stricken Jewish ghetto of New York City, so beloved by later generations of Jewish Americans, appalled contemporary American writers ranging from Henry James ("There is no swarming like that of Israel") to Edith Wharton to Rev. A. E. Patton, a respected Protestant leader, who saw at Ellis Island "the Jewish hordes, ignorant of all true patriotism, filthy . . . stealthy [and] . . . lazy" to F. Scott Fitzgerald in

The Great Gatsby to Thomas Wolfe ("swarming, shrieking . . . tides of dark amber Jewish flesh").[3]

The upsurge in communism, radicalism, anarchism, bombings, strikes, violence, and labor unrest led to widespread fear of *all* immigrants, who were seen by most Americans as threats to the nation's social and political stability. The Bolshevik Revolution of November 1917 and Communist uprisings in other countries terrified Americans.[4] The average citizen of the United States shared few beliefs with the Jewish anarchist Alexander Berkman, who shot Henry Clay Frick, an executive of Carnegie Steel, during the steel strike of 1892, or with Berkman's wild-eyed girlfriend the Jewish Russian and Communist agitator Emma Goldman, or with the hundreds of thousands of New York Jewish Communists, Socialists, and anarchists.[5]

Antialien hysteria reached a peak in the "Red Scare" of 1919–20. Socialist and Communist organizations, many led by Russian, Polish, and German-speaking foreigners, proliferated in major American cities populated by immigrants, many of whom did not even speak English. Homegrown Communists such as John Reed (made famous by the movie *Reds*) hoped and believed that a Communist-led revolution was impending in the United States. A general strike paralyzed Seattle. Mail bombs were sent to government officials around the country. On June 2, 1919, bombs exploded in eight different cities at the same hour, one at the home of Attorney General A. Mitchell Palmer in Washington, D.C. Coincidentally, Franklin and Eleanor Roosevelt were in Palmer's neighborhood when the bomb went off. FDR was then serving as Woodrow Wilson's assistant secretary of the navy.[6]

Palmer and other governmental officials reacted with an over-whelming show of force. A police strike was broken in Boston, and Massachusetts governor Calvin Coolidge became a national hero, saying "There is no right to strike against the public safety by any-body, anywhere, anytime." Steel mill and mine strikes led in part by radicals and Communist Party members were ruthlessly sup-pressed. Palmer rounded up thousands of alien and immigrant socialists, anarchists, and Communists, many of whom were Jews. Hundreds were deported, including Emma Goldman and Alexander Berkman. In 1920 Nicola Sacco and Bartolomeo Vanzetti, two Italian immigrant anarchists, were convicted of rob-bery and murder and sentenced to the electric chair. The judge referred to them as "those anarchist bastards." Many liberals believed that Sacco and Vanzetti had been unjustly convicted because they were Italians and anarchists. Their case became an international cause célèbre. Although Felix Frankfurter aided in their legal defense, Sacco and Vanzetti were executed in 1927.[7]

While the Red Scare subsided in the 1920s, most Americans were convinced that immigrants were threats to the American way of life, especially leftists from Eastern and Southern Europe and Jewish Communists. Thus, long before the advent of Nazism, these events had triggered congressional enactment of highly restrictive immigration laws that had the overwhelming support of the Amer-ican people. By 1924 Congress had radically changed America's formerly generous immigration policy to exclude Italians, Poles, Slavs, Jews, Chinese, Japanese, and other non–Anglo-Saxons believed to be threats to the nation.

Antisemitism played a major role in this legislation. White Protestant Americans also feared Catholics, Bolsheviks, anarchists and revolutionaries of all kinds and colors. In 1921 one senator made hay out of a statement the director of the Hebrew Immigrant Aid Society (HIAS) made in a memorandum: "If there were in existence a ship that would hold three million human beings, the three million Jews of Poland would board it to escape to America."[8] The eugenicist movement added more ammunition. The distinguished anthropologist of the American Museum of Natural History Madison Grant wrote in *The Passing of the Great Race* (1916) of "the Jew, whose dwarf stature, peculiar mentality, and ruthless concentration on self-interest are being engrafted upon the stock of the nation." Foreign Service bureaucrat Wilbur J. Carr reported to Congress in 1920 that Jewish emigrants were "filthy, most un-American . . . often dangerous . . . [and] mentally deficient."[9]

The Jewish congressman from Brooklyn Emanuel Celler fought a losing battle against anti-immigration legislation. "When I finally rose to talk, I knew it was in vain," Celler recalled. They did not want as prospective citizens 'wops,' 'dagoes,' 'Hebrews,' 'honkies,' 'bulls,' and others known by similar epithets." The Chinese were denied entry by congressional acts from 1882 to 1902. President Warren G. Harding signed the provisional Quota Act of 1921, the first of several laws designed to restrict immigration by use of quotas. Later, the harsher Johnson-Reed Immigration Act of 1924 based immigration quotas upon two principles, the racial supremacy of British and Nordic people, and the ethnic makeup of the United States in 1890, prior to the massive Eastern and Southern European immigration. It limited the number of immigrants to 150,000 per year. The vote was 326 to 71 in the House and 62 to 6 in the Senate.

The era of mass Jewish, Eastern European, Slavic, Polish, and Italian immigration closed, and an epoch in American history came to an end. The immediate impact of the new laws fell on "the vast tormented reservoir of Polish, Romanian, and Ukrainian Jews." In 1924 and 1925 barely 10,000 Jewish immigrants entered the United States. "The Statue of Liberty would still stand in New York harbor," Maldwyn Allen Jones observed, "but the verses on its base would henceforth be but a tribute to a vanished ideal."[10]

By 1933 many liberals and Jewish Americans supported restrictive immigration laws to protect scarce American jobs and keep wages high. Most Jewish labor unions and other Jewish groups recognized the futility of fighting the legislation. Roosevelt's views on immigration in the 1920s were conventional. He was certainly no friend to Communists, anarchists, and revolutionaries. Like most Americans, he thought the nation had taken in more immigrants than it could digest. For example, he believed Asians could not assimilate into American society and should be excluded altogether.[11]

The Depression exacerbated America's xenophobia. In 1930 President Herbert Hoover ordered the State Department to slow down immigration administratively by having American consulates strictly interpret the "likely to become a public charge" (LPC) clause of the Immigration Act of 1917. The House passed a bill that reduced quotas by 90 percent. Because Democrats gained seats in the 1930 election, a Jewish congressman, Samuel Dickstein, chairman of the Immigration Committee, was able to bottle up legislation to *limit* immigration. The political consensus was nearly unanimous that times were too tough to let in more immigrants. There the matter stood *before* Hitler came to power and *ten years before* the Final Solution began in 1941. The 1924 Immigration Act, enacted to keep Southern and Eastern Europeans, Communists, and radicals out of the United States, guaranteed that the United States would not offer a limitless haven to victims of the Holocaust.[12]

But immigration laws, Hitler, Nazism, pogroms, antisemitism, and European Jewry were the farthest things from Franklin Roosevelt's mind when he took the oath of office on March 4, 1933. "The brief period from 1929 to 1945," historian C. Vann Woodward wrote, "is unique in American history for its complexities of change and violence of contrasts. People who lived through the years of the Great Depression, the New Deal, and the Second World War . . . experienced more bewildering changes than had several generations of their predecessors." The stock market crash of October 1929, economic collapse, near starvation in some places, industrial and class warfare, open rebellion against state and local authorities, and the rise of demagogues such as Huey Long and Father Charles Coughlin were unimaginable four years earlier, when Herbert Hoover became president. A cloud of economic uncertainty and fear descended on the nation. The world economy was in shambles. The governments of Western Europe could not pay their war debts. On the day of Roosevelt's inauguration, "the nation was in a state of shock."[13]

Life in the United States in the early 1930s presented a dismal picture. "In the long-blighted countryside," David M. Kennedy wrote, "unmarketable crops rotted in fields and unsalable livestock died on the hoof. . . . In towns and cities across the country, haggard men in shabby overcoats, collars turned up against the chill wind, newspapers plugging the holes in their shoes, lined up glumly for handouts at soup kitchens." The unemployed traveled the country seeking work. "Hoovervilles," small, makeshift villages of shacks, abandoned cars, and packing boxes, sprung up in dreary parts of towns. Women scavenged on garbage heaps searching for food. "It has been," Jane Addams of Hull House recalled, "like a disaster or flood, fire or earthquake, this universal wiping out of resources." Never had the nation experienced such mass unemployment. "We have gone to the bottom of the barrel," a Kansas editor wrote. American Jews shared their compatriots' privations. Jewish New Yorkers were devastated by a run on the Bank of the United States founded by East European Jewish immigrants. Many of the 400,000 Jewish depositors lost their life savings, and Jewish businessmen went bankrupt. In 1931 Jewish welfare agencies increased by 42 percent their aid to destitute Jews. In some cities the increase was 100 percent. Construction of synagogues ceased. Yeshiva University almost closed.[14]

As governor of New York, Franklin D. Roosevelt had at least done *something*. He had championed unemployment insurance and old-age pensions. When he took the presidential oath of office, he was determined to act. His first job was to give the American people confidence. This "great nation will endure as it has endured, will

Rabbi Stephen S. Wise addresses the crowd at a mass meeting in Battery Park to protest the Nazi persecution of German Jews. The meeting followed a protest march through lower Manhattan in which an estimated 100,000 people took part.

Courtesy of Bettman/Corbis

revive and will prosper," he reassured Americans. "The only thing we have to fear is fear itself—nameless, unreasoning, unjustified terror which paralyzes needed efforts to convert retreat into advance." The great task before him was "to put people to work" and to "putting our own national house in order." The new president made it clear that he intended to put foreign affairs a distant second.[15]

The New Deal meant as much, if not more, to African Americans as it did to Jews. Racism, white supremacy, segregation, and lynching had gone unchallenged through the twentieth century. FDR and ER began chipping away at this massive evil. The Roosevelts opened the door to the most mistreated of America's minorities. Black leaders were welcomed at the White House, to the consternation of racists everywhere. ER developed close friendships with Walter White of the NAACP and activist Mary McLeod Bethune, who was the head of an unofficial "black cabinet." ER agitated for the appointment of black women to government positions. FDR appointed the first black federal judge and brought blacks into the federal government in unprecedented numbers.[16]

ER was involved in the bitter campaign to enact a federal law designed to end the lynching of blacks. There were twenty-eight lynchings in 1933 alone. The Wagner-Costigan bill held local officials accountable if they failed to protect their citizens from lynching. FDR publicly deplored lynching, but he would not support the bill. He feared offending his powerful Southern allies in Congress. "I did not choose the tools with which I must work," FDR told Walter White. "Had I been permitted to choose them I would have selected quite different ones. But I've got to get legislation passed by Congress to save America. The Southerners by reason of the seniority rule in Congress are chairmen or occupy strategic places on most of the Senate and House Committees. If I come out for the anti-lynching bill now, they will block every bill to keep America from collapsing. I just can't take that risk."[17] FDR's Faustian bargain with segregationist Southern Democrats was something of a preview of the "deals with the devil" he had to make with Joseph Stalin and other villains of history to defeat Hitler and Nazism.

In his history of the New Deal, William E. Leuchtenburg titled his chapter on foreign affairs "A Farewell to Arms." Appeasement and pacifism were nearly as prevalent in the United States as in Europe and Great Britain, and Roosevelt acceded to the popular mood of isolationism, nonintervention in European affairs, and economic nationalism. "Opinion leaders publicly avowed their guilt for leading the country into war in 1917 and resolved they would never again so abuse the trust people had placed in them," Leuchtenburg concluded. Many Americans sympathized with Hitler's seemingly legitimate demands that ethnic Germans living in other countries, such as Austria and Czechoslovakia, be allowed to join the German Fatherland. Nor were Jewish Americans immune to pacifism, appeasement, and isolationism. "I would as little support a war to crush Hitlerism as a war for the strengthening of Jewish claims in Palestine," Rabbi Stephen Wise wrote in 1932. This was the overwhelming sentiment of the American, British, and French people in the 1930s. "Of the hell broth that is brewing in Europe," Ernest Hemingway wrote in 1935, "we have no need to drink." World War I had taken so many young lives that the Western democracies were determined it would not happen again. There would be "peace in our time," as Neville Chamberlain would proudly assert after accepting Hitler's demands at Munich in 1938. Americans hailed him as a hero, just as the British did. "To hell with Europe and the rest of those nations!" Senator Thomas Schall of Minnesota said in 1935.[18]

In January 1936 Japan walked out of the London Naval Conference. On March 7, 1936, Adolf Hitler rose in the Reichstag to proclaim the remilitarization of the Rhineland. The Versailles treaties forbade Germany from stationing troops or erecting fortifications on the left bank of the Rhine. Hitler abrogated the treaty. He had witnessed Benito Mussolini's foray into Ethiopia and was emboldened to act. Hitler gambled that the democracies would not stop him. The Japanese, too, were on the move. In 1937 Japan invaded China and landed soldiers and businessmen to take over the country.

The Spanish Civil War, from 1936 to 1939, was a prelude to World War II. Democrats, liberals, socialists, union members, Communists, and Jews had applauded FDR's recognition of the Soviet Union in 1934 and welcomed the leftist republican government in Spain. Catholics opposed recognizing a regime dedicated to eradicating religion from the globe. The Civil War pitted a right-wing rebellion, led by General Francisco Franco of the Falange Party and supported by the Catholic Church, Nazis, and Italian Fascists against the popularly elected leftist government allied to the Soviet Union. The war drove another wedge between Jews and Catholics. Nazi airplanes bombed civilians at Guernica, Spain, on April 26, 1937, while aiding Franco's troops. American Jews rallied to the Loyalist side and founded the Hollywood Anti-Faccist League. The American Catholic press excoriated Jews. "It is rather galling to find vociferous and misrepresentative Hebrews championing Stalin and Caballero while they denounce Hitler," one archdiocesan newspaper, the *Brooklyn Diocese Tablet*, wrote in March 1937. To Father Coughlin, the "radio priest," the Spanish Civil War was "a battleground of communism versus Christianity." FDR said American neutrality would be enforced. There was nothing to be gained by losing Catholic votes, although FDR secretly tried to aid the Loyalist government.[19]

In the summer of 1936 Roosevelt advocated a Jewish homeland in Palestine and asked the British to permit increased Jewish immigration to that destination. Riots and killings in Palestine alarmed the friends of Jewish aspirations. British officials blamed the Jews for the disturbances and urged an end to Jewish immigration. The Warburgs counseled peace. The Ben-Gurions counseled armed resistance. Rabbi Wise called on FDR at Hyde Park after returning from a meeting of the World Jewish Congress in Geneva. He asked Roosevelt to intervene, which he did. FDR asked the British not to curtail Jewish immigration, and the British acceded to his request. According to Wise's biographer Melvin Urofsky, FDR's request allowed fifty thousand Jews from Germany and Austria to enter Palestine, "men, women, and children who would undoubtedly have perished had the 1939 White Paper [closing Palestine to Jews] been issued three years earlier."[20]

The plight of Palestine and European Jewry was only a small blip on the radar screen of American politics in 1935 and 1936. The forces of radicalism from the right and the left were palpable. Millions were still suffering from the Depression. Many were angry with the government, banks, and capitalists generally. Some were angry with FDR. Huey Long, the "Kingfish" of Louisiana, was also called "the Messiah of the Rednecks." Father Coughlin was "rising on a mighty tide." "You can laugh at Father Coughlin, you can snort at Huey Long," Hugh Johnson, former director of the National Recovery Agency

(NRA) said March 4, 1935, on a nationwide radio broadcast, "but this country was never under a greater menace." Huey Long was assassinated by a secular Jew in 1935, but the country was harangued by other demagogues, and some observers foresaw the collapse of the American economic and political system. In his January 1936 State of the Union message to Congress, FDR blasted big business: "We have earned the hatred of entrenched greed," he roared, declaring war on the too-rich and the too-powerful.[21]

Franklin D. Roosevelt en route to Municipal Stadium to make his "Green Pastures" address, Charlotte, NC, September 10, 1936

Courtesy of the Franklin D. Roosevelt Library

The 1936 election, like the 1932 election, was about jobs, the Depression, and the economy. The Republicans nominated Governor Alf Landon, the "Kansas Coolidge." The Townsendites, Coughlin, and Long's followers coalesced into the Union Party, which nominated William Lemke, a Republican congressman from North Dakota.[22]

Racism bubbled beneath the surface. Roosevelt worked hard to keep together his unlikely political coalition, which included Southern whites and Northern blacks. The Democrats nominated Roosevelt, but even the party convention posed problems. Simple courtesies, such as having a black clergyman deliver the invocation or asking the black congressman from Chicago Arthur Mitchell to second his nomination, roused some Southerners to denounce the president. The racist senator from South Carolina "Cotton Ed" Smith theatrically walked out of the convention during the invocation, declaring, "By God he's as black as melted midnight! . . . This mongrel meeting ain't no place for a white man!" German Americans knew that Roosevelt was no friend of Germany. The German American Bund, a small crackpot group, announced that a vote for Roosevelt and his "Jewish dictatorship" was a vote for communism. But many ordinary German Americans turned against Roosevelt as well. FDR tried but failed to hold on to some of the German ethnic vote, which was historically Republican. He even sent a bland letter of greeting celebrating German Americans, contributors to the nation, to an American Nazi rally at Madison Square Garden in 1934.[23]

Foreign policy played a minor role in the election. FDR had not allowed the internationalism of his heart to affect his head, but he knew that America might soon play a crucial part in the affairs of nations. "I cannot, with candor, tell you all is well with the world," he told a cheering crowd of Democrats at Philadelphia's Franklin Field. "Clouds of suspicion, tides of ill-will and intolerance gather darkly in many places."[24]

But Roosevelt had not come to the Democratic convention to discuss Hitler, Mussolini, or Hirohito. He had come to declare war on the economic tyranny of big business and unrestrained capitalism. "The royalists of the economic order have conceded that political freedom was the business of the Government," he thundered, likening Republicans to the British in 1776, "but they have maintained that economic slavery was nobody's business." He

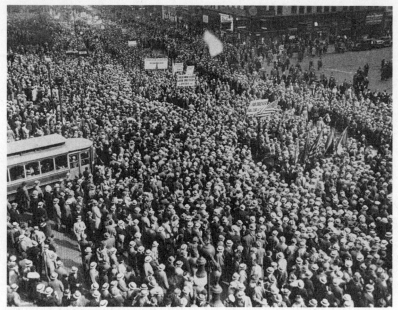

More than 100,000 demonstrators gather in front of Madison Square Garden on May 10, 1933, to take part in an anti-Nazi protest march through lower Manhattan.

Courtesy of the United States Holocaust Memorial Museum

challenged his opponents to allow average Americans equal opportunities in the marketplace. The convention exploded in cheers. "There is a mysterious cycle in human events. To some generations much is given. Of other generations much is expected. This generation of Americans has a rendezvous with destiny." The roar of the crowd, the festive occasion, and the war on entrenched greed enveloped these prophetic words.[25]

There was more. At Madison Square Garden on October 31, the president was blunt. "Never before in all our history have these forces [of "organized money," "financial monopoly," and "reckless banking"] been so united against one candidate as they stand today. They are unanimous in their hate for me—and I welcome their hatred. I should like to have it said of my first administration that in it the forces of selfishness and of lust for power met their match. . . . I should like to have it said," the crowd roared, clapped, and shouted its approval. "Wait a moment!" Roosevelt yelled. "I should like to have it said of my second administration that in it these forces met their master." Madison Square Garden had never seen anything like this before. "Rarely in Roosevelt's political career was there such a night," Arthur Schlesinger noted. But some former friends and old allies quit the campaign in disgust. Al Smith compared the New Deal to communism and said, "There can be only one capital, Washington or Moscow." Raymond Moley, a former New Dealer, was stunned "by the violence, the bombast, the naked demagoguery of these sentences."[26]

FDR's Jewish supporters and advisers were a campaign issue. A doggerel rhyme of the day had Franklin telling Eleanor:

> *You kiss the niggers,*
> *I'll kiss the Jews,*
> *We'll stay in the White House*
> *As long as we choose.*

Of course, Jews overwhelmingly supported FDR.[27]

While the 1936 presidential campaign was under way, Germany and Japan entered the Anti-Comintern Pact. The Democratic Party divided deeply on foreign affairs. Southern and border state Democrats were internationalists. Western and Midwestern Democrats were isolationists. Roosevelt sought all of their votes to win renomination and reelection. He saw that democracy was at war with fascism. "We are fighting," he said on June 27, 1936, "to save a great and precious form of government for ourselves and for the world!"[28]

Roosevelt defeated Alfred Landon and William Lemke by a landslide, the biggest victory in American history, carrying every state except Maine and Vermont. Democrats controlled the House 334 to 89 and the Senate 75 to 17. Roosevelt won a resounding victory in the immigrant wards of the big cities, where turnout increased a third over 1932, and the vote for FDR was overwhelming.[29]

At Hyde Park on election night, Franklin Roosevelt sat jubilantly in his dining room by the teletype machines and telephones, tallying the votes amid relatives, friends, and campaign workers. According to Sam Rosenman, when he learned he had carried hostile New Haven, Connecticut, by 15,000 votes, he "leaned back in his chair, blew a ring of smoke at the ceiling, and exclaimed, 'Wow!' He knew it was over."[30]

Chapter 3

"The Old Roosevelt Magic
Has Lost Its Kick"

I n early 1937 Franklin Roosevelt thought he was politically invincible. He believed he could intuit the will of the people, outfox his opponents, manage his unwieldy coalition, keep his enemies at bay, and rally the public to his banner. But unlike his first inauguration, when an occasional ray of sunlight pierced the gloom, a cold rain drenched these festivities. It was an omen Roosevelt did not heed. "The Constitution of 1787," he said, as seven of the nine Supreme Court justices listened, "did not make our democracy impotent." Millions of families were living on incomes "so meager that the pall of family disaster hangs over them day by day. . . . I see one-third of a nation ill-housed, ill-clad, ill-nourished." He was determined to make every American citizen "the subject of his country's interest and concern; and we will never regard any faithful, law-abiding group within our borders as superfluous." The last sentiment was lifted verbatim from a letter written by Rabbi Stephen Wise, which "came just in the nick of time," FDR wrote the rabbi.[1]

"Spectacular victory in the 1936 election," Frank Freidel observed, "emboldened Roosevelt to embark upon policies equally spectacular." He decided to tame his nemesis, the Supreme Court, to modernize the government, and to purge the Democratic Party of hidebound conservatives. "I owe nothing to anyone," he said. He failed in all of these endeavors, although he salvaged much from the wreckage. However, these political disasters weakened Roosevelt's ability to save European Jewry. Presidential hubris in 1937 and 1938 was forced to give way to presidential caution in 1939 and 1940.

FDR took up battle with the Supreme Court, an institution he believed was out of touch with the American people. He secretly devised a plan requiring that for every justice over seventy, the president could appoint an additional justice. If the plan worked, FDR could immediately add six New Deal justices to the Court. "The answer to a maiden's prayer!" he said with a laugh when told of the idea by Charles Wysanski, a colleague of Justice Frankfurter. His flimsy public justification for the "Court-packing" scheme was that the Court's workload was too heavy, and he wanted to improve the efficiency of the government. No one, including Roosevelt's friends, believed him. Everyone saw the ploy for what it was, a scheme to alter the Court's political makeup so it would approve New Deal legislation.[2]

Reaction to the Court-packing plan was overwhelmingly negative. "We were shocked," Emanuel Celler recalled. Even Governor Herbert Lehman opposed the plan. The president had taken no congressional leaders into his confidence, and many read about this political bombshell in the newspapers. Hatton W. Sumners of Texas, the Democratic chairman of the House Judiciary Committee, said, "Boys, here's where I cash in my chips." Vice President John Nance Garner, surrounded by senators, held his nose and gestured "thumb's down" in the lobby of the Senate. Republicans and the press were outraged. While Republicans did not have the votes to defeat the plan if the Democrats supported FDR, tinkering with the Supreme Court was too much for Southern and Western Democrats and for liberals who cherished the Court's independence on civil liberties. And it was too much for the country. Pent-up concern about Roosevelt's arrogance played a role. Still, the president had large majorities in Congress.[3]

Roosevelt pressed on. Chief Justice Charles Evans Hughes appeared before a Senate committee with a message approved by Justice Brandeis that the Court was current in its work. In a dramatic turnabout, the Court approved important New Deal legislation. Justice Owen J. Roberts switched his vote and, in 5-to-4 opinions, the Court upheld the constitutionality of minimum wage laws, the National Labor Relations Act, and the Social Security Act. These were fatal blows to Roosevelt's plan. "The switch in time"—Roberts's change of his vote—"that saved nine" also (in Hughes's words to Roberts) saved the Court.

Vice President Garner visited the president in July. "Do you want it with the bark on or the bark off, Cap'n?" the Texan asked the president. After explaining that "with the bark off" was telling the plain truth, Garner told Roosevelt, "All right. You are beat. You haven't got the votes." The Court-packing bill died in the

Senate. FDR nominated Hugo L. Black, a loyal New Dealer, to replace a retiring justice, and the controversy was over. Roosevelt had suffered one of the greatest losses of his political life. It was, Freidel wrote, "a staggering setback from a Congress top-heavy with Democrats. He had expended a large part of his political capital on a failed enterprise." Roosevelt was depressed for months, deeply hurt, shaken, and angry.[4]

In September 1937 FDR traveled to the Midwest, greeting crowds of supporters along the way. Hitlerism and international aggression were on his mind, and at Chicago on October 5, he made a dramatic speech. Alluding to the turmoil in Spain and China, he said that "peace-loving nations" must stand up to aggressors. He called for "a quarantine" of belligerents but added that he was determined "to adopt quickly every practicable measure to avoid involvement in war." Internationalists approved, but Hull, party leaders, isolationists, Republicans, and the press did not. For them, the Neutrality Act was holy writ. A "quarantine" was inconsistent with neutrality. Pacifists called the president a warmonger. Even the American Federation of Labor (AFL) chided him. "It's a terrible thing to look over your shoulder when you are trying to lead," FDR told Rosenman, "and to find no one there." It was a mistake he would not make again.[5]

The president's bad news was far from over. The country's economic recovery stalled. The stock market fell. Visions of the 1929 crash loomed in investors' heads. "We are headed into another depression," Morgenthau told Roosevelt. The president had no idea how to handle the situation. There were eleven million people unemployed in 1938. He wanted to balance the budget and decrease government spending, but many economists urged the opposite: massive government spending. A special session of Congress failed, divided by the furor over an antilynching bill. Roosevelt simply could not afford to challenge Southern power brokers on the lynching bill, not even for beliefs he held dear or for people he knew were oppressed. By December the president was despondent.[6]

On December 7, 1937, events in China exploded. The Japanese invasion of China had continued throughout 1937. Newsreels graphically depicted the ruthless Japanese war on Chinese civilians. FDR was amazed at the success of "the German-Italian-Japanese combination," the "three bandit nations." Publicly he said little. His "quarantine" speech had been a bust. Japanese airplanes sank the USS *Panay*, a naval vessel anchored near Nanking that had sheltered American officials and citizens fleeing Japanese aggression. Two American flags, fourteen by eighteen feet in size, were painted on the deck, and the Japanese planes attacked survivors as they went ashore. This was no mistake by Japanese pilots. It was a test of American will, and America failed the test.[7]

Horrific events occurred fifteen miles away in Nanking, the capital of Nationalist China. While historians disagree about the number of those killed in "the rape of Nanking," all agree it was an atrocity on a monstrous scale. Chinese civilians were mowed down by machine guns, decapitated, used for bayonet practice, burned alive, and tortured. They were buried alive, disemboweled, nailed to wooden boards, frozen in icy ponds, ripped apart by vicious German shepherd dogs. Thousands of Chinese women were raped and murdered. Chinese soldiers were executed. Piles of corpses were left in full public view. The Yangtze River literally turned red with blood.

The Nanking outrage was described in the American press and contributed to American anti-Japanese sentiments. But Japanese countered press reports with effective propaganda, and many Americans believed the atrocity reports to be exaggerated. Most Americans were unconcerned with what the Japanese were doing to the Chinese. "The Rape of Nanking was front-page news across the world," historian Iris Chang concluded, "and yet most of the world stood by and did nothing while an entire city was butchered."[8]

Americans opposed war with Japan or even retaliation for the bombing of the *Panay*. Senator William Borah said he was "not prepared to vote to send our boys into the Orient because a boat was sunk that was traveling in a dangerous zone." The public's reaction dampened FDR's desire for a naval blockade. In the end, the *Panay* incident was resolved. The Japanese formally apologized. But their militarists learned that the United States was not about to start a war in the Pacific.[9]

Hitler, meanwhile, had long preached the unification of the German people into a single nation. His first step was *Anschluss*, the union of Germany and Austria in March 1938. The Austrian government was overthrown by a Nazi fifth column inside the country. "All [tank] drivers should be sure to wear goggles," Colonel Alfred Jodl jokingly told his officers. "Otherwise, they might be blinded by the flowers thrown at them." The Austrians were happier than the

Germans. They tossed flowers and chanted *"Ein Volk, ein Reich, ein Führer"* as Nazi troops marched into Vienna.

The *Anschluss* caught Roosevelt by surprise. Austrian Jews were suddenly under Hitler's thumb, and many fled, creating a major refugee problem. The abusive treatment of Austrian Jews, especially the aged Sigmund Freud, who lived in Vienna, shocked Americans. The Germans seized his passport and impounded his money while Nazi thugs raided his home at night. The Germans launched an orgy of violence against Jews. "It was," a British reporter wrote, "an indescribable witches' sabbath." Roosevelt was furious. Felix Frankfurter's beloved eighty-two-year-old uncle, Dr. Solomon Frankfurter, chief librarian at the University of Vienna, was sent to a concentration camp. He was released through the good offices of his nephew's British friend Lady Nancy Astor. While many Americans agreed with Senator Borah that the Nazi takeover was "not of the slightest moment" to the United States, reactions were, according to Saul Friedlander, sharper in Washington than in London or Paris."[10]

Like Roosevelt, Winston Churchill was one of the few people who realized the gravity of the situation. Chamberlain had foolishly rejected Roosevelt's counsel, and his appeasement policy drove Anthony Eden to resign as foreign secretary. "I must confess that my heart sank, and for a while the dark waters of despair overwhelmed me," Churchill wrote. "I . . . saw before me in mental gaze the vision of Death." *Anschluss* confirmed Churchill's worst fears. "The gravity of the events of the 11th of March cannot be exaggerated," he told the House of Commons. Many members, however, greeted Churchill's speech with derision.[11]

After the *Anschluss*, two Jewish congressmen from New York—Samuel Dickstein, chairman of the House Immigration Committee, and Emanuel Celler—tried to convince Congress to amend the immigration laws. Dickstein proposed that unused quotas be filled by refugees. Celler's proposal included a variety of exemptions for refugees and allowed the president to enlarge the quotas. The bills died. Despite Americans' disdain for German persecution, they were unwilling to open the floodgates of immigration. After the Évian Conference in July 1938, Celler introduced another bill, but abandoned it in the face of massive opposition. Dorothy Thompson, a liberal pro-immigration columnist and wife of Sinclair Lewis, said raising the issue of quotas was "political dynamite." Condemnation of aliens, one senator said in 1940, was "the best vote-getting argument in present-day politics." Numerous bills to end or greatly restrict immigration were introduced at each session. Senator Robert Reynolds of North Carolina, leader of the anti-immigration forces in Congress, introduced a bill in 1939 to reduce quotas by 90 percent, and it was given serious consideration.[12]

In March 1938 Roosevelt again responded to the plight of Jewish refugees. He ordered that full use of the German and Austrian quota could be made by Jewish immigrants. The political risk he took was significant. The great increase in Nazi oppression in 1938 coincided with the depths of the "Roosevelt Recession." Unemployment soared to between eight million and ten million. Restrictionists pointed out credible evidence that every refugee who entered the United States and found employment put an

American out of work. In response, Jewish-owned department stores issued public statements denying that they replaced native workers with Jewish immigrants.

Despite the unpopularity of helping Jewish refugees, Roosevelt persisted. Eleven days after the *Anschluss*, Roosevelt instructed Hull to invite friendly governments to join the United States in setting up a special committee to facilitate emigration from Austria and Germany. Two days later, on March 25, he announced that he was calling an international conference. "The announcement," Henry Feingold wrote, "must have confounded many people," given the political risk it entailed. American Jews were thankful. "Splendid," wrote Governor Lehman. "I only wish I could do more," replied FDR.[13]

The president's options were limited by American antisemitism and opposition to immigrants from Eastern Europe. Anti-Jewish propaganda was widely distributed, some of it secretly financed by the Germans. Media mogul William Randolph Hearst was feted by Hitler. The German-American Bund, active in states with large German American populations, was loudly pro-Nazi. While the great majority of German Americans rejected the Nazi message, a vociferous minority caused the administration a great deal of anxiety. William Dudley Pelley's Silver Shirts sold a million publications alleging that Jews controlled the federal government. Pelley's *Libertarian* magazine vilified FDR, the "Kosher New Deal," "communistic Jewish Reds," and published a regular feature titled "News Behind the Jews and Jews Behind the News." Father Coughlin had 3.5 million regular listeners to his radio program, and his magazine, *Social Justice*, reprinted long excerpts from *Protocols of the Elders of Zion*. Friends reminded Jewish groups that "latent racial and religious antagonism" could burst into flames. Anti-Jewish letters and telegrams to FDR fill bulging files at the Roosevelt Library.[14]

Herbert Feis, a high-ranking Jewish State Department specialist in international trade, went to work to aid Austrian Jewry. He suggested merging the Austrian and German quota, which FDR did, and streamlining the cumbersome affidavit process, but this met bureaucratic resistance. FDR himself raised the issue of helping Austrian Jewry at a cabinet meeting on March 18, 1937. "After all," Morgenthau quoted Roosevelt as saying, "America had been a place of refuge for so many fine Germans in the period of 1848 and why couldn't we offer them again a place of refuge at this time." Roosevelt asked the cabinet whether Congress would agree to increase the German quota. Garner replied that if Congress could vote by secret ballot it would end *all* immigration. Roosevelt later told Morgenthau and Sumner Welles, under secretary of state, that increasing the quotas was a political impossibility, but he would liberalize his own immigration procedures and ask South American countries to take in more refugees. FDR's use of the full German-Austrian quota was well in advance of American public opinion.[15]

The United States had no special responsibility to German or Austrian Jewry for the crisis created by Hitler. But FDR was concerned. He had been looking for ways to isolate the Nazi regime, and an international conference would highlight German barbarity even if it failed to solve the refugee crisis. The president called a thirty-two-nation conference for July 1938 in Évian, France. The idea originated in conversations among Roosevelt, Sumner Welles, George Messersmith, and Morgenthau. The idea of a presidential advisory committee on refugees also came out of these discussions. Benjamin V. Cohen, an administration lawyer, stated that even if the Évian Conference were a failure and negotiations with the Nazis came to nothing, the world would see the Germans as villains.[16]

Needless to say, the invitations were accompanied by a statement that "no country would be expected or asked to receive a greater number of immigrants than is permitted by its existing legislation." The president's call for the conference and combination of the Austrian-German quotas flew in the face of settled immigration policy and were vociferously criticized by the Veterans of Foreign Wars (which called for an end to *all* immigration), the American Coalition of Patriotic Societies ("stop the leak" they said, "before it becomes a flood"), and several Catholic newspapers. Members of Congress denounced the conference. Representative Thomas A. Jenkins said that Roosevelt had gone "on a visionary excursion. . . . He forgets the cold winds of poverty and penury that are sweeping over the 'one-third' of our people who are ill clothed, ill housed, ill fed."[17] Two-thirds of the American people disagreed with Roosevelt's actions. Americans disliked Hitler's policies, but 72 percent remained opposed to allowing more German Jews to immigrate. "Don't we have enough of that [Jewish] scum here already?" one letter writer asked the president. Jews were well aware of the impossibility of changing the immigration laws and discouraged agitation to increase the quotas lest an irate Congress curtail immigration altogether. Despite the laws, the United States was already accepting more Jewish refugees by far than any other country in the world.[18]

A formal statement by Myron C. Taylor, a Roosevelt friend and former chairman of U.S. Steel, to the Évian Conference reviewed the history of immigration and placed the blame for the current situation—forced migration, the uprooting of men and women of every race and creed from their long-established homes—squarely on Germany. "We must admit frankly, indeed, that this problem of political refugees is so vast and complex," he continued, "that this meeting could only begin a process to ameliorate the conditions of the unfortunate human beings caught up in it." He chided Germany for its "disregard of elementary human rights" and "accepted standards of civilization."[19]

In April 1938, contrary to the advice of the State Department, Roosevelt formed the President's Advisory Committee on Political Refugees (PACPR) to be a liaison between private refugee agencies and the international body he hoped would emerge from the Évian Conference. He asked a distinguished group to serve on the PACPR, including several Jews: Paul Baerwald, chair of the prestigious rescue agency American Jewish Joint Distribution Committee or the "Joint," Henry Morgenthau Jr., Bernard Baruch, and Rabbi Wise. The president prevailed upon Myron Taylor to serve as the chief American representative at the Évian Conference in July. Hitler was pleased with the concept of other countries taking in Jews. "We are ready to put all these criminals at the disposal of these countries . . . even on luxury ships," he said with a sneer.[20]

The Évian Conference accomplished little of substance, although Roosevelt did succeed in putting the Jewish refugee question on the international agenda and putting the spotlight on Germany's inhumane policies. The President of the United States at least had recognized that a solution must be found. American representatives pointed out that the United States took in more than twenty-five thousand German refugees a year under the existing quota and that if there were an orderly exodus of Jews from Germany, the United States would do its fair share. The conference established a permanent body, the Intergovernmental Committee on Refugees (IGCR), to seek opportunities for resettlement and, as Roosevelt saw it, as a way to aid Jews escaping Nazi Germany. It was a rational reaction to what later turned out to be an irrational situation. "Roosevelt," Friedman wrote, "could not conceal his disappointment." No nation was willing to accept unpopular and impoverished Jewish refugees whose assets had been looted by Germany and who would compete with native-born citizens for jobs. Palestine was excluded by Great Britain because the British were pro-Arab and nervous about an Arab uprising and their oil supply. Taylor had asked the various governments to "act and act promptly." "Most government representatives acted promptly," *Newsweek* concluded, "by slamming their doors against Jewish refugees." FDR's ability to influence foreign governments in 1938, it turned out, was extremely limited.[21]

Taylor nevertheless believed that a start had been made and concluded the conference on an optimistic note. Goldie Meyerson (later Golda Meir) publicly hoped she would live long enough for the Jewish people not to need any more expressions of sympathy. Ira Hirschmann criticized Évian as a "facade behind which the civilized governments could hide their inability to act." In retrospect, Évian highlighted the dilemma later faced by the democracies. No one then realized the lengths to which the Nazis would go. Both Romania and Poland sent observers to discover ways by which they could imitate Germany by ejecting their large Jewish populations and expropriating their property. There was no consensus on what to do among twenty-one Jewish rescue organizations present at the conference. One Jewish publication called Évian a "spectacle of Jewish discord and disruption."[22]

Most countries did nothing after Évian. Latin American countries even further restricted immigration. George Rublee criticized the "indifference of the participating governments" and said that except for the United States and Great Britain, "doors have been systematically closed everywhere."[23] Latin American nations feared German retaliation, their own German-speaking minorities, the loss of lucrative trade agreements with Germany, prejudice against Jews, and an influx of Jewish businessmen.

Many Jews were disillusioned with the conference. Some believed it actually hurt Jews in Poland and Romania. Polish diplomats hinted at pogroms if they would speed up Jewish emigration. The State Department continued to support restrictive U.S. immigration laws. Congressman Celler described the consular service as having "a heartbeat muffled in protocol." The Nazis were delighted. "We are saying openly that we do not want the Jews," one German newspaper gloated, "while the democracies keep on claiming that they are willing to receive them—and then leave the guests out in the cold! Aren't we savages better men after all?"[24]

As the "Roosevelt Recession" continued into 1938, the president's popularity declined. In an era of fascist dictatorships, the growing power of the federal government worried many Americans. "The next two years really don't count," a dejected Roosevelt told Morgenthau, "they are over the dam." Roosevelt felt he would be out of office in 1940 but might make a comeback, as Grover Cleveland had done. He was detested by the rich and beloved by the poor, the blacks, the Jews, labor unions, the unemployed, and many others. "It takes a hungry man to appreciate Roosevelt," a Washington cabdriver said. "All the passengers in the parlor cars are against you," a Pullman car porter reported to Roosevelt, "all the passengers in the day coaches are for you—and our train has two parlor cars and nine day coaches."[25]

Congress was in revolt. Ickes thought the president "a beaten man." "Who does Roosevelt think he is?" Senator Burton K. Wheeler asked a White House aide. "He's like a king trying to reduce the barons" of Capitol Hill. Most representatives and a majority of senators came from safe districts. They did not owe their seats to FDR, nor did he cultivate the rank and file. Many perceived this as arrogance. Chairmen of powerful committees could defeat the president's initiatives, and some delighted in doing so. Despite the admonition "For God's sake, don't send us any more controversial legislation!," the president fought for reform measures. He wrangled a watered-down wages and hour bill from a reluctant Congress. This law was "the last of Roosevelt's basic New Deal measures to pass Congress," Burns observed.[26]

Roosevelt suffered more indignities. His plan to reorganize the executive department, a "good government" measure formulated by public administration experts, was defeated. His enemies and a public wary of dictators assembled a coalition to defeat even this modest proposal. The president was forced to state that he had "no inclination to be a dictator." He had "none of the qualifications which would make me a successful dictator" and "too much historical background and too much knowledge of existing dictatorships" to want to become one. He tried to compromise but lost on a 204 to 196 vote in the House as his opponents cheered. "The old Roosevelt magic has lost its kick," General Hugh S. Johnson, Roosevelt's onetime director of the National Recovery Administration and now a fiery anti–New Deal columnist, exclaimed.[27]

The president's next 1938 indignity was his failure to rid himself of the conservatives in his own party. For Roosevelt to embark on a purge of conservative Democrats was a sign of desperation. The president wanted the party to support his liberal agenda and was angry at those who had opposed his Supreme Court plan. He therefore set out to defeat nine of twenty-nine Democrats seeking reelection. These men included Walter George of Georgia; Ellison D. "Cotton Ed" Smith of South Carolina; Guy Gillette of Iowa; Millard Tydings of Maryland; and John J. O'Connor of New York, chairman of the House Rules Committee. "Roosevelt Declares War on Party Rebels," the newspapers exclaimed. FDR especially detested Tydings, who ran "with the Roosevelt prestige and the money of his conservative Republican friends both on his side."

He pressed his friend Breckinridge Long, a wealthy Maryland Democrat, to raise money for Tydings' opponent.[28]

Upset by the drama of the SS *St. Louis* incident (to be discussed in chapter 5), Morgenthau brought up the issue of refugees with FDR on June 19, 1939. "Now, Mr. President," he said, "a year has passed and we have not got anywhere on this Jewish refugee thing. What are we going to do about it?" Roosevelt thought quite a while. "I know we have not," he said. Even Sam Rosenman "has got his eyes open that it isn't so easy. The whole trouble is England." Roosevelt told Morgenthau he had talked to the president of Paraguay about taking five thousand Jews and that he could not

Franklin D. Roosevelt with Eleanor Roosevelt, Marguerite LeHand, Grace Tully, Mrs. Rosenman, Samuel Rosenman, and Rosenman's son.

Courtesy of the Franklin D. Roosevelt Library

"make any headway." Then he suggested that if Morgenthau would give him a list "of the thousand richest Jews in the United States I am willing to tell them how much they should give and "even call it the Roosevelt Plan." Morgenthau reminded Roosevelt that before he talked about money, he must have a plan. He then said, "If you don't mind, I would like to keep after you." "I don't mind at all," Roosevelt replied. Morgenthau noted in his diary that Roosevelt "is really tremendously interested. The great trouble is there is nobody who is following him on the program."[29]

From Roosevelt's perspective, Jewish Americans were divided on what to do about European Jewry. His analysis would have placed Jewish voters in a category of ethnic blocs that, like the Irish, Poles, and Italians, had an attachment to their people abroad but were Americans first. They would not fault him for acting in America's national interest as long as the national interest was clear. Jewish Americans, he knew, came in many varieties. He was well aware that the Morgenthaus, Sulzbergers, Lehmans, and Proskauers believed in accommodation and assimilation. Zionism was an unpleasant issue for them. They wanted to be and were "100 percent Americans." He also knew that Rabbi Wise and members of the American Jewish Congress held different views; that Eastern European Jews would hold rallies, stage boycotts, and speak out publicly. Roosevelt also knew that neither he nor the State Department nor any Jewish organization had any plan likely to free German Jewry from Hitler's grip. He heard a variety of suggestions from different Jewish groups, friends, and advisers and was anxious to help. In the early 1930s, the AJ Committee and

American Jews of German ancestry, respecting the wishes of German Jews themselves, counseled against public demonstrations. Rabbi Wise and the AJ Congress went ahead with denunciations of the Hitler regime, rallies, and a boycott.

Roosevelt counted on Jewish votes in the House of Representatives. There, the same spectrum of Jewish opinion appeared. Representative Sol Bloom, chairman of the House Foreign Affairs Committee, was an accommodationist and cooperated with the State Department's cautious approach. Emanuel Celler, congressman from Brooklyn, urged a more proactive policy. Samuel Dickstein, congressman from the Lower East Side and chairman of the House Committee on Immigration, was somewhere between Bloom and Celler. According to Breitman and Kraut, all of the Jews in Congress (there were ten in the first session of the Seventy-fifth Congress and six in the second) "walked a tightrope on issues of concern to Jews, lest they be vulnerable to the charge of using their positions to advance Jewish causes at the expense of the national interest."[30] After the *Anschluss*, Celler and Dickstein proposed resolutions urging unrestricted immigration for victims of religious and political persecution. The major Jewish organizations, including the AJ Committee, the AJ Congress, and the National Council of Jewish Women, opposed these efforts for fear of an antisemitic backlash and cooperated with the State Department in pressuring the congressmen to abandon their efforts.[31]

Roosevelt, like the American Jewish leadership, undoubtedly felt that he had done the best he could with the tools he had been given. And, indeed, much had been done by the democracies. By the

71

end of 1939, 126,000 Austrian Jews of a total of 185,000 had emigrated. Twenty-six thousand Czechs escaped between April and
September 1939. The United States under Roosevelt had done its
part in this remarkable humanitarian shift in populations. "In both
1938–39 and 1939–40," Rubinstein concludes, "Jews comprised
more than one-half of *all* immigrants admitted to the United States
. . . and were the largest single group identified by the Immigration
Department in every year from 1936–37 until 1941–42."[32]

The congressional midterm election of 1938 was a disaster for
FDR. Despite a few successes (O'Connor was defeated), his purge
failed. Walter George and Millard Tydings won by large margins.
Smith won in South Carolina. Race played a prominent role. "You
ask any nigger on the street who's the greatest man in the world,"
one white Georgia Democrat said, "nine out of ten will tell you
Franklin D. Roosevelt." George called FDR's opposition to him
the "second march through Georgia." The number of Republicans
in the House almost doubled, from 88 to 170. Republicans won 12
governorships. In New York, Lehman barely defeated Thomas E.
Dewey. When asked if Roosevelt were not his own worst enemy,
"Cotton Ed" Smith quipped bitterly, "Not as long as I am alive."[33]

Chapter 4

"I Myself Could Scarcely Believe That Such Things Could Occur"

Despite his travails in 1938, Roosevelt was concerned about Jewish Americans and saving European Jewry. When the AJ Congress proposed to hold a referendum of all American Jews on the issue of who should speak for American Jewry, the AJ Committee assailed the Congress as giving ammunition to Hitler. "So there *was* an international Jewish conspiracy after all," antisemites would say. Rosenman told Wise that "the Chief" said "the whole thing is loaded with dynamite." "Won't this enable Americans to say that the fellows who wrote the *Protocols of the Elders of Zion* had some justification?" Roosevelt asked Rosenman.[1]

In October 1938 FDR tried to secure Neville Chamberlain's help on the Jewish refugee crisis. He wrote the prime minister that the IGCR had avoided an emotional approach to the problem and that, "while it may be too much to expect an early change in the basic racial policy of the German Government," the Germans ought to assist other governments by permitting orderly emigration and allowing Jews to take with them a reasonable percentage of their property. He urged Chamberlain to explain to Hitler that "the present German policy of racial persecution" had done more harm than any other to the estimate of Germany held by Americans. Chamberlain, the man who had so misjudged Hitler, also misjudged Roosevelt. He refused Roosevelt's request.[2]

Hitler set his sights on Czechoslovakia. Three million ethnic Germans lived in the westernmost section of Czechoslovakia known as the Sudetenland. They had been made part of Czechoslovakia when that nation was created in the aftermath of World War I. Many German Czechs wanted to be part of the Fatherland, and Hitler used their aspirations to create a warlike atmosphere to demand "justice" for the Sudeten Germans. Neither the British, the French, nor the Russians wanted a war with Germany. Chamberlain effected a compromise in which Czechoslovakia surrendered the Sudetenland. The infamous bargain was sealed at Munich on September 29, 1938. Chamberlain returned to London bringing, he said, "peace with honor. I believe it is peace for our time." Nazi troops marched into the Sudetenland while FDR battled to defeat Senator Millard Tydings in Maryland.

FDR had always had misgivings about appeasement. "We cannot stop the spread of Fascism," he told Ambassador Anthony Biddle, "unless world opinion realizes its ultimate dangers." He privately compared the "outrage" committed by Britain and France against the Czechs with Judas Iscariot's betrayal. Yet he diplomatically cabled "Good man" to Chamberlain. He realized Britain was too weak to stand up to Hitler alone. Churchill said, "we have sustained a total and unmitigated defeat." Roosevelt began meeting with Hull, William Bullitt, Biddle, and Welles to develop a strategy to meet emerging danger. As David M. Kennedy wrote, "the American president was a powerless spectator at Munich, a weak and resourceless leader of an unarmed, economically wounded, and diplomatically isolated country." But Roosevelt told his son Elliott, "Sooner or later there'll be a showdown in Europe." He knew he had to stop Hitler.[3]

Even before Munich the president had arranged for greater production of arms and had secretly aided the British and the French. Roosevelt's policy was to deter Hitler through an enormous production of armaments and airplanes. In November he ordered the manufacture of ten thousand combat aircraft a year at a time when the air corps had nine hundred planes. He secretly ordered Bullitt in France and Biddle in Poland to quietly urge resistance to Hitler's aggression in the face of Chamberlain's appeasement policy.[4]

The 1938 elections were barely over when the Nazis staged Germany's first modern pogrom. On the night of November 9, 1938, ostensibly in retaliation for the killing of a Nazi diplomat in France by a young Jew, Herschel Grynszpan, well-orchestrated anti-Jewish riots spread across Germany. Nazi storm troopers, the SA, the SS, and antisemitic mobs smashed, looted, and burned Jewish businesses, homes, and most of Germany's synagogues. Thousands of Jews were arrested and sent to concentration camps. The event was later called *Kristallnacht*, the Night of Broken Glass. Austrian Nazis joined in, burning all twenty-one of Vienna's synagogues.[5]

After *Kristallnacht* the Nazi regime assessed an "atonement fine" against all German Jews of a billion Reichsmarks for the damage done, closed all Jewish retail businesses, and announced the liquidation of real estate, securities, and industrial firms owned by Jews. The "civilized world," a British diplomat observed, "is faced with the appalling sight of 500,000 people about to rot away in starvation." It was now clear to the whole world that the Jews of Germany could no longer live in their own country.[6]

Americans were outraged. Across the political spectrum, from John L. Lewis to Herbert Hoover, Americans denounced the Nazis. Even the notorious antisemite Henry Ford publicly criticized the Nazis. American public opinion, the German ambassador wired Berlin, "is without exception incensed against Germany." Assistant Secretary of State George Messersmith sent a memo to Hull strongly recommending that this "irresponsible and mad act" be condemned. Roosevelt called the American ambassador to Germany home for "report and consultation" and said, "the news of the past few days from Germany has deeply shocked public opinion in the United States. . . . I myself could scarcely believe that such things could occur in a twentieth-century civilization." No U.S. ambassador returned to Germany until the Nazis were overthrown. After *Kristallnacht*, it was clear that Roosevelt was the Nazis' "Enemy of Peace Number One."[7]

Roosevelt was the only important world leader to criticize Germany. Chamberlain did not want to upset his delicate peace and equated the pogrom with "the senseless crime committed in Paris," the killing of the German diplomat. French leaders were silent.

When Ickes denounced Hitler as "a brutal dictator who . . . is robbing and torturing thousands of fellow human beings," the German chargé sent a protest. The State Department refused to accept it. According to two leading historians of *Kristallnacht*, withdrawing the American ambassador "was a dramatic move that could not be misread by the German government. It was one step from breaking off relations with Germany." The Nazis believed Roosevelt was controlled by the Jews. He "seemed to me," Ribbentrop told one diplomat, "to be strongly influenced by Jews." Roosevelt took the pogrom as a personal affront, even a threat to his Jewish friends. Why, he asked Rosenman, did not some Jew assassinate Hitler?[8]

Roosevelt denigrators give him no praise for his reaction to *Kristallnacht*. "The symbolic withdrawal of Ambassador Wilson and the president's brief verbal chastisement of Germany," Arthur Morse whined, "comprised the total American response to the *Kristallnacht*." Others called Roosevelt's action a mere gesture. It was, however, a great deal more than the response of any other nation and an important diplomatic statement. There was nothing else Roosevelt could do except sever diplomatic relations with Germany. A PBS documentary, *America and the Holocaust: Deceit and Indifference*, shows the viewer a Jewish leader thanking Roosevelt: "You spoke alone among the world leaders."[9]

Kristallnacht shocked both Franklin and Eleanor Roosevelt. "This German-Jewish business makes me sick," ER wrote to Lorena Hickok on November 14. On December 6 she made an appeal for funds to settle Jewish refugees in Palestine. She bypassed the State

Department and worked, at times covertly, to help Jewish refugees. FDR asked Isaiah Bowman, president of Johns Hopkins University and a renowned geographer, to find places where Jews could live. For two years Bowman and a State Department team studied the problem. Sumner Welles suggested appropriating the Baja peninsula of Mexico for a Jewish homeland in exchange for a settlement of a United States–Mexican oil controversy. Henry Morgenthau encouraged FDR but pointed out the difficulties inherent in his chief's grandiose visions. "The world," Chaim Weizmann observed, "is divided into two groups of nations, those which want to expel Jews and those which do not want to receive them."[10]

Roosevelt sought Brandeis's advice. Both Frankfurter and Brandeis urged Roosevelt to pressure the British on Palestine. "Visibly shaken," Howard Sachar wrote, "Roosevelt informed [Brandeis] that he had just asked the British ambassador 'to help open the doors of Palestine.'" He had a plan to relocate one hundred thousand Jewish families to Palestine, but neither the British nor the Arabs would budge. Roosevelt then announced on November 18 that twelve thousand to fifteen thousand visitors' visas for German Jewish refugees would be extended. "The gesture," Breitman and Kraut noted, "was a significant bending of immigration regulations." Roosevelt also ordered Myron Taylor to London to press serious negotiations with the Germans and issued instructions allowing Taylor to bypass Ambassador Joseph P. Kennedy, who was unfriendly to Jewish immigration.[11]

It was clear to Roosevelt that war between Great Britain and Germany was likely. He sent a secret reassuring message to

Chamberlain and decided against making a public statement at that time about Jews. He realized that it was far more important to persuade the American public that the survival of Great Britain was paramount. Rosenman and Messersmith agreed. "There are things in the world today which are of even greater importance than the refugee problem," Messersmith wrote a fellow diplomat. A Gallup poll indicated that 94 percent of Americans disliked Hitler's treatment of German Jews, but 77 percent opposed allowing Jewish exiles into the United States. Nevertheless, the State Department made some administrative changes which eased entry into the country.[12]

By January 1939 Roosevelt was convinced that America's security was threatened by events in Europe. He had already ordered the military to prepare plans in the event of a violation of the Monroe Doctrine. He had sent William Bullitt on a secret mission to shore up the alliance against Hitler. "All about us," he told the nation in his State of the Union speech, "rage undeclared wars—military and economic. All about us are threats of new aggression." He urged his countrymen to prepare. He began a long and difficult campaign to educate Americans that a war against Nazism was a war to save religion, freedom, and democracy. But he knew the country would not yet follow him. When an American bomber aircraft crashed in California and the body of a French official was found in the wreckage, isolationists professed outrage.[13]

In an attempt to bring the Senate leadership into his confidence, Roosevelt invited members of the Military Affairs Committee to an off-the-record meeting where he tried to convince them that Germany, Italy, and Japan were attempting to dominate the world. His description of Hitler was vivid:

> But if this wild man . . . who conceives himself to be, as [Kurt von] Schuschnigg [the former Austrian chancellor] said after the famous visit to Berchtesgaden, he said that Hitler, walking up and down the room for about eight hours, pounding the table and making speeches, only mentioned two people in his entire conversation, one was Julius Caesar and the other was Jesus Christ. He kept on talking about these people in such manner as to indicate that he believes himself to be a reincarnation of Julius Caesar and Jesus Christ. What can we do about a personality like that? We would call him a "nut." Now if he insists on going ahead to the westward . . . and the French and the British . . . decide to fight, then you come to a question of arms. . . . It is a fifty-fifty bet that they would be put out of business and that Hitler and Mussolini would win. . . . Then the next step, which Brother Hitler suggested in the speech yesterday, would be Central and South America. . . . Those are things you ought to regard. . . . Do not say it is chimerical; do not say it is just a pipe dream. Would any of you have said six years ago . . . that Germany would dominate Europe? . . . This is the gradual encirclement of the United States by the removal of our first lines of defense.

The president said, in confidence, that war was imminent and that the safety of the Rhine frontier was America's business. One senator leaked to the press that FDR had said, "our frontier is on the Rhine," which Roosevelt vehemently denied. "Some boob got that off," he quipped.[14]

The president, it appeared, could not even have a confidential meeting with the Senate leadership. Republican senator Hiram Johnson of California, a liberal Republican, had said Roosevelt "wanted . . . to knock down two dictators in Europe, so that one may be firmly implanted in America." The State Department was staffed by cautious men such as Hull, whom FDR had appointed for political reasons. It was riddled with "Old School" antisemites, some of whom, at this time, sympathized with the Nazis. Ambassador Joseph Kennedy said the "Jew media" wanted to "set a match to the fuse of the world." Roosevelt, according to Gillman, "was never again so candid in discussing military strategy" with Congress. Thereafter, he gave Biddle and Bullitt assignments he could not entrust to the State Department, and to Morgenthau tasks he could not entrust to the War Department. In 1939 Secretary of the Treasury Morgenthau arranged for the French and the British to procure modern military aircraft.[15]

In February 1939 Roosevelt was fed up with Chamberlain's indecision. He wrote his old Harvard history professor that he wished the British would "stop this 'We who are about to die, salute thee' attitude. . . . What the British need today is a good stiff grog." On the Ides of March 1939 Hitler invaded the remnant of Czechoslovakia. Why, Chamberlain whined, should England risk war for "a far-away country of which we know very little?" Chaim Weizmann wondered if this was the way the Czechs were treated, what could the Jews expect? Japan was on the move in the Pacific. Generalissimo Francisco Franco marched into Madrid, and Benito Mussolini marched into Albania. Great Britain guaranteed Polish independence. Roosevelt was shaken. "Never in my life have I seen things moving in the world with more cross currents or greater velocity," he wrote a friend. He realized neutrality had been a mistake and that U.S. negligence had played a role in Franco's victory in Spain. He publicly expressed his disapproval of German aggression and went to work to repeal neutrality laws. Tentatively and discreetly, he assumed leadership of an international anti-Nazi coalition.[16]

On April 15, 1939, Roosevelt sent a telegram to Hitler and Mussolini asking them bluntly, "Are you willing to give assurances that your armed forces will not attack or invade the territory of the following independent nations?" FDR listed thirty-one countries, including Poland, France, Russia, Britain, and Palestine. He asked for a commitment that none of the countries would be invaded for twenty-five years. His efforts were met with ridicule. Hermann Göring thought "Roosevelt was suffering from an incipient mental disease," and Mussolini said the message was the "result of infantile paralysis."

On April 28, in the longest speech of his life, Adolf Hitler mocked Franklin Roosevelt. For two hours, in a speech filled with sarcasm and invective, the Führer pointed out that Americans talked about resolving problems at the council table but repudiated the League of Nations, that the western United States had been occupied by force, that none of Roosevelt's thirty-one countries asked for his help and instead had told the German government that they did not feel threatened by Germany. Hitler gave FDR sarcastic assurances that Germany did not intend to invade the United States. "The paunchy deputies rocked with raucous laughter," William L. Shirer recalled, "as the Fuhrer uttered with increasing effect his seemingly endless ridicule of the American President." Isolationist senators were ecstatic. "He asked for it," Senator Nye said.[17]

By early 1939 the only two men Hitler feared were Winston Churchill and Franklin Roosevelt. Roosevelt was educating the American people by putting "the bee on Germany." In May the ever-alert German chargé Hans Thomsen warned that FDR had a "pathological hatred for the leaders of Germany and Italy" and would "personally . . . endeavor to come to the aid of our opponents" by "creating the conditions" for America's entry into the war. The president's European policy from spring 1939, Robert Herzstein wrote, "was predicated upon a commitment to destroying Hitler and all his works." The Führer, one journalist concluded in 1939, "must clearly understand that President Roosevelt is his most dangerous opponent."[18]

After the horror of *Kristallnacht*, an interdenominational group of social workers, jurists, and other activists, including Rabbi Wise's daughter Justine Polier, a juvenile court judge in New York, came up with an idea to allow twenty thousand child refugees from Germany to enter the United States outside of the quota. The Non-Sectarian Committee for German Refugee Children was organized. Judge Polier conferred with ER who, in turn, asked FDR how to proceed. "Franklin gave the bill the green light," according to Joseph P. Lash. "My husband says that you had better go to work at once and get two people of opposite parties in the House and Senate" to sponsor the bill, ER wrote Polier on January 4, 1939. He advises that "you choose your people rather carefully and, if possible, get all the Catholic support you can." The State Department would not interfere if Congress acted. As a consequence, and following FDR's political advice, Democratic senator Robert F. Wagner of New York and Republican Edith Rogers of Massachusetts introduced a bill that would have allowed an additional twenty thousand German refugee children to come to the United States. This was the first serious effort in fourteen years to amend the immigration laws.[19]

The Wagner-Rogers bill had support from clergy, labor leaders, prominent New Dealers in the administration such as Secretary of Labor Frances Perkins, Governor Lehman of New York, and other prominent Jews. Southern educators such as Frank Porter Graham, president of the University of North Carolina, well-known individuals such as Herbert Hoover, and others publicly endorsed the bill. Jewish organizations were afraid to support it vigorously because they believed it would not help the situation for Jews to plead for special treatment for their coreligionists. For strategic reasons, Rabbi Wise tried to steer a middle course. "After all," he told a congressional committee, "we cannot take care of all of them. Germany has a population of five or six hundred thousand Jews." Leading the forces against the bill were the American Legion, with one million members, the American Coalition of Patriotic Societies (representing 115 organizations totaling 2.5 million members), and the Junior Order United American Mechanics.[20]

Nativism and prejudice against Jews played a major role in defeating the Wagner-Rogers bill. The "subtle and effective argument," the *Nation* opined, "is the *sotto voce* contention that this is a Jewish bill." The president of the United Daughters of 1812 explicitly based her opposition on the children being Jewish. Laura Delano, FDR's first cousin and wife of the immigration commissioner, said that "twenty thousand charming children would all too soon grow into twenty thousand ugly adults." The Depression also played a role. The poor children of America should be helped first; the bill would break up families; it was the first wedge in opening immigration to all; the bill was backed by foreigners and Communists. Two-thirds of Americans opposed the measure, according to one poll. The bill was amended to death and its sponsors abandoned the fight.[21]

The Roosevelt administration was divided over the bill. In fact, the Jewish community had been divided. Opinion polls in the late 1930s showed that half of all Americans had a low opinion of Jews. Thirty-five percent believed that European Jews were responsible for their own oppression. Seventy-seven percent said "no" to the question "Should we allow a larger number of Jewish exiles from Germany come to the United States to live?" Eighty-three percent of all Americans opposed increasing quotas. "With his personal popularity already at an all-time low," Friedman concluded, "Roosevelt could only have suffered politically" from a fight for the Wagner-Rogers bill.[22]

More importantly, Roosevelt was secretly developing a coalition to obliterate Nazism from the face of the Earth. He was, at that very moment, at work revising the Neutrality Act to arm Hitler's opponents. He could not allow his sympathy for Jewish refugees to interfere with this critical task. As Robert Dallek pointed out, "A fight on the Wagner-Rogers bill would have crippled his main objective." His strongest allies in his war against Hitler were Southern Democrats, and they were the most vocal opponents of liberalizing the immigration laws. Southern congressmen had voted 127 to 0 for the restrictive Johnson Immigration Act of 1924, but Southern House members voted 106 to 3 to revise the neutrality laws in 1939. Roosevelt needed this Southern bloc to fight Hitler, and dared not alienate them by supporting a liberalization of the immigration laws.[23]

Frances Perkins, Ben Cohen, and Harold Ickes supported the Wagner-Rogers bill. The State Department opposed it. According to Monty N. Penkower, *Kristallnacht* "galvanized Mrs. Roosevelt into action." She privately backed the Wagner-Rogers bill, meeting with Ben Cohen, Rabbi Wise, and Clarence Pickett of the American Friends Service Committee to discuss strategy. She said a kind word about the bill at a press conference. She committed herself to help Jewish refugees. FDR himself took no further action, although, according to ER, he "was anxious to see the bill go through." Wise understood the political difficulties and kept a low profile. Rosenman, a member of the AJ Committee, wrote Myron Taylor: "I do not believe it either *desirable* or *practicable* to recommend any change in the quota provision of our immigration law." On December 5, 1938, Rosenman sent a memo to FDR warning him that allowing more refugees into the country would "create a Jewish problem in the U.S." On February 22, 1939, ER confidentially telegraphed FDR at sea. "Are you willing I should talk to Sumner [Welles] and say that we approve passage of Child's Refugee Bill?" On February 28, 1939, ER wrote to Judge Polier explaining that if FDR came out for the bill and "was defeated it would be very bad" and that the bill might cause opponents to cut the quota by 90 percent "and that, of course, would be very serious."[24]

Roosevelt critics have used the Wagner-Rogers bill to demonstrate FDR's alleged indifference toward Jewish refugees. In the PBS documentary *America and the Holocaust: Deceit and Indifference*, viewers were told that when FDR was asked to support the Wagner-Rogers bill, he responded with the words "File no Action" on a memo. However, in reality, Roosevelt not only favored the bill but also was involved in the strategy to enact it. The bill was clearly destined for defeat, and people of goodwill such as Welles and James G. McDonald, chairman of the PACPR, thought the president's support might backfire and cause Congress to *reduce* the quotas. One Roosevelt critic acknowledged that it was politically impossible for FDR to publicly support the Wagner-Rogers bill, yet criticized him for abdicating "his leadership role."[25] David Wyman, another critic, blamed the Roosevelt administration for failing to support the bill, although members of the administration *did* support the bill. He blamed Roosevelt for his "impartial silence" and related the "File No Action FDR" story. FDR's memo was in response to a request from Representative Caroline O'Day of New York asking the president to give his view of the bill. But Wyman omitted the rest of the story, namely FDR's advice to Rabbi Wise's daughter Judge Justine Polier and the political context in which the bill arose.[26]

Father Charles E. Coughlin, the "Radio Priest," was at the height of his career as a right-wing, antisemitic rabble-rouser. He attacked Jews as both Communists and capitalists, moneylenders and crooks. He blamed the Jews for foisting communism on Russia and for the suffering of the German people. Nazism, he said, was "a political defense mechanism" against the Jewish invention of communism. Winter 1938 saw the rapid growth of Coughlin's Christian Front. Chapters sprung up in New York, Boston, Philadelphia, Baltimore, Chicago, and Detroit, cities where most American Jews lived.[27]

Speakers on Coughlin's radio program urged their followers to "liquidate the Jews in America." Jews were ridiculed as warmongers. FDR was called "Rosenfelt" or "Rosenvelt" or other Jewish names. Hitler was "the savior of Europe." It was as vicious an antisemitic movement as America has ever seen. Christian Fronters, like their Nazi role models, picketed Jewish businesses, desecrated synagogues, and attacked Jews on the streets of New York and Boston where, Leonard Dinnerstein wrote, "sympathetic policemen of Irish background allowed the outrages to continue." The German-American Bund held a "patriotic" rally at Madison Square Garden on George Washington's birthday, February 22, 1939, where thousands of American Nazis cheered and saluted speakers who denounced Jews, Communists, Roosevelt, Morgenthau, Baruch, and Lippmann. Aping German Nazis, George Froboese called for a "Jew-free America." Fritz Kuhn, the portly American Bundesführer, blamed the Jews for FDR's "warmongering."[28]

Brazen antisemites in the House and Senate denounced Jews. Representative Louis McFadden of Pennsylvania denounced the "Jew-controlled New Deal," and Senator Robert Reynolds of North Carolina contended that the Jews would not have been forced out of Europe if they "had not impoverished those lands . . . or . . . had not conspired against their governments."[29]

Supreme Court justice Benjamin Cardozo died in July 1938. Despite the upsurge in antisemitism, the drubbing he took in the November election, and American xenophobia, Roosevelt nominated his friend Felix Frankfurter to the vacant Supreme Court seat. Some prominent Jews, including Arthur Sulzberger, publisher of the *New York Times*, thought it unwise to nominate a second Jew to the Court (Brandeis was still serving), and they let the president know their opinions. Frankfurter's name, *Time* magazine charged, had "come to symbolize Jewish radicalism in the New Deal." But Roosevelt disagreed. He wrote Judge Julian W. Mack:

I feel it is peculiarly important—just because of the waves of persecution and discrimination which are mounting in other parts of the world—that we in this country make it clear that citizens of the United States

> *are elected or selected for positions of responsibility*
> *solely because of their qualifications, experience, and*
> *character, and without regard to their religious faith.*

Frankfurter was confirmed by the Senate and became the third Jew to serve as a U.S. Supreme Court justice. During the confirmation hearings, Hitler was destroying the Austrian Jewish community from which Frankfurter had sprung.[30]

Chapter 5

"Our Gratitude Is as Immense as the Ocean:" The Voyage of the SS St. Louis

On May 27, 1939, the SS *St. Louis* arrived in Havana Harbor with 936 European Jews seeking asylum. The passengers believed they would find temporary haven in Cuba and, like tens of thousands of German Jews before them, would ultimately immigrate to the United States. Cuba had previously welcomed Jewish refugees: 1,500 in 1938 alone. But the political situation in Cuba had changed dramatically in the few months prior to May 1939. A new immigration law enacted in a political battle between President Laredo Brú and Manuel Benitez Gonzalez, the corrupt director-general of immigration, caught the *St. Louis* passengers in a vexing web of local politics and international diplomacy.

The Jewish population of Cuba exceeded six thousand and was located conspicuously in Havana. Cuba's economy was depressed; businessmen and labor unions complained about competition from aliens, especially Jews. "Cuba is not all rum and rumba," one writer noted; "all the worries of the world can be found here in miniature." The German embassy in Havana, a native Cuban Nazi Party, provocateurs sent by Germany, and local antisemites had begun agitating to ban Jews. The pro-Nazi editor of Havana's oldest daily newspaper, *Diario de la Marina*, claimed that they were Communists.[1]

Many Cubans thought that their country was being overrun by Jewish refugees. Instead of immigration leveling off at 1,500 a year, 500 refugees were coming in the early months of 1939. To make matters worse, two other refugee ships, the British *Orduna* and the French *Flanders*, arrived in Havana at the same time as the *St. Louis*. Within a twenty-four-hour period more than 1,200 refugees arrived from three European ports. The Cubans allowed forty-eight refugees with proper visas to disembark from the *Orduna* and thirty-two refugees from the *Flanders*. This coincidence exacerbated Cubans' apprehensions that they were being overwhelmed. Protected by military strongman Colonel Fulgencio Batista, Manuel Benitez had become wealthy from bribes. According to conflicting reports, officials in the Cuban government wanted either to end the corruption or a cut of the illegal money. Benitez refused to cease his extortions or to share his ill-gotten gains. Hence Brú's government issued Decree 937 on May 5, 1939, which ended the director-general's power to issue landing certificates.[2]

The arrival of the *St. Louis* brought to a head the agitation of Cuban antisemites, business and labor leaders, and Cuban officials fighting over power, bribes, and government reform. The Cuban government had alerted shipping companies to the new regulation, but only twenty of the *St. Louis*'s passengers had complied. Some probably knew they carried illegal landing certificates, but most did not. When the ship arrived at Havana on May 27, President Brú refused to permit the passengers to disembark. Worldwide press coverage and front-page newspaper headlines in the United States related the heart-wrenching story.[3] But Brú's action was popular with Cubans. Colonel Batista could have intervened but did nothing. His party was facing a difficult election, and he dodged the issue, claiming to be ill with the grippe.[4]

The United States government's role in the *St. Louis* episode was both delicate and positive. The American consul-general in Havana, Coert DuBois, and Ambassador J. Butler Wright worked closely with Jewish aid groups. They urged Cuban officials to admit the refugees on humanitarian grounds. Constrained by Roosevelt's Good Neighbor Policy and American interests in keeping Cuba in the anti-Nazi camp, the State Department would not bully the Cuban government. However, both DuBois and Wright assisted the Joint and Lawrence Berenson, its representative in Cuba. As DuBois confided to Secretary of State Hull, the "illegitimacy of the collections [of bribes] and the magnitude of the sums collected are the crux of the whole '*St. Louis* incident.' " The State Department knew that behind-the-scenes fights for control of Cuba's immigration policy and for a lot of money were going on, but the United States could not take sides. To force Brú to admit the *St. Louis* passengers would have put a stamp of approval on Benitez's corruption. As late as May 26, the day before the *St. Louis* arrived, Benitez stated unequivocally that it would land.[5]

What happened next was part farce and part tragedy. Lawrence

Berenson, a successful Jewish New York lawyer, was sent by the Joint to negotiate with the Cuban government. Harvard-educated, former president of the Cuban Chamber of Commerce in the United States, and a major player in Cuban politics, Berenson appeared to be the right man for the job. He had previously purchased one thousand visas used by German Jews to immigrate to Cuba. He was close to Batista and may even have been his attorney. Berenson was confident that he could negotiate the freedom of the *St. Louis* passengers. He arrived in Havana with a briefcase full of cash, prepared to bribe Cuban officials and conduct business as usual.[6]

But Berenson miscalculated. Batista refused to meet with him. Public opinion backed Brú. The sale of landing permits had been too open and notorious, and violations of Cuban laws by foreign steamship companies had been too "flagrant and defiant." Benitez had lost his power to issue permits. A clandestine meeting at Benitez's *finca* (ranch) in Piñar del Rio (or as the Cuban Jews called it *reparto judio*, the suburb built with Jewish money) would not avail Berenson this time.[7]

Local Nazis inflamed antisemitic sentiment by manipulating the media and using Havana as a center for coordinating Nazi espionage in the United States. On May 25, 1939, the Joint learned from its agents that the Cuban Immigration Department had begun "a house-to-house check of all German refugees" and that pogroms were being organized.[8]

Despite the work of the Cuban Jewish community and offers by the Joint to guarantee support of the immigrants, Brú ordered the *St. Louis* out of Cuban waters. He was angry at the Hamburg American Line and Berenson because both knew in advance that the *St. Louis* passengers would not be admitted, yet the ship had sailed to Havana anyway. From Brú's point of view, Berenson was complicit with Benitez. The State Department also knew of this situation. "Evidently," DuBois reported, "Berenson elected to disregard the warning and play the game of Colonel Benitez and the Hamburg American Line."[9]

The Joint offered to post a $500 cash bond for each passenger. This amounted to nearly $500,000 donated by American Jewry to help the victims of Nazism. But it was to no avail. On June 2 the *St. Louis* was ordered out of Havana Harbor, its destination undetermined. For two days it steamed northward. American immigration officials announced that the ship could not land in the United States and that the State Department could not interfere in Cuba's internal affairs. Many American newspapers, including the *New York Times*, criticized this refusal to help beleaguered refugees. Others condemned Germany and Cuba. Some, like the *Christian Science Monitor*, blamed the Jews for being too selective in their destinations. The *St. Louis* was four miles off the coast of Florida when on June 4 President Brú relented. He agreed passengers could land if, within forty-eight hours, the Joint posted bonds of $650 per passenger.[10]

Berenson then made a major blunder. Brú had told Berenson on June 1 that he sympathized with the passengers but had to "maintain the prestige of the Cuban government vis-à-vis the Hamburg American Line." However, he was willing to listen to alternatives

SS St. Louis *passengers line the rails of the ship after being denied entrance to Cuba.*

Courtesy of United States Holocaust Memorial Museum (AP/Wide World Photos)

after the ship left Havana. Had Berenson met Brú's conditions, all of the passengers might have disembarked. Instead Berenson tried to bargain with Brú and told the Joint leaders that he could save them "a considerable amount of money." He counteroffered less money and asked Brú to permit the refugees on the other two ships to land as well. Brú was not interested in bargaining, and to Berenson's amazement, on June 6 the Cuban government declared that the *St. Louis* could not return to Cuba. DuBois told Berenson that morning that he and "his coreligionists in New York" had erred in getting the matter "off the plane of humanitarianism and on the plane of horse-trading."[11]

Samuel Rosenman and Henry Morgenthau took a personal interest in the plight of the *St. Louis* passengers. On June 5 Morgenthau told Hull that his friends in New York—doubtless, the Joint—had stated that if funds were needed, Jewish organizations would respond immediately. Hull, too, had spoken with FDR and Ambassador Wright moments earlier about the *St. Louis*. He had considered issuing tourist visas to the Virgin Islands as a temporary solution, but was advised that to do so was illegal. "The Cuban ambassador," Hull said, "talked like the main thing was the financing . . . that he believed it would be worked out as long as there was no publicity." Hull was aware that the Jewish organizations handling "the money end of this" had representatives in Havana. He assured Morgenthau that the situation would work out if finances were truly available, and advised him to tell his friends to send a representative to Cuba "who knows how to dicker. . . . That's the main thing."

Morgenthau, a substantial contributor to the Joint, was clearly working with the rescue organization on a solution. The next day Hull informed Morgenthau that both parties were driving a hard bargain and that it did not look promising. When Hull stated that "they don't know where the boat is," Morgenthau asked if it was appropriate "to have the Coast Guard look for it?" Hull feared that a search by the Coast Guard, which was under the jurisdiction of Morgenthau's Treasury Department, might end up on the front page. Morgenthau assured him it would not. Minutes after their conversation, Morgenthau called the Coast Guard commander in Florida and asked him to ascertain clandestinely the location of the *St. Louis.*

Many in the Roosevelt administration were concerned about the passengers. Morgenthau spoke with Sumner Welles the next day. He assured Morgenthau that Ambassador Wright was "seeing the president of Cuba at seven o'clock tonight." Welles undoubtedly guided FDR through the morass of Cuban politics. He had been assistant secretary of state for Latin American affairs and ambassador to Cuba and was sympathetic to the plight of Jewish refugees.[12] The Joint had other close contacts in the administration. J. C. Hyman, the executive director of the Joint, wrote his chairman, Paul Baerwald, on June 27 that "We had Eddie [Edward S.] Greenbaum [a high-ranking military officer in the War Department] on this thing and Sam Rosenman."[13]

The *St. Louis* turned back toward Germany. The passengers, their supporters, and many others pleaded with Roosevelt to permit the *St. Louis* and the other two ships to land in the United States, but he had no authority to violate the popular immigration laws. FDR also may have known that the Joint was concerned about the fate of six thousand German Jewish refugees already living in Cuba. Half of that number were at risk because they did not have legal papers or were being supported by Joint funds. Many of these refugees had the same "Benitez landing cards" the *St. Louis* passengers had. They could be expelled, not to mention the threat of pogroms.[14] Morgenthau and Rosenman doubtless apprised Roosevelt that the Joint was working to prevent the passengers' return to Germany. Politically, the president was too weak to fight on this issue. "What could he have said?" Ronald Sanders concluded in *Shores of Refuge* (1988). "The Atlantic Ocean was at that moment teeming with boatloads of refugees."

The president and his administration aided the passengers by assisting the Joint. When James N. Rosenberg, acting chairman of the Joint, cabled Brú that he had deposited $500,000 in a Havana bank and guaranteed that "none of these refugees will become public charges," Ambassador Wright telephoned Welles for instructions. "After consulting with Roosevelt," Gellman wrote, "Welles instructed the ambassador to speak with the Cuban president stressing the humanitarian aspects of the case." The Cuban president, however, refused to discuss the issue.[15]

The American press sympathized with the *St. Louis* passengers. Newspapers blamed Germany and Cuba. Walter Winchell said that the refugees' troubles were not caused by a failure to touch Cuban hearts, but "a failure of touching Cuban palms. And we don't mean trees." However, American newspapers, even those that supported the Wagner-Rogers bill, opposed admitting the refugees into the United States. One exception to the law of the land was sure to be "followed by other shiploads," and it would set a "dangerous precedent," as one editorial commented. Indeed, many other ships carrying refugees were then at sea.[16]

American Jews were anxious and angry about the plight of the *St. Louis* passengers. The files of the Joint are full of letters and telegrams from Jewish leaders, organizations, and individuals demanding that the Joint take strong action. A typical letter of June

7, 1939, from the president of the Jewish Federation of St. Louis, Missouri, read: "As you can imagine, I am besieged with requests for information as to what the JDC is doing." The Joint regional chairman, Herbert Mallinson, wrote, "I have never seen the people in this section so distressed as they have been over this refugee ship." He called New York to tell the Joint "our people are just wild about the Cuban thing." The Joint decided to put up the $500,000 it ultimately spent because of the pressure from American Jewry.[17]

Americans were eager to help the passengers. "The feelings of sympathy for the passengers, and indignation against the German authorities," recorded the Joint's minutes, created "a mandate to the JDC to exert every possible effort to help land these passengers, at whatever cost." "You know *St. Louis* caused tremendous excitement here," Rosenberg wired Morris C. Troper in Paris on June 10. "Hysterical uninformed people criticizing JDC." Hyman replied, "Extraordinary emotion sweeping throughout country respect tragedy *St. Louis* . . . we [are] flooded with proposals. . . . Time is of essence." The Joint felt it was being blackmailed by the Cubans. Some board members opposed putting up $500,000 because it would have to do the same for the next boat and the one after that. Benitez, through his agents, urged the JDC to fight the Brú government's decree.[18]

The legal and political impossibility of the United States admitting the *St. Louis* passengers was well understood at the time, especially by rescue advocates. Robert Balderston of the American Friends Service Committee (Quakers) explained to the passengers in Antwerp "the reasons why the US couldn't make an exception for them when they were in sight of our shores under what were really false representations."[19]

The Roosevelt administration was sympathetic from the beginning of the episode. The State Department worked behind the scenes to ensure that none of the refugees was returned to Germany. Ambassador Wright met personally with the Cuban secretary of state to urge him to help the *St. Louis* passengers. Morris C. Troper, the Joint's European chairman, lobbied European relief agencies and guaranteed the maintenance costs of the passengers. The Joint appealed to the Jewish Agency in Palestine, which refused to allot immigration certificates to the *St. Louis* passengers. Coincidentally, when Cuba decided not to admit the refugees, Joint chairman Paul Baerwald was in London to establish the Coordinating Foundation, which was created to assist German Jewish refugees. Baerwald and Ambassador Joseph Kennedy went to work to secure British help.

On June 10 Kennedy wired Hull that he and Sir Herbert Emerson, the League of Nations high commissioner of refugees, were working to find temporary refuge for the *St. Louis* passengers.[20] Baerwald met with Robert Pell of the IGCR and with British Home Office and Foreign Office staff. A meeting with Ambassador Kennedy was "quickly arranged." Baerwald described Kennedy as "extremely amiable." Kennedy telephoned Home Secretary Sir Samuel Hoare and told him that he expected to see Sir Samuel that evening "to support the recommendation" that the British accept several hundred passengers.[21]

Kennedy and Baerwald endeavored to convince the British to take in three hundred passengers on condition that other countries took their shares. Max Gottschalk, the Joint's Belgian representative, lobbied the king and the prime minister of that nation, while Morris Troper lobbied in Paris. In the end, 288 went to Great Britain, 181 to the Netherlands, 224 to France, and 214 to Belgium.[22]

One condition on which the passengers were permitted to enter these four countries was that their stay would be temporary and that efforts would be made to effect their permanent immigration to another country. More than 700 of the refugees had affidavits and other documents for visas to the United States, and many already had their quota number to enter. They would have come to America but for the advent of war in September 1939.[23]

In this difficult, potentially tragic situation, American Jewry and the Roosevelt administration were spectacularly successful. Those involved in the rescue effort believed that the *St. Louis* passengers would ultimately immigrate to the United States. George Baker told the JDC Board that it was "merely going to bridge a time between the acceptance by the United States of these people, when they may officially be admitted." At a meeting on June 10, a JDC member telephoned the French Consul in Tangier and requested temporary asylum until the passengers "were able to sail for the United States." "The JDC's monumental work in rescuing the 907 unfortunate wanderers . . . has been hailed with joy by everyone," the Joint's press release exulted. "This deed will be inscribed in golden letters in the history of the JDC, and Jews everywhere will be grateful."[24]

A total of 936 Jewish refugees had left Hamburg for

Havana; 29 disembarked at Havana; 907 sailed back to Europe; 288 disembarked in England and lived through the Holocaust. The remaining 619 went to France, Belgium, and Holland. The leading authorities on the SS *St. Louis* estimate that 392 of the 619 who disembarked at Antwerp survived the war (the remaining 227 likely were murdered by the Nazis). The U.S. Holocaust Memorial Museum acknowledges that "the majority survived the war." Thus more than two-thirds of the passengers of the SS *St. Louis* likely survived the Holocaust.[25]

The passengers knew that the Joint had saved them. "Our gratitude is as immense as the ocean on which we are now floating," they wired Troper. Three years later, after Hitler had conquered the Netherlands, France, and Belgium and initiated the Final Solution, approximately 227 of the *St. Louis*'s 936 Jewish passengers were murdered in concentration camps. Of course, in June 1939, no one foresaw this tragedy.[26]

Belgium and the Netherlands were safe havens at that time. Ominously, there was an antisemitic demonstration in Antwerp when the *St. Louis* docked. "We, too, want to help the Jews," a pro-Nazi National Youth Organization handbill read; "if they call at our offices each will receive gratis a piece of rope and a strong nail." But the Dutch were relatively tolerant of their Jewish refugee population. The Anne Frank story had begun to unfold by 1939. Otto and Edith Frank of Frankfurt moved to Holland in 1933. Anne Frank attended the Montessori School in Amsterdam. She and her sister adapted to Dutch life, while their parents hoped to return to Germany. Relatives came through Amsterdam on their way to strange places such as Peru. In 1935 Anne visited Switzerland with her parents. Her Uncle Walter was arrested on *Kristallnacht* and later released. In 1939 the Franks wondered if they should move again. But where should they go? Certainly not Palestine. Life there was poor and brutal. "Sanne Ledermann's father had been there in 1934," Melissa Müller wrote, "hoping to establish business connections," but returned to Amsterdam. "Nothing but flies and Arabs there," he had said with a groan, "absolutely unbearable."[27]

Chapter 6

"Not a Question of Money, but Lives:" FDR Tries to Ransom German Jewry

Hitler's persecution of the Jews and the refugee crisis he created were unremitting. One positive result of the Évian Conference had been the creation of the Intergovernmental Committee on Refugees (IGCR) and the appointment of George Rublee, a prominent New York lawyer and a classmate of Roosevelt's at Groton, as the first director of the IGCR. Rublee, persuaded by Roosevelt to undertake the onerous assignment, established his office in London in August 1938, and spent months trying to arrange meetings with the Germans with little help from the British or the French. The Czech crisis and the Munich agreement intervened, but eventually, after FDR asked Chamberlain to personally intercede with Hitler, preliminary negotiations began in October. *Kristallnacht* in November 1938 delayed matters further. The political situation in the upper echelon of the German government was fluid and unpredictable, which made negotiating for Jewish lives next to impossible.

In December 1938 Rublee finally met with Dr. Hjalmar Horace

Greeley Schacht, president of the Reichsbank and a well-known German financier, on a plan to permit 150,000 German Jews of working age to leave Germany over three years, another 250,000 dependents to follow, and the Germans to guarantee the safety of those elderly Jews who remained. Under the Schacht Plan, the Nazi regime would have taken Jewish property, put it in trust, robbed German Jewry of their wealth, and then proceeded to extort huge sums from Jews worldwide. The plan involved increased sales of German goods abroad in return for the release of German Jewish hostages by the German government. Schacht stressed, however, that on acceptance of the plan, the persecution of Jews would cease and that Hitler had approved Schacht's mission.

Jewish leaders were outraged and refused to meet and discuss the plan. "I was shocked by its malevolence," Kuhn, Loeb, & Company banker Lewis Strauss recalled. To cooperate with such extortion was to create the very "international Jewish conspiracy" Hitler claimed ruled the world and to strengthen the Nazi economy as well. American liberals, the liberal press, and the AJ Congress denounced the ransom plan. "I did not think that I was as much hurt by Hitler's measures," an outraged Nahum Goldmann of the World Jewish Congress said, "as by the attitude of the Washington foreign office and those of other democracies." Joseph Tenenbaum, chairman of the AJ Congress Joint Boycott Council, told Rabbi Wise such "procedures make the Jewish victims agents of the Nazi Government."[1]

Roosevelt, however, was very interested in the progress of these negotiations and encouraged them. He sensed the danger ahead.

He knew Hitler was no ordinary antisemite. Beating, abusing, and robbing innocent people and forcing them out of their native land was beyond the traditional European Jew-hatred with which the world was long familiar. Roosevelt had confidential reports from the American consul-general in Berlin, Raymond Geist, who was both well connected to German sources and sympathetic to the plight of German Jewry. Geist was already warning that the Nazis had embarked on a program of "annihilation" of the Jews and that their sights extended beyond Germany.[2]

Thus FDR supported both the Rublee negotiations and utopian proposals of Herbert Hoover and Bernard Baruch for a "United States of Africa." Lewis Strauss believed a new nation could be established in sparsely settled British colonies in Africa where millions of refugees could rebuild their lives. Strauss, Baruch, Rosenwald, and other wealthy Jewish Americans were prepared to raise a sum, in Baruch's words, "far exceeding $300 million." The president, working privately with Welles, wrote down a scheme of his own to save five hundred thousand German Jewish refugees, with the United States taking thirty thousand a year (the approximate American quota) of the one hundred thousand to leave Germany and Austria annually. This memorandum, in FDR's own handwriting, is at the Roosevelt Library.[3]

Roosevelt was not just concerned with Jewish refugees; he was also besieged by numerous groups and thousands of petitioners. The files at the Roosevelt Library bulge with letters of all descriptions seeking help for refugees. ER urged FDR in April 1939 to help "important leaders trapped in Madrid" after receiving a telegram from Albert Einstein and Dorothy Thompson, Sinclair Lewis's wife. Socialist Party leader Norman Thomas wrote him to "lay before you a terrible plight, not only of Jews but of Social Democrats and other anti-Nazis in the Sudeten areas."[4]

FDR was incredulous at the German mistreatment of Jews. He was astonished when told of a meeting at which Foreign Minister Joachim von Ribbentrop raved and ranted that Jews should leave Germany penniless because they were all criminals. He asked Welles to confirm that von Ribbentrop had actually said these things. "If there is any truth to it, the time will come when we can bring it out for the benefit of humanity," he told Welles. FDR thought the Schacht proposal sickening. He told Myron C. Taylor, chief American delegate to the Évian Conference, that Hitler was "asking the world to pay a ransom for the release of hostages in Germany and barter human misery for increased exports." Roosevelt, however, saw that there was no other choice. He urged his negotiators to keep trying.

FDR and Jewish leaders worried that if Germany could extort money for Jewish lives, so would Poland, Hungary, and Romania. Polish officials, in fact, did formally request that the IGCR extend its activities to Poland, which, like the Nazis, also sought to force their Jewish population out of the country. "I do not believe that the migration of seven million persons from their present homes and their resettlement in other parts of the world is either possible or essential to a solution of the problem," FDR wrote to Hull.[5]

In retrospect, if Jewish leaders and communities around the world had paid Hitler the ransom he demanded, more Jews may have survived. But then the Führer may have reneged on the deal. The moral issue of whether the Jews should have cooperated in the ransom scheme is a post facto one. In early 1939 no other means of rescue existed. Yet the volatility of Hitler's regime and its unlikely adherence to an agreement to allow emigration for the next three years—a period that witnessed the German invasion of Poland, France, Russia, and the bombing of Great Britain—made it improbable that the United States could accomplish anything more. And American antisemites let Roosevelt know that, as one telegram stated, his plan to "facilitate influx of 30,000 Jewish Communists" was "a betrayal of American workers." The American people would "block this pernicious Jewish immigration."[6]

Despite his distaste for the negotiations, Rublee persisted. Everyone recognized that it was a ransom scheme and that Germany was using human beings to sell German goods. On the other hand, summary rejection would exacerbate the plight of German Jewry. "The attack on the Jewish community in Germany on the one hand and the indifference of the participating governments to the fate of the victims on the other," Rublee wired Hull on November 14, "has brought the affairs of the Intergovernmental Committee to a critical state where, in our opinion, immediate action is required if the President's initiative is to lead to a positive result." Schacht told a delegation of American Quakers in December, "Be quick, for nobody knows what happens in this country tomorrow."

Administration officials vainly sought Mussolini's help in relocating European Jews to Ethiopia and Kenya and in influencing his German ally. On January 3, 1939, Ambassador William Phillips paid a personal call on Mussolini, delivered a letter from the president, and read to the Duce a memorandum he had been instructed to present with the letter. Phillips made it clear that Germany's methods of forcing the Jews out of Germany had shocked public sentiment in America. Mussolini expressed his dislike for the Jews, his belief that "they would all have to go," and that continual condemnation of Germany's action had only made the situation worse. The conference was a failure. Mussolini wrote to FDR on January 11, pointing out that the Jews were not welcome in Italy or anywhere in Europe and that the Jews ought to have their own state somewhere (but not in Palestine).[7]

In January and February 1939 Rublee was in Berlin with two assistants talking to Schacht and, after Schacht's dismissal, to Hermann Göring's agent Helmut Wohlthat. Rublee was told that his presence was an embarrassment to the German government, but he persisted. He urged the Germans to come up with a specific plan. Rublee believed at one point that he had the support of Göring and other, more moderate Nazi leaders who demonstrated an entirely new attitude toward "the Jewish problem."

From these talks, the Rublee Plan emerged. The plan would have created a trust fund derived from 25 percent of Jewish assets in Germany, which would in turn pay for transportation, German equipment and goods, the emigration of 150,000 Jewish workers, then 250,000 dependents, and the formation of the international corporation to put the plan into effect. It specifically addressed the emigration of Jews, as Jews, from Germany and used the definition of "Jew" from the Nuremberg laws. The fund would then purchase German goods in other countries to equip the emigrants. The plan also called for massive funds to be raised from wealthy American, British, and French Jews. The *Nation* magazine called it "an undisguised ransom scheme." The AJ Congress rejected it, as did the Jewish Labor Committee. Refugee organizations were appalled, but Rabbi Wise urged that it be given "careful and thorough consideration." All Jewish organizations ultimately denounced it. The State Department and the ICGR approved it.[8]

Events within the German government delayed implementation of the Rublee Plan. Hitler equivocated on the scheme, and his intentions were unclear. On January 30, 1939, he infamously declared that "if international finance Jewry should succeed once more in plunging nations into another world war, the consequence will not be the Bolshevization of the Earth and thereby the victory of Jewry, but the annihilation of the Jewish race in Europe." Hitler knew exporting Nazism abroad was difficult, but spreading anti-semitism by flooding the world with impoverished Jews was much easier. Jewish leaders were reluctant to participate in this morally dubious plan. The internal political situation in Germany was unstable. "The Jewish question," the American chargé Prentice Gilbert observed, "is so wrapped up with National Socialist politics that I do not believe anyone in Germany can give insurances regarding either Jewish emigration or the treatment which would be accorded the Jews remaining in Germany."[9]

Encouraged by FDR, the feeling in the administration was that the Rublee Plan could work and that "the release of all, or nearly all, Jews from concentration camps would be a considerable achievement." The PACPR, together with the IGCR and Myron Taylor, began work on an international corporation to be called the Coordinating Foundation to implement the plan. In February 1939 Rublee reported to the IGCR that as unpalatable as it was, he had negotiated a solution with the German government and that, in his opinion, there was a possibility of a radical change in the condition of the Jews in Germany and the release of Jews from concentration camps. Rublee was well aware of the immorality of the German position, but he told the IGCR that "questions of punctilio and pride should be subordinated so far as possible" to humanitarian purposes to save hundreds or thousands who looked to the IGCR as their savior. Rublee, feeling he had accomplished all he could and anxious to return to his law practice, resigned.

But the more radical Nazi factions decided to seize *all* Jewish property in Germany. The Rublee Plan became a Nazi political football, kicked in several directions by Hitler, Göring, von Ribbentrop, and others. Jewish leaders in America were torn between going along with a plan that approved Nazi confiscation of Jewish assets in Germany and abandoning the Jews of Germany to a worse fate. It was, like many situations the Nazis created, a true Hobson's choice.[10]

Roosevelt resisted the notion that the refugee problem was solely a Jewish problem. To agree to the uniqueness of the Jews' predicament was to let Hitler frame the issue. FDR insisted that Nazi oppression of *all* people, not just Jews, must be opposed. He questioned Rublee extensively about why the agreement was limited to Jews. He insisted on defining the crisis as one of all "political refugees" to garner as much political support as possible. To do so would avoid riling up antisemites and help non-Jews as well as Jews.

Acknowledging that Jews were the sole or even the chief victims of Nazism accomplished little in terms of marshaling opposition to Hitler at home or abroad. An expert politician, FDR knew he needed to bring as many people as possible under the tent of refugee rescue if he were to succeed. To Roosevelt, singling out the Jews as the chief victims of the Nazis showed poor political judgment and alienated numerous other victims of Nazism and their supporters for no purpose. Czechs and Czech Americans, for example, could justly claim that they, in fact, were the chief victims of Hitler's aggression, not to mention Poles and Polish Americans after September 1939.[11]

Despite the bleak prospects for the Rublee Plan, a statement of agreement was completed in February. The Roosevelt administration pressured the British to close the deal. But the IGCR, the British, the French, and Latin American countries were unenthusiastic. The Nazis put increased pressure on Jews, requiring them to deliver their valuable possessions to the government and forcing hundreds to leave the country to speed up the IGCR's work. When Hitler invaded the remnant of Czechoslovakia in March 1939, he brought 350,000 Czech Jews under his control. The supervisor of the Central Reich Office for Jewish Emigration, Adolf Eichmann, went to work forcing Jews out of that captive country.

Sumner Welles continued to believe the Rublee Plan might work and pressed for its acceptance. Reinhard Heydrich's Gestapo, meanwhile, began rounding up Jews in Germany at random, and the illegal sale of visas became big business, especially among South American consuls. It was in this atmosphere that the dramatic voyages of the *St. Louis*, the *Orduna*, and the *Flanders* occurred.[12]

Roosevelt was anxious to put the Rublee Plan into operation as soon as possible. According to Yehuda Bauer, "a most extraordinary campaign was waged by the president, the State Department, and Taylor, to press American Jewish organizations into accepting the Rublee Plan." To complement the Rublee Plan, Myron Taylor organized the Coordinating Foundation. Rosenman was chairman of a group of seventy prominent Jews who agreed to serve. A meeting of the group was held on April 15 in Rosenman's chambers in New York. But American Jewish organizations were unable to pay the astronomical sum demanded by the Nazis and could not agree on a plan to raise the money.

In April Raymond Geist, who had dealt personally with both Himmler and Heydrich, predicted the Nazi program of placing Jews in work camps, confiscating their wealth, and forcing as many Jews as possible out of the Reich would end in the murder of those Jews who remained in Germany. This possibility was shocking enough to worry Geist and FDR. In early May Geist warned Washington that if a settlement was not reached soon, it would be too late for German Jewry.[13]

On May 4, 1939, Roosevelt asked this group, which included Paul Baerwald, Henry Ittleson, Lewis L. Strauss, Joseph Proskauer, Sol Strook, and Rosenman, to meet with him. He informed the group of Geist's warning and urged immediate action. But these men were unhappy with the Rublee Plan. They held back from organizing the Coordinating Foundation or raising funds. Lewis Strauss recalled that the leaders had to make "the most agonizing decisions we ever faced." Roosevelt, however, was adamant. He knew from Geist what could lie ahead and insisted on quick action. The warnings from the Berlin embassy were "sound and not exaggerated," Roosevelt told them. "It was not so much a question of the money," he warned, "as it was of actual lives."[14] The president personally badgered and cajoled the leaders of the Joint to send a representative to London to put the Rublee Plan into effect.[15]

An agreement between American and British Jewish leaders was soon reached, but differences developed with the British government. The British were far less interested than the Americans in freeing Jews, who might wish or be forced to go to Palestine. The Balfour Declaration, that "His Majesty's Government view with favour the establishment in Palestine of a national home for the Jewish people," had been issued on November 2, 1917, as a war measure to rally Jewish support for the British cause in World War I. After the war, the League of Nations gave Great Britain a mandate to govern Palestine. For more than twenty years, the British government had tried to balance its conflicting interests in Jews, Arabs, and oil.

Immigration had increased the Jewish population of Palestine from 192,000 to 355,000. But by early 1939, with war on the horizon, and soldiers garrisoned in several Arab and Muslim countries, Great Britain was more interested in Middle East tranquillity than in meeting its wartime commitments to the Jews. Moreover, the British Empire's crown jewel, India, was home to the world's largest Muslim population, and many Muslims served in the British military. Britain would not fight Arabs and Germans simultaneously. By 1936, Jewish immigration to Palestine had already caused an Arab revolt, a general strike, and a boycott of British goods. The region was in a virtual state of rebellion. Two hundred ninety Jews and seventeen hundred Arabs had been killed in domestic violence in 1938. The British army put down the revolt, but to calm the region they issued a diplomatic White Paper on May 17, 1939, that in effect shelved the Balfour Declaration and severely limited Jewish immigration.

FDR was incensed with the British policy and thought it illegal. He instructed Secretary of State Hull, Ambassador Kennedy, and other diplomats to oppose restrictions on Jewish immigration to Palestine and spoke directly to Prime Minister Neville Chamberlain about the issue. He even pressured the British to adopt a plan to remove two hundred thousand to three hundred thousand Arabs from Palestine and resettle them in Iraq to make room for more Jewish immigrants. The British grudgingly allowed reduced Jewish immigration to Palestine.

But Roosevelt could only do so much. He could not undermine Britain's strategic position in the Arab world on the eve of war. The coming war could be won or lost based on access to oil. The British could maintain an army in the Middle East to suppress Arab uprisings or fight the Nazis. They could not do both. Despite misgivings by FDR and later by Winston Churchill, the 1939 White Paper remained official British policy until the end of World War II.[16]

Even with its restrictions, the White Paper proved important to the survival of the Jews of Palestine, the Middle East, and North Africa. The British policy of preserving the Arabs' and the Muslims' nonbelligerent status (partly by siding diplomatically with them against the Jews) and defending British influence in the Middle East meant that millions of Jews in the region (Syria, Iraq, Iran, Egypt, French Northwest Africa, the Arabian peninsula, and Palestine) were saved from the Holocaust. In fact, the British Eighth Army, which defended Palestine, included several Indian divisions in which two-thirds of the men were Muslim.[17]

Roosevelt's Coordinating Foundation and the Rublee Plan moved ahead. On June 6, at Roosevelt's instigation, the Joint agreed to fund the foundation to aid German Jewish refugees with or without participation by British Jews. There should be no uncertainty, James N. Rosenberg of the Joint said, "as to our readiness to carry through a commitment which in effect was desired by Mr. Taylor and the president."[18] Baerwald of the Joint negotiated with Wohlthat in London. The JDC signed a charter for the foundation in late July. The trustees included prominent Britons and Americans, such as attorney John W. Davis, a former presidential candidate, the president of Swarthmore College, and Lessing J. Rosenwald of Sears, Roebuck, among other luminaries. Dr. Paul von Zeeland, former prime minister of Belgium, agreed to serve as director without pay.[19]

The Germans abandoned the Rublee Plan and reverted to forcing Jews out of Austria and Germany with little more than the clothes on their backs. Robert Pell of the State Department, who succeeded Rublee on the IGCR and served as its vice director, engaged in negotiations throughout the spring and summer of 1939 to salvage the plan, which now potentially included the Jews of Czechoslovakia.[20]

Roosevelt was convinced that there had to be a pragmatic solution to the Jewish problem. He was anxious, within the confines of American political constraints, to help implement some kind of plan to ransom Hitler's hostages. He wrote to Taylor in June 1939:

> *[In] the absence of drastic changes in the government and attitudes, if not human nature, in Europe, the problem in its larger aspects appears almost insoluble except through a basic solution such as the development of a suitable area to which refugees would be admitted in almost unlimited numbers. . . . I am convinced, nevertheless, that every effort must continue to be made to attain a practical solution along these lines.*

Roosevelt made those efforts. By July 20, 1939, the Coordinating Foundation was in business, with a million-dollar grant from the Joint. FDR was concerned that the rescue effort was bogging down and decided to present his own plan for resettlement at a meeting of the executive committee of the IGCR in Washington in October 1939. However, Germany's invasion of Poland in September signaled the start of World War II and put an end to the Rublee Plan and all other peacetime rescue schemes.[21]

Chapter 7

"Well, Bill, It's Come at Last"

. . . the President wants to talk to the American
people about Hitler. So far as he is concerned, there is
absolutely nothing important in the world today but
to beat Hitler.
—Harry Hopkins to Robert E. Sherwood, October 1940[1]

In June 1939 King George VI and Queen Elizabeth made a triumphal visit to the United States. After a tumultuous welcome in New York City, the royal couple visited the Roosevelts at Hyde Park. There FDR told the king in the strictest of confidence his global strategy, one he had not even disclosed to Prime Minister Neville Chamberlain. On the evening of July 18, 1939, the president met with the Senate leadership. Could he confide in senators as he had the king of England? "I've fired my last shot," he told them. "I think I ought to have another round in my belt." Senator William Borah and his colleagues dismissed Roosevelt's pleas to lift the arms embargo. Roosevelt was furious. "[W]e ought to introduce a bill for statues of Vandenberg, Lodge, and Taft to be erected in Berlin and put the swastika on them," he said in private. In July Roosevelt presciently told the Soviet ambassador that "as soon as Hitler had conquered France, he would turn on Russia." He saw clearly what others could not see at all. Senator Borah said there would be no war. "Germany isn't ready for it," he asserted. But Roosevelt and his key ambassadors, William C. Bullitt and Anthony J. D. Biddle, were secretly working to build an anti-Nazi coalition.

On August 25, 1939, Great Britain signed a treaty of alliance with Poland. For five days, Hitler hesitated. Churchill was at Chartwell writing history when Hitler invaded Poland late on the evening of August 31, 1939. Churchill heard the news over the telephone at 8:30 A.M. on September 1 from the Polish ambassador. By the afternoon, Chamberlain had asked Churchill to join a war cabinet. "We are fighting to save the whole world from the pestilence of Nazi tyranny," Churchill told the House of Commons, "and in defense of all that is most sacred to man." Chamberlain appointed Churchill first lord of the Admiralty. "Winston is back," the Board of Admiralty signaled all British ships.[2]

Otto Frank, father of Anne Frank, was always an optimist. He knew that Holland had remained neutral in World War I. Hitler, a master of disinformation, had stressed Dutch neutrality in his August 31, 1939, war directive. Anne Frank was ten years old and considered herself to be Dutch. Her fourteen-year-old sister Margot wrote her American pen pal that living in "a small country we never feel safe."[3]

"Is Hitler mad enough to choose war?" Rabbi Wise wrote to

Judge Julian Mack on August 31. At ten minutes to three on the morning of September 1, William Bullitt called the president from Paris with the news of the German invasion. "Well, Bill, it's come at last," FDR said. "God help us all." And he went back to sleep until six-thirty. More calls came from Bullitt in Paris and Kennedy in London. Britain and France would go to Poland's aid. That night, the president spoke to the American people. He patiently explained that while Europe was far away, "every ship that sails the sea, every battle that is fought, does affect the American future." While America would remain neutral, he said, "I cannot ask that every American remain neutral in thought as well. . . . Even a neutral cannot be asked to close his mind or his conscience."[4]

On September 3, Ambassador Kennedy telephoned Roosevelt to report on Chamberlain's speech in Parliament. In a voice choked with emotion, Kennedy whimpered, "It's the end of the world . . . the end of everything." Later, at an embassy dinner, Kennedy said that Great Britain would be "badly thrashed in the present war." But, as James MacGregor Burns wrote, Roosevelt then "set into motion long-laid plans for the emergency. . . . Now the crisis hours seemed not strange to him, but more like picking up an interrupted routine" from twenty years ago, when Woodrow Wilson was his chief. On September 11 Roosevelt sent a secret letter to Churchill letting this tenacious foe of Hitler know "how glad I am that you are back again at the Admiralty" and that he should "keep me in touch personally with anything you want me to know about." Roosevelt had serious doubts about Chamberlain's ability to fight Hitler.[5]

The British would not be thrashed. It was not the end of the world, but it was the beginning of the end of European Jewry. The coming of the war sealed the fate of Hitler's hostages as he waged a race and ideological war to remake Europe. The Jewish Telegraphic Agency reported only three months later that Nazis entered Ostrovic near Warsaw and "forced all the Jewish men to dig a large pit and then . . . shot them down from behind with machine guns."[6]

The "death watch over Europe," as Adolph Berle called it, ended on September 1, 1939. Franklin Roosevelt faced a European war of potentially gigantic proportions as he presided over a nation sympathetic to the democracies and disdainful of Nazism, but overwhelmingly opposed to joining the conflict. He was committed to all-out aid to France and Britain short of war, but he had no fear of war and had already begun to prepare for it. For six years he had known that Adolf Hitler was a madman. He had warned Joseph Stalin that Germany was a threat to both the Soviets and to the Americans. Roosevelt did not want war at that moment, but he worked diligently to create a coalition to wage war against Hitler.

Sometime between September 1939 and December 7, 1941, Roosevelt's determination to keep the nation out of war went into reverse. The American people were not privy to his thoughts and neither are historians. While Roosevelt was "captain of the ship of state," Burns observed, "many hands reached for the tiller, and a rebellious crew manned the sails." Roosevelt's nightmare was that Hitler would conquer Europe and the Soviet Union before he could convince his stubborn fellow Americans, led by a flock of isolationist ostriches, to go to war.[7]

Complicating matters further, the president's second term ended on January 20, 1941. Would he run for a third term? Who would succeed him if he did not? No president had ever run for a third term. His party was riven with conflict. Congress was in open revolt against his leadership. Southern Democrats detested his wife and her liberal friends, black and white. The Roosevelt recession had abated, but America's economic ills remained, and his opponents charged that he was becoming a dictator. After his clumsy attempt to pack the Supreme Court, even some of his friends were uneasy.

There was a strong possibility that FDR would be out of office in January 1941, only sixteen months away. "I want to go home to Hyde Park. I want to take care of my trees. . . . I want to finish my little house on the hill," Roosevelt told the president of the Teamsters Union in early 1940, and, according to Roosevelt's friends, he was serious. Rosenman and Robert Jackson, for example, were convinced Roosevelt would not run. According to others, he was dissembling.[8]

The conquest of Poland was swift. The German *blitzkrieg* (lightning war) lasted four weeks. Poland's outdated army and air force crumbled before the Wehrmacht's modern tanks and the Luftwaffe's bombers. The Soviet Union invaded eastern Poland. Warsaw fell to the Nazis. Massive air raids on civilian populations made their debut on the world stage. Polish cities suffered enormous damage, and the Germans waged "a merciless and systematic campaign of biological destruction" of Poles, who were treated by the Nazis as subhuman. Some Polish children were abducted so they could be "Germanized." Great Britain and France declared war on Germany on September 3, 1939.[9]

In Poland Hitler exterminated enemies of the Reich, hereditary

123

nobles, professors, schoolteachers, intellectuals, bishops, and priests. Villages were burned and civilians massacred by the thousands. In November ninety-six Polish schoolteachers were murdered in Rypin. A few months later 6,000 intellectuals, lawyers, civil servants, and clergymen were killed. "It is the Führer's and Göring's intention," a Nazi colonel wrote, "to destroy and exterminate the Polish nation." Polish Jews were prominent victims of this campaign against civilians. Savagery had become a way of life in Europe.[10]

Despite the new barbarity, the Final Solution had not yet begun. Jews were forced into labor camps and sent to ghettos, but not singled out to be murdered in large numbers. For the time being Jews were treated more or less like Poles and Czechs, thousands of whom were forced into the Nazi slave labor system, where many died. The 160,000 Jews of Lodz, for example, were locked in a closed ghetto. "In the period 1939–1941," Richard C. Lukas found, "Poles were even more exposed than Jews to arrest, deportation, and death. Most Jews during this period had been herded into ghettos."[11]

The Nazis aimed to stamp out all resistance in Poland. To that end, they turned a former cavalry barracks into a "quarantine" camp for rebellious Poles. Located on the outskirts of Oswiecim, it became known by its German name, Auschwitz. Polish and German Jews were prisoners, not refugees. "Once war began," Gilbert wrote, "escape became virtually impossible, as Greater Germany's frontiers were sealed." After September 1939 Greater Germany included western Poland, with its capital moved to Cracow from Warsaw.[12]

124

One step in FDR's plan to rid the world of Hitler was to repeal the Neutrality Act of 1935, which prevented him from sending arms to countries at war. Acting behind the scenes, the president lobbied a suspicious Congress to repeal the act. "I am almost literally walking on eggs. . . . I am at the moment saying nothing, seeing nothing and hearing nothing," he told the governor-general of Canada. By November, after a bruising debate, Congress modified the Neutrality Act to allow the president some latitude to sell arms on a cash-and-carry basis to the Allies. "It is a great and well-deserved victory for you," Emanuel Celler wrote him. Roosevelt wrote William Allen White that his problem was to get the American people to see the danger without scaring them into thinking that they would be dragged into war. He talked about defense, but he worked to encircle Hitler's Germany. "Roosevelt," Hans Thomsen, the German chargé in Washington, reported, "is determined to go to war against Germany, even in the face of resistance in his own country."[13]

The American political landscape shifted dramatically when Hitler invaded Poland. Republican internationalists, Eastern businessmen, Southerners, and pro-British conservatives who detested Roosevelt and the New Deal saw the president in a new light. Here was a strong leader who was willing to stand up to Hitler. Republican Henry Luce, the powerful publisher of *Time* magazine and producer of "The March of Time" newsreels, supported repeal of the Neutrality Act and began to see Roosevelt as the leader of the free world who could make America a world power. Public opinion against the Nazis hardened, but the American people were adamant that they would stay out of Europe's war at any cost.[14]

FDR tried to win the celebrated aviator Charles Lindbergh over by offering him a secretaryship of air. Lindbergh was opposed to American aid to the Allies, a viewpoint shared by millions of Americans, including prominent leaders in Congress; right-wing publishers; former New Dealers; and pacifists such as Norman Thomas, the nation's leading Socialist. The European war, Lindbergh argued, was just "a continuation of the old struggle among Western nations for the material benefits of the world." The Germans, British, and French all wanted territory and power, and there was no good or bad nation in the squabble. What concerned Lindbergh and his supporters was that white Europeans were fighting each other when they ought to be fighting people of color and "the Asiatic hordes."[15]

Roosevelt saw airpower as the instrument to defeat Hitler while keeping the war away from America. Had the United States a sufficient number of airplanes, "Hitler would not have dared to take the stand he did," he told his military chiefs. As early as September 19, 1939, Hitler alluded to "a weapon [with] which we ourselves could not be attacked." The Germans began planning to build an atomic bomb. In October, at the request of Albert Einstein, Roosevelt met with an old supporter, the financier Alexander Sachs, who educated the president about nuclear fission and the Germans' plan to build a fission bomb. "Alex, what you are after is to see that the Nazis don't blow us up." "Precisely," Sachs replied. From this meeting emerged the Manhattan Project.[16]

Roosevelt had already decided to aid the French and British as much as possible. His military advisers vehemently disagreed with his decision to send the British "three out of eight units" of American

Franklin D. Roosevelt and Henry Morgenthau, Jr. February 9, 1934.

Courtesy of the Franklin D. Roosevelt Library

war production. But the president ignored his military chiefs and gave Secretary of the Treasury Henry Morgenthau the authority to allow the Allies to purchase arms. Morgenthau was as dedicated as FDR to fighting the Nazis. Morgenthau helped the Allies procure modern aircraft and took the heat for the president when an American bomber crashed near Los Angeles with a Frenchman aboard. Everyone in Washington knew the secretary of the treasury could be counted on to assist any anti-Nazi endeavor. He warned of the Nazi threat more often than any other cabinet member and managed an efficient department. When FBI director J. Edgar Hoover was stymied by the attorney general in his counterespionage work against Nazi spies, he went to Morgenthau to lobby FDR. Hoover got what he needed, permission to expand wiretaps against suspect citizens.[17]

The start of the war did not deter Roosevelt from trying to save German Jewry. The White House and the State Department had investigated possible places to which Jewish refugees could flee. All sorts of harebrained ideas were considered. The State Department actually pursued the notion of Jewish homelands in Angola, British Guiana, and the Dominican Republic. But Jewish Americans were divided on what to tell the president. More conservative leaders such as Paul Baerwald and Lewis Strauss thought that if Germany lost the war, the Jews would return home. Zionists, led by Wise, demanded that Palestine be opened to settlement. In October 1939 Roosevelt met again with Justice Brandeis. They discussed creation of a resettlement agency for Jews headed by Bernard Baruch. The acerbic Brandeis told the president, "Baruch would be more likely to consider colonization of Jews on some undiscovered planet than Palestine." At one point Roosevelt hoped to settle Jewish refugees in the Orinoco River Valley of Venezuela. Congress urged Great Britain to admit Jews into Palestine. Even antisemites agreed that Jews should go "somewhere else." Nothing came of these schemes.[18]

David Ben-Gurion worried as early as January 1934 about a Nazi massacre of the Jewish people. He had read *Mein Kampf* in 1933 and predicted Hitler would start a war in Europe and kill Jews during the conflict. With the war under way Ben-Gurion knew that Britain alone could not defeat Germany. "Tens and hundreds of thousands in Poland are doomed to slaughter," he said.

There was "no guarantee that the angel of death will not visit the neighboring countries." Ben-Gurion knew about the early murder of Jews in Poland. "Hitler is a preying beast," Ben-Gurion said, "who wants to devour . . . the Jews all over the world."[19] "The Executive," Ben-Gurion wrote in the fall of 1939, "should do all it can, as if we ourselves were inside this inferno." He vowed to speed up creation of a Jewish homeland.[20]

A small group of Palestinian Jews believed that they should revolt against the British. While most Zionists believed in the moral discipline of *havlagah* or self-restraint in the face of Muslim terrorism, Abraham Stern and members of the underground terrorist organization Irgun Z'vai Leumi (the National Military Organization) embarked on an armed terror campaign. The Zionist movement, including Ben-Gurion, Weizmann, Brandeis, and virtually all American Zionists, opposed the terrorists. Indeed, world opinion sympathized with the Jews of Palestine because of their refusal to resort to terrorism. In May and June the Irgunists blew up government buildings. In August they killed more than seventy Arabs in retaliation for attacks on Jews. On August 26, 1939, Stern and his fellow terrorists murdered two British police officers, to the horror of American Jewry.[21]

Closer to home, Secretary of the Interior Harold Ickes championed plans to open Alaska to Jewish refugees or to admit them as "temporary visitors" to the Virgin Islands. In August 1939 the Department of the Interior released a report urging new settlements in Alaska made up of unemployed Americans and "skilled labor from the four corners of the Earth." The report attracted widespread opposition from anti-immigration forces and most Alaskans, including the territory's delegate to Congress. Roosevelt sympathized with Ickes on this issue, but Undersecretary of State Sumner Welles convinced the president that allowing immigrants into Alaska "would lead to a breakdown in our whole system of protective immigration laws." Even the Jewish director of the Division of Territories and Island Possessions, Ernest Gruening, attacked the bill because the territory was not treated as an equal to the states, and he did not want Alaska to become a "virtual concentration camp." Felix S. Cohen, a Jewish Department of the Interior attorney, made an impassioned plea for the bill. But Roosevelt's old nemesis Senator Millard Tydings of Maryland, chairman of the Committee on Territories and Insular Affairs, killed it. The bill, correctly perceived as liberalizing the immigration laws, suffered the fate of all such legislation.[22]

Referring to the George Rublee Plan that FDR had championed, Henry Feingold wrote: "To those familiar with the elaborate murder apparatus conceived by Nazis in 1942, it seems incredible that barely two years before, the Nazi regime was party to an agreement for an orderly exodus of the Jews of Germany." But the war changed everything. The State Department felt that these ideas were now a dead letter and that any justification for the IGCR to exist ceased after the invasion of Poland. The president disagreed. In fact, he insisted on going forward with the October 1939 meeting of the IGCR despite the invasion of Poland, the opposition of the State Department and the British Foreign Office, and just about every participant. The meeting opened in Washington on

October 16 under a cloud. Delegates were concerned about the survival of their nations, not refugees.[23]

Prior to the formal meeting Roosevelt entertained the delegates at a luncheon at the White House. It was clear in March 1938, he told the delegates, that private agencies alone could no longer deal with the refugees who "had been driven from their homes . . . [and] were beating at the gates of any nation which seemed to offer them a haven. Most of these fellow human beings belonged to the Jewish Race, though many thousands of them belonged to other races and other creeds." The president delivered the main address and predicted the war would create a massive refugee problem. His solution was resettlement in one of the "many vacant spaces of the Earth's surface." Roosevelt sought a dramatic, large-scale solution involving many countries, not just Palestine. He said:

> *Gentlemen, that is a challenge to the Intergovern-*
> *mental Committee. It is a duty because of the pressure*
> *of need. It is an opportunity because it gives a chance*
> *to take part in the building of new communities for*
> *those who need them. Out of the dregs of present dis-*
> *aster we can distill some real achievements in human*
> *progress. This problem involves no one race group—no*
> *one religious faith. It is the problem of all groups and*
> *all faiths. It is not enough to indulge in horrified*
> *humanitarianism, empty resolutions, golden rhetoric,*
> *and pious words. We must face it actively if the demo-*
> *cratic principle based on respect and human dignity is*

*to survive, and if world order, which rests on security
of the individual, is to be restored.*[24]

Although nothing came of the IGCR meeting, Roosevelt continued to study resettlement and the possibility of a "supplemental
Jewish homeland." In 1940 he initiated the secret "M" project and
brought Henry Field of the Chicago Museum of Natural History
to Washington to survey all resettlement possibilities. Six hundred
sixty-six sites were studied before 1945. The State Department
continued to disagree with him. In February 1940 Robert Pell suggested that the IGCR be "put quietly to sleep," as all the delegates
did was "make pretty speeches" and hold large banquets. Roosevelt sent an angry reply: "Even if this proposed meeting [of the
IGCR] makes 'pretty speeches,' it is worthwhile keeping this committee very definitely alive."[25]

American Jews reacted unfavorably to Roosevelt's efforts at
resettlement outside of Palestine. Zionist sentiment was growing,
and to propose Jewish settlement elsewhere was a betrayal. Roosevelt assured Brandeis privately that he had not lost interest in
Palestine. On the other hand, some Jewish philanthropists and the
Joint saw the wisdom of simply getting Jews out of Europe.
Stephen Wise and Chaim Weizmann were willing to listen.[26]

Meanwhile, the Germans informed the United States that they
were willing "to continue to cooperate with the Intergovernmental
Committee with respect to emigration of Jews from Germany,"
although the Nazis had repudiated the Rublee Plan. The Nazis even
flirted with resettlement schemes of their own, such as transporting

fifteen million Jews to Guinea or Madagascar. In October 1939 they talked about "a sort of Jewish reservation" in Lublin, Poland. In fact, by January 1940 seventy-eight thousand Jews had been sent to Lublin.[27]

The Nazis wavered between expulsion and extermination. Roosevelt was the most powerful enemy of the Reich, and Hitler believed the president was controlled by Jews. After the invasion of Poland, even as they held out hope of a ransom deal, the Nazis began murdering Jews, Poles, Communists, intellectuals, and others. "Until 1941," Wyman wrote, "the main purpose of Nazi persecution of the Jews was to force them to leave Germany, not exterminate them, a fact which warrants repetition because all postwar reflection upon Germany and the Jews is filtered through knowledge of the extermination policy." Roosevelt vacillated between hope that the world could solve the colossal refugee problem the war would soon create and despair that human depravity would prevent anything from being done.[28]

The administration used the immigration quotas to the fullest from September 1939 through July 1940 and the fall of France. The German quota was 95 percent filled; the Hungarian, 100 percent. The State Department tightened some of its requirements. For example, the German quota was largely filled by German Jewish refugees who had previously fled to England, Cuba, and other countries. Many more Jews arrived from Belgium, Britain, France, and the Netherlands.[29]

Secretary of the Interior Ickes was given free rein by the president. When the Alaska plan was defeated in Congress, Ickes and his Jewish lawyer, Nathan Margold, turned their attention to the U.S. Virgin Islands, which were administered directly by the Interior Department. The Interior Department argued that under existing laws it could admit refugees as "temporary visitors." The State Department disagreed. A presidential order allowed the governor of the Virgin Islands to admit alien visitors without visas in emergencies, and the island's legislature voted to admit refugees. However, according to federal immigration regulations, when an immigrant secured a temporary visitor visa, he lost his right to apply for permanent immigration. The Interior and Labor Departments agreed to exempt the Virgin Islands from this regulation, but State and Justice argued that only Congress could amend the law. Typical of the Roosevelt administration, inconsistent policies were advanced by different groups.

From September 1939 until the eve of the Democratic Party convention in July 1940, Roosevelt publicly withheld judgment whether he would run again. He encouraged others to run, but he also plotted to keep some delegates in his pocket. He kept his options open. At times he said he had no desire to run. At other times he was as silent as the Egyptian sphinx. Indeed, reporters at the 1940 Gridiron Dinner much enjoyed a huge papier-mâché sphinx decoration complete with a long cigarette holder protruding from a grinning mouth.[30] The most powerful president since Abraham Lincoln had to decide whether to run for an unprecedented third term at a time when he was at his politically weakest. Republicans, anti–New Deal Democrats, and ambitious men of all stripes who wanted to be president saw 1940 as their chance to knock Roosevelt off his pedestal.[31]

FDR was at his wiliest in 1940. His strategy was to watch and wait, to pit his Democratic rivals Postmaster General James A. Farley, the Roman Catholic chairman of the Democratic Party; Vice President James Nance Garner of Texas, who despised his boss; and his indecisive secretary of state, Cordell Hull, against each other. He led people to believe he would not run. Despite his coyness, he would never countenance the nomination falling to an anti–New Dealer or a candidate not committed to destroying Nazism. To assure that his legacy would not be erased by his own party, he manipulated people and events so that the Democratic Party would *beg* him to accept a draft. He would then, with a display of reluctance, run for a third term. He simply would not permit Garner to be president. When the vice president announced his candidacy, FDR quipped, "I see that the Vice President has thrown his bottle—I mean his hat—into the ring." (Garner was a heavy drinker.)[32] The Democratic Party convention was scheduled to convene in Chicago on July 15, 1940, and the general election was on November 5. The president had to play his political cards carefully until the election was over. Every event of 1940 must be seen in light of these two dates and Roosevelt's determination to be reelected.

The war in Europe was hard to find in the winter of 1939–40. Isolationist senator William Borah dubbed it the "Phony War," a name that stuck. Others called it "Sitzkreig" (sitting war) or the "bore war." The consensus was that it would be a long, drawn-out affair, like World War I. Men would fight in trenches. The British and French military planned for a war of attrition. They instituted an effective blockade of Germany, preventing imports of food, fuel, and other necessities. Roosevelt sent Sumner Welles on what he dubbed a fact-finding trip to Europe and a secret mission to convince Italy's Il Duce to stay out of the war. While the mission polished Roosevelt's image as a peacemaker, his real goal was to buy time to help the Allies rearm.[33]

The Nazis were well aware of Roosevelt's efforts to stiffen the resolve of the Poles, the French, and others. High German officials mounted a secret propaganda effort in the United States to prevent Roosevelt's renomination, to influence Catholics and the Vatican against him, and ultimately to defeat him in the election. The German embassy financed anti-Roosevelt and isolationist books, speeches, and articles. It paid writers, supported the America First Committee, helped isolationist congressman to attend the Republican convention, and collaborated with Quaker opponents of war. When they occupied Warsaw, the Germans discovered compromising documents at the Polish foreign ministry that proved that Bullitt and Biddle had stated that the United States would enter the war. The Nazis published these Polish documents to embarrass FDR and manipulated their isolationist friends to defeat Roosevelt. FDR and Hull said that the documents were forgeries.[34]

On April 9, 1940, Germany invaded Denmark and Norway. The Phony War was finished. Chamberlain's hope that a blockade would strangle Germany's economy evaporated. FDR made it plain on April 18 that he believed Hitler aimed to conquer the world. The Polish documents became old news, and cries went up for Chamberlain to resign. "In the name of God, go!" one member of Parliament shouted at Chamberlain. On May 10 Winston Churchill became prime minister, and his cabinet agonized whether to make peace with Hitler or commit the nation to total war. Churchill publicly defied Hitler. "You ask what is our policy? I will say: It is to wage war . . . against a monstrous tyranny, never surpassed in the dark, lamentable catalogue of human crime. That is our policy," he told the House of Commons on May 13, 1940.[35]

Despite Churchill's declaration, his cabinet wrestled from Friday through Tuesday, May 24–28, over the decision to wage war. This course of action, which appears inevitable today, was not inevitable in May 1940. Many people around the world misunderstood Hitler. "I do not consider Hitler to be as bad as he is depicted," the Indian leader Mahatma Gandhi wrote in May 1940. Many in Britain and the United States sought to accommodate Hitler another time because they desperately wanted to avoid war. Hitler represented antisemitism and resistance to communism, "the wave of the future." Chamberlain told Ambassador Kennedy that "America and the world Jews had forced England into the war." Gandhi alleged that the Jews "wanted America and England to fight Germany on their behalf." John Lukacs wrote in *Five Days in London, May 1940* (1999) that "then and there Adolf Hitler came closest to winning the Second World War." In those five days Churchill did his part in saving the democracies. "I hope it is not too late," Churchill told his bodyguard with tears in his eyes. "I am very much afraid it is."[36]

On May 10 German soldiers parachuted into Belgium and the Netherlands to seize their airfields. Dive bombers attacked, and massive German armor and infantry invaded the Dutch and Belgian homelands. Allied troops rallied to defend Belgium and were defeated by superior Nazi armies. Ambassador Bullitt wired Roosevelt that "unless God grants a miracle . . . the French army will be crushed utterly." There was panic in the United States. Roosevelt canceled his May 16 appointment to discuss refugee matters with Baruch, Lessing Rosenwald, and Van Zeeland.[37]

By May 15 the German army, to the amazement of the French government, had invaded France through the Ardennes Forest and captured northern France. "The scene has darkened swiftly," Churchill wrote FDR. "The small countries are simply smashed up, one by one, like matchwood." Churchill warned of a "Nazified Europe established with astonishing swiftness." He asked Roosevelt for forty or fifty old destroyers, hundreds of modern aircraft, antiaircraft weapons, and steel loans to keep "that Japanese dog quiet in the Pacific." Five days later he warned Roosevelt that if Britain were defeated, the British fleet would become part of the German navy. Roosevelt feared that Germany would soon have the power to threaten the United States. The French surrendered on June 22. Their swift defeat and the British escape at Dunkirk did not portend British victory against Germany. Indeed, according to Williamson Murray and Allan R. Millett, the German victory represented one of the great military triumphs of history.[38]

By the summer of 1940 most Americans realized that the war had come to threaten their own national interests. But not all understood. A thousand Dartmouth undergraduates wired Roosevelt to "keep the U.S. out of the war!" Roosevelt told his radio listeners to look at a map of the world and ponder the range of German airpower. The president convinced Congress to appropriate nearly a billion dollars for defense and promised that the nation would build a two-ocean navy and fifty thousand airplanes a year. However, he decided, against the advice of his military and diplomatic advisers, to grant many of Churchill's aid requests. FDR bucked General George C. Marshall to send airplanes to England. "I might guess wrong," Roosevelt told Ickes, but he stuck with what David Kennedy described as "his high-stakes gamble" that Britain and France could hold out. He "refused to abandon Great Britain to her fate," Friedlander concluded, "whatever the risks."[39]

In a fireside chat the president pointed out the futility of isolationism; the need for national defense; and the dangers of spies, subversives, and internal divisiveness. He could not send troops or the navy to aid Great Britain because Congress and the public would not have stood for it. But Roosevelt was also determined to lead the American people another step toward the defeat of Hitler.[40]

On June 4 Churchill told the House of Commons that Great Britain would fight on the beaches, on the landing grounds, and in the streets against Nazi Germany.

We shall go on to the end, we shall fight in France,
we shall fight on the seas and oceans . . . we shall

defend our island, whatever the cost may be . . . we shall never surrender . . . until in God's good time, the New World, with all its power and might, steps forth to the rescue and the liberation of the Old.

He eloquently acknowledged his and Roosevelt's monumental challenge to rescue Western civilization.[41]

Chapter 8

"The President Had Said That He Would Wage War but Not Declare It"

The president had said that he would wage war but not declare it, and that he would become more and more provocative. If the Germans did not like it, they could attack the American forces.

—Churchill reporting to his war cabinet, August 1941[1]

In a speech at the University of Virginia, despite his need for big-city ethnic votes in the coming election, FDR served notice on Mussolini. Referring to Italy's declaration of war against France that very day, he said, "On this tenth day of June 1940, the hand that held the dagger has struck it into the back of its neighbor. On this tenth day of June 1940, in this university founded by the first great American teacher of democracy, we send forth our prayers and our hopes to those beyond the seas who are maintaining with magnificent valor their battle for freedom."[2] Many were horrified by Roosevelt's warlike statements, including his defeatist friend Breckinridge Long, who confided to his diary his belief that Roosevelt had gone too far. "If we are not very careful we are going to find ourselves the champions of a defeated cause." If England were defeated, FDR would lose the election. The German ambassador correctly understood Roosevelt's remarks as evidence of his "fanatical hatred" of the Nazis.[3]

France crumbled. On June 16 the French premier, Paul Raynaud, resigned, and Marshal Henri Philippe Pétain formed a new French government, which promptly surrendered to the Germans and created the pro-Nazi Vichy regime. Americans were shocked at newsreels of German troops marching into Paris. "The Battle of France is over," Churchill told the House of Commons. "I expect that the Battle of Britain is about to begin. Upon this battle depends the survival of Christian civilization." If the British failed to defeat Hitler, he said, "the whole world, including the United States . . . will sink into the abyss of a new Dark Age." England "will have her neck wrung like a chicken," Pétain predicted.[4]

Events in Europe transformed the American political landscape. Roosevelt had become a tower of strength in an uncertain world. Roosevelt slates in California and Texas won in Democratic primaries. John Nance Gardner's challenge evaporated. The anomaly of a third term paled in comparison to a Second World War. Democratic Party regulars realized Roosevelt was their only chance to remain in power and that he could be elected to a third term. Domestic politics, New Deal legislation, and help for Jewish or non-Jewish refugees took backseats to the defense of the American homeland, aid to the Allies, and Roosevelt's reelection.[5]

Roosevelt knew that it would take time to defeat Hitler and was forced to set new priorities. "He was," Burns wrote, "simply operating on his old political rule that he could exert leadership on only one front at a time, and he was husbanding all his strength for the crucial political problems involved in the situation abroad." Saving the Jews of Europe could not be a priority except as an integral part of his most important job, saving Great Britain and Europe from Nazism.

Roosevelt acted decisively. As commander in chief, he ordered the military to do his will over strenuous objections from cabinet members, generals, and ambassadors. He organized political and propaganda campaigns to drum up support for military aid to Britain. His political friends organized the Committee to Defend America by Aiding the Allies. Roosevelt warned Pétain not to surrender the French fleet to the Germans. When Pétain failed to heed him, Roosevelt secretly approved the British destruction of the French fleet at Toulon and the killing of twelve hundred French sailors. He told the American people that South America, the Caribbean, and Mexico were targets of Nazi aggression and that he would expand American naval power to enforce the Monroe Doctrine. He also played on American fears of subversion by the Nazis to convince the American people that the fight against Hitler was their fight.[6]

Roosevelt was keenly aware of the need for bipartisan support of the Allies. He laid the groundwork by bringing leading Republicans into his cabinet. He made an overture to Alf Landon, his Republican opponent in the 1936 election, but Landon insisted that Roosevelt forgo a third term. Neither Henry L. Stimson, a former Republican secretary of war, nor Frank Knox, a former Rough Rider and Landon's running mate in 1936, cared about party politics.

Both joined FDR's cabinet, Stimson as secretary of war and Knox as secretary of the navy, on the eve of the Republican convention in June to help Roosevelt fight a more important battle. It was not a coalition government on the British model, but it was "the closest thing to it in the history of the United States before or since."[7]

The Republican convention nominated an attractive, articulate newcomer to politics, Wendell Willkie, on June 28, 1940. Roosevelt continued his charade of pretending he did not want to run, but let Hull and James Farley know that the pressure of a draft was becoming irresistible. Hull accepted the inevitable; Farley did not. He was angry and hurt by FDR's duplicity. He met with the president at Hyde Park in July and gave him fair warning that he would continue to seek the nomination. Farley was true to his word. He did everything in his power to defeat his former boss. "Jim," Roosevelt told his postmaster general and former political adviser, "if nominated and elected, I could not in these times refuse to take the inaugural oath, even if I knew I would be dead within thirty days."[8]

When navy lawyers said his plan to transfer destroyers to Britain was illegal, Roosevelt told the secretary of the navy to do "what I told you to do." In June he began shipping arms to Britain. Army chief of staff George C. Marshall and the chief of naval operations, Admiral Harold Stark, told the president officially and in writing that Britain would likely be defeated, and both opposed sending arms. Roosevelt stuck to his guns.[9] Donald Nelson, head of industrial mobilization, later recalled:

> *Who among us except the president of the United*
> *States really saw the magnitude of the job ahead?* . . .
> *None of us—not one that I know of except the presi-*
> *dent—saw that we might be fighting Germany and Japan*
> *all over the world. He took his stand against the advice*
> *of some of the country's best minds, but his foresight was*
> *superior than theirs, and this foresight saved us all.*[10]

In the sweltering July heat of Chicago, Franklin Roosevelt successfully pulled off his ploy. He continued to pretend that he would
not accept the nomination. Alben W. Barkley stunned the delegates
by telling them that "at the specific request and authorization of
the president" he was making it clear that the president had no
desire to run or to be nominated. All of a sudden, the loudspeakers
blared "We want Roosevelt!" and the delegates began a noisy
hour-long demonstration and parade showing their hero that they
insisted he run. The whole scene was orchestrated by boss Ed
Kelley, mayor of Chicago. In his July 18 acceptance speech, Roosevelt warned the country against "appeaser fifth columnists who
charged me with hysteria and warmongering" and against turning
the government over to "untried hands."[11]

Willkie proved to be Roosevelt's most formidable opponent. A
former New Deal Democrat from the Midwest, Willkie was literate, articulate, energetic, and charming. A lawyer-businessman
who still kept his country-boy sincerity, he was an effective candidate and critic of the New Deal. Booth Tarkington called him "a
good, sturdy, plain, able Hoosier." Willkie was an internationalist

who said that any man who thought that the war in Europe was of no consequence was "a blind, foolish, and silly man."[12]

The nation began the massive task of rearming. "Against Europe's total war," *Time* reported in May 1940, "the U.S. Army looks like a few nice boys with BB guns." The United States Army numbered 504,000, smaller than those of the Netherlands and Belgium. Germany had an army of 6.8 million. In March 1940 the military brass refused to comply when the French and the British ordered five thousand airframes and ten thousand engines, but the president forced them to act. By June Roosevelt had concluded that the United States would soon be in the war but with naval and air forces only. While Roosevelt distrusted the Japanese, he did not view Tokyo as a threat to the United States, and certainly not a military threat to the American homeland. The Tripartite Pact of September 1940, which allied Germany, Italy, and Japan was a major mistake by the Japanese. Their alliance with Nazi Germany made them absolute enemies in FDR's eyes.[13]

The fall of France emboldened Japan to consider an invasion of Dutch and French colonies in Asia and Hitler to covet their Caribbean colonies. Hitler decided to invade England, and Churchill begged Roosevelt for destroyers. "Mr. President," Churchill cabled Roosevelt on July 31, "with great respect I must tell you that in the long history of the world this is a thing to do *now*." Roosevelt's advisers did not believe Britain would survive.[14]

In August 1940 Hitler attacked Great Britain. The long-expected Battle of Britain had begun. By August 15 1,800 German warplanes were bombing England. The American public was infuriated. They admired the courage of their English cousins and demanded action to help the British. However, isolationist congressmen and newspaper publishers violently opposed sending destroyers, which they said meant declaring war on Germany. A bill to enact a peacetime draft was percolating in Congress. Roosevelt, as commander in chief, created "a new government within a government" to protect the hemisphere and aid the Allies. He ignored Congress and established an Office of Emergency Management by executive order, bypassing the War and State Departments, which did not endorse his quasi-war against Hitler and which he did not absolutely control.[15]

The impasse ended in the nick of time when, on September 13, the president decided without congressional approval to trade destroyers for British bases. The act might have cost him the election. Wendell Willkie, the Republican candidate, secretly approved the trade but hypocritically labeled it "the most arbitrary and dictatorial action ever taken by any president in the history of the United States."[16] Willkie did not cease his political opportunism. He trailed Roosevelt in the polls, and Ickes ridiculed him as "a simple barefoot Wall Street lawyer." But Willkie had an issue: Roosevelt was leading the country into war. The president had signed the Selective Service Act in September, and the first drawing was a week before the election. American boys would soon be dying overseas, Willkie claimed. "If his promise to keep our boys out of foreign wars is no better than his promise to balance the budget," Willkie wailed, "they're already almost on the transports."[17]

The Battle of Britain and the "Blitz," the Nazi bombardment of

London, galvanized American support for the beleaguered British. Speaking of young Royal Air Force pilots, Churchill told the House of Commons, "Never in the field of human conflict has so much been owed by so many to so few." Edward R. Murrow's reports created sympathy for "the little people who live in those little houses, who have no uniforms and get no decoration for bravery." The press publicized the heroism of the British people. American movies such as *The Man I Married* and *Foreign Correspondent* portrayed Germans as evil aggressors. But not everyone agreed that Hitler was evil or the enemy of America.[18] Aviator Charles Lindbergh, "the Lone Eagle," dragged his socialite wife and author, Anne Morrow Lindbergh, into the fray with him. In the fall of 1940 she published *The Wave of the Future*, a best-seller in which she argued that the war in Europe was not between good and evil, but a conflict between the "Forces of the Past" (British and American democracy) and the "Forces of the Future" (Nazism, Fascism, Communism); that it was futile to fight this "wave of the future"; and that America should stay out of Europe.[19]

Many Irish, Italian, and German Americans turned against Roosevelt because of his defense of Great Britain. The Republic of Ireland was no friend of Britain. It remained neutral in the war and refused to allow British warships in its ports. Willkie made blatant appeals to Irish and Italian American voters that he would not "fight anybody else's war." Their votes might swing the election in key states such as New York, Massachusetts, and Illinois. A substantial minority of Jewish voters also opposed aid to Britain. The prominent Reform rabbi and Zionist leader Abba Hillel Silver supported Willkie against

Roosevelt. The Battle of Britain was stalled. Late polls showed Willkie cutting into Roosevelt's lead. CIO president John L. Lewis came out against the president but did not support Willkie. Even the *New York Times* endorsed Willkie. Certainly the Axis hoped for Roosevelt's defeat, and the Nazis sent money to influence the election. The German government released "the Potocki report," documents on Roosevelt's alleged intervention in Polish affairs. Göring sent $160,000 to delegates to the Democratic convention.[20]

Roosevelt went out to fight Willkie in the last two weeks of the campaign. He told the voters that the Republicans were playing politics with national defense. "Your boys are not going to be sent into foreign wars," he said. "Your President says this country is not going to war." The two parties were in a death grip. Republican radio messages were merciless: "When your boy is dying on some battlefield . . . crying out, 'Mother! Mother!—don't blame Franklin D. Roosevelt because he sent your boy to war—blame YOURSELF, because YOU sent Franklin D. Roosevelt back to the White House!"[21]

Election eve at Hyde Park was tense. A supporter had put up a sign that read "Safe on third," but the president did not feel safe. He broke into a heavy sweat and asked to be alone. His bodyguard, Mike Reilly, quickly carried out his order. FDR smoked his cigarettes in his famous cigarette holder and studied the numbers. One report had reached him that in New York only the Jews were solidly for him. But by midnight, the returns improved and victory was in the air.

Roosevelt defeated Willkie, 27,243,466 to 22,304,755, in an election in which a record 50 million people voted. Roosevelt's anti-Nazi stance had cost him much Italian, Irish, and German American support, but it won him Jewish votes. Ninety out of one hundred Jews voted Democratic, even though neither Roosevelt nor Willkie supported revision of the immigration laws. Roosevelt also gained Polish American votes. The American people chose Roosevelt because they trusted him to lead them if war came. The Nazis now knew where they stood. They, too, had lost the election, despite what one historian described as "one of the most massive interferences in American domestic affairs in history." "It is," William Shirer wrote in his Berlin diary, "a resounding slap for Hitler and Ribbentrop and the whole Nazi regime." Hitler and his generals realized that war with the Americans was likely. "The supreme law of [Roosevelt's] actions," the German chargé, Hans Thomsen, wired Berlin, "is his irreconcilable hostility to the totalitarian powers." Rosenman wrote FDR that the election "has saved, for a time at least, the kind of America I want my children to live in—perhaps the only kind in which they would be permitted to live at all."22

Roosevelt used his third inauguration to call his countrymen to their next historic mission, the defeat of Hitler and the preservation of democracy. The sun was shining and the sky was clear. Roosevelt was confident. George Washington's task, he told the American people, was to create the nation; Lincoln's was to preserve it from disruption from within. The people's task now was defeat of "disruption from without." In an answer to Anne Lindbergh's *Wave of the Future*, Roosevelt said, "There are men who believe that democracy . . . is limited or measured by a kind of mystical and artificial fate—that, for some unexplained reason, tyranny and slavery have become the surging wave of the future—

and that freedom is an ebbing tide. But we Americans know that this is not true." He quoted Washington's first inaugural: "The preservation of the sacred fire of liberty" was entrusted "to the hands of the American people," and they would not let it "be smothered with doubt and fear. . . . We do not retreat."[23]

In December 1940 Churchill had sent Roosevelt a letter that starkly described the likelihood of a Nazi victory if the United States did not abandon its "cash and carry" policy on supplying arms to Britain. The Chamber of the House of Commons had been destroyed. Massive German bombing had desolated Coventry and Bristol. Hitler knew that sinking merchant vessels was more important than attacks on enemy warships. The United States would take years to gear up for war, and Britain might not survive. Churchill told Roosevelt that the United States must protect the Atlantic sea lanes and finance the British war effort.[24]

With the election over, Roosevelt had four years to fight Hitler. He was rested and ready for battle. One evening, Hopkins recalled, "he suddenly came out with it—the whole program," later known as Lend-Lease. He answered Churchill's confidential entreaties at a December 17 press conference. He simplified his aid policy to Britain by comparing it to lending a garden hose to a neighbor whose house was on fire.

> *I don't say to him before that operation, "Neighbor, my garden hose cost me $15; you have to pay me $15 for it." What is the transaction that goes on? I don't want $15—I want my garden hose back after the fire is*

*over. All right. If it goes through the fire all right,
intact, without any damage to it, he gives it back to me
and thanks me very much for the use of it.*[25]

The essence of Lend-Lease was that if the United States supplied Britain now, the American homeland would be protected
from the Nazi arsonists next door. Rosenman and Sherwood went
to work on the "Arsenal of Democracy" speech that Roosevelt
delivered in a fireside chat on December 29, 1940. This address
was his first direct, sustained public attack on the Third Reich.
"The Nazi masters of Germany," he told the American people,
sought to "enslave the whole of Europe" and "dominate the
world." "No man can tame a tiger into a kitten by stroking it," he
told his huge radio audience. Hitler had proclaimed that there
were "two worlds that stand opposed to each other," but America
would not allow Germany to act like "a gang of outlaws" surrounding the United States and demanding tribute. The people of
Europe did not want Americans to fight. Instead, the United States
must supply ships, guns, and airplanes in record quantities at
record speed. "We must be the great arsenal of democracy," the
president urged. Lend-Lease was a substitute for declaring war. In
his address Roosevelt attacked appeasers with gusto. "There are
also American citizens, many of them in high places, who unwit-
tingly in most cases, are aiding and abetting the work of [Axis]
agents." The State Department wanted him to delete the phrase
"many of them in high places." Roosevelt laughed and wrote,
"many of them in high places, including the State Department,"

but his speechwriters deleted his addition. The speech galvanized the anti-Nazi world. "I believe that the Axis powers are not going to win this war," he concluded, ". . . our common cause will greatly succeed."[26] The Germans bombed London the night of FDR's fireside chat. It was their heaviest attack of the whole war.[27]

Americans fiercely debated H.R. 1776, the Lend-Lease bill, with no apparent thought that in 1776 the United States had fought Great Britain. Senator Robert Taft said Lend-Lease was a farce. "Lending war equipment," he quipped, "is a good deal like lending chewing gum. You don't want it back." Mothers asked Congress to "Kill Bill 1776, not our sons." Lend-Lease was insurance against war, FDR told the American people. Any "talk about sending armies to Europe" was a "deliberate untruth." Whether Roosevelt believed what he said is debatable. The Nazis secretly lobbied against Lend-Lease. Thomsen organized a letter-writing campaign, and the German embassy contributed funds to publications of the America First Committee.[28]

Lindbergh testified in Congress against Lend-Lease. Unmoved by the plight of France and Britain, the American celebrity was completely out of touch with political reality. He and his anti-Roosevelt friends on the America First Committee trumpeted the idea that a strong Germany was in America's interest as a bulwark against communism. Remarkably, many in America agreed. Thousands of students at Yale cheered Lindbergh when he spoke in October 1940. The Nazis, of course, supported the efforts of the America First Committee.[29]

American Jews mobilized to support Lend-Lease. Sol Bloom,

chairman of the House Foreign Affairs Committee, worked diligently for Lend-Lease, as did Henry Morgenthau. Senator Burton
K. Wheeler called the plan "the New Deal's triple 'A' foreign
policy—it will plough under every fourth American boy." Roosevelt was livid with rage: "I regard [Wheeler's remark] as the most
untruthful, as the most dastardly, unpatriotic thing that has ever
been said. Quote me on that."[30]

Roosevelt used his January 6, 1941, State of the Union message
to continue to educate the public on Hitler's method of conquest, his
use of "treachery and surprise," "secret agents and their dupes—
and great numbers of them are already here, and in Latin America."
He pointed out that the United States could not stand alone against
a Nazified "Europe, Asia, Africa, and Australasia . . . dominated by
the conquerors." He articulated the war aims of a country still at
peace: the "four essential freedoms . . . freedom of speech and expression—everywhere in the world . . . freedom of every person to wor-
ship God in his own way—everywhere in the world . . . freedom
from want . . . and freedom from fear." The world he envisioned was
the "very antithesis of the so-called new order of tyranny which the
dictators seek to create." He stood before Congress, which had the
sole authority to declare war, and declared his own war on Adolf
Hitler. "There can be," he concluded, "no end save victory."[31]

While isolationists such as Wheeler bellowed that Roosevelt
should force Britain to negotiate with Hitler, Roosevelt did exactly
the opposite. He and his military advisers made plans for American entry into the war. Admiral Harold R. Stark prepared Plan D
or "Plan Dog," which set forth an Atlantic "first" (defeat Germany

first), Pacific "second" (defensive war with Japan) strategy. He dispatched Robert Murphy to North Africa to try to woo the local Vichy regime away from the Nazis. "Don't bother going through the State Department," Roosevelt told Murphy, knowing that many department bureaucrats disagreed with his anti-Nazi policies and might sabotage them. Roosevelt sent Admiral William A. Leahy as ambassador to Vichy France to make it clear to the French government "that it can count on full support from the United States" if it turned on Germany. Roosevelt's spymaster William Donovan went to the Balkans to stiffen resistance to Hitler with the promise of American support.[32]

Roosevelt's next step was the clearest illustration yet that he had no faith in the State Department. Unable to meet with Churchill personally, he sent Harry Hopkins on a ten-day tour to take the measure of the prime minister and to gauge firsthand the British situation. Roosevelt trusted Hopkins. In the background Felix Frankfurter warned Churchill through intermediaries to be tactful with Hopkins and coached the mercurial leader how to handle Roosevelt's emissary. Frankfurter desperately wanted Churchill and Roosevelt to get along. So did Hopkins. "I suppose," he told Edward R. Murrow, "you could say that I've come here to try to find a way to be a catalytic agent between two prima donnas."[33]

Churchill sought to ingratiate himself with the former social worker by talking about modernizing slum cottages. "Mr. Churchill," Hopkins said, "I don't give a damn about your cottagers. I've come over here to find out how we can help you beat this fellow Hitler." "The president," Hopkins told Churchill, "is determined that we should win the war together . . . at all costs and by all means he will carry you through." The climax of Hopkins's trip was a dinner in Glasgow. "I suppose you wish to know what I am going to say to President Roosevelt on my return," he told the audience in off-the-record remarks. He said he would quote a verse from the Bible: "Whither thou goest, I will go; and where thou lodgest, I will lodge; thy people shall be my people, and thy God my God." Hopkins hesitated and said, "Even to the end." Churchill wept.[34]

The war was, Churchill recalled in his memoirs, "to be the defeat, ruin, and slaughter of Hitler, to the exclusion of all other purposes, loyalties, or aims." Roosevelt asked Churchill to deliver a major speech to help passage of Lend-Lease. "What is the answer that I shall give, in your name, to this great man, the thrice-chosen head of a nation of a hundred and thirty million?" Churchill asked over the radio. "Give us the tools," Churchill concluded, "and we will finish the job."[35]

The Italians had invaded Egypt in September 1940 but were thrown back by the British. In January 1941 the British capture of Tobruk in Libya forced the Italians to surrender but convinced Hitler to send a German army to North Africa under General Erwin Rommel. The great prize was the Suez Canal, which allowed the British fleet freedom of movement from the Indian Ocean to the Mediterranean Sea and ultimate control of the Mediterranean itself. Roosevelt's envoys encouraged Vichy France's neutrality, and kept the pressure on Pétain to refrain from anti-Jewish measures.[36]

After a bitter debate in which Willkie supported FDR ("He is *my* president now"), Lend-Lease passed the House in February by a vote of 260 to 165 and passed the Senate in March by a vote of 60 to 31, with an amendment that forbade the navy to convoy or escort merchant vessels. It was a declaration of limited war, an expression of the will of the American people at that moment. Roosevelt talked about avoiding war and undoubtedly hoped against hope to do so. However, as his sympathetic biographer Frank Freidel pointed out, "only in his most optimistic moments could Roosevelt have believed that the Axis could be overthrown without ordering millions of American soldiers and sailors into combat." Roosevelt's alter ego Hopkins became administrator of Lend-Lease. FDR's undeclared war against Hitler had taken a great stride forward. "Thank God!" one Londoner exclaimed. "The tanks are coming."[37]

In early 1941, Chaim Weizmann visited the United States to drum up support for greater Jewish immigration to Palestine. The American Palestine Committee received massive support from prominent Americans, including Senator Robert Wagner of New York, Al Smith, Willkie, and 150 congressmen. Secretary of the Treasury Henry Morgenthau Jr., sensitive to the plight of European Jewry since the SS *St. Louis* incident, enthusiastically joined the Zionist cause. He met with Bernard Joseph of the Jewish Agency and visited the JDC's refugee settlement in Santo Domingo. Morgenthau was so enthusiastic that Weizmann had to restrain the secretary's idea that three hundred thousand Jews enter Palestine "immediately" lest he embarrass Churchill. Roosevelt was noncommittal and acted cautiously.[38]

The situation in the Middle East was volatile in the spring of 1941. A pro-Nazi revolt erupted in Iraq in March, and a Vichy regime ruled Syria. Rommel's army might attack Palestine from

North Africa while the Arabs of Iraq and Syria attacked from the north. Such actions meant the death of Palestinian Jewry. Jewish leaders talked of mass suicide in the Yishuv (Jewish Palestine). Led by Wise, Brandeis, and others, American Jews worked tirelessly for the right of Jews in the Yishuv to arm and defend themselves. Morgenthau lobbied Hopkins to support a Jewish self-defense army. The British recovered Iraq and Syria in June, but not before the pro-Nazi Arabs murdered 140 Jews and injured 700 more in Baghdad.[39]

Roosevelt focused on defeating Nazism. "It tore Eleanor's heart up," one of ER's friends said, "that Harry [Hopkins] could forget the hungry and unemployed."[40] Jewish New Dealers were thrilled. Both Frankfurter and Morgenthau were actively involved in Lend-Lease. Ben Cohen left for England as legal adviser to Ambassador John G. Winant. Halifax cabled home that Cohen was a "left-wing New Dealer . . . [but] is more interested in winning the war." Frankfurter pushed hard for maximum aid to Britain. "Mr. Justice Frankfurter," Jay Pierrepont Moffat recorded in his diary, "has, I am told, virtually become the lawyer for the British case and argues for them on all occasions, even against the State Department, which is the guardian of American interests." There was still no unity in Congress or the nation on how far the United States should go in protecting transports. "The President," Admiral Stark said, "has on his hands at the present time about as difficult a situation as ever confronted any man anywhere in public life."[41]

Fortunately for Roosevelt, powerful Southern Democrats shared his views of the war in Europe. James F. Byrnes of South Carolina, Carter Glass of Virginia, Tom Connally and Sam Rayburn of Texas, and Claude Pepper of Florida were in the forefront of military preparedness. Southerners opposed liberalizing immigration laws, but they provided the critical margin in both houses to enact Lend-Lease. They were Roosevelt's "legislative bastion." Byrnes managed Lend-Lease on the Senate floor. Southerners, Glass said, favored "doing everything possible to bring about the downfall of Hitler and his gang." Instituting a draft was essential, Alabama's Luther Patrick said, "to keep our Southern boys from filling up the army." Most importantly, Senator Walter F. George of Georgia, chairman of the Senate Foreign Relations Committee, supported Lend-Lease and gave Roosevelt a valuable working concept. George was not ready, he said, "to abandon the principle of the freedom of the high seas." This gave the president a guidepost to confront Hitler's U-boats within the boundaries of the law, public opinion, and congressional sentiment.[42]

Hitler responded to Lend-Lease by invading Yugoslavia in April and killing seventeen thousand civilians. Greece was next, then Libya. Britain was being strangled by U-boats, but Roosevelt would not order armed convoys. Stimson, Knox, Ickes, and interventionists were thoroughly disgusted by Roosevelt's caution, but isolationists were hard at work in opposition. "There will be revolution . . . if the Administration gets us into this damnable war," Senator Burton K. Wheeler of Montana charged. "I am unalterably opposed to convoys. Convoys mean shooting and shooting means war," the respected Senator Robert A. Taft warned.[43] John Cudahy, former ambassador to Belgium and a Lindbergh intimate, visited Ribbentrop and Hitler in May in Berlin and urged the Nazis to declare publicly that armed convoys meant war. Roosevelt's health deteriorated. Missy LeHand, his secretary, said, "what he's suffering from most of all is a case of sheer exasperation." Eliot Janeway's analysis was that "the President was in bed . . . feeling there was nothing he could do except let the tides fall."[44]

"The hour of fascist totalitarianism seemed to have struck," T. R. Fehrenbach observed. "Everywhere, the democratic effort was always too little and too late. Hitler, always moving first, had become invincible. He had conquered all Europe except Russia and Spain, and he had a working agreement with both totalitarianism nations. His legions threatened Suez and the entire Middle East. India, which had eluded Napoleon, seemed suddenly within his reach." And Americans were still opposed by a wide margin to stopping Hitler. A Gordon Gallup public poll on April 1, 1941, showed 79 percent of citizens opposed sending American troops overseas, for any reason. The American military staff was dispirited and pervaded with defeatism all through 1941.[45]

Yet, on May 27, Roosevelt took another step, announcing an "unlimited national emergency" in a radio address. The Nazis, he said, were conducting "a world war for world domination," but Hitler would not threaten the Western Hemisphere. American policy was to resist actively "every attempt by Hitler to extend his Nazi domination to the Western Hemisphere," to "give every possible assistance to Britain" by drawing a line at Iceland and Greenland, and to create the machinery for civilian defense. "For almost an hour, a whole nation here stilled itself to listen to his words," the *Times* noted. The nation was one step closer to war.[46]

160

Chapter 9

"We Will Help to End the Curse of Hitlerism"

As Roosevelt heated up his war against Hitler, the Führer stepped up his war against the Jews. Like criminals, the Nazis hid their murderous activities. Hitler's *Nacht und Nebel* (Night and Fog) decree of December 1939 had allowed authorities to seize "persons endangering German security." People began to "vanish without a trace into the night and fog." But Hitler also made public threats, such as his December 30, 1939, New Year's message that "the Jewish-capitalistic world will not survive the twentieth century." Some of the terror visited on the Polish people and the Jews in Poland was not secret. Thousands of professors, intellectuals, doctors, and businessmen were murdered. "The Poles," Hans Frank said, "do not need universities or secondary schools." The Polish government-in-exile publicized these atrocities, particularly the imprisonment and murder of Roman Catholic priests. But the Nazis kept a great deal secret. In 1940, when two thousand Jews from Radom, Poland, were sent away to die as slave laborers, no one at the time knew what had happened to them.[1]

"After the war," Goebbels wrote on June 6, 1940, "we shall deal quickly with the Jews." Hitler talked of shipping European Jewry to the French island of Madagascar. By the fall, the Jews of France were marked for separation from society and the Jews of Warsaw were forced to live in a crowded ghetto. Millions of Jews under German rule "had no means of escape," Martin Gilbert observed.[2]

After *Kristallnacht* German Jews sought visas to any country that would accept them. Rabbi Leo Baeck's daughter went to England, while the rabbi stayed in Berlin to tend his flock. He sent an emissary to Lodz, Poland, to tell the Jews in that large ghetto to volunteer for German work groups. Advised by Mahatma Gandhi that all the Jews should commit mass suicide, Baeck disagreed. "We Jews know that the commandment of God is to live . . . I shall be the last to leave. . . . As long as a *minyan* exists in Berlin, here is my place." His American admirers arranged for a position for him as rabbi at a temple in Cincinnati. As a rabbi he would have been admitted outside the quota, but Baeck stayed. He preached in his synagogue through April 1941. The last public Yom Kippur service in wartime Berlin was in the fall of 1941. The Nazis ordered all Jews to turn in their radios on that day, the holiest of the Jewish year, which was a sacrilege. Baeck did not hand over his radio until the holiday ended.[3]

FDR wrestled with increasing antisemitism as the number of anti-Roosevelt, antiwar, and radical right-wing organizations grew in proportion to Roosevelt's toughening stand against Nazism and Fascism. Congressman John E. Rankin of Mississippi charged that "Wall Street and a little group of our international Jewish brethren" wanted war. With Nazi support, Father Charles Coughlin had reprinted *Protocols of the Elders of Zion* and denounced American Jews for leading the nation into a war with Germany to aid Great Britain. Many in his Irish Catholic audience despised Britain and agreed with the radio priest. Retired General Van Horn Moseley urged the sterilization of refugees (and later all Polish Jews) and denounced Roosevelt and Jewish warmongers trying to "take over the world." The German-American Bund held a "patriotic" rally at Madison Square Garden on George Washington's birthday, February 22, 1939, where thousands of American Nazis cheered and saluted speakers who denounced Jews, Communists, Roosevelt, Morgenthau, Baruch, and Lippmann. Aping German Nazis, George Froboese called for a "Jew-free America." Fritz Kuhn, the portly American Bundesführer, blamed the Jews for FDR's "warmongering."[4]

That antisemitism had some influence in State Department thinking and the actions of some of its personnel there can be no doubt. Many in the department thought communism worse than Nazism and that Bolshevism was a Jewish phenomenon. William Bullitt, former ambassador to France, called a Russian official "a wretched little kike." In 1941 the *New Republic* accused the department of antisemitism, charging that "petty bureaucrats" sabotaged the president's program to help refugees "just because it is his," and lambasted the "little nest of antisemites" at State.

Some consuls abroad blatantly obstructed Jewish refugees coming to the United States. Others, such as Harry Bingham, the vice consul in charge of visas in Marseilles, went to heroic lengths to save Jews and other victims of the Nazis. There were, however, few Jews in the State Department, and the antialien, nativist sentiments of many active in refugee affairs cannot be overlooked.[5]

Unfortunately, the State Department was not unique in American government or society. Antisemitism was rife in the United States Army during Roosevelt's administration. Army intelligence kept files on prominent Jewish Americans; some top officers were vocal antisemites. Indeed, three retired generals chaired the America First Committee. The Military Intelligence Division (MID) had long been a hotbed of antialien, antisemitic thinking. Office of Naval Intelligence (ONI) personnel believed that Jewish organizations such as the Joint and the Hebrew Immigrant Aid Society (HIAS) obtained privileged treatment for Jewish refugees and were vehicles for espionage and sabotage for the Nazis. The army investigated Rabbi Wise, B'nai B'rith, and FDR's Jewish advisers Rosenman and Niles, and counterintelligence officers followed four hundred Orthodox rabbis who came to see FDR in 1943.[6]

Roosevelt's response to American antisemitism was to equate antisemitism with disloyalty. He gave FBI director J. Edgar Hoover enlarged powers to fight antisemitic groups. Walter Winchell, a Jew, was an influential syndicated columnist and radio commentator. He relentlessly excoriated Hitler and his sympathizers in the United States, whom he labeled "swastinkas" and "Hitler rooters." FDR arranged for Winchell to receive tips from Hoover, and Winchell gave Hoover the publicity he loved by portraying him as a patriotic enemy of Nazism and Fascism. Representative Rankin called Winchell "a little slime-mongering kike." But none of this deterred Winchell, who went after General Moseley, William Dudley Pelley and his Silver Shirts, Lindbergh, and the Christian Mobilizers.[7]

Other groups battled American Fascism and Nazism. Leon G. Turrou's best seller *The Nazi Spy Conspiracy in America*; the movie *Confessions of a Nazi Spy*, starring Edward G. Robinson; Congressman Martin Dies of Texas and the House Un-American Activities Committee; and investigations by Congressman Dickstein contributed to the suppression of Nazism in the United States. In November 1939 Thomas E. Dewey, the New York County district attorney, charged Fritz Kuhn of the German-American Bund with grand larceny and forgery, and a jury convicted him.[8]

Acting secretly and cautiously at first, but with increasing determination, Roosevelt and Hoover discredited and destroyed the antisemitic right and the American Fascist and Nazi movements by portraying them as fifth columnists, dupes of foreign powers, and traitors. Ickes formed a group that included Dorothy Thompson, George Gallup, Henry Luce, and the theologian Reinhold Niebuhr. Luce was particularly helpful, as his "March of Time" movie newsreels and other media promoted Roosevelt's intervention policies.

Roosevelt and Hoover took on Father Coughlin. FBI agents infiltrated the Christian Front, and fourteen men were indicted for sedition. When Coughlin defended them, he lost credibility even though they were all acquitted. Other Catholics revealed that Coughlin was financed by the Nazis. Harassed by federal agents and finally abandoned by the Catholic Church hierarchy, the Radio Priest was driven off the radio by 1942.

Other right-wing antisemites eventually met the same fate, including "the Lone Eagle," Charles A. Lindbergh. Roosevelt had had enough of Lindbergh a year earlier. "If I should die tomorrow, I want you to know this," Roosevelt told Morgenthau. "I am absolutely convinced that Lindbergh is a Nazi."[9]

On April 25, 1941, Roosevelt compared Lindbergh to Clement L. Vallandigham, Lincoln's "Copperhead" opponent. "Well, Vallandigham, as you know, was an appeaser. He wanted to make peace from 1863 on because the North 'couldn't win?' " And "there were an awful lot of appeasers that pleaded with [George] Washington to quit, because he 'couldn't win.' " Lindbergh said that if his commander in chief thought he was disloyal, he should and did resign his colonel's commission in the Air Corps Reserve.[10] FDR's New Dealers; anti-Nazis; interventionists; and, of course, Jews were appalled by the famous pilot. Dorothy Thompson called him a "somber cretin" and "pro-Nazi." Winchell called him the "Lone Ostrich." Harold Ickes called Anne Morrow Lindbergh's *The Wave of the Future* "the Bible of every American Nazi, Fascist, Bundist, and appeaser."

In 1938 Lindbergh had accepted a medal, the Service Cross of the German Eagle, from Hermann Göring and a proclamation signed by Hitler. Ickes lambasted this "knight of the German Eagle" and called him "a menace to this country and its free institutions."

On Bastille Day, July 14, 1941, Ickes ridiculed Lindbergh at a meeting sponsored by France Forever. No one had ever heard Lindbergh utter "a word of horror at, or even aversion to, the bloody career that the Nazis are following," Ickes charged. "No, *I* have never heard Lindbergh utter a word of pity for Belgium or Holland or Norway or England. *I* have never heard him express a word of pity for the Poles or the Jews who have been slaughtered by the hundreds of thousands by Hitler's savages. *I* have never heard Lindbergh say a word of encouragement to the English for the fight they are so bravely making for Lindbergh's right to live his own life in his own way, as well as for their own right to do so."[11]

Lindbergh wrote Roosevelt a letter defending his acceptance of the Nazi medal at a dinner at the American embassy. Ickes demolished the pathetic former hero. "If Mr. Lindbergh feels like cringing when he is correctly referred to as a knight of the German Eagle," Ickes wrote, "why doesn't he send back the disgraceful decoration and be done with it? Americans remember that he had no hesitation about sending back to the President his commission in the United States Army Air Corps Reserve. In fact, Mr. Lindbergh returned his commission with suspicious alacrity and with a total lack of graciousness. But he still hangs on to the Nazi medal!" In Des Moines, Lindbergh made a blatantly antisemitic speech, accusing Ame-rican Jews of being prowar and anti-American.[12]

Lindbergh got what he deserved, "a Niagara of invective." According to Scott Berg, "Few men in American history had ever been so reviled." He had gone from "Public Hero No. 1" to "Public Enemy No. 1." Roosevelt's press secretary said Lindbergh's message was straight out of Berlin. He was denounced by Republican leaders Wendell Willkie and Thomas A. Dewey, by theologians and ministers of all faiths, and *Time* denounced the America First Committee as antisemitic. *Liberty* called Lindbergh "the most dangerous man in America." The Jewish community was vocal in its denunciation. But the victory over Lindbergh, America First, isolationists, antisemites, and Nazi sympathizers belonged to a man who had said nothing officially or in public, the president of the United States.

In June 1941, Democratic congressman John R. Rankin of Mississippi launched an antisemitic tirade about "warmongering international Jewry." New York representative Michael Edelstein rebutted Rankin's "scurrilous demagoguery" and was so angered by the Southerner's remarks that he collapsed and died of a heart attack in the Capitol lobby. But Rankin was not alone. He was joined at times by illustrious senators such as Robert M. LaFollette and George Norris and by less illustrious men such as Burton K. Wheeler, Gerald Nye, and Ernest Lundeen, who denounced the "Baruchs and Morgenthaus," "international bankers," and the "Rothschilds, Sassoons, Warburgs, and Kuhn Loebs." The *Chicago Tribune* warned American Jews not to agitate for war, "to think and act as Americans . . . [to] be wholly American and not members of any racial group."[13]

On June 22, 1941, Hitler invaded the Soviet Union. Believing he could quickly defeat the Soviets and then turn his attention to Britain before the United States could gear up for war, the Führer unleashed Operation Barbarossa, the most massive military assault in world history. More than three and a half million German troops in 153 divisions, 3,300 tanks, 2,700 aircraft, and 600,000 motor vehicles attacked north and south. By September the Germans had captured two million Soviet prisoners.[14]

Churchill, the quintessential anti-Communist, was quick to offer aid to his former enemy. "If Hitler invaded Hell I would make at least a favourable reference to the Devil in the House of Commons," he quipped. Roosevelt's cabinet and the American public were divided. Most felt the Soviet Union would collapse quickly. The invasion set off a new wave of isolationism, as Hitler had foretold. Many agreed with Missouri Democrat Bennett Clark that "Stalin is as bloody-handed as Hitler." Harry Truman said that if Germany "is winning we ought to help Russia, and if Russia is winning, we ought to help Germany, and that way let them kill as many as possible."

Roosevelt, however, wanted to whip Hitler first and foremost. On June 24 he said, "of course we are going to give all the aid we possibly can to Russia." As he had sent Hopkins to evaluate Churchill, Roosevelt sent him to Moscow to take the measure of Joseph Stalin. The Soviet Union, like Britain, relied heavily on America's industrial power to assist their war effort. Roosevelt fought bitterly with his own War and State Departments, which were slow to obey his orders to aid the Russians.

Despite FDR's resolve, the United States was ill prepared to help the victims of Nazi aggression. "The national effort," Langer and Gleason wrote, "was still but a half-hearted one . . . the administration of the war production program remained chaotic."

Meanwhile, the Germans continued to bomb England. "You do your worst," Churchill challenged Hitler in a speech on July 14, "and we will do our best." British bombs soon began to fall on German cities.[15]

In 1940 Hitler and his top officials had been undecided how to solve the "Jewish Question." At that time they had even considered sending millions of Jews to Madagascar, off the coast of Africa. Poland had been an "experimental playground" of mass killings. But Operation Barbarossa brought to full flower Hitler's concept of "a war of annihilation" against the homeland of "Jewish Bolshevism." The Russian invasion gave new meaning to Hitler's genocidal dreams. "We must forget the concept of comradeship between soldiers," the Führer told his senior officers in March 1941. "A Communist is no comrade before or after the battle. This is a war of annihilation." Hitler told Goebbels, "when we have won, who will ask us about the methods?" By the summer of 1941 Hitler had decided to deport European Jews to Poland and Russia, which he believed would soon be defeated. As enslaved laborers the Jews would gradually die there from starvation, overwork, and exposure.[16]

The war against the Russians was as barbaric and genocidal as the war against the Poles. The Nazis murdered Soviet civilians without remorse, including "all Bolshevist leaders or commissars," the "Jewish-Bolshevik intelligentsia," Jews generally, Russian POWs, and partisans. The German army calculated that their policies would kill thirty million people. The infamous Commissar Order of June 6 explicitly required German soldiers to murder "all grades of political commissars." Four specifically selected SS military units or *Einsatzgruppen* (task groups) of six hundred to a thousand men each, accompanied the Wehrmacht into Russia as did more numerous battalions of *Ordnungspolizei* (German Order Police). Their mission was to murder civilians and prisoners of war. Nazis believed in the racial inferiority of the Slavs ("a rabbit family"), the Ukrainians ("idle, disorganized"), and the Russians, in addition to the Jews. The murder of millions of Jews could be hidden in this war on Russia.[17]

Three thousand Poles were murdered at Auschwitz by March 1941. The Germans created concentration camps and prisons to house political prisoners, Poles, Jews, and homosexuals. They murdered Jews and Serbs in Yugoslavia. Hundreds of thousands of Russian prisoners of war were also shot, beaten, starved, and killed by exposure, exhaustion, and forced marches. Some Latvians, Romanians, Lithuanians, Ukrainians, and others who delighted in persecuting Jews joined in their murderous activities. By July, Jews were being murdered on a large scale in Poland and in Russia. Ten thousand Jews were massacred in Kishinev. Twenty-three thousand six hundred Hungarian Jews were deported to Russia and shot. Churchill told the British people in August that "scores of thousands" of Russians were being murdered by ruthless Germans. "We are in the presence," he said, "of a crime without a name."[18]

The Holocaust was still in its infancy, but it had become the Final Solution. If Hitler underestimated the restraints on FDR and the unwillingness of the American people to go to war, the House of Representatives made it perfectly clear in the summer of 1941. The Selective Service Act of 1940 expired in 1941, and draftees were required to serve only twelve months. Men in the army were threatening to "go over the hill by October," writing "OHIO" on their barracks walls. After strenuous efforts by Stimson and Marshall, the House passed a bill extending the draft by a single vote, 203 to 202.[19]

On Sunday, August 3, 1941, Roosevelt left the White House to go fishing on the *Potomac*, his presidential yacht. He sailed to Cape Cod; then, in the dark of night, he secretly boarded the heavy cruiser USS *Augusta*. He met Churchill at Argentia Harbor on the Newfoundland coast. In a historic meeting, the president of the United States, a neutral country, met with the prime minister of a nation at war to plan joint military strategy and to announce "certain common principles," that is, their war aims. The Atlantic Charter, a mimeographed press release, promised that the Anglo-Americans sought no territory but only the "right of all peoples to choose the form of government under which they will live." It assumed "the final destruction of the Nazi tyranny and a just peace." Public reaction to the Atlantic Charter was predictable. Republicans charged Roosevelt with warmongering and secret deals. The *Chicago Tribune* called Roosevelt a true British Tory, and the Nazis blamed the Jews. Hitler blamed everything on "the Jewish clique surrounding Roosevelt."[20]

Despite his defiance of aggressors, Roosevelt did not want war with Japan in 1941 or 1942. He remained adamant, however, that

Franklin D. Roosevelt and Churchill on board the Prince of Wales, *at the Atlantic Conference at Argentia Harbour, Newfoundland, August 10, 1941.*

Courtesy of the Franklin D. Roosevelt Library

Japan withdraw from China. His weapon was an economic embargo, and he gradually restricted trade with Japan to slow their military buildup and to stop Japanese aggression. In July 1941 he froze Japanese assets in the United States but allowed trade to continue, overseen by a government committee. "He conceived the freeze on assets," Kennedy concluded, "as a temporary and complicating device, one more click of the trade-sanction ratchet." Hard-liners wanted more aggressive action, but Roosevelt demurred. He thought it best "to slip the noose around Japan's neck and give it a jerk now and then." The freeze went into effect as Roosevelt left to meet with Churchill at Argentia. To suit their stronger anti-Japanese aims, State Department staffers interpreted his policy as a *total* freeze of *all* Japanese assets. They forced his hand, but the president could not back down later when he learned what had happened.[21]

Hitler *did not want* war with the United States—at least not until he had defeated Russia and could turn his full attention to Britain. He ordered his admirals to avoid at all costs hostile incidents with the United States Navy. But Roosevelt *did want* war with Nazi Germany. Burns believed Roosevelt crossed the threshold of war in July. "There is little doubt," Joseph P. Lash believed, "that in the autumn of 1941, Roosevelt was seeking to provoke an undeclared war with Germany because he knew that he could not get a declaration of war from Congress." On September 4, 1941, a German U-boat appeared 165 miles off Iceland. The World War I–era destroyer USS *Greer* steered a course toward the U-boat so that the British could attack it. Although not escorting a convoy, the captain of the *Greer* had very broadly interpreted his orders to protect American ships from Nazi submarines. The British attempted to bomb the U-boat but missed. The submarine commander, believing the *Greer* had attacked him, retaliated by firing torpedoes, which missed the ship.[22]

Roosevelt used the *Greer* incident to stoke hatred of Nazi Germany. "I am sure that even now the Nazis are waiting to see whether the United States will by silence give them the green light to go ahead on their path of destruction." Roosevelt warned Hitler that he dare go no farther. "One peaceful nation after another has met disaster because each refused to look the Nazi danger squarely in the eye until it actually had them by the throat. The United

States will not make that fatal mistake." "This was piracy," he told the nation, "piracy legally and morally." "Hitler's advance guard—not only his avowed agents but also his dupes among us— have sought to make ready for him footholds and bridgeheads in the New World." Roosevelt insisted that he did not seek war with Germany. "But . . . when you see a rattlesnake poised to strike, you do not wait until he has struck before you crush him." From now on, the president warned, German or Italian warships entering American waters would be attacked.

FDR was exhausted by the game he was playing with Hitler but did not waver in his resolve. He, alone in the world, *both* understood the Nazi menace *and* had the power to do something about it, if only he could bring his reluctant countrymen to understand. On October 9, in a secret meeting with Vice President Henry Wallace and others, Roosevelt placed development of the atomic bomb in the hands of the army.[23]

Roosevelt had described the *Greer* incident to the nation on September 11 as an unprovoked attack. Isolationists charged that FDR was scheming to stage an incident to provoke war. The German Foreign Office, knowing Congress opposed war with Germany, saw to it that a communiqué protesting Roosevelt's reaction to the *Greer* incident was delivered to the leading isolationist members of Congress, Hitler's allies in America. The Germans knew that a formal diplomatic protest to the State Department would be dismissed. The Nazis told their agents in Washington to expose "Roosevelt's warmongering policy" in "a suitably confidential manner."[24]

With the German conquest of the Netherlands in May 1940,

the refugee Frank family was trapped. They had left Germany to escape the Nazis, but the Nazis were now back in control of their lives. They could not escape this time. A family with two young daughters and a sick, elderly grandmother could not just walk across the border. They had no car. In the beginning, German rule lay lightly on the Dutch people. Life went on more or less as it had. Books by Jewish authors and kosher practices were banned, and Jews were ordered to register with the government. But the new rulers seemed relatively benign. Otto Frank's business improved. In December 1940 he moved his offices to 263 Prisengracht near the Westerkerk, Amsterdam's most famous landmark. Anne continued to play at the office, type on the typewriters, and telephone from room to room.[25]

Franklin D. Roosevelt and Eleanor Roosevelt returning to the White House after his third inauguration, January 20, 1941.

Courtesy of the Franklin D. Roosevelt Library

FDR's domestic war on antisemites and isolationists continued. He could not attack the far-right antisemites, discredit isolationists, harass and arrest fifth columnists, American Nazis, and Fascists, and hold together his New Deal coalition of Catholics, Jews, blacks, and other ethnic factions *and* single-handedly reform the immigration laws to admit imperiled Jewish refugees. He needed the help of some of his bitterest critics to do that.

Senator Gerald Nye of Wisconsin, Lindbergh, and other anti-semites tried to divert the growing anti-Nazi attitude of the American public by attacking the Hollywood movie studios as Jewish "war propaganda machines" run by aliens, with names such as Cohn, Mayer, Warner, and Goldwyn. According to Nye, films such as *Sergeant York* starring Gary Cooper (1941); Charlie Chaplin's *The Great Dictator* (1941), which ridiculed Hitler; and *The Man I Married* (1940) aimed to arouse "war hysteria." Nye, chairman from 1934 to 1936 of a Senate committee investigating the role of American businesses in the United States' entrance into World War I, believed Roosevelt was manipulating Hollywood to turn out anti-Nazi propaganda. He railed against "Jewish radio commentators, columnists, and publications." Jews had "inborn hatreds" of Germans and harbored "vengeful spirits." Senator Charles W. Tobey of New Hampshire, a Nye committee member, had called Sol Bloom "a Jew with all it implies; very able and always makes everything play for his own aggrandizement."

The movie moguls consulted with Roosevelt aides and decided to stare down the committee. They retained Wendell Willkie as counsel. He blasted the committee as antisemitic and un-American. Harry M. Warner testified that Jews were businessmen, not propagandists, but he *was* in favor of Roosevelt's foreign policy and opposed to Nazism. "I, Harry Warner, head of a motion-picture company, hating Nazism, will do everything in the world to incite the people against Nazism," he declared. In case the committee was still confused, Willkie told them that if it intended "to inquire whether or not the motion-picture industry, as a whole, and its leading executives, as individuals, are opposed to the Nazi dictatorship . . . there need be no investigation. . . . We abhor everything which Hitler represents."

The president ridiculed Nye's committee at a press conference. He read a telegram he claimed had been sent to the committee: "Have just been reading book called Holy Bible," Roosevelt told the press. "Has large circulation in this country. Written entirely by foreign-born, mostly Jews. First part full of warmongering propaganda. Second part condemns isolationism, with faked story about Samaritan. Dangerous. Should be added to your list and suppressed."26

By now, the American public was fed up with Nazi bullying and persecution. While many Americans disliked Jews, they detested Nazis. The press, led by Luce's *Life* magazine, condemned Nye and called his committee a "kangaroo court." When the committee adjourned on September 26, 1941, "the hearings were in disarray."27

In 1941, the Nazi puppet government tightened the noose on the Jews of Amsterdam. In January, Jews were banned from movie theaters. The next month, the Jewish quarter was cordoned off and hundreds of Jews were arrested and bullied. Demonstrations and a general strike in support of the Jews were ruthlessly suppressed. Jews were required to deposit their money with a Jewish banking house controlled by the government. In the summer Jews were banned from beaches, parks, and hotels. But in July the Franks traveled fifty miles outside Amsterdam to visit relatives. Otto and Anne stayed in a hotel, despite the regulations, on a trip to the country in September. Jewish children were told in September that they were going to separate schools. Anne had to leave her classmates and knew no one in her new class. By October 1941 a decree allowed Nazi functionaries to deprive Jews of their jobs and "Aryanize" Jewish businesses. Otto Frank transferred his business to his non-Jewish friend Jan Gies.[28]

Despite its slow pace in capturing Western Europe, the flames of the Holocaust were engulfing Russia. In August Germans used poison gas to murder Russian POWs and later killed Poles and Jews. In September at Babi Yar near Kiev, 33,771 Jews were murdered and another 35,782 "Jews and Communists" in two other cities. Thousands of Russian POWs were killed in the Sachsenhausen concentration camp. The new plan, murder by gas, would, Martin Gilbert wrote, "ensure that most future killing would be done behind a mask of secrecy," but by late 1942 the Nazis had already murdered one million Jews without the use of gas or death camps.[29]

Hitler hoped to kill every Jew in the world, not just European Jewry. On November 28, 1941, he met with Haj Amin el-Husseni, the grand mufti of Jerusalem. The Muslim leader told the Führer that the Arab world was firmly convinced the Germans would be victorious because of German military might and "because Allah could never grant victory to an unjust cause." Hitler reminded el-Husseni that he was "fighting the Jews without respite" and that this "naturally entailed a stiff opposition to the Jewish homeland in Palestine where the Jews want to establish . . . a central government for their own pernicious purposes." Germany wanted to liberate the Arabs from the British. After that, "Germany's only remaining objective in the region would be limited to the annihilation of the Jews living under British protection in Arab lands."[30]

The Atlantic naval incident Roosevelt hoped for never occurred. The USS *Kearny* was torpedoed in October and eleven sailors were killed, but that failed to pull the trigger. On Navy Day, October 30, 1941, Roosevelt made a warlike speech claiming he had a Nazi map of South America showing five nations targeted for subjugation. He excoriated Hitlerism and Nazism. "We have wished to avoid shooting," Roosevelt warned, "but the shooting has started. And history has recorded who fired the first shot. In the long run, however, all that will matter is who fired the last shot." He told his audiences that Hitler planned to abolish all existing religions. Hitler sought to impose an "International Nazi Church" upon the whole world. *Mein Kampf* would be Holy Writ "and in the place of the cross of Christ will be put two symbols— the swastika and the naked sword." Nazi cruelty was hard for Americans to understand. "It has not been easy for us Americans to adjust ourselves to the shocking realities of a world in which the principles of common humanity and common decency are being mowed down by the firing squads of the Gestapo," Roosevelt told the nation. The march of Hitlerism would be stopped, he told his enthusiastic listeners. "Very simply and very bluntly—we are pledged to pull our own oar in the destruction of Hitlerism. . . . And when we have helped to end the curse of Hitlerism," he promised, "we shall help to establish a new peace."[31]

Congress debated revision of the neutrality laws and allowed the arming of cargo ships by slim margins. On October 30, the date of FDR's rousing speech, a U-boat torpedoed the *Reuben James*, killing 115 sailors, but Americans were *still* not ready for war. Roosevelt met the loss "with fatalistic resignation." The Nazi press disclosed that Roosevelt had appointed William J. "Wild Bill" Donovan head of a spy agency: "The Jew-Roosevelt," the *Völkischer Beobachter* headlined, "Names Warmaker Donovan as Super Agitator." "He had no more tricks left," Robert Sherwood recalled. "The bag from which he had pulled so many rabbits was empty." But there was no question in anyone's mind that, as *Time* magazine stated on November 10, 1941, Roosevelt was "waging the first great undeclared war in U.S. history."[32]

The Japanese dropped the lighted match into this smoking tinderbox when the Imperial Air Force attacked the American fleet at Pearl Harbor. Roosevelt was "completely calm," ER wrote. "His reaction to any event was always to be calm." "Yesterday," Roosevelt told the Congress, "December 7, 1941—a date which will live in infamy—the United States of America was suddenly and deliberately attacked by naval and air forces of the Empire of Japan." He recounted Japanese treachery and the empire's attacks on other countries. "No matter how long it may take us to overcome this premeditated invasion, the American people in their righteous might will win through to absolute victory."[33]

But this was not the war Roosevelt wanted. It was, FDR had said to Churchill in August, "the wrong war in the wrong ocean at the wrong time." He and Churchill had mapped out a Germany

Pearl Harbor, December 7, 1941.

Courtesy of the Franklin D. Roosevelt Library

first, Japan second strategy. Despite the tragic loss of life and ships at Pearl Harbor, and despite the American people's near-unanimous desire to retaliate against Japan, Roosevelt's chief enemy was Adolf Hitler. Hitler did not have to declare war on the United States. The United States had no reason to declare war on Germany. Roosevelt waited.

On December 11, 1941, Hitler declared war on the United States. Despite the Führer's misgivings about having to wage a two-front war, he knew that Roosevelt was his mortal enemy and would do whatever was necessary to rescue Great Britain. He now had the Japanese navy on his side. Thus he wanted to make certain that the United States was also ensnared in a two-front war. He believed Roosevelt was controlled by the Jews; that war with America was inevitable, and that Germany may as well strike at a time of Japanese ascendance in the Pacific. Finally, he had nothing but contempt for the weak, "decayed . . . half Judaized, half Negrified" irresolute Americans.[34]

Roosevelt had gotten the better of Hitler in their war of nerves. His verbal attacks and secret machinations had infuriated Hitler and clouded his judgment. In a rambling speech to the Reichstag, Hitler lashed out at Roosevelt. The American president had started the war to cover up his failures. Backed by millionaires and Jews, Roosevelt was "responsible for the Second World War. . . . I consider him mad, just as Wilson was. . . . Roosevelt comes from a rich family. . . . I was the child of a small, poor family. . . . [Roosevelt] was strengthened in dissemblance by the Jews around him . . . The full diabolical meanness of Jewry rallied around this man, and he stretched out his hands."[35]

Roosevelt made it plain in his brief message to Congress requesting recognition of a state of war between the United States and Germany that he viewed the struggle as one of "the forces of justice and of righteousness over the forces of savagery and barbarism." He had no illusions about the mad leader and murderous regime he was determined to destroy.[36]

Churchill relished the events of December 1941. "Many disasters, immeasurable cost, and tribulation lay ahead," he said, but the United States was now at Great Britain's side. The war would be won. "England would live; Britain would live." Churchill later recalled, "Hitler's fate was sealed." But European Jewry did not live. Their fate also was sealed. On December 8, 1941, one day after "the date which would live in infamy," hundreds of Polish Jews were secretly gassed in an experimental, specially designed building in Chelmno.[37]

Chapter 10

"Spies, Saboteurs, and Traitors Are the Actors in This New Tragedy"

Roosevelt had worked and schemed hard after the fall of France to prepare the American people to join the Allies' great crusade against the Nazis. In the last days of December 1941 he had his war. The tripartite Axis of Germany, Italy, and Japan threatened global domination, but the Allies knew they must first save Europe, then the rest of the world. But what had FDR done to save nonbelligerent refugees of Europe? So many people—Poles, Russians, and Jews—had been targeted for death by happenstance of birth, faith, and ethnicity.

Roosevelt was deluged with requests to help European refugees. There were hundreds of thousands of non-Jewish refugees in flight from Poland, Finland, France, Belgium, and the Netherlands. In June 1940 Freda Kirchwey, editor of the *Nation*, telegraphed Roosevelt asking him to save "valuable lives of leading anti-Fascists now in France." He replied that he was deeply sympathetic, but the problem was "formidable and difficult." ER sought a passport for Varian Fry of the Emergency Rescue Committee to go to France to rescue political and intellectual refugees. FDR's reply to his wife was cautious. (Fry went.) Roosevelt was besieged with requests for visas for British refugee children. In reply to a request from G. Ashton Oldham, Episcopal bishop of Albany, New York, he explained the quota system, the need for affidavits, the strict immigration laws, and how the government was doing its best. Harold Ickes wrote him about the Spanish Refugee Rebel Campaign because of "the urgency of the situation." FDR replied in detail, explaining the restrictive laws, and concluded, "I am convinced that everything practicable, consistent with the existing law, is now being done." To give more aid to refugees, he told Ickes, Congress would have to change the laws.[1]

By 1940, no one doubted Hitler's ruthlessness. The British were at war with Germany; therefore German refugees, including German Jews, were enemy aliens. All of these "aliens" would have to be interned when they entered England. The British could not understand why Germany drove skilled citizens out of the country in wartime, even if they were Jews, except to infiltrate the host countries or overwhelm them with poor, dependent refugees. German Jews did not doubt that their coreligionists were used as hostages and unwilling spies. Rabbi Leo Baeck's biographer described Adolf Eichmann's fury when he learned that Martha Hirsch's in-laws had emigrated in June 1941. "Relatives in Germany could be hostages; relatives outside of Germany were of no value to the Nazis."[2]

In the summer of 1940, many in Europe and the United States

believed that Nazism *was* the wave of the future. Roosevelt received alarming reports about Nazi activities in South America. Many Europeans happily collaborated with the Nazis. Senator Key Pittman of Nevada, chairman of the Senate Foreign Relations Committee, called on the British government to abandon the British Isles. "This will end Hitler's ambition for world conquest," he asserted. "Germans of future generations will honor Herr Hitler as a genius," Mahatma Gandhi wrote in an Indian newspaper in June. The aga khan said that he and the khedive of Egypt "will both drink a bottle of champagne when the Fuhrer sleeps in Windsor Castle." The Germans believed the war was over. "The final victory of Germany over England," Alfred Jodl wrote, "is only a question of time."[3]

But Franklin and Eleanor Roosevelt did not see the Nazis as invincible. ER wrote of the plight of European Jewry in her newspaper column "My Day." The day after the invasion of Poland, she condemned Hitler for mistreating minorities, "not only Jews, but also Christians." She lauded the efforts of Mrs. Stephen Wise and the Women's Division of the American Jewish Congress to house all refugees, Jewish and non-Jewish. She criticized the Christian Front for its antisemitic antics and wrote frequently about the evil of intolerance. "Perhaps the wave of antisemitism is our greatest manifestation of intolerance today," she wrote in *Cosmopolitan* in February 1940, "though in some places anti-Catholicism runs a close second, and in others fear of the Negro's aspirations is paramount." In June 1940, with the election looming in November, she publicly urged revision of immigration laws to admit opponents of Nazism and Fascism.[4]

Jewish organizations and leaders were actively engaged in sur-
veilling Nazi groups in the United States. Congressman Dickstein
openly denounced American pro-Nazi groups and served as vice
chairman of a committee to investigate Nazi subversion. He
received pro-Nazi hate mail in return. One letter writer condemned "hoodlums, mainly Jewish" who interrupted a German-
American Bund meeting in New York and decried "Yiddsher
bedlam which has so conspicuously characterized our Jew Deal."
The American Jewish Congress created a "Bureau of Investigation," a youth division of the Congress to spy on pro-Nazi groups.
Young New York Jews infiltrated meetings of the German-American
Bund, the American Nationalist Party, and the Citizens Committee
of 500 and reported on meetings of more than forty subversive
organizations.[5]

With Hitler and Mussolini in control of most of Europe, many
in the American government became concerned about internal
subversion by immigrants from Europe, the so-called "fifth
column" or "Trojan horse." Speaking before a joint session of
Congress on May 16, 1940, the president said bluntly, "These are
ominous days—days whose swift and shocking developments force
every neutral nation to look to its defenses." He asked Congress to
examine the dangers that confronted the American people. "We
have seen the treacherous use of the 'fifth column' by which persons supposed to be peaceful visitors were actually a part of an
enemy unit of occupation." Attacks on factories and munition
works were now a "part of the new technique of modern war." He
asked for a large appropriation for defense and said, "Our

defenses must be invulnerable, our security absolute." He meant it. FDR brought his message to the American people on May 26, 1940, when he told them in a fireside chat that "spies, saboteurs, and traitors are the actors in this new tragedy. With all of these we must and will deal vigorously."[6]

Breckinridge Long argued for cutting off *all* immigration as a security measure, but Roosevelt disagreed, fearing Congress would overreact. On June 29, 1940, the State Department instructed its officers to withhold permanent visas from anyone about whom they had "any doubt whatsoever." The decision to limit immigration prevented many Jews from fleeing Germany, Poland, France, and other countries, but not all Jews were trying to flee in 1940.[7] German and Austrian immigration visas to the United States fell from 27,370 in 1939 to 4,883 in 1942.

The fall of France, with an army of 1.5 million soldiers and its famed Maginot Line of fortifications, made no sense to most Americans in 1940. The only explanation was that a "fifth column" of German spies and traitors within France had aided its collapse. Many Americans believed that German Jewish refugees played a role in the defeat of France, willingly or under duress as a result of Nazi threats against their families in the Fatherland. Americans viewed European Jews as radicals, Communists, and socialists who could not be counted on as loyal Americans in this hour of crisis. (The phrase "fifth column" came from the Spanish Civil War when the Fascist general General Emilio Mola said that he had four columns of troops encircling Madrid and a "fifth" column of collaborators already in the city.)[8]

The United States was beset by near-hysteria over fifth colum-nists, a hysteria abetted by many people for many reasons, including the president's stoking of anti-Nazi feeling and because it made good copy for radio and newspapers. Representative Samuel Dick-stein, a New York Democrat, introduced legislation to investigate Nazi activities in the United States. Minority citizens who refused to salute the flag were beaten. In one poll, 71 percent of Americans believed that Germany had "already started to organize a 'fifth column' in this country." Magazines featured stories such as "Hitler's Slave Spies in America" and "Enemies within Our Gates." Edward G. Robinson starred in the movie *Confessions of a Nazi Spy.* "Fifth-Column Lessons for Americans" appeared in newspa-pers. People were warned to be on the alert around "German waiters" who might be "snoopers" for Hitler. Breckinridge Long was concerned about the thousands of aliens in the United States, "some of them known to be active German agents."

William C. Bullitt, former ambassador to France, erroneously stated in a public speech that "more than one half the spies cap-tured doing actual military spy work against the French army were refugees from Germany." William Allen White reported in 1940 that Joseph Goebbels had told Cornelius Vanderbilt in 1939: "[W]hen we get good and ready, we expect to take your imperti-nent nation from within."[9]

Germans were not the only potential enemies. Roosevelt had long apprehended the infiltration of the Americas by foreign powers, including the Japanese. As early as 1934 he asked the State Department to investigate Japanese espionage. The American government was concerned about the loyalty of Japanese Hawaiians, and prepared a report on the issue in 1933. In fact, there were "pro-Japanese sentiments among Japanese Americans in Hawaii."[10] Roosevelt made plans to round up suspected Japanese Americans in Hawaii to protect the American military presence. By 1940 Roosevelt viewed Japanese Americans as potential "enemy aliens" even though they were American citizens.

State Department officials, some of them antisemites and others prejudiced against refugees from Eastern and Southern Europe, closed the gates of immigration. By June 1940 all consuls were instructed not to issue a visa "if there is any doubt whatsoever concerning the alien." George Messersmith, Sumner Welles, and Adolf Berle, all sympathetic to Jewish concerns, expressed deep anxieties about the fifth-column threat.[11] Congress was as determined as the president to control subversive and terrorist activities. The Alien Registration Act of 1940, commonly known as the Smith Act, outlawed as "subversive" activities such as advocating the overthrow of the government. It expanded the grounds for the deportation of aliens and required all aliens in the United States over age fourteen to register and be fingerprinted.

Many diplomats overseas were concerned about exactly who was coming to America and why. Undersecretary Welles wrote FDR that the United States could not allow Germany to get away with forcing Jews into France because the Germans would then force more Jews out and inaugurate a " 'reign of terror' against the Jewish people." Herbert C. Pell, minister in Portugal, wrote Hull in September 1940 that while he sympathized with the goals of the president's Advisory Committee on Political Refugees (PACPR), the system was not working properly. In his opinion, political influence and bribery resulted in visas being granted in many cases to "the least desirable element and those against whom there is evident ground for doubt." Those who had the backing of "racial" organizations (i.e., Jewish groups) got ahead of more desirable individuals, sometimes bragging about their political influence on the State Department. Pell asked for an investigation, as he believed doubtful individuals were being allowed to enter the United States. "The matter is already a subject of general Lisbon gossip and may become an open scandal," he wrote.[12]

Roosevelt did not quibble about civil liberties when he perceived that the nation's security was at risk. He believed that security came before all else. FDR knew a great deal about spies and sabotage. He had been assistant secretary of the navy in 1916, when German saboteurs blew up the National Storage Plant on Black Tom Island near New York City. That subversive act killed seven workers and destroyed valuable munitions destined for the Allies. In 1919, as he and Eleanor parked their car on R Street in Washington, a would-be assassin accidentally blew himself to pieces and damaged Attorney General A. Mitchell Palmer's house. Roosevelt also knew the value of espionage. He planned to use it extensively himself and expected Hitler to do the same.[13]

Despite assertions by Roosevelt critics among Holocaust historians to the contrary, the threat of German sabotage and espionage in the United States was real. The *Abwehr*, the German spy agency, had made America a high-priority target and was inactive before

December 1941 only because of Hitler's desire to keep America out of the war. The FBI ultimately arrested *Abwehr* agents, but not before they stole the Norden bombsight; aided pro-Nazi groups; and provided technical information on ships, aircraft, and equipment, and convoys to Britain.[14]

FDR understood the influence of German Americans and their potential ability to thwart his plans to defeat Hitler. Nazi propaganda had been aimed at ethnic Germans throughout the Americas since 1933. In 1937, Hermann Göring told William C. Bullitt that there were people in his government who "believe that we should attempt to organize Germans, especially of the Middle West, who if war came might prevent the United States entering such a conflict." Nazi propagandists in the United States had many tools to employ. They manipulated Americans' traditional isolationism, the dislocations of World War I, the German ethnic roots of many Americans, and prejudice against Germany's East European enemies Poles and Slavs.[15] In the summer of 1940, Hans Thomsen, the German chargé, spent at least $20,000 promoting isolationist books and articles. He hired one publicist to write articles debunking the threat of a fifth column. Clearly the Nazis themselves wanted to protect their American spies and fifth columnists.[16]

President Roosevelt himself had a close call with espionage in May 1940. Scotland Yard arrested Tyler Kent, a clerk in the U.S. embassy in London, for taking hundreds of documents, including secret correspondence between Roosevelt and Churchill. If revealed, these documents, might have compromised the president's efforts to aid Britain and may even have cost him the 1940 election. Kent was an antisemite and Roosevelt-hater. He explained to his friends that Roosevelt was trying to draw America into this "Jew's war." He had stickers on his office filing cabinet that stated "THIS IS A JEW'S WAR." Kent passed the documents to the Italian embassy and then to the Nazi foreign office. He was tried in secret and went to prison. However, the Germans had secured some U.S. codes, and Roosevelt was rattled. "From this point on," Breitman noted, "FDR could hardly overemphasize the Fifth Column danger."[17]

The president was so concerned about spies that he asked Congress to transfer the Immigration and Naturalization Service from the Labor Department to the Justice Department. American visa policies were now a matter of grave concern, and State Department officials "stiffened their resolve not to allow a misplaced humanitarianism to interfere with their duty." Roosevelt and other government officials feared that Nazi or Soviet agents were infiltrating the United States disguised as refugees. This official policy of suspicion quashed any hopes that Roosevelt would open wide America's doors to European Jews. The United States, Louis De Jong concluded, "had lost their unshakable faith in their absolute safety."[18]

Another reason for the new restrictions on immigration was FDR's appointment of Breckinridge Long to be special assistant secretary of state in charge of emergency war matters. Long was a friend of the president, a Woodrow Wilson Democrat descended from two aristocratic Southern families, the Breckinridges of Kentucky and the Longs of North Carolina. He had been assistant secretary of state under Wilson and an unsuccessful candidate for the

U.S. Senate from his native Missouri. Long had been a major contributor to Roosevelt's campaigns and was a floor manager at the 1932 Democratic convention. Now a Marylander, he had helped Roosevelt in the bitter 1938 campaign against Senator Millard Tydings and helped raise funds for FDR's presidential library.[19]

After the German invasion of Poland in 1939, Roosevelt had appointed Long special assistant secretary in charge of emergency war matters. After Pearl Harbor Long became head of the State Department's Special War Problems Division. In that post he became the chief American government official in charge of refugees. Long was overwhelmed by the job. He frequently described in his diary events following "one another so fast" that it was hard to appreciate "the rate of speed at which we are proceeding." To Long, Hitler appeared to have outdone Alexander the Great, Julius Caesar, Genghis Khan, and Napoleon. "No one knows what will happen next," Long worried.[20]

Like Roosevelt, Long was a wealthy elitist and a loyal Democrat, but unlike Roosevelt, not much of a humanitarian. He was conservative, a nativist, and a fervent believer in a restrictive immigration policy. He viewed himself as guarding the gates of America against spies, saboteurs, Nazis, and Communists, as he simultaneously fended off well-meaning but mistaken "wild-eyed elements" and other misguided altruists and bleeding hearts. In January 1940 Long opposed aid to Finland and he opposed aid to the Poles in March 1940 because of "political repercussions." He was especially insensitive to the difficulties facing Jewish refugees.[21]

Long's pessimism and caution consistently led him to take the most defeatist and restrictive positions on refugee matters. Even though he was a political appointee among State Department bureaucrats, he became a zealous convert to the bureaucratic mind-set. When asked to handle the evacuation of children out of England, he felt "under our laws we are limited." He perceived many reasons why helping the English children would be difficult. There were too many children; each case had to be handled individually; and refuges must be found. Enthusiasm for bringing them might wane, and it would be cruel to the children if they got to the United States and were not properly cared for. Later he described the emotion over the British refugee children as "an enormous psychosis," and thought the surest road to war would be the sinking of an American ship with "two thousand babies on it." In fact, in August 1940 he thought the British would be defeated.[22]

Long was incensed over the *Quanza* incident in the summer of 1940. The SS *Quanza* left Lisbon, Portugal, on August 9, 1940, with 317 passengers. One hundred ninety-six passengers disembarked in New York City on August 19, and the ship sailed to Veracruz, Mexico. The remaining passengers were refugees who had Mexican visas but were denied entry. The ship headed back to the United States to take on coal at Norfolk, Virginia, before sailing back to Lisbon. Friends of the refugees began to lobby ER to let the refugees enter the United States. These friends retained a Jewish lawyer in Norfolk, Jacob L. Morewitz, to file a suit on their behalf in federal court. The ship landed on September 11, in the middle of the election campaign.[23]

Roosevelt sent Patrick Malin of the PACPR to Norfolk. Malin

ruled on the spot that 35 people had valid travel documents and that the rest of the passengers were political refugees so they could all come ashore. Long was livid when he learned of the events in Norfolk. He was determined that future violations would not occur. "Franklin," Eleanor told FDR about Long, "you know he's a Fascist." FDR was displeased. "I've told you, Eleanor," he replied, "you must not say that." She said, "Well, maybe I shouldn't say it, but he is." The refugees sent Roosevelt roses "with everlasting gratitude for your humane gesture, from the refugees of the SS *Quanza*."[24]

Roosevelt and Long clearly shared some beliefs, especially about security issues. After 1940, Roosevelt worried about saboteurs and spies coming into the country disguised as refugees. Like Long, FDR deferred to congressional prerogatives on the immigration issue, although his deference was based more on practical politics—constitutionally he could do nothing in that arena. Long's desire to exclude all foreigners was part of his nativist values. Some rescue advocates believed, as one wrote in 1940, "FDR doesn't want any more aliens from Europe—refugees have been implicated in espionage." Long felt that Roosevelt would back him up in his conservative approach to immigration policy, and to some degree he was correct.[25]

Long's relationships with Jews depended on the individual. He had a warm relationship with Bernard Baruch, whom he had known and socialized with since Woodrow Wilson's administration. Long had similar feelings about Ambassador Laurence Steinhardt, "an able man" who "has decisiveness and courage." Steinhardt, a wealthy, assimilated Jew, had an even more negative attitude than Long toward East European immigrants, including Jews.

Long disliked liberals, idealists, and "sentimentalists" of all stripes, including ER and her friends. He detested Harold Ickes and disliked Rabbi Stephen Wise, who not only disagreed with him but also battled him publicly on the refugee issue. Long correctly believed that many of his critics hated him personally and "would throw me to the wolves in their eagerness to destroy me." He described Benjamin Cohen, a lawyer, as "a very able protégé of Felix Frankfurter." When FDR sent Cohen to London in 1940 as legal adviser to the ambassador, Long saw it as Roosevelt's sending "a representative of his racial group and philosophy" to work on behalf of Jews. His assessment may have been partially true.[26]

Long was not Roosevelt's adviser on foreign policy. He was a functionary. Undersecretary of State Sumner Welles was Roosevelt's closest adviser in the State Department, and Welles was entirely sympathetic toward Jews. Long was not a confidant of Roosevelt's or a member of his inner circle, nor could Roosevelt have given Long's opinions much weight. Long attended the 1940 Chicago convention to work for Roosevelt's nomination but was excluded from any important decision-making, especially about foreign policy. "I had less to do with it than any convention I have attended since 1912," he lamented. His diary entry for Roosevelt's fourth inauguration, on January 20, 1945, verged on the pathetic. Not invited to the event, he ruminated at every slight. "*Something* happened—several years ago—to estrange me from the White House. What it was I do not know." He blamed his fall from grace on Harry Hopkins.[27]

Roosevelt employed Long primarily as a troubleshooter to pacify the conservatives in Congress. He was Roosevelt's emissary to men such as the volatile Martin Dies, chairman of the House Un-American Activities Committee; ambassador to Britain Joseph P. Kennedy; Georgia senator Walter George; and others. Long had good political instincts, or so it appeared to Hull and Roosevelt prior to 1944.[28]

In customary Roosevelt fashion, the president created several agencies with similar missions, and the differences in their views began to emerge. Long's opinions differed radically from those of the PACPR, appointed in what then seemed simpler times. Long embarked on a course of restricting the flow of refugees at the same time that the PACPR, the Justice Department, and the first lady were trying to increase it. Throughout 1940, a policy battle raged within the administration. The PACPR and Jewish groups lobbied intensely to admit Jews fleeing Nazi persecution. Some were admitted. For example, Long approved visas for hundreds of rabbinic scholars from the Baltic region. But from the beginning the State Department was obstructive. It did not issue visas that by law it should have issued, and it narrowly construed immigration laws to exclude classes of refugees.[29]

James G. McDonald, chairman of PACPR, was outraged at Long's machinations and demanded a meeting with Roosevelt. He and George L. Warren, PACPR executive secretary, wrote the president on October 8, 1940, complaining that few visas had been issued and that people cleared by their committee were no threat to the United States. The Spanish border was closed, and many who had reached Lisbon were still being refused visas. "To close this last avenue of escape is to condemn many scientists, scholars, writers, labor leaders, and other refugees to further sacrifices for their belief in democracy and to bring to an end our tradition of hospitality to the politically oppressed." McDonald was supported by ER, who urged FDR to think of "these poor people who may die at any time and who are asking only to come here on transit visas." But Long persuaded the president that the PACPR, Rabbi Wise, and other refugee advocates let their sympathy for Hitler's victims get the better of their judgment. Articles had appeared with titles such as "War by Refugee," and Long successfully appealed to Roosevelt's cautious nature when it came to internal security. Long was backed by many in the State Department and many in the field, including Laurence Steinhardt, a Jew and ambassador to the Soviet Union.

To Steinhardt, Long, and many others, admission to the United States was a privilege, not a right. Steinhardt wrote Long in May 1941, "I feel strongly that when our country is facing perhaps the greatest crisis in its history, its security from foreign machinations is of a great deal more importance than the entry of this, that, or the other immigrant, no matter how good a case he or she can make out on humanitarian grounds." Steinhardt was convinced that spies and saboteurs had already been admitted to the United States and that admitting refugees on a large scale was "likely to result in extensive sabotage and the loss of American lives and property and the crippling of our national defense program." The ambassador noted that his embassy had obtained direct evidence that a substantial portion of refugees from the Soviet Union were approached by the Soviet spy agency, the State Political Directorate (GPU), "to act as its agent in the United States." Varian Fry, the agent of the Emergency Rescue Committee in Marseilles, "had to be careful not to help a fifth columnist."[30]

Long's arguments had merit. Consuls abroad, he told Roosevelt, had a better chance to ferret out spies and subversives than a committee of liberal laymen in the United States. Roosevelt took the fifth-column threat very seriously and needed little convincing by Long. German spies *were* in the United States, and Long was well acquainted with the subversive infiltration of the State Department by spies and with the steps spies had taken to compromise the Foreign Service itself.[31] However, Roosevelt also listened to refugee advocates. In October 1940 he met McDonald, who felt the president knew the issues and was sympathetic to his position. The president wanted his subordinates to work out a compromise. He asked McDonald to work with the Justice Department to devise a screening procedure acceptable to both the State Department and his committee. The election was one month away, and the president likely did not want the refugee question to become a political issue.[32]

At that time, the idea of using the U.S. Virgin Islands as a temporary haven came to a head. Harold Ickes and his Interior Department lawyers, some of whom were Jewish, believed the immigration laws could be interpreted to admit refugees into the Virgin Islands as "temporary visitors" not subject to quota limits. The governor-general had publicly announced that some refugees would be admitted temporarily even though they had no State Department visas. But Roosevelt had to make the final decision. He knew Ickes and Nathan Margold, his staff attorney, had their hearts set on using the Virgin Islands as a refuge, but Roosevelt could not let the department or the governor-general determine foreign policy. Ickes' legal position was weak, and the Virgin Islands had its own social and economic problems. Breckinridge Long and the State Department adamantly opposed the plan. Roosevelt concluded that he could not bypass the immigration laws, which meant antagonizing Congress, and told Ickes not to proceed. Ultimately he could not approve the plan over the objections of the Departments of State and Justice.[33] Yet he was disturbed by the situation. In a confidential memorandum to Ickes, he wrote:

> *Do you mind my being perfectly frank in regard to the proposed proclamation by the Governor of the Virgin Islands in regard to the admission to this Island of certain refugees?*
>
> *I yield to no person in any department in my deep-seated desire to help the hundreds of thousands of foreign refugees in the present world situation. . . . If the Interior Department could find some unoccupied place not now a social and economic problem where we could set up a refugee camp . . . that would be treated with sympathy by the State Department and by me.*

He concluded on a personal note with obvious sincerity:

> *Tell Margold that I have every sympathy but that if he has some better plan to come and tell me about it*

and I will give it really sympathetic consideration. I cannot, however, do anything which would conceivably hurt the future of present American citizens. The inhabitants of the Virgin Islands are American citizens.[34]

The State Department and the president contended that the United States was doing all it could for refugees consistent with public safety. By the spring of 1941 the State Department cited the danger of foreign subversion when it instructed consuls to reject immigrants if they had siblings, spouses, or children living under Nazi control. Roosevelt signed the Bloom-van Nuys Act in June, which authorized consular officials to withhold a visa if the official knew or had any reason to believe that an applicant might "endanger the public safety" once in the United States. The FBI began to screen applicants for visas. Long even undermined FDR's pet project the Intergovernmental Committee on Refugees (IGCR) by cutting its budget and personnel. The State Department let South American countries know that the United States was closing its doors to suspicious refugees, and this decision caused a decrease in immigration to the entire Western Hemisphere.[35] In any event, by late 1941 Hitler was no longer allowing Jews to escape from Europe. As Gulie Ne'eman Arad observed, "the American quota became immaterial; Nazi restrictions on legal exit from the German-controlled territories rendered it meaningless."[36]

Whether Roosevelt believed and encouraged the fifth-column hysteria or not, the effect was the same. Americans were concerned about foreigners coming to the United States. The president could not and did not ignore this tidal wave of antialien, antirefugee sentiment. Whether or not he agreed with that sentiment, he actively used it to turn public opinion against Hitler and to secure the safety of the American homeland.[37] As late as September 1941 Roosevelt was trying to accommodate refugee advocates as best he could, consistent with national security. He agreed with McDonald, Attorney General Francis Biddle, and Rabbi Wise to modify the screening procedure proposed by Breckinridge Long to allow more protection for refugees' procedural rights.[38]

Hitler, as usual, was one step ahead of his enemies. He was using refugees as weapons of war. The Western nations were facing a flood of five million Jews from the East. It was, as Deborah Dwork and Robert Jan van Pelt observed, a " 'form of blackmail' to which the west would not succumb." Even the liberal, pro-Jewish *New Republic*, which was highly critical of the State Department, recognized in April 1941 that while subordinates in Washington were blind, "President Roosevelt sees the problem clearly," and that "Germany's 'war by refugees' " was "an essential part of Hitler's coldly calculated strategy to confuse his opponents. It is brutal exploitation of human misery in order to add to the burdens of his opponents at a time when he is about to attack them with his armed forces."[39]

- - *Chapter 11* - -

"We've Got to Go to
Europe and Fight"

"It must be borne in mind," Mark S. Watson, the official army historian of World War II wrote, "that President Franklin D. Roosevelt was the real and not merely a nominal Commander in Chief. Every president has possessed the constitutional authority which that title indicates, but few presidents have shared Mr. Roosevelt's readiness to exercise it in fact and in detail and with such determination."[1] The president brought to the prosecution of this massive global war the full measure of his talents, energy, intellect, power, and personality.

He was determined to keep the American people united in a war without mercy against Japan and a war to extinguish Nazism. There was never any doubt in Roosevelt's mind about demanding the unconditional surrender of the Nazi regime. He was determined to win at all costs. The temporary suspension of civil liberties, a harsh code of drumhead justice, the creation of the world's first atomic weapon, and the massive bombing of German or Japanese civilians did not much concern Roosevelt. "He was never theoretical about things," wrote Francis Biddle, of the president's insistence on the primacy of military defense over issues of civil liberties. Nor was "the President . . . a dreamer," wrote Robert Jackson, FDR's attorney general and a Nuremburg tribunal judge. He was a practical war leader, with a clearly defined mission. He was confident of his ability to execute a global strategy to win the war *he* intended to fight *as quickly as possible* with as little loss of *American* lives as possible. These were Roosevelt's goals, and he achieved them all brilliantly. To do so he was forced by his enemies, his allies, and events to make hard choices that shattered the lives and cost the deaths of millions.[2]

The attack on Pearl Harbor dealt the United States a serious blow, but the Japanese juggernaut had only begun. Within hours of the attack, the Japanese bombed the largest American air base in the world, Clark Field on the Philippine island of Luzon. B-17 Flying Fortresses and P-40s, the pride of the U.S. Army Air Force, were destroyed on the ground. On December 10 the Japanese air force sank the greatest warships of the British navy, HMS *Prince of Wales* and *Repulse*. Battleships at sea had never before been sunk by aircraft. "I was thankful to be alone," Churchill recalled. "In all the war, I never received a more direct shock." The Japanese occupied Thailand, invaded Burma and Malaya, and threatened Singapore. Hong Kong, Guam, and Wake surrendered. Japanese soldiers murdered British and Canadian prisoners of war—by shooting, bayoneting, or beheading them—throughout the Pacific theater. General Douglas MacArthur's troops were defeated in the Philippines. MacArthur escaped to the island of Corregidor in Manila Harbor, where he held out for several months before fleeing to Australia. "I shall return," he promised. Roosevelt faced the crisis with equanimity "in psychological uniform as Commander in Chief." In addition, he said good-bye to his sons James and Elliott, who were in the service. ER wept. The president did not.[3]

Supreme Court justice Robert Jackson recalled that the country's mood was somber. "A very deep pessimism" replaced "foolish optimism" about the invincibility of the American navy. American intelligence services had "let us down at every point. . . . We had enormously underestimated the strength and striking power of Hitler. We had overestimated the staying power of France . . . England [and] Belgium." It looked to many like a long, hard, costly war. "There was talk about a war of a decade . . . spirits were pretty low here."[4]

On December 22, 1941, Churchill arrived at the White House with his staff, his map room, and a mission to ensure that the United States did not turn its attention to Japan and ignore Germany. "I clasped his strong hand," Churchill wrote of FDR, "with comfort and pleasure." Thus began the most critical phase of their historic partnership. The two men worked day and night to plan the war against the Axis powers. Churchill need not have worried. A weaker president might have turned his attention to retaliation against Japan, but Roosevelt's chief enemy was always Adolf Hitler. Decisions were made about Singapore, Australia, American bombers in Britain, and troops in Northern Ireland. Roosevelt and Churchill agreed that the war would be run from Washington. FDR created the Joint Chiefs of Staff and relied heavily on its members: Army general George C. Marshall; Admiral Ernest J. King, chief of naval operations; and General Henry H. ("Hap") Arnold of the army air corps, soon to be called the army air force.[5]

On December 26 Churchill addressed Congress. He electrified his audience by lambasting the enemy. "What sort of people do they think we are?" he growled. "Is it possible they do not realize that we shall never cease to persevere against them until they have been taught a lesson which they and the world will never forget?" Churchill traveled to Ottawa to address the Canadian Parliament. "When I warned [the French government] that Britain would fight on alone whatever they did," he told his delighted audience, "their generals told their prime minister and his divided cabinet: 'In three weeks England will have her neck wrung like a chicken.' Some chicken! Some neck!"[6] He and FDR announced a "Declaration by United Nations" pledging "complete victory" over the Axis powers and Hitlerism to preserve human rights, liberty, and religious freedom. They discussed an invasion of French North Africa, a second front in Europe, and the war in Russia even as the German army approached Moscow.[7] On January 6, 1942, a determined FDR told the Congress in his State of the Union message:

> *For the first time since the Japanese and the Fascists and the Nazis started along their blood-stained course of conquest they now face the fact that superior forces are assembling against them. Gone forever are the days when the aggressors could attack and destroy their victims one by one without unity of resistance. . . . The militarists of Berlin and Tokyo started this war. But the massed, angered forces of common humanity will finish it.*

He promised that America would produce 60,000 airplanes in 1942; 125,000 in 1943; 25,000 tanks in 1942; and 75,000 in 1943. "No compromise could end the conflict," he concluded. "There never has been—there never can be—successful compromise between good and evil. Only total victory can reward the champions of tolerance, and decency, and freedom, and faith."[8]

The White House became a military command center. Anti aircraft guns were placed on the roof. Soldiers stood guard. Tourists were banned. A bomb shelter was constructed underneath the Treasury Department, but Roosevelt would not go to see it. He admired Churchill's mobile map room so much that he had his own map room constructed on the ground floor of the White House. Large-scale charts of the Atlantic and the Pacific were affixed to the walls; pins showed the location of ships. Top-secret dispatches arrived around the clock to three shifts of officers. Only Hopkins, Marshall, King, and Admiral William Leahy, FDR's chief of staff, and the president had access to the room.[9]

In February Roosevelt made a difficult decision about the Philippines. It was obvious that the American and Philippine forces could not stop the Japanese onslaught. Manuel Quezon, the Philippine president, proposed immediate independence from the United States, withdrawal of all American and Japanese forces, and Philippine neutrality. The panicky MacArthur wired that it "might offer the best possible solution of what is about to be a disastrous debacle." To fight meant the certain capture or death of American soldiers and the mass murder of Filipinos. The decision, Stimson said, was "ghastly in its responsibility and significance." But it was a decision FDR made quickly. "We can't do this at all," he replied to the Quezon proposal. "I immediately discarded everything in my mind I had held to his discredit," General Marshall said of Roosevelt. "I decided he was a great man." Firm resistance to Japanese aggression meant substantial loss of American life, but the American forces were ordered "to keep our flag flying in the Philippines." Roosevelt, Stimson, and Marshall were well aware that the American garrison was being abandoned to its fate. The "battling bastards of Bataan" knew it, too.[10]

By March 1942 the Japanese had captured Singapore, Rangoon, Sumatra, Timor, New Guinea, New Britain, and the Solomons. India and Australia were next. The British defeat at Singapore and sur-render of 130,000 British troops was "the greatest disaster to British arms which our history records," lamented Churchill. Roosevelt's popularity dipped. Isolationists, well aware that Roosevelt's first priority was to defeat Hitler, exclaimed "Pacific First" and urged the president to "send ships to MacArthur." They criticized supplying Russia and Britain instead of the U.S. Navy in the Pacific. Some— "the KKK crowd," "some wild Irish," right-wingers, defeatists— wanted to negotiate peace with Hitler.[11]

During those dark months of Japanese victories, Roosevelt signed an order interning Japanese Americans. While the American Civil Liberties Union and others railed against the order, the public approved overwhelmingly. Citizens on the West Coast had become hysterical about the Japanese living in their midst. Some claimed they saw signals and strange lights sent or set up by Japanese Americans. Racial hatred and fear of the Japanese exploded. Law enforcement officials, politicians, the governor, California attorney general Earl Warren, the army general in charge of the West Coast, and Secretary Stimson all clamored for action. With the Philippines and Singapore about to fall, Roosevelt viewed the decision of little importance and signed the internment order.[12] Roosevelt was also concerned about German aliens in America. In a note to Hull Roosevelt asserted that "*all* German aliens in America are potential, if not actual spies." "I don't care about the Italians," FDR told Attorney General Biddle. "They are a lot of opera singers. But the Germans are different. They may be dangerous."[13]

Americans did not know where Japanese aggression would end. They were so fearful of Japanese sabotage that the 1942 New Year's Day Rose Bowl game was moved from Pasadena, California, to North Carolina. Barbed wire was strung along West Coast beaches. Many in America saw the war against Japan as a race war that Americans must win. The Hearst newspapers described Japan as a "racial menace." Even Fiorello LaGuardia, the liberal mayor of New York, called Mikado a "yellow rat." It is easy to forget, John W. Dower wrote in *War without Mercy*, "the visceral emotions and sheer race hate that gripped virtually all participants in the war. . . . Race hate fed atrocities, and atrocities in turn fanned the fires of race hate." Most Americans detested the Japanese far more than the Germans. Arthur Miller, the future playwright working in the Brooklyn Navy Yard during World War II, recalled that his coworkers did not comprehend what Nazism meant. "We were fighting Germany essentially because she had allied herself with the Japanese who had attacked us at Pearl

Harbor." "Probably in all our history," historian Allan Nevins observed in 1946, "no foe has been so detested as were the Japanese." This was the overwhelming sentiment of the American public throughout the war.[14]

Americans could distinguish between "good Germans" and "bad Germans." They believed that the atrocities committed by Germany were "Nazi" crimes. The German people were not all bad, but the atrocities committed by Japan were those of "Japs" and "yellow bastards." Indeed, admirals, generals, and congressmen referred to the Japanese as "Japs," a derogatory epithet. "A Jap is a Jap," one general said. The victims of Japanese aggression were Americans, Britons, Australians, and "good" Asians, Filipinos and Chinese. To some Americans the Germans were murdering alien, "inferior," and even dangerous people—Russian Communists, Poles, Slavs, and Jews—but the Japanese had humiliated and defeated English-speaking people and chopped off the heads of Caucasian prisoners of war and civilians. The American thirst for vengeance for Pearl Harbor and Japanese atrocities knew few bounds.[15]

The Japanese waged an anti-white, anti-Anglo-American campaign in Asia, promising "Asia for the Asians" and independence for European colonies. They appealed to Muslims in Southeast Asia and, according to Burns, "raised the specter of an ultimate appeal to Islam and to antiwhite feeling in the Middle East." Roosevelt urged Churchill, in the strongest language he ever used with the prime minister, to grant India some type of independence. Churchill would not hear of it.[16]

"The Pacific situation is now very grave," Roosevelt wired

Churchill after the Allies lost the Battle of the Java Sea in February 1942. The men "Dugout Doug" MacArthur (his nickname while hiding out on the island of Corregidor) left behind suffered starvation, illness, torture, and death. Eighty thousand American and Filipino troops and twenty five thousand civilian retreated to the Bataan Peninsula. The Americans at Bataan surrendered on April 9, and in early May General Jonathan M. Wainwright sent his last message to the president from Corregidor: "With broken heart and head bowed in sadness but not in shame, with continued pride in my gallant troops, I go to meet the Japanese commander."[17]

The Japanese army, like the SS, had no regard for human life and took sadistic delight in torturing and murdering "inferior races." In the infamous Bataan Death March, the Japanese murdered 5,000 Filipinos and 750 American soldiers. American and Filipino soldiers who were sick, thirsty, and starving were beaten and whipped, their canteens, food, and personal items stolen. Japanese guards cut off the fingers of American officers to steal their West Point rings. Prisoners were bayoneted and shot to death for fun. Filipinos who gave food to American soldiers were murdered. Sick Americans were buried alive. The Japanese amused themselves by cutting off the heads of American soldiers.[18]

The American public learned about Bataan a year later. But Japanese atrocities were foremost in the minds of the American public from the beginning of the war. Soldiers and nurses who surrendered in Malaya were bayoneted and shot. The Japanese murdered five thousand Chinese civilians in Singapore. One hundred twenty Australian prisoners of war were executed by sword or bayonet. The Japanese, unlike the Germans, executed, tortured, starved, humiliated, and mistreated Allied prisoners of war.[19]

The Germans, meanwhile, were well aware that the United States was no direct threat to Germany. "Now it is impossible for us to lose the war," Hitler gloated. "We now have an ally who has never been vanquished in three thousand years." The Japanese navy was a worthy adversary of the United States. Hitler predicted, on another occasion, "I don't see much future for the Americans. It's a decayed country." The Führer now felt free to exterminate his enemies.[20]

After America entered the war, Hitler began to construct massive coastal fortifications from Norway and Finland to the Bay of Biscay, between France and Spain. He intended to prevent an Allied invasion of Fortress Europa. Called "the Atlantic Wall," these formidable defenses contained massive concrete and steel fortifications stretching over twenty-four hundred miles of shoreline. An extensive railway system allowed troops, heavy guns, and supplies to be moved rapidly, and obstructions on the beaches and flooded areas inland thwarted airborne soldiers. The Organization Todt, a military public works agency, employed slave labor from conquered countries and volunteers to work day and night for years to build an impregnable defense system. The strength of the Germans' Atlantic Wall was convincingly demonstrated on August 19, when the Allies attempted a raid at Dieppe on the French coast. Fifty percent of the troops were killed or captured.[21]

The Battle of Midway in June 1942 demonstrated to the Japanese that victory was not going to be easy. Admiral Isoroku Yamamoto's armada of 165 ships confidently set out to destroy the remainder of the American Pacific Fleet. The stakes were enormous. "Victory," John Keegan wrote, "seemed to lie only one battle away." The Americans, having broken the Japanese code, soundly defeated the Imperial Navy at this western end of the Hawaiian chain. Admiral Chester Nimitz attacked the Japanese fleet and destroyed four aircraft carriers, three hundred and seventy two aircraft, and killed thousands of Japanese sailors. The battle restored the balance of naval power in the Pacific, but the Japanese still commanded a massive fleet, superior in many ways to the American fleet. The short war the Japanese sought had become a long war instead.[22]

But the victory at Midway was just short of miraculous. Gordon W. Prange's classic history is titled *Miracle at Midway*. Everything went right for the Americans and wrong for the Japanese, including the weather. What Keegan called the "most stunning and decisive blow in the history of naval warfare" almost failed, and Roosevelt knew it. Had the Battle of Midway been lost, Yamamoto could cut the supply line to Australia and attack Hawaii and even California. Roosevelt would then have been forced to bring American forces back from the Atlantic and Europe to concentrate on Japan.[23]

Japanese atrocities at the Battle of Guadalcanal enraged the American public because American boys were dying horrible and unnecessary deaths at the hands of the beastlike Japanese. But Americans were not fighting in the European theater. "I have never heard or read of this kind of fighting," Major General Alexander A. Vandegrift wrote to his superiors in 1942 about the fighting on Guadalcanal. "These people refuse to surrender. The wounded will wait till men come up to examine them, and blow themselves and the other fellow to death with a hand grenade."[24]

The Soviets pressed Roosevelt for more matériel and a second front, in Western Europe. "We've got to go to Europe and fight," General Marshall's war planner, Dwight D. Eisenhower, argued, if "we're to keep Russia in, save the Middle East, India, and Burma." Roosevelt agreed that the United States should launch a massive invasion of Western Europe as soon as possible. Soviet foreign minister Vyacheslav Molotov arrived at the White House for a conference in May. It was said that Molotov spoke only four words in English: "yes," "no," and "second front." Roosevelt wanted to keep the Russians in the war at all costs and promised a second front. He was extremely concerned about the possibility of a Soviet defeat.[25]

Churchill, justly worried that Roosevelt had his own agenda, returned to the United States in June, where he learned of the British army surrender at the Libyan port of Tobruk. The battle for North Africa, which the Germans saw as a sideshow, had seesawed. The Mediterranean was critical to the British strategy of protecting its interests in Egypt and the Suez Canal and its ally Greece. General Rommel had forced the British to retreat toward Alexandria. The fall of Tobruk meant the end of a second front in 1942. Thirty thousand British troops surrendered, and the undersupplied German army captured essential vehicles, gasoline, and rations. Rommel and Hitler agreed to pursue the Allies to Egypt, and Rommel entered Egypt on June 23. The Jews of Palestine were terrified. The Germans captured Sevastapol in June and by August had crossed the Don to within a hundred miles of Stalingrad.[26]

The most serious threats to the Allies were the German U-boats, which were winning the war in the Atlantic. In March 1942 273 merchant ships were sunk. It was the "Happy Time" for the submariners of admirals Erich Raeder and Karl Doenitz. All along the American east coast, U-boats sank ships of all kinds, including tankers, "silhouetted against the lights of Miami and Atlantic City." In April the United States was losing 500,000 tons of shipping a month. Four hundred ships were sunk and five thousand lives were lost.[27] The president's top priority was building ships, setting incredible goals, and forcing the nation to meet them. American shipbuilders such as Henry J. Kaiser responded with record-breaking production. Cargo vessels called "Liberty ships" rolled out of American shipyards.[28]

The raising and training of an army, navy, and air force of millions of men and women created massive political problems. Forts, naval bases, training camps, and airfields had to be built. Arms and equipment had to be manufactured. Specialized medical care was needed as the terrors of modern warfare unfolded. American industry produced new kinds of ships for amphibious warfare and transporting men and matériel: the LSD (landing ship, dock), the LST (landing ship, tank), and the LCI (landing craft, infantry), the Liberty ship, and the Victory ship. Bauxite, aluminum, chromium, and other imports had to be safely brought to the United States.[29]

For FDR, the State Department and its quibbling about immigration restrictions receded. Cordell Hull was ill with tuberculosis and diabetes and temporarily ceded control of the department to his rival Sumner Welles. Taking morphine (or more likely codeine), the ailing secretary of state had been exhausted by the events surrounding Pearl Harbor. He was so ill in early 1942 that he went to Miami to recuperate. Roosevelt relied on Welles to handle "crucial secondary matters" such as the atrocities against the Jews of Europe.[30]

Mannheim was bombed on May 19, 1942. On May 30 the RAF sent 1,000 bombers to destroy Cologne's chemical and machine tool industries, leveling much of the city and killing 469 German civilians. "We hope," Churchill told Stalin, "to shatter almost every dwelling in almost every German city." The British were determined to bomb the Germans into submission. While the British began bombing German industrial centers and cities, Roosevelt made plans for the biggest bomb ever made. He was determined to build a nuclear fission bomb and created the secret Manhattan Engineering District within the Army Corps of Engineers. Hence the atomic bomb project was called the Manhattan Project.[31]

In July Churchill and Roosevelt agreed to invade French North Africa. Called Operation Torch and commanded by General Eisenhower, the plan was to land troops at Oran and Algiers on the Mediterranean and Casablanca on the Atlantic coast of Morocco. But Rommel pushed the British back to El Alamein, and Mussolini sought to conquer Egypt. The Jews in Palestine prepared to defend Haifa. Arabs chanted *"Bissama Allah oua alard Hitler"* (In Heaven Allah, on Earth Hitler) and marked the houses in Tel Aviv they would occupy when all the Jews were killed. The British considered abandoning Egypt and moving their forces to the Persian Gulf, but the loss of these oil fields might cost Britain 20 percent of its military capacity.[32]

Jewish Americans fervently supported the war effort. Rabbi Wise put aside his pacifism and urged his friend the Reverend John Haynes Holmes to open his eyes: "Hitler has permitted his horrors of war upon lesser peoples to culminate in a world war against freedom and Democracy. . . . I wish you could see eye to eye with me." Jewish members of the Roosevelt administration devoted their energies to the war effort. Morgenthau headed the Treasury Department's efforts to finance the war, keep inflation under control, tangle with Congress, and handle controversial special projects for the president. Abe Fortas became Undersecretary of the Department of the Interior.[33] Benjamin V. Cohen went to England in 1941 to assist Ambassador Winant. Between 1943 and 1945, Cohen was general counsel in the Office of War Mobilization (OWM). Herbert Lehman went to the State Department to work on international relief operations and in 1943 became director of the United Nations Relief and Rehabilitation Administration (UNRRA). The labor leader Sidney Hillman became associate director-general of the Office of Production Management and worked tirelessly for Roosevelt in the political battles of the 1940s. David Lilienthal put the TVA to use in the war effort by providing power to the atomic energy installation at Oak Ridge, Tennessee.[34]

Winning the war and aiding FDR on the home front was Justice Felix Frankfurter's top priority. His opinions gave unqualified support to the war effort. He dissented in *West Virginia Board of Education v. Barnette*, 319 U.S. 624, when the Supreme Court struck down a law mandating the saluting of the U.S. flag even if it violated a student's religious beliefs. He worked tirelessly behind the scenes to further the war effort, assisting Henry Stimson, and counseling Roosevelt on appointments. Frankfurter urged Roosevelt to appoint the Republican Harlan Stone chief justice instead of the president's first choice, Robert Jackson. "Few things would contribute as much to confidence in you as a national and not a partisan President," he told FDR. Frankfurter remained active behind the scenes promoting Zionism.[35]

More important by far than the activities of American Jewish leaders was the commitment of ordinary American Jews to the war. "Everybody knew the war was going badly," Stella Suberman, a young Jewish woman from Miami Beach recalled, "especially the war we considered 'our' war, the war in the Pacific. The papers carried no good news, only reports of defeats, one after another." Jewish men and women enlisted in droves in the army, navy, army air force, and coast guard. Tens of thousands were drafted. Life for American Jews, like life for all Americans, focused on the war effort. There were American Jewish servicemen in all aspects of the war. Synagogues and community centers opened their doors and American Jews opened their homes to Jewish servicemen. Military service, war bonds drives, Jewish USO's (United Service Organizations, which provided entertainment and assistance to American servicemen), and volunteering for war-related causes became part of American Jewry's daily life. Stella Suberman's new husband, Jack, and his close friend Irv Rubin enlisted in the army air force. " 'Contributing to the war effort' was now everybody's goal," she explained.[36]

Chapter 12

"No Force on Earth Can Stop Them"

At some point in 1941 the German leadership decided to undertake the genocide of European Jewry. Implementation of the plan began with the start of the Russian campaign in June 1941. The phrase "Final Solution" was first used in May 1941 and soon became code words for the annihilation of the Jews. By the fall of 1941 Jews were being transported to camps to be gassed. In December 1941 Hans Frank made it clear that the war would be only a "partial success if the Jewish clan survived it." The Final Solution, already official policy, was introduced to even more branches of the German government on January 20, 1942, at Wannesee, near Berlin. Reinhard Heydrich called the meeting of top German officials to explain the annihilation of "some eleven million Jews" of Europe, including all the Jews of Britain, Turkey, Switzerland, the Irish Republic, Ukraine, Russia, Poland, Hungary, France, Morocco, Algeria, and Tunisia. Technical obstacles were ironed out and "a complex system of subterfuge" created to convince the Jews and the world that the goal of the Nazis' relocation of millions of Jews was resettlement.[1]

Deception and disinformation were central to the plan. The Germans deceived their Jewish victims to avoid resistance. European Jews and most people outside of Europe believed that Jews were taken to labor camps. When Jews escaped and warned other Jews, they were not believed. The massacres of 1941 were concealed and denied. Jewish ghettos were sealed off from the world and from each other. Even at their last moments, many prisoners at Auschwitz did not believe they were going to die. Lilli Kopecky from Slovakia was an Auschwitz survivor. "This," she said, "is the greatest strength of the whole crime, its unbelievability."[2]

FDR's first knowledge of German bloodthirst was their mass killings of Poles, Christians, and Jews. The Polish government-in-exile had made it clear to the British and American government in 1940 and 1941 that atrocities were under way against Polish civilians. General Wladyslaw Sikorski, the Polish leader, visited Washington in March 1941 with information. He returned in March 1942, when he asked the Americans to declare a policy of reprisals against the Germans. But, Roosevelt and other officials were suspicious of atrocity stories. Few Americans had any love for the Stalinist Soviet Union, so they treated reports of German mass murder as a case of the "pot and the kettle." False atrocity stories were common during World War I. The desperation of Soviet and British governments and especially of French and Polish governments-in-exile argued against the credibility of their genocide stories. Finally, the intrinsic incredibility of genocide gave American government officials pause. For all these reasons Americans were instinctively skeptical.[3]

American Jews were not the only people who argued that more should be done to succor their kinfolk and coreligionists. "The Polish people," Richard C. Lukas writes in *The Forgotten Holocaust* (1986), "were unhappy with the silence of the world to the calamity in Poland." What was the benefit of liberation, the Poles asked, if most of the Polish nation were dead? Sikorski asked Churchill to allow the Polish air force, which was operating with the RAF, to launch retaliatory air strikes against German targets. In the United States, Polish representatives lobbied General George Marshall to send the army air force to bomb German targets in Poland.[4]

Deborah E. Lipstadt observed that it is "important to remember that the Nazis treated the mass murder program quite differently from their other antisemitic campaigns." The Nazis' successive actions—the 1933 boycott, the 1935 riots, the Nuremberg Laws, *Kristallnacht*, and rounding ups of some Jews—were done openly, but the Final Solution was clandestine. In addition to their secrecy the Germans conducted a deliberate disinformation campaign. The words "Final Solution" were code words used in top-secret communications between high-level German officials. For example, some Jews in concentration camps were forced to send reassuring postcards to friends and family. The SS made strenuous efforts late in the war to dispose of corpses and to destroy evidence of death camps. In September 1943 the Nazis sent 5,007 prisoners to live in 30 stables at Auschwitz that were named "Work Camp Birkenau." Inmates sent postcards to relatives and friends and for a while even received Red Cross food parcels. Because the Auschwitz-Monowitz complex eventually housed more than 70,000 Jewish laborers, the adjacent gas chambers and crematoriums were not identified for some time.[5]

The war was much bigger news than atrocity stories. After Germany invaded Poland in 1939, the American public read dramatic stories of war and conquest, the fall of Western Europe, and the climactic struggle in Russia. So many events crowded out news of the persecution of the Jews. Nazi antisemitic policy was only part of general wartime suffering. And after Pearl Harbor, Americans focused on the Japanese. Therefore, it must be kept in mind that in the early years of the conflict the persecution and massacre of European Jews (no one used the word "Holocaust," as we do today) was one story among many tales of woe all over the globe.[6]

The *Struma* incident is a good case in point. The *Struma* was an old cargo vessel filled with desperate Jewish refugees trying to reach Palestine in December 1941. It left Romania and ended up in Istanbul. The passengers were forbidden to disembark, and the ship was not allowed to make needed repairs. On February 23, 1942, the Turks towed the *Struma* out to sea, where it was sunk by a Russian submarine, killing 768 passengers. It was an outrage. But Pearl Harbor had been attacked on December 7. Americans were in a panic and arguing about interning Japanese Americans. American ships were being sunk and merchant seamen killed by U-boats within sight of New York and other East Coast cities. The Japanese had sunk the battleships *Prince of Wales* and *Repulse*, killing 730 British sailors. American troops were fighting in the

Bataan Peninsula after the fall of Manila. Rommel was on the offensive in North Africa. Singapore surrendered on February 15. And on February 19, the Japanese attacked Darwin in northern Australia, killing 172 and causing widespread panic. The *Struma* tragedy was a small story by comparison.[7]

While news of the slaughter of Jews, Poles, and Russians was widespread in the fall of 1941, reporters remained cautious. News stories used qualifying words such as "purported" and "alleged." The terror inflicted on German Jews—the yellow star, impoverishment, and closing synagogues—was widely reported. But the Nazis denied stories of mass murder. Jews were needed as laborers, the Nazis claimed, and were sent to labor camps.[8]

Despite global skepticism, mass murder was hard to keep secret. During 1942 it gradually became clear to many that the Nazis were bent on an official policy of killing Jews. Refugees from Germany brought with them explicit descriptions. United Press correspondents told of an "open hunt" on Jews and Poles, that two hundred thousand to four hundred thousand Jews had already been killed. The firing squads, the SS, and the mass graves were revealed and published to the world. And some Americans were outraged over events such as the sinking of the *Struma*, whose passengers had been barred from Palestine. ER urged Sumner Welles to help Jewish refugees enter Palestine. They "certainly will help us rather than the Axis," she said. Welles agreed. The episode was one of the "most shocking tragedies . . . in a tragic year," he replied. "This British policy is so cruel," ER wrote Welles, "that, if it were generally known in this country, it would increase the dislike of Great Britain, which is already too prevalent." But in February 1942 FDR was watching helplessly as the Japanese conquered the Philippines and the Pacific.[9]

Throughout 1942 the Final Solution was in high gear. Victorious Nazis sent Jews from all of occupied Europe to secret death camps in Poland. Jews in Warsaw were starving to death. Many were sent to Belzec by trains that traveled at night throughout the Lublin and Galician regions. The Jews of central Poland and Warsaw were sent to Sobibor, Auschwitz, Chelmno, and Treblinka. In August 1942 alone, four hundred thousand Jews were killed.[10]

The Polish Jewish socialist organization the Bund issued a report through the London-based Polish government-in-exile in June 1942 describing the slaughter of Jewish men, women, and children. The Bund estimated that seven hundred thousand were already dead. It broke the story of the use of poison gas and of the Nazis' coordinated plan to annihilate the Jews of Poland. The BBC broadcast a summary on June 2, and the British press reported the story forcefully. Headlines such as "GREATEST POGROM— ONE MILLION JEWS DIE" ran in the *Daily Mail*. The American press reacted cautiously, placing the stories on inside pages and omitting the systematic nature of the murders. Nevertheless, some newspapers did tell the story fully, and CBS Radio broadcast the essential facts on June 29 in New York. "The pattern of subdued, almost repressed treatment of much of the news of the Final Solution continued," Lipstadt writes, "even as the pace and scope of the news increased." The number of victims, one million, was too immense to be believed.[11]

In Germany, Rabbi Leo Baeck's circle of friends became smaller and smaller. He wore a yellow Star of David. Jewish services were forbidden, but he had his students until June 30, 1942, when the Nazis closed the school and began rounding up the few remaining Jews of Berlin. His days were taken up writing letters to those who had escaped and encouraging those who had stayed. A few brave anti-Nazi Germans gave him food and hope. The Allies bombed Berlin. "One must live to survive," he said, "as if there will be a tomorrow."[12]

Anne Frank enjoyed her Jewish school, friends, teachers, new cat, and new best friend. Her former best friend, Lucia, had joined the *Jeugdstorm* or Youth Storm, a Nazi youth group. The Franks insisted that Margot, Anne's older sister, read the German classics. Anne acted in plays staged for family and friends as Jews were banned from all cultural events. By April 1942 all Jews were forced to wear the yellow star, with the word *Jood* printed in black. Otto Frank was certain the Americans would arrive soon. For her thirteenth birthday, Anne's father bought her a red-and-light-green checkered cloth diary. Although rumors circulated about Jews being deported, Anne enjoyed going out for ice cream and flirting with the boys. Then on July 5, 1942, the Franks received a written summons ordering Margot to a labor camp and informing them in detail of what she was allowed to take with her. The Franks entered their secret hiding place as the Nazis began hunting Jews down to fill their quotas for the trains to the "labor camps."[13]

On July 17, Morgenthau again brought up the issue of Palestine to FDR. Roosevelt charmed Chaim Weizmann, who was visiting the United States, but also told him that "this was positively no time to bring up this matter; that only three days ago the English thought that there was going to be an Arab uprising and that the English were terrifically worried about having the Arabs stab them in the back. . . . I told Weizman I have to look after the diplomatic end." Mideast oil could not be allowed to fall into Germany's hands. FDR wanted the Jews in Palestine to fight with the Allies but "we need fifty thousand rifles and ten thousand machine guns and where are you going to get them from? We haven't got them." The United States' first consideration was to make sure the British could keep Alexandria and Cairo from falling to the German army. "You know, Mr. President," Morgenthau told Roosevelt, "they [the Jews of Palestine] make magnificent fighters and they have demonstrated their courage." Roosevelt said, "I know that, but we have just got to wait." For the time being, Morgenthau noted in his diary, "there is nothing that I can do," FDR told Hull. "If we pat either Arab or Jew on the back, we automatically stir up trouble."[14]

To Roosevelt it was clear that Britain could not afford a civil war in Palestine. But so great was the Jewish opposition to British policy that a small radical group plotted armed insurrection in Palestine. In 1941 a member of terrorist organizations, first the Irgun Z'vai Leumi and then the LEHI (Lohamei Herut Yisrael or Fighters for the Freedom of Israel), Avraham Stern, had concocted a scheme to join forces with the Nazis against the British to establish a Jewish state in Palestine. He approached a Nazi emissary in Vichy Syria with this wild plan, which obviously failed. Both the

British and the Palestinian Jewish leadership turned on the Stern Gang, which then resorted to robbing banks and murdering civilians. The Stern Gang's terrorist legacy later impeded the Irgun and one of its young leaders, Hillel Kook, also known as Peter Bergson, in their efforts to influence American policy.[15]

During the summer the American press began to run stories on the shootings, mass graves, and mysterious deportations to the East. In June the World Jewish Congress held a press conference in London. Its spokesman put the Jewish death toll at more than a million (it was actually greater) and called Eastern Europe a "vast slaughterhouse for Jews." Jewish organizations, including the American Jewish Congress and B'nai B'rith, held a mass demonstration in New York City on July 21, 1942, at Madison Square Garden. Roosevelt's name "was the signal for an ovation." Twenty thousand people inside and thousands outside cheered New York governor Herbert Lehman, Rabbi Wise, Mayor LaGuardia, and others as they denounced the Nazis and urged the Allies to defend the Jews of Palestine.[16]

The president sent a message to the rally that the American people "will hold the perpetrators of these crimes to strict accountability in a day of reckoning, which will surely come. . . . Americans who love justice and hate oppression will hail the solemn commemoration in Madison Square Garden as an expression of the determination of the Jewish people to make every sacrifice for victory over the Axis powers." The front-page headline in the next day's *New York Times* was "Nazi Punishment Seen by Roosevelt." Winston Churchill reiterated his and Roosevelt's commitment "to place retribution for these crimes among major purposes of this war. The Jews were Hitler's first victims," Churchill wrote, and "ever since they have been in the forefront of resistance to Nazi aggression." The meeting declared its "trepidation for the fate of our people in Palestine" and fear of the "deadly enemy . . . knocking at its gates." Protests also were held in Chicago, Los Angeles, and other cities, where political leaders and Christian clergy denounced the mass murder of European Jews. The Synagogue Council of America designated July 23 a day to remember the slain.[17]

We will never know the exact date when FDR first knew about the Holocaust and what he knew of it. However, as early as August 22, 1942, he said at a press conference:

> *the communication which I have just received . . . gives rise to the fear that as the defeat of the enemy countries approaches, the barbaric and unrelenting character of the occupational regime will become more marked and may even lead to the extermination of certain populations.*

As Walter Laqueur pointed out, the "certain populations" were not "the people of the Netherlands and Luxembourg from whose government-in-exile he had received information." Henry Morgenthau stated in 1947 that "We knew in Washington, from August 1942 on, that the Nazis were planning to exterminate all the Jews of Europe." But FDR may not have believed the effect of the massacres as late as September, when he told Felix Frankfurter not to worry, that the Jews were being used to build fortifications on the Soviet frontier.[18]

Why did Americans, Jewish and non-Jewish, not see at the beginning of the Holocaust, what was actually happening? First, the Germans kept it a secret. Thousands were sworn to silence. The killing sites were in remote locations. The images of piles of corpses that shocked the world in 1945 and thereafter were not seen until after the war. There were no news reports from the con-centration camps. Second, it was part of a jumble of dramatic and contradictory events. The Nazis' treatment of its foes disguised the systematic extermination. In one widely publicized massacre, the Germans killed the entire adult population of the Czech village of Lidice in reprisal for its aid to the assassins of SS general Reinhard Heydrich. Third, false World War I atrocity stories prejudiced hearers against stories so grotesque that they tested credibility. Genocide was literally beyond belief. Finally, the Allies saw nothing to gain by emphasizing the murder of Jews over non-Jews. The reason was obvious at the time: Hitler tried his best to turn the war into "the Jews' war." The Jews and the division of mankind into conflicting racial groups were central to his worldview. But Jews and those friendly to the Jewish people were already com-mitted to the defeat of Germany. Major segments of American, British, and British Empire populations did not care about Jews and, indeed, were antisemitic themselves. They were unwilling to fight to save Jews, but they were willing to fight to free humankind from Nazi oppression. Ambassador William Bullitt was saying as late as 1943 that "the Roosevelt administration's emphasis on the European war as opposed to the Asian one was the result of Jewish influence."[19]

In the summer of 1942, General Sikorski and other European leaders in exile proposed to retaliate against the Germans for their war crimes against Poles, Jews, and other captive people. Sikorski's requests were rejected. The Allies' position was that attacks on civilians and cities were illegal except for military objectives, which included industrial targets. The Allies were bombing "industrial sites" in German cities and would not stop even if Hitler stopped killing Jews. In fact, Hitler and Goebbels publicly blamed the bombing of their cities on American and British Jews. Goebbels threatened "mass extermination of Jews in reprisal for the Allied air bombings of German cities." The British chief of the air staff, Sir Charles Portal, wrote Churchill, "we should almost certainly be overwhelmed with requests from all the other Allies that we should also redress their grievances in the same way. This would result in nothing but a series of 'token' reprisals, which would . . . be completely ineffective as deterrents." Marshall told Sikorski in March 1943 that the proposed bombing operations would disrupt military efforts in Europe and Africa. They were impractical from a technical standpoint. Finally, the Germans would exact retribution against captured air crews.[20]

There was no campaign to rescue the civilian victims of German atrocities because it was a military impossibility. The purpose of the war was to destroy Hitler, Nazism, and the German armed forces, and to free all of the oppressed people of Europe from German tyranny. For Americans, winning the war *meant* the rescue of Europe, *including* the Jews. And, in any event, during 1942 Allied victory was uncertain. Public morale had to be sustained. Some newspapers charged that the government was withholding bad news. Announcing a war to save the Jews would have hurt the war effort, not helped it.[21]

Roosevelt had no illusions about Adolf Hitler. Roosevelt understood him well and knew that there was no reasoning or negotiating with him. From many sources over a period of eight years, Roosevelt perceived Hitler as a monomaniac, an emotional, occasionally irrational tyrant whose will was law in Germany and occupied Europe. Roosevelt undoubtedly saw, as those close to Hitler saw, the Führer's incredible determination, his rage and fury, his instinct to go for broke. He had no reason to doubt that Hitler was murdering every enemy he could get his hands on—Jews, Poles, and Russians foremost.[22]

The deportation of the Jews of Vichy France in the summer of 1942 dramatically illustrated German cruelty to the world. Many witnesses in France and segments of French society, especially the clergy, protested what was happening. Roman Catholic clergy denounced Nazi treatment of French Jews. American relief organizations were overwhelmed with anguished requests. The American diplomat, Pinkney Tuck, conveyed to Pierre Laval, the chief of government of Vichy France, the United States' protest against the "revolting" and "inhuman" treatment of the victims. Sumner Welles described the protest as "the most vigorous representations possible." The *New York Times* headline read: "U.S. Rebukes

Vichy on Deporting Jews." Cordell Hull personally delivered a message condemning the "revolting and fiendish" deportations to the Vichy ambassador.

Tuck was outraged at the barbaric treatment of Jews in Vichy France. On September 11, 1942, he wired Hull that the United States should immediately rescue five thousand to eight thousand Jewish children left behind in France when their parents were deported. Well aware that the intention of the Nazi authorities was that the parents "should not survive," Tuck pressed the State Department and the Vichy government. By September 28, Hull approved the issuance of a thousand visas. Vichy officials stalled because the Germans claimed that if five thousand Jewish children were released, the United States would use the rescue in anti-German propaganda. "I had difficulty restraining my anger," Tuck wired Hull on October 3. Roosevelt himself authorized the State Department to issue visas for the five thousand Jewish children, but according to Breckinridge Long, "desired that there be no publicity in connection therewith." It is hard to know if Roosevelt was complying with Vichy blackmail demands not to use the children for propaganda purposes or if he was fearful of congressional reaction. It was probably both.

On October 9 Tuck met with Laval and assured him that he would recommend to the department that the arrival of the children should not be made the occasion for propaganda or demonstrations. Laval agreed to release the children. But France broke off diplomatic relations with the United States on November 8, 1942, following the Allied landing in North Africa, and the children never left France.[23]

Meanwhile, Breckinridge Long was concerned that special treatment of Jewish refugees would play into Hitler's hands by proving that the United States had gone to war "at the instigation and direction of our Jewish citizens." Long was accused at the time of being "a narrow, limited man" with no sympathy for the oppressed. But he had a compassionate side in individual cases and endorsed the plan to rescue the French Jewish children. The "appeal for asylum," he wrote in his diary in September . . . was "irresistible to any human instinct and the act of [Nazi] barbarity just as repulsive."[24]

Throughout 1942 the Nazis denied that massive deportations of Jews were anything other than for labor service in the East or repatriation. But more reports came out of Europe. The gassing of Jews at Chelmno was disclosed in August by the Polish underground. But even Jewish publications in America would not print the story because their editors did not believe it. Gerhart Riegner, representative of the World Jewish Congress in Geneva, may have been the first Jew outside of Nazidom to see the complete picture. A German industrialist, Eduard Schulte, who knew of the extermination plan, sent the information to a contact in Switzerland through a Jewish friend with orders to keep his name a secret. Riegner obtained the story and met with the American vice consul to get word of the mass killings to the outside world.[25]

Richard Lichtheim, the head of the Geneva office of the Jewish Agency for Palestine, had been reporting the horrors of Nazi persecution and murder of Jews for years. By August 1942 he had information that women, children, the old, and sick were being deported to unknown destinations as well as able-bodied men. On September 3, 1942, he concluded that "the intention cannot be to get labour supply but simply to kill off the deportees." All the relief organizations in Europe were in despair, he wrote, because "no force on earth can stop them." On August 8, 1942, Riegner had already telegraphed the London and New York offices of the World Jewish Congress: "Received alarming report that in Führer's headquarters plan discussed and under consideration according to which all Jews in countries occupied or controlled Germany number 3 to 4 million . . . be exterminated at one blow to resolve once for all the Jewish Question in Europe." But Riegner was not certain. "We transmit information with all necessary reservation," he added.[26]

Chapter 13

"This Bestial Policy of Cold-Blooded Extermination"

Roosevelt warned the Germans on August 21, 1942, that war criminals would face "fearful retribution" when the war ended. He issued a press release that reminded the Nazis that mass killings were the acts of "desperate men who know in their hearts that they cannot win." The front-page headline in the *New York Times* on August 22 read "President Warns Atrocities of Axis Will Be Avenged." In September 1942 Harry Hopkins prepared a memorandum for FDR proposing a United Nations Commission on Atrocities, the purpose of which, according to Hopkins, was "to deter those committing the atrocities by naming their names and letting them know that they are being watched by the civilized world, which will mete out swift and just punishment on the reckoning day." Ben Cohen drafted an extremely confidential radical plan to create a Jewish state in Palestine.[1]

On October 7, Roosevelt told the Nazi ringleaders that he was aware that the "commission of these crimes continues" and that it was "the intention of this Government that the successful close of the war shall include provision for the surrender to the United Nations of war criminals; and that the criminals would receive sure and certain punishment." The ringleaders, he warned, would be subjected to "just and sure punishment" for their atrocities. The statement made it clear that the Allies would not resort to general reprisals against German citizens. Roosevelt made these statements "to deter those committing the atrocities by naming their names and letting them know that they are being watched by the civilized world," to keep the American people informed of their enemies; and to encourage the Allies to persevere to defeat Germany.[2]

Congressman Emanuel Celler wrote FDR a strong letter on October 10, 1942, denouncing Vichy France's "pogroms and persecutions of helpless Jews." He alleged that Premier Pierre Laval had promised Hitler to deliver the 170,000 Jews in unoccupied France to be interned. "They are to be deported to Germany or Axis-controlled lands, there to linger in a slavery worse than death." Celler reported suicide, children snatched from parents, and huge fines. He asked Roosevelt to call Laval to task while the United States still had an embassy in Vichy. It was evident that Celler, a Jewish congressman from Brooklyn, did not know or did not believe as late as October 10, 1942, what exactly was taking place in France. Like others, he was still talking about pogroms, persecutions, and slave labor camps.

Roosevelt replied that Celler had raised a question "that has given me deep cause for thought. The end we have in view is identical and there only remains a question as to how best we can relieve the persecutions and sufferings of these unhappy refugees." He reviewed his previous actions of withdrawing the U.S. diplomats in France and making strong protests. "Our representative also stressed the fact," FDR told Celler, "that the world, and the people of France, would one day pass judgment on Laval for this callous act." Hull had directly confronted Vichy's ambassador. The American attitude, Roosevelt continued, was well known. Unfortunately, the damage was done, and the wise course was to concentrate on quietly assisting those who could be rescued, including children who were scheduled to come to America. At that moment Tuck was negotiating to get departure permits for Jewish children. While its actions were of limited success, the United States had done all it reasonably could in Vichy France under the circumstances.[3]

In the fall of 1942 America and the other Allied nations were on the move. On October 23 General Bernard Montgomery began his assault on Rommel at El Alamein. The continued existence of the Yishuv (Jewish Palestine) depended on Montgomery's success. At the same time the Western Naval Task Force left Hampton Roads in the first amphibious military operation to cross an ocean. The first lady traveled to Britain. Greeted by the king and queen, Foreign Minister Anthony Eden, and General Eisenhower, ER charmed the British public and American servicemen alike.[4]

Hitler's deep hatred of Roosevelt grew as the war progressed. In a rambling speech on September 30 at the Berlin Sport Stadium, he called Roosevelt "the chief warmonger of this war" and warned that the "hour shall come when we will reply. Let us hope that by then these two chief war criminals [Roosevelt and Churchill] and their Jewish Strawmen refrain from whining and baaa-ing" when England is defeated. Hitler blamed the war on international Jewry and recalled his September 1939 warning that if the Jews made war on Germany "Jewry will be eradicated."[5]

In late 1942 Roosevelt was preoccupied with the Pacific war. On October 24 he instructed the Joint Chiefs to hold Guadalcanal. FDR had a personal interest in Guadalcanal: his son James was fighting there. The American public wanted action against Japan, and victory on Guadalcanal became a major American priority. A fierce naval battle went on for three days, from November 12 to November 15. The Air Force gradually wrested control of the air from the Japanese. By December there were 60,000 Americans on the island. The U.S. Navy and Marines held the island and won a decisive victory in November and December 1942. But the campaign had cost the American military its greatest number of casualties to date.[6]

Meanwhile, Gerhart Riegner's information confirming the worst news about the Holocaust reached the State Department in August. Department officials dismissed the atrocity stories as unbelievable and delayed passing them on. Rabbi Stephen Wise, however, received the information from London. Riegner had reported his information to the British Foreign Office, which gave it to Samuel S. Silverman, a Jewish member of Parliament. Silverman forwarded it to Wise. Not knowing that the State Department had Riegner's report, the rabbi sent it to Sumner Welles, who asked Wise to keep it secret until the report could be verified. Welles did what any responsible government official would have done: he checked the information. After all, Riegner's telegram stated, "we transmit information with all necessary reservation as exactitude cannot be confirmed."[7]

Riegner's telegram was only a first step. He "hedged his message with qualifications," and much of it was wrong. Thus the State Department's delay was understandable. Sumner Welles, too, found the atrocity stories unbelievable. He, like many others, thought it illogical that the Germans, desperate for laborers, would kill Jews, and he knew that atrocity stories had been fabricated in the last war. Stories of the use of corpses to make soap, for example, were a staple of British propaganda during World War I, although they were false and the British knew it. Thus Welles reassured Wise that the stories could not be true. Nevertheless, Welles gave the reports the highest priority and set about having them investigated.[8]

Wise asked Welles and Frankfurter to tell Roosevelt, and he gave Frankfurter Riegner's cable. Other information about the mass extermination began appearing in the Jewish press. Overcome with grief, Wise met with Jewish leaders to figure out what to do. By November Welles had secured sufficient corroboration to conclude that an extermination program was indeed under way.[9]

From Roosevelt's perspective, everything was done that could reasonably be done for European Jewry. He had met with Chaim Weizmann in July at Churchill's request to discuss Palestine. He had issued public warnings of retribution in August. Myron Taylor pressed to have the pope speak out. Roosevelt tried his best to save French refugees from "those human butchers." On October 7

Welles announced establishment of a United Nations Commission for the Investigation of War Crimes to punish those who committed war crimes. Amending the immigration laws was an impossibility. It was, of course, not absolutely clear to Roosevelt, prior to Welles's November report, that the systematic murder of Jews was taking place.[10]

Hitler helped the investigators by declaring in his September 30 public address in Berlin that he had warned "Jewry" in 1939 that if they "plotted" another world war "to exterminate the Aryan peoples of Europe, it would not be the Aryan peoples which would be exterminated, but Jewry . . . I shall be right also in that prophesy." But Hitler had been threatening to kill Jews since the 1920s, and few believed that Germany would actually do it.[11]

On November 24 Welles asked Wise to come to the State Department. After an investigation by Leland Harrison and his staff at Bern, Switzerland, which included interviews with Riegner, Richard Lichtheim of the Jewish agency, the Red Cross, the Vatican, and others, corroboration of their sources, and sworn statements of witnesses, Welles was convinced that the reports of systematic killings were true. Welles's decision to inform Wise was contrary to the thinking of most State Department personnel, who thought the stories exaggerated and that the United States could do nothing, even if they were true, to relieve the suffering of the Jewish people. Political pressure to take action would be unpleasant and could only result in rescue proponents' disappointment in the administration.[12]

Welles and Roosevelt disagreed with the State Department. "I regret to tell you, Dr. Wise," Welles told the rabbi, "that these [reports] confirm and justify your deepest fears. There is no exaggeration." Welles urged Wise to make the information public, which he soon did. Wise told the press that 2 million Jews in occupied Europe had been killed (it was closer to 3.5 million) in an "extermination campaign," that corpses had been used for "soap fats and fertilizers" (which was not true), and that his sources had been "confirmed by the State Department." The American press carried the story, some on the front page. Welles doubtless acted with FDR's blessing.[13]

The result was a wave of denunciations and demonstrations against Germany. A Day of Mourning was held on December 2, 1942, and given broad coverage in the press. The *New York Times* denounced the Nazis' "homicidal mania." Special services, radio broadcasts, and a ten-minute work stoppage were held in New York City. NBC radio broadcast a memorial service to the nation. Services were held all over the country. According to Doris Kearns Goodwin, ER, in New York on December 2, realized for the first time "the enormity of the slaughter." Wise requested a meeting with the president on December 2, 1942.[14]

On December 8, Rabbi Wise and a group of Jewish American leaders visited FDR at the White House. They gave him a memorandum, "Blueprint for Extermination," and requested him to warn the Nazis that they would be held to strict account for their crimes and to form a commission to investigate German actions and make a public report. According to notes made by Adolph Held of the Jewish Labor Committee, Roosevelt said that the "government of the United States was very well acquainted with most of the facts you are now bringing to our attention. Unfortunately, we have received confirmation from many sources." He told the group that they could prepare a statement for his signature and that "we shall do all in our power to be of service to your people in their tragic moment." Roosevelt was clear that the rescue of the Jews would be difficult. We "cannot treat these matters in normal ways," he said. "We are dealing with an insane man— Hitler, and the group that surrounds him represent an example of a national psychopathic case."

Roosevelt wanted to make it clear that Hitler, not the German people, was the enemy. It was not "in the best interests of the Allied cause to make it appear that the entire German people are murderers or are in agreement with what Hitler is doing." Wise told the press after the meeting that the president was "profoundly shocked" at the news and that the Nazi criminals would face "a day of reckoning which will surely come."[15]

Two days after Rabbi Wise's announcement, FDR met with Vice President Henry Wallace and House Speaker Sam Rayburn to discuss loosening immigration restrictions. Rayburn explained the political impossibility of achieving that goal. On December 3 Morgenthau talked with FDR about Palestine and told him he was having a meeting at his home that night at the suggestion of Sam Rosenman. Roosevelt advised Morgenthau to "go easy on that because I have pretty well made up my mind as to what I am going to do." Roosevelt said he "would call Palestine a religious country . . . leave Jerusalem the way it is and have it run by the Orthodox

Greek Catholic Church, the Protestants, and the Jews—have a joint committee run it." He "would put a barbed wire around Palestine . . . begin to move the Arabs out," and "provide land for the Arabs in some other part of the Middle East." Palestine would be 90 percent Jewish and an independent nation. As for the Jews in Europe, Roosevelt said he had been working with Isaiah Bowman, studying many places in the world, and had recently talked with the president of the Republic of Colombia.[16]

A formal Allied declaration on the Nazi extermination of the Jews had been in the works for several months. The British government had been under intense pressure from an outraged public, including the archbishop of Canterbury, to speak out. The United Nations Declaration on Jewish Massacres was issued on December 17, 1942, nine days after Wise and his delegation requested it. Signed by the United States, Great Britain, the Soviet Union, and eight occupied countries, it denounced "in the strongest possible terms this bestial policy of cold-blooded extermination." It condemned the German government's "intention to exterminate the Jewish people in Europe. . . . None of those taken away are ever heard of again. . . . The infirm are left to die of exposure and starvation or are deliberately massacred in mass executions."[17] The impact of this Declaration was considerable. It received wide publicity in the American press and, more importantly, committed the Allies in the eyes of the world to prosecute war crimes against European Jewry.[18]

This declaration is barely quoted and hardly discussed by the Roosevelt critics in academe. Henry Feingold, for example, left readers with the impression that the few public statements issued

11 ALLIES CONDEMN NAZI WAR ON JEWS

United Nations Issue Joint Declaration of Protest on 'Cold-Blooded Extermination'

Special to THE NEW YORK TIMES.

WASHINGTON, Dec. 17 — A joint declaration by members of the United Nations was issued today condemning Germany's "bestial policy of cold-blooded extermination" of Jews and declaring that "such events can only strengthen the resolve of all freedom-loving peoples to overthrow the barbarous Hitlerite tyranny."

The nations reaffirmed "their solemn resolution to insure that those responsible for these crimes shall not escape retribution and to press on with the necessary practical measures to this end."

The declaration was issued simultaneously through the State Department here and in London. It was subscribed to by eleven nations, including the United States, Britain and Russia, and also by the French National Committee in London.

The declaration referred particularly to the program as conducted in Poland and to the barbarous forms it is taking.

TEXT OF DECLARATION

The attention of the Belgian, Czechoslovak, Greek, Luxem-

Continued on Page Ten

Front page story, New York Times, December 18, 1942, on Joint Declaration condemning Germany's "bestial policy of cold-blooded extermination" of the Jews.

were done so reluctantly. He belittled the declaration by dismissing it as "a joint Anglo-American statement" and "the December 17 'solemn resolution,'" which was worse than nothing because it "showed clearly" that there would be "little effort to prevent the Final Solution while the war was in progress." The "precedent of saying nothing, so perplexing to later observers, was firmly established in 1942," Feingold wrote in *Alice in Wonderland* fashion without regard for the undeniable fact that FDR said everything that could be said at the time. Roosevelt, as we have seen, said everything Jewish leaders asked him to say. Many other historians have inexplicably ignored the declaration.[19]

In December 1942 there was absolutely nothing Franklin Roosevelt and the Allies could do to save European Jewry. A map of Europe demonstrates why. Jewish leaders and organizations offered no realistic plan to rescue Hitler's victims because there was none to offer. The Germans were the unchallenged masters of Europe. The Jews were prisoners of the

Germans. They were captives right in the middle of Nazidom, in occupied Poland. They could not flee. No army, navy, or air force in the
world could reach them. They had, as Martin Gilbert wrote, "no
means of escape." Proposals by American Jews to create havens in
neutral or Allied countries, for example, were fantasies. By order of the
German government, Jews were forbidden to emigrate. In August the
Allies attempted to land at Dieppe, France, and suffered a disastrous
defeat. In October there was fierce fighting in Guadalcanal, Stalingrad, and North Africa. Fortress Europa was impervious to Allied
attack, and Hitler's victims were far behind the walls of his fortress.[20]

American Jews disagreed among themselves about what to do
to save European Jewry. The bitterness of these disagreements was
intensified by the utter helplessness of those who wanted to help.
The AJCommittee and assimilationist, non-Zionist Jews in the
Roosevelt camp (notably Morgenthau, Rosenman, Frankfurter,
and Lehman) preferred quiet diplomacy. The Zionist AJ Congress
and its affiliate the World Jewish Congress led by Rabbi Wise
marched and held mass meetings to urge more government action.
There was a plethora of other groups: the Jewish Labor Committee
(mostly anti-Zionist, prodemocratic, and socialist); B'nai B'rith, a
nonpolitical fraternal organization that gradually became more
political and pro-Zionist; the Synagogue Council of America (a
religious group representing all branches of Judaism); the
Orthodox Agudath Israel of America; the American Joint Distribution Committee, (the "Joint") which had historically rescued
Jews in Europe; the Zionist Organization of America; and the
American Zionist Emergency Committee, among others.[21]

In May 1942 American Zionists met in an extraordinary conference at the Hotel Biltmore in New York City. Hundreds of Jewish leaders heard Chaim Weizmann, the grand old man of Zionism, describe the horrors inflicted on European Jewry and the perfidy of the British, who had reneged in the 1939 white paper on promises made in the post–World War I Balfour Declaration. The conference demanded that "the gates of Palestine be opened" and "that Palestine be established as a Jewish Commonwealth . . . then and only then will the age-old wrong to the Jewish people be righted." The Biltmore Declaration was new and militant, and new fire-eating leaders had emerged with it: David Ben-Gurion, chairman of the Jewish Agency Executive in Palestine, and Rabbi Abba Hillel Silver of Cleveland. Jewish congressmen such as Emanuel Celler were vocal Zionists. Most of the Jews close to FDR, including Sam Rosenman, supported the Biltmore Declaration.[22]

Many American Jews, particularly leftists and conservative assimilationists, were appalled by the Biltmore Declaration. They argued that it antagonized the Arabs but did not help Europe's Jews. Some saw the declaration as "a declaration of war by Jews on the Arabs." Because of the difficulties faced by the British, FDR opposed any action that would stir up the Arabs or endanger Allied oil supplies, and he opposed congressional resolutions that were pro–Biltmore Declaration. Many Arab leaders were vocal supporters of the Nazis, and neither Roosevelt nor Churchill wanted to create another front in the Middle East.[23]

German victories in North Africa in 1942 and antisemitic propaganda aimed at both Europeans and Arabs convinced

American military planners and diplomats that it was unwise for the Allies to talk about the Nazi war against the Jews. There were strong feelings in the War and State Departments as well as in the Office of War Information (OWI) that Arabs and Muslims were potential allies. But while government officials knew that Roosevelt would never abandon the Jews of Palestine, the president's military concerns about North Africa and the Middle East were genuine. He deferred to the British in this area of historic British influence, and Eisenhower, Marshall, and Stimson were nervous about riling up twenty-five million Arabs in North Africa.[24]

President Roosevelt, in hindsight, appeared all-powerful. But in 1942 the American people and Congress knew better. The congressional elections of November 3, 1942, were a political disaster for the president. Republicans gained forty-four seats in the House and nine in the Senate. The war news was depressing. The Japanese were killing American soldiers at Guadalcanal, and the Germans were advancing on Stalingrad. There was no progress on the second front. Roosevelt had ordered the invasion of North Africa, but it was still a secret on Election Day. Wartime rationing was unpopular.[25]

The anti-Roosevelt coalition did not wait for Congress to convene to slam the president. The Third War Powers bill, which permitted the president to suspend laws restricting the "free movement of persons, property, and information into and out of the United States," became a target of the Roosevelt-haters. The bill would allow the president to bypass laws hampering the war effort, but his opponents perceived it as a back-door method to allow European refugees, particularly Jews, into the country. It was tabled in committee, 24 to 0. "The ugly truth is," *Newsweek* reported, "that antisemitism was a definite factor in the bitter opposition to the President's request for power to suspend immigration laws for the duration." Had there been even a glimmer of hope that Congress would change its mind and allow Jewish refugees into the United States, these hopes were dashed after the November 1942 elections.[26]

In the fall of 1942 Roosevelt knew that the Allies lacked the military strength to launch a second front in Europe, but they had to reassure the Soviets that an Anglo-American offensive was in the offing and convince Americans that the United States was striking at the Germans. French North Africa (Morocco and Algeria) was the logical soft spot. The Vichy government, heretofore collaborating with Hitler, might be persuaded to join the Allies' cause or offer less resistance than the Germans. Roosevelt directed the secret negotiations and overrode Marshall, Eisenhower, and his top military advisers when he decided to invade North Africa. Roosevelt sent Robert Murphy, his personal emissary, to lay the groundwork with local Vichy officials, some of whom did cooperate. Murphy utilized twelve Allied consuls who were basically spies. Bill Donovan and his new espionage agency, the Office of Strategic Services (OSS), also went to North Africa and reported directly to Roosevelt. The loyalty of the Arab Muslim population to the French government was an essential part of Roosevelt's plan, and several hundred thousand French-trained Muslim troops were a prize worth fighting for.[27]

Operation Torch was supposed to have begun before Election

Day, November 3, 1942. Roosevelt desperately wanted a successful amphibious landing by American troops to lift morale and, hopefully, to elect more Democrats to Congress. But it did not occur. Although FDR, holding up his hands in mock prayer, had asked Marshall, "Please make it before Election Day," Eisenhower postponed the invasion until November 8.[28]

To succeed in the North Africa campaign, Roosevelt was forced to make deals with unsavory characters such as Admiral Jean-François Darlan, a notorious Nazi-collaborator and commander of all Vichy military forces. But Roosevelt's gamble paid off: Operation Torch succeeded brilliantly. General George S. Patton's men went ashore near Casablanca. A worried FDR received the news at Shangri-La, his hand shaking as he picked up the telephone receiver. "Thank God. Thank God," he said. "That sounds great. We have landed in North Africa," he told his guests. "Casualties are below expectations. We are striking back." Marshall realized the wisdom of Roosevelt's decision. "We failed to see that the leader in a democracy has to keep the people entertained. . . . The people demand action," he wrote.[29]

Montgomery's decisive victory at El Alamein the first week in November and the Americans' landing in North Africa ended the Nazi threat to the Yishuv. Half a million Palestinian Jews would survive the Holocaust. But Roosevelt was not worrying solely about Palestine. His worries were global: Franco in Spain might jump in on the Nazi side; Pétain and Darlan might fight to the death. A storm of protest broke over Roosevelt's head because he had cooperated with a Nazi-collaborator.[30] "Prostitutes are used," the editor of the *Nation* wrote of the Darlan deal, "they are seldom loved." Roosevelt replied with what he claimed was an old Orthodox Bulgarian proverb: "My children, it is permitted you in time of grave danger to walk with the devil until you have crossed the bridge." "Of course I'm dealing with Darlan," he shouted at Free French emissaries, "since Darlan's giving me Algiers!" Roosevelt said that the Darlan deal was "only a temporary expedient, justified solely by the stress of battle." He demanded the liberation of all imprisoned anti-Nazis and "the abrogation of all laws and decrees inspired by Nazi governments or Nazi ideologists." Roosevelt was bitter at his critics. Rosenman recalled that Roosevelt showed more resentment over criticism about Darlan than at any other time he knew about.[31]

The Allies quickly captured Morocco and Algeria. Tunisia and Libya were a different story. The Germans and Italians under Erwin Rommel, the "Desert Fox," fought tenaciously. The Luftwaffe's superiority and friendly weather were too much for the Allies. Well into February 1943, the Germans believed they could halt the Allied advance. At the Battle of Kasserine Pass in mid-February 1943 the Afrika Korps and the 10th Panzer Division wiped out an American infantry regiment, an armored regiment, and inflicted six thousand American casualties in an attempt to divide the Allied armies. Eisenhower replaced the American commander at Kasserine Pass with General George S. Patton.[32]

Despite their successes, the Allies were far from victory. The invasion across the English Channel was still up in the air. Churchill said he favored it, but did all he could to delay it. Nazi deception about the Holocaust continued unabated. Tragically, most of Polish

Jewry was dead by March 1943. Belzec was closed. Majdaneck was still gassing victims. Three million Jews were already dead.[33]

"The relentless killing missed no day," Gilbert wrote, "and took no rest." Jews were trapped in the Warsaw ghetto in January. But they began to resist. On Passover, April 18, German troops entered the ghetto, and twelve hundred Jews resisted with a few guns, hand grenades, and incendiary bottles. It took the German army several weeks to subdue the ghetto. On the Eastern Front, deportation of Jews increased even as German soldiers retreated. Secrecy was still maintained. In September Jews in the Lodz ghetto did not believe Jews were being liquidated. The crimes of the Holocaust were well concealed. Corpses at many camps from Chelmno to Treblinka were dug up and burned. In September Treblinka was destroyed, the site plowed under, and a farm built on it. Other sites, including Ponar near Vilna and Babi Yar near Kiev, were dug up so that tens of thousands of corpses could be burned.[34]

It was unclear in 1943 that the German satellite countries would cooperate in the murder of the Jews. In March 1943 the Bulgarians resisted and released Jews already in custody. Finland, Italy, and Hungary also refused to cooperate. Hitler personally urged the Hungarian leader, Admiral Miklos Horthy, to "resettle" his nation's Jews, and Horthy refused. In North Africa, the German occupation of Tunisia in May meant plunder and slave labor for the Jews, but not extermination.[35]

But European antisemitism also had to be reckoned with. The Germans were hardly alone in their hatred of Jews. "If you can't kill Serbs or Jews," the Croatian interior minister, Andrija

Artukovi, said in 1941, "you are an enemy of the state." German propaganda claimed Jews had started the war. This strategy succeeded in Europe and the Middle East. American propaganda was tailored to European audiences. It urged opposition to the Nazis but did not mention the slaughter of the Jews because they were Jews. Unfortunately, "to defend or champion the Jewish cause vigorously," an American military attaché observed in 1942, would hurt the Allied cause in occupied Europe because many of Hitler's victims were as antisemitic as the Führer.

Nor would Roosevelt allow the Germans to make World War II into a "Jews' war." Jews were, or should have been, according to Roosevelt's viewpoint, citizens of their respective nations, entitled to equal treatment as Poles, Hungarians, Russians, or Frenchmen. More importantly for FDR, this viewpoint reflected political reality. Americans would not fight a war for European Jewry or for any other oppressed minority. Thus, for both domestic and foreign policy reasons, Roosevelt could not permit the United States to be perceived as giving Jews special leniency or aid.[36]

Hitler had met with the grand mufti of Jerusalem, Haj Amin al-Husseni, on November 28, 1941, to discuss their mutual opposition to the British, the Communists, and the worldwide destruction of the Jews. Germany, the Führer told the charismatic Muslim leader, would occupy southern Russia; "liberate" the Middle East from British rule. The German army, in fact, made preparations to invade the Middle East in conjunction with Arab groups in pursuit of Hitler's dream of the annihilation of world Jewry.[37]

Chapter 14

Placating Moroccans
and Killing Japs

On January 7, 1943, Franklin Roosevelt addressed a cheering Congress. "I cannot prophesy. I cannot tell you when or where the United Nations are going to strike next in Europe." It may be in Norway or France or Sicily, he said, but "we and the British and the Russians will hit them from the air heavily and relentlessly. Yes, the Nazis and the Fascists have asked for it—and—they are going to get it." But the Nazis and the Fascists were not alone. In the dramatic 1944 movie *The Purple Heart*, one of the condemned Doolittle raiders says to his Japanese captors, "This is your war—you wanted it—and you asked for it. And now you're going to get it—and it won't be finished until your dirty little empire is wiped off the face of the earth." Roosevelt agreed. All three barbaric creeds—Nazism, Fascism, and Japanese militarism—would be utterly destroyed.[1]

Two days later, FDR secretly left Washington and traveled by train with a small entourage to Florida. In an exhausting five-day journey, he flew to Brazil, across the Atlantic to British Gambia, and finally to Casablanca, where he met with Churchill and the military brass to map out a blueprint for victory. Roosevelt's priorities at Casablanca were to defeat the U-boats in the Atlantic; to aid the Russians; and to plan the Combined Bomber Offensive against Germany that many hoped would defeat the Nazis without a land campaign. Finally, he sought a greater emphasis on the war against Japan. Roosevelt and Churchill called for the unconditional surrender of Germany. "This is not the end," Churchill said. "It is not even the beginning of the end. But it is, perhaps, the end of the beginning."[2]

Roosevelt's machinations in North Africa involved him in local politics. Antisemitic Frenchmen remained in power in North Africa. The Supreme Command pledged to leave the French administration in control. This was the price Roosevelt paid for a less costly victory in that region. Roosevelt tried to meliorate what he saw as a temporary problem by convincing Admiral Darlan to announce the relaxation of anti-Jewish laws. Darlan's assassination in Algiers on December 24, 1943, proved fortunate for Roosevelt, but discrimination against Jews continued. A five-star resident general, Auguste Noguès, governed Morocco. Some American commanders, notably Patton, were happy to cooperate with Noguès because his authoritarian Vichy government made easier the Americans' military mission, pacifying the country and freeing up Allied soldiers to fight Germany.[3]

Roosevelt's main goals at Casablanca were military. The Allies' highest priority was to defeat the enemy's submarines. German U-boats controlled the Atlantic even as Roosevelt and Churchill were meeting. The North African campaign was at a critical stage, and Roosevelt wanted American soldiers attacking Germans, not serving as an occupation army. He wanted DeGaulle, General Henri Giraud, and other squabbling French officials to resolve their differences and fight Germans instead of each other, and he wanted to bring Arabs and Muslims into the Allied camp. On the day the Free French leader DeGaulle arrived at Casablanca for his "shotgun wedding" with General Henri Giraud, Darlan's successor as high commissioner, Roosevelt gave a dinner in honor of the sultan of Morocco. The purpose of the dinner was to demonstrate that the United States was not an imperial power and favored Moroccan independence. FDR's conversation with the sultan outraged Churchill and French leaders, who intended to restore their nations' empires, not dismantle them.[4]

Jewish-American soldiers in Algiers protested vigorously to Ambassador Robert Murphy about what they perceived as his failure to relieve the suffering of Algerian Jews in early 1942. Some suggested that Murphy return to America. (Here was yet another example of the Roosevelt critics' cowed, meek, silent American Jews! Their "silence" was heard clearly by Ambassador Murphy.) Eisenhower detailed Major Paul F. (Piggy) Warburg, of the Jewish banking family, to advise Murphy on Jewish affairs. Henry Morgenthau was also angry about Vichy's mistreatment of Jews in North Africa in early 1942. Morgenthau visited Algiers and met with thirty local Jewish leaders at Murphy's residence. There he learned that while the Jews of North Africa had been exiled and victims of discrimination and occasional loss of their businesses, they had not been physically molested. Indeed, Morgenthau discovered that "the most extreme antisemitic decrees had not been enforced in North Africa." This experience may well have demonstrated to Morgenthau that the facts on the ground were not always reported accurately during the war.[5]

Roosevelt met Noguès, the governor of Morocco, to iron out their differences. The resident general had refused to betray Vichy but now sided uncomfortably with the Allies. Murphy had earlier met Noguès and trusted him enough to inform him of the possibility of invasion. He believed Noguès to be a "capable and intelligent officer and administrator . . . with several decades of experience in Morocco, familiar with all the intricate problems of the region," and undoubtedly so informed FDR.

By the time Roosevelt met with Noguès, it was clear that governing North Africa could be fraught with difficulties. Murphy knew of the age-old segregation of Algerian Jews, but he believed it was in the United States' interest to placate Frenchmen, Arabs, and Muslims, many of whom were antisemites.[6] Great care must be taken, Murphy believed, to prevent racial uprisings detrimental to the Allied campaign. This meant caution in addressing Nazi laws revoked by General Giraud on March 14, 1943.[7]

Thus, when Roosevelt met Noguès, he told the resident general:

> *[T]he whole Jewish problem should be studied very carefully. . . . In other words, the number of Jews engaged in the practice of the professions (law, medicine, etc.) should be definitely limited to the percentage*

that the Jewish population in North Africa bears to the whole North African population. Such a plan would therefore permit the Jews to engage in the professions, and at the same time would not permit them to over-crowd the professions, and would present an unanswerable argument that they were being given their full rights. To the foregoing General Noguès agreed generally, stating at the same time that it would be a sad thing for the French to win the war merely to open the way for the Jews to control the professions and the business world of North Africa. The President stated that his plan would further eliminate the specific and understandable complaints which the Germans bore towards the Jews in Germany, namely that while they represented a small part of the population, over 50 percent of the lawyers, doctors, schoolteachers, college professors, etc., in Germany were Jews.

Roosevelt's goal at Casablanca was to solve several problems: to reach an accommodation with the Vichy resident general, who governed millions of Muslims and Frenchmen; to meliorate, in a "fair" way, local discrimination against Jews; and to blunt Nazi propaganda aimed to divide the Allies, the Muslims, and the French. As he did with Noguès, Roosevelt frequently left his visitors convinced that he agreed with their point of view. FDR had long believed that quotas for minorities were sometimes a necessary evil. His allusion to the high percentage of lawyers and doctors in

Germany was mistaken, but in fact the percentages of Jews in the professions in prewar Berlin and Warsaw, respectively, were 40 percent and 50 percent, and this was Noguès's perception. According to Murphy, Roosevelt could see that Allied success in North Africa depended upon how well the French maintained order in the Maghreb.

Noguès, Rooosevelt told the press, "is all for one party . . . He is for Noguès. And . . . he is no more pro-Hitler than I am . . . he is pro-Noguès . . . Well, it's much better in the rear of our armies to keep a perfectly nice, quiet position in Morocco than it is to go chasing rainbows as to the future of France." Neither DeGaulle's ambitions, nor French imperialism, nor antisemitic laws in North Africa would deter Roosevelt from his mission to defeat Hitler.[8]

After Casablanca, Roosevelt and Churchill informed Stalin of their plans to defeat Germany in 1943. But Stalin was displeased when he learned that no date had been set for the second front. Roosevelt took great pains to convince the Soviet leader of America's sincerity, and that supplying the Red Army was one of the president's highest priorities. But FDR did have an immediately higher priority, namely the Battle of the Atlantic. Losses outpaced ship construction by a million tons. The situation was so desperate that Churchill and Roosevelt agreed to postpone convoys to Russia, a step that infuriated an already suspicious Stalin.[9]

In Stalin's view, Russians were fighting and killing Germans and dying by the hundreds of thousands while Americans and Britons dallied in North Africa. Sevastopol had fallen to the Nazis in July, and the German army continued its advance during the summer and fall of 1942. Rostov-on-Don was captured in July. Stalingrad was under siege. Bombed by one thousand German aircraft and heavily damaged by artillery and tanks, the Red Army refused to surrender Stalingrad. The Nazis juggernaut stalled, and by late November 1942, as cold weather set in, 250,000 German troops were encircled by the Russians. By late December the Germans were retreating. In January 1943 the Soviets reclaimed Stalingrad at a cost of 1 million casualties.

The German forces around Stalingrad surrendered in February 1943. The Russian victory was a significant turning point in the war, but Hitler refused to give up his attempt to conquer Russia. The Germans' counteroffense at Belgorod and Kharkov demonstrated that the war was far from over. Hitler planned new offensives and put renewed emphasis on the U-boat war and new weapons soon to be available. Gas warfare was to be used against London; pilotless airplanes, the V-1 and V-2 rockets; and a long-range cannon, the V-3. The German counteroffensive after Stalingrad and the failure of the Allies to establish a "second front" in Europe led the Soviets to secretly pursue a separate peace with Germany. Still confident of victory, the Germans rejected all peace feelers from Moscow. For Roosevelt and American military planners, Stalingrad meant a change in strategy. Russia would not collapse. Now, less manpower but "bombers in fantastic numbers" would defeat Germany.[10]

In North Africa, progress against the Germans was slow. Rommel's army was attacked front and rear and bombed mercilessly, but held out into May. In May Americans attacked Japanese forces on Attu in the Aleutian Islands with heavy casualties. The Japanese abandoned Kiska. There was a lull in the Pacific war as American military chiefs studied how best to proceed. They decided to continue the assault on the Solomon Islands. Future president John F. Kennedy lost his PT boat in one of these actions.[11]

It was also a time of labor unrest and strikes at home. Roosevelt's old nemesis John L. Lewis continued to rail at the president. He led a national strike of coal miners and boycotted the War Labor Board. Roosevelt reminded the strikers in a fireside chat that they had "sons who at this very minute—this split second—may be fighting in New Guinea, or in the Aleutian Islands, or Guadalcanal, or Tunisia, or China, or protecting troops ships and supplies against submariners on the high seas." Roosevelt called upon the miners' patriotism but made it clear that the "war is going to go on. Coal will be mined no matter what any individual thinks about it." Strikers were drafted. When railroad workers went on strike, the War Department seized and ran the railroads until the issues were resolved. But the coal strike hurt the economy and slowed production of guns and tanks. The public was livid, and Congress seized the opportunity to roll back the power of the union movement. The Smith-Connally Act of June 25, 1943, dealt harshly with strikers and was vehemently opposed by organized labor. Still the New Dealer, Roosevelt vetoed the bill, but Congress overrode his veto.[12]

The Battle of the Atlantic raged in early 1943 as it had from the beginning of the war. Upon the success or failure of their efforts depended the Anglo-American return to Europe. Churchill later admitted that the U-boat peril was "the only thing that really frightened me during the war." Admiral Doenitz "considered the months January through March 1943 the peak of submarine achievement." Dramatic, costly, and deadly sinkings of American ships occurred in spring 1943. In March 1943 a vast nor'easter slammed two convoys together. German U-boats sunk twenty-two merchantmen in the havoc. The situation became critical when the Germans coordinated a blitz attack on Allied shipping. U-boats sank forty-one ships from March 1 to March 10 and forty-four ships in the second ten days of March for a total of 500,000 tons of shipping. The famous sinking of the USS *Dorchester*, in which four chaplains of different faiths, including Rabbi Alexander Goode, gave others their life jackets and perished, occurred on February 3, 1943.[13]

While it was clear in hindsight that the Allies turned a corner in the spring of 1943, contemporaries were unsure. The U-boat was Germany's best hope to defeat the Anglo-Americans. "The Germans never came so near to disrupting communication between the New World and the Old as in the first twenty days of March 1943," the Admiralty staff concluded. Ernie Pyle, the well-known war correspondent, "gloomed with the desperate belief that it was actually possible for us to lose this war." Germany built more and bigger submarines and searched for newer weapons. The German snorkel breathing device, which allowed German submarines to remain submerged for longer periods, came on line in 1944. One hundred ninety-eight U-boats were built between May and December 1943. "From the Allied point of view," historian Samuel Eliot Morison observed, "victory was not even in sight."[14]

On the other side of the world, progress, in the Pacific was slow. The global death toll was growing impossibly obscene. Led by MacArthur, the United States Army gradually conquered the Solomon Islands and invaded New Guinea, where fighting conditions were a deadly mix of heat, rain, disease, snipers, and boredom. The Japanese massacres of millions of innocent people infuriated Americans. Their claims to be an Asian "master race" destined to rule all inferiors were virtually identical to the Nazis'. Like Hitler, Japanese leaders believed that Americans were racial inferiors, barbarians, too decadent and materialistic to fight. Japanese racism extended to Jews. Like the Nazis, they associated Roosevelt with the "Jewish plutocracy" and mindlessly adopted Nazi antisemitic doctrines. As practitioners of Shinto, Japanese were vicious anti-Christians as well. They published cartoons denigrating Christianity and depicting a crucified Franklin Roosevelt stabbed with Japanese swords.[15]

Like the Nazis, the Japanese believed in their "peoplehood" or *minzoku*, the equivalent of the Nazi *Volk*. Japanese writers cited German racial theories and deliberately ignored Hitler's anti-Japanese statements in *Mein Kampf*. In fact, these passages were deleted in the Japanese translation. The Japanese believed they were destined to rule the world, or at least a great part of it. They accepted the Nazi-like notion of *Lebensraum* ("expansion of living space") so that the "Yamato race" could occupy Asia and beyond. All the great oceans would be renamed the "Great Sea of Japan."[16]

Thus Americans hatred of the Japanese was easy to understand, and American attention to horrors in the East understandably took precedence over horrors in Europe. Japanese atrocities included contests between Japanese officers to decapitate the most Chinese civilians, rape and murder of Christian nuns in Hong Kong, the binding and bayoneting of fifty British officers in Hong Kong, and the frequent use of bayonets to kill prisoners of war and civilians. The duplicity of the Japanese military, which lied when it claimed that it adhered to international law in the treatment of prisoners, inflamed American opinion. The Japanese kidnapped thousands of Korean and Chinese girls and women and forced them to become prostitutes for Japanese soldiers. They drowned victims and doused others with gasoline and burned them alive. They enslaved their victims, Asian and white, and worked them to death. The building of the notorious Burma–Siam "railroad of death" (recalled in the motion picture *The Bridge on the River Kwai*) took the lives of tens of thousands, including 60,000 Asians of various nationalities and 15,000 Allied POWs. No wonder Admiral William "Bull" Halsey said "Kill Japs, kill Japs, kill more Japs." Many historians have compared Japanese atrocities with those of the Nazis.[17]

But most importantly, for our story, was the abuse of American POWs. John W. Dower concluded in *War Without Mercy* that of 235,473 American and British prisoners captured by Germany and Italy together, only 9,348 (4 percent) died in captivity. These figures compared with the Pacific war, where of Japan's 132,134 Anglo-American POWs 35,756 (27 percent) died. The Japanese murdered 34 percent of their American prisoners. In April 1943 the American public was infuriated when it learned that the Japanese had decreed death for the Doolittle raider air crew members and executed several after torturing them. The 1943 movie

Bataan, starring Robert Taylor, portrayed Japanese soldiers as cowardly "monkeys."

The Japanese gratuitously murdered 250,000 Chinese civilians in Chekiang Province in reprisal for the Doolittle bombers landing there. The American public knew full well by 1943 that the Japanese were torturing and decapitating American POWs and mutilating corpses. By January 1944 the American public learned about the Bataan Death March of April 1942. The horror stories of American POWs being tortured, crucified, buried alive, nailed to trees, and used for bayonet practice enraged Americans, who vowed that Japan would pay dearly for its barbaric behavior.[18]

Indeed, American rage against the Japanese knew practically no bounds. The British ambassador reported to the Foreign Office in January 1944 a "universal 'exterminationist' anti-Japanese feeling here." Some American writers, columnists, military leaders, and political figures called for the annihilation of the Japanese people. One consequence of Japan's racist war polices was that the lives of Japanese civilians came to mean very little to Americans. In a speech to Congress, Churchill called for the laying of Japanese cities in ashes. The killing of Japanese POWs by Americans, the fire-bombing of Japanese cities, and the nuclear bombing of Hiroshima and Nagasaki were undoubtedly influenced by American fury at the Japanese. By April 1945 Paul V. McNutt, chairman of the War Manpower Commission, publicly advocated "extermination of the Japanese in toto."[19]

Chapter 15

Disappearing in the Bermuda Triangle

I n early 1943, the major U.S. Jewish organizations combined their relief efforts and created a new organization, the Joint Emergency Committee on European Jewish Affairs (JEC). The JEC included the American Jewish Committee, American Jewish Congress, B'nai B'rith, Jewish Labor Committee, Synagogue Council of America, Agaduth Israel of America, Union of Orthodox Rabbis, and American Emergency Committee for Zionist Affairs, among other organizations. Its aim was to represent virtually all points of view held by American Jews, although the JEC refused to include the Committee for a Jewish Army, a front group for the Palestinian terrorist group Irgun.

The JEC instigated mass meetings throughout the United States. Working with organized Jewish communities and Christian church groups, the Federal Council of Churches, and AFL and CIO unions, the JEC held forty rallies in twenty states. Thousands of people attended and learned about the mass murders in Europe.

The JEC lobbied for a congressional resolution condemning the Nazis' "brutal and indefensible outrages." This resolution passed both houses unanimously, but JEC efforts failed to secure the inclusion of a paragraph urging specific action to rescue the Jews.[1]

Jewish congressman met with FDR and asked the president to simplify the procedures for admission into the United States. Roosevelt arranged a meeting among Breckinridge Long, Congressman Celler, Dickstein, and Bloom. The president stated that perhaps visitors' visas would again be issued. Later, ten members of the Interdepartmental Visa Review Committee went over possibilities for simplifications of the procedures. Celler requested and the Joint Emergency Committee agreed to draft the recommendation. Celler did not bring up to FDR the question of shipping food through the blockade.[2]

The JEC lobbied the Roosevelt administration. On March 4 Rabbi Wise wrote FDR about the "tragic fate which has overtaken the Jewish people in Nazi-occupied Europe. . . . I beg you, Mr. President," Wise pleaded, "to initiate . . . action which, if it cannot end the greatest crime ever perpetrated against a people, may yet save that people from utter extinction by offering asylum to its remnants in Sanctuaries to be created under the aegis of the United Nations." In reply Roosevelt assured Wise that the government "has moved and continues to move, so far as the burden of war permits, to help the victims of the Nazi doctrines of racial, religious, and political oppression." On March 27 Wise and Proskauer met with British foreign secretary Anthony Eden and then with Sumner Welles. Eden was no friend of the Jewish people.

His private secretary wrote of him: "He loves Arabs and hates Jews." Eden told Wise and Proskauer in no uncertain terms that His Majesty's government would not beg Germany to release Jews. It was, he said, "fantastically impossible."[3]

From the archbishop of Canterbury to Mayor Fiorello LaGuardia, from the House of Commons to the House of Representatives, Americans and Britons demanded action to save the Jews of Europe. Both the State Department and the Foreign Office were pressed to report some positive steps. The result was what the State Department termed a "preliminary refugee conference," which met on April 19, 1943, in Bermuda. Breckinridge Long, wary of British attempts to dump "responsibility and embarrassment for the refugee problem" in the State Department's lap, viewed the conference with suspicion. Before the meeting, both the State Department and the Foreign Office made it clear publicly that the Allies' options for rescuing Jewish victims were limited. The solution to the refugee problem was to win the war, declared William Dodds, chair of the American delegation and Long's close friend. Little came from the Wise/Proskauer meeting with Welles in March, but he did promise that the JEC's views would be represented at the upcoming Bermuda conference.[4]

While some historians have deplored the callousness of the British and American governments in not asking Hitler to release the Jews in 1943 and not offering to send food through the blockade, the situation was complicated. First, Hitler would never have complied. The Allies had publicly and repeatedly condemned to no avail the Nazi regime for the atrocities. In reality the Allies feared that, if through some miracle Hitler agreed to liberate them, hundreds of thousands or maybe millions of starving refugees would overwhelm them, disrupt military operations, and Hitler's "war by refugee" would succeed. No nation in the midst of total war, they believed, could take on the responsibility to assist a large, unknown number of sick and destitute immigrants. Finally, Eden represented the Churchill government's firm resolve to prevent massive Jewish immigration to Palestine, lest that event trigger another Arab revolt.[5]

Felix Frankfurter spoke with Supreme Court justice Robert Jackson, Roosevelt's choice to head the Bermuda delegation. Given the international situation, "far too little has been done to make the issue of the conference a very promising one," Frankfurter wrote in his diary. "Robert said he supposed there is very little we can do except make the right kind of gesture, but the gesture is important." Those who attended the conference faced the political reality that neither British nor American public opinion favored unlimited Jewish immigration, even if it helped them to escape the Nazis.[6]

Long saw to it that the business of the Bermuda Conference would be circumscribed. He sent his personal friend and ardent opponent of immigration Robert Borden Reams to act as secretary to the U.S. delegation. Jewish organizations were not allowed to send advocates. Welles agreed that Judge Proskauer could recommend the names of three technical experts to attend. George Backer, president of the American Organization for Rehabilitation through Training (ORT), a Jewish group, and George Warren,

Map of Europe, 1942.

Author's collection (map by Tim Belshaw)

executive secretary of the PACPR, both of whom were sympathetic to Jewish concerns, participated. The JEC viewpoint also was represented by Congressman Sol Bloom of New York, who unsuccessfully advocated an aggressive rescue policy.[7]

As the Bermuda Conference on refugees convened, the Germans still fought in North Africa, and their successful submarine campaign against North Atlantic shipping continued unabated. The war in the Pacific was in its beginning stages. Although the United States was victorious at Guadalcanal, the Japanese mounted a massive air offensive on Henderson Field just as the

Bermuda Conference began. On April 18, the day before the Bermuda Conference convened, U.S. Navy reconnaissance crews learned that Admiral Isoroku Yamamoto, the architect of the attack on Pearl Harbor, was flying to Bougainville to rally the air assault on Guadalcanal. American fighters intercepted his plane and shot it down.[8]

The Bermuda Conference was an exercise in futility. If the Allies could barely send men and war matériel across the Atlantic Ocean, they had no prospect of landing an army near Germany or Poland. In April 1943 they possessed no airplanes capable of reaching the concentration camps from their most forward bases. There was nothing that could be done militarily to rescue the Nazis' Jewish prisoners. Consequently Roosevelt showed little interest in the conference before it convened, as nothing of practical value could come from it.[9]

The Bermuda Conference began on April 19 and lasted twelve days. Long and his staff prepared a tightly restricted memorandum to guide the delegates, cautioning them against overemphasizing the Jewish nature of the refugee problem; warning them not to pledge any funds; and, most importantly, not to propose changes to U.S. and British immigration laws. Delegates discussed ways to encourage neutral countries to accept more refugees and to set up temporary havens for refugees and how to rejuvenate the IGCR.

The Joint Emergency Committee's views and Jewish voices were heard at the Bermuda Conference. Wise sent a detailed memorandum to Welles, who saw to it that the delegates were informed of the committee's views. The chief suggestion was, in Judge Proskauer's words, "the implementation of some method of approach to the Nazi and Nazi-dominated governments to get the Jews out of Germany and Austria and Poland and other such places." Congressman Bloom argued at considerable length on this issue. George Backer informed the delegates about the situation European Jewry faced. "Insofar as this conference is concerned," Backer stated, "it would never have been necessary to call it" except to help Jews. With persistence and eloquence, Backer urged efforts to rescue Jewish children from Romania and Bulgaria. Saving the Jews, he said, "is an act of moral force; it is an act against reason, if you like, that these who are now helpless and can harm no one will be saved from disaster."[10]

The Jewish leaders' frustration with their government's policies was palpable. The JEC memorandum reminded the delegates that the "systematic mass extermination of Jews in Nazi-occupied territory" had been authenticated; that more than two million Jews had been killed; and that "the holocaust of murder continues unabated." It emphasized that while Jewish Americans sympathized with "all peoples suffering from the hardships of Total War . . . *the Jews are the only people who have been singled out and marked for total extermination by Nazi Germany.*" The memorandum argued that those "Jews who remain in Europe are *de facto* prisoners of war . . . and . . . therefore should be entitled to the Red Cross aid which goes to war prisoners."[11] Even to characterize Jews as prisoners of war would be of little practical value, for at that time the British were having great difficulty dealing with

Hitler to exchange military POWs and the Germans were murdering Russian POWs.

One group that was not represented in the JEC, the PACPR, and especially not at the Bermuda Conference was the Committee for a Jewish Army, the Irgun front group. While the conference was under way, Irgunists ran advertisements in American newspapers that many Americans, Jewish and non-Jewish, viewed as crackpot, wild-eyed, and utterly impractical. The advertisements urged open immigration to Palestine and the "creation of a Jewish army of *Stateless and Palestinian Jews*, including 'Suicide' Commando Squads which will raid deep into Germany and Air Squadrons for retaliatory bombing."[12] American Jews, of course, were neither stateless nor Palestinian and were already fighting the Germans and the Japanese as members of the American military. American Jews had never supported a Jewish army. FDR was not about to divert military resources (presumably the United States would give this imaginary army the "Air Squadrons") from the hard-pressed Russian, British, and American armed forces to equip a Jewish army commanded by the Irgun. American Jews were well aware that money raised by Peter Bergson, leader of the Irgun cell in the United States, would likely end up buying weapons for the Irgun to use against the British in Palestine.[13] Finally, unrestricted Jewish immigration would have pushed millions of Nazi-sympathetic Arabs into Hitler's arms. The Middle East would become another war front.

The Irgunist proposal to raise a Jewish army infatuated a few naive Americans, but it fooled very few others, especially the

British, who knew exactly what the Jewish army would be used for in the immediate future. Vladimir Jabotinsky had successfully lobbied to create a Jewish legion in World War I and had fully intended those soldiers to become the core of an army of the future Jewish state. Churchill, a friend of Jewish aspirations, scotched the idea of a Jewish army even in the darkest days of Dunkirk.[14] State Department documents reflected a genuine fear that special efforts to rescue only Jews would play into the hands of Nazi propagandists. Since the onset of the massacres, the department consistently argued that references to the refugee problem should contain the deliberately vague mention of "unfortunate peoples whose plight also warrants our more earnest consideration."[15]

Rescue advocates recognized that the Jews of Europe were prisoners, not refugees. The difference was critical, because a refugee is a person fleeing his homeland, while a prisoner cannot flee. The Jews were not ordinary prisoners. They were, as Rubinstein described them, "prisoners of a psychopath whose life's mission consisted in killing every last one of them and who happened to be the absolute dictator of most of Europe." For the Allies to accede to the JEC resolution and the pleas of rescue advocates to negotiate with Hitler was a recipe for disaster. If they did secure the release of refugees and were then unable or unwilling to provide asylum, the Allies' credibility would be destroyed throughout the world. The U.S. Congress would never allow millions of refugees, Jewish or not, to come to the United States.

Allied war policy and the Allies' view of the war was to strangle Germany's economy, starve her army and her people, and destroy her will to fight as quickly as possible, not move or feed millions of people who had a right to remain in their homelands, free of Nazi tyranny. Contemporaries well remembered that the British blockade of Germany had helped win World War I. The Germans were keenly aware that food shortages had crushed the morale of the German home front. Indeed, food was a weapon of war. An army, as Napoleon quipped, marches on its stomach. Lack of it brought Britain close to defeat in 1941. America's production of it was a major factor in the Allied victory. Germany starved Europe to feed itself. To ease Germany's plight by taking off their hands the Jewish prisoners their abhorrent policies had created or to send food to the enemy would give Hitler victory in his "war by refugee." Relieving Germany's economic problems flew in the face of an essential war strategy.[16]

The Bermuda delegates also knew that the Battle of the Atlantic was at a critical juncture. The year 1942 had been catastrophic: U-boats had sunk six million tons of Allied merchant shipping. The winter of 1942–43 was one of the harshest on record. Allied losses in March 1943 were so high that some planners suggested abandoning the convoys that protected merchant ships. The invasion of Italy lay in the future. Experts ruled out the use of Allied ships to transport refugees across the Atlantic. Senator Scott Lucas pointed out "the present limitation on shipping, submarine warfare . . . this country straining every point in order to get men and food and supplies to the North African frontier." Breckinridge Long also had instructed the delegates not to seek vessels for transportation that must be diverted from military shipping.[17]

The idea of negotiating with Adolf Hitler for the release of the Jews was considered absurd. Hitler's contempt for diplomacy and treaties was well known to everyone who had observed Munich, the conquest of Czechoslovakia, and the Nazi-Soviet nonaggression pact. "We cannot rely on anything he would promise," stated Richard Law, the chief British delegate to Bermuda. We could not embark on solutions such as these, he said, "without jeopardizing the course of the war." Obviously the Nazis would only release Jews if there were some advantage to them, and the Allies were not going to assist Nazi Germany. They would not take any risk, however slight, that German saboteurs might enter England or the United States disguised as refugees. Nor would the Allies allow the Nazis to use Jewish immigration for propaganda purposes in the Middle East or elsewhere. American war policy was grounded on the unconditional surrender of Germany and no negotiation with Hitler.

A full and frank discussion among the American delegates took place on Sunday, April 25. Senator Lucas said, "I listened with tremendous interest and profound sympathy for the great mass of Jewish people that are now stranded in these Axis-controlled countries." He had read the Wise memorandum and wanted to know if 3.5 million were still alive. Backer told the delegates there were no longer such large numbers of Jews in occupied Europe and that the Jews of Hungary and Italy were not in danger of extermination. There were, in Backer's estimation, about 1,750,000 Jews left in Europe, excluding the 740,000 Jews of Hungary. When Backer had been told that 90 percent of Polish Jewry was dead, he replied somberly that it was "rather difficult, almost incredible, to believe that figure."[18]

In a poignant exchange of views, Senator Lucas expressed his sincere desire to help as many European Jews as possible, but he thought the JEC asked for the impossible. If Hitler did release 100,000 Jews, many would starve and die before they could be rescued. The massive effort involved in caring for 100,000 refugees would "stop this man's war." Backer disagreed, and stated that if 100,000 Germans soldiers offered to surrender "we would find some way to get them out."[19]

Senator Lucas reminded Backer that there were Jewish soldiers and sailors at the front and "plenty more going." To divert resources to aid massive numbers of refugees would prolong the war and would endanger the lives of "our own boys." If that happened, he said, "you will have a pretty serious problem on your hands." Indeed, the senator continued, "plenty of boys right from the Jewish families now raising this issue" could be killed. Backer agreed with Lucas and the hard-nosed Robert Borden Reams that the Allies could not negotiate with Hitler. Realistically Backer had "no great hopes" that Hitler would let out any Jews, but Backer continued to urge negotiations with the Romanian and Bulgarian governments, which were technically independent of Germany. Senator Lucas was convinced that if Hitler freed 150,000 refugees "he would only be doing it for military reasons. I think you will agree, that he is not going to let Jews out unless it helps Mr. Hitler in some way."[20]

The Bermuda Conference concluded with a confidential report

that recommended no negotiation with Hitler, the use of neutral shipping to transport refugees, consideration of Cyrenaica and Madagascar as refuges, negotiations on refugees in Spain, and the expansion of refugee camps in North Africa. They recommended a postwar declaration of the rights of all refugees to repatriation, and reinvigoration of the IGCR. Some of these recommendations addressed Jews specifically but did not amount to a plan to rescue European Jewry. The Bergson group's proposal to create a Jewish army was never discussed, presumably because it was viewed as unrealistic. Publicly the delegates reported only that "a number of concrete recommendations" were submitted to their governments but had to be kept confidential, as they involved military considerations. The delegates candidly admitted that any recommendation must pass two tests: Would it "interfere with or delay the war effort?" and Was it "capable of accomplishment under war conditions?" The final press release said only that concrete recommendations would be sent to government officials.[21]

Despite their unrealistic expectations, many Jewish leaders were disappointed with the Bermuda Conference. Rabbi Wise and Joseph Proskauer wrote Sumner Welles on May 13, 1943, to convey "the sense of despair of the American Jewish community" at the American government's continued inaction in the face of genocide. A commission on war crimes, they reminded Welles, was promised in December 1942 but was not yet established. They believed that the Bermuda Conference was a total failure for many reasons, but especially because "no effective action was taken to save the Jews of Europe by arranging for their exit from Nazi-occupied

Europe." Congressmen Dickstein and Celler condemned the conference in the House. Representative Bloom responded, "I as a Jew am perfectly satisfied with the results of the Bermuda Conference. . . . The security of winning the war is our first step. We as Jews must keep this in mind." Celler and Wise denounced Bloom for his candid reply.

The conference was roundly criticized by rescue advocates and many Jewish leaders, organizations, and publications. "To 5,000,000 Jews in the Nazi Death-Trap Bermuda Was a Cruel Mockery," the Irgunists advertised in the *New York Times*. Representative Celler called it a "diplomatic mockery." The Bergson group called Bloom the State Department's *shabbas goy* (a gentile who performs chores forbidden to Jews on the Sabbath). Rabbi Israel Goldstein expressed the Jewish leadership's views best: "The job of the Bermuda Conference apparently was not to rescue victims of Nazi terror, but to rescue our State Department and the British Foreign Office." But Jewish leaders realistically knew that, as Morris D. Waldman, of the American Jewish Committee stated, "Nothing will stop the Nazis except their destruction. The Jews of Europe are doomed whether we do or don't. Setting up the machinery of tribunals won't stop them."[22]

The Irgunists were roundly criticized in the U.S. Senate for their inflammatory advertisement. Fellow senators were mortified at Bergson's unwarranted criticism of Senator Lucas. Bergson's national chairman, Senator Edward Johnson, warned Bergson to use greater caution in the future. Senator Harry Truman, who had lent his name to the Bergson group, declared:

*I am very certain that there is not a senator on that
list who knows anything about the advertisement or
had anything to do with it. The reason my name is on
the list is that I was laboring under the delusion that
this was an organization for a Jewish army to help win
the war. If it is the intention to use the committee for
any other purpose, it can no longer have my support or
the use of my name.*[23]

For many, the Bermuda Conference was a disappointing
episode in American history. It was arranged by people in the State
Department and British Foreign Office who had little if any desire
to help the Jews of Europe. Cynical, antisemitic American and
English diplomats saw the conference as a sop to what they privately called the "sob sister" crowd and "those wailing Jews."
Even pro-Roosevelt Jewish Americans were disturbed by the lack
of effort for rescue.

But the question still remained: Was rescue of European Jewry
possible in April 1943? Could the Bermuda conferees tell the
world that the Allies were losing the Battle of the Atlantic, had no
hope of invading occupied France and Germany for at least
another year, and that the bombing of German cities, fuel plants,
and military factories was not winning the war? Was there anything they could say or do that would change the course of the
Holocaust? The answer was certainly "no." "Rescuing the European Jews was," Lucy Dawidowicz wrote, "an unachievable task."
The JEC and Irgunist proposals "conceived in hopelessness and

helplessness" were unrealizable. The Bermuda Conference failed because it "forced both the Jewish community and the Allied governments . . . to . . . answer the question of 'do what?' What could, realistically, be done? Since this question . . . had no answer, it is not surprising that the conference was a failure."[24]

Chapter 16

"The President Was Deeply Moved by the Situation"

B usy with warfare in Russia, North Africa, and the Pacific, and preparing for the invasion of Italy, FDR gave the Bermuda Conference a low priority. The Jewish congressmen he had met with recognized that little could be done to rescue European Jewry. Other Jews agreed. Sydney Silverman, a Jewish member of Parliament, acknowledged in the House of Commons on February 25, 1943, that there was "no great hope" until an Allied victory, but that "by the time the Allied nations have concerted their plans there will be nobody left to save." Yitzhak Zuckerman, a member of the Jewish resistance in Warsaw, wrote on November 26, 1943, that he knew no one could save them and that they only wanted "such assistance as would enable us to die with honour."[1]

On June 29, Roosevelt wrote Hull to notify American representatives in North Africa to protect Jewish property in the area. On June 30 Roosevelt wrote Churchill that the need to assist refugees, "in particular Jewish refugees, has not grown less since we discussed the question, and all possible outlets need to be kept open. Of these the most practical still is North Africa." He acknowledged privately to the prime minister that "our immediate facilities for helping the victims of Hitler's Anti-Jewish drive are so limited at present that the opening of the small camp [in North Africa] proposed for the purpose of removing some of them to safety seems all the more incumbent on us." On July 8 Roosevelt followed up with Churchill on provisions for Jewish refugees in Spain. He asked Eisenhower to find a place of temporary residence. He wrote Churchill: "I will arrange for the transportation of these refugees by land. . . . You will arrange for their sea transportation . . . I will request the American military authorities to make available cots and tents . . . a temporary reception center." When Britain agreed to accept four thousand Bulgarian Jewish children but asked the United States to share the cost of chartering ships, Roosevelt ordered $500,000 spent from his emergency fund. But the ships never became available and the Nazis refused to release the children.[2]

By May 1943 the war was "slowly, and almost imperceptibly" tilting in the Allies' favor. The Japanese grudgingly abandoned Guadalcanal; the Germans surrendered Stalingrad on February 2, 1943. In January the USAAF bombed a German target, Wilhelmshaven, for the first time. The Eighth Army entered Tunisia in January, and Allied soldiers damaged the Nazi atomic research facility at Rjukan, Norway, in March. But none of these actions was decisive. The European continent and vast expanses of Southeast Asia were still under Axis hegemony. For all their successes, the

Allies confronted immense regions and still-powerful forces capable of tenacious defense and counterattack. At the same time, the Allies had, at best, an uneasy alliance. Stalin was furious at Anglo-American broken promises. The Russians had lost millions of lives while they believed Churchill dallied in the Mediterranean. Roosevelt sought a man-to-man conference with Stalin, but Stalin refused.[3]

Roosevelt and Churchill met again in May, at the Trident Conference in Washington. "The enemy," Churchill told a joint session of Congress on May 19, 1943, "is still proud and powerful. He is hard to get at. He still possesses enormous armies, vast resources, and invaluable strategic territories. . . . No one can tell what new complications and perils might arise in four or five more years of war."[4] Roosevelt's top priority was to keep faith with the Russians and to set a date to invade France. Churchill's priority was to invade Italy. "I only crossed the Atlantic for this purpose," he told Lord Moran. But it was not to be. Overall control of the Allied cause belonged to Roosevelt, who wanted to attack Germany directly as soon as possible and give Stalin his second front.[5]

On May 7, before Churchill's visit, Hull sent Roosevelt a summary of the "program of positive action . . . to alleviate the plight of European refugees." These proposals included the evacuation of five thousand persons from Bulgaria to Palestine, transfer of twenty thousand refugees from Spain to North Africa, and reactivation of the Intergovernmental Committee. Roosevelt agreed with Hull that the United States could not "give unlimited promises" but would cooperate with Britain to assist their evacuation projects. The United States should contribute to the cost of transporting refugees to North Africa and suggested that the money "come out of Lehman's funds"—that is, the United Nations Relief and Rehabilitation Administration (UNRRA). Roosevelt approved instructions to Ambassador John G. Winant to meet Eden and speedily implement the Bermuda recommendations. Clearly Roosevelt believed that some definite, if limited, steps might be taken as a result of Bermuda and that "we have already brought in a large number" of "temporary visitors."[6]

In May Rommel raced for Tunis but was defeated. Two hundred seventy-five thousand Germans surrendered on May 13. May also brought a dramatic shift in the Battle of the North Atlantic. The British broke the German naval Enigma communications code, which allowed Allied aircraft to locate submarines and attack them with air-to-sea rockets. On May 24 Admiral Dönitz withdrew his U-boats from the North Atlantic but promised to return.[7]

The State Department's hidebound, sometimes antisemitic bureaucracy had its own agenda: to keep out as many refugees as possible and to limit the United States' involvement in rescue activities. The department had the support of its natural ally the Republican congressional leadership. But FDR had little use for the State Department on this issue. In 1943 Hull was a weak leader in poor health, and he relied on Breckinridge Long to administer the department's policies on refugees. But as we have seen, Long saw himself as the chief defender of America's immigration laws. His xenophobia and desire to protect the department and the president from criticism led him to undermine even the modest rescue efforts FDR believed to be in place. Long had the support of a powerful conservative clique: Robert Border Reams, Long's point man at Bermuda; Ray Atherton, Visa Division chief; and Wallace Murray and Elbridge Durbrow, Middle East and European specialists, respectively. Long's allies, especially Durbrow and Atherton, did not want the department to confirm the truth of Hitler's atrocities by rescuing his victims.[8]

Several officials decided that one way to prevent criticism of the department was to stop information about the Holocaust from entering the country via diplomatic cables and pouches. On February 27, 1943, Leland Harrison, the American minister at Bern, Switzerland, was instructed not to accept for diplomatic transfer private communications to the United States except under extraordinary circumstances. This meant that cables from Jewish refugee advocates such as Gerhart Riegner of the World Jewish Congress stationed in Switzerland would not be forwarded via diplomatic pouches to American Jewish leaders such as Rabbi Wise. Although Welles signed this infamous Cable 354, historians have agreed that he signed it as a matter of routine without knowing what it said. Indeed, Cable 354, drafted by Elbridge Durbrow, contradicted Welles's previous instructions to transmit Riegner's cables from Europe. When he learned the effect of Cable 354, Welles attempted to rescind it.[9]

Roosevelt was personally sympathetic with several rescue efforts that were either sabotaged by the State Department or failed to come to fruition. The first involved the Jews of Romania. Seventy thousand Romanian survivors of the 1941 deportations to Transnistria were still alive in February 1943 when the Romanian government offered to relocate them in exchange for a financial payment, essentially ransom. The *New York Times* ran a story on the offer, and Morgenthau immediately sought FDR's support. Roosevelt sent him to Welles. The State Department dragged its feet on the proposal, fearing that it was an Axis blackmail scheme, and worse, from the department's viewpoint, that the plan might succeed and saddle the United States with seventy thousand Jewish refugees. The Treasury Department, which enforced the Trading with the Enemy Act, had no objection to the rescue plan, because the funds would remain in a blocked account in Switzerland until the war was over. On July 16 Treasury agreed to issue the necessary license.[10]

Rabbi Wise saw FDR on July 22 to discuss the Romanian proposal and a second plan, to rescue French Jewish children. Roosevelt readily agreed to help. He informed Morgenthau of his support and confirmed his approval in a letter to Wise on August 14. The plan failed because the Romanians demanded one hundred million dollars and the Germans vetoed it. The Nazis said that it contravened Hitler's agreement with the Arabs. The Arabs apparently pressured the German Foreign Office, and Eichmann pushed the Romanians to call it off.[11]

The second plan involved the rescue of Jewish children in France. Gerhart Riegner of the WJC reported in April that a group of people in Romania and occupied France would advance funds to support Jewish children in hiding or help them escape. When Wise asked Welles to help, the undersecretary sent the rabbi to the Treasury Department. On July 22, when Wise met with FDR, he told him about Riegner's proposal. "Stephen," the president said, "why don't you go ahead and do it?" Wise worried aloud that Morgenthau might not cooperate. Roosevelt called Morgenthau on the telephone and said, "Henry, this is a very fair proposal which Stephen makes about ransoming Jews." Treasury immediately approved both the French and Romanian operations. Morgenthau wrote Secretary of State Hull, who concurred. "The president," Henry Morgenthau recalled in 1947, "was deeply moved by the situation" and "could not have been more receptive." Remarkably, the State Department bureaucracy was not to be persuaded by Welles, Hull, or even by FDR himself.

After Roosevelt agreed with Wise on the proposal to send money to blocked accounts to help rescue Jewish children, Herbert Feis, a Jewish expert at State on international economic affairs, personally took the telegram approving the project to Hull for his signature. Long and his clique, however, delayed action until Hitler sabotaged the plan.[12]

Roosevelt, unlike Churchill, believed that at this point in time the Allies could afford to send food and medicine into Nazi territories. "Roosevelt reportedly did his best to persuade Churchill to allow further humanitarian exceptions to the blockade of Europe," Breitman notes, "but with no success." Francis Sayre, a State Department official, reported at the time that "The public reason given is that Germany would probably interfere, but the actual reason is not that. It is Churchill's insistence on the primacy of the military consideration." Churchill and Eden believed in the traditional British strategy of tightening a ring around German-held territories and using the blockade to starve Germany into surrender.[13]

Roosevelt also met with Zionist leader Chaim Weizmann, in June 1943. The president was candid about the difficulty of establishing a Jewish state during the war, his fears of a Nazi incursion in Iraq, and the lack of responsible Arab negotiating partners. Relying on a firsthand report from his personal emissary, Colonel Harold Hoskins, Roosevelt was cautious about making promises he could not keep. Nevertheless, after his talk with Weizmann, FDR dispatched Hoskins to arrange a meeting between Weizmann and Ibn Saud. Saud refused to cooperate. FDR personally intervened to help restore property to the Jews of Tunis. In July Roosevelt informed Churchill that he had asked Eisenhower to locate a site in North Africa for the Jewish refugees then in Spain, and requested that the two governments share the cost of transporting them. On July 30 Roosevelt issued a statement warning neutral nations not to harbor war criminals. "One day Hitler and his gang and Tojo and his gang will be trying to escape from their countries."[14]

The Allied Combined Bombing Offensive directed at Western Germany commenced on June 10, 1943. American aircraft conducted daylight "precision" raids, while British airplanes bombed at night. The Eastern Front Battle of Kursk, the greatest tank battle in history, involving two million men and 6,000 tanks, began on July 5. Two hundred fifty thousand British and 230,000 American soldiers landed in Sicily on July 9. Roosevelt and Churchill focused their attention on the Italian campaign. On July 24 the Allies began their deadly bombing campaign against Hamburg, which Joseph Goebbels called "a catastrophe of hitherto inconceivable proportions."[15]

The bombing of cities and deliberate killing of civilian populations was a new and horrible tactic tested during the Spanish Civil War. The Germans initiated it against Warsaw in 1939 and continued over Rotterdam and London in 1940. The British and Americans bombed civilians to retaliate for Germany's air war on Allied cities and for Japanese atrocities generally.[16] On June 12 Düsseldorf suffered the most massive air raid of the war to date. Cologne was heavily bombed on June 28. The USAAF bombed Rome on July 19, targets in Norway on July 25, and the Ploesti (Romania) oilfields on August 1. Forty-two thousand German civilians were incinerated in the Hamburg bombings, more than all British civilians killed in the entire Blitz.[17]

On July 25 Mussolini was dismissed from office and the king appointed Marshal Pietro Badoglio, one of Mussolini's confederates, as prime minister. To his liberal critics, livid that Fascists were still running Italy, Roosevelt replied that his first goal was "the end of armed opposition" and his second "to avoid anarchy. . . . In other words, common sense." Unconditional surrender was an important goal, but Badoglio had control of the Italian fleet, the Italian government, and part of the army. He also had 74,000 British POWs. Like the Darlan deal in North Africa, to make some arrangement with Badoglio did not offend the ever-practical FDR. Tragically, Mussolini's fall proved to be a disaster for Italian Jewry and Jews in Italian-occupied countries.

Roosevelt undoubtedly believed that his policies, which included some relief for Jewish refugees within the immigration laws, were being carried out. His knowledge of the State Department's activities, however, was controlled by Breckinridge Long, whom Roosevelt trusted. The president received written memorandums nominally from Hull but written by Long, and he was briefed by Hull in person after Long had talked to Hull.[18]

Long misled Roosevelt about essential facts and told exaggerated accounts of the State Department's rescue efforts. He told FDR that the United States had admitted 580,000 refugees between 1933 and 1943, when in fact this was the number of visas issued or authorized, not people who actually came into the United States. Only 210,732 people were actually admitted. Roosevelt was told that the IGCR, which he had championed since 1938, would be rejuvenated, but Long did little to effect it. The State Department and its consuls abroad interpreted the visa provisions more strictly than the law required, needlessly delayed applications, and sabotaged military efforts to help transport refugees from North Africa to the United States. Long and his allies in the department worked surreptitiously to thwart Roosevelt's efforts.[19]

Morale in the United States and abroad had been damaged by strikes, race riots, conflicts within the administration, and rancor in Congress. "The whole world is watching our domestic troubles," the *New York Times* lamented. On July 27, when Roosevelt told the press that his major speech the next day would be about the war, a reporter quipped, "Abroad or at home, sir?" "I hoped you would ask that question just that way," Roosevelt replied and proceeded to give the press a preview, explaining that when "we send an expedition to Sicily," it begins on the farms and in the mines of America. There "is just one front, which includes at home as well as abroad."[20]

On July 28, 1943, Roosevelt met with the Polish ambassador and a Polish soldier, Jan Kozielewski (Karski), who had seen first-hand the Warsaw ghetto and the Belzec death camp. Karski's mission was to educate the president on the needs of the Polish underground and the Polish government-in-exile, and to affirm their ability to revolt against German rule. He sought to convince Roosevelt that Soviet and Communist agents in Poland were disloyal and destructive, and finally to publicize his eyewitness account of the extermination of the Jews.

The president, according to Karski, was "amazingly well informed about Poland and wanted still more information." He spent most of his time with Karski asking detailed questions related to the war. "He was anxious to learn the techniques for sabotage, diversion, and partisan activity." Roosevelt did ask Karski if the published casualty figures of Jewish deaths were true. Karski listed the concentration camps by name, including Auschwitz. "I am certain," he told FDR, "that many people are not aware of the horrible fate to which the Jewish population is subject." He told the president that 1.8 million Polish Jews had been killed and that there was "a difference between the system of German terror directed against the Poles and the Jews." The Germans sought to kill each and every Jew. Polish Jewry would cease to exist within months without Allied intervention. Roosevelt wanted to know if the Polish underground cooperated with the Jews. Karski said that it did, but that aid was limited due to the terrible condition of the Jews and the German policy of killing not only those who aided Jews but also their families. Only the Allies could help Polish Jewry, preferably by retaliating against German civilians wherever they could be found.[21]

Roosevelt or one of his advisers realized after meeting Karski that his credible eyewitness accounts of the Holocaust would be helpful to American Jewish leaders. Within hours, a White House messenger delivered to the Polish embassy a list of prominent Americans the president thought Karski should contact. Karski met with most of the major Jewish organizations and many Jewish leaders, including Wise, Goldmann, and Waldman of the World Jewish Congress, and labor leaders David Dubinsky and Sidney Hillman. Karski convinced the Joint to contribute five hundred thousand dollars to assist Polish Jewry.[22]

Karski went on to become an effective spokesman for both the Polish and the Jewish cause throughout the war. But he did not succeed with Supreme Court justice Felix Frankfurter. After hearing Karski's story for more than twenty-five minutes, Frankfurter paced back and forth and said, "A man like me talking to a man like you must be totally frank. So, I say I am unable to believe you." Frankfurter's friend the Polish ambassador was startled. "Felix, you cannot tell this man to his face that he is lying. The authority of my government is behind him." "Mr. Ambassador, I did not say that this young man is lying. I said that I am unable to believe him. There is a difference." He then put both of his arms out and waved his hands as if to make the unbelievable news disappear, murmured "No, no," turned around, and left the room.[23]

On the evening of July 28, Roosevelt delivered a major fireside chat. "The massed, angered forces of common humanity," he told

Americans, "are on the march . . . . The first crack in the Axis has come. The criminal, corrupt Fascist regime in Italy is going to pieces. The pirate philosophy of the Fascists and Nazis cannot stand adversity." "We are still far from our main objectives in the war," he told the American people, but the plans "we have made for the knocking out of Mussolini and his gang have largely succeeded. But we still have to defeat Hitler and Tojo on their own home grounds. No one of us pretends that this will be an easy matter." Millions of Americans took heart and were reassured that America would triumph over Nazism. But Roosevelt and Churchill knew that avoiding defeat was not victory. The German military might still grant its Führer a stalemate.[24]

At their Quebec meeting on August 17–24, 1943, Roosevelt and Churchill agreed that Operation Overlord, the D-Day invasion, would take place on May 1, 1944. They confirmed myriad details about the landing, from naming an American as supreme commander to the building of artificial ports (Mulberry harbors). It was to be the greatest amphibious military invasion in history. For FDR, the key to victory over Nazi Germany lay in a frontal assault directly across the English Channel. The British did all they could to avoid it. In an angry exchange with Stimson, Churchill warned of a "channel full of corpses." For the British leader, horrific memories of Passchendaele, Dunkirk, and Gallipoli caused him to hesitate. Marshall and Roosevelt had no such memories to dull their resolve.[25]

Roosevelt believed that America's relationship with the Soviet Union was critical to victory and that postwar peace rested on

Soviet-American friendship. Delay of the second front and bitter controversy over Poland threatened that relationship. Stalin had withdrawn his ambassadors from Britain and the United States. What if Stalin made a separate peace with Hitler and the Anglo-Americans faced Germany alone? What if the Soviet Union defeated Germany without American assistance? Roosevelt's highest priority was to keep the uneasy alliance on track toward the D-Day invasion. We will, Roosevelt said at Ottawa on August 25, 1943, communicate the decision made at the Quebec Conference to Germany, Italy, and Japan "in the only language their twisted minds seem capable of understanding."[26]

Roosevelt and Churchill also agreed at Quebec that the issue of Palestine had to be put on the back burner. A stable Middle East was critical to Allied plans in 1943. Any time the president touched the issue—even by merely receiving Zionists—he triggered explosive reactions in Egypt, Syria, and Saudi Arabia. Churchill consistently opposed any action that would affect the military situation in the Middle East by antagonizing Muslims or Arabs. Supporting a Jewish state not only stirred up local Arabs but also riled up Muslims around the world, some of whom were fighting in British armies.[27]

American and British troops advanced in Italy as the Soviets drove westward against the Germans. An August air raid on the Ploesti oilfields in Romania cost 54 aircraft and killed 532 Allied airmen. A secret Italian surrender was negotiated in early September, and the Italian fleet capitulated. Hitler sent commandos to rescue Mussolini, who declared from the safety of Germany that he was still the leader of Italy. The German army entered Italy, slowing the Allied advance, but in late September the Allied capture of airfields at Foggia placed many targets in Eastern Germany and Poland—including the Auschwitz/Bergen-Belsen death camps—within USAAF bombing range.[28]

Roosevelt hoped that airpower could win the war without great loss of American lives. In a message to Congress of September 17, he mocked Hitler as the Führer once mocked him. Hitler, he said, "started boasting that he had converted Europe into an impregnable fortress. But he neglected to provide that fortress with a roof. . . . The British and American air forces have been bombing the roofless fortress with ever-increasing effectiveness." And he told the American people that their air force was not bombing "for the sheer sadistic pleasure of killing, as the Nazis did," but rather striking factories, shipyards, and military targets. Losses had been sustained, but more planes would be produced. The Allies' air superiority was growing every minute. "But we have no minutes to lose."[29]

When ER returned from a trip to the Pacific she told her husband that the one thought on the minds of American servicemen was to win the war quickly and return home. She was deeply affected by the suffering of American GIs, the thousands of young men dead, wounded, and crippled. By October she was in a deep and paralyzing depression. Like all Americans, she and FDR desperately wanted a speedy end to the war.[30]

But the war did not end. Neither did the murder of European Jewry. The Holocaust went on without respite seven days a week.

By August 1943 four million Jews were dead. On October 4 Heinrich Himmler reminded his SS officers of the Nazis' "unwritten and never-to-be written page of glory" in Germany's history. "Among ourselves," he told his fellow murderers, "it should be mentioned quite frankly, and yet we will never speak of it publicly." Despite Hitler's talk about the extermination of the Jews, deception was still the order of the day. Secrecy was, Penkower wrote, "the most fiendish ingredient in accomplishing the Nazi murder plan." After all the news and even after the Allied declaration of December 1942, the majority of Jews in Romania, Bulgaria, and Denmark ignored accurate information that they were in great peril. As late as 1944 Hungarian Jews did not believe couriers of the Zionist youth movement sent to warn them of their danger.[31]

There was disbelief during Christmas 1942 even at Treblinka. Signboards were erected at the railroad station inscribed with spurious names—"Restaurant," "Ticket Office," "Telegraph," "Change for Eastbound Trains"—to deceive and thereby pacify arriving victims. Germans assured Zionist youth groups that they were going to Palestine. In July 1943 a Nazi official, Martin Bormann, issued instructions that whenever the Jewish question was "brought up in public . . . there may be no discussion of a future overall solution. It may, however, be mentioned that the Jews are taken in groups for appropriate labor purposes." When the German Foreign Ministry suggested keeping 30,000 Jews "in reserve" for exchange purposes, the SS reply was that "the mass shootings [would become] known abroad." Even though reports of the Holocaust were many and accurate, Nazi efforts at deception continued well into the autumn of 1943. As late as October 1943, Jews told they were going to freedom in Switzerland were shocked when they arrived at Auschwitz.[32]

The Warsaw Ghetto uprising of April 19–May 16, 1943, surprised the Nazis. It was the first armed uprising in an occupied European city and the first by Jews. Other revolts followed. The Nazis redoubled their efforts to kill Jews as soon as possible.[33] Some historians, notably Arno J. Mayer, have argued that as the war began to turn against Hitler, he increased his efforts to exterminate European Jewry and win the one war he could still win, the war against the Jews. Thus the closer the Allies came to victory, the faster European Jewry was murdered. On November 3, 1943, the Nazis began a "harvest festival" and killed 18,000 prisoners at Majdanek, Poland, in one day.[34]

Anne Frank and her family were hiding in "the secret annex," small rooms totaling fifty square meters in the midst of Amsterdam, their only "outings" being to the attic, where they could look out at the neighboring backyard. There were 20,000 to 30,000 Jews in hiding in Holland awaiting the Allied invasion.[35] In early 1943 Leo Baeck was sent to Theresienstadt, the "showplace" concentration camp the Nazis could show to visiting dignitaries and representatives of the Red Cross. Prominent and well-known Jews, World War I heroes, and some who bought their way in were at Theresienstadt. Conditions, however, were poor. In 1942 60,000 Jews lived in buildings designed for 10,000. Death and disease from unsanitary conditions and hunger were prevalent. From time to time inmates were shipped off to Auschwitz. Here Baeck, age seventy, survived and ministered to his fellow Jews.[36]

Congressional interest in the plight of European Jewry blew hot and cold. Prior to the Bermuda Conference, Senator Edwin Johnson, national chairman of the Irgunist CJA, sought Senate approval for a resolution in favor of speedy rescue. The Senate took no action. In June a bill to simplify the naturalization process for *resident aliens with children in the American armed forces* was defeated overwhelmingly. In September Congressman Dickstein's bill to allow refugees to enter the United States temporarily but leave within six months of the war's end never got out of committee. The mood of Congress slowly changed as news of Nazi atrocities sank in and prospects of victory brightened. The CJA worked, cajoled, ran advertisements, and lobbied. Mainstream Jewish organizations and Zionists pushed for a Jewish homeland and open immigration to Palestine.[37]

Allied airplanes were effectively bombing the Ruhr, Hamberg, and Berlin. Kassel was bombed in October. Americans touted their "precision bombing" of German military targets, while the British, who knew from experience that precision bombing was a comforting myth, bombed German civilians at night. Despite the Allied campaigns, Nazi Germany remained master of Europe. The Allies had no way to rescue those Jewish communities on the continent that had not yet been deported to death camps. Indeed, because of the bombing, Himmler *increased* security at the camps to prevent escape and constructed *more* factories near Auschwitz because it was out of the range of Allied bombers. Allied strategy was the progressive destruction and dislocation of the German military system and the destruction of the morale of the German people.

Roosevelt had no qualms about bombing German civilians. Submarine bases, construction and manufacture of transport vehicles, airplanes, submarines, ball bearings, oil, and rubber were all targets, and the loss of nearby civilians' lives was an acceptable cost of success. If Operation Pointblank, as the bomber offensive was called, succeeded, the long-awaited second front could be opened in the summer of 1944. Ironically, while the Allies declined to bomb German targets as reprisals for the murder of the Jews, the Nazis claimed they were liquidating the remaining ghettos and killing Jews as reprisals for the Allied bombing of German dams.[38]

The bloody campaign continued in Italy. General Mark Clark's Fifth Army landed at Salerno in September and was nearly defeated by Albert Kesselring's German troops. Naples fell to Allied troops on October 1, and U.S. forces attacked Wake Island in the middle of the Pacific. But the "precision bombing" air war was not going well. Too many American planes were shot down and too many airmen lost for too few results. In mid-October the USAAF lost one in five of its aircraft on a raid against Schweinfurt and ceased unescorted daylight sorties.

On October 13, 1943, Italy was liberated and declared war on Germany. The news was improving on every front in early November, but the fighting was fierce. The war in Italy cost 188,000 American casualties. The Russians withstood a Nazi counteroffensive and captured Kiev on November 6. Four hundred RAF bombers struck Berlin, but Hitler had no intention to quit the war.

In June 1943 he inspected his secret rocket facility at Peenemünde and redoubled his efforts to build missiles, pilotless planes, and very-long-range cannons. The British had no defense against these advanced weapons, and in August Churchill ordered Peenemünde destroyed regardless of the casualties.[39]

In November the House Foreign Affairs Committee deliberated a resolution urged on Congress by Bergson and the Irgunists, now calling themselves the Emergency Committee to Save the Jewish People of Europe. The resolution called on the president to create a commission to devise a plan to rescue the surviving European Jews. Witnesses

Franklin D. Roosevelt visits US Army troops at Teheran Conference, December 2, 1943.

Courtesy of the Franklin D. Roosevelt Library

testified to the State Department's bad faith. Long's misleading testimony and cross-examination by Representative Will Rogers Jr., cosponsor of the rescue resolution, verified that the State Department had vastly exaggerated its actions to rescue Hitler's victims. Long told the House committee what he had told FDR, that 580,000 refugees had been admitted to the United States since 1933, instead of 210,732. Long's number was based on the number of visas issued, not people actually admitted. He claimed that the IGCR could negotiate with the Axis when it clearly could not. Emanuel Celler demonstrated that Long had misled the committee and was shedding "crocodile tears" for the Jews.[40]

On November 11 Roosevelt left Washington for a nine-day sea voyage to Oran, Algeria, and then to Cairo to confer with Churchill, Chiang Kai-shek, and others. Roosevelt then went to Teheran, where he and Churchill met Joseph Stalin for the first time. Churchill still resisted the cross-Channel invasion plan. But to Roosevelt, nothing was more important to postwar world peace than Soviet-American cooperation, and the price for future cooperation was the second front in Europe. The president flew over Cairo and the Nile. Seeing the Pyramids from the air, he said, "man's desire to be remembered is colossal." The problems presented by the Soviet behemoth were also "colossal."[41]

The Big Three met face to face at Teheran to discuss global military strategy; Muslim Turkey's entrance into the war; the fates of postwar Germany and Poland; and Roosevelt's "supreme ambition," creation of an international peacekeeping organization. His poor health was beginning to show. "Have you noticed that the president is a very tired man?" Churchill asked Lord Moran, his physician. "His mind seems closed; he seems to have lost his wonderful elasticity." But Roosevelt worked diligently to placate Stalin, cajole Churchill, and hold the alliance together. The prime minister waffled on D-Day until the very end. Roosevelt met privately with Stalin about Poland and the support he might need of Polish-American voters if he ran for reelection in 1944.[42]

Roosevelt returned to the White House, in December, peaceful and satisfied, but he discovered a city in a bitter, divisive, partisan, racist frame of mind. "There is a terrific tension on the Hill," one New Dealer observed. Party and sectional politics boiled over. Conservatives were furious at Roosevelt's "unholy alliance" with Stalin. "The president has come back to his own second front," Max Lerner wrote.[43]

Positioning himself as a candidate in the 1944 election, Roosevelt implied that the New Deal was finished and transferred "Dr. New Deal's" duties to "Dr. Win-the-War." Asked by a journalist if this was a declaration for a fourth term, FDR replied, "Oh, now, we are not talking about things like that now. You are getting picayune."[44] One thing was certain: Roosevelt would never give up his war against Hitler or hand its direction to another. Only death removed him from leadership of the Allies.

American Jewish Patriots, Palestinian Jewish Terrorists, and "the Irgunist Hoax"

Ikey, Mikey, Jakey, Sam
We're the boys that eat no ham.
We're all in the Army now
So we're eating ham for Uncle Sam.
　　　　　　　　—New York Jewish basketball cheer

Ich bin ein jude *(I am a Jew)*
　　—American Jewish paratrooper (101st Airborne) to cap-
　　tured German soldiers during the Battle of the Bulge[1]

"We are now in this war," President Roosevelt said in his broadcast to the nation on December 9, 1941. "We are all in it—all the way. Every single man, woman, and child is a partner in the most tremendous undertaking of our American history."[2] Jewish-Americans could not have agreed more. They were, like all Americans, preoccupied with the war. It powerfully affected their immediate and daily lives. "As in the population as a whole,"

Nazi propaganda poster picturing Franklin Delano Roosevelt, Winston Churchill, and Joseph Stalin, titled "Who is to blame for war?" The poster holds the three leaders guilty of beginning the war, but claims that behind them stand the Jews.

Courtesy of the United States Holocaust Memorial Museum

Deborah Dash Moore wrote, "scarcely a Jewish family existed that did not have a son or a brother, a father or an uncle, in the service. Quite a few had sisters or daughters in uniform as well." Five hundred and fifty thousand Jewish Americans—11 to 12 percent of the nation's Jewish population—served in the United States military. Eight percent of all Americans in uniform were Jews, about twice their proportion of the population as a whole. Thirty-six thousand received medals and citations for bravery. There were 35,157 casualties, and 8,000 Jewish Americans were killed in action. The highest priority of American Jewish communities was the war and their men and women in uniform. Jewish communal efforts were directed toward supporting these servicemen and servicewomen, helping grieving and needy Jewish families, and supporting the war effort generally.

The Jewish Welfare Board, a USO agency, worked to meet the social, cultural, and religious needs of "Jewish fighters for America" and supplied chaplains, prayerbooks, kosher food, and Jewish literature. Rabbis urged their congregants to work for victory, ministered to those affected by the war, helped organize community projects, and enlisted as chaplains. Rabbi Abba Hillel Silver encouraged America's Jews to "fling themselves resolutely into the fight with Amalek," the biblical enemy of the Israelites. Three hundred forty thousand Jewish women served as nurses and in a variety of other capacities. Twelve graduated in the first class of commissioned officers in the Women's Auxiliary Army Corps.[3]

Jewish Americans experienced World War II, not the Holocaust. In July 1943, Stella Suberman, a young Jewish girl from Miami Beach, was excited about the invasion of Sicily.

> *Just before we left for Kansas, there was big news on the world scene: the Allies had invaded Sicily. It was a clear indication that Italy was about to fall, and my father wrote, "Mussolini must be kicking himself that he joined up with that* momser *[bastard, Hitler]. What a* schlemiel.*"*

A popular song during the war looked forward to the day "when those little yellow bellies meet the Cohens and the Kellys."

The Normandy invasion stirred the souls of Jewish Americans and raised their hopes of early victory. Suberman recalled:

> *In early June, D-Day, as the momentous event was called, finally happened. Again I got the news from someone waking me and shaking a newspaper at me. This time it was [her father-in-law], and the newspaper headline said that Allied forces had landed at Normandy. "It's the second front!" Alex yelled at me. "The second front!" In a man so careful to minimize excitement, this was a tremendous show of it. And who could blame him? This was not the standard news item, not the report of just another battle. It was weighty, and so breathtaking in its promise that I felt sure that our enemies would be surrendering before you could say "Up with Ike."[4]*

American Jewish communities united as never before to defeat Germany and Japan. By 1943 in Richmond, Virginia, for example, seven hundred Jewish men and women had served in the armed forces. Ten were killed, including Major Milton Joel of the army air force, who received the Silver Star. Lewis L. Strauss became a commodore in the navy. Two of Richmond's rabbis enlisted as chaplains. Beth Ahaba synagogue managed a serviceman's center or USO and ministered to more than 150,000 servicemen and servicewomen of all denominations.[5]

This story was repeated throughout the United States from

New York City to Los Angeles. Temple B'nai Israel in Amarillo, Texas, held services for soldiers stationed there. The sisterhood of Congregation Adath Yeshurun in Houston entertained at the soldiers' Service Bureau. Louis Stein, a young man from Brownsville, Texas, was killed in action near Strasbourg.[6]

Jewish servicemen had been killed at Pearl Harbor. Sergeant Meyer Levin, son of a Brooklyn tailor, was a bombardier on the Flying Fortress that bombed the Japanese battleship *Haruna* on the first day of war. Its pilot, Captain Colin Kelly, was killed and became one of World War II's first heroes. Levin was awarded the Distinguished Flying Cross and Silver Star and was later killed in action. Expressing the sentiments of the typical Jewish-American serviceman, Lieutenant Raymond Friedlander of New York wrote home from the front: "No matter how much easier and more pleasant it would be to be elsewhere at this moment, I still want to be here. This is the summit of human achievement—carrying the fight for all I've learned to love and all that's good in the world, carrying the fight with all its dangers to the enemy I hate." At age twenty-four, Friedlander was killed in action over Italy on January 27, 1944. Many a Jewish-American boy left home for the European theater promising his parents that he "was gonna stop Hitler."[7]

In his book *The Curtain Rises*, author and war correspondent Quentin Reynolds related a story that occurred in a quiet London club in 1943. A self-important English "gentleman" and club member had asked him where he lived, and Reynolds replied that his home was in New York.

*"How awful!" he said, looking at me sympatheti-
cally. "All you see there are Jews."*

*"I'm used to being with Jews," I told him. "Where
I've been lately the place is full of them."*

"Where have you been?" he asked.

*"I have been with the First Division in Sicily," I
said. "It's full of Jews. It will please you to know a hell
of a lot of them were killed."*

*He looked at me and blinked, not understanding,
and I walked away. I was a little afraid I might get sick
or slug him.*[8]

Bernard Barshay of Perth Amboy was aboard the first LST, loaded
with infantry and tanks, to hit the Normandy coast on D-Day. Private Edward Frindel of New York was a paratrooper who jumped
out of his transport plane over a blacked-out France. First Lieutenant
Frances Y. Slanger, a Jewish army nurse from Roxbury, Massachusetts, waded ashore on a Normandy beachhead on D-Day plus four.
She became the first American nurse of World War II to die under the
Nazi guns. Lieutenant Slanger wrote a famous letter to the United
States Army newspaper *Stars and Stripes* hours before her death:

*Sure we rough it, but in comparison to the way you
men are taking it we can't complain, nor do we feel that
bouquets are due us. But you, the men behind the guns,
the men driving our tanks, flying our planes, sailing our
ships, building bridges, and to the men who pave the way*

*and to the men who are left behind—it is to you we doff
our helmets. To every GI wearing the American uniform,
for you we have the greatest admiration and respect.*

The letter and Slanger's heroic death was a moving wartime
story in future editions of *Stars and Stripes*.[9] The 3rd Armored
Division commander, Major General Maurice G. Rose of Denver,
Colorado, was the son of an aged immigrant rabbi and immigrant
mother. A World War I veteran and career army officer, he led his
division through the block-by-block fighting in Metz, into

At Fort Bragg, North Carolina, shortly before the 45th Field Hospital
shipped out to England, the nurses posed in front of one of the cookie-cutter
barracks. Frances Slanger is fourth from the left, both hands in pockets.

Cologne, and into the Ruhr Valley. General Rose was killed on a reconnaissance patrol in March 1945, reaching for his pistol rather than be captured by Germans.[10]

Jewish chaplains ministered to Jewish GIs and sailors. They celebrated the Jewish holidays as the GIs fought the Axis. They were well aware that they fought as Jews and as Americans. General Harry Collins' Haggadah used by Jewish soldiers in the 42nd ("Rainbow") Division in Germany read, "You too are engaged in a battle for freedom against a modern Pharaoh who has sought not only to enslave your people, but to make slaves of the whole world."[11] When the USS *Dorchester* sank in February 1943, four chaplains drowned in the frigid waters of the North Atlantic. Among them was Rabbi Alexander Goode, who, like his three fellow chaplains, gave his life jacket to others as the ship sank from Nazi torpedoes.[12]

Generalizations, of course, are just that. Many Jewish families dreaded the army and the draft and the possibility of sons being killed in a war some did not fully understand. Author Norman Podhoretz, who grew up in Brooklyn, recalled his poor, barely literate in English, Yiddish-speaking grandmother's reaction upon hearing "Uncle Sam Needs You" on the radio: *"Ver iz er, der Uncle Sam? Im hob ikh extra in dr'erd!"* (Who is he, that Uncle Sam? Him I would especially like to send six feet under!) Grandma Esther viewed her son Maxie's being drafted into the army as a great calamity. So "preoccupied was she with her private troubles and woes," Podhoretz observed, "that it is entirely possible she knew nothing about the war and its connection with the fate of the Jews." But the young men of Podhoretz's neighborhood, the Brownsville section of Brooklyn, wound up in uniform, as did a dozen or more of Podhoretz's cousins, a brother-in-law, and two uncles. "Never in my young life," Podhoretz wrote, speaking for practically all American Jews of that era, "had I ever felt so pure a love for anything or anyone as I did for America during the war."[13]

These stories could be repeated endlessly throughout World War II. Native-born American Jews, immigrants, children of immigrants, refugees from Germany and Nazi-occupied Europe, Orthodox, Reform, and Conservative, traditional or secular—they all agreed that the most important thing they could do to destroy the Nazis was to serve the United States of America.

The children of the wealthy and influential, such as Henry and Robert Morgenthau, sons of the secretary of the treasury, served in the army and navy, respectively, and Felix Warburg's sons served in the army. Henry Morgenthau III served with Patton's Third Army in Normandy, and Bob Morgenthau's destroyer, the USS *Landsdale*, was sunk in the Mediterranean. (Bob survived to become a renowned New York County district attorney.) Hundreds of thousands of poor and middle-class, ordinary Jewish men and women served their country in uniform, becoming a part of the Greatest Generation. But not every Jew living in the safety of America was an American citizen dedicated solely to American war aims. A group of young Palestinian Jews stranded in the United States agitated for the overthrow of the British in Palestine. Some, like their leaders, Peter Bergson and Samuel Merlin, sat out the war, preferring to agitate rather than enlist and fight the Nazis themselves. Others, such as Eri Jabotinsky were found to be physically unfit, but would have served in the American armed forces. Still others, notably Yitshaq Ben-Ami and Alexander Rafaeli, served honorably in combat, Ben-Ami in the Battle of the Bulge and Rafaeli in the invasion of Southern France.[14]

Hillel Kook, who used the alias Peter Bergson (to protect his family in Palestine) came to America in July 1940 to raise money for his Palestinian political organization, the Irgun Zeva'i Le'umi (National Military Organization) or Etzel (its Hebrew acronym) and drum up support for a Jewish army. Bergson was more radical than his mentor Vladimir (Ze'ev) Jabotinsky, founder of the radical Revisionist Zionist movement from which the Irgun sprang. The Revisionists and Irgun insisted that the future Jewish state in Palestine must include all of the land of the biblical Kingdom of Israel, including Transjordan (formerly known as Eastern Palestine and now Jordan) and Jerusalem. The Betar, the Revisionists' militant youth wing, taught young Jews to fight, drill, and use firearms. Menachem Begin, an Irgun leader and later prime minister of Israel, began his career as a Betar leader. Bergson went to Europe in 1939 as a member of the Irgun to organize an armed struggle against the British for an independent Jewish state in Palestine.[15]

The Irgun bought guns and ammunition in Europe as early as 1939 to resist the British White Paper that limited Jewish immigration to Palestine and to promote Aliya Bet (immigration to Palestine in defiance of the British quotas). In 1939, the Irgun sent Aliya Bet fundraisers to the United States and formed a front group, the American Friends of a Jewish Palestine, to advocate armed conflict with the British and to aid illegal immigration. Bergson was a key player in this intrigue. He showed his early penchant for publicity when he staged a news conference at the Zionist Congress in Geneva and announced the objective of concentrating in Palestine one hundred thousand fighters for Jewish sovereignty. By that time Jabotinsky had decided that the Irgun should stage an armed revolt in Palestine.[16]

Jabotinsky, the Revisionist movement, and the Irgun were anathema to most American Jews. The Revisionists opposed the powerful Zionist trade union the Histradrut. In Palestine they were antiunion strike breakers whose actions sometimes provoked violence. Most American Jews, by contrast, were a strong component of the prolabor New Deal Democratic coalition. Jabotinsky urged military action (or illegal vigilante justice, depending on one's point of view) against Arab civilians. American Jews and the Zionist movement opposed this radical tactic. Milton Handler, a Jewish lawyer in FDR's administration who agitated for the rescue of European Jewry described the Bergson group as "notorious for its advocacy of terrorism, its divisiveness, its lack of discipline, and its disunifying attitude and effect."[17] Jewish philanthropists refused to donate to Revisionist causes. In the United States the Revisionists appealed mainly to unacculturated Orthodox and immigrant Jews at a time when most Jews were becoming more middle-class, more Americanized, and were abandoning Orthodoxy. By 1930, the Jewish workforce was becoming "white-collar," and few new immigrants arrived after 1924.

There was a strong undercurrent in the Revisionist movement of condemnation of secular and Reform Jews. Bergson readily admitted that he had little support from Reform Jews. Thus Revisionist organizations had few members in relation to mainstream organizations. At their 1930 national convention there were forty delegates. Jabotinsky himself failed to draw large crowds when he visited the United States in May 1940. "Revisionism," Aaron Berman observed, "did not win many adherents in the United States and existed only on the fringes of the American Zionist community."[18]

The Irgun, many Jewish Americans knew, had emerged from a series of violent events in Palestine that had begun with an Arab massacre of 133 Jews in 1921 and continued throughout the 1930s as Arab terrorists attacked Jewish farmers and other civilians. Innocent Jews were murdered as they left movie houses, in their homes, and as they went to the marketplace. The Jewish leadership of the Yishuv (Jewish Palestine), including David Ben-Gurion, refused to engage in terrorist retaliation, calling instead for a policy of restraint or *havlaga* (self-defense).[19]

But not all Jews in the Yishuv agreed with Ben-Gurion and the Zionist leadership. Hard-line Revisionists and their supporters established the Irgun in 1937 as its military arm. The Revisionists modeled themselves on Fascist movements complete with a "poetry of blood sacrifice, the uniforms . . . monster parades" and speeches by the charismatic Jabotinsky. The Zionist mainstream, which leaned left in its politics, saw the Revisionists and Irgunists as Fascists. "To a degree," J. Bowyer Bell concluded, "they were right: such ideas molded in such forms had become vastly popular." According to one Israeli historian, the Irgunists "ambushed and killed Arabs; they threw bombs into Arab coffeehouses and marketplaces, causing dozens of deaths." Thus began a fierce, bloody, and deadly struggle for the heart and soul of Zionism, Jewish Palestine, and ultimately the State of Israel.[20]

Ben-Gurion, the Jewish Agency, and the Haganah did not countenance the murder of innocent Arab men, women, and children in retaliation for the murder of innocent Jews. The Irgunists believed in retaliation and exercised it. Like the Irish terrorists of the Irish Republican Army (IRA), on whom they modeled themselves, the Irgun terrorists detested the British, whom they saw as illegal occupants of the Jewish homeland. The Jewish Agency leadership, the mainstream Zionist movement, and American Jewry, on the other hand, believed that Britain would ultimately do justice to the Jewish people and create a Jewish homeland of some kind. Regardless of what happened in Palestine, because American Jews abhorred terrorists who killed innocent Arab civilians and the Irgun had minuscule support among Jewish Americans, Jabotinsky's Fascist-sounding, alarmist rhetoric turned off most American Jews. His slogan "If you will not liquidate the Diaspora, the Diaspora will liquidate you" was anathema to patriotic American Jews. Thus those American Jews who supported Zionism identified with what they considered the legitimate Jewish leadership, Ben-Gurion of the Jewish Agency and Chaim Weizmann, president of the World Zionist Organization. The Jewish Agency leadership cooperated with British authorities in tracking down and capturing Jewish terrorists.[21]

In 1938, the British brought in Major General Bernard Montgomery to quell Arab and Jewish violence. The parallel between Palestine and Ireland, wrote Colonial Secretary William George

Arthur Ormsby-Gore, is "singularly complete." Between the May 1939 issuance of the White Paper and the outbreak of war in September, the Irgun attacked British government installations and, by its own account, murdered one hundred, thirty people.[22]

When the war began in September 1939, the Irgun temporarily suspended its terrorist campaign, but some Irgun diehards continued. Avraham Stern created LEHI (*Lohamei Herut Yisrael, or* Fighters for the Freedom of Israel), known to the British and American Jewry as "the Stern Gang," which continued to assassinate British police officers and officials during the war. To the Allies and American Jewry, the Irgunists were terrorist militants. Ben-Gurion called them Nazis. One Zionist group in New York denounced the Revisionists as "Fascisti, Hitlerites, Blackshirts." Wise denounced the movement as "Fascism in Yiddish or Hebrew." Albert Einstein, too, publicly denounced the Revisionists.[23]

It was a mistake to view opposition to the right-wing Irgunists as coming from the "conservative" Jewish establishment, which, in fact, was "liberal" in its politics and uniformly anti-Fascist. Opposition to Jewish terrorism in Palestine came from *all* Jewish quarters. Golda Meir, later prime minister of Israel, was adamant in her opposition to the Irgun. Unalterably opposed to terror of any kind, she believed the Irgunists "were wrong (and thus dangerous to the *Yishuv*) from start to finish." The left-wing intellectual Hannah Arendt, who escaped Germany and made her way to New York in May 1941, supported Bergson's Committee for a Jewish Army until she realized that it was a Revisionist front group. She denounced the Revisionists as "Jewish Fascists" in March 1942. The left-wing

Die jungjüdische Gruppe (The Young Jewish Group), organized by Hannah Arendt and Joseph Maier in New York, denounced Jewish terrorists attacks on the British and the Arabs in 1942. Even Rabbi Abba Hillel Silver, a Zionist militant who sometimes agreed and cooperated with him, said Bergson and his group were "charlatans and racketeers." Thus American Jewish leaders agreed with and heeded Ben-Gurion's and the Jewish Agency's wishes that they boycott Irgunist activities in America.[24]

FDR opposed a Jewish army in Palestine because the British "in their Near Eastern campaign . . . must of necessity have the support of not only the Jews in Palestine, but also of a far greater number of Arabs in Transjordan, Sa'udi Arabia, and in the northern Arab states."[25] The Revisionists thereafter allied themselves with Roosevelt's political enemies, anti-Roosevelt isolationists such as Senators Burton K. Wheeler and Gerald P. Nye, on the theory that if these conservatives did not want European Jews in America, they "must find for us a State somewhere."[26]

No one who knew Bergson's background and understood the Irgun had any doubt that his sole purpose in America was to raise money to wage war on the British. Despite the man's disingenuous public denials at the time, funds raised by the Bergsonites in the United States were secretly transferred to the Irgun. Their first front group was called, appropriately, the Committee for a Jewish Army of Stateless and Palestinian Jews. All of the leaders were Irgunist, including Samuel Merlin; Alexander Rafaeli; Yitshaq Ben-Ami; and Eri Jabotinsky, son of the founder of the Revisionist movement. As Rafael Medoff points out, the leadership of the anti-Roosevelt

Revisionist fringe groups were not even American citizens.[27] FDR's bitterest critics among historians claimed that Bergson cut all ties to the Irgun to work exclusively to rescue European Jewry, and they describe him as "a Zionist emissary." However, Bergson only ceased mentioning the Irgun as he continued his efforts to create a Jewish army to fight the British. In later life Bergson readily admitted lying (he called it "weaseling") about his Irgun connections.[28]

Bergson revealed to his chief American supporter and fundraiser, Ben Hecht, as early as 1941 that his goal was to overthrow British rule in Palestine. Hecht was a well-known playwright and Hollywood screenplay writer. He had salvaged the script for David O. Selznick's *Gone with the Wind* and wrote the screenplay for Alfred Hitchcock's *Notorious*. "If you get a Jewish army organized," Hecht told Bergson, "you'll have a big military force with which to fight the Arabs, after the war is over. And, who knows, maybe the British, too. Obviously, that's the reason the British are opposed to putting such an ally in the field today. It might mean their losing Palestine tomorrow." "You have said the truth, Mr. Ben Hecht," Bergson's assistant Samuel Merlin piped up. According to Hecht, Bergson smiled and said, "One thing at a time. First step—a Jewish army in Africa. Then—next step—the opening of the ports of Palestine and moving in the Jewish refugees from the massacre. Then—third step—Palestine and the liberation."[29]

Bergson's technique was to draw in famous supporters, celebrities, intellectuals, Hollywood personalities, and Park Avenue sponsors, most of whom did not understand his real goals. For example, the best-selling author and Dutch expatriate Pierre van Paassen chaired the CJA campaign and drew large crowds to

Bergson's rallies. But when van Paassen realized what Bergson's actual goals were, he quit.

In an article titled "The Irgunist Hoax" in *The Protestant* in April 1944, van Paassen pointed out that the same four or five young Irgunists operated all the front groups from the Committee for a Jewish Army to the Emergency Committee to Save the Jews of Europe, and that the Irgun, a "numerically insignificant group in Palestine," was modeled on the Social Revolutionary Party of tsarist Russia. The Irgun, van Paassen reported, was proscribed in Palestine because of its Fascist methods and use of terror against Jewish opponents—Arabs and Britons alike. The Jews of Palestine "have no truck or trade with the Irgun," van Paassen continued.[30]

Bergson had brought into the organization a number of persons "notorious for their reactionary past in American public life"—his congressional allies Wheeler and Nye. According to van Paassen, the Irgun also refused to collaborate with established Jewish and non-Jewish bodies and organizations "of a progressive, reputable and democratic character. Like the Irgun in Palestine, the Irgunist directors of the Committee for a Jewish Army wanted to play and did play a lone hand." The committee had neither the means, the facilities, "nor, I declare, the intention to save Jews."

> *To speak bluntly, that "Committee to Save the Jewish People of Europe" is a hoax, in my judgment a very cruel hoax perpetrated on the American public, Jewish and non-Jewish alike. That committee and its directors have but one aim in view; to increase the*

*prestige of the outlawed political group in Palestine
known as the Irgun and the glorification of the Irgun's
self-styled "dynamic" missionaries in this country.*[31]

Van Paassen closed by describing the Irgun as "fascist" and "terrorist." He deeply regretted that some well-meaning people had joined and supported these groups because he was a member: "If people knew what was really involved they would have kept the committee at a considerable distance."

None of the FDR decriers explained that van Paassen thought Bergson and the Irgun were a hoax and a fraud. They downplayed the Irgun to readers who therefore were at a loss to understand why Jewish leaders and FDR did not support this nice young man from Palestine. The Dutch writer's detailed exposé was even missing from *Militant Zionism in America* (2002), Rafael Medoff's otherwise-scholarly book on the Revisionist movement.[32]

Bergson avoided mentioning the British, the ultimate target of his Jewish Army, but he fooled few people. "A Jewish Army," the British Foreign Office noted privately, "cannot be disassociated from Jewish Nationalism." Bergson's strongest congressional supporter was Andrew L. Somers, the son of a militant Irish nationalist, and a vigorous opponent of Great Britain. Years later Bergson admitted that the main purpose of the Jewish Army was to overthrow the British in Palestine. Jewish Americans were overwhelmingly pro-British, anti-Irgun, and out to defeat Hitler and the German Army, not plotting a Zionist revolt in Palestine.[33]

American Jews knew what Bergson was up to. Ben Hecht,

starstruck by Bergson and deeply moved by the plight of European Jewry, invited a group of prominent Hollywood Jews to a fundraising meeting at the Twentieth Century–Fox studio. Harry Warner and Charlie Chaplin were there. After hearing diatribes against the British in Palestine, people began stalking out of the place. Hecht obtained nine thousand dollars instead of the millions Bergson hoped to raise.[34]

Bergson realized that the only way he could raise funds among American Jews was to hide his real goals. He was successful when he professed that the CJA's aim was to create a Jewish army to fight Nazis and to rescue European Jews. American Jews were aroused by the publicity surrounding the Allied declaration of December 17, 1942, and other revelations of Nazi atrocities. Mainstream groups organized rallies and demonstrations. On February 13, 1943, the *New York Times* ran a story that the Romanian government was willing to free 70,000 Jews if certain amounts of money were paid. Four days later the Irgunists ran an advertisement in the *Times*:

> *FOR SALE to Humanity*
> *70,000 Jews*
> *Guaranteed Human Beings at $50 apiece*

The advertisement created the impression that funds given to the Committee for a Jewish Army, the Irgunist front group, would be used to ransom the Romanian Jews, which they never were, because the Romanian Jews were never ransomed. Indeed the Germans had killed the plan before the story ran in the *New York Times*.[35]

The American Jewish leadership charged Bergson with

deceptively implying that each fifty-dollar contribution would save a Romanian Jew, and accused him of irresponsible and unethical behavior, something "very close to fraud." When Morris D. Waldman of the AJCommittee met with members of the State Department Division of Near Eastern Affairs in January 1944, he told them that the Bergson group's activities and their advertisement implying that the Transnistrian Jews could be rescued at fifty dollars a head were "little better than racketeering."[36]

But America-bashing Roosevelt decriers were not to be diverted by mere facts. "The main issue," David Wyman informed us, "is not whether the plan might have worked." The crucial point was that the Americans and the British "*almost* cursorily dismissed this first major *potential* rescue opportunity." First, there was no rescue opportunity to miss. Second, the Romanians were allies of the Germans fighting the Soviets at Stalingrad. Obviously Americans could not give their enemies money to continue killing Allied soldiers. "In Yiddish," Dawidowicz quipped, "we would say to this: 'If Grandma had wheels, she'd be a streetcar.' "[37]

On March 1, 1943, the American Jewish Congress, joined by the AFL and the CIO, the Church Peace Union, and many Jewish organizations, staged a huge "Stop Hitler Now" rally at Madison Square Garden. Twenty thousand people filled the Garden, ten thousand to fifteen thousand gathered outside, and thousands were turned away. Speeches by Mayor LaGuardia, AFL president William Green, Rabbi Wise, and Chaim Weizmann, telegrams from distinguished people such as the archbishop of Canterbury, and an eleven-point rescue plan convinced many, including the

New York Times editorial writers, that "the United Nations governments have no right to spare any efforts that will save lives."

The rescue proposals advanced at the rally depended on Hitler's agreement to stop murdering Jews and to permit them to emigrate. Such proposals seemed realistic at the time to many who were uninformed about the true nature of the Holocaust. Critics demanded that FDR and his administration do something and not, as one editorial charged, "stolidly stand by and do nothing in the face of one of the world's greatest tragedies." Already the charge was made by some that "in this country, you and I and the president and the Congress and the State Department are accessories to the crime and share Hitler's guilt." Rabbi Wise and others criticized the administration's "rescue through victory" policy. "We are told that the best way to save the Jews is to win the war," Wise declared, "but what hope is there that victory will come in time to mean survival of European Jews?"[38]

In early 1943, Ben Hecht worked with Bergson and the Irgunists to convince a group of American Jews, this time New York writers, to produce a theatrical production, *We Will Never Die.* Thirty famous writers came to George and Beatrice Kaufman's home to hear him out. When Hecht began ranting how "our great keeper of the rights of man—Roosevelt" and "England's great humanitarian, Churchill" had let the Jews down, six of the guests walked out. "Who is paying you to do this wretched propaganda," Edna Ferber demanded, "Mr. Hitler? Or is it Mr. Goebbels?" For the rest of his life Hecht never comprehended that FDR stood between the Jews and Hitler. He did not understand what had gone wrong at the meeting. Beatrice Kaufman tried to explain: "You

"We Will Never Die" Pageant, March 9, 1943, Madison Square Garden. In front of a backdrop of two towering tablets inscribed in Hebrew with the Ten Commandments, a rabbi opened a performance dedicated to the murdered Jews of Europe. The event was the brainchild of members of the Committee for a Jewish Army headed by Peter Bergson and some of the most prominent Jews in show business, including scriptwriter Ben Hecht.

Courtesy of the American Jewish Archives

asked them to throw away the most valuable thing they own—the fact that they are Americans." With the help of producer Billy Rose and director Moss Hart, Hecht finally got *We Will Never Die* off the ground.[39]

On March 9, 1943, Madison Square Garden hosted *We Will Never Die*, another huge Irgun-sponsored protest and a star-studded pageant against the destruction of European Jewry. It was written by

Hecht and starred Paul Muni and Edward G. Robinson. Kurt Weill wrote the musical score. Later productions included Marlon Brando, Frank Sinatra, Sid Caesar, Jerry Lewis, Dean Martin, and Danny Thomas. It got the nation's attention. There were performances in Washington, Philadelphia, Chicago, Boston, and Hollywood. The event was broadcast over the radio. Eleanor Roosevelt attended the Washington performance, as did three hundred senators and representatives, members of the cabinet, and six Supreme Court justices.

Calling themselves the Emergency Committee to Save the Jewish People of Europe, the Irgunists held a conference in New York in July 1943. Established Jewish organizations refused to participate. At the request of Max Lerner, ER sent a message emphasizing the importance of a realistic plan of rescue. "It is hard to say what can be done at the present time, but if you are able to formulate a program of action," she felt sure FDR would support it. Morgenthau apparently had an open mind about Bergson's call for action. "It is my earnest hope," he wrote Max Lerner, "that out of your Emergency Conference will come a specific plan to relieve the critical situation which exists among the Jewish people.... With so substantial a group of outstanding people backing your efforts, I feel confident that some plan and some action will certainly result." Like ER, Morgenthau wanted to present FDR with a realistic rescue plan.[40]

A coalition of Jews and non-Jews, the Hearst newspaper chain, Herbert Hoover, Harold Ickes, Will Rogers Jr., Fiorello LaGuardia, and many others agitated for rescue. Bergson met with ER in August, and she gave a copy of the committee's recommendation to her husband. In her column the next day she wrote that the percentage killed among European Jews "far exceeds the losses among any of the United Nations." She later wrote a message for the committee to use in a broadcast reflecting FDR's views that "everything possible that can be done was being done" and that the best way to save people was "to win the war as rapidly as possible."[41]

Rescue efforts were shelved as hopeless. It was, Rabbi Silver observed, "a situation which we cannot help." By August Gerhart Riegner and Richard Lichtheim reported that four million Jews were dead and only one and one-half million to two million were still alive in Europe. The "Ark of Death," Silver lamented, bearing two million dead Jews, was "leading us . . . through the wilderness to Palestine!"[42] During 1943 and early 1944, American Jewish groups coordinated their efforts to secure a congressional resolution endorsing a Jewish commonwealth in Palestine. Zionist fervor and American sympathy for European Jewry led to widespread support in Congress for a resolution urging that "the doors of Palestine . . . be opened" for "a free and democratic Jewish commonwealth." In January 1944, while D-Day was in its planning stages, the resolution was introduced in Congress. However, the War Department asked congressional committees to desist. It feared that Arab uprisings would follow the resolution and require the diversion of Allied troops to the region. Roosevelt supported his military advisers and reinforced this request. Hull told Halifax in November 1943 that the administration was under pressure from Jewish Americans and unless something happened the "Jewish extremists would get control." Halifax wired Eden that Hull was "anxious to forestall what he expected to be 'a Jewish blast.' "[43]

The Irgunists organized a protest "pilgrimage" to Washington, D.C., by four hundred mostly immigrant Orthodox rabbis on October 6, 1943, three days before Yom Kippur. Rosenman, Wise, and mainstream Jewish leaders were outraged at Bergson's "stunt" and asked FDR to avoid the protesters. The demonstration and the appearance of the "greenhorn" participants embarrassed many American Jews, who had adopted American behavior and dress, abandoning "old country" ways, speaking English, not Yiddish, and becoming "real" Americans. Most American Jews had abandoned Orthodox Judaism, with its strict kosher laws, long beards, foreign garb, and the wearing of yarmulkes and tsitsit (fringes) in public. Orthodoxy demanded the physical separation of men and women in the synagogue, strict attendance to the Jewish Sabbath on Saturday, and the observance of a multitude of holidays and laws that interfered with everyday life in America. Americanized Reform and Conservative Jews had abandoned these practices. Indeed many Americanized Orthodox Jews had also. Most American Jews drove their cars on Saturday and attended Conservative synagogues and Reform temples, where they could understand the English and Hebrew service and sit with their wives, daughters, and mothers.

Thus most American Jews in 1943 did not view bearded, foreign-looking, and Yiddish-speaking Orthodox rabbis in their long black velvet coats, big hats, and Hasidic garb as their representatives to Washington. Samuel Rosenman spoke for much of American Jewry when he referred to the Orthodox rabbis as "a group of rabbis who just recently left the darkest period of the medieval world." Arthur Hertzberg, a participant at age twenty-two in the march, describes these immigrant Orthodox rabbis as follows:

> *These rabbis were not clean-shaven or well-dressed. They were avowedly East European. They represented not "American types" from the posh synagogues. On the contrary, they might just as well have been the rabbis whom Hitler was then putting in death-camps along with their congregants.*[44]

The *American Hebrew* chided the Irgunists: "The spectacle is enough to make the angels weep . . . many people cannot but come to the conclusion that some of the groups are exploiting the situation for reasons of their own."[45] Wise publicly blasted the demonstration in *Opinion*, as did pro-Zionist American Jewish leaders and Jewish members of the administration.

The Irgunists had been informed earlier that the president would not meet with the rabbis, although they did meet with Vice President Henry A. Wallace and some congressmen at the Capitol. Knowing the president was not available, Bergson nevertheless directed the group to the White House to embarrass FDR. There, a delegation presented a petition to Marvin McIntyre, one of the president's secretaries.[46]

Roosevelt did not meet with the rabbis because he followed the advice of American Jewish leaders, not Palestinian Irgunists. He did not want to raise the stature of the Irgun and oppose the great

American Jewish soldiers in the China-Burma-India Theater of Operations during World War II.

Courtesy of the Museum of American Jewish Military History

majority of Jews in America. He listened to Jewish congressmen (who unanimously tried to prevent the Irgun demonstration), Rosenman, Rabbi Wise, and leaders he and American Jewry respected. These men represented the overwhelming opinion of American Jewry. FDR meant no disrespect to the rabbis, who were manipulated by Bergson, but he refused to be pressed to aid the Irgunists.[47]

Wyman recounted this episode as follows in *America and the Holocaust: Deceit and Indifference*, his anti-Roosevelt PBS documentary: "In October [the Bergson Group] held an unprecedented demonstration in Washington. Four hundred Orthodox rabbis arrived from around the nation two days before the most holy day in the Jewish year to present the petition [for a rescue agency] to the *president*, but Jewish leaders opposed to the Bergson Group advised Roosevelt against it. White House spokesmen claimed the president was too busy, but a look at his appointment calendar reveals he was free that afternoon." The words were accompanied by sinister music, film of tearful rabbis, and a zoom into Roosevelt's calendar that day, as if a big secret had just been revealed. Wyman's account sounded like that of a Bergson camp follower who, forty years later, still had an ax to grind with FDR. He failed to tell viewers who was behind the rabbis' visit, how controversial Bergson, the Irgun, and the "Emergency Committee" were, that Bergson knew the president had declined beforehand to meet the delegation, that every Jewish congressman and the entire American Jewish leadership opposed the march, and that the immigrant Orthodox rabbis represented a small segment of American Jewry.

There also was an undercurrent in the anti-FDR, pro-Irgun, American-bashing version of history that Reform Jews, who made up a large percentage of Jewish Americans, did evil to believe in traditional American and Jewish emancipationist values of Jewish acculturation. Penkower criticized Wise and Rosenman, who, he noted, were "both of the Reform persuasion," for advising FDR not to receive the Orthodox rabbis. Hecht belittled "the Americanized Jew who ran newspapers and movie studios."[48] This undercurrent came to the surface in *Shake Heaven and Earth* (1999) by Louis Rapoport, who apparently wrote the family-authorized biography of Bergson. His demonization of Stephen

Wise was complete. Wise was "a showman of the synagogue," an adulterer, a plagiarist, unintelligent, and egocentric. Not content with savaging Wise, he condemned his religious practice: "But in the Reform synagogue, where Judaism took on trappings of the Protestant churches, the people loved Dr. Wise's dramatic, showy sermons accompanied by solemn music." (Instrumental music is forbidden in Orthodox services.) Ben Hecht detested Stephen Wise and was well aware that his own and Bergson's activities were roundly denounced in Reform synagogues.[49]

The Irgunists were publicly hostile to the Roosevelt administration and opposed by virtually every major American Jewish organization.[50] They ran ads critical of Roosevelt's lack of rescue efforts, and on November 1, 1943, held a rally honoring Sweden for its role in rescuing Danish Jews. Leon Henderson, a disgruntled former director of the Office of Price Administration, lambasted Roosevelt and Churchill and accused them of "moral cowardice." These tactics did not endear Bergson or his front groups to FDR or American Jewish leaders. As it turned out, the State Department had urged Sweden to help the Danish Jews.[51]

On February 1, 1944, four months before the Normandy invasion, the Irgun, led by Menachem Begin, former head of the Betar youth movement and Bergson's comrade, declared war on the British in Palestine. Begin called on "the Hebrew nation in Zion" to rise in revolt against Great Britain, to stop paying taxes, and to engage in a general strike. The Irgun began attacking and killing British policemen and bombing government buildings, railroads, and arsenals. The Stern Gang murdered Lord Walter Guinness Moyne, the

British minister for Middle East affairs on November 6, 1944, which infuriated Churchill and briefly turned him away from assisting the Zionist cause. Palestinian Jews and the Haganah cooperated with the British in rounding up the Jewish terrorists. "We shall repay you, Cain," the defiant Begin told the Zionist majority. (Begin and the Irgun blew up the King David Hotel in July 1946, killing twenty-eight British, forty-one Arabs, seventeen Jews, and five others.)

In 1944, the Irgun not only made war against the British authorities but also attacked Jewish leaders, "vilifying them," in the words of Tom Segev, "as false, cowardly, imbecilic, and traitorous." In response the Haganah and the Jewish Agency joined forces with the British army and police to hunt down and kill Irgun terrorists. The breach in Zionism, wrote Paul Johnson, "was envenomed by abuse." Revisionists leaders accused Mapai, the mainstream Socialist labor party, of collusion with the British and treason to the Jewish cause.[52] It is this banner and ideology the Roosevelt decriers continue to carry into their histories.

Bergson was elated. The war *he* wanted to fight, the war against the British, not the Nazis, had begun. The defeat of Japan and Germany, the welfare of American servicemen, and the interests of the United States were of no concern to Hillel Kook, aka Peter Bergson. Those were somebody else's problems. Bergson had a different mission. Indeed, two of the Irgunists who had worked with Bergson and criticized FDR, Arieh Ben Eliezer and Eri Jabotinsky, left the United States immediately for Palestine to join Begin.[53]

Despite these well-known facts, some of the anti-Roosevelt historians portrayed the Revisionists, the Irgunists, and Bergson as heroic champions of the rescue of Europe's Jews fighting against the cowardly American Jewish establishment, which included every major Jewish leader and organization, including almost all Zionists led by Wise, Silver, and others. In this fairy tale version of history, the young, cosmopolitan, honest, sincere, idealistic "Bergson Boys" were pitted against the old, stodgy, corrupt, self-hating American Jewish Congress, the American Jewish Committee, the Zionist Organization of America, Hadassah, B'nai B'rith, the Jewish War Veterans, Chaim Weizmann, president of the World Zionist Organization, as well as the "court Jews" (Frankfurter, Rosenman, and Morgenthau) and *shatladim* (self-appointed intercessors) such as Proskauer and Lehman. In other words, against virtually all of American Jewry. These historians also ignored the Jewish American Greatest Generation, the Jewish men and women in the Normandy invasion and in bombers over Nazi Germany and in the Pacific war.[54]

Irgunists had nearly no American constituency. American Jews contributed to Bergson's front group because they wanted to save European Jewry, but these contributors had no say in Bergson's activities or where their dollars were spent. The Irgunists represented the views of a small minority of Palestinian Jewry, as Bergson admitted, and depended on sensationalism to raise funds. Their anti-British stance was incomprehensible to Jewish Americans, many of whose sons and daughters were at that very moment fighting the German army in Europe alongside their beleaguered British allies. The defeat of the Japanese, who had bombed Pearl Harbor, not Tel Aviv, and the Germans, who sought to destroy freedom all over the world, may not have been of any concern of Peter Bergson and the Irgunists, but it was the number one priority of American Jews and Franklin Roosevelt.

One of Bergson's top lieutenants, Yitzhak Ben-Ami, correctly observed in his memoir: "The United States was at war with ever greater numbers of casualties. As was only natural, the President, and the people of the United States, were out to win the war in the shortest time possible, with the least casualties, and this was what occupied their thoughts."[55]

Chapter 18

"One of the Blackest Crimes of All History" and the American War Refugee Board

In his January 11, 1944, State of the Union address, Roosevelt gave one of the most radical speeches of his life. He condemned "selfish pressure groups," "bickering and self-seeking" partisans, and cynical lobbyists who "seek to feather their nests while young Americans are dying." To those who felt that the war was won, "the dangerous folly of that point of view can be measured by the distance that separates our troops from their ultimate objectives in Berlin and Tokyo—and by the sum of all the perils that lie along the way." He called for an economic bill of rights, which included tax laws to combat unfair profits and price fixing for food. American citizenship encompassed the right to a remunerative job, adequate clothing, a decent home, medical care, and education. The president's liberal New Deal agenda "fell with a dull thud" in Congress.[1]

Roosevelt had much on his plate, but one issue agitated his old friend Henry Morgenthau as nothing had agitated him before: the State Department's treachery in failing to provide even the modest assistance to European Jewry the president believed to be under way. Roosevelt's information on refugees came mainly from Breckinridge Long via Secretary of State Cordell Hull. Either deliberately or negligently, Long had misled the president when he reported that the United States had admitted 580,000 refugees since 1933. In fact, 166,843 had been admitted through normal channels and 43,889 on emergency visas for a total of 210,732.[2]

As we have seen, in November 1943, there had been a slim chance to save seventy thousand Romanian Jews in Transnistria, a portion of the Ukraine under Romanian control, if Gerhart Riegner at the World Jewish Congress could obtain some funds. At the Treasury Department Morgenthau believed that aid was forthcoming to the refugees. However, the State Department had surreptitiously collaborated with the British Foreign Office to block the license needed to transfer the funds. Morgenthau was shocked to learn that the Foreign Office had sent a message that their real concern was "the difficulties of disposing of any considerable number of Jews should they be rescued." In other words, the British did not object to trading with the enemy; they resisted rescuing *any* Jewish refugees who might want to go to Palestine or some other inconvenient place. Compounding the duplicity, State Department personnel hid two cables about the extermination of European Jewry and tried to prevent Riegner and the WJC from using diplomatic channels to communicate with Rabbi Stephen Wise.[3]

Henry Morgenthau was livid. The Foreign Office message, he fumed, was "a satanic combination of British chill and diplomatic double-talk, cold and correct and adding up to a sentence of death." Morgenthau's staff—general counsel Randolph Paul, Foreign Funds Control Chief John Pehle, assistant general counsel Josiah DuBois Jr., and Ansel Luxford, a departmental lawyer—were incensed. DuBois investigated the antirescue clique at State. Oscar Cox and Benjamin Cohen had inquired who in the State Department was in charge of refugee matters. Pehle replied that it was Long and his staff. DuBois pointed out that "[Herbert] Feis and [Bernard] Meltzer [two Jews], we know, are the only two men in the State Department who have been doing anything on this, and they were opposed by Breckinridge Long and that whole crowd."[4] Dubois wrote a confidential report to Morgenthau titled "Report to the Secretary on the Acquiescence of This Government in the Murder of the Jews." It charged the State Department with "wilful failure to act and wilful attempts to prevent rescue efforts. . . . The attitude [of the British Foreign Office] to date is no different from Hitler's attitude."

On January 13, Morgenthau told his staff he did not think Harry Hopkins would be of any use to press the issue but "I do think that to save time it would be useful to have Rosenman and Cohen." Rosenman had doubts about bringing the dispute to FDR, about adverse publicity, and about Morgenthau's secret Saturday meeting ("whether when you talk about refugees, you want to have three Jews," namely Cohen, Rosenman, and Morgenthau). Morgenthau was angry. "I don't think you have any conception of how serious this thing is," he told Rosenman. "Well, I'm sure I have," Rosenman retorted. "Well, if you have I don't see how you can keep the President out of it." Rosenman wanted everything off the record. "Don't worry about the publicity. What I want is intelligence and courage—courage first and intelligence second," Morgenthau told him.

Rosenman realized Morgenthau was serious. When he hung up, Morgenthau exclaimed, "My God! Sam Rosenman—would there be any publicity?" Morgenthau knew that Rosenman was closer to Roosevelt than he was and could defeat the plan, although he thought "fellows like Ben Cohen and the rest will cut his throat." "In the final analysis," Morgenthau said, "Rosenman is a fine person. . . . He will be all right." Of course, in the climate of the times, a front-page news story about a Morgenthau, Rosenman, and Cohen meeting called to help foreign Jews could not have been helpful either to FDR's political fortunes or the cause of European Jewry.[5]

Henry Morgenthau met his staff at his home. He called on Jewish New Dealers Sam Rosenman, Ben Cohen, and Oscar Cox to develop a strategy to convince the president to create a separate American rescue organization and to get the State Department out of the Jewish refugee business. The idea of a separate *American* rescue agency, not an Allied or "intergovernmental" body, emerged during 1943. The Irgunist Emergency Conference to Save the Jewish People of Europe promoted the idea, and Rabbi Wise of the JEC had called for it at the March 1, 1943, "Stop Hitler Now" rally.[6]

Morgenthau's diaries and transcriptions of his conversations reveal that these Jewish officials viewed Roosevelt as a victim of State Department intrigue. "The president," Morgenthau told his staff, "hasn't had anybody who really feels like you people do about this thing." Once the facts were laid before him, Morgenthau believed Roosevelt would do the right thing. For example, Roosevelt had "worked on the visa thing . . . and got nowhere." The president "has been hammered so on that child visa thing. . . . The President himself, I know, has tried." Morgenthau's Jewish assistant, Harry Dexter White, disagreed and said Roosevelt would never "pay any attention to the problem, unless he is brought to the point where he has to make a decision." White believed Roosevelt allowed Britain too much latitude and that he was ultimately responsible for the situation. Morgenthau defended FDR. He told his war council on January 15, "I know that the man did everything possible that he could." In 1947, Morgenthau wrote that FDR had been "deeply moved" by Rabbi Wise's plea to help the Jews of France and Romania. He had listened sympathetically to him on the issue of the War Refugee Board and "gave us his blessing."[7]

Morgenthau's biggest concern was how to circumvent Cordell Hull without creating discord. The president disliked bickering in his cabinet and insisted that subordinates resolve their differences. Morgenthau knew how touchy Hull was about his department's failures. When Hull and Breckinridge Long met Morgenthau on December 20, 1943, they realized that Morgenthau knew the department had sabotaged rescue efforts approved by the president. Hull apologized and blamed his "people down the line." He had little knowledge of the refugee situation and did not even know the names of the men in charge, other than Long. Morgenthau met Hull a second time, on January 12, 1944, but the meeting was inconclusive. Morgenthau later wrote, "It was time to go to FDR."[8]

As Morgenthau's plans developed, Rosenman paved the way behind the scenes by briefing the new undersecretary of state, Edward R. Stettinius, Jr. Ben Cohen and Oscar Cox also helped behind the scene. Cox was a highly respected insider in the administration who was instrumental in drafting the Lend-Lease Act, the legal opinions concerning Japanese-American internment and had served as a prosecutor of the captured German saboteurs who slipped into the United States during the war. He served as a lawyer with the Federal Office of Economic Administration, the successor to the Lend-Lease Administration, as well as assistant solicitor general. Morgenthau called him a "smart operator." He was born and raised a Jew by his Russian immigrant parents Jacob and Sarah Cox of Portland, Maine, but married a Presbyterian and hid his Jewish past from his children and others. He was held in high esteem in the Roosevelt administration and by the president himself.[9]

Cox was "haunted by the suffering of refugees." He and his assistant in the Lend-Lease Administration, Milton Handler, another Jewish New Deal lawyer, had drafted a plan for an interdepartmental agency to rescue Jews in June 1943 and had discussed the plan with Morgenthau at least as early as June 16, 1943. Roosevelt had supported it, but the State Department had opposed the plan. Cox and Handler apparently originated the idea of the War Refugee Board. Certainly Cox had been forcefully agitating for such an agency within the administration. Now was the time to marry Cox's plan to Treasury's initiative.[10]

One of Morgenthau's priorities was to remove Long from any responsibility for refugees and replace him with his trusted lieutenant John Pehle. But Morgenthau worried about Roosevelt. "Roosevelt wouldn't move on Hull, he never has; and Hull wouldn't move on Long," he told his staff. As long as you work for Roosevelt, you do not need an old-age pension, he told his staff; "he never fired anybody." Morgenthau's war council knew that Long was nervous. Long knew that FDR was sympathetic to Jewish refugees. He had approved the Transnistria license to Riegner because he was told Roosevelt favored it. When he learned of the Treasury Department's impending attack on his department, Long tried to cover his tracks. He sent a telegram to Winant expressing "astonishment" at the position of the Foreign Office. Long had misled the House Committee on Foreign Affairs in his testimony about refugees when it was considering a resolution to create a rescue agency. His "conscience bothers him terribly," White said. "He knows he is vulnerable, he knows the thing is dynamite, and that he might lose his job."[11]

On the other hand, Morgenthau's staff was concerned that their boss had poor command of the facts and that he might back down when he confronted Roosevelt. He changed the title of the report from "Acquiescence of the Government" to "A Personal Report to the President," but the contents were the same. Morgenthau's advisers recommended that the president issue an executive order to create a rescue board. They knew that Congress might act on the Irgunist rescue resolution if the president did not. The Senate Foreign Relations Committee had unanimously reported out a resolution calling for a rescue commission. However, Sol Bloom, chairman of the House Foreign Relations Committee, delayed the resolution because he viewed it as an Irgunist ploy, a slap in the face of the Bermuda Conference, and an attack on the president.[12]

Had Morgenthau not taken the lead when he did, it is doubtful the rescue agency proponents would have succeeded. Morgenthau's anger at the State Department was so intense that he was emboldened to go to Roosevelt, criticize State, and ask the president to act in a matter that FDR had avoided. "Some of these people have died because of inaction," Morgenthau told his staff. Cox had already been in touch with Jewish organizations, mainly the Joint, about funding the new board. "I checked with both organizations and individuals," he told Morgenthau, "and you won't have any question."[13]

On January 15, 1944, Cohen and Cox joined Morgenthau's staff in reviewing the political situation and the secretary's "Personal Report to the President" line by line and how to approach FDR. The report began: "One of the greatest crimes in history, the slaughter of the Jewish people in Europe, is continuing unabated." In nine pages, it detailed the procrastination, misrepresentation, suppression of facts, deliberate interference with rescue efforts, and antisemitism of State Department officials, especially Breckinridge Long. It set out in detail the obstruction of the French and Romanian licenses, the cover-up of the obstruction, and Long's concealment of the State Department cable that ordered the suppression of information about the Holocaust. "Indifferent, callous, and perhaps even hostile" officials could not rescue the Jews from extermination, the report concluded. The preface made it clear that, in Feingold's words, the information in the report "had all the earmarks of a nasty political scandal." Cox urged Morgenthau to tell Hull "you need a new deal on this thing." Morgenthau agreed that the issue had become "a boiling pot on the Hill."[14]

Rosenman undoubtedly briefed FDR prior to his meeting with Morgenthau. Cox and Cohen also were one step ahead of Morgenthau. Cox had been urging the rescue commission since June 1943. He sent a draft of a press release and executive order to Morgenthau on December 20, 1943. He pressed Morgenthau again in late December. Cox's assistant, Milton Handler, and Ben Cohen drafted the legal documents. Cox also sent a draft to Rosenman. Cox knew on January 15 that Stettinius had already talked to the president about the idea of a rescue agency while Hull was in Moscow. "The President thought it was fine," according to Cox.[15]

Ben Cohen reminded Morgenthau's Treasury Department staff that it was a political year and "all the politicians were trying to explain the value of minority groups"—that is, Republicans were appealing to Jewish voters and that this factor "which you don't want to put in the memorandum" [to FDR] would influence the president. Cox also pointed out that "in terms of the president that is basic here . . . is you also have . . . a domestic political problem."[16]

Roosevelt met Morgenthau, Pehle, and Paul for twenty minutes on January 16, 1944. The president preferred to hear a summary, not to read the report. He was unwell but listened attentively. Morgenthau stated that he was deeply disturbed when Pehle revealed the details of the State Department's deceptions. All three accused the department of failing to prevent the extermination of Jews. They had hidden their "gross procrastination" behind window dressing such as "intergovernmental organizations" and had suppressed reports on German atrocities. Congress was presently debating the Irgunist-inspired Rescue Resolution, and if the State Department's actions became public, a "nasty scandal" could ensue.[17]

The president was impressed. The implications of an election-year scandal were certainly not lost on the president. He agreed to create the agency and talked about getting refugees into Turkey, Spain, and Switzerland. He suggested that Morgenthau consult Stettinius who would be sympathetic, and he wanted Rosenman, the Jewish adviser Roosevelt most trusted, to be involved. The president was not inclined to believe that Long wanted to stop effective action but that he had "soured" on the problem when Rabbi Wise led him to approve entrance of a long list of "bad" people into the country. The president gave Morgenthau's plan his blessing. Long would no longer supervise refugee matters at State.

Compared to other political battles of the moment, it was an easy decision. The war was being won; the climate of both congressional and public opinion on helping Jews was changing; the efforts of the Emergency Committee publicized the plight of Hitler's victims; a potential political scandal could be averted; all of his close Jewish advisers favored the idea; and the president's July 23, 1943, meeting with Jan Karski may have influenced his thinking. John Pehle, the first director of the War Refugee Board, believed that Karski had shocked the president with his credible firsthand account of the crematoriums and that this information had changed his attitude. He "at once asked for the creation of the American Refugee Board," according to Karski. Cox said that Roosevelt favored such a body even before the rescue resolution was introduced in Congress. In any event, Roosevelt had no desire to sidestep the rescue issue now that *Congress* would not stand in the way, as it had previously, over the mere possibility of Jewish refugees entering the United States.[18]

DuBois had told Morgenthau, "If it means anything and if you want to, you can tell the president if he doesn't take any action on this report, I'm going to resign and release the report to the press." Henry Morgenthau III believed that his father's tactic was "to play up the politically explosive nature of the problem." The Personal Report, he noted, retained all the implications in the original report "that a nasty political scandal was in the offing."[19]

FDR's health was deteriorating in January 1944. He was sick when he returned from Teheran. Roosevelt said he was suffering from the flu or the grippe, but Rosenman missed the "rescue" meeting at Morgenthau's home because he had to meet with the president, who had slept late because he was not well. "I'm worried about the boss," Rosenman told Morgenthau on January 15.[20]

On January 22, 1944, while World War II was far from over, the president issued Executive Order 9417 to establish a War Refugee Board (WRB), consisting of the secretaries of treasury, state, and war. The order declared, "It is the policy of this government to take all measures within its power to rescue victims of enemy oppression in imminent danger of death" and to provide "relief and assistance consistent with the successful prosecution of the war." Congressman Celler wrote to congratulate Roosevelt on January 25, 1944. "Your glorious action has cleared the atmosphere. It is like a bolt of lightning dispelling the storm."[21]

Morgenthau's tough-minded assistant, John Pehle, was named acting director and later director. The president gave one million dollars from his emergency fund to operate the board and permitted private (i.e., Jewish) organizations to contribute funds. Despite the rescue resolution then in the House, everyone knew Congress would not appropriate a single dime. "The last thing I think you want to do is go to Congress," Pehle told his staff. In May the WRB received an additional four million dollars, which it shared with the IGCR. In all, twenty million dollars were donated by private groups for rescue efforts, fifteen million of it by the Joint.[22]

The WRB was a sincere, forceful demonstration that Americans were parting company with the British on the rescue issue and would henceforth do all they could to save European Jewry. "The board," Morgenthau wrote in 1947, "was made up of crusaders, passionately persuaded of the need for speed and action." The WRB developed plans for the rescue, transportation, and relief of Hitler's victims. It had authority to establish temporary havens and to enlist the cooperation of foreign governments. It had the enthusiastic support of Secretary Morgenthau, who, in turn, had the president's endorsement.[23]

FDR expected the WRB to do its best to rescue European

Jewry, and he ordered the military to cooperate. On February 11, 1944, staff officers met in the secretary of war's conference room to write a cable to theater commanders concerning the WRB's function. One officer argued against sending the cable lest it create confusion among the commanders. He asserted that nothing more could be done for the Jews than what was being done through army civil affairs. "We are over there to win the war and not to take care of refugees," the officer asserted. "The President doesn't think so," Colonel Harrison A. Gerhardt, assistant secretary of war and John McCloy's executive assistant, replied. "He thinks relief is a part of winning the war."[24]

It was never contemplated that the WRB would use military force to rescue Jews. The president's executive order charged the WRB to rescue those in imminent danger of death "consistent with the successful prosecution of the war." The president knew that the American people would support efforts to rescue Jews as long as victory was not delayed and the lives of American servicemen were not expended on any goal but the earliest possible Allied victory. Pehle informed the British that "it is not contemplated that combat units will be employed in rescue operations unless the rescues are the direct result of military operations." Indeed, General George Marshall and the Joint Chiefs of Staff had a standing policy to reject any and all civilian rescue operations.[25]

Those who resisted America's active involvement in rescuing European Jewry continued to believe that such a mission was detrimental to the war effort. "That Jew Morgenthau and his Jewish assistants like DuBois are trying to take over this place," the powerful State Department official James Dunn exclaimed, even though DuBois was a Protestant. Despite such sentiments, the State Department issued cables explaining the mission of the WRB and the change in American policy. "You should do everything possible to effectuate this policy," the instructions informed embassies and missions, "bearing in mind that time is of the essence." The War Department issued similar instructions. The State Department telegrams effectively changed "the whole government policy," according to Pehle.[26]

While the Irgunists felt that they had forced FDR to create the WRB, the British believed the scheme was a political ploy to garner New York votes in the 1944 presidential election. They were embarrassed by it. Anthony Eden wrote to a cabinet committee that the WRB was formed to placate "the large Jewish vote" and to spike "the guns of Congress." Long thought the creation of the WRB "a good move" because "there are four million Jews in New York and its environs who feel themselves related to the refugees and because of the persecution of the Jews, who have been demanding special attention and treatment." It was clear that failing to mention the Jews by name had not worked. The WRB changed that policy. Only the Jews had been singled out for extermination, and only the Jews had no nation to protect them. The WRB sought and soon obtained a tough presidential declaration condemning the genocide, promising American aid, and threatening American retribution. The British could stew in their own juices. The Soviets, of course, never lifted a finger to rescue one Jew, but millions of Jews were saved by being behind the Soviet front lines.[27]

Powerful elements in the administration fought the WRB. R. Borden Reams warned that the Germans would claim that the Allies were fighting for the Jews. Others asserted that the WRB's activities would result in more Jewish deaths. But Morgenthau stayed the course. Myron Taylor, of the IGCR, tried to derail the WRB, believing it encroached on his committee's territory. But he retreated in the face of Morgenthau's strong support of the rescue agency. Everyone knew, or quickly learned, where Roosevelt stood.[28]

Meeting of War Refugee Board: Secretary of State Cordell Hull, Secretary of the Treasury Henry Morgenthau, Jr., Secretary of War Henry Stimson, and John Pehle, Director of the War Refugee Board, Washington, D.C., March 21, 1944.

Hungary became a major battleground of the Holocaust. Germany invaded its now nominal ally Hungary on March 19, 1944, in part because the Hungarians were making peace overtures to the West and in part to exterminate the largest surviving Jewish population in Europe, about 750,000 people. Morgenthau convinced Roosevelt to issue a strong statement written by the WRB staff, on March 24, which denounced the "systematic torture and murder of civilians in Europe and in Asia."

> *In one of the blackest crimes of all history—begun by the Nazis in the day of peace and multiplied by them a hundred times in time of war—the wholesale systematic murder of the Jews of Europe goes on unabated every hour. As a result of the events of the last few days hundreds of thousands of Jews, who while living under persecution have at least found a haven from death in Hungary and the Balkans, are now threatened with annihilation as Hitler's forces descend more heavily upon these lands. That these innocent people, who have already survived a decade of Hitler's fury, should perish on the very eve of triumph over the barbarism which their persecution symbolized, would be a major tragedy.*[29]

Roosevelt again promised swift punishment of the Nazis. "The United Nations has made it clear," he said, "that they will pursue the guilty and deliver them up in order that Justice be done. It is therefore fitting that we should again proclaim our determination that none who participate in these acts of savagery shall go unpunished." That warning applied not only to the leaders but also to their subordinates in Germany and in the satellite countries. "All who knowingly take part in the deportation of Jews to their death in Poland or Norwegians and French to their death in Germany are equally guilty with the executioner. All who share the guilt shall share the punishment." He urged the German people to show the world by their actions that in their hearts they did not share Hitler's "insane criminal desires." He urged those under Nazi rule to conceal Hitler's victims. Roosevelt also asked them to "record the evidence, to convict the guilty." He called on "the free people of Europe and Asia" to temporarily open their frontiers to the victims of oppression. "We shall find havens of refuge for them, and we shall find the means for their maintenance and support until the tyrant is driven from their homelands and they return."[30]

"Roosevelt Warns Germans on Jews," read the front-page headline in the *New York Times* on March 25, 1944. "Says All Guilty Must Pay for Atrocities and Asks People to Assist Refugees."[32] The president's statement was widely disseminated in many languages throughout Europe. It circulated through underground channels, neutral radio stations, and newspapers across Axis Europe. Copies were dropped by air over Hungary and other occupied countries. The BBC broadcast it. The statement may very well have encouraged German officials and officers to slow down the killings or consider Hitler's overthrow.[32]

FDR was pleased with Pehle's handling of the WRB. On March 7, 1944, Roosevelt told Morgenthau that he was trying to persuade the British to state publicly that they would let Jewish survivors immigrate to Palestine. He said, "They don't want to change the white paper, but I want to get them to say publicly, if I am successful through the Refugee Committee in bringing any Jews out of Europe, [that] they will let them go to Palestine. . . . I want them to mention Palestine by name." A few minutes later he told Morgenthau, "You know, the Arabs don't like this thing." Morgenthau kept the president apprised of the activities of the WRB. On March 11, 1944, he sent Roosevelt a "very encouraging cable from Mr. Ira Hirschmann in Ankara. . . . Things at last are beginning to move."[33] Eden continued to blame American domestic politics and Roosevelt's humanitarianism for WRB activities that raised prospects of more immigration to Palestine. For that reason the Foreign Office even opposed the issuance of another United Nations declaration condemning the extermination of the Jews. Another British diplomat wrote that the creation of the WRB was the result of Jewish pressure and "first-rate importance" of New York in the presidential election.[34]

While the establishment of the War Refugee Board renewed the hopes of Jewish groups, the possibility of rescuing Jews remained slight. By January 1944, two million Jews had been killed at Chelmno, Belzec, Treblinka, and Sobibor. A total of five million were already dead. Factories near Birkenau, part of the Auschwitz complex, gave the impression that the entire camp was a slave labor facility, when in fact it was the most gruesome of all the Nazi death camps.[35]

The WRB was in constant communication with Jewish groups

of all viewpoints and facilitated communications overseas by cable between Jewish groups. Representatives of the World Jewish Congress held regular meetings with WRB staff members. The WJC files at the American Jewish Archives are filled with letters to a variety of WRB staffers and memorandums of numerous meetings. The same is true for the Joint, the Irgunists, and the Orthodox organization Agudat Israel and Vaad Hatzalah. Jewish leaders discussed and debated many proposals with WRB staffers. For example, Jewish leaders discussed a proposal to have the United States proclaim that all Jews remaining in Europe be protected as far as their safety was concerned and that any infringement upon this safety be dealt with as if American citizens were concerned. WRB staff member Lawrence Lesser pointed out that such warnings to the Germans had had no effect on the mistreatment of actual Jewish-American citizens in Hungary who had been purposely removed to places exposed to Allied bombings and killed as a result of such bombings.[36]

The WRB worked diligently to save Jewish lives. Morgenthau believed it was instrumental in helping thousands of Jews escape through the Balkans in 1944 and 1945, in ferrying refugees across the Baltic to Sweden, and in negotiations with Himmler to get several trainloads of refugees out of Germany. The WRB, he wrote, "did a good deal to redeem before the world the moral position the United States lost through the procrastination and worse of the delinquent officials in the State Department." Writing in 1947, Morgenthau's claims for the success of the WRB were modest. He blamed the State Department for the failure to rescue "thousands of Hitler's victims," not hundreds of thousands. "The hope . . . was to get a few of them out—a few women, perhaps a few children." The board itself, in its official history, claimed to have rescued "tens of thousands."[37]

Roosevelt kept pressure on the British to admit more Jewish refugees into Palestine and to help others to escape. In May he ordered Robert Murphy to see that "as many [Jews] as possible" were sent to Palestine. Also in May, at Morgenthau's request, Roosevelt personally rescinded an army restriction forbidding military assistance to stateless refugees (mainly Jews) crossing the Adriatic to occupied Italy. The WRB persuaded the State Department to change its visa policy to encourage other nations, notably Latin American countries, to honor fraudulent passports previously issued to Jewish refugees still alive in concentration camps. It convinced the State Department to honor lapsed visas of those in enemy-controlled territory.

After the Normandy invasion, the board lobbied General Eisenhower to issue a statement warning the Nazis not to exterminate camp inmates. Roosevelt approved a draft warning Germans not to harm civilians "whether they were Jewish or otherwise." Eisenhower amended the language to "no matter what their religion or nationality may be."[38] The final statement from the Allies' supreme commander was simple and crystal clear:

Germans! You have in your midst a great many men
in concentration camps and forced labor battalions.
Germans! Do not obey any orders, regardless of their

*source, urging you to molest, harm or persecute them,
no matter what their religion or nationality may be.*

*The Allies, whose armies have already established a
firm foothold in Germany, expect, on their advance, to
find these people alive and unharmed. Heavy punishment awaits those who, directly or indirectly, and to
whatever extent, bear any responsibility for the mistreatment of these people.*

*May this serve as a warning to whoever at present
has the power to issue orders.*

The WRB worked to help refugees escape from danger, and
once they had escaped to move them out of harm's way to neutral
countries such as Spain, Portugal, and Turkey. In Hungary the War
Refugee Board worked with the governments of Sweden and
Switzerland in a major rescue effort. In early March, with many in
the Hungarian government seeking a way out of the war, the WRB
convinced the U.S. government to warn Hungary that its participation in "Hitlerite persecutions" was viewed "with great serious-
ness." Roosevelt mentioned Hungary by name in his March 24
statement.[39]

Hitler, however, was determined to kill as many Jews as possible no matter what the Allies said or did. On March 19, Germany took over the Hungarian government and sent Adolf
Eichmann to Budapest to bring the Final Solution to Hungary. The
WRB broadcast Roosevelt's March 24 statement into Hungary and
dropped leaflets by airplane. On May 27, Roosevelt warned that

"Hungary's fate will not be like that of any other civilized nation . . . unless the deportations are stopped."[40] Members of Congress and clergy issued public warnings. But the German leadership was so obsessed with killing Jews that deportations from Drancy in France, 150 miles from the battlefield, occurred three weeks after the Normandy invasion.[41]

The United States again demanded that Hungary recognize passports of dubious legality previously issued (or sold) by Latin American diplomats. At the board's instigation, the Swedish government sent a native Swede, the businessman Raoul Wallenberg, to Budapest to rescue Jews by bribing officials with funds provided by the Joint. The board urged the Vatican to speak out.

On July 14, 1944, Secretary of State Hull declared:

> *The number of victims of these fiendish crimes is great. The entire Jewish community in Hungary, which numbered nearly 1,000,000 souls, is threatened with extermination.*
>
> *The horror and indignation felt by the American people at these cold-blooded tortures and massacres has been voiced by the President, by the Congress and by hundreds of private organizations throughout the country.*
>
> *It may be futile to appeal to the humanity of the instigators or perpetrators of such outrages. Let them know that they cannot escape the inexorable punishment which will be meted out to them when the power*

of the evil men now in control of Hungary has been broken.

"Hull Again Scores Nazi 'Massacres' " read the headline in the *New York Times* of July 15, 1944. "Punishment Is Certain for 'Savage Crimes' in Hungary and Greece, He Declares."[42]

Christian Americans of Hungarian descent held a special service and protest in the Bronx against the persecution of Jews in Hungary. Both Protestant and Catholic Hungarian Americans protested in New York, Chicago, Milwaukee and other cities. These protests were rebroadcast to Hungary by the Office of War Information, as was the message of Archbishop Francis J. Spellman, which unequivocally denounced the massacres as contrary to Christian doctrine.[43]

Germany was losing the war, and Admiral Horthy worried about Soviet occupation and Allied retribution. Deportations from Budapest were delayed, but Hitler held the German forces and Fascist collaborators in Hungary firm. On June 16, the United States had confronted the Hungarian government with its responsibility for the "infamous treatment visited upon the Jews," questioned it about future treatment, and reiterated in the words of the official WRB history, "the grave view which this Government took regarding the persecution of Jews and other minorities." The WRB requested neutral nations to inform Germany and Hungary that the United States would accept all Jews allowed to emigrate.[44]

The British reluctantly agreed to cooperate "to the extent of British resources" and publicly joined with the United States in its declaration, while secretly demanding that the United States not insist that Britain take in Jewish refugees or permit them to go to Palestine. The United States took most of the responsibility for finding places of refuge. Thousands of visas were authorized for children and Hungarian relatives of American citizens, but the Germans and their Hungarian collaborators refused to allow the Jews to escape. Wallenberg issued Swedish protective papers and, with the help of Swiss and Red Cross representatives, may have saved as many as seventy thousand Jews. The massive Soviet summer and fall offensive, Operation Bagration, which began on the third anniversary of Barbarossa, stunned the Germans. Belorussia and much of Poland were liberated. The Romanians were desperate to quit the war. On August 23, King Michael had Ian Antonescu arrested and announced that Romania was switching sides. The Jews of neighboring Hungary might soon be saved. Therefore in the fall of 1944, the Germans made strenuous efforts to kill the Jews of Budapest. They were losing the war, however, and miraculously because of the Soviet and Anglo-American offensives, many of the Jews of that city survived.[45]

The WRB facilitated the movement of refugees to safer areas. If reliable temporary havens could be established for those who had already escaped the Holocaust, perhaps Turkey, Spain, liberated Italy, and other countries could be persuaded to take in more refugees. Morgenthau's "Treasury boys" and the Irgunists agitated for temporary American havens, and the WRB staff worked hard to create them.[46]

While the WRB staff and rescue advocates favored temporary

refugee camps on American soil, neither board members nor the president shared their enthusiasm. Americans were not fighting and dying in the deadliest war in American history to bring tens of thousands of Jewish refugees to America. Indeed, opposition to allowing more refugees into the United States did not abate. In 1943, when Breckinridge Long testified that 580,000 refugees had come into the country, the *Chicago Tribune* subtitled its report: " 'Open Door' Policy Bared; Quotas Disregarded." Secretary of War Stimson saw the proposal for refugee camps as extremely controversial and had a long talk with Pehle about it. In Stimson's view Congress would never permit Jewish refugees to immigrate in large numbers, given the "long history of the Jewish problem in this country." Morgenthau and congressional leaders recognized the controversy such a proposal would generate and the political impossibility of altering the immigration laws. Little had changed in the minds of many Americans since the immigration legislation of 1924 and the Smith Act of 1940.[47]

In April and May 1944, Roosevelt acted with customary caution. The secret D-Day invasion was fast approaching, and he was totally focused on it. He was unwilling to risk any adverse effect on morale and exacerbate his battered relationship with a Congress ever jealous of its prerogatives with regard to immigration laws. He was, however, willing to test the political waters with one refugee facility provided it was, or appeared to be, justified by a real emergency. That emergency conveniently materialized in occupied Italy, where the Allies encountered a flood of refugees. FDR personally lobbied for an experimental haven in the United States, calling congressional leaders of both parties to the White House. He publicly applauded the idea of "free ports"—places where refugees, like goods in transit, could be housed before being sent back overseas after the war.

On June 8, two days after the Normandy invasion, Roosevelt approved creation of the Oswego Emergency Refugee Shelter in a muted letter of instruction. The name itself emphasized the temporary nature of the project. But Roosevelt was enthusiastic. "Fort Ontario is my camp," he told Morgenthau and Pehle. "I know the fort very well. It goes back to before Civil War times and is a very excellent place." Four days later, Roosevelt explained the Oswego experiment to Congress and promised that the refugees would return home after the war. "As the hour of the final defeat of the Hitlerite forces draws closer, the fury of their insane desire to wipe out the Jewish race in Europe continues undiminished," he told Congress. In praise of the WRB, he said that it had "succeeded in saving the lives of innocent people" and "brought new hope to the oppressed peoples of Europe." But he was candid in explaining the reality of the situation.

> *Notwithstanding this Government's unremitting efforts, which are continuing, the numbers actually rescued from the jaws of death have been small compared with the numbers still facing extinction in German territory. This is due principally to the fact that our enemies, despite all our appeals and our willingness to find havens of refuge for the oppressed peoples, persist in*

their fiendish extermination campaign and actively pre-
vent the intended victims from escaping to safety.[48]

The Oswego camp received 982 refugees in August 1944. FDR exercised caution in operating the shelter. The refugees would not be granted visas; they were treated as temporary internees, not as immigrants; immigration laws would be respected; and the army would see to it that there were no escapes. The camp would house mostly women and children, he said.[49]

The Oswego experiment was a failure. The refugees were unhappy, bitter, and quarrelsome. Many did not realize that they would be housed like prisoners in a barracks behind a guarded fence. Logistical problems were myriad: uncomfortable lodging, extremely cold weather, employment issues, schools for children, emotional problems among refugees, religious divisions between Orthodox and secular Jews and between Jews of different nationalities. In addition, demands from the refugees and their supporters that they be "released," despite Roosevelt's contrary assurance to Congress, wrecked the experiment. The idea that refugees who had escaped the Holocaust and had been free in Italy would return to internment, living behind a barbed-wire fence in a freezing cold New York town, proved to be unrealistic. Congress took no action on bills proposing additional camps or free ports.[50]

Despite his customary caution, the president was much criticized for attempting to circumvent the immigration laws, for misleading Congress on the male/female ratio of refugees, and for bringing Communists and intellectuals instead of "laboring men" to the United States. On June 14, 1944, Senator Robert R. Reynolds wrote the attorney general inquiring "as to just what ground the President based his authority . . . permitting refugees or anyone else to enter this country outside of our quotas or in violation of our present immigration statutes." Antisemites wrote bitter letters to FDR and Morgenthau. Even the editors of *Life* magazine were shaken by nasty mail in response to a photo story on the arrival of the Oswego refugees. Liberals, on the other hand, thought the Roosevelt administration too stingy. The leftist author and editor, Isadore F. Stone, called Oswego "a kind of token payment to decency, a bargain-counter flourish in humanitarianism."[51]

Meanwhile, the WRB had to contend with unhappy refugees demanding privileges and exceptions that the administration dared not grant. Roosevelt was well aware of the widespread opposition to releasing the internees. On January 17, 1945, he wrote a note to Attorney General Francis Biddle that declared that he wanted the refugees to remain at Oswego as promised and to return to Europe as soon as the journey could safely be arranged.

Unhappy as they were with their situation, the Oswego refugees shared with most American Jews the belief that Roosevelt's heart was in the right place. They realized at the time that he had much bigger problems than housing refugees who had escaped the Nazis and that he was in "a deadly Zoroastrian battle with evil incarnate." After the war, the inmates remained in America after all.[52]

Chapter 19

"What Is the Job before Us in 1944?"
D-Day and a Dying President

The year 1944 is loaded with danger.
—Churchill to FDR, October 27, 1943

O f all the political issues before Congress in early 1944, few were as divisive as a proposed bill permitting soldiers to vote in federal elections by absentee ballot when their home state laws did not provide the ballots. Southerners feared that black soldiers, disfranchised in their home states, would be able to vote in federal elections. Representative John Rankin of Mississippi blamed the bill on Communists and Jews. He called Walter Winchell a "little kike," to the applause of many colleagues. Republicans wanted FDR to pledge not to run for reelection. The soldiers' votes would have guaranteed his victory. The bill, as envisioned by FDR, failed.[1]

The tax bill was equally divisive. In February Roosevelt proposed a bill that would have heavily taxed "unreasonable" profits. When Congress ignored him and enacted a bill more to the liking of big-business interests, Roosevelt vetoed it in searing language. He said that the bill provided relief "not for the needy but for the greedy." The next day "hell broke out in the Senate." Senator Alben Barkley of Kentucky, the Democratic majority leader and Roosevelt's loyal friend, was irate. He lambasted the House bill and resigned as majority leader. He was immediately reelected and the president's veto held firm in the Senate, but the fight left much bitterness.[2]

Many Americans believed the war would soon end. Roosevelt did not. The Italian campaign was not going well. The surprise landing at Anzio Beach on January 22, 1944, succeeded, but the invasion bogged down at a cost of many American lives. To American GIs, Italy was "an endless road of sticky mud dotted with minefields . . . mountain crags filled with almost inaccessible gun pits; murky, freezing rivers." The Italian stalemate continued through April. "We have got a long, long road to go," FDR said in March 1944. "We are going to win the war—it is going to take an awfully long time." Berlin was bombed in daylight raids as American warplanes struck ball-bearing plants and other military targets. In late February the Eighth Air Force launched "Big Week," a seven-day bombing campaign that destroyed 70 percent of Germany's aircraft plants.[3]

The Germans held on tenaciously in Italy even as the Russians neared Romania. In a March 30 raid on Nuremberg, the RAF suffered its worst losses of the war. Ninety-six of 795 aircraft and one in ten American aircraft were lost in daylight raids over Berlin. The Germans retaliated by bombing London well into 1944. Amid this desperate carnage, training exercises began for D-Day. Allied raids over France were choreographed to convince the Germans that the invasion would take place at Calais, not Normandy.[4]

Roosevelt and Churchill worried about Hitler's new secret weapons. The Führer had given the highest priority to his "pilot-less airplanes," the V-1 and V-2 rockets. The Germans invented these first modern missiles in a desperate attempt to achieve a stalemate. Hitler's team of scientists, including Wernher von Braun, labored to develop missiles capable of attacking the United States. German rockets attacked England in June 1944 with heavy loss of life and property. The Allies bombed every suspected rocket facility they could locate, including ski sites in France. Eisenhower worried that if the Germans rocket-bombed the Portsmouth-Southampton area, the Normandy invasion might have to be scotched.[5]

The Russian military juggernaut moved relentlessly westward. In late January 1944, the Red Army broke the Leningrad blockade. In February, they reached Estonia, and, by March, the Bug River in Poland and the Dniester. They liberated Odessa in April and recaptured Sevastopol the next month. Bombing raids over France and the Netherlands in May paved the way for D-Day.

Roosevelt's hard-nosed attitude toward Germany never wavered. The Joint Chiefs of Staff asked him to retreat from his stand on unconditional surrender. Nazi propagandists were stiffening the German people's will to fight by claiming that the Allies were bent on extinguishing their nation. Roosevelt replied in March 1944, "I am not willing at this time to say that we do not intend to destroy the German nation." He detested German militarism and would root it out if it took two generations. There would be no Third World War caused by Germany. To some degree, Roosevelt's harsh attitude may have been affected by the agony of Jews.[6]

Roosevelt's health had seriously deteriorated by March 1944. He was constantly tired. At times he had difficulty concentrating and even breathing. He nodded off in meetings and had to work fewer hours each day. On March 28 military doctors diagnosed his advanced cardiovascular disease, hypertension, and high blood pressure. Dr. Howard G. Bruenn later said that the president's condition was "God-awful." The doctors prescribed digitalis, which undoubtedly extended Roosevelt's life, but the drug was new and the doctors were concerned about damaging his heart with an overdose. The president had to rest and avoid stress.[7]

His doctors recommended a vacation. On April 8 Roosevelt repaired to Hobcaw Barony, Bernard Baruch's plantation in low-country South Carolina, where he rested for twenty-eight days. He returned to Washington on May 6. "I had a really grand time at Bernie's," Roosevelt wrote Harry Hopkins. FDR knew he had a serious illness and agreed to limit his activities when he returned to Washington. His new schedule consisted of two hours for appointments from 11:00 A.M. to 1:00 P.M. and two hours after lunch for paperwork. His medical condition was carefully hidden from the public.

Franklin Roosevelt was no longer the vigorous leader of the New Deal years. He was a dying man surrounded by a protective staff. Ben Cohen and Sam Rosenman were very concerned about the president's health. Cohen urged Roosevelt to forgo a fourth term. Democratic Party bosses adamantly opposed Vice President Henry Wallace's renomination because the next vice president might very well become president. Wallace was so unpopular that his presence on the ticket might defeat the Democrats. The true state of Roosevelt's health remained one of the best-kept secrets of World War II.[8]

Roosevelt's illness did not shield him from the dramas unfolding in 1944. In April Sewell Avery, president of Montgomery Ward and inveterate opponent of the New Deal, refused to honor contracts with the federal government that required a minimum wage and recognition of labor unions. Because a slowdown in the production of goods threatened the war effort, Roosevelt ordered the army to take over the company. The company chairman was carried from his office by soldiers with rifles and fixed bayonets. The event was front-page news and engendered howls of protest over Roosevelt's dictatorial behavior. Most Americans, however, approved.

Roosevelt returned rested from Hobcaw on May 7, 1944. Harry Hopkins was in the hospital. His eighteen-year old son, Stephen, a marine, had been killed in the Marshall Islands in February. The death of young Hopkins devastated Roosevelt, who soon faced one of the greatest ordeals of his life, D-Day and the Normandy invasion. Everyone, ER recalled, lived "suspended in space, waiting for the invasion, dreading it and yet wishing it could begin successfully." Her husband, the man who had pledged the "utter destruction" of Hitler and Nazism, braced himself for the climax of the global war he had led.[9]

Hitler knew the cross-Channel invasion was imminent. At one point he accurately predicted its location, but he would be ready everywhere along the French coast. He assigned his best general, Erwin Rommel, to lead the defense of Fortress Europa. Sixty divisions, many combat-hardened, stood ready to throw back the Allied invasion. Beaches were fortified with steel piles, wooden stakes, mines, and barbed wire. The Atlantic Wall boasted reinforced bunkers and myriad artillery. Hitler knew the wall was "the most decisive factor that there is" and had demanded construction of 15,000 permanent defensive positions by the spring of 1943. By July 1944 the Germans had poured 17.6 million cubic meters of concrete on the coasts of Holland, Belgium, and France. Hitler believed Roosevelt would be defeated in the November election and, "with luck, would finish up somewhere in jail."[10]

According to Carlo D'Este, the Normandy invasion was the most massive and complex military operation ever conceived. It embraced the largest fleet ever assembled—6,483 vessels of all kinds, including landing craft. "The destinies of two great empires," Churchill said with a growl, "seem to be tied up in some Goddamned things called LSTs." It was the largest combined operation of the war and the greatest amphibious invasion in history. Could the Americans and the British defeat Hitler's seasoned army? Could the Führer's Fortress Europa be successfully invaded? One American military historian later wrote that there was one big question "whether we could make it against the big leagues. Till then we'd been fooling around the periphery. Now we were going into the center of things. Beneath the bravado, there was an under-current of concern, even fear."[11] There was, Steven Casey wrote in *Cautious Crusade* (2001) "an alarming increase in support for a negotiated peace" if the German army overthrew Hitler. The failure and cost of the Italian campaign did not bode well for a cross-channel invasion.

Roosevelt had planned to be in England on D-Day. "Our friend-ship is my greatest standby amid the ever-increasing complications of this exacting war," Churchill wrote FDR on June 4. "How I wish you were here." But the president's health would not permit him to travel. Instead, he went to the home of his aide General Edwin "Pa" Watson, in Charlottesville, Virginia, to prepare a speech. Eleanor remained in Washington. "I feel as though a sword were hanging over my head, dreading its fall and yet knowing it must fall to end the war," she wrote him. The invasion, set for June 4, was post-poned due to bad weather. The Allies captured Rome on June 4, 1944. Roosevelt returned to Washington, calm and collected. He had learned from his bout with polio, ER recalled, "that if there was nothing you could do about a situation, then you'd better try to put it out of your mind and go on with your work at hand."[12]

Allied soldiers stormed the beaches of Normandy on June 6. Americans awoke to "the most exciting moment in our lives," according to Fiorello LaGuardia, and "the hour for which we were born," according to the *New York Times*. But beneath the elation lay widespread dread of enormous casualties and defeat. Roosevelt spoke to the American people over the radio. He prayed for "our sons, pride of our nation. . . . Give strength to their arms, stoutness to their hearts, steadfastness in their faith. They will need Thy blessings. Their road will be long and hard, for the enemy is strong. He may hurl back our forces. Success may not come with rushing speed, but we shall return again and again."[13] General Eisenhower was so concerned about possible failure that he prepared beforehand a statement in case the operation failed:

> *Our landings in the Cherbourg-Havre area have failed to gain a satisfactory foothold and I have withdrawn the troops. My decision to attack at this time and place was based upon the best information available. The troops, the air and navy did all that bravery and devotion to duty could do. If there is any blame or fault attached to the attempt, it is mine alone.*[14]

The German defense was tenacious. "The news couldn't be better," Hitler said, "As long as they were in Britain we couldn't get at them. Now we have them where we can destroy them." But Allied naval firepower and airpower were overwhelming. "You used the word 'stupendous,' " Churchill wired FDR. "I must admit that what I saw could only be described by that word."

Roosevelt was exhausted and depressed in the weeks following D-Day. "I cannot live out a normal life span," he told Eleanor. "I can't even walk across the room to get my circulation going." He talked to Sam Rosenman about a small memorial in Washington to him after he died and to Grace Tully about Margaret Suckley,

The Normandy Invasion. Chaplain Meyer holds Jewish services on board Ancon, flagship of Force "O," in early June.

Courtesy of the National Archives

his favorite cousin, taking care of his dog, Fala, after his death. James Roosevelt found his father autographing books and assembling mementos for his children and grandchildren. "His mind," Doris Kearns Goodwin observed, "seemed preoccupied with intimations of death."[15]

The Normandy invasion succeeded, but at a slower pace than its planners had hoped. Rommel's troops fought bravely, and German tanks proved superior to the Allies'. One thousand American bombers and another thousand fighter escorts raided Berlin on June 21. The Germans held Cherbourg until June 26. July and August brought Allied victories, but at a heavy price. Caen fell on July 9. The famous fight for Saint-Lô demonstrated continued Nazi determination to resist. The Red Army advanced into Poland and Belorussia. But a massive V-1 rocket attack on London killed nearly three thousand people, and the advance in France was slowed by terrain unfriendly to armored divisions. The Lufwaffe downed thirty B-24 Liberator and four fighters over Leipzig on July 7.[16]

Because Britain postponed general elections during World War II, Churchill did not have to answer to the electorate until the war was over. But in the United States, where the Constitution mandated a presidential election every four years, Roosevelt ran for a fourth term with a global war raging and in a domestic atmosphere filled with economic discord, racial strife, and bitter personal animosity toward him. He faced Republican Thomas E. Dewey, the uncharismatic forty-two-year-old governor of New York.

Roosevelt sought a fourth term to see the war through to the end. "All that is within me cries out to go back to my home on the Hudson River," he wrote his supporters, "but the future existence of the nation and the future existence of our chosen government are at stake." He threw open the nomination for vice president because he did not have the strength to face a replay of the controversy of 1940. To insist on keeping the left-wing Henry Wallace on the Democratic ticket might, he brooded, "kill our chances for election this fall and if it does it will prolong the war."[17]

His health precarious, suffering from terrible pain and fatigue,

Roosevelt accepted his party's nomination on July 21, but hid his medical condition from the electorate. In his acceptance speech he said, "What is the job before us in 1944? First, to win the war— to win the war fast, to win it overpoweringly." But his vigorous rhetoric was not matched by his physical strength. An Associated Press photograph of an exhausted president, his mouth open, his eyes glassy, flashed across the country. Republican newspapers ran it, enlarged, on the front page. After the death of one of his most trusted assistants, Missy LeHand, in late July, Roosevelt's health declined further. He suffered a major angina attack in the middle of a speech in August. On another occasion, in the company of his son James, his face turned white with pain. "Jimmy, I don't know if I can make it," he said with his eyes closed. Yet he went on to campaign for reelection.[18]

In August it seemed the war in Europe might end quickly. A group of German officers led by Klaus von Stauffenberg had tried but failed to assassinate Hitler on July 20. The Allies landed in the south of France on August 15 and raced up the Rhone Valley. Allied troops liberated Paris on August 25. In eighty days (June 6 to August 25) forty German divisions had been destroyed. "The joy that entered the hearts of all civilized men and women can only be measured by the gloom which settled there one June day four years ago when German troops occupied the French capital," Roosevelt told his fellow Americans.

The Red Army had entered Poland in July and was moving rapidly on the Eastern Front. Roosevelt was under enormous pressure from Polish Americans to ensure that Poland would be free from

Soviet domination. But Stalin's army controlled the ground, and Roosevelt had no power to alter the Communist chief's determination to rule Poland. According to the military historian Williamson Murray, for "all of August, well into mid-September 1944, it had appeared to Allied commanders that they were on the brink of bringing the war to a successful close." The "dizzying pace" of the Allied campaign "induced a kind of euphoria," Kennedy wrote. The invasion had "brought the end of the war in Europe in sight, almost within reach," one intelligence report claimed.[19]

Juggling military and civilian problems, Roosevelt dealt decisively with a strike of transportation workers in Philadelphia in August. In the midst of a global war about human freedom, a thousand white employees of the Philadelphia Transit Company walked off their jobs to protest the promotion of eight blacks to motormen. Because racial discrimination violated an executive order, the Fair Employment Practices Commission (FEPC) intervened. The strike paralyzed one of the nation's largest war-production centers. Roosevelt ordered the army to take over the company, operate the transit system, and break the strike.[20]

American antisemitism was at high tide. The voices of the far right were still heard. Roosevelt encouraged Attorney General Biddle to indict "the seditionists," and he complied. The leader of the Christian Mobilizers, Joseph E. McWilliams, who called Roosevelt the "Jew King," was indicted along with James True, who claimed to have patented a club he dubbed the "Kike Killer." But the extremists were not alone. A poll taken in 1945 showed that 58 percent of Americans believed Jews had too much power. In

1944, 24 percent believed that of all the ethnic, religious, or racial groups in America, the Jews were the greatest menace. Roving gangs of hoodlums, especially Irish Catholics, terrorized Jewish neighborhoods in Boston. Some conservative congressmen attacked Jews as Communists. Congressman John A. Flannagan of West Virginia stated on the floor of the House that he did not want "any Ginsberg" to lead his son in battle. Despite their solid military record, American Jews were accused of not fighting while urging others to go into battle for them.[21]

Throughout the summer and fall, Roosevelt was not only running for president but also working hard to create the future United Nations. Woodrow Wilson's humiliating failure over the League of Nations was always before him. He met Churchill and the combined chiefs again in Quebec in September. They had reasonable hope, based on intelligence, that the Germans would have to surrender by mid-December 1944. "Optimism was at its height," army historians noted. On September 28, some of General Omar Bradley's officers sent him a captured bronze bust of Hitler with a message: "With seven units of fire [seven days' supply of ammunition] and one additional division, First U.S. Army will deliver the original in thirty days." But it was not to be. The Germans still had too much fight in them. "German morale on this front," Eisenhower reluctantly acknowledged, "shows no sign of cracking." By late September it was clear there would be, in Bradley's words, "a bitter-end campaign."[22]

At this time, FDR discussed with Henry Morgenthau the latter's punitive postwar peace for Germany, which called for partition of the country, dismantling industry in the Ruhr and the Saar, binding the German economy to agriculture, and control of the German education system. The president concurred with Morgenthau that the German people must be taught a lesson they would never forget.[23] Roosevelt's hatred of Germans and Nazism did not mellow as the war continued. Roosevelt sent Stimson a memo on August 26 stating, "The German people as a whole must have driven home to them that the whole nation has been engaged in a lawless conspiracy against the decencies of modern civilization." In September Roosevelt told Stimson and McCloy that he was inclined to let the Germans eat from "soup kitchens."[24]

Rumors circulated about Roosevelt's precarious health, and Republicans were optimistic that they could defeat the "tired, old men" in Washington. Anti-Roosevelt newspapers emphasized his age and infirmities. But the champion of campaigners had one more race in him. He captivated audiences with his charm and wit. He lambasted Republicans as hypocrites. "We have all seen many marvelous stunts in the circus," he told a partisan labor union dinner in September, "but no performing elephant could turn a handspring without falling flat on its back." Not content with "attacks . . . on me, or my wife, or on my sons. No, not content with that," he chided Republicans, "they now include my little dog Fala." His audiences roared with laughter. "The old master still had it," *Time* reported. He campaigned in freezing rain at Brooklyn's Ebbets Field and in an open limousine driving through New York City to dispel charges that his health was too poor for him to govern.[25]

The campaign had a nasty undercurrent. Republicans seized on Roosevelt's relationship with Sidney Hillman, a high-profile New York Jewish labor leader with a left-wing background. In discussing Harry Truman's nomination as vice president, Roosevelt had allegedly said "Clear it with Sidney." The Republicans charged that everything had to be "cleared with Sidney," and "Clear Everything with Sidney" placards appeared at political rallies. "Communists are seizing control of the New Deal," Dewey charged. Roosevelt responded with ridicule and a defense of religious and ethnic tolerance. In the 1928 election, he told a Democratic crowd in Boston, "all the bigots . . . were gunning for Al Smith. . . . Today in this war . . . our fine boys are fighting magnificently all over the world and among those boys are the Murphys and the Kellys, the Smiths and the Joneses, the Cohens, the Carusos, the Kowalskis, the Schultzes."[26]

Roosevelt's age and health were the chief issues in the campaign. Dewey said the administration was run by "old, tired, and quarrelsome men . . . the most wasteful, extravagant, and incompetent" in history. But FDR used his remaining strength to make brilliant speeches outdoors in cold and rainy weather to prove he was strong enough to serve as president.[27]

Roosevelt's last campaign ended in victory, albeit the slimmest margin of victory of his four presidential elections. The scene at Hyde Park was familiar. The guests included the Morgenthaus and the Rosenmans among family, old friends, and supporters, except that John and FDR Jr. were in the Pacific, Elliott was in Europe, and Jimmy was in Hawaii. Roosevelt knew he had won by 11:00 P.M., but "the graceless Dewey" would not concede until 3:16 A.M. "I still think he is a son of a bitch," Roosevelt told his secretary William D. Hassett, on his way to bed.[28]

"The First Victims Would Be the Jews:" Why FDR Did Not Order the Bombing of Auschwitz

After the Normandy invasion in June 1944, the Allies were clearly winning the war, but the Jews of Europe were still in danger. The Anglo-Americans' inability to rescue European Jewry, even as their armies rolled toward Paris, resulted from the unwavering commitment of Adolf Hitler and the agencies of the Nazi government to kill as many Jews as possible before Germany was defeated, and the Soviet refusal to help the Jews in any way.[1]

Five million European Jews were dead by the summer of 1944. Treblinka, Sobibor, and Belzec, having finished their work, were closed, and special SS units were charged with covering up the crimes. But 750,000 Jews remained alive in Hungary. In March Hitler had occupied Hungary and replaced President Miklos Horthy with a pro-Nazi puppet government. In April the Nazis, led by Adolf Eichmann and aided by Hungarian collaborators, began to round up Hungarian Jews. "Hungary's Jewry has been struck," the WJC noted in its "Report on Rescue Problems," "with a suddenness, speed and ruthlessness of which there has been no parallel, even in our recent martyrology."

As these events unfolded, the Allied bomber offensive against Germany, Operation Pointblank, destroyed German oil storage depots, synthetic oil plants, and factories. In the spring of 1944 the Allies had secured the Italian air base at Foggia, Italy, which became home to hundreds of heavy bombers and fighter escorts. The USAAF finally was capable of bombing the Auschwitz (Oswiecim) area in Silesia, Poland, 620 miles from Foggia. As early as January 21, 1944, the Allies had targeted the nearby I. G. Farben chemical and rubber ("buna") plant in their campaign to destroy German war-making industry. These efforts intensified in May in preparation for D-Day, just as news broke of the roundup of Hungarian Jews.[2]

The WRB had intensified its efforts at psychological warfare. It had broadcast Roosevelt's statement promising punishment for those involved in genocide. Prominent Americans had issued stern warnings. American Protestant and Catholic clerics had beseeched the Hungarian people to protect the Jews. Nothing had worked. As the situation in Hungary grew more desperate, Isaac Sternbuch of the Union of Orthodox Rabbis in Switzerland urged his organization exiled in New York to request air raids upon the towns that were railway junctions for trains deporting Hungarian Jews to Poland. In May Sternbuch realized that railway lines could be easily repaired and urged that "bombing should be repeated at short intervals to prevent rebuilding."[3]

Operation Frantic began on June 2, four days before D-Day.

American bombers flew from Britain and Italy to the Soviet air base at Poltava and from there to targets in Poland, Hungary, Romania, and Germany. The operation continued for four months, and flights passed over the rail lines to Auschwitz and over Auschwitz itself. But stern military necessity forced the Allies to prioritize their targets. In late June the Germans bombed the Poltava airport, destroying forty-three B-17s and damaging 26, destroying 15 Mustang fighter escorts, and blowing up 450,000 gallons of aircraft fuel. Operation Frantic was suspended in July.[4]

On June 7, the day after D-Day, Yitzak Gruenbaum of the Jewish Agency met with L. C. Pinkerton, American consul in Palestine. Gruenbaum requested Americans to warn the Hungarian government against killing Jews, to bomb railway lines, and "that the American air forces receive instructions to bomb the death camps in Poland." Pinkerton agreed to report the first two requests but balked at the third. "Won't bombing the camps also cause the death of many Jews?" he asked Gruenbaum. Gruenbaum replied that the Jews in the death camps were destined to die anyway and might be able to escape in the confusion. The camps' destruction might disrupt the killing process. Apparently appalled at the idea of killing Jewish prisoners, Pinkerton advised Gruenbaum to present in writing his suggestion to bomb the death camps.[5]

On June 11 Gruenbaum handed his proposal to the Executive of the Jewish Agency at Jerusalem. The motion to bomb the camps was overwhelmingly rejected. "We do not know the truth concerning the entire situation in Poland, and it seems that we will be unable to propose anything concerning this matter," David Ben-Gurion opined. "It is forbidden for us to take responsibility for a bombing that could very well cause the death of even one Jew," another member, Dr. Emil Schmorak, noted. A third member opposed asking the Americans to bomb the camps "and thus cause the murder of Jews." Yet another said "we cannot . . . cause the death of a single Jew." Ben-Gurion summarized the vote: "The opinion of the Jewish Agency's Executive Committee is not to propose to the Allies the bombing of sites in which Jews are located."6

Gruenbaum was disappointed in his colleagues. "They do not want to take such responsibility upon themselves," he lamented. Thus the Jewish Agency never went on record in favor of the bombing and never asked FDR or the American government to bomb Auschwitz. Because Chaim Weizmann and Moshe Shertok (head of the JA Political Department) presented an aide-mémoire to the British government on July 6, 1944, suggesting the bombing of Birkenau and other places (it was seventh on a list of priorities), many historians concluded that the agency must have changed its mind after the June 11 vote. It may have, but there is no record of such a vote, and the JA never took an opportunity to lobby the U.S. government to act.7

On June 18, Jacob Rosenheim, president of the Orthodox Agudas Israel World Organization, wrote Henry Morgenthau, chairman of the WRB, imploring the United States to bomb the railroads between Hungary and Poland. "Every day of delay," Rosenheim wrote, "means a very heavy responsibility for the human lives at stake." Morgenthau sent Rosenheim's letter to John

Pehle, who contacted John J. McCloy, assistant secretary of war. Pehle told McCloy that he had "several doubts" about the proposal, including (1) the propriety of using military airplanes for this purpose; (2) "whether it would be difficult to put the railroad line out of commission for a long enough period to do any good"; and (3) "even assuming that this railroad line were put out of commission for the same period of time, whether it would help the Jews in Hungary." Pehle made it clear to McCloy that he was not "at this point at least, requesting the War Department to take any action on this proposal other than to appropriately explore it."[8]

Pehle kept McCloy apprised of the situation. In a June 29 memorandum, Pehle enclosed a copy of a cable from Leland Harrison, U.S. minister to Switzerland, describing the deportation of Jews from Hungary to Poland to be killed, but not requesting the War Department to bomb the camps or railway lines. On the same day, Benjamin Akzin, a young Jewish WRB staffer and Zionist activist, recommended that the camps be bombed. This "*might* appreciably slow down the systematic slaughter *at least temporarily*," he wrote. In addition to destroying the camps, Akzin believed the action was a matter of principle "as the most tangible—and perhaps only tangible—evidence of the indignation aroused by the existence of these charnel-houses." Akzin acknowledged that "a large number of Jews in these camps may be killed. . . . But such Jews are doomed to death anyhow." Pehle never gave Akzin's memo to McCloy, because he did not agree with it. Even Akzin felt that the strongest statement he could make was that bombing the installations *might* slow down the slaughter at least *temporarily*.[9]

Leon Kubowitzki met with WRB representatives on June 28 and wrote to Pehle on July 1 asking him to consider the destruction of the Auschwitz gas chambers. But Kubowitzki and the WJC adamantly *opposed* the bombing of the camps and urged instead that the camps be destroyed by Soviet and Polish troops.

> *The destruction of the death installations cannot be done from bombing from the air, as the first victims would be the Jews who are gathered in these camps, and such a bombing would be a welcome pretext for the Germans to assert that their Jewish victims have been massacred not by their killers, but by the Allied bombings.*[10]

Kubowitzki, Nahum Goldmann, and others proposed that the Soviets send paratroopers and that the Polish Home Army attack and dismantle Auschwitz. The Soviets were in a position to do something about Auschwitz. Their western offensive reached Poland in July, and the army captured Lublin, one hundred, sixty miles from Auschwitz, on July 24, 1944. But Pehle did not pass Kubowitzki's request on to McCloy because he likely thought it impractical and a prelude to a request for American troops.

Pehle, Kubowitzki, and Goldmann were in good company on the bombing issue. On June 27, Jacob Fishman, a Zionist leader and columnist, wrote in the New York Yiddish-language *Morgen Journal* of the pros and cons of bombing the camps. The victims would be Jews, but Jews had escaped from Treblinka after a revolt there. "I am still thinking about the idea," he concluded. Thus by the end of June 1944 most Jewish public and private opinion either opposed bombing Auschwitz or was divided on the issue.[11]

By this time there was no doubt in the minds of many in the American government that Hungarian Jews were being sent to Auschwitz. On May 10, the *New York Times* reported that the Hungarian government "is now preparing for the annihilation of Hungarian Jews." On July 3, the *Times* carried a story on page 3 headlined "Inquiry Confirms Nazi Death Camps" and which stated that 1,715,000 Jews had been killed at Auschwitz and Birkenau.[12]

Churchill responded favorably to Weizmann's and Shertok's request to bomb Auschwitz, but the RAF did not approve the operation. They knew that it was a difficult mission, of no military value, and that the war was far from over. Churchill never pressed the plan. On the July day Weizmann and Shertok met with Anthony Eden, Churchill informed the House of Commons that 2,752 British civilians had been killed by German rockets in the preceding three weeks.[13] To military men, risking valuable airplanes and pilots on hopeless civilian rescue operations would only delay victory. On the other hand, if Germany's war-making capability was destroyed, the war would end and all civilians, including Jews, would be saved. The British secretary of state for air, Sir Archibald Sinclair, studied the bombing request and concluded that the distances were too great for British night bombers. Such an attack "might be carried out by the Americans by daylight," he reported, but it would be dangerous and costly. He doubted that the victims would be helped, even if the plants were destroyed.[14]

On July 4, McCloy responded to Pehle's June 29 letter about bombing the railway lines:

> *The War Department is of the opinion that the suggested air operation is impracticable. It could be executed only by the diversion of considerable air support essential to the success of our forces now engaged in decisive operations and would in any case be of such very doubtful efficacy that it would not amount to a practical project.*

This response was consistent with the bedrock American policy that the most effective relief for victims of enemy persecution—and indeed, American prisoners of war—was the speedy defeat of the Axis. Historians have debated the truthfulness of this and subsequent letters from McCloy. Martin Gilbert accepted the letter at face value: "The principal 'decisive operations' mentioned in this letter," Gilbert noted, "remained the Allied attempt to destroy all of Germany's war-making powers based upon the manufacture of synthetic oil."[15]

In July 1944, the Germans held 28,867 American POWs— 12,274 army soldiers and 16,593 pilots, navigators, and gunners—as well as more than 200,000 British and Commonwealth POWs. The POWs were scattered over 57 different stalags (camps), but the vast majority of Americans were held in just

3056

An aerial reconnaissance photograph of Auschwitz.

Courtesy of the United States Holocaust Memorial Museum

eight main camps, all in eastern Germany, to deter escape through France. There was no plan to rescue these men, even though the War Department was aware that they were being deprived of food and medicine and that as the war progressed, they were in danger of being held as hostages by Hitler or murdered by the SS or the Gestapo. But the priority of Allied commanders was to win the war. There were decisive operations under way. Pleas by POW families and officers within the military were rejected in language similar to the president's executive order creating the WRB, and army group commanders were ordered to help POWs "provided that such actions are not at the expense of the main operations." One British naval officer's proposal to use gliders and para-troopers to rescue POWs at Marlag Nord, near Bremen, was sum-marily rejected as "not considered practical" and "not considered advisable." The plan would be considered "if and when consistent with operations."[16]

The Jewish Agency sent two telegrams to Roosevelt on July 11, 1944, on a related matter, the Brand mission, but did not request FDR to bomb the camps or the railway lines. The agency believed that direct negotiations with the Gestapo, which the Brand mission represented, were more likely to save Jews than bombing the camps.[17] The Irgunist Emergency Committee urged the bombing of both railway lines and the extermination camps in a letter to FDR. Professor Johan J. Smertenko claimed that the bombing "would enable the Hebrew people gathered in these camps to escape" and join the resistance. Roosevelt's secretary William D. Hassett sent the letter on to the WRB and the State Department. Preoccupied with the invasion of Europe, the president would not interfere with Eisenhower's critical mission to liberate Europe. And the opinions of Bergson and the Irgun likely carried no weight with him.[18]

Events in Hungary overtook the discussion about bombing the camps. By June 7, 289,357 Hungarian Jews had been deported, and by July 9, a total of 437,402 Jews had been sent to Auschwitz and murdered. The Hungarian government ceased the deportations on July 8, bowing to pressure from the Allies, Swedes, Swiss, and the Vatican, and an Allied bomb attack on Budapest. The requests to bomb the railway lines and the camp were too little, too late for nearly five hundred thousand Hungarian Jews. The July 2 Allied raid on Budapest appeared to be, but was not, in retaliation against the Hungarians for deporting the Jews. The Hungarians had intercepted Allied telegrams requesting the bombing of collaborating Hungarian and German agencies, and they believed the bombings aimed to stop the Jewish massacre. In reality, the raids were part of the Allies' systematic bombing campaign. Three hundred thousand Jews in and near Budapest still lived in July thanks to those Allied raids.

The cessation of Hungarian deportations became public on July 19. Auschwitz, however, continued to murder Jews from elsewhere in Europe until January 1945.[19] The bombing of Germany was so effective that "Jewish labor was now judged essential if the munitions factories of the Reich were to be kept in operation." In the summer of 1944, Jewish slave laborers were sent from Auschwitz to other camps and factories in Germany, thereby improving their chance to survive.

Anne Frank spent much of 1944 writing and revising her famous diary. On March 28, 1944, she heard a speech over the radio by an exiled Dutch leader calling on the Dutch people to document the crimes of the German occupying army. She also began writing short stories. On D-Day, June 6, 1944, exactly twenty-three months after the Franks had gone into hiding, the eight residents of the annex hugged one another and wept. But on August 4, the Gestapo arrived. Someone had betrayed the Franks. They were sent to Westerbork, a transit camp, and then to Auschwitz.[20]

In May, Adolf Eichmann dispatched Joel Brand, a Jewish-Hungarian businessman and civic leader, on a mission to learn if the Allies might trade the lives of a million Jews for ten thousand trucks and other supplies—the "blood for goods" deal. Both Roosevelt and McCloy evinced strong interest in the Brand mission and kept up with its progress. In fact, Roosevelt personally intervened in the affair. The British refused to negotiate with Brand, but according to Ira Hirschmann, the president was "alert to an opening through which lives might be saved," and sent Hirschmann to intercede. Hirschmann met personally with FDR, who admonished the young diplomat to "keep talking. Cable back everything you hear. While you talk, these people still have a chance to live." Indeed, Hirschmann carried a letter from the president that conveyed his personal interest in Brand's mission.[21]

The State Department telegraphed Ambassador Laurence Steinhardt in Turkey that "every effort should be made to convince the Germans that this government is sufficiently concerned with this problem that it is willing to consider genuine proposals for rescue and relief of the Jews and other victims." Hirschmann advised Washington "to keep the pot boiling" and allow Brand to return to Hungary with some kind of proposal to gain time. He met with Brand in Cairo on June 22 and flew to London, where Eichmann's offer was being debated.[22]

Churchill put the kibosh on Brand's mission. "On no account," he minuted Eden on July 7, "have the slightest negotiations, direct or indirect, with the Huns." The Jewish Agency, which had invested all its rescue efforts in the Brand mission, sought help from Roosevelt. It wanted the WRB to aid Brand's return to Budapest to tell Eichmann that the Allies were considering the deal. This telegram could have, but did not include, a request to bomb Auschwitz.[23]

Obviously the Allies could never have seriously negotiated with the Nazis to supply the dying Reich with trucks for the Eastern Front. The key to victory was for the Allies to remain united at all costs. The WRB found these "fantastic" proposals for saving the Jews of Hungary "of dubious reliability," which they clearly were. While the British worried that the WRB would cave in to Jewish-American political pressure, the U.S. government was not about to risk its alliance with the Soviets over such a far-fetched deal. Eventually the Brand mission was found to be a Nazi ruse to keep the Jewish leadership pacified with "secret negotiations" or an attempt to negotiate a separate peace with the Anglo-Americans and divide the Allies. Patriotic American Jews, dedicated to their nation's victory, had no intention of endorsing such an absurd plea. According to the WRB's official history, "the Germans were attempting to use the Jews in their hands not only as pawns for possible economic and personal benefit but also as a means to create dissension between the United States and Great Britain."[24]

Despite rejecting the Brand mission and requests to bomb the camps, the Allies agreed to broadcast public warnings to German and Hungarian officials and railwaymen and published a declaration expressing their readiness to admit Jewish escapees from Hungary. The British and American governments issued a joint declaration on August 17 agreeing to the Hungarians' offer to release certain categories of Jews if the Allies would accept them. The British demanded that the United States take all the responsibility.[25] On August 9 Kubowitzki again wrote to McCloy.

> *My dear Mr. Secretary:*
>
> *I beg to submit to your consideration the following excerpt from a message which we received under date of July 29 from Mr. Ernest Frischer of the Czechoslovak State Council [in exile] through the War Refugee Board:*
>
> *"I believe that destruction of gas chambers and crematoria in Oswiecim by bombing would have a certain effect now. Germans are now exhuming and burning corpses in an effort to conceal their crimes. This could be prevented by destruction of crematoria and then Germans might possibly stop further mass exterminations especially since so little time is left to them. Bombing of railway communications in this same area would also be of importance and of military interest."[26]*

Contrary to its characterization by numerous historians and the U.S. Holocaust Memorial Museum as a request by the World Jewish Congress to bomb Auschwitz, this letter did not endorse the bombing but merely passed on a message from another party without comment. Kubowitzki, in fact, was on record in July *opposing* the bombing. Indeed, Kubowitzki wrote Pehle a similar letter on August 8, 1944, containing the same quotation from Frischer, but specifically reminded Pehle of his earlier July 1 letter opposing the bombing. As Richard Levy observed, "the language suggests that he was taking care of an obligation in the most perfunctory way." Kubowitzki wrote Frischer on August 2, 1944:

> *I think you know that we are not in favor of the bombing of the extermination installations in Oswiecim and Birkenau, because we believe in hayei shaa [saving those currently living, literally "life of the hour"], and we are afraid for the Jewish victims of such bombings and of giving the Germans an alibi: that the Jews were killed by the Allied bombs and not by the Nazis' fiendish inventions.*[27]

McCloy responded much as he had to Pehle in July:

> *This War Department has been approached by the War Refugee Board, which raised the question of the practicability of this suggestion. After a study it became apparent that such an operation could be executed only*

by the diversion of considerable air support essential to the success of our forces now engaged in decisive operations elsewhere and would in any case be of such doubtful efficacy that it would not warrant the use of our resources. There has been considerable opinion to the effect that such an effort, even if practicable, might provoke even more vindictive action by the Germans.[28]

When the Hungarians ceased deportations in July, the Allies were unsure if the requests to bomb Auschwitz were still on the table. On August 16, representatives of all the major American Jewish organizations met with Pehle in Washington. The organizations had united to expedite rescue measures in Hungary. Pehle was "extremely skeptical that any Jews would be permitted to leave Hungary." The Nazis, he said, "might destroy them on the spot." According to a memorandum of the meeting, Pehle "flatly rejected as unfeasible the proposal that the extermination installations in Oswieczym [Auschwitz] and elsewhere should be destroyed by bombing or parachutists." "A proposal to bomb the facilities," Pehle noted, "had been objected to by Jewish organizations because it would result in the extermination of large numbers of Jews there." The alternative was to send an underground detachment, but he expressed doubt "that the Poles could muster the strength for such engagements."

After this meeting, these groups sent a memorandum outlining their requests for rescue. It did not include a request to bomb Auschwitz, nor did any of the representatives at the meeting request that Auschwitz be bombed. Pehle felt that public reaction would be unfavorable to a diversion of military forces "from present crucial military activities" for any reason. American Jewish leaders obviously agreed or had serious reservations about bombing the camps as well.[29]

Kubowitzki persisted in his plan to seek help from the Polish underground to destroy "the instruments of death" at Auschwitz. In late August, he transmitted to Pehle a letter from a member of the Polish National Council to the Polish Prime Minister, Stanislaw Mikolajczyk, on the subject. On August 30, Kubowitzki wrote directly to McCloy. He told the assistant secretary, "We know how strongly this country and the Administration feel about the annihilation of the Jewish people in Europe." He pointed out in no uncertain terms that the WJC "did not ask for the destruction of the death installations by bombing from the air. We asked that the destruction be done either by Soviet paratroopers or by the Polish Underground."[30]

In this same letter, Kubowitzki informed McCloy that the WJC had suggested the use of volunteer Allied (presumably Anglo-American) paratroopers. McCloy replied on September 3 that a decision to use Allied paratroopers at Auschwitz must be made by the commanders in the area. "I am sure [the Allied Mediterranean commander] would do anything he felt he could to check these ghastly excesses of the Nazis. Perhaps an alteration in the tactical situation may make it possible for him to take some effective steps along the lines you propose." Leaders of the WJC and its supporters continued to debate the bombing of Auschwitz. Ernest

Frischer continued to favor bombing and believed the destruction of the extermination installations by Russian paratroopers or the Polish underground "absolutely impossible."[31]

Rescue advocates were grasping at straws. The Soviets would not help. The Polish underground could not help. The U.S. Army refused to consider sending paratroopers to rescue American POWs who were in danger, it was thought at the time, of being murdered by the SS and the Gestapo. Kubowitzki noted in a confidential memorandum to the WJC office committee that WRB staffer Lawrence Lesser "did not expect much from the Russians who had written off their war prisoners in German camps."[32] Of course, Jewish leaders knew that help from the Poles was unlikely. The Poles were as anti-semitic as the Germans. Members of the WJC believed in October 1944 that "the attitude of the Polish population was always bad against the Jews and that was why the Germans have chosen Poland to become the cemetery of Jews. They could do it in no other country." Letters and telegrams from the WJC to the Soviets requesting the use of Russian paratroopers were ignored.[33]

On September 2, Benjamin Akzin tried again to convince Pehle to meet with Roosevelt and request that the camps be bombed. "I am certain," Akzin urged Pehle, "that the President, once acquainted with the facts, would realize the values involved and, cutting through the inertia-motivated objections of the War Department, would order the immediate bombing of the objectives suggested." Pehle disagreed. The WRB, according to the minutes of the WJC, "has no plan at all" and are "showing a complete air of helplessness."[34]

The limits of Allied airpower were dramatically illustrated in August and September, when Allied pilots, including Polish volunteers, flew a mission to drop supplies to the Polish resistance in Warsaw. The American Eighth Bomber Group flew the last Operation Frantic missions on September 18–20 and dropped 1,284 containers of arms and supplies over Warsaw. These efforts were futile and costly. Less than 100 containers reached the Polish Home Army. The Germans captured the rest, and, on September 20, shot down 5 of 20 Allied aircraft. Two hundred Allied air crew members were killed over Warsaw. The WJC continued to promote their alternative plan, a raid on Auschwitz by Soviet and Polish troops.[35]

Kubowitzki wrote Pehle again on October 1, 1944, letting Pehle know he had contacted Soviet authorities. On October 3, Pehle informed McCloy that the death camps were increasing their pace of murder and asked that consideration be given to bombing the camps. Again, Pehle was performing a perfunctory task. As the WJC office committee minutes noted on October 20, 1944, "Pehle had never felt very keen" on the subject of bombing the camps. McCloy's executive assistant, Colonel Harrison A. Gerhardt, opposed the bombing because the region was within the sphere of Russian responsibility. Nahum Goldmann, president of the World Jewish Congress and a representative of the Jewish Agency, claimed thirty-six years later that he visited McCloy to urge that the camps be bombed, even though this request was in conflict with WJC policy. "McCloy indicated to me," Goldmann wrote Martin Gilbert, "that, although the Americans were reluctant about my proposal, they might agree to it, though any decision as to the target of bombardments in Europe was in the hands of the British." Goldmann also went to see General John Dill, the senior British representative on the Combined Chiefs of Staff, whose attitude was totally negative. Apparently the WJC, like the JA, both supported and opposed the bombing of Auschwitz.[36]

In September and October 1944, the War Department Operations Division and the Air Force Operational Plans Division reviewed the bombing request. General Frederick Anderson, General Carl "Tooey" Spaatz's deputy for operations, recommended against it. Spaatz was in command of the United States Strategic Air Forces in Europe. His common sense telegram read:

> *Do not consider that the unfortunate Poles herded in these concentration camps would have their status improved by the destruction of the extermination chambers. . . . There is also the possibility of some of the bombs landing on the prisoners as well . . . And in that event the Germans would be provided with a fine alibi for any wholesale massacre that they might perpetrate . . . Therefore recommend that no encouragement be given to this project.*[37]

Although Hungarian Jewry received a brief reprieve, the remnant of European Jewry did not. Tens of thousands of Jews were transported from all over Europe to Auschwitz from August to November 1944. The Jews of Lodz, Poland, the largest remaining

Jewish ghetto in Europe, were murdered during September, October, and November. On October 10, Jewish groups, the Polish government-in-exile, and others pressured the British and the Americans to warn the Germans that if their plans for "mass execution at Oswiecim and Brzezinky" were carried out, those responsible "from the highest to the lowest" would be brought to justice. The German Telegraph Service denied the truth of the reports even as the exterminations continued.

Anne Frank and her family were still alive in October 1944. Rumors spread at Auschwitz that the Russian army was only sixty miles away. In late October or early November, with the Russian army fast approaching, Anne and her sister, Margot, were sent from Auschwitz to Bergen-Belsen. Their mother, Edith, lingered at Auschwitz and died on January 6, 1945, but Anne's father, Otto Frank, survived, freed by the Russians on January 27, 1945.[38]

The best-known episode in the War Refugee Board's campaign to rescue European Jewry was under way at this time. From July 9, 1944, to January 17, 1945, Raoul Wallenberg worked frantically to save the Jews of Budapest. When Eichmann returned to Budapest on October 17, Wallenberg was still there. He was helpless to prevent the renewed deportations, killings, and shootings even as the Red Army, massed in Poland and Romania, drew closer. With the help of the Hungarian Arrow Cross Party (Nyilas) Fascists, the Nazis slaughtered thousands of Jews in Budapest. Yet, 120,000 Jews survived as late as December 1944. After waiting in vain for the Red Army, thirty thousand Jews were marched by Arrow Cross gangs in November toward the Austrian border.

Thousands died. On January 17, 1945, Wallenberg was captured by the Soviet army and never seen again.[39]

It was clear that Jews remaining at Auschwitz would be killed before the Germans retreated. By November 8, 1944, Pehle read the report of two escapees from Auschwitz, Rudolph Vrba and Alfred Wetzler, eyewitnesses to the Holocaust, and changed his mind on the bombing issue. He told Ira Hirschmann that this report was "convincing in a way in which other reports have not been, as you know it is not easy to believe that such things take place." Pehle wrote McCloy that he was now convinced the camps ought to be bombed and enclosed copies of the Vrba-Wetzler report, which gave shocking details of conditions at Auschwitz. No previous report "has quite caught the gruesome brutality of what is taking place in these camps of horror."[40]

But McCloy was unmoved. The General Staff Operations Division concluded that bombing was "not feasible from a military standpoint." The camp was beyond the range of medium bombers, dive bombers, and fighter-bombers. Heavy bombers must be used, but these aircraft were fully engaged in destroying industrial targets. They could not be diverted from that role. McCloy ignored the Allied air base at Foggia (round-trip, 1,300 miles) when he erroneously claimed that Auschwitz could only be attacked by American heavy bombers traveling 2,000 miles over enemy territory from bases in Britain. But he accurately reflected the views of the army air force commanders. Major General J. E. Hull considered the plan "of very doubtful feasibility" and "unacceptable from a military standpoint at this time." It was a diversion from the strategic bombing campaigns, and the results would not justify the cost in men and aircraft. McCloy likely never read the Vrba-Wetzler report and returned it to Pehle.[41]

In any event, it was too late. By early November, the Russian army was approaching Auschwitz, and the inmates were being shipped to Germany or marched to death. On

Campaign tour near Hyde Park with Henry Morgenthau, Jr., November 6, 1944.

Courtesy of the Franklin D. Roosevelt Library

November 25, 1944, Pehle released to the press the Vrba-Wetzler report on the death camps. "U.S. Board Bares Atrocity Details Told by Witnesses at Polish Camps," the *New York Times* front-page headline read on November 26. "It is a fact beyond denial," the WRB press release stated, "that the Germans have deliberately and systematically murdered millions of innocent civilians—Jews and Christians alike—all over Europe. . . . So revolting and diabolical are the German atrocities that the minds of civilized people find it difficult to believe that they have actually taken place."[42]

That same day, November 26, Heinrich Himmler ordered the crematoriums at Auschwitz dismantled. The machinery was sent to other killing facilities. Allied bombers attacked factories near Auschwitz and Monowitz on December 18 and 26. The plants and slave labor camps attached to the abandoned death camps remained in operation until January 8, 1945. Much of the physical evidence of industrialized murder at Auschwitz—corpses in mass graves, fences, and guard towers—was removed during December and January. Only the approach of the Red Army in January 1945 caused the Nazis to close Auschwitz. On January 18 and 19, the Gestapo "evacuated" 65,000 prisoners from Auschwitz into Upper Silesia by marching them in freezing weather. Thousands died. Soviet troops arrived at Auschwitz on January 27, 1945. They found 7,600 survivors.[43]

In all likelihood, Roosevelt knew little or nothing of the requests to bomb Auschwitz. They were most actively pressed during the summer and fall of 1944, when the president was both ill and extremely busy. He focused his limited energy on D-Day, the progress of the war in Europe and the Pacific, the imminent collapse of Germany, conferences with Churchill and Stalin, and the November election. These monumental tasks pressed on him. The president never received formal requests to bomb Auschwitz from any credible person or group he respected, and there was no convincing evidence that his close advisers—Morgenthau, Rosenman, Byrnes, or Hopkins—approached him with such a request. Nor did notable or important Jewish leaders or organizations in America or Palestine request that American forces bomb Auschwitz at a time when bombing might have accomplished something.[44]

Until recently, skeptics had not contended that Roosevelt knew about the request to bomb Auschwitz. In 1983, Morton Mintz of the *Washington Post* interviewed John McCloy, then 88 years old.

McCloy told Mintz that he had never talked to Roosevelt about it but that he had spoken to Harry Hopkins, who said, "the Boss was not disposed to" the bombing. McCloy stated to Mintz that he told Rosenman of air force general Henry H. "Hap" Arnold's negative appraisal of the idea, gave it to Rosenman and "that was the end of that." Even FDR critic David Wyman told Mintz that there was no documentary evidence "that the bombing question ever came to Roosevelt. FDR didn't care enough about the whole issue of rescue to let that issue or any aspect of it become a deep concern." Wyman doubted that Hopkins was involved either, given his poor health in the spring and summer of 1944. McCloy's biographer, Kai Bird, flatly stated that "there is no evidence that Roosevelt was ever approached about the matter." And, according to Bird, no records of discussions with Hap Arnold or Harry Hopkins could be found.[45]

In 1986, Henry Morgenthau III interviewed ninety-one-year-old McCloy. "They came to me and wanted to order the bombing of Auschwitz," McCloy told Morgenthau. At first, he told Morgenthau that neither his father nor FDR was involved in that issue. Then he said the president opposed the bombing because it would have done no good. The president made it clear, McCloy said, that the United States "would have been accused of destroying Auschwitz, bombing these innocent people. This isn't right . . . he took it out of my hands. We didn't want to get involved in this diversion." McCloy then said that FDR was irate at the idea of bombing Jews in the camps to make a gesture. "He said why the idea, they'll say we bombed these people, and they'll only move it down the road a little way and bomb them all the more. . . . If it's successful, it'll be more provocative and I won't have anything to do [with it] . . . we'll be accused of participating in this horrible business."[46]

The only firsthand evidence that Roosevelt was ever informed about the request to bomb Auschwitz was John McCloy's interview at age ninety-one. This is hardly reliable evidence that FDR was told of the proposal. Prior to 1986 and for the previous forty years, McCloy claimed that Roosevelt never knew about the bombing request, nor did McCloy ever say that he had discussed it with FDR.

The debate whether FDR knew or did not know of the request to bomb Auschwitz, however, is a tempest in a teapot. He would likely have treated a decision about bombing Auschwitz as a military, not a political, matter. It was unlikely that Roosevelt knew about the request to bomb Auschwitz. But McCloy's description of Roosevelt's attitude rings true even if it were never expressed. His alleged reaction complements everything we know about Roosevelt's mind-set, his keeping his eye on the speediest victory possible, and his likely revulsion at bombing "places where there are Jews." At this stage of the war, Roosevelt almost always deferred to military decision-makers and rarely considered political objectives more important than military ones. For example, he did not discipline General George S. Patton for his highly publicized indiscretions or involve himself in the politics of selecting generals. "War," as Louis Morton wrote of Roosevelt, "was an aberration, a nasty business to be got over with. . . . Beat the bully and bring the boys home—that was the American approach to war."[47]

FDR Attempts to Create a Jewish State for the Victims of "Indescribable Horrors"

Tragically, the war against Germany did not end in the middle of December, as Roosevelt's military chiefs believed it would. On a bitterly cold December 16, 1944, the Germans mounted a final, desperate, massive counteroffensive to push the Allies out of Belgium. The Battle of the Bulge resulted in seventy thousand American casualties and the surrender of ten thousand American soldiers to the Wehrmacht. In one episode in the battle Germans massacred a hundred American POWs. There was panic in the Allied armies. Eisenhower, however, remained cool and sent General Patton to relieve the American garrison that barely held the line at Bastogne, France. When the skies cleared on December 22, Allied airpower sent the Germans reeling. "Brad, this time the Kraut's stuck his head in a meat-grinder. And this time I've got hold of the handle," Patton told General Omar N. Bradley. By the second week of January 1945 the battle ended in Allied victory. For Roosevelt, according to Frances Perkins, these were "weeks of great decisions in the war, with the Battle of the Bulge adding to the terrible strain of uncertainty." Roosevelt never questioned Stimson's, Marshall's, or Eisenhower's leadership. "In great stress," Marshall said, "Roosevelt was a strong man." Stimson agreed. "He has really exercised great restraint," the secretary noted in his diary.[1]

By January, Berlin and many other German cities lay in ruins. Tokyo was being bombed mercilessly. General Spaatz's U.S. Strategic Air Forces and British Bomber Command had decimated German oil and transportation targets. The Reich's economy was in shambles. But the pale, drugged Führer raved and ranted and pushed his forces to fight on. Yearning to end the war quickly, Eisenhower approved the firebombing of Dresden. Like Hitler, the Japanese militarists fought on. More kamikazes were readied as the Japanese people prepared to fight the Americans to their own certain deaths.[2]

Roosevelt's health was precarious. Perkins thought his "face looked thin, his color was gray, and his eyes were dull." Some days he was the old FDR; other days his appearance scared those around him. "I was frightened. I had never seen him like that," Perkins recalled. Roosevelt did not have the strength for a traditional inauguration and scaled back the event to a brief ceremony at the White House. His January 20 inaugural address, delivered from the south porch of the White House in bitter cold, was five minutes long, the briefest in American history. "The President," Katherine Marshall recalled, "was pale and drawn, his hands trembled constantly, his voice appeared weak." He was in so much pain before the reception that he needed a large glass of straight whiskey before he greeted his guests.[3]

Nevertheless, two days later he was off to meet Churchill and Stalin at Yalta. On January 30 he celebrated his sixty-third, and last, birthday en route. At Yalta, Roosevelt's priorities were securing Russian assistance in the war against Japan, which Roosevelt believed would cost many American lives, and agreement on the organization of the United Nations. He was successful on these issues, but he paid a price. The military reality of Soviet occupation forced him to accept Russian hegemony in Poland and elsewhere in Eastern Europe. He acceded to Stalin's demands regarding Japan and China. In his toast, Stalin saluted Roosevelt as "the man with the broadest conception of national interest . . . he had forged the instruments which led to the mobilization of the world against Hitler." Churchill's doctor, Lord Moran, called Roosevelt "a very sick man . . . I give him only a few months to live." Roosevelt's fragile world was battered again when Harry Hopkins, having reached the limit of his physical endurance, declined to make the nine-day return voyage across the Atlantic with Roosevelt and flew home. It was their last and sadly unfriendly farewell.[4]

On February 14, 1945, on his way back to the United States, Roosevelt stopped at Great Bitter Lake in the Suez Canal to meet King Abdul Aziz Al Saud, better known as Ibn Saud, the leader of Saudi Arabia. Roosevelt had promised his Jewish friends he would try to solve the problem of Palestine when the war was over. He conferred with Rabbi Wise and told his cabinet before he left for

Franklin D. Roosevelt at Great Bitter Lake where he received King Ibn Saud of Saudi Arabia on board the USS Quincy, *at 11:30 A.M., February 14, 1945, after the Yalta Conference*

Courtesy of the Franklin D. Roosevelt Library

Yalta that he would meet Saud and "try and settle the Palestine situation." He discussed the concept of a Jewish homeland with Stalin at Yalta, told the Soviet leader that he was a Zionist, and asked if he, too, was one. Stalin replied warily: yes, in principle, but he recognized the difficulty of solving the Jewish problem. When Stalin asked Roosevelt if he planned to make concessions to Saud, Roosevelt joked that he might offer "to give him the six million Jews in the United States." The war was still going on and bombs were still being dropped on Cairo and the Suez Canal.[5]

Because of the physical danger to Roosevelt, his meeting with Saud was so secret that it was hidden even from British intelligence. Roosevelt told only Churchill and then only on the evening before they separated at Yalta. Churchill was as infuriated as Roosevelt knew he would be. The British long had a monopoly on the Middle East as a sphere of influence, a monopoly that Americans had assiduously respected. Indeed, the whole problem of Palestine and Jewish refugees reflected American deference to British policy. Churchill was so concerned about Roosevelt's change in policy that he decided to follow in Roosevelt's footsteps to preserve British power and prestige in the area. Roosevelt met three kings: Farouk of Egypt, Ibn Saud of Saudi Arabia, and Haile Selassie of Ethiopia. Only the meeting with Saud had any significance. Roosevelt had previously agreed to a congressional subsidy for Saudi Arabia, and hoped to reduce the tension in Palestine and to convince Saud to allow the Jews to create a state or homeland of some kind.[6]

The president arrived in his cruiser, the USS *Quincy*, at 10:00 A.M. on the morning of the fourteenth. Saud had arrived earlier with a party of four and spent the night on the USS *Murphy*, awaiting FDR. He brought along one hundred sheep he intended to kill and cook so that all on board could be his guests. The king, three princes, and two ministers crossed the gangplank and went to meet Roosevelt, who was sitting in his wheelchair on the deck of the *Quincy*. Roosevelt and Saud talked for an hour and a quarter. When lunch was announced Roosevelt took the elevator while Saud was accompanied to the president's private suite. Roosevelt pressed the red emergency button to stop the elevator between decks so that he could smoke two cigarettes out of the presence of the strict Wahhabi Muslim king. The king was miffed when he learned that Roosevelt had to depart at 3:30 P.M. and could not join him for the banquet he had planned on the *Murphy*. Roosevelt agreed to drink a cup of Arabian coffee served by two resplendent coffee servers brought along by Saud.[7]

The two men labored to charm each other. Saud told the president that they were twins because they were both the same age, both were heads of state with grave responsibilities, were both farmers at heart, and they both bore in their bodies grave physical infirmities. (The king walked with difficulty because of wounds in his legs.) Respecting their physical handicaps, the president said to the king: "You are luckier than I because you can still walk on your legs and I have to be wheeled wherever I go." To this the king replied: "No, my friend, you are the more fortunate. Your chair will take you wherever you want to go and you know you will get there." The president then made the king a gift of the wheelchair he was sitting in.[8]

The old campaigner turned on all of his charm for Saud. Throughout the meeting, according to his aide Colonel William A. Eddy, "President Roosevelt was in top form as a charming host, witty conversationalist, with the spark and light in his eyes and that gracious smile which always won people over to him whenever he talked with them as a friend. . . . With Ibn Saud he was at his very best." Roosevelt asked the king for advice about a serious problem for which he felt "a personal responsibility," namely the Jewish victims of the Holocaust who had suffered "indescribable horrors at the hands of the Nazis: eviction, destruction of their homes, torture, and mass murder." Saud replied that the Allies should give "them and their descendants the choicest lands and homes of the Germans who had oppressed them." Roosevelt replied that the Jewish survivors had a sentimental desire to settle in Palestine and feared remaining in Germany. The king rejoined that he had no doubt that the Jews had good reason not to trust the Germans, but "surely the Allies will destroy Nazi power forever and in their victory will be strong enough to protect Nazi victims. If the Allies do not expect firmly to control future German policy, why fight this costly war?" Saud could not conceive of leaving an enemy in a position to strike back after defeat, he told Roosevelt. He gave the president a long dissertation on the basic attitude of the Arabs toward the Jews.[9]

FDR returned to the attack, saying that he counted on Arab hospitality and on the king's help in solving the problem of Zionism, but the king reiterated that the enemy and the oppressor should pay: "Amends should be made by the criminal, not by the innocent bystander. What injury have Arabs done to the Jews of Europe? It is the 'Christian' Germans who stole their homes and lives." Later, when Roosevelt returned to the subject, complaining that Saud had not helped with his problem, the king lost patience and observed that American "oversolicitude for the Germans was incomprehensible to an uneducated Bedouin with whom friends get more consideration than enemies." Saud's final remark on the subject was to the effect that it was Arab custom to distribute survivors and victims of battle among the victorious tribes in accordance with their number and their supplies of food and water. Palestine, he said, was a small, land-poor country "and had already been assigned more than its quota of European refugees."

Roosevelt had tried to convince Saud, but to no avail. The "Arabs would choose to die," Saud told the president, "rather than yield their land to the Jews." Roosevelt tried economic aid, irrigation projects, and improved living standards, but Saud was adamant. Ibn Saud's calm and sincere statements had a profound effect on Roosevelt. His meeting with Saud was his one complete failure, FDR later told Eleanor. "I most gloriously failed where you are concerned," he reported to Rabbi Wise on his return. Roosevelt had no solution to the issue of Palestine except to place it before the soon-to-be-established United Nations Security Council. On the voyage home, Roosevelt's military aide "Pa" Watson died. The president was devastated. His life was slipping away.[10]

Roosevelt told Edward Stettinius that "he must have a conference with congressional leaders and reexamine our entire policy in Palestine." Stettinius noted that Roosevelt "was now convinced that if nature took its course there would be bloodshed between the Arabs and Jews. Some formula, not yet discovered, would have to prevent this warfare."[11]

On March 1, the exhausted president apologized to Congress for remaining seated as he addressed a joint session. He found it difficult to stand with "ten pounds of steel on the bottom of my legs," he said to great applause. He reported on agreements reached with Churchill and Stalin and described his meeting with Ibn Saud. Roosevelt ad-libbed a sentence that shocked the Jewish community and puzzled his advisers. "On the problem of Arabia," he said, "I learned more about that whole problem, the Moslem problem, the Jewish problem, by talking with Ibn Saud for five minutes than I could have learned in the exchange of two or three dozen letters." According to Rosenman, it must have just "popped into his head, for I never heard him say anything like that on the way home." Hopkins noted wryly that "the only thing he learned, which all people well acquainted with the Palestine cause knew, is that the Arabs don't want any more Jews in Palestine." Until he had heard it himself from Saud, Roosevelt could not bring himself to believe it.[12]

FDR later reported to Wise:

> *There was nothing I could do with him. We talked for three hours and I argued with the old fellow up hill and down dale, but he stuck to his guns. He said he could see the flood engulfing his lands, Jews pouring in from Eastern Europe and from America, from the Riviera and from California, and he could not bear the thought. He was an old man and he had swollen ankles and he wanted to live out his life in peace without leaving a memory of himself as a traitor to the Arab cause.*[13]

FDR was now frightened for the Jews in Palestine, Judge Joseph Proskauer recalled, believing that "either a war or a pogrom would ensue." Jewish statehood was now out of the question. "Joe, you know I go out on a limb for my friends and I have done so here," Roosevelt replied, "you must help."[14] Colonel

Hoskins later recalled that ER said that she thought the Zionists were "much stronger, and were perhaps willing to risk a fight with the Arabs." "Mr. Roosevelt agreed that this was a possibility," Hoskins reported, "but reminded her that there were fifteen or twenty million Arabs in and around Palestine and that, in the long run, he thought these numbers would win out."[15]

How was it that the same man, who, according to his critics, did not care one whit about Jewish people, tried his best in the final weeks of his life to establish a Jewish homeland for the victims of the Holocaust? Roosevelt faced no election. He had no obligation to see Saud. Yet he did. Why?

The obvious explanation was that Roosevelt was sincere in his desire to help the Jews of Europe, or perhaps he felt a moral obligation to deliver on his 1944 campaign promise to help create a Jewish state. He naively believed that he could sit down face-to-face with the leader of the Muslim world, work out a solution to the problem of Palestine, and provide a homeland for Hitler's victims. Roosevelt had wanted to solve the problem of a Jewish homeland, or at least to settle Jews safely *somewhere*, ever since Hitler began his antisemitic crusade. He had spent hundreds of hours in the 1930s searching for places on the globe where Jews might live. He had called the international conference at Évian. He had set up the President's Advisory Committee on Refugees. His heart had always been in the right place. To him, it was the difficulty of what he often called "the ways and means"—that is, the method and manner of accomplishment, not solely the rightness of the cause.

According to Peter Grose, author of *Israel in the Mind of*

America (1984), Roosevelt was and remained committed to the Zionist vision of a Jewish homeland in Palestine from the early 1930s to the end of his life. Influenced by Brandeis, Frankfurter, and Benjamin Cohen, all of whom he respected, Roosevelt's views on Zionism were "stranger and more complex than either critics or defenders suppose."[16]

Like all American presidents, FDR was influenced by his religious upbringing and was fascinated with the history of the Jewish people. Roosevelt believed wholeheartedly in a Jewish homeland in Palestine. He knew well the importance of the Balfour Declaration in post–World War I Europe and was incensed when he learned of

In 1944, in occupied Germany, NBC Radio, together with the American Jewish Committee, broadcast the first Jewish service since the rise of Hitler.

Courtesy of the American Jewish Committee

417

the British White Paper of 1939. He believed that the solution to the Jewish-Arab problem was to transfer the entire Arab population of Palestine to another country, and he discussed such a plan with Brandeis and with British representatives. He had the same discussion with Chaim Weizmann in 1940. He always believed the issue could be settled "with a little baksheesh" (bribery).[17]

It is true that during the early years of the war, he put the notion of a Jewish homeland on the back burner, but that was because, as with so many other critical issues, he knew that the Allies must concentrate on winning the war before anything could be done in Palestine. He refused to meet Ben-Gurion in 1942 and told Hull that "we should say nothing about the Near East or Palestine or the Arabs at this time. . . . If we pat either group on the back, we automatically stir up trouble." In 1942, he told Morgenthau that he would designate Palestine a religious country and have a joint committee of the major religions govern Jerusalem. If necessary, "I would provide land for the Arabs in some other part of the Middle East." Naturally, if the Jewish population was in the majority, they would govern the country, he told Morgenthau.[18]

Despite the impossibility of getting Arabs, not to mention his own State Department, to agree to a Jewish homeland, Roosevelt stayed his course. He listened to his pro-Arab advisers such as Colonel Harold B. Hoskins, but disagreed with them. In 1943, Roosevelt told Eugene Meyer, publisher of the *Washington Post*, to tell Jewish leaders that "he and Mr. Churchill between them would see them through" when the war was over. It is true that he courted Jewish voters in the 1944 election and had Rabbis Wise and Silver as White House guests for political reasons, but after the election he told Under secretary of State Edward Stettinius in a private, off-the-record conversation that "Palestine should be for the Jews and no Arabs should be in it." He was not for coexistence or a binational state. Palestine "should be exclusive Jewish territory." Yet Roosevelt believed that the half million Jews in Palestine were no match for the millions of Muslims who, he wrote Senator Wagner privately, "want to cut their throats the day they land. The one thing I want to avoid is a massacre."[19]

Roosevelt discussed these issues with Rabbi Wise in January 1945. Wise assured him that the Arabs would not fight and the Jews would not try to take more land. "The President feels confident . . . he will be able to iron out the whole Arab-Jewish issue" at Yalta, Wise told Stettinius and Emanuel Celler. Roosevelt informed Stettinius that he would convince Saud to agree to Palestine for the Jews and independence and economic development for the Arabs. He would take out a map and point out to Saud "what an infinitesimal part of the whole area was occupied by Palestine," Stettinius recorded in his diary. "President Roosevelt said to some of us privately he could do anything that needed to be done with Ibn Saud with a few million dollars," recalled his aide David Niles a year or so later.[20]

Experts and diplomats vainly tried to temper FDR's enthusiasm. "You must be warned," wrote economist James M. Landis in January 1945, "Ibn Saud both personally and as a political matter feels very intensely about [Palestine]." Compromises were always rejected. Recently, Landis went on, "he threatened in the presence of one of my people to see to the execution of any Jew that might seek to enter his dominion." It is true that Roosevelt was shocked by what he heard at his meeting with Saud. But as Wise recalled later, this was "a momentary sense of failure." The Arabs, FDR told Wise in their last meeting, would have to be over-ruled. Roosevelt hoped until his last day on Earth to see a Jewish homeland in Palestine. "I think Eleanor and I will go to the Near East [after the war]," he told Frances Perkins, "and see if we can manage to put over an operation like the Tennessee Valley system that will really make something of that country."21

The United States First Army had crossed the Rhine at Remagen on March 7. Patton's infantry crossed the Moselle. The Allied air forces roamed the skies of Germany at will. Just after Pearl Harbor, Roosevelt had told the American people that the United States could "accept no result save victory, final and complete."22 He had not changed his mind: "Practically every German denies the fact they surrendered in the last war. But this time, they are going to know it!"23 Roosevelt had high hopes that after the war ended, the United Nations would bring peace and stability to the world. He planned to go to the San Francisco Conference on April 25, 1945, to formally establish the new world organization.

Rabbi Leo Baeck was still alive and still ministering to his fellow Jews at Theresienstadt in April. The camp would be liberated by the Soviet army in May, and, on July 5, 1945, the long-suffering rabbi would be reunited with his family. David Ben-Gurion continued his political ascent in the Yishuv. His Mapai Party would continue to dominate Palestinian Jewish politics. By this point in the war, the inmates of Bergen-Belsen were not being executed or gassed. They died a slow, agonizing death from hunger, thirst, exposure, and infectious diseases. Anne and Margot Frank died of typhus between the end of February and mid-March 1945. British troops arrived at the camp on April 15.[24]

On March 24, Roosevelt met with Robert E. Sherwood, who had just returned from a fact-finding mission in the Pacific theater that had included a meeting with MacArthur. Roosevelt told Sherwood he planned to be at the San Francisco Conference "at the start and at the finish, too." He asked Sherwood to find him some quotations for his April 14 Jefferson Day speech. Sherwood found his boss in much worse condition than he had ever seen him. "I thought it was a blessing that he could get away for a while to Warm Springs."[25]

On March 29, 1945, Roosevelt traveled to Warm Springs for the last time. He enjoyed himself as he relaxed in the company of his old friend Lucy Rutherford, Lucy's painter friend Elizabeth Shoumatoff, and his two cousins Margaret Suckley and Laura Delano. His mind was focused on the United Nations. He told his companions that he was thinking of resigning from the presidency and heading the United Nations "if I can get the job." Henry Morgenthau stopped in for a visit on his way from Florida to Washington.[26]

On April 11, 1945, Allied armies liberated Buchenwald. The world would shortly learn what the Final Solution actually was. It

Franklin D. Roosevelt, Warm Springs, GA, April 11, 1945, the day before his death.

Courtesy of the Franklin D. Roosevelt Library

also was the last full day of FDR's life. On the morning of April 12, he went through his correspondence. Among the letters he signed were messages to Arab leaders similar to a letter he had sent Ibn Saud reiterating his assurances about Palestine. He was cheerful and relaxed. Referring to one draft of a letter prepared for his signature he quipped, "A typical State Department letter—it says nothing at all."[27]

At one o'clock he seemed to be looking for something. His cousin Margaret asked him "Have you dropped your cigarette?" He looked at her, his forehead in pain, and tried to smile. "I have a terrific pain in the back of my head," he said, and slumped forward. Shortly thereafter he lost consciousness and died at 3:35 P.M. Margaret Suckley wrote in her diary, "Franklin D. Roosevelt, the hope of the world, is dead."[28]

But for Adolf Hitler, Roosevelt's death was a sign that all his problems were over. Joseph P. Goebbels, the Führer's dwarflike propaganda minister, was ecstatic. "My Führer!" he told Hitler, "I congratulate you. Roosevelt is dead. It is written in the stars that the second half of April will be the turning point for us. This is Friday, 13 April. It is the turning point!" "Here, read this!" Hitler told Albert Speer. "Here! You never wanted to believe it. Here! . . . Here we have the great miracle that I always foretold. Who's right now? The war is not lost. Read it! Roosevelt is dead!" Frederick the Great, Goebbels told his master, had been saved by the death of Tsarina Elizabeth in the Seven Years' War. Field Marshal Kesselring recalled that this was the "miraculous salvation" Hitler clung to "like a drowning man to a straw."[29]

When Robert Sherwood heard the news he thought "It finally crushed him. He couldn't stand up under it any longer. The 'it' was the awful responsibility that had been piling up for so many years. The fears and the hopes of hundreds of millions of human beings throughout the world had been bearing down on the mind of one man, until the pressure was more than mortal flesh could withstand." Senator Robert Taft lamented, "He dies a hero of the war, for he literally worked himself to death in the service of the American people."[30]

Surrounded by his family and friends and Harry Truman, the new president of the United States, and other distinguished mourners, Franklin Delano Roosevelt was buried on April 15, 1945, at Hyde Park, his family home on the Hudson River. West Point cadets acted as a guard of honor. A squad of cadets fired three volleys of musketry, the traditional last tribute given to a soldier. Newspapers around the country added the president's name to their lists of local soldiers and sailors killed or missing in action:

ROOSEVELT, Franklin D. Commander in Chief U.S. Armed Forces, at Warm Springs, Georgia.[31]

Near midnight on April 29, 1945, trapped in his besieged, claustrophobic, subterranean Berlin bunker, Adolf Hitler dictated his "Private Testament." In it, he blamed "international Jewry" for World War II and gloated about his having killed "the real culprit" in the death of millions of "Europe's aryan peoples." On April 30 at 3:30 P.M., eighteen days after Franklin Roosevelt's death, Hitler shot himself in the right temple with his 7.65mm Walther pistol and died. His body was burned in the garden of the Reich Chancellery.[32]

Chapter 22

The Verdict

"God," Samuel Butler quipped, "cannot alter the
past. That is why he is obliged to connive at the
existence of historians."[1]

Everything's got a moral, if only you can find it.
        —*Alice in Wonderland,* Chapter X

What is the verdict on Franklin Roosevelt's efforts to save the Jews during the Holocaust and World War II? The word "verdict" derives from the two Latin words *verus* (true) and *dictum* (speech). It connotes something more than a mere "judgment." It means a true, just, and fair judgment. A verdict in the legal system, as countless judges have charged innumerable juries, must "speak the truth." When we say that a person "stands before the bar of history" or is subject to the "judgment of history," we should at a minimum use the same criteria, the same sense of justice, impartiality, and fairness that courts, judges, and juries are supposed to use. Did a person act reasonably under all of the known circumstances given his realistic choices and in accordance with accepted rules of behavior?

The Holocaust and the Final Solution were conceived in the deranged minds of Adolf Hitler and his followers. It progressed on a twisted path from insult and injury in the 1930s to the monstrous acts of wartime Auschwitz. As Adolf Hitler degraded Jews in Germany, Franklin Roosevelt brought them fully into American political life. As Hitler enacted the Nuremberg Laws, invaded Austria, and persecuted Austrian Jewry, Roosevelt appointed an Austrian-born Jew to the U.S. Supreme Court. No two men in the world differed so dramatically and publicly on the twentieth-century version of the "Jewish question."

Even as Hitler brutally conquered Europe, one-third of the Soviet Union, and the Mediterranean littoral of North Africa, Americans were determined to stay out of war. Wary of Europe's endless quarrels, disillusioned by the First World War, and emerging from the Great Depression, Americans overwhelmingly opposed sending Americans boys overseas to fight Germany. While the United States remained aloof, Hitler became the undisputed master of Europe. At the height of his power in 1942, the Führer controlled nations from the Atlantic to the gates of Moscow, from Norway to Morocco. His Japanese allies controlled vast areas of Asia and the Pacific Ocean. This totalitarian military power allowed Nazi Germany to murder six million Jews.

Miraculously, the British and the Russians, led by their indomitable leaders Winston Churchill and Joseph Stalin, contained the Nazi threat in 1940 and 1941. They did this only because Franklin Delano Roosevelt, America's indomitable leader, defeated powerful forces of isolationism and selfishness at home to create an "arsenal of democracy" that supplied the Allies with desperately needed war matériel. While much of his nation looked the other way, FDR waged a secret, undeclared war against Germany. Patiently and cautiously, he taught the American people to see that the defeat of Nazi Germany was the most critical task facing mankind. The Japanese attack on Pearl Harbor was the starting gun in the American leg of the relay race to smash the Axis across the world. Thanks to Roosevelt's leadership, courage, and vision, the thousand-year Reich was defeated in less than four years after America's entrance into the war.

To defeat Hitler and his Fascist allies and collaborators, Roosevelt was forced to make many difficult, morally distasteful life-and-death decisions. The most difficult was an early, unwavering decision to concentrate on winning a massive land war against Germany quickly and decisively, even if it meant significant loss of American lives, giving a lower priority to the war against Japan, liberating the Philippines and rescuing American POWs held by the Japanese, building a strong government in China, and aiding the captive peoples of Europe and Asia. Late in the war, to protect American POWs in Soviet hands, Roosevelt was forced to return to the Soviet Union—and to certain death—anti-Communist Russian POWs who had deserted the Soviet army. He made unpalatable decisions at home. He abandoned his reform politics and brought in his domestic nemesis Big Business to run the war efficiently; interned loyal Japanese Americans; kept out desperate refugees; suppressed antiwar publications; ignored racial segregation in the armed services; and put on hold the issue of creating a Jewish nation until the war was over. His life was expended and all of his values subordinated to defeat the Nazis.[2] As he said many times, he worked with the tools he was given.

FDR never fully understood or knew Hitler's insane, half-secret war against the Jews or the Holocaust the way we do now. Richard Breitman has observed that in the Nazi view of the world, Jews were the cause of all of Germany's troubles. Therefore, from the Nazis' perspective, military setbacks or even losing the war was no reason to stop the Final Solution. Rather, it was a reason to continue it. This viewpoint would have been incomprehensible to FDR.[3] He never saw the films and photographs of Buchenwald, Bergen-Belsen, or Auschwitz. Had he lived to see them, even with what he knew, he, like most Americans, would have been shocked.

On the day FDR died, April 12, 1945, Generals Dwight Eisenhower and Omar Bradley visited the Ohrdruf-Nord concentration camp near Gotha, Germany. SS guards had murdered everyone before fleeing to prevent the inmates from testifying. Bodies were everywhere; the stench was unbearable. Bradley was speechless. George S. Patton vomited and refused to enter a room containing the corpses of men starved to death. Eisenhower was stunned. The atrocities were "beyond the American mind to comprehend," he said. That night he declared, "I can't understand the mentality that would compel these German people to do a thing like that."

The next day the supreme commander visited Buchenwald. "I

While touring the newly liberated Ohrdruf camp, General Dwight Eisenhower and other high-ranking U.S. Army officers view the bodies of prisoners who were killed during the evacuation of the camp, April 12, 1945.

Courtesy of the American Jewish Committee

never dreamed that such cruelty, bestiality, and savagery could really exist in this world! It was horrible," he wrote his wife, Mamie. Some American officers wept. "The things I saw beggar description," Eisenhower wrote Marshall. "I made the visit deliberately, in order to be in a position to give firsthand evidence of these things if ever, in the future, there develops a tendency to charge these allegations merely to 'propaganda.' "[4]

Why were Eisenhower, Bradley, and Patton shocked by what they saw? The Allies had denounced the extermination of the Jews 2 1/2 years before, and Eisenhower himself had issued a warning to the Germans. But reports of extermination and finally seeing and understanding it were entirely different things. Franklin Roosevelt had faced a human tragedy the scale of which was new to history—"a crime without a name," as Churchill called the Holocaust. People refused to believe it. It was unprecedented. It was unexpected. Hannah Arendt, an early German refugee from Nazi persecution and later author of *The Origins of Totalitarianism* and *Eichmann in Jerusalem*, stated that well into 1943 neither she nor her husband believed reports about the Holocaust. It just "couldn't be," she recalled. It was "militarily unnecessary and uncalled for," her husband told her. "Don't listen to any of these fairy tales, they couldn't do that," he said.[5]

When the massacre of the Jews was first publicized by Rabbi Stephen Wise in November and December 1942, there was general disbelief. An American journalist recalled:

> *There were many things happening in Washington and many things happening in the world. . . . I went to a press conference with Stephen Wise and he talked about mass murder of Jews in Europe. And he had what he said was evidence of that. There were perhaps five or six other reporters at the place. There were many other events happening at the time. Did I write a story about it? Yes. Did it make one of the wires? Yes. Did papers pick it up? Yes. Did anybody believe it? I doubt it. Did I believe it? Yes, perhaps halfway I believed it. I believed a little bit of it. I didn't believe all*

of it. It was beyond the comprehension of everybody in this country.[6]

Until late 1942, Ben-Gurion and his colleagues visualized large-scale pogroms, not the Final Solution. In January 1944, he said, "None of us . . . myself included . . . knew that the catastrophe was so near and so great." His biographer Shabtai Teveth wrote, "as must be repeated forever, such annihilation was far beyond his grasp and that of his generation." He foresaw destruction, but not the Holocaust. Ben-Gurion was not alone. When a survivor of Transnistria, fifteen-year-old Jona Scharf, arrived in Palestine in August 1944, no one, including her own brother, believed her story of concentration camps. "They didn't believe that people were made to dig their own graves, and were then shot to death. I suppose it was really too horrible to believe."[7]

There was disbelief even among those privy to information about the Final Solution and most emotionally invested in the victims. Leon Kubowitzki told the WJC that in June 1943, "a year ago"—after the Bermuda Conference—"we did not know the appalling dimensions of the exterminations. We knew that hundreds of thousands had been killed. We did not know that we had lost two-thirds of the Polish Jews. We did not know that the immense majority of the Jews of occupied Russia had been murdered." Disbelief continued into 1944. "So revolting and diabolical are the German atrocities that the minds of civilized people find it difficult to believe that they have actually taken place," a November 1944 WRB press release stated.[8]

Assistant Secretary of War John J. McCloy "could not shake his disbelief" that the Holocaust was taking place as late as December 1944. He told Kubowitzki, "We are alone. Tell me the truth. Do you really believe that all those horrible things happened?" Kubowitzki concluded years afterward that McCloy's "sources of information . . . were better than mine. But he could not grasp the terrible destruction."[9]

Arthur Koestler, a Hungarian Jewish refugee and a journalist, wrote in the *New York Times Magazine* in January 1944:

> *I have been lecturing now for three years to the troops, and their attitude is the same. They don't believe in concentration camps, they don't believe in the starved children of Greece, in the shot hostages of France, in the mass graves of Poland, they have never heard of Lidice, Treblinka or Belzec; you can convince them for an hour, then they shake themselves, their mental self-defense begins to work and in a week the shrug of incredulity has returned like a reflex temporarily weakened by a shock.*[10]

Clearly there was information, but as Yehuda Bauer, Walter Laqueur, and others point out "information did not mean knowledge."[11] As Peter Novick observed, there was a natural will to disbelieve atrocity stories. "Who after all, would want to think that such things were true?" The U.S. Office of War Information concluded that even if the facts were true, they would be thought to be exaggerated and the agency would lose credibility by disseminating them. War is about killing and hardening one's heart to death and destruction and turning away from unpleasant thoughts, especially when it comes to civilians who are citizens of other countries.[12] Louis de Jong, an eminent Dutch historian and a Holocaust survivor, reminded his audience in 1989 at a lecture at Harvard University:

> *[There is] an aspect of the Holocaust which is of cardinal importance and which can never be sufficiently underlined: that the Holocaust, when it took place, was beyond the belief and the comprehension of almost all people living at the time, Jews included. Everyone knew that human history had been scarred by endless cruelties. But that thousands, nay millions, of human beings—men, women and children, the old and the young, the healthy and the infirm—would be killed, finished off, mechanically, industrially so to speak, would be exterminated like vermin—that was a notion so alien to the human mind, an event so gruesome, so new, that the instinctive, indeed the natural, reaction of most people was: it can't be true.*[13]

Tragically, it must also be recognized that life during World War II was fragile. The Germans captured 5,700,000 Soviet prisoners (about the size of the entire U.S. Army overseas), and about 3,300,000 died in captivity. These deaths occurred mostly in 1941 and 1942 under horrifying circumstances, including starvation, cannibalism, typhus, and exposure. Germany targeted civilians in Allied cities. The Allies retaliated, killing 600,000 German and more than nine hundred thousand Japanese civilians before the war was over.[14]

What did Franklin Roosevelt do in the face of the Nazi threat? First and foremost, he led the Allies to victory. There can be little debate that his leadership was a critical factor, perhaps the most critical factor, in the defeat of Nazi Germany. Historians generally agree that he was an architect of victory in World War II. He stood steadfastly against Hitler and for Britain and the Soviet Union. Without Roosevelt's leadership, Hitler could easily have killed twice as many Jews as he did. The defeat of Britain and Russia, or even a stalemate governed by a Pax Germanica, would have resulted ultimately in the extermination of all of the Jews of the Soviet Union, the Middle East, and probably Great Britain had it been occupied by Germany. How can any right-thinking person conclude otherwise?

Roosevelt's contemporaries correctly believed he was their savior from the Nazi onslaught. Churchill's military aide, General Hastings Ismay, found Roosevelt to be the perfect coalition chairman, "wise, conciliatory, paternal." "Above all, he was absolutely fearless," Isaiah Berlin wrote of Roosevelt. "In a despondent world which appeared divided between wicked and fatally efficient fanatics marching to destroy, and bewildered populations on the run . . . he believed in his own ability . . . to stem this terrible tide. He had all the character and energy and skill of the dictators, and he was on our side."[15] Beginning in 1933, he consistently defined and defended liberal, democratic values that protected Jews. His moral authority had no parallel. Politics, we are told, is the art of the possible. Even in the face of most of America's hostility to European immigrants, the fact of the Great Depression, and substantial antisemitism at home, Roosevelt held firm to his beliefs. From 1933 to 1940 he worked within the immigration laws—laws he was powerless to change—to provide as much relief as he could to Jewish refugees, consistent with political reality.

"The stricken people in the Balkans have one and one hope only, and that is 'President Roosevelt,' " Hirschmann wrote Isador Lubin on April 20, 1944. "I heard this again and again. As I spoke to the refugees, somehow they all seemed to know of the President's order [creating the WRB]. 'Thank God for your Great President,' they keep saying to me."[16]

"They won the war, didn't they?" the Polish courier, Jan Karski, told one interviewer. "They crushed Germany. If it were not for this victory, all of Europe would be enslaved today. That I know." Gerhart Riegner of the WJC kept a picture of FDR on his office wall at the office of the World Jewish Congress. In 1942, he called FDR "one of the most farsighted statesmen of our time" and "one of the most comprehensive friends of our people." "We needed inspiration," Riegner told Richard Breitman in the 1990s. "FDR's image served that purpose—even if it was a disappointment to learn later that FDR was also another politician. Still, I will give him credit; he had a strategy to win the war." Indeed, Peter Bergson said that Roosevelt was among "our staunchest friends."[17]

A Jewish sergeant, Alan S. Maggin, wrote his wife on April 13, 1945:

> *When I got up this morning, the sun was shining and I felt in a swell mood. Right now however I feel like crying . . . Lieutenant Walston told me that President Roosevelt had died last night . . . He was a great man, honey, and only the history books in the future will appreciate how truly great he was . . . He fought and died for his country, while others with less foresight just sat back and wanted to wait while we hung on the brink of disaster.*[18]

"Men will thank God on their knees a hundred years from now that Franklin D. Roosevelt was in the White House," the often hostile *New York Times* opined at the time of his death.[19] "More than any other man of his time, Roosevelt radiated faith in the survival of democracy and decency," Lucy Dawidowicz observed in 1982. "American Jews loved him for his good works and ideals, but most of all for his hatred of the Nazi regime."[20] Roosevelt turned America from a wary looker-on into Hitler's strongest foe. His persistent attacks on isolationists as "narrow, self-serving, partisan, conservative, antidemocratic, antisemitic, pro-Nazi, fifth columnist, and even treasonous" (in the words of historian Wayne S. Cole) rallied Americans to fight Germany. "No wonder the Jews loved Roosevelt," Dawidowicz pointed out.[21]

Roosevelt helped to win the war and defeat Hitler, but why did he not do more to save the Jews? While the charges against FDR of indifference or the laughable charge of complicity in the Holocaust are many and varied, the chief accusations concentrate on six issues: United States immigration laws, the SS *St. Louis* incident, failure to denounce the Holocaust, the Bermuda Conference, the War Refugee Board, and most frequently the Allies' decision not to bomb Auschwitz. A just reckoning on these charges requires an accurate description of each and a careful examination of each of them before one, two, or even six verdicts can be rendered by scholars and interested readers.

United States Immigration Laws

James MacGregor Burns called FDR a lion and a fox. Roosevelt decriers accused him of "political expediency" and a "politics of gestures." A lion relies on strength, but a fox must sometimes resort to subterfuge and expediency. Indeed, Roosevelt famously said of himself, "You know I am a juggler and I never let my right hand know what my left hand does." The critical point is that, overall, given the reality of the political situation and Americans' strong opposition to allowing in more immigrants, security issues, and world war, Roosevelt's policies saved as many Jews as could realistically be saved. It is extremely doubtful that any other leader could have saved more lives. Before the Final Solution, when saving Jews was possible, the United States took in more refugees than any other country. When Hitler unloosed his genocidal war, Roosevelt chose the cautious approach of protecting the American homeland and limiting immigration.[22]

Charges by revisionist historians in the 1980s and 1990s that FDR deliberately failed to liberalize American immigration laws in the 1930s and early 1940s can quickly be dismissed. As we have seen, he simply did not have the political clout to accomplish this. Since the era of World War I the U.S. Congress and the American people were committed to a highly restrictive immigration policy. The Great Depression and European military aggression doomed immigration reform in all of the Western nations. "The importance of security questions in public debate over immigration affairs at this time cannot be overestimated," J. Bruce Nichols concluded. The political consensus underlying the immigration laws was so profound that even Senator Robert Wagner of New York, sponsor of the 1939 Wagner-Rogers Bill, did not advocate a change. Wagner received thousands of requests from constituents of many nationalities seeking help for relatives and friends. His 1938–39 "Alien Files" fill ten archival boxes. But he routinely replied that he "cannot advance people on the lists."[23]

In June 1940, when sympathy for France and Great Britain was strong, there was considerable opposition to allowing even children to come to the United States temporarily. Seven different congressional bills allowing special visitors' visas to French children and other European children stranded in France were defeated. Despite opposition by some congressmen, British children were given special treatment by virtue of the large British quota and the fact that these children would return to Britain when the war was over. Even with this favorable treatment, few British children actually came to the United States because no vessels could be found, as the Germans refused safe conduct and actually sank ships with British children aboard.[24]

Some historians have disparaged Roosevelt's calling of the international conference at Évian, France, in 1938. Apparently unaware that Congress, not the president, enacts immigration laws, Herbert Druks wrote, "The President refused to have the immigration laws changed and sought to solve the problem by initiating a world conference on refugees." According to Henry L. Feingold, the Évian Conference was an empty political gesture, not a genuine effort to solve the problem. Évian was an example of "the vacillating, contradictory character" of Roosevelt's policies, a mere "policy of gestures." For Robert S. Wistrich, Évian was not merely a "farce," it also *increased* the Nazis' brutal policies by demonstrating that the Western nations were unwilling to accept Jewish refugees. David Wyman faults FDR because his administration "did not attempt to bypass the law to rescue any sizable number of refugees," although at the same time he conceded that such a move "undoubtedly would have been both futile and dangerous."[25]

These historians are guilty of the worst kind of judgment by hindsight. The evidence demonstrated that Roosevelt did all he reasonably could with the limited power he possessed. Even his critics acknowledge that America's immigration laws were politically impossible to change. The chances of changing the immigration laws were, according to Wyman, nonexistent.[26] As to the Évian Conference, Wyman conceded that a "humanitarian motivation on Roosevelt's part may by no means be ruled out"; that Roosevelt "stood to lose more by taking the lead in calling the conference than he could gain"; and that it exposed him to strong criticism. In plain English, by calling the Évian Conference, Roosevelt did all he could and at considerable political risk. He put the issue on the international agenda. He highlighted Nazi hatred of Jews and its impact on the rest of the world.[27]

As to the Roosevelt administration's record on admitting refugees into the United States, it is instructive to look in two stages: what Roosevelt did before the fall of France in 1940, an event that shocked Americans, and what he did thereafter. America admitted tens of thousands of German and Austrian Jewish immigrants between 1933 and 1938. The exact figures are not known, but William Rubinstein estimated the number at 46,000. Another work estimates it at 102,000.[28] In fact, revisionist historians' misreading of history was nowhere better illustrated than in their failure to describe fairly the rescue of German and Austrian Jewry. Feingold wrote that "the failure of Évian to produce concrete results made Jewish leaders . . . realize that no Western country intended to be a haven for the Jews of Germany and Austria, no matter how dire the conditions became for Jews in Nazi-controlled territories."[29] Rafael Medoff in *The Deafening Silence* (1987) and Saul Friedman in *No Haven for the Oppressed* (1973) elaborated on America's and Roosevelt's alleged failings (Medoff's chapter titles include "As Heartless as It May Seem" and "However Imminent Be Their Peril") but never informed their readers that 72 percent of German and Austrian Jews found a haven in the Western democracies, including 83 percent of German Jewish children and youth. According to Rubinstein, it "constituted one of the most successful and far-reaching programs of rescue of a beleaguered and persecuted people ever seen up to that time."[30]

World War II began in September 1939. By then Hitler had power over the Jews of Germany, Austria, and Czechoslovakia, but not the Jews of Poland and Russia, who later became his chief victims. The Jewish population of Germany in 1933 was about 500,000 (525,000 if the Saar is included after 1935). Rubinstein estimated that at most, 24,700 Jewish children and youth remained within the pre-1933 boundaries of Germany in September 1939. Most Austrian Jews also survived. Of the 185,000 Jews in Austria at the time of the *Anschluss* (March 12, 1938), 126,000 emigrated by the end of 1939. Sixty-eight percent of Austrian Jewry fled within 21 months. The start of the war sealed the fate of those Germans, Austrians, and Czechs who stayed behind. Rarely in history have so many escaped certain persecution so quickly.[31]

From 1938 to 1940, the United States responded positively to the crisis. In that period of restrictive immigration laws and widespread antisemitism, Jews comprised half of *all* immigrants admitted to the United States. The democracies had a small window of opportunity to take in the bulk of the Reich's Jews and they succeeded, even given the difficult circumstances. While it is true that the United States had a strict quota system established in the 1920s, the quota for Germany (25,957 per year) was the highest for any country other than Britain (65,721). It was much higher than Italy (5,802), Ireland (17,853), or Spain (252), and ironically, German and Austrian Jews benefited from the German quota. It is well to remember that, of the nearly six million Jews who were murdered in the Holocaust, 4,565,000 were Polish and Russian and 125,000 were German. The United States accepted about twice as many refugees as the rest of the world combined, 200,000 of 300,000.[32]

FDR tried to do even more. He held his nose and vigorously pursued a ransom scheme, the Rublee Plan, with the Nazis in 1938 and 1939 through the IGCR, which failed only because the Nazis would not agree to let the Jews go. His willingness to support this scheme came from the fact that he was far ahead of the rest of the world, including the American Jewish leadership, in seeing what might lay ahead if the Jews of Germany were not ransomed.[33]

After the war began in 1939 and especially after the fall of France in 1940, Roosevelt clamped down on immigration for fear of subversion, spies, and terrorists. He had vivid recollections of the Red Scare of the 1920s and German espionage in the United States, particularly the 1916 "Black Tom" incident, in which German saboteurs destroyed munitions on Black Tom Island, New Jersey, near New York City. His first priority was, as it should have been, the protection of the American homeland. Security, Roosevelt believed, came first. Congress and the American people were vehement in keeping the doors closed to any aliens who might be potential provocateurs and terrorists. Roosevelt was preparing for a possible war, and he wanted national unity above all else. Liberalizing the immigration laws was political dynamite, not a political balm.

As Novick points out, we know that technical and military obstacles are sometimes intractable (fleets of American transport planes could not sweep down and rescue concentration camp prisoners), but we somehow believe that all attitudinal or political obstacles can be overcome. Yet we also know that "dramatic reversals in mass attitudes toward immigration . . . [were] impossible and absurd." Because FDR appeared so powerful, because he was so admired by American Jews, and because he gave so much hope to the Jewish people, his inability to change the immigration laws now seems inexplicable. But even Franklin Roosevelt could not accomplish the impossible.[34]

The SS St. Louis Incident

As we have seen, the charge against FDR of indifference to the fate of the SS *St. Louis* refugees is also unfounded. The Joint Distribution Committee, with the active help of the Roosevelt administration, saved the passengers on the SS *St. Louis* from returning to Germany. Despite this undeniable fact, many people erroneously believed the "ill-fated ship" returned to Germany and that all of its passengers were sent to concentration camps. As we have seen, at least two-thirds of the passengers on the *St. Louis* survived the war. Revisionist historians asserted that FDR turned a deaf ear to their pleas because he was either an antisemite or a coldhearted coward. It was a myth that the United States Coast Guard was sent to keep the passengers from swimming ashore when Treasury Secretary Morgenthau ordered them to track the ship to help the passengers. Some scholars claimed that American Jews were scared and silent in the face of this outrage, when they obviously were not. Why are people asked to believe these myths?

The reason is simple. Scholars, historians, and journalists who wrote about the *St. Louis wanted* to establish that everyone, particularly Americans, bore some responsibility for the Holocaust.[35] After all, if everyone is to blame, Roosevelt, the most powerful man on Earth, must be especially at fault. The basic indictment of all "bystanders" to the *St. Louis* tragedy—the Roosevelt administration, American Jewry, and indeed all Americans—was concocted by a sensationalist former CBS News reporter named Arthur D. Morse in 1967. His best-selling book *While Six Million Died: A Chronicle of American Apathy* (1967) had all the virtues and defects of yellow journalism: exciting disclosures ("for the first time"), reckless allegations of supposed misdeeds by high government officials, the "inside story" by a reporter with an eye for news, no opportunity for the accused to respond, interesting characters, and a one-sided verdict. It was everything a tabloid newspaper publisher could want. Morse's account of the *St. Louis* was based primarily on interviews with Lawrence Berensen, the lawyer who, sadly, botched the passengers' case in Cuba. Morse failed to interview most of the other participants, such as Henry Morgenthau, or examine the records of the Joint. Despite its baleful effect, the book influenced recent Roosevelt biographers such as Kenneth S. Davis, who based his treatment of the *St. Louis* on Morse's work.[36] Whether or not history repeats itself, historians surely repeat each other.

Morse's newspaper-story-as-history only works if FDR and

the American Jewish leadership are portrayed as apathetic, cowardly, indifferent, or even complicit with the Nazis, which is, of course, the opposite of the truth. In Rabbi Haskel Lookstein's *Were We Our Brothers' Keepers?* (1985), the story of the *St. Louis* moves from incomplete facts to sermonizing. In the preface to Lookstein's book Elie Wiesel claimed that "Everyone knows: if its passengers cannot disembark they will be delivered to the executioner," as if the death camps—not yet built and probably not yet planned in June 1939—were already in operation. Wiesel damned American Jews for not taking to the streets "to vent their anger at Roosevelt." But he did not seem to appreciate what the American Jewish leadership and the Roosevelt administration actually did. American Jews had no reason to "vent their anger" at Roosevelt, because they were not angry with the man whose administration was cooperating with the Joint to save the passengers and who was emerging to the world as its only hope to stop Hitler.[37]

This story needs a villain at the highest level. Who better than Roosevelt himself? Virtually everyone who has written on the *St. Louis* has condemned Roosevelt for his failure to reply to telegrams from the passengers. He "did not reply to or even acknowledge the two telegrams sent to him by the passenger committee on the *St. Louis*," Gordon Thomas and Max Witts wrote in *Voyage of the Damned* (1994), the only book-length treatment of the *St. Louis* incident.[38] But the only truthful telegram Roosevelt could have sent was:

> *Dear Passengers: I cannot violate the immigration laws of the United States enacted by an overwhelming majority of the Congress fifteen years ago, and therefore I cannot allow you to disembark in the United States. I am, however, encouraging my State Department to help the Joint bribe governments in Cuba and Europe to allow you to enter. I could make the* St. Louis *a big issue but that might well derail my secret plan, which I have not shared with Congress or the American people, to help France and Great Britain stand up to that Jew-hating Hitler. P.S. Please do not tell anyone I am involved in a secret war against Hitler. FDR.*

Had Roosevelt sent a telegram telling the passengers why he could not help them and wishing them luck, he would have long ago been skewered for sending a bland, insensitive, politically motivated message designed to garner Jewish votes.

Revisionist historians have ignored the embarrassing fact that all of the passengers on the *St. Louis* were actually *saved* from going back to Germany at that time. Geoffrey Perrett in *Days of Sadness, Years of Triumph, the American People, 1939–1945* (1973) told his readers that "the governments of Britain, France and the Netherlands agreed to take most, but not all, of the refugees in. The rest (no one knows exactly how many there were) sailed to Hamburg, to torture and death." Arthur Hertzberg wrote in *The Jews in America: Four Centuries of an Uneasy Encounter . . . A History* (1989) that the "desperate passengers . . . telegraphed the President, but he ignored them. The ship had no choice but to go back to Hamburg; most of its passengers ultimately perished in Nazi-held Europe." The *ship* returned to Hamburg but the *passengers* did not. Rafael Medoff, author of *The Deafening Silence*, tells us histrionically, if not historically, that the *St. Louis* "chugs slowly back toward Hitler's inferno," but death camps, ovens, and crematoriums did not exist in June 1939. The fact was that according to the U.S. Constitution, only Congress, by amending the statutes on immigration, could allow the *St. Louis* passengers to enter the United States. The president of the United States—even FDR—could not change laws enacted by Congress by issuing dictatorial decrees.[39]

The story of the *St. Louis* as it is currently told has become a modern fairy tale. Like all fairy tales, it has an important "lesson" to teach. The moral is that "bystanders," namely Americans (especially Jewish Americans) and the antisemitic Franklin D. Roosevelt, failed to help the victims of Nazism. By their sins of omission, these alleged "bystanders" were therefore accomplices of the Nazis. (The fact that Americans rescued the passengers somehow disappears from the story.) *Newsweek* magazine, in a story on evil in American society, told the *St. Louis* fairy tale this way.

> *When Hitler saw that the 900 Jews fleeing Germany in 1939 on the ship* St. Louis *had been turned back by Cuba, refused entry by every other country and had returned to the Third Reich, "he took that as a rationalization," says Dr. Carl Goldberg, a psychoanalyst at*

the Albert Einstein College of Medicine in New York.
"See, the world doesn't care about these people. We can
do with them whatever we like." [Emphasis added][40]

Historians knew the truth but chose to emphasize Roosevelt's
alleged failure to save the *St. Louis* passengers from returning to
Germany at the time. Wyman's *Paper Walls* (1968) fails to tell the
story of the *St. Louis* in depth, and omits the critical roles of the
State Department and the Joint. Wyman apparently was not interested in relaying the positive accomplishments of his bêtes noirs,
the Roosevelt administration and the American Jewish leadership,
because the *St. Louis* episode contradicts his charges of America's
"abandonment of the Jews." In a later preface (1985) he repeated
the *New York Times* story that the Coast Guard patrol boat was
sent to prevent attempts by refugees to jump off when he had to
have been aware of Morgenthau's conversation with Hull about
sending the cutters to keep track of the ship so it could return to
Cuba. The necessary evidence existed in Morgenthau's diary,
which Wyman quoted, but only when it served his purpose.

To call Roosevelt an antisemite and condemn his administration as accomplices of the Nazis with regard to the SS *St. Louis* is
contrary to the known facts. Obviously it was a human tragedy of
the first order that people, so close to freedom, were returned to
Europe, where some would become victims of the Holocaust. But
Roosevelt had no way of seeing three years into the future. Roosevelt knew, through Welles, Hull, Morgenthau, and Rosenman,
that the Joint was doing all that could be done for the *St. Louis*

passengers and that his confidant Sumner Wells was assisting in that effort. Roosevelt thought it wiser not to do anything publicly. He understood and approved bribery and behind-the-scenes diplomacy and knew that the Joint with the active cooperation of his administration saved every passenger on the SS *St. Louis* from going back to Germany.[41]

Stella Suberman, the young Jewish woman from Miami Beach whose husband, Jack, served in the army air corps, recalled seeing the SS *St. Louis* off the coast of Florida. "I did not know that in time this ship would become a cause célèbre . . . [but] I was confident that our government was in some unpublicized way seeing to those Jews." Years later, Stella was told and consequently believed that the ship was denied the right to land by President Roosevelt and "the Voyage of the Damned" ended tragically in Europe. But, as it turns out, the belief of the young Stella, the one who naively thought that "our government was in some unpublicized way seeing to those Jews," was correct.[42]

Failure to Denounce the Holocaust

When World War II began on September 1, 1939, Roosevelt faced the same challenge that George Washington met at Valley Forge and Abraham Lincoln after Fort Sumter: how to convince the American people to fight and stay the course to victory. Whatever Hitler said or did about the Jews of Europe was of small moment in the bigger picture of what the Allies would do to defeat the Axis juggernaut. Without victory over Hitler, Mussolini, and Tojo on the battlefield, the world faced a future full of Holocausts. By

1941, millions of innocent Jews, Poles, Russians, Czechs, Belgians, and Chinese were being murdered by design. Roosevelt embarked on what Steven Casey has called a "cautious crusade," defeating the Nazis while holding a difficult coalition of disparate races, religions, ethnic groups, and nations together and keeping others—Muslims, Arabs, and Irish—quiet.

Roosevelt had spoken out eloquently and forcefully about Nazi aggression and crimes against humanity generally and against Jews specifically since the late 1930s. Alone among world leaders, he had publicly rebuked the German government for *Kristallnacht* in November 1938 and recalled the American ambassador, never to return. Of course, Roosevelt was not speaking out against the Final Solution because it had not yet begun. As Arno J. Mayer pointed out, this "intensified persecution was not a prelude to . . . predetermined mass murder." It was "more an echo of the pogroms" of the past. Nevertheless, FDR and his administration were among Hitler's most vociferous critics. Roosevelt was well aware early on that talking and threatening had no effect on Hitler. In his fireside chat of September 11, 1941, before Pearl Harbor, he had said, "I assume that the German leaders are not deeply concerned, tonight or any other time, by what we Americans or the American government say or publish about them. We cannot bring about the downfall of Nazism by the use of long-range invective."[43]

The Final Solution began with the mass shooting of Jews, among others, in Russia by the *Einsatzgruppen* and *Ord-nungspolizei* in June 1941. Even Roosevelt's critics concede that

Hitler was able to do whatever he wanted in occupied Russia and Poland. The United States was not even a belligerent (and Roosevelt had failed to provoke Hitler into starting a war in the Atlantic) until the Japanese bombed Pearl Harbor on December 7, 1941, after the Final Solution had begun.

By late 1942, when Hitler was at the height of his power, the Allies knew that the Germans were massacring Jews. Roosevelt, along with Churchill, Stalin, and ten Allied governments-in-exile, denounced the German atrocities in a published and widely disseminated declaration condemning the "German Policy of Extermination of the Jewish Race." Not content with "denying to persons of Jewish race . . . the most elementary human rights," the declaration began, the Germans "are now carrying into effect Hitler's oft-repeated intention to exterminate the Jewish people in Europe." The declaration continued:

> *From all the occupied countries Jews are being transported in conditions of appalling horror and brutality to Eastern Europe. In Poland, which has been made the principal Nazi slaughterhouse, the ghettos established by the German invader are being systematically emptied of all Jews except a few highly skilled workers required for war industries. None of those taken away are ever heard of again. The able-bodied are slowly worked to death in labor camps. The infirm are left to die of exposure and starvation or are deliberately massacred in mass executions. The number of*

victims of these bloody cruelties is reckoned in many hundreds of thousands of entirely innocent men, women, and children.

The above-mentioned Governments and the French National Committee condemn in the strongest possible terms this bestial policy of cold-blooded extermination. They declare that such events can only strengthen the resolve of all freedom-loving peoples to overthrow the barbarous Hitlerite tyranny. They reaffirm their solemn resolution to ensure that those responsible for these crimes shall not escape retribution and to press on with the necessary practical measures to this end.[44]

This explicit declaration was front-page news in the *New York Times* and throughout the world. Those who condemn Roosevelt's failure to speak out ignore this declaration and claim he was part of a "conspiracy of silence." Michael Beschloss in his bestseller *The Conquerors* (2002) titles his chapter on the subject "The Terrible Silence." But there was no such conspiracy, and Roosevelt was not silent.

Many Roosevelt critics ignore the declaration and omit it from their rendition of history. Robert S. Wistrich's *Hitler and the Holocaust* (2001) leaves it out of his chapter titled "Britain, America, and the Holocaust." Beschloss claims that FDR's references to the extermination of the Jews were "vague and seldom" prior to 1944 and that he "did not mention the subject . . . except in the most oblique fashion in his public statements." His description of the declaration follows the anti-FDR, America-as-bystander line: "On December 17, 1942, at the initiative of the British, the Allies issued a declaration against 'exposure and starvation' and 'mass executions' imposed by the Nazis on "many hundreds of thousands of innocent men, women, and children." This is a pale paraphrase and selective quotation from the declaration. Beschloss unaccountably omits the explicit, dramatic, public, front-page condemnation of the German government's "bestial policy of cold-blooded extermination." He never mentions the critical word "extermination," which was used three times in the statement.[45] Other Roosevelt critics also downgrade the declaration to an unimportant statement. Deborah E. Lipstadt refers to it dismissively as "the December 1942 statement confirming the Nazi policy of exterminating the Jews." Feingold belittles the declaration.[46]

With the declaration issued and the Germans publicly warned of eventual retribution, the Allies utilized massive propaganda and psychological warfare to demoralize the enemy, urge the captive people of Europe to join the Allied cause, influence the outcome of specific battles and campaigns, and deceive the enemy. While this effort was designed to win the war, not focus on the Holocaust, it regularly denounced Nazi atrocities against *all* Europeans in order to convince *all* Europeans to join the resistance. "That the Nazis were the enemy of the Jews was well known; there was no rhetorical advantage in continuing to underline the fact," Novick observes. "The challenge was to show that they were everyone's enemy, to broaden rather than narrow the range of Nazi victims."[47]

Roosevelt and the U.S. government spoke out against Nazi

atrocities throughout the war. Winston Churchill's Moscow Declaration on Atrocities of November 1, 1943, resulted from frustration with the Allies' response to the Holocaust. That declaration warned future participants in genocide that the Allies had received "from many quarters evidence of atrocities, massacres, and cold-blooded executions." While the brutalities of "the Hitlerite forces" were "no new thing . . . [w]hat is new is that many of these territories are now being redeemed" by Allied armies. "The recoiling Hitlerite Huns are redoubling their ruthless cruelties." Therefore the Allied powers declared that lists of the "abominable deeds" would be compiled "in all possible detail," from all Nazi Europe, "the three Allied powers will pursue [every guilty German] to the uttermost ends of the earth and will deliver them to their accusers in order that justice may be done." In keeping with Allied strategy and philosophy that Jews were not, as Hitler claimed, a separate nation or race, Jews were not always specifically mentioned but "the slaughters inflicted on the people of Poland" and "in the territories of the Soviet republic" that included Polish and Russian Jews were specified.[48]

Some Jewish leaders were outraged by the Allies' failure to mention Jews by name. On November 4 David Niles, an FDR aide, sent a note to the president's press secretary asking him to inform Roosevelt that "our American enemies" (the Irgunists) were interpreting the omission as "an invitation to Mr. Hitler to continue his atrocities against Jews. I tried to point out [to them] that the Moscow Conference did not mention any religious group, like Catholics or Protestants." Niles suggested having someone ask the president to declare publicly that crimes against Jews were included in the declaration. As a result, Cordell Hull appeared before a joint session of Congress and stated that "bestial and abominable" Nazi crimes had been perpetrated "against people of all races and religions, among whom Hitler has reserved for the Jews his most brutal wrath. Sure punishment will be administered for all these crimes." Hull regularly denounced the Nazi crimes against the Jews during 1944.[49]

On March 24, 1944, at the instigation of the War Refugee Board, Roosevelt issued his well-known statement about "one of the blackest crimes of all history . . . the wholesale systematic murder of the Jews of Europe." The U.S. Holocaust Memorial Museum ignored this statement and claimed that the WRB unsuccessfully pressed for a presidential condemnation of Nazi genocide. Of course, to speak out or to fail to speak out about the Holocaust is an emotional issue of the first magnitude. Failure to publicly condemn the Nazi genocide would have been morally reprehensible. But the whole debate misses the point. First, FDR *did* publicly condemn the Germans. Roosevelt knew, as he said in 1941, that the German leaders were not "deeply concerned . . . by what we Americans or the American government say or publish about them." Winning the war was the only response to the Nazi genocide, the only message Hitler understood. Even though FDR did so, speaking out did not stop or even slow down the Holocaust. In fact, it may have increased Hitler's determination to kill more Jews.

"The World Jewish Congress had repeatedly insisted from the

outset of the extermination process on the immense value of solemn, specific, and reiterated warning," the WJC's "Program of Relief and Rescue of Jews" submitted to the WRB on March 3, 1944, read.[50] While Jewish leaders and rescue organizations hoped and believed that "solemn warnings" from Roosevelt and Churchill would deter the Nazis, they were proven wrong. Indeed, FDR's Declaration of December 17, 1942, not only failed to deter the Nazis, it also may have spurred the Germans on to even greater efforts at genocide.

In his broadcast to the German people on February 18, Hitler's propaganda minister Goebbels, made this reference to the protest of the United Nations:

> *If hostile foreign countries raise a sanctimonious protest against our antisemitic policy and shed hypocritical crocodile tears over our measures against Jewry, that cannot prevent us from doing what is necessary. Germany in any case has no intention of yielding to this Jewish threat, but intends rather to exercise against Jewry our prompt and, if necessary, our complete and most radical suppression.*[51]

Even FDR's bitter critic Irgunist Ben Hecht conceded that "speaking out" was a waste of time. "The outcry [against the German murder of the Jews] seemed to make little sense and hold less victory. It had reached German ears and done no good. My theory had been wrong. The Germans, made aware that the murder of the Jews was humanly distasteful to the world, had not stayed their reddened hands. They had continued killing Jews." The composer Kurt Weill, who collaborated with Hecht on the pageant We Will Never Die, said that it had "accomplished nothing . . . all we have done is make a lot of Jews cry, which is not a unique accomplishment."[52]

Roosevelt had no power over the actions of genocidal maniacs except to hunt them down and kill them. He knew Hitler was insane, a "wild man" and a "nut." In short, he knew that winning the war as quickly as possible was the only solution, and he did it.

The Bermuda Conference

If speaking out was not the answer, then what about rescuing the Jews from the Holocaust? Why did FDR not implement a plan of rescue? Why did the conference designed to come up with such a plan, the Bermuda Conference, fail?

The Bermuda Rescue Conference of April 1943 took place at a time when the Allies were losing the Battle of the Atlantic and a year before the Normandy invasion. American merchant mariners were dying in the frigid waters of the North Atlantic while trying to deliver tanks, weapons, and ammunition to England. A rescue operation in occupied Poland was out of the question. Nevertheless, the Bermuda Conference was certainly a depressing episode in American history. The State Department and British Foreign Office personnel who organized the conference shamefully had little if any desire to help the Jews of Europe. Cynical, antisemitic diplomatic careerists and political appointees saw the conference as a sop to the "sob sister" crowd and "those wailing Jews." Even pro-Roosevelt Jewish Americans were angered and disturbed by the lack of rescue efforts.

But the questions remain: Was rescue possible in April 1943? Could the conferees announce to the world that the Allies were losing the Battle of the Atlantic; that they had no hope of invading Continental Europe for another year; and that the bombing of German cities, fuel refineries, and military factories had so far failed to win the war? Was there anything the conferees could say, do, or request that would have changed the course of the Holocaust? The answers are "no." As Professor Rubinstein observed, the Bermuda Conference failed because it "forced both the Jewish community and the Allied governments . . . to . . . answer the question of 'do what?' What could, realistically, be done? Since this question . . . had no answer, it is not surprising that the conference was a failure."[53]

Revisionists have shrilly denounced the Bermuda Conference. Feingold's chapter title in *The Politics of Rescue* (1970) called it "The Bermuda Conference: Mock Rescue for Surplus People." Volume 3 of Wyman's documentary history *America and the Holocaust* is titled "The Mock Rescue Conference: Bermuda." Feingold and Wyman portrayed the conference as a deliberate public relations fraud arranged by the British and latched on to by Breckinridge Long and the State Department. For Feingold the "calling of the Bermuda Conference in mid-1943 marks the fullest development of what might be called a politics of gestures."[54]

Wyman claims the conference was not intended to help the

trapped Jews "but to give enough of the *appearance* of action to quiet the pressures" for rescue building in the United States and Britain. He calls it a "hoax" and a "ruse" and claims American Jewish leaders were "cast into despair" by the indifference of the two great democracies. Other critics claim the conference "would reveal that the Allies had abandoned European Jews to their fate." Penkower says the conference was used only for "cosmetic effect."[55]

These highly charged accusations, however, fail to recognize the giant elephant sitting in the middle of the room: What could the delegates have advised the Allies to *do* to stop the Holocaust? Saul Friedman lauds Congressman Sol Bloom for standing up for the proposition of negotiating "with the Nazis for the release of great numbers of Jews. Only Bloom tried to force the conferees into serious discussions on the prospect of trans-blockade feeding of Jews." Monty Penkower touts "approaches to the German government and its satellites to permit Jewish emigration [and] . . . UN financial guarantees for feeding and rescue." In other words, according to Roosevelt's critics, the Bermuda Conference would have *succeeded* if the delegates had recommended that the Allies politely ask Herr Hitler to stop his genocidal war against the Jews and sent food from Americans' rationed cupboards to Nazi gangsters who would promise to use this precious commodity to feed Jews they intended to murder instead of easing their own food shortage! This is, to be polite, nonsense. As Dawidowicz points out, these proposals boiled down to begging Hitler to let the Jews go.[56]

Richard K. Law, undersecretary for foreign affairs and head of the British delegation, stated unequivocally that victory provided the only real solution to the refugee problem and that persecuted people "should not be betrayed . . . into a belief that aid is coming to them, when, in fact, we are unable to give them immediate succor." United States assistant secretary of state Adolf Berle, who was sympathetic to the plight of European Jews (and even supported Bergson on some issues), said in a speech soon after the conference that "nothing can be done to save these helpless unfortunates except through the invasion of Europe, the defeat of the German arms, and the breaking of German power. There is no other way." Both were correct.[57]

On the third day of the conference, Law reported confidentially to Anthony Eden that it was as much in the Americans' interest "as ours that there should be some positive result" but "you can look at the map for hours on end and still there seems to be no solution." "If we here can define the problem in terms of practical possibilities . . . and if we can put in train some machinery which will exploit those limited possibilities . . . we shall have done something."[58] Clearly the contemporary evidence is that the delegates hoped to accomplish *something* and that the conference was not "a facade for inaction." The fact that little was accomplished is not evidence that all of the delegates were acting in an elaborate, cynical charade.

Despite these documentary records, Law's testimony has been distorted. He was quoted by virtually every writer as saying twenty-two years later, 1965, that the Bermuda Conference was "a conflict of self-justification, a facade for inaction. We said the results of the conference were confidential, but in fact there were no results that I can recall." But the *only* source of this quotation is Arthur D. Morse in *While Six Million Died*. The footnote says "interview with author." Thus we were expected to rely on Morse—and him alone—for the accuracy of this quotation. By 1965, Law may very well have, with hindsight and after the war was won, regretted that more was not attempted at Bermuda. But Law's putative statement does not support a sweeping conclusion that the delegates and the Allies had no interest in a rescue plan, no matter how modest, if one could have been devised.[59]

Finally and unfortunately, the main murder process was over by August 1943, several months after the Bermuda Conference. Russian Jews were murdered between June 1941 and October 1942. Polish Jews were killed between March 1942 and August 1943, Western European Jews between July 1942 and August 1943. "By the summer of 1943," Yehuda Bauer observed, "there were only remnants left of Jewish communities in the East." Until the fortunes of war changed dramatically in 1944, the rescue of European Jewry was an impossibility. Even in 1944, rescue proved to be nearly impossible.[60]

The War Refugee Board

By late 1943 and early 1944, the tide of war favored the Allies, and the Nazis' grip on their remaining Jewish prisoners could possibly be loosened. In January 1944, Roosevelt created the War Refugee Board, a separate American governmental agency, funded in part by American taxpayers and in part by Jewish organizations, to attempt to rescue foreign Jews from the Holocaust. There is no comprehensive history of the WRB, and as with other issues in America's response to the Holocaust, there are vast differences of opinion among historians about its effectiveness. What is not in dispute, however, is that the WRB was a vigorous, sincere effort by the Roosevelt administration to save the surviving Jews of Europe and led by a director, John Pehle, Jr., whom all agree was a man of integrity, energy, and commitment. "For rescue advocates," Feingold wrote, "a more propitious appointment could hardly be imagined." In his report to the WJC in November 1944, Kubowitzki paid "sincere tribute . . . to the fervor, daring, and perseverance of [the WRB's] leading officers and workers." Most of Roosevelt's critics agree that the WRB waged an incessant and vigorous psychological warfare campaign to save the Jews of Hungary, Bulgaria, and Romania by issuing numerous statements, threats, and demands to those governments and encouraging other nations, the Vatican, and organizations to do so as well. According to Breitman, the board had considerable impact on the actions of neutral countries and those countries allied with Germany.[61]

Now that the war was being won and the genocidal activities of the Nazis were more clearly understood, the WRB convinced the State Department to liberalize American visa procedures, allowing more refugees to enter the United States. With the help of Ambassador Laurence Steinhardt, the flamboyant WRB agent, Ira Hirschmann, streamlined visa procedures for refugees entering Turkey from the Balkans. Hirschmann's efforts are credited by some historians as saving the Transnistrian and Bulgarian Jews from the Holocaust. The board convinced the War and State

Departments, over strenuous British objections, to allow food packages to be sent to civilians in German internment camps and cleared the way for millions of dollars (mainly from the Joint) to pay for relief supplies and rescue operations. Whether any of this effort saved any of Hitler's Jewish victims is open to debate. The WRB pressured foreign governments and financed small efforts to rescue Jews and assist refugees in the Balkans, Spain, Portugal, Switzerland, and Sweden. After the success of the Normandy invasion at least these rescue efforts could be attempted.[62]

Oscar Cox told Hirschmann "to see that you do not work in a vacuum out there, we are going to put teeth into your efforts." Pehle supported him enthusiastically. Hirschmann met with Hopkins, Morgenthau, Frankfurter, Benjamin Cohen, and Isador Lubin. FDR personally supported Hirschmann's efforts. Lubin, United States commissioner of labor statistics and at this time special statistical assistant to the president with an office in the White House, obtained a letter from the president to give to Hirschmann to further his work. Lubin warned him that the British "run things in the Middle East" and would cause trouble. "If you get into a jam, cable this word to me at the White House. Perhaps I will be able to get the boss to help." It proved to be a magic word, Hirschmann recalled later, which cleared up snarls and opened doors in the months to come.[63]

When Hirschmann needed assistance from the White House, help was forthcoming. Once, when a group of Jewish refugees stranded on a ship in Istanbul Harbor needed visas to enter Palestine, Hirschmann used the code word in a cable to Lubin, and results were instantaneous. British recalcitrance turned to speedy cooperation. Later, in Washington, Hirschmann learned how his message had worked. As soon as Lubin received Hirschmann's cable he "went directly to the president, who communicated immediately with Churchill."

On another occasion the State Department ordered Hirschmann to provide signed receipts for cash given as "baksheesh"—bribes—to Turkish officials. He futilely explained that this was impossible. The problem then disappeared. He learned that Morgenthau had intervened and taken the issue to the president, who resolved the issue. After that episode Hirschmann had unlimited access to money and gold from both the State Department and Jewish organizations. Revisionist historians knew of Roosevelt's personal efforts to assist Hirschmann because they have utilized Hirschmann's memoir *Caution to the Winds* (1962) when it suited their purpose. However, they unanimously omit its favorable references to FDR.[64]

And what of Raoul Wallenberg? He is revered as "a Swedish diplomat," not as an agent of the War Refugee Board and the Roosevelt administration. But Wallenberg would never have gone to Hungary had it not been for the WRB and the Joint Distribution Committee. The WRB's Swedish representative, Iver Olsen, was instrumental in selecting Wallenberg, who had worked in Palestine and was therefore well acquainted with Jews. The board furnished Wallenberg with detailed plans of action and funding. The World Jewish Congress, the Joint, the State Department, and the WRB persuaded the Swedish Foreign Ministry to send Wallenberg to

Budapest. He arrived on July 9, 1944—after Hungarian deportations to Auschwitz had ceased as a result of Allied bombings and Roosevelt's warnings. Wallenberg worked through diplomatic channels, and while the numbers can be disputed, bribed local officials with money from the Joint to save as many Jews as he could.

Wallenberg was heroic, and his memory is justly honored. But it is important to remember that the American rescue policy initiated by the WRB set him on his path and provided him with the plan and the resources to succeed. Enormous sums of money from the Joint paid for his efforts at protecting, freeing, feeding, and housing tens of thousands of Jews.[65] Americans honor Raoul Wallenberg the Swedish diplomat, not the agent of the American government, which is what he actually was.

The revisionists have had a difficult time explaining the War Refugee Board. If the Irgunists, Morgenthau, and the young men of conscience at Treasury heroically convinced FDR to create the WRB, then their and the WRB's successful rescue of some undetermined number of Jews must redound, at least in part, to the president. But this logical *quod est demonstrandum* is unrecognized by revisionists. For Herbert Druks, the WRB was a farce. Druks claims that he "discloses the fakery of F.D.R.'s last-minute rescue efforts through the War Refugee Board." It saved only "a few Jews" and failed to provide these Jews with a place to go.[66] For Rabbi Lookstein the WRB was "a relatively small operation that came on the scene rather late." While its creation marked "a significant shift in American policy" and it may have saved 200,000 lives, the WRB was a failure because it might have saved millions had it been created two years earlier. "No military resources whatever were diverted to it, and it succeeded in obtaining the admission of no more than one thousand refugees," according to Wistrich.[67]

Arthur Morse could not make up his mind about the board. He details in five breathless chapters the heroic work of the board. He agreed that its staff was dedicated and pressured the Axis satellites. He contended that Hirschmann saved the remnants of the Jews in the Transnistrian camps and influenced the course of events in Bulgaria and Romania. Morse even praised FDR's March 24, 1944, statement on Nazi criminality, which was "not a polite pronouncement couched in diplomatic terms and released into the empty air and forgotten." Indeed, Morse claimed with his usual flair for exaggeration, that in "little more than a year the War Refugee Board was responsible for the direct rescue of several hundred thousand men, women, and children and the sustenance of additional thousands."[68]

On the other hand, the WRB that Feingold and Morse praised was, nevertheless, part of a "policy of gestures" and "humanitarian rhetoric . . . substituted for action." "The War Refugee Board represented a small gesture of atonement by a nation whose apathy and inaction were exploited by Adolf Hitler . . . the people of the United States remained bystanders."[69]

What do the Roosevelt decriers mean by these criticisms? They seem to live in perpetual denial that World War II and the Holocaust were interrelated, simultaneous events. In 1944, thousands of hardened murderers working for a deranged madman were

killing innocent, unarmed, unpopular, and hated civilians, protected by a powerful German military machine, ferociously
defending the German homeland from certain defeat, and Roosevelt should have done what? Stopped the war in its tracks in a
quixotic attempt to save Jewish prisoners of the Nazis? Diverted
the military resources needed to end both World War II and the
Holocaust in a futile attempt to save European Jews? That
undoubtedly would have suited Hitler, and perhaps that was part
of his strategy.

Revisionists have argued that the WRB was "too little, too late."
But this is only a valid criticism if the WRB could have saved the
Jews in Polish death camps in 1942 or 1943. Yet the Allies were
stalled in a hard and bitter ground war in Italy, were losing the
Battle of the Atlantic until mid-1943, and had no success on the
ground in Western Europe until D-Day, June 6, 1944. The air war
was costly, deadly, and had failed to end the war. On the Eastern
Front the Soviets were locked into a two-year struggle to the death
with an implacable enemy. They refused all requests to save Jews
from the Holocaust, no matter how modest, and even abandoned
three million of their own POWs to murder by the Nazis.[70]

Wyman argued that the WRB should have been established in
1942, yet few historians believe the Allies had the power to stop
the Holocaust in 1942. "So long as [Hitler] commanded the European Continent from the Atlantic Wall to the gates of Moscow and
Leningrad, the fate of the Jews in his grip depended on his, Hitler's,
will," Lucy Dawidowicz observed. In December 1942, the Allies
verbally threatened the Germans with retribution for the murder

of the Jews, but Hitler was understandably unfazed. His military machine was still preeminent in Western Europe. Stalingrad was not yet lost.

"We now know," Dawidowicz continued, "that Hitler would never have let the Jews go, though no one knew it then." Despite diplomatic dissembling, Hitler never abandoned his goal of destroying European Jews. The Germans' implacable policies of industrial-style murder could not be moderated by appeals to humanity. No matter how much the revisionists wish it were otherwise, no one could stop Hitler from exterminating Jews in 1942 or 1943. To imply that the Allies could have done so ignores the reality of the war at the time.[71]

Some Hungarian and Romanian Jews were saved in 1944, and the chief cause of their salvation was the Soviet offensive, Operation Bagration, and Roosevelt's strategy of winning the war quickly. While thousands of American and British pilots and millions of Soviet troops and thousands of Soviet tanks make no appearance in the Roosevelt critics' version of Holocaust history, it was these men who saved tens of thousands of Jews in Hungary and Romania. Had the Allies' effort flagged; had the Normandy invasion been postponed; had precious men, war matériel, and airpower been diverted to futile rescue attempts, the Fascist leaders of Romania and Hungary would have had no incentive to resist Hitler or aid the Jews. Franklin Roosevelt, Winston Churchill, Joseph Stalin, Dwight Eisenhower, Georgi Zhukov, and the Allied armed forces *as well as* Wallenberg, Hirschmann, and the WRB saved those Jews of Central Europe who survived the Holocaust.[72]

The Allies' Decision Not to Bomb Auschwitz

And finally there is Auschwitz. How does one judge the Roosevelt administration on the issue of bombing Auschwitz? To attempt a judgment it is important to put the question into both perspective and context. Even Roosevelt's critics agree that the window of opportunity to bomb Auschwitz was both small and late in the war—about six months in the summer and fall of 1944. The first unequivocal request to bomb Auschwitz was on June 24, 1944, and addressed to the WRB in Bern, Switzerland. More than five million Jews were already dead. This window closed in November, when the Nazis ordered Auschwitz destroyed.[73]

The power and precision of World War II's aerial bombardment were mythical, and the American military knew it. Only one in five bombers got within *five miles* of its designated target. In 1942 the British bombed German cities because they were large enough to locate from the air. "More USAAF bombs landed in fields and killed cows than hit German factories," one Eisenhower biographer concluded. Aerial bombardment entailed ponderous moral consequences. At the beginning of the war, Americans insisted that they would not engage in the bombing of cities or civilians. The B-17 bomber and the Norden bombsight, many believed, made bombing quite precise and helped mitigate the consequences of these acts. Those beliefs were part of the myth.[74]

There was, however, no question that with the application of sufficient willpower and effort, the Allies *could* have bombed Auschwitz. The Fifteenth Air Force accidentally bombed the camp on September 13, 1944, in sorties against a plant at Monowitz. Bombing "the camps," however, did not necessarily mean destroying the gas chambers, crematoria, and ditches used in the Final Solution. However, bombing the camps necessarily meant killing many Jewish inmates. The airplanes that struck the fuel and rubber plants around Auschwitz were heavy bombers dropping bombs over a wide area from a high altitude. Hundreds if not thousands of prisoners would have perished in a rain of steel, incendiaries, and high explosives directed against the camp buildings. Low-altitude raids by large bombers guaranteed huge losses of aircraft and crew as well.[75]

The risk that could not be taken was that bombing would kill Jewish inmates but fail to halt the extermination process. As Rubinstein points out, Allied bombs could fall on barracks rather than on gas chambers. In 1944, there was strong likelihood that this would happen, given the inaccuracy of Allied bombing and the relatively small area occupied by the crematoria as compared to the many acres of barracks. "I am perfectly confident," intelligence officer and later Supreme Court Justice Lewis F. Powell recalled in 1985, "that General [Carl] Spaatz would have resisted any proposal that we kill Jewish inmates in order temporarily to put an Auschwitz out of operation."[76]

Stubborn advocates of bombing Auschwitz wore blinders to the fact that World War II was at its crisis in June–November 1944 and seem to have imagined that airpower was readily available for any task that contemporaries or advocates might wish done. But an apocalyptic struggle was under way in Western Europe, and strategic bombing was a key to victory or defeat. In January 1943, at Casablanca, Roosevelt and Churchill had agreed to a bombing strategy: the USAAF would bomb industrial targets during the day, and the RAF would bomb the surrounding area at night. The real effectiveness of the air war was still uncertain. In 1943, the United States Eighth Air Force had, according to Williamson Murray, "flirted with absolute defeat in the skies over Germany." It lost thirty percent of its crews almost every month. Not until May 1944 did American bomber losses begin to decline. The battle for air superiority was a close-run contest well into 1944, and the outcome was uncertain to the Allies. The British and American military were prepared to let their POWs die at the hands of the SS rather than divert men, matériel, and airpower from the war effort.[77]

Allied air force commanders resented "diversionists," who proposed shifting airplanes to other targets and meddled in their grand strategy of winning the war by strategic aerial bombardment. "There are a lot of people who say that bombing can never win a war," Air Chief Marshal Arthur "Bomber" Harris, commander of RAF Bomber Command, said in 1943. "Well, my answer to that is that it has never been tried yet. And we shall see."[78] They believed the war could be won more quickly by concentrating on bombing Germany's industrial and transportation infrastructure. Political authorities rarely injected themselves into targeting decisions because, in historian Tami Davis Biddle's words, "such decisions were complex, dependent on contingent factors (like weather), and subject to special types of technical knowledge and expertise." Roosevelt, whose philosophy this late in the war was to let the military brass make military decisions, was "noninterventionist."[79]

The strategy of concentrating on industrial targets was modified somewhat as D-Day approached. An Allied failure to defeat the Lufwaffe might have proven fatal to the invasion. Thus the Allies made an all-out effort in the winter of 1943 and spring of 1944 to eliminate the German air force.[80] As hard as it may be to believe, army air force commanders vigorously resisted even *that* diversion of airpower *to aid in the preparation for D-Day.* The air campaign preceding D-Day, called the "Transportation Plan," became the focus of rancorous debate. Churchill fought Eisenhower, who was forced to turn to Roosevelt and Marshall for support. Eisenhower threatened to "pack up and go home" if he were not given *temporary* control of the air force from mid-April to mid-September to bomb continuously the German transportation and communication networks that served Normandy.[81]

Civilians' and politicians' wishes to bomb a concentration camp in Poland or even to rescue Allied POWs paled into insignificance when measured against the tasks of preparing the Normandy invasion; supporting Allied armies after the landings; ferrying supplies; paving the way for more landings in southern France; relieving the miserable, costly ground war in Italy; and destroying launch sites that hurled deadly V-1 and V-2 rockets into London. "This new form of attack," Churchill wrote after the war, "imposed upon the people of London a burden perhaps even heavier than the air raids of 1940 and 1941." According to Biddle, during July and August 1944, the Allied air forces sent 16,566 sorties and one-fourth of the two months' bomb tonnage against V-weapon sites. The fear that German science could pull a rabbit out of a hat was not unfounded, as the late deployments of the jet plane and missiles demonstrated. "We shall not allow the battle operations in Normandy . . . to suffer" despite the "grievous suffering" of many people, Churchill told the House of Commons.[82]

Even if Allies could pinpoint bomb the killing operations at Auschwitz, the Nazis did not need that horrible facility to kill Jews, and everyone knew it. Millions of Jews had been murdered by shootings, forced marches, exposure, and starvation. An illustration of that truism is the extermination of Hungarian Jewry itself. In July 1944, Horthy ordered a halt to the deportations. The roundup of 150,000 Budapest Jews was suspended, and they were relatively safe until October 15, 1944, when Ferenc Szalasi's pro-Nazi, antisemitic Arrow Cross movement took over the country. Eichmann and the SS returned to Budapest. Jews were mercilessly killed by roving bands of Arrow Cross soldiers in Budapest. Auschwitz ceased operations by November 21 but Ravensbruck and Mauthausen continued on, murdering thousands. A forced winter march to Austria killed thousands more. On December 22, 1944, as the Soviet army neared, Eichmann fled Budapest, but the Arrow Cross was still killing hundreds of Jews in January 1945.[83]

According to Hitler's close confidant, economic planner, and minister for armaments and munitions, Albert Speer, if the Auschwitz-Birkenau gas chambers were destroyed, "Hitler would have hit the roof. . . . He would have ordered the return to mass shooting. And immediately, as a matter of top priority." In a 1972 interview, Speer said that if the Allied bombing of German cities had been announced as retaliation for the Holocaust, Hitler would have diverted more of his dwindling manpower and resources to the murder of the Jews. Three hundred "little Auschwitzes" would have been created, or the SS would have reverted to shooting its victims, as the *Einsatzgruppen* had done in Russia. By 1944, Nazi murderers were both hardened and experienced. They were proud of their achievements and preferred killing civilians to being sent to the Eastern Front. "The idea," Weinberg concluded, "that men who were dedicated to the killing program, and who saw their own careers and even their own lives tied to its continuation, were likely to be halted in their tracks by a few line-cuts on the railways or the blowing up of a gas chamber is preposterous."[84]

With regard to the narrower issue of bombing the railroad lines, even Roosevelt's critics agree that it was a chimera. To succeed would have been extremely difficult at the distances involved, and trains could divert to other routes, as numerous lines ran between Hungary and Auschwitz. Destroyed lines would require daily bombing to keep them out of service for any length of time. After the war "Bomber" Harris said that cutting the lines would have achieved no effective result, except for a few days "unless a totally impracticable (numerically) effort was applied virtually continuously to that end." Even the Confederate Army could quickly repair railroad lines during the Civil War. That is why General William Tecumseh Sherman had his troops take pains to tear up, heat, and bend railroad iron to prevent rebuilding damaged lines.[85]

Wyman, Roosevelt's most sincere and indefatigable critic, is forced to acknowledge that cutting the railway lines would have necessitated "close observation of the severed lines and frequent rebombing, since repairs took only a few days." But, even on this obvious point, Wyman cannot bring himself to concede that the U.S. military took the correct course. "In the case of railroad lines," he claims, "the answer is not clear-cut." But it was clear-cut to every air war expert then and now. One lesson of the Normandy invasion was that every transportation resource—from tracks to stations, yards, and locomotives—had to be bombed continuously to be effective. Even Feingold concedes that "when the possibility of rescue through bombing is closely scrutinized, its possibility of saving lives seems remote."[86]

Most importantly, in 1944 no American civilian, soldier, politician, or organization with any clout or credibility was willing to take the moral responsibility of pushing Washington to bomb Auschwitz. Few prominent individuals and no American Jewish group of any consequence asked the Roosevelt administration to bomb Auschwitz. Even the Jewish Agency executive in Palestine voted against it in June 1944 and never took another vote. Yitzhak Gruenbaum never wrote to L.C. Pinkerton, as the American diplomat suggested, requesting the bombing of Auschwitz. Dr. Leon Kubowitzki, head of the Rescue Department of the World Jewish Congress, consistently and vociferously opposed the action and proposed a different idea, an attack by Soviet paratroopers. At the August 1944 meeting of Jewish representatives with John Pehle, there was no dissent on the decision not to bomb the camps. Pehle himself adamantly opposed it.[87]

Some Jewish leaders wanted Auschwitz bombed but fretted about the moral dilemma so much that they would not commit their organizations to it. According to David Ben-Gurion's biographer Shabtai Teveth, "the dread of ever being charged with moral responsibility for massacre of Jews . . . continued to guide the JAE," even as it closed its eyes to requests to bomb Auschwitz from its representatives in London, Weizmann and Sharett (later Shertok). The JAE like the World Jewish Congress, *transmitted requests by others* to bomb but would not commit themselves publicly and officially to the request. Thus the JAE and the WJC had it both ways. They both did and did not request that Auschwitz be bombed.[88]

The ethical dilemma posed by bombing Auschwitz and the likely consequent killing of thousands of innocent Jews was very real for those Jews who faced the actual decision in 1944. Indeed, the killing of an innocent person is strictly forbidden by Talmudic law. The Talmud commands a Jew to die himself rather than kill an innocent person. "Allow yourself to be killed rather than commit murder," the Talmud teaches. "Who knows that your blood is redder? Perhaps his blood is redder," the sages said. According to the Jerusalem Talmud, if a group of Jews is commanded to deliver under threat of death to all, one of its members to an enemy who intends to kill him, all must die rather than kill one innocent. This explains Dr. Emil Schmorak's comment at the June 1944 meeting of the Jewish Agency Executive: "It is forbidden for us to take responsibility for a bombing that could very well cause the death of even one Jew."[89]

It is easy in this moral quagmire to blame John McCloy for failing to authorize or even to investigate bombing Auschwitz. He certainly is a convenient target for the Roosevelt critics. As part of the Eastern WASP establishment, he lived in a world full of genteel antisemitism. But, as we have seen, the roundup of Hungarian Jews began in April 1944 and McCloy, who greatly respected Pehle, never received a request to bomb the camps from Pehle until it was too late, in November. And McCloy had every right to rely on Pehle. No one doubted Pehle's commitment to saving Jews. Pehle first detected the duplicity of the State Department in sabotaging relief operations. Accompanying Morgenthau, he explained the situation to Roosevelt himself.[90]

Most historians believe that Pehle's hands were tied because the War Department insisted that the armed forces would not be employed for rescue operations unless in conjunction with operations whose objective was defeating the enemies' armed forces. Pehle had agreed with this interpretation of the WRB's authority based on the president's executive order that the WRB's efforts must be "consistent with the successful prosecution of the war."[91] However, the implication that Pehle believed he had no right to request military assistance is belied by both Pehle's and Morgenthau's actions. First, both men were committed to cutting red tape—military or otherwise—when it suited their purposes. For example, Morgenthau convinced FDR to countermand a military order that hindered Jewish refugees from crossing the Adriatic to escape from Yugoslavia into occupied Italy.[92] Second, there is nothing in the correspondence between Pehle and McCloy to suggest that Pehle acted improperly or beyond the scope of the WRB's jurisdiction when in November 1944 he suggested bombing Auschwitz. In its reply the military refused but did not tell Pehle that the request was not the legitimate business of the WRB. Third, Pehle *did* request the bombing when he was convinced it was the right thing to do. Finally, experience reveals that Morgenthau would have gone to FDR to insist on the bombing of Auschwitz had he strongly favored it.[93]

McCloy relied on Pehle and probably believed in August 1944 that the war would soon be over. Like his friend Felix Frankfurter and others in the government, McCloy harbored doubts about the accuracy of reports on the extermination of the Jews, which he thought grossly exaggerated. The official, unpublished WRB history notes that "because of the immensity of the catastrophe being visited upon the Jews of Hungary, the board gave serious consideration to all rescue proposals advanced. . . . It was suggested that concentration and extermination centers be bombed in order that the resultant confusion might enable some of the persons held to escape and hide. . . . These particular proposals were not referred to the War Department because the board did not feel justified in asking at that stage of the war that any measures be undertaken involving the diversion or sacrifice of American troops." The board itself would not take on the moral responsibility of requesting bombing until November 1944. By then it was too late.[94]

In sum, for many weighty reasons the United States and its Allies refused to destroy Auschwitz by bombardment. The chief reason was the moral dilemma of deliberately killing hundreds or even thousands of innocent men, women, and children in a futile effort to stop the killing of others marked for death. That is why there was little discussion of bombing Auschwitz at the time, and no credible American Jewish leader or organization asked Roosevelt to bomb the camps. The issue was essentially created by historians years after the actual events. Historian Richard Levy has pointed out a July 11, 1944, note in the Jewish Agency archives that represents "the most closely argued contemporary Jewish viewpoint available to us." The bombing, it said, was "hardly likely to achieve the salvation of the victims to any appreciable extent." While the plant and personnel would be destroyed and the "dislocation of the German machinery for systematic wholesale murder may possibly cause delay in the execution of those still in Hungary . . . it may not go very far, as other means of extermination can be quickly improvised." The main purpose of the bombing, according to this contemporary record, "should be its many-sided and far-reaching moral effect," namely the Allies waging direct war against the extermination of the Jews. It would give the lie to Nazi assertions that the Allies were indifferent to or not displeased with the murder of the Jews; it would dissipate the incredulity that persisted about reports of extermination; and it would demonstrate to the Germans that the Allies were serious about punishing the guilty. This note, however, was never presented to the American government.[95]

Conclusion

Did Franklin Roosevelt make mistakes in his war against Hitler? Certainly he did. Were there things he could have done to save millions of European Jews that he failed to do? Absolutely not. Could he have saved more than he did? It is possible that more could have been done to save a small number of European Jews, just as more could have been done for American POWs, Poles, Filipinos, Chinese, and many other victims of Axis murder. Undoubtedly, with the luxury of hindsight, an excellent plan could be devised by an enterprising historian to rescue American POW survivors of the Bataan Death March in 1944 instead of 1945. But impartial historians believe Roosevelt's ability to save substantial numbers of Jews was quite limited. "There were some minimal possibilities of rescuing Jews," Weinberg concluded, "but they were minimal." It is also fair to ask if more Jews would have been saved if the war had ended two weeks or two months sooner, as FDR hoped. Rubinstein argues flatly that the Allies could not have saved any more Jews from the Holocaust than they did. Ben-Gurion saw that no rescue that could make a real difference was possible. "We shall not engage in futile acts," he said. "Nothing can be done to check them," Nahum Goldmann told fellow members of the WJC. "We can only work for victory."[96]

Even Roosevelt's severest critics do not claim he could have prevented the Holocaust from happening. Feingold conceded that even if Roosevelt could have made the rescue of the Jews one of the Allies' primary war aims, "there would still have been almost insurmountable roadblocks." The Nazis were in "physical control of the slaughter" and it was "not in the power" of the Allies "for the first years of the war" to come to the rescue of the victims.[97] No matter what Roosevelt or anyone else said or did, Hitler would have killed more than five million Jews.

Those historians who argue that Roosevelt and the American people were "complicit" in the Holocaust can be forgiven their rhetorical excess. These historians do not really claim that FDR and the American people conspired with the Nazis to kill Jews. An "accomplice" is a person who participates in and is guilty, morally and legally, of a crime. An "accomplice" is a coconspirator who acts to further the conspiracy. "Complicity" is defined by *Webster's* as "partnership or involvement in wrongdoing." To assert that FDR and Americans were accomplices is an affront to common sense, logic, a willful distortion of truth, and a hateful slander. The "complicity" argument is beneath contempt. Observing this phenomenon among Jewish historians, Yehuda Bauer concluded:

> *The wrath and frustration of the Jewish people finally turned against itself. . . . The Nazis murdered the Jews—everyone knows that. . . . But who was really responsible? In accordance with "good" Jewish tradition, many Jewish historians, writers, and journalists blamed Chaim Weizmann, Stephen Wise, David Ben-Gurion, Nahum Goldmann, Yitzhak Grünbaum, Moshe Shertok, and all the rest of the Jews who tried to rescue their fellows. They were responsible because*

*they had failed. This suicidal tendency in historio-
graphy is typical of a frustrated public refusing to recognize its essential helplessness in the face of
overwhelming force.*[98]

The argument is ridiculous but Wyman, who was deeply hurt
and wounded by the horrors of the Holocaust and America's
failure to save the victims, makes it nevertheless on the first page
of *The Abandonment of the Jews* (1984): "The Nazis were the
murderers, but we were the all too passive accomplices."[99] And
Wyman is not alone in his bizarre charge of American complicity
in genocide. Reevaluating, denigrating, and debunking the American government, its leaders, institutions, and society has blos-
somed since the 1960s and the advent of the civil rights movement,
the feminist movement, and the Vietnam War. Historians have
confronted racism, slavery, discrimination against women, and the
exploitation of Native Americans, among many other failures of
American society. And historians, such as Wyman who have
immersed themselves in the horrors of the Holocaust, are deeply
affected by their vicarious involvement in it.

This victimology atmosphere and the trauma of the Holocaust
provided a hospitable environment for erroneous and exaggerated
accounts of America's alleged failure to provide a haven for the
oppressed and failure to rescue European Jewry. Rafael Medoff,
apparently unaware that American Jewish men and women were
busy fighting the Japanese and the Germans, informs us that
during World War II, Jewish leaders were "on vacation" or

"lunching at the regular hour at their favorite restaurant" instead of protesting. "What exactly *were* they doing?" Medoff asks. "Vacations were seldom sacrificed," Wyman informs us in a rare lapse from his factual account. To these historians it is as if the Holocaust happened but World War II did not. Maybe they believe Jewish Americans were vacationing on the Pacific islands of Guadalcanal and Iwo Jima and lolling on the beaches of Normandy and at the Battle of the Bulge![100]

FDR is held responsible for the Holocaust by this same group of myopic historians because he failed to prevent the Holocaust, even though he was unable to prevent it. In hindsight, FDR may have missed opportunities to rescue some people. The number, if any, can be debated, but it was small in relation to six million murdered, and minuscule in relation to the thousands, or tens of thousands, who would have perished if victory were delayed. Roosevelt, like everyone else in the Allied camp at the time, failed to see the Holocaust and the Final Solution for what it actually was in its monstrous totality. As he was fighting World War II all over the globe, he arguably should have taken firmer control of the immigration policies of the State Department and shaken up State Department personnel earlier than he did. In hindsight, he should not have relied on Breckinridge Long for as long as he did, and he should arguably have given more aid and encouragement to neutral countries' efforts to rescue Jews. Henry Morgenthau believed that "America has no cause to be proud of its handling of the refugee problems." State Department officers procrastinated when modest rescue proposals were put forth, suppressed information, and interpreted the immigration laws too narrowly. They were overly cautious, and at times some did this with a specific goal of keeping Jewish refugees out of the United States.

But, as the old adage goes, "we must never forget that there was a time when events now in the past were still in the future." Was fiddling with immigration regulations more important than getting war matériel to Churchill or building the arsenal of democracy that led to Hitler's downfall? According to Saul Friedman, Benjamin Cohen told him in an interview long after the war, "When you are in a dirty war, some will suffer more than others. . . . The question was whether you could reduce the suffering without a sacrifice on your part. Things ought to have been different, but war is different, and we live in an imperfect world. . . . To imagine that Roosevelt could come up with a magic wand to solve the Jewish problem might be expecting too much." Roosevelt did not abandon the Jews of Europe any more than he abandoned the many other victims of Axis genocide. Parents have not abandoned a child kidnapped and murdered by a criminal. War demands brutal and heart-wrenching decisions of leaders, and those who mourn their victims have every right to be bitter. Indeed, Nichol and Rennell in *The Last Escape* (2003), a history of Allied POWs, entitle one of their chapters "Abandoned to Their Fate."[101]

In his gargantuan struggle with Nazi Germany, Roosevelt succeeded admirably where all others had failed. On June 10, 1940, Adolph Berle met with Roosevelt. "I observed," Berle wrote in his diary, "that as the situation now stood, it seemed to me that there were only two men left in the world, himself and Hitler. That, said the President, is a terrible responsibility."[102]

No one knows what Franklin Roosevelt felt in his heart of hearts about the Holocaust. But we do know what he said and what he did. Prior to 1941, no one believed the Germans would try to exterminate all of European Jewry. Wyman emphasizes that until 1941 "the main purpose of Nazi persecution of the Jews was to force them to leave Germany, not to exterminate them, a fact which warrants repetition because all postwar reflection . . . is filtered through knowledge of the extermination policy." Thus Roosevelt's reaction to the Hitler regime—his condemnation of the *Kristallnacht* pogrom, his combining the Austrian-German quota, his loosening of visa restrictions before the fall of France, his opposition to the British white paper—demonstrate his commitment to help European Jewry. Ultimately his masterful handling of the American entrance into the war with Germany and his effective leadership as a war president led to the extinction of the Third Reich.[103]

To Franklin Roosevelt, the American people, and Jewish Americans, destroying Hitler meant saving the Jews of Europe. The Holocaust, regardless of how Roosevelt decriers portray it today, was part and parcel of World War II as it occurred. Roosevelt gave his life both in the cause of winning that war and saving the Jews from Hitler. The two goals were inseparable. Because he felt "a personal responsibility" for Hitler's Jewish victims, in the last weeks of his life he went to see King Ibn Saud of Saudi Arabia to try to convince him that those who had suffered "indescribable horrors at the hands of the Nazis" deserved to live in a new Jewish homeland in Palestine.

Jewish Americans knew what they had lost when FDR died. With all his faults and failures—and some Jewish Americans were disappointed in his handling of the Holocaust at the time—they knew he had saved their country and the world from the most powerful, successful, and deadly Jew-hater in all recorded history. Rabbi G. George Fox spoke truly for American Jewry in his remarks on the president's death:

> *Among those whose tears for the departed are among the most sincere, are the Children of the Household of Israel—not only the Jews of America, but the Jews of the world. They found in him a friend and a protector—a fearless battler for human rights everywhere. His early denunciations of the bestialities of Hitler when others held their peace; his courageous and forthright condemnation of Nazi inhumanity at a time when the rest of the world . . . refused to take note of them . . . his overpowering drive to break the unholy yoke of Nazism and Fascism, have made the Jews throughout the world regard him as their outstanding friend; and he was their friend. . . . The uprooted, blasted, wounded lives, wherever they are, will never forget the tender concern for their welfare shown by the man who dared to challenge the jungle fury of the brutal beasts of Europe.*[104]

Postscript

"No, no!" said the queen. "Sentence first—verdict afterwards."

—*Alice in Wonderland*, Chapter XII

Where does history—the compilation and interpretation of facts about the past—end and politics, morality, philosophy, ideology, and religion begin? The answer to that question depends entirely on who is recording history and for what purpose. To the ancients one of the purposes of history was to teach moral lessons regardless of the veracity of the story that bore the moral lesson. In his *Germania, Histories* of Rome, and *Annals*, the Roman historian Tacitus (c.55–c. 120 C.M.), for example, intentionally and systematically distorted events of history by representing them as clashes of characters, exaggeratedly good with exaggeratedly bad, symbols of virtue or vice. "This I regard as history's highest function," he wrote, "to let no worthy action be uncommemorated, and to hold out the reprobation of posterity as

487

a terror to evil words and deeds." This has been a common use of history from ancient times. Enlightenment historians such as Edward Gibbon, author of *Decline and Fall of the Roman Empire*, did the same thing; they wrote history to teach moral lessons. According to this view, history is "philosophy teaching by example." "It is not easy," Herbert Butterfield wrote, "to resist the temptation to personify and idealise history." But preaching history does have limits if one also is interested in telling the truth.[1]

Philosophers and historians have vigorously debated whether the writing of history should be influenced by moral judgments, but in fact, philosophers notwithstanding, we all make moral judgments about historical events and people. Indeed, to learn moral lessons from the past is one reason why we read and write history books. We are creatures influenced by our moral beliefs. "Let us . . . reject the notion of the historian as a hanging judge," E. H. Carr and other philosophers of history have argued. But no one listened. Public hangings have always drawn crowds, and modern historians who lynch the dead and smear their reputations attract a large readership.[2]

History is also an integral part of all revealed religions and has a special place in the Jewish religion. "Remember the days of old, consider the years of many generations: ask thy father, and he will show thee; thy elders, and they will tell thee," Moses said in his farewell to the Israelites. "In many lands and ages Amalek and his cruel descendants have risen up against us," the modern American Jewish Reform prayerbook, *Gates of Prayer* (1975), reminds Jewish worshippers, "and untold suffering has been our lot." To remember

Chaplains at war, Kobler Field, Saipan, Marianas, 1944.
National Jewish Welfare Board, Military Chaplaincy Records, nd, 1917–1984.

Courtesy of the American Jewish Historical Society

the actual, historical suffering and martyrdom of the Jewish people
is an essential part of Judaism. From slavery and the killing of the
firstborn in Egypt to the genocidal machinations of Haman in the
Book of Esther, Jews are taught that they have traveled a painful
path but survived oppression, exile, and death. It is little wonder
that remembrance of the Holocaust has become part of Jewish religious practice as well as a signal event of modern history.[3]

One delicate issue in discussing the history of the Holocaust is
that remembrance of the Holocaust (*Shoah* [the catastrophe] in
Hebrew) has become, for many Jews, part of the Jewish religion. It

is remembered on a date, Yom Hashoah (Holocaust Remembrance Day) in April, like other Jewish holy days and holidays. It is mentioned in Jewish prayerbooks. "Our foes were not content," one Reform prayerbook reads, "to give us pain; their dream was darker still: a world without Jews, a world that would forget our very name!" It is hard to tell, Peter Novick observed, "where 'civil religion' leaves off and 'the real thing' begins." A minority of rabbis and Jewish theologians have argued for including the Holocaust in the Talmudic commandments (making 614 instead of the historic 613) and seeing it as a "revelatory event" like Sinai and the Exodus. Comparing the Holocaust to any other genocide is blasphemy, according to at least one rabbi. Holocaust services pointedly condemn those who were "overcautious" and "hesitating" and the sin of "too much patience," "silence," "indifference," and "the closing of borders." Prayers of thanks to the liberators, the leaders, and to the GIs, sailors, and airmen who killed Amalek are few and far between. How can one impartially discuss the facts of history in such a context?[4]

While not a historian, Elie Wiesel, the Nobel Prize–winning poet and chairman of the commission that built the United States Holocaust Memorial Museum, has had an enormous impact on the popular view of the Holocaust and consequently our view of FDR. For Wiesel, the Holocaust is "equal to the revelation at Sinai." Any attempt to "desanctify" or "demystify" it is perceived to be a subtle form of antisemitism, an attempt to interpose a barrier between mankind and this numinous, horrific event. Any survivor, according to Wiesel, "has more to say than all the historians combined about what happened." Wiesel goes so far as to claim that "Auschwitz cannot be explained. . . . The Holocaust transcends history. . . . [It is] the ultimate mystery, never to be comprehended." The Holocaust for Wiesel is a "mystery religion."[5]

Thus, to write Holocaust history puts a burden on a historian that writing about Thomas Jefferson's quarrels with Alexander Hamilton or the presidency of Benjamin Harrison does not. "Historical research in the area of the Holocaust is beset with problems of no ordinary kind," Henry Feingold concluded after years of study. "It seems as if the memory of that human-made catastrophe were as deadly to the spirit of scholarship as was the actual experience to those who underwent its agony."[6] The anger and passion of many Holocaust historians, themselves deeply affected by their work in this field, their desire to teach a moral lesson of transcendent importance and to judge and punish all the living and dead who failed to save six million martyrs is understandable. And worse still, similar forces of evil are at large in our world today that must be identified for what they are. Thus the need to fix blame on as many people as possible for as many misdeeds as possible is a moral imperative to historians of this stripe. "Better be unjust to dead men," Lord Henry Acton wrote, "than give currency to loose ideas on questions of morals." Or as radical historians of the 1960s said, paraphrasing Karl Marx, "The historians have interpreted the world; the thing, however, is to change it."[7] For many historians of the Holocaust, not to mention politicians and activists, understanding what actually happened and why takes a backseat to preventing it from happening again. Perhaps they are right. What is the value of telling the truth if you can skew the story to save future victims of murderers like Hitler?

Anti-Roosevelt revisionists write with righteous anger at the senseless murder of six million innocent people. The possibilities of rescue are exaggerated to teach lessons about indifference. As the title of Henry Feingold's book of essays on the Holocaust, *Bearing Witness* (1995), demonstrates, Feingold uses religious terminology in describing historic events. Feingold is a well-respected historian, but, like many of his colleagues, seemingly blames everyone in the world for the monstrous deeds of the Nazis and their fellow criminals, ignoring the obvious fact that not only was everyone not guilty, but also many millions were fighting to stop those who were. Feingold's essay "Who Shall Bear Guilt for the Holocaust?," published in the scholarly journal *American Jewish History*, misdirects indictments against people he and other prominent critics insist on describing as "bystanders" and "witnesses" to the Holocaust, which, of course, implies moral culpability.[8] Nowhere in this twenty-page essay does the author mention the names of Adolf Hitler, Reinhardt Heydrich, Heinrich Himmler, Martin Bormann, and other actual murderers of six million Jews. FDR, Winston Churchill, Pope Pius XII, Allied war leaders, John J. McCloy, the U.S. Congress, Henry Morgenthau, and the International Red Cross endure passionate reproaches, as if *they* were guilty of murdering Jews instead of the Nazis. To characterize as "witnesses" Franklin Roosevelt and Winston Churchill, the men who defeated Hitler and ended his murderous campaign to kill every Jew in the world, has an *Alice in Wonderland* quality about it. Were the

American soldiers fighting and dying on Normandy beaches "witnesses" to the Holocaust, or were they "bystanders," or were they both? Holocaust research, as Feingold says, is beset with problems of no ordinary kind, but there is no problem identifying the guilty.[9]

"The terrible finality of the murder of the European Jews and their disappearance from history darkens our memories and clouds our vision of the past," Lucy Dawidowicz observed. Righteous anger, sincere remorse, a soul wounded by the study of murdered innocents, and the urgent need to instruct future generations are understandable emotions, but they neither change basic facts nor excuse the writing of unfair history. Elie Wiesel to the contrary notwithstanding, the Holocaust *is* a part of history. The events and facts *are* knowable, insofar as anything in history is knowable. Indeed, we know a great deal about the Holocaust. The events of the Holocaust happened within the context of World War II. They happened because Hitler and his henchmen had both the will and the power to commit atrocities of incredible magnitude, not unlike the Japanese mass murder of twenty million Asians. Franklin Roosevelt grappled for real power and fought a deadly war that expended real people's lives and fortunes. It may all appear mystical, unknowable, inauthentic, and mysterious to some, but it was quite real and unmystical as it was lived.[10]

Counterfactual history that makes a moral statement is a perfectly acceptable way to make a point—if it is fair. But historical "what ifs?" can be used in any way a historian wishes. In promoting his argument for the bombing of Auschwitz, for example, Wyman claims that if the Auschwitz mass-killing machinery had been destroyed by August 20, 1944, the train transporting Anne Frank and her family "very likely would not have left Holland, because most of its passengers were bound for the Auschwitz gas chambers." Despite his deep hope for a better result, where does Wyman think the train would have gone?[11]

Here is another, more probable counterfactual interpretation with a different moral: Anne Frank and her family were taken into custody on August 4, 1944, and shipped to Auschwitz in early September. Anne and her sister Margot were sent to Bergen-Belsen in late October or early November. Her mother and father remained

As American troops arrived, a homemade American flag was raised by the prisoners of Dachau prison camp. As it waved in the breeze, it seemed to reflect the joy of inmates who realized freedom for the first time in many years.

in Auschwitz. If Auschwitz had been bombed in September or October, the United States Air Force would have killed Anne Frank and her entire family. Her father, Otto, who survived the war and publicized Anne's diary afterward would have died and the famous diary likely would have never become the phenomenon that it did. Bombing Auschwitz would have likely killed Anne Frank and kept from public view the most famous diary of the Holocaust. Which is it? Can we truly know? Can we really condemn those who chose not to bomb Auschwitz?

Neither FDR nor the leaders of American Jewry were perfect. As we have seen, Americans looked across the Pacific Ocean after Pearl Harbor and saw a monstrous enemy who had murdered masses of innocents and attacked Americans without warning. Anger, bigotry, and thirst for revenge colored their views of the war against the Japanese. They looked across the Atlantic Ocean and saw the most powerful and brutal military machine in the history of mankind poised to conquer Britain and the Soviet Union. It is inaccurate at best and mendacious at worst to portray Franklin Roosevelt, Jewish Americans, and Americans generally as mere "witnesses" and "bystanders" to a war they won at great cost.

Roosevelt had sworn to utterly destroy the Axis war machine. He promised speedy punishment for war criminals. Bystanders and witnesses are passive; they do not fight and die. They do nothing. FDR and millions of American soldiers, sailors, and airmen fought and died to *stop* Hitler's Holocaust permanently. Bystanders do not leave their farms in Iowa or their neighborhoods in the Bronx, enlist in the army, fight at Normandy, and die in the Battle of the

Bulge. The Greatest Generation of Americans did not inhabit the same moral universe as the Nazis, their collaborators, and the true bystanders: French, Dutch, Romanian, Hungarian, and Ukrainian collaborators, Swiss bankers, and Franco's Spaniards who were pleased to let Jews die in concentration camps and do nothing to stop Hitler. Anyone who claims Franklin Roosevelt and those American troops did nothing is either a fool or a knave.

Until revisionist historians rewrote history Tacitus-style to teach lessons they thought more important than to record events, Roosevelt was nearly universally regarded as a savior of mankind from the scourge of Nazism. "More than any other man of his time, Roosevelt radiated faith in the survival of democracy and decency," Lucy Dawidowicz observed in 1982. "American Jews loved him for his good works and ideals, but most of all for his hatred of the Nazi regime." "His enemies accused him of being a friend of the Jews," Rabbi Abraham Feldman said. "It is one of the glorious boasts of modern Jewry that Franklin Roosevelt was our friend." Long before others, Rabbi Feldman continued, FDR saw the dangers of Nazism and "when the sword was finally forced into our hands, he, as Commander in Chief, proved himself . . . one of the supreme strategists of history." Americans had a right and a moral duty to defend themselves and to place the imperative to win the war ahead of all other considerations.[12]

Revisionist historians also have heaped scorn on Jewish Americans of the Holocaust era who supported Franklin Roosevelt. And they blame Roosevelt for relying on American Jewish leaders. Although veiled in righteous rhetoric, one of the key assumptions of the Roosevelt decriers is that American Jews *ought* to have placed loyalty to European Jewry *ahead* of loyalty to America. This judgment is in stark contrast to both reality and morality, and to the feelings and beliefs of Jewish Americans in the 1940s, when American Jews *unequivocally* put loyalty to America ahead of loyalty to European Jewry and when most had put the evils of Europe behind them as well. Feingold describes "Jewish voters who viewed themselves as patriotic American citizens rather than victimized Jews," as if they bore guilt for their patriotism and the fact that they had become Americans. "For most American Jews, winning the war—not the rescue of their brethren—received priority," Feingold complains, as if American Jews did something wrong when they rightly placed winning the war and defending their homeland from Germans and Japanese ahead of rescuing European Jewry. They and their parents had left Europe because, as Philip Roth recalled, "life [there] was awful, so awful . . . it was best forgotten."[13]

Robert S. Wistrich, who teaches at Hebrew University, follows this line in *Hitler and the Holocaust*. "What united most American Jews much more than links across the ocean," he writes with exquisite condescension, "was the desire to prove their newfound American patriotism." What can Roosevelt decriers possibly mean by these accusations? American Jews are and always have been Americans first and Jews second. Their duty to defend America and fight for American goals was *never* subordinated to any other cause, including saving the Jews of Europe. The *National Jewish Monthly* of B'nai B'rith spoke for American Jews when it said, "there is only one way to stop the Nazi massacres, and that is by crushing the Nazis in battle, wholly, completely, and irrevocably. . . . Everything for victory!"[14]

And what was "newfound" about the patriotism of American Jews? Jewish Americans, unlike their ghetto and shtetl-dwelling ancestors and a few Jewish immigrants, aliens, and foreigners in their midst in the 1940s, had sought and mostly achieved equality in the United States the same way that all immigrants had done. They fought and died in the American Revolution, the Civil War, the Spanish American War, and World War I. They built homes, businesses, synagogues, schools, and lives as other American immigrants had done before them and loved America for all it had done for them, their children, and the Jewish people.[15]

FDR and Jewish Americans should be honored for their actions during World War II, not defamed. The moral of the story of FDR and the Holocaust is that a great man and a generous nation did the best they realistically could in an extreme, extraordinary, and unprecedented situation. I would change Lord Acton's dictum to "Better to be just to dead men and women than give currency to loose interpretations of history based on hindsight, blind and misguided moral outrage, and political agendas."

Afterword

The pendulum of history swings in wide arcs, but the pendulum of historians—indeed of most concerned citizens who evaluate history—often swing in even wider arcs. For academics and writers, historical revisionism is the road to tenure, to Pulitzers and to praise. If journalism is the first draft of history, then revisionism is the second. Typically third and fourth drafts are required to set the record straight.

The history of FDR's role in the Holocaust is currently undergoing this process. Robert Rosen's carefully researched and beautifully written book may well prove to be the final draft. I recall vividly the first draft: Roosevelt as saint. I had the unenviable task, as a seven year old, of breaking the news of Roosevelt's death to my immigrant grandmother. I had never before seen her cry. She had lost her president, her father, her rabbi, her friend. Although Judaism prohibits graven images, the photograph of "our" president—cut out of a magazine and placed in an inexpensive frame—hung proudly on the wall of my grandmother's home and those of many of her friends. He was our hero, our savior, our secular "moshiach." He had been sent by God to defeat Hitler, to save the Jews and to end the Depression. He could do no wrong in our community. The rumors that he had Jewish roots—that his name was originally Rosenfeld—were circulated with pride in our community. Maybe, just maybe, there was a kernel of truth. (When I told this to FDR's granddaughter Laura, who is a neighbor and friend on Martha's Vineyard and is married to a Jewish man, she laughed and said that Roosevelt is, in fact, the Dutch version of Rosenfeld.) No one blamed Roosevelt for Hitler's mass murder. By preparing the American people for war, despite domestic objections, he had hastened Hitler's defeat and saved the remnants of European Jewry. With the help of his Jewish Secretary of the Treasury, Henry Morgenthau, he had established the War Refugee Board, that received and gave asylum to many (though certainly not enough) Jews.

At the time of Roosevelt's death, we knew that many Jews had been killed by the Nazis—our own relatives among them—but we had no idea of the scope of the tragedy. We were more aware of the enormity of the victory that Roosevelt had helped to achieve over the forces of evil.

This was the first draft reported by the general and the Jewish press and accepted by the Jewish community. It remained the conventional wisdom throughout my childhood and into my early adulthood.

Then came the first revisionists. The book *While Six Million*

Died: A Chronicle of American Apathy (1967) by Arthur D. Morse and later books by Henry Feingold, David Wyman and others were greeted by a combination of shock, chagrin, and intellectual curiosity. Our tradition began, after all, with Abraham shattering idols. We have always been an iconoclastic people who revel in debunking and challenging the conventional wisdom. A part of me welcomed this second draft. Roosevelt, after all, was not *my* hero. He was my parents' and grandparents' hero. Part of the process of growing up is to reject your parents' heroes—to shatter their idols, as Abraham had done.

I could never bring myself, however, to buy into the entire revisionist account of Roosevelt as villain. I could accept the imperfections of the hero, because I had come to realize that there were no flawless personages in history. Even Abraham, Moses and David were deeply flawed characters. I knew that Thomas Jefferson, who had declared that all men are created equal, had refused to free his own slaves, that Abraham Lincoln, who had finally freed the slaves, had expressed racist attitudes toward black people, and that many of Americas greatest heroes—from Thomas Edison to Henry Ford to Charles Lindbergh—had been virulent antisemites. But much of the revisionism with regard to Roosevelt lacked nuance, context and perspective. It was almost as if Roosevelt did not want to save as many Jews as possible—that he, like Stalin, was happy to see the Nazis reduce the population of the world's most longstanding troublemakers.

Robert Rosen proves that nothing could be further from the truth. Roosevelt was a man with considerable, but certainly not unlimited, power to influence the course of events in Europe. And he prioritized the use of that power in what he believed was the most effective manner: win the war as quickly as possible and save as many Jews as was consistent with the first priority and the political realities that limited his options.

Reasonable people can debate specific decisions, indecisions, actions and inactions. Roosevelt's failure to fire Breckinridge Long, who was instrumental in delaying visas and causing the deaths of so many Jews, seems inexcusable to me, even in retrospect. There are other decisions as well that warrant criticism. But Rosen proves that no one should question Roosevelt's motives or good will toward the Jewish victims of the world's worst human atrocity. From now on no serious scholar of Roosevelt's role in the tragic events of the early 1940s can fail to take into account Robert Rosen's masterful and balanced analysis of the choices of evil faced by the man who remains one of the greatest presidents in our history.

Alan M. Dershowitz
Cambridge, Massachusetts
April 2006

Timeline

January 30	President Paul von Hindenburg appoints Adolf Hitler Reich chancellor.
February 27	The Reichstag in Berlin is set on fire.
March 4	Franklin D. Roosevelt is inaugurated as president of the United States.
March 20	The first concentration camp is opened at Dachau, near Munich.
April 1	Nazi boycott of Jewish-owned businesses.
July 20	Nazi Germany and the Vatican sign a concordat guaranteeing the rights of the Catholic Church in Germany.
August 25	German officials and Zionist representatives sign the "Haavra (Transfer) Agreement."
	Boycott of Germany by Jewish groups in the United States.
	Anti-Nazi rally in New York City.

| December 5 | Otto and Edith Frank move their family to Amsterdam. |

1934

| June 30 | "Night of the Long Knives;" Hitler has his Nazi rivals murdered. |
| August 2 | Hindenburg dies. |

1935

March 1	Germany occupies the Saar.
May 27	NRA declared unconstitutional.
August 14	Social Security Act passed.
September 15	The Nuremberg racial laws are announced at a Nazi Party rally in Nuremberg.
December	Otto and Margot Frank visit Switzerland.

1936

March 7	Hitler repudiates the Versailles and Locarno treaties as German troops occupy the Rhineland.
April 19	Outbreak of Arab Revolt in Palestine (1936–1939).
May 5	Fall of Ethiopia to Italy.
July 16	The Spanish Civil War begins. It continues until 1939.

October 25	Germany and Italy establish the Rome-Berlin Axis.
November 7	FDR re-elected president for a second term.
November 25	Germany and Japan sign the Anti-Comintern Pact, directed at the Soviet Union.

1937

February	FDR's Supreme Court-packing plan.
July 7	Japanese forces invade northern China.
July 16	Buchenwald concentration camp opens.
August	Hundreds of attacks on Jews in Poland.
December 28	Antisemitic government installed in Romania.

1938

March 12	The German army marches into Austria and the formal union (*Anschluss*) of Austria with Germany takes place.
April	FDR forms the President's Advisory Committee on Political Refugees (PACPR).
April 26	The "Decree Regarding Registration of Jewish Property" requires all Jews in Germany to register their assets.
May 16	First Jews begin forced labor in Mauthausen concentration camp.
July 6–15	Évian Conference on Refugees.

August	FDR begins trying to ransom German Jewry.
September 29–30	Germany, Great Britain, France, and Italy sign the Munich Agreement, approving Germany's annexation of the Sudetenland.
November	FDR's attempted "purge" of conservative Democrats.
November 7	Herschel Grynszpan assassinates Ernst vom Rath.
November 9–10	The Night of Broken Glass (*Kristallnacht*) pogrom takes place throughout Germany and Austria.
December	Establishment of Mossad for Aliyah B (illegal immigration to Palestine).

1939

....

January	Debate over the Wagner-Rogers immigration bill.
January 17	Felix Frankfurter confirmed by a unanimous Senate vote to the United States Supreme Court.
January 30	Hitler speaks to the Reichstag, threatening the annihilation of the Jews in Europe in the event of a war.
March 15	German forces occupy Prague, Bohemia, and Moravia.
March 28	Franco marches into Madrid. Fascists are victorious in Spanish Civil War.
March 31	Great Britain and France guarantee the sovereignty of Poland.
April 15	FDR's telegram to Hitler and Mussolini asking for assurances of non-aggression.

May 15	Establishment of Ravensbrück concentration camp for women.
May 17	The British White Paper on Palestine establishes a limit on Jewish immigration.
May and June	Over nine hundred Jews attempt to emigrate from Germany on board the steamship SS *St. Louis* in May, but are forced to return to Europe in June.
July 20	The Coordinating Foundation is established.
August 23	The Nazi-Soviet Nonaggression Pact is signed in Moscow.
September	FDR continues his efforts to ransom German Jewry by supporting the Rublee Plan and insisting on the Coordinating Foundation.
September 1	Germany invades Poland. The beginning of World War II in Europe.
September 3	Great Britain and France declare war on Germany.
September 12	Bombing of Warsaw by Luftwaffe.
September 17	Soviet forces enter eastern Poland.
September 21	Germany orders the expulsion of Poles, Jews, and Gypsies from the Polish territories to be incorporated into the Reich.
September 27	Warsaw surrenders.
October 1	German authorities begin the deportation of Jews.
October 8	First Jewish ghetto established.

1940

January 4	The first gassing of disabled patients by the Nazis.
February 8	Lodz ghetto established.
April 7	Germany invades Denmark and Norway.
April 27	Himmler orders the establishment of a concentration camp at Auschwitz (Oswiecim, Poland).
May 10	Germany launches its offensive against the Low Countries and France. Rotterdam bombed by Germans.
	Neville Chamberlain resigns as British prime minister and is replaced by Winston Churchill.
May 15	The Netherlands surrender to the Germans.
May 16	FDR tells Congress "These are ominous days . . . we have seen the treacherous use of the 'fifth column'."
May 17	Germany invades France.
May 24–28	British cabinet wrestles with the decision to continue the war against Germany.
June 10	Roosevelt's speech at the University of Virginia warning Mussolini.
June 14	German troops enter Paris.
	The first prisoners, more than seven hundred Poles, arrive at Auschwitz.
June 22	France surrenders.

August 13	The German bombing campaign against England, the Battle of Britain ("the Blitz"), begins.
August 15	Madagascar Plan.
September 2	The United States agrees to provide Great Britain with fifty destroyers in return for bases.
September	SS *Quanza* incident at Norfolk, Virginia.
September 27	Tripartite (Axis) Pact between Germany, Italy, and Japan.
October 12	Warsaw ghetto established.
November 7	FDR reelected president for a third term.
November 15	Warsaw ghetto sealed.
December 29	FDR's "Arsenal of Democracy" speech.

1941

January 6	FDR's "Four Freedoms" speech.
	Charlie Chaplain's *The Great Dictator*.
March 11	The Lend-Lease Act is signed by President Roosevelt.
May	Spy Tyler Kent is arrested in London.
May 20	The Germans stop all Jewish emigration from Belgium and France.
May 27	FDR announces "unlimited national emergency."
	Rommel advances in North Africa.

June 22	"Operation Barbarossa," the German invasion of the Soviet Union, begins.
June 23	*SS Einsatzgruppen* and *Ordnungspolizei* units begin exterminating Jews and Gypsies in the Soviet Union.
June 27	Hungary joins the Axis and enters the war.
June 29	State Department tightens visa procedure.
July	Franks travel to visit relatives.
August 1	United States oil embargo of Japan.
August 9–14	British prime minister Winston Churchill and United States president Franklin D. Roosevelt meet aboard a warship and sign the Atlantic Charter.
August 23	Himmler issues a directive ordering a halt to all Jewish emigration.
September 3	About nine hundred people, mostly Russian prisoners of war, are gassed at Auschwitz. Vilna ghetto established.
September 8	Siege of Leningrad begins.
September 19	Fall of Kiev.
September 29–30	SS *Einsatzkommando* murders more than thirty-three thousand Kiev Jews at Babi Yar.
October	Otto Frank's business in Amsterdam is "Aryanized." He transfers business to Jan Gies.
October 12	The German army reaches the outskirts of Moscow. Warsaw ghetto established.
October 15–23	All Jewish emigration from Germany is prohibited. Mass deportations of German Jews begins.

November 1	Construction of the Belzec extermination camp begins.
November 24	Theresienstadt "model camp" established.
November 30– December 1	First transports arrive at Majdanek.
December 7	Japan bombs the U.S. naval base at Pearl Harbor, Hawaii.
December 8	Japan attacks the Philippines.
December 7–8	The SS opens the first extermination camp at Chelmno, near Lodz in western Poland. First use of mobile gas vans.
December 10	*Prince of Wales* and *Repulse* sunk.
December 11	Germany and Italy declare war on the United States.
December 22	Churchill and FDR meet in Washington.
December 25	British troops in Hong Kong surrender to the Japanese.

1942

December 8	Breckinridge Long becomes special assistant secretary of state in charge of emergency war matters.
January	Rationing begins in the United States.
January 2	Manila, capital of the Philippines, surrenders to the Japanese.

January 2	Executive order 9066, signed by President Roosevelt, orders all Japanese Americans living on the West Coast of the United States into internment camps.
January 13	The St. James Palace Declaration on war crimes.
January 20	The Wannsee Conference in Berlin to coordinate the Final Solution.
February 15	Singapore surrenders.
February 23	The *Struma* sinks off the Turkish coast.
March 1	Construction begins on the Sobibor extermination camp.
March 19–20	The Belzec extermination camp begins killing Jews deported from Lvov.
March 20	Mass gassings of Jews from Upper Silesia begin at Auschwitz-Birkenau.
March 27	The first Jews are deported from France to Auschwitz.
April	The Franks are required to wear yellow star. Anne Frank buys her diary.
April 9	American forces surrender to the Japanese at Bataan. Bataan Death March begins.
May 6–11	Biltmore (Zionist) Conference in New York City demands establishment of Jewish commonwealth.
May 7	Opening of Sobibor extermination camp.
May 7	Battle of the Coral Sea.
May 29	Jews in occupied France are required to wear the yellow badge.

June 2   Polish Bund and BBC report seven hundred thousand Jews killed in Poland (*New York Times* carries report on July 2).

June 4–7   The U.S. Navy defeats the Japanese fleet at the Battle of Midway.

June 10   German forces murder all the men and some women in the village of Lidice, Czechoslovakia.

June 21   Surrender of British at Tobruk.

July 5   Anne Frank and her family move into a secret annex constructed in the top stories of her father's office building in Amsterdam.

July 15   The deportation of Jews from Holland to Auschwitz begins.

           The Treblinka death camp begins receiving Jews from Warsaw. It is the last of the three camps, along with Belzec and Sobibor, created to exterminate Polish Jews.

July 21   Mass demonstration at Madison Square Garden and in New York City sponsored by AJ Congress and B'nai B'rith against Nazi massacres of Polish Jews.

July 23   The mass murder of Jews at Treblinka begins.

August 8   Riegner's telegram to Rabbi Wise describing his belief in Final Solution.

August 19 The Battle of Stalingrad begins.

           Battle for Guadalcanal.

August 21 FDR warns Germans that war criminals would face "fearful retribution."

September 13	Germany begins its attack on the Soviet city of Stalingrad.
September–October	Efforts by FDR and State Department to save five thousand Jewish children in France.
October 7	FDR warns Germans again and United States announces creation of United Nations Commission for the Investigation of War Crimes to prosecute the guilty.
October 23	The battle of El Alamein in Egypt begins.
October 27	Japanese withdraw at Guadalcanal.
November 2	British victory at El Alamein.
November 7–8	Operation Torch, the invasion of North Africa, begins as Allied troops land in Morocco and Algeria.
November 11	Germans occupy Vichy France.
November 24	Welles confirms massacre of Jews to Wise; Wise makes facts public that two million Jews were dead. Actually, approximately three and a half million Jews were dead.
December 2	Day of mourning in major American cities for the Jews of Europe.
December 8	Rabbi Wise and four other Jewish leaders meet with FDR.
December 17	United Nations Declaration on Jewish Massacres issued by FDR, Churchill, Stalin, and Allied governments-in-exile.

1943

January	German rabbi Leo Baeck is arrested and sent to the Theresienstadt concentration camp in Czechoslovakia, where he remained until after the camp is liberated by the Soviets at the end of World War II.
January 14–24	Roosevelt and Churchill meet at Casablanca. FDR's conference with Noguès.
February 2	The German Sixth Army at Stalingrad surrenders to Soviet forces; Battle of the Atlantic is raging.
March 9	"We Will Never Die" rally at Madison Square Garden.
April 13	The discovery of mass graves at Katyn containing the bodies of thousands of Polish officers massacred by the Soviet Union.
April 19	Bermuda Conference on Refugees convenes.
April 19–May 16	Warsaw Jewish ghetto uprising.
April 30	The Bergen-Belsen concentration camp is opened.
May 7	Tunis falls to the Allies.
May 12	Trident Conference in Washington, FDR meets with Churchill.
June 1	Liquidation of Lvov ghetto begins.
June 23	Peenemünde rocket site discovered by Allies.
June 28	All five crematoriums completed at Auschwitz-Birkenau.
July 4–22	The Battle of Kursk.

July 9	Allies invade Sicily.
July 22	Rabbi Wise meets with FDR on proposals concerning Romanian and French Jews.
July 25	Mussolini is dismissed as head of government in Italy and arrested.
July 28	FDR meets with Jan Karski.
	August Gerhart Riegner and Robert Lichtheim report four million Jews are dead.
August 1	USAAF raids on Ploesti oil fields.
August 17	Peenemünde bombed.
September 3	The Allies land in southern Italy.
September 9	The German army occupies parts of Italy.
September 23	Vilna ghetto liquidated.
October 1	Rescue of Danish Jews.
October 6	March of four hundred Orthodox rabbis in Washington.
October 20	United Nations War Crimes Commission established.
November 3	Nazi authorities launch Operation Harvest Festival. By the end of November the three extermination camps used in Operation Reinhard—Sobibor, Treblinka, and Belzec—are closed.
November 28– December 1	Churchill, Roosevelt, and Stalin meet in Teheran.

1944

January 16	Morgenthau and Treasury staff meet with FDR.
January 22	President Roosevelt creates the War Refugee Board.
	Allies land at Anzio.
February 1	The Irgun declares war on the British in Palestine.
February	Primo Levi is sent to Auschwitz.
March 6	First large-scale daylight bombing of Berlin by USAAF.
March 19	German forces occupy Hungary; Horthy arrested.
March 24	FDR condemns the massacre of the Jews as "one of the blackest crimes of all history" and promises swift punishment of the Nazis.
April 5	Ploesti bombed by USAAF based at Foggia, Italy.
April 25	"Blood for Goods" deal offered by Eichmann to Joel Brand.
April 27	German authorities begin the deportation of Jews from Hungary to Auschwitz.
May 19	Joel Brand arrives in Istanbul.
June 4	U. S. troops enter Rome.
June 6	D-Day. The Western Allies land in Normandy in France.
June 8	FDR approves Oswego shelter.
June 11	Jewish Agency Executive votes 11 to 1 not to request bombing of Auschwitz.

June 13	First V-1 missiles hit England.
June 18	Rosenheim requests bombing of Auschwitz.
June 22	Operation Bagration along an 800-mile front in White Russia (now Belarus). The Soviets inflict immense losses on the Germany army and drive them back almost four hundred miles.
	Kubowitzki writes Pehle opposing bombing of Auschwitz.
July 9	Horthy orders a halt to the deportation of Jews from Hungary to Auschwitz; 437,402 Hungarian Jews killed at Auschwitz; Raoul Wallenberg arrives in Budapest.
July 20	A small group of German army officers, eager to end the war, unsuccessfully attempts to assassinate Adolf Hitler.
July 25	Soviet forces liberate Majdanek.
August 1	Polish uprising against the Germans in Warsaw.
August 4	After living undetected for 25 months, Anne Frank and her family, and the four others hiding in the secret annex, are reported to the Nazis. The annex dwellers are all sent to the Auschwitz concentration camp.
August 15	American forces land in southern France.
August 24	Paris is liberated.
August 25	Antonescu is overthrown; Romania declares war on Germany.
September 8	First V-2 missiles hit London.

September 17	Operation Market Garden.
October 2	German troops crush Warsaw Polish uprising.
October	Industrialist Oskar Schindler is granted permission by the Nazis to establish a munitions factory in Czechoslovakia.
	United States general Douglas MacArthur returns to liberate the Philippines from Japanese control.
October 9	Moscow Conference.
October 15	Horthy announces a truce with the Allies. The Horthy government is overthrown by the Fascist Arrow Cross Party with German support.
October 23–26	The largest naval battle in history, the Battle of Leyte Gulf, in the Philippines, ends in almost total destruction of the Japanese fleet.
November 2	The gassings at Auschwitz are stopped.
November 5	Eichmann deports Jews from Budapest on foot in death marches to Austria.
November 7	FDR is reelected president for a fourth term. Lord Moyne is assassinated by the Stern Gang.
November 25	Destruction of the crematoriums at Auschwitz by Germans begins.
December 16	Battle of the Bulge, a major counteroffensive by the Germans against the Allies.

1945

January 12	Soviets launch an offensive along the entire Polish front, entering Warsaw on January 17 and Lodz two days later. By February 1 they are within 100 miles of the German capital of Berlin.
January 17	Russian troops liberate Warsaw.
January 18	Sixty thousand Auschwitz prisoners are sent on death marches to camps in the West.
January 27	Soviets liberate Auschwitz.
February 4–11	Allied leaders Churchill, Roosevelt, and Stalin meet in Yalta in the Soviet Union to discuss strategies for ending the war and to plan future forms of government for Germany and other parts of Europe.
February 13	Allied bombing of Dresden.
February 14	FDR meets with Ibn Saud.
February 19	American marines land on Iwo Jima.
March 7	American forces cross the Rhine at Remagen.
April 1	American troops land on Okinawa, beginning the largest land battle of the Pacific War; Japanese forces there are defeated by June.
April 11	United States general George S. Patton and his Third Army liberate the Buchenwald concentration camp in Germany. American reporter Edward R. Murrow broadcasts his impressions of Buchenwald a few days later.
April 12	President Roosevelt dies of a cerebral hemor-

	rhage in Warm Springs, Georgia.
April 22	Soviet troops enter Berlin.
April 25	The United Nations meets in San Francisco.
April 28	Italian partisans execute Benito Mussolini. Final gassing at Mauthausen.
April 29	Dachau liberated by U. S. Third Army, saving thirty thousand inmates.
April 30	Hitler commits suicide.
May 2	German forces in Berlin and Italy surrender.
May 3	German authorities turn over Theresienstadt to the Red Cross.
May 7	Unconditional surrender of Germany to Eisenhower.
May 8	The war in Europe officially ends.
August 6	Bombing of Hiroshima.
August 9	Bombing of Nagasaki.
August 15	Japan surrenders.
November	Nuremberg trials.

Acknowledgments

First and foremost, I want to thank my wife, Susan, who has now suffered through both the Civil War and World War II. Second, I want to thank my agent, Al Zuckerman, of Writer's House who made the publication of this book possible, and my old friend Dorothea Benton Frank, who made Al Zuckerman possible. I am honored by Gerhard Weinberg's Foreword and his willingness to read and review my manuscript. My thanks also to our mutual friend and accomplished historian, Andrea Mërhlander of Berlin, who introduced me to Professor Weinberg. I am honored again by Alan Dershowitz's Afterword. Professor Dershowitz challenged me to write a better book, and I hope I did not fail him.

My editor Alexander Moore of Charleston, South Carolina, did yeoman's work in helping me organize, reorganize, edit, and condense this book. His intelligent, wry, sympathetic, and untiring efforts made a huge difference.

I want to acknowledge my debt to Lucy Dawidowicz, whom I

met in the 1980s and found to be one of the most honest, delightful, and brilliant people I have ever known. I also want to pay tribute to the great Roosevelt biographers Arthur M. Schlesinger Jr., William E. Leuchtenberg, James MacGregor Burns, Warren Kimball, Ted Morgan, Doris Kearns Goodwin, and especially Frank B. Freidel, a wonderful man who was one of my teachers at Harvard.

My typist and copy editor Yurie Lee worked diligently day and night over many months to produce the manuscript. Without her dedication and incredible ability to keep things straight, I would have not been able to complete the task. Claudia Pugh, formerly Claudia Kelley, my administrative assistant for more than thirteen years was, as always, there when I needed her, and, I trust, always will be.

I have been fortunate in having good and honest friends who have read and critiqued the manuscript without pity or sympathy for the author. I particularly want to thank the following: David Popowski, Esq., of Charleston, South Carolina, an accomplished lawyer and the son of Holocaust survivors, who sensitized me to many issues and made innumerable and important suggestions; Mark Wine, Esq., of Washington, a devotee of Sir Winston Churchill, a brilliant lawyer with a sharp mind, a sharp pencil, and a big heart; and my cousin Marvin Cohen, another Harvard man whose brilliance and insights have impacted both my life and this book.

Close friends, like family, live, often uncomfortably, with the research and writing of a book. I am indebted to my good friends Michael Levkoff, Harriet and Steve Steinert, Dottie and Franklin

Ashley, Catherine Hay, Dottie and Peter Frank, Tom Houck, Richard and Belinda Gergel, Bob Schindler, John Jakes, Jerry Kaynard, Alvin Hammer, and Marty Perlmutter.

I imposed on several accomplished historians, who disagreed with some of what I had to say, to read parts of the manuscript. I very much appreciate Warren Kimball, a highly respected Roosevelt biographer and now a fellow Charlestonian, who read and evaluated several chapters, and Richard Breitman, who also generously read several chapters and took time out of his busy schedule to meet with me, as did Alan Kraut. William D. Rubinstein graciously reviewed the manuscript and shared his thoughts and broad knowledge of the field with me. Steven Casey, the distinguished Roosevelt scholar, critiqued several chapters and offered valued advice.

My staff at the Rosen Law Firm has patiently listened to my stories and helped me in numerous ways: Marcia Jones, Lisa Magnan, Susan Patton, Stephenie Driver, Amy Temkin, Danielle Walker, Ashley Lambert, Lindsay Foreback, Evan Gault, and Emily Covill. Special thanks to Susan Patton for securing the photographs and illustrations in record time, and Lindsay Foreback for stepping up to the plate in the ninth inning.

It is amazing how many people, including friends, fellow historians, and lawyers, are passionately interested in FDR and the Holocaust. I wish to thank Pete Fuge, Dr. Alan Nussbaum, Marion Slotin, James McLaren, Barry Gumb, Mark Andrews, Jon Mersereau, Mel Frumkes, Lynn Gold-Biken, Lewis Regenstein, Blanche Weintraub, Barbara Ellison, Judy Grossman, Tom Tisdale,

Alex Sanders, and Peggy Jalenak. My rabbi, Anthony D. Holz of
K.K. Beth Elohim in Charleston, South Carolina, Rabbis David
Radinsky and Ari Sytner of Brith Sholom Beth Israel, and Jerry
Zucker helped me with Hebrew, biblical, and Talmudic references.
Carol Handler advised me on her father's papers. Several people
helped me track down Oscar Cox's life story, including Eunice
Cox, his daughter-in-law; Rabbi Carolyn Braun; and Cantor Ruth
Ross of Temple Beth El, Portland, Maine.

I have been fortunate in having the assistance of several
research assistants, chief among them Professor F. Kennon Moody
at the FDR Library, whose excellent work I wish to acknowledge.
Jennifer G. Priest and Eve Cassat conducted research at the
National Archives, and Daniel Gourvitch and Ali Rosen at the
Library of Congress. Several researchers worked at the College of
Charleston and Charleston County Library, including Joseph
Nussbaum and LaRisha Porter.

Special thanks to Sol and Sara Breibart, Ted and Dale Rosen-
garten, Lenore Weitzman, Henry Morgenthau III, Ambassador
William J. Vanden Heuvel, accomplished historians and friends,
for their kind assistance. Gerald Granston, a very young passenger
on the SS *St. Louis*, read my chapter on the famous voyage and
offered excellent advice.

I also have been fortunate in having the support of the splendid
staff at the American Jewish Archives in Cincinnati, including
Kevin Profitt and Camille Servizzi as well as Gunnan M. Berg and
Fruma Mohrer at the YIVO Institute. The research staff at the
Charleston County Public Library also has been particularly helpful.

I want to acknowledge the help of Maren Read and Nancy Hartman of the U.S. Holocaust Memorial Museum, Adam Rosenthal of the Museum of Jewish Heritage, the staffs at the Library of Congress, the FDR Library, the National Archives, and Christopher M. Laico of the Columbia University School of Law Library.

I would like to acknowledge Stanley Fishtine's unpublished manuscript critiquing David Wyman's *The Abandonment of the Jews* at the FDRL. I read it with great interest and picked up some interesting points.

My extended family was, as usual, wildly supportive and blindly enthusiastic. I wish to thank my ever-supportive mother-in-law, Joyce Ann Corner, Leon Rosen, Dutch Cohen, Willie Adler, Carolyn Cohen, Sandy and Chuck Marcus, Julie Hoover, Mark Tanenbaum, Phyllis and Lou Tanenbaum, all of the Feldmans (especially Stuart), Alison and Al, Sue and Buzz Corner, and Louise Waring.

The people who suffer the most when an author is writing a book are his family. My children, Annie, Ali, and Will, have been supportive each in her or his own way: Annie by her good humor, enthusiasm, emotional support, and always "seizing the day"; Ali by inspiring this book, assisting in the research, agreeing with the author, and dragging her boyfriend, Daniel, into the venture; and Will by being there every day "through thick and thin," going to World War II movies and pretending to like them, and bringing joy into my life. I am the luckiest father I know. But I am also a lucky brother in having the unconditional love, constant help, and support of my sister, Debra.

Bibliography

Primary Sources

Manuscripts and Manuscript Collections
American Jewish Archives, Cincinnati, Ohio
    Benjamin V. Cohen Papers
    Dickstein Papers
    World Jewish Congress Papers
Arthur W. Diamond Law Library, Columbia University, New York, NY
    Handler Papers
Columbia Oral History Collection, Butler Library, Columbia University, New York, NY
Franklin D. Roosevelt Presidential Library, Hyde Park, NY
    Adolf Berle Papers
    Benjamin V. Cohen Papers
    Oscar Cox Papers
    Ira Hirschmann Papers
    Isador Lubin Papers
    Morgenthau Diaries
    Morgenthau Presidential Diaries
    Presidential Press Conferences of Franklin D. Roosevelt
    Franklin D. Roosevelt Papers
    Samuel Rosenman Papers
    War Refugee Board Records
American Jewish Joint Distribution Committee Archives, New York City
    SS *St. Louis* files
Library of Congress, Manuscript Division, Washington, D.C.
    Wilbur Carr Papers
    Benjamin V. Cohen Papers
    Breckinridge Long Papers

National Archives, Washington, D.C., and College Park, Maryland
   Ira Hirschman Papers
   U.S. State Department Records
   YIVO Institute Archives, New York City
   Waldman Papers

Published Diaries, Memoirs, Letters, and Speeches

Ben-Ami, Yitshaq. *Years of Wrath, Days of Glory: Memoirs from the Irgun.* New York: Shengold, 1982.

Berlin, Isaiah. *Personal Impressions.* Princeton, NJ: Edited by Henry Hardy. Princeton University Press, 1998.

Biddle, Francis Beverley. *In Brief Authority.* Garden City, NY: Doubleday, 1962.

Black, Allida M., ed. *Courage in a Dangerous World, The Political Writings of Eleanor Roosevelt.* New York: Columbia University Press, 1999.

Bloom, Sol. *The Autobiography of Sol Bloom.* New York: G. P. Putnam's Sons, 1948.

Blum, John Morton, ed. *From the Morgenthau Diaries.* 3 vols. Boston: Houghton Mifflin, 1959–67.

Bohlen, Charles E. *Witness to History: 1929–196.* New York: W. W. Norton, 1973.

Bradley, Omar N. *A Soldier's Story.* New York: Modern Library, 1999.

Butcher, Harry C. *My Three Years with Eisenhower: The Personal Diary of Captain Harry C. Butcher, USNR, Naval Aide to General Eisenhower, 1942 to 1945.* New York: Simon and Schuster, 1946.

Byrnes, James F. *All in One Lifetime.* New York: Harper & Brothers, 1958.

Campbell, Thomas, and George Herring, eds. *The Diaries of Edward R. Stettinius, Jr.* New York: New Viewpoints, 1975.

Celler, Emanuel. *You Never Leave Brooklyn: The Autobiography of Emanuel Celler.* New York: John Day, 1953.

Chadakoff, Rochelle, ed. *Eleanor Roosevelt's "My Day."* New York: Pharos, 1989.

Dawidowicz, Lucy. *From That Place and Time, A Memoir, 1938–1947.* New York: W.W. Norton & Co., 1989

Dodd, Martha, and William E. Jr., eds. *Ambassador Dodd's Diary, 1933–1938.* New York: Harcourt, Brace, 1941.

Dubois, Josiah E. Jr. *The Devil's Chemists.* Boston: Beacon Press, 1952.

Eddy, William A. *F.D.R. Meets Ibn Saud.* New York: American Friends of the Middle East, Inc., 1954.

Freedman, Max, ed. *Roosevelt and Frankfurter: Their Correspondence, 1928–1945.* Boston: Little, Brown, 1967.

Fry, Varian. *Surrender on Demand.* 1945. Reprint, Boulder, CO: Johnson Books, 1997.

Goldmann, Nahum. *Memories: The Autobiography of Nahum Goldmann.* New York: Weidenfeld & Nicolson, 1969.

Gunther, John. *Roosevelt in Retrospect.* New York: Harper & Brothers, 1950.

Hassett, William D. *Off the Record with FDR, 1942–1945*. New Brunswick, NJ: Rutgers University. Press, 1958.

Hecht, Ben. *A Child of the Century*. New York: Simon and Schuster, 1954.

Hirschmann, Ira. *Caution to the Winds*. New York: David McKay, 1962.

———. *Life Line to a Promised Land*. New York: 1946.

Hull, Cordell. *The Memoirs of Cordell Hull*. 2 vols. New York: MacMillan, 1948.

Hunt, John Gabriel, ed. *The Essential Franklin Delano Roosevelt*. New York: Gramercy Books, 1995.

Ickes, Harold L. *The Secret Diary of Harold L. Ickes. vol. II, The Inside Struggle, 1936–39*. New York: Simon and Schuster, 1954.

———. *Vol. III, The Lowering Clouds, 1939–1941*. New York: Simon and Schuster, 1954.

Israel, Fred L., ed. *The War Diary of Breckinridge Long*. Lincoln: University of Nebraska Press, 1966.

Jackson, Robert H. *That Man: An Insider's Portrait of Franklin D. Roosevelt*. Edited by John Q. Barrett. New York: Oxford University Press, 2003.

Karski, Jan. *Story of a Secret State*. Boston: Houghton Mifflin, 1944.

Kleiman, Max, ed. *Franklin Delano Roosevelt: The Synagogue's Tribute, 1882–1945.* New York: Bloch, 1946.

Lash, Joseph P. *Eleanor Roosevelt: A Friend's Memoir*. Garden City, NY: Doubleday, 1964.

———. *From the Diaries of Felix Frankfurter*. New York: W.W. Norton and Co., 1975.

Leahy, William D. *I Was There*. New York: Whittlesey House, 1950.

Lilienthal, David E. *The Journal of David E. Lilienthal, Vol. I, The TVA Years, 1939–1945*. New York: Harper and Row, 1964.

Meir, Golda. *My Life*. New York: G.P. Putnam's Sons, 1975.

Murphy, Robert. *Diplomat among Warriors*. Garden City, NY: Doubleday, 1964.

Perkins, Frances. *The Roosevelt I Knew*. New York: Viking, 1946.

Podhoretz, Norman. *My Love Affair with America: A Cautionary Tale of a Cheerful Conservative*. New York: Free Press, 2000.

Polier, Justine Wise, and James Waterman Wise. *The Personal Letters of Stephen Wise*. Boston: Beacon Press, 1956.

Rabin, Yitzhak. *The Rabin Memoirs*. Berkeley: University of California Press, 1996.

Roosevelt, Eleanor. *This I Remember*. New York: Harper and Brothers, 1949.

Rosenman, Samuel I. *Working with Roosevelt*. New York: Harper and Brothers, 1952.

———. ed. *The Public Papers and Addresses of Franklin D. Roosevelt*. New York: Harper and Brothers, 1950.

Suberman, Stella. *When It Was Our War: A Soldier's Wife on the Home Front*. Chapel Hill, NC: Algonquin Books of Chapel Hill, 2003.

Sulzberger, C.L. *A Low Row of Candles: Memoirs and Diaries, 1934–1954*. New York: MacMillan, 1969.

Ward, Geoffrey, ed. *Closest Companion: The Unknown Story of the Intimate Friendship Between Franklin Roosevelt and Margaret Suckley*. Boston: Houghton Mifflin Company, 1995.

Weizmann, Chaim. *Trial and Error: The Autobiography of Chaim Weizmann*. New York: Harper, 1949.

Wheeler-Bennett, Sir John, ed. *Action This Day; Working with Churchill. Memoirs by Lord Norman Brook, et al.* London: Macmillan, 1968.

Wise, Stephen Samuel. *Challenging Years: The Autobiography of Stephen Wise*. New York: G. P. Putnam's Sons, 1949.

Other Published Primary Sources

Abzug, Robert H. *America Views the Holocaust, 1933–1945: A Brief Documentary History*. New York: St. Martin's Press, 1999.

Louchheim, Katie, ed. *The Making of the New Deal: The Insiders Speak*. Cambridge, MA: Harvard University Press, 1983.

Mendelsohn, John, ed. *The Holocaust: Selected Documents in Eighteen Volumes*. New York: Garland, 1982.

U.S. State Department. *Foreign Relations of the United States*. Volumes for 1933–1945. Washington: Government Printing Office, 1933–45.

Wyman, David S., ed. *America and the Holocaust: A Thirteen-Volume Set Documenting the Editor's Book "The Abandonment of the Jews."* New York: Garland, 1990.

SECONDARY SOURCES

Dictionaries, Encyclopedias, and Reference Works

Carruth, Gorton and Eugene Rich, eds. *American Quotations*. New York: Wings Books, 1988.

Graham, Otis L., Jr., and Meghan Robinson Wander, eds. *Franklin D. Roosevelt, His Life and Times: An Encyclopedic View*. Boston: G. K. Hall, 1985.

Laqueur, Walter, ed. *The Holocaust Encyclopedia*. New Haven, CT: Yale University Press, 2001.

Overy, Richard. *The Penguin Historical Atlas of the Third Reich*. New York: Penguin Putnam, 1996.

Books

Adams, James Truslow. *The March of Democracy: A History of the United States, Volume VI, Second Part of Annual Chronicle*. New York: Charles Scribner's Sons, 1943.

Arad, Gulie Ne'eman. *America, Its Jews, and the Rise of Nazism*. Bloomington, IN: Indiana University Press, 2000.

Atkinson, Rick. *An Army at Dawn: The War in North Africa, 1942–1943*. New York: Henry Holt, 2002.

Bailey, Thomas A. and Paul B. Ryan. *Hitler vs. Roosevelt: The Undeclared Naval War*. New York: Free Press, 1979.

Baker, Leonard. *Days of Sorrow and Pain: Leo Baeck and the Berlin Jews*. New York: Macmillan, 1978.

Barenblatt, Daniel. *A Plague upon Humanity: The Hidden History of Japan's Biological Warfare Program*. New York: HarperCollins, 2004.

Bauer, Yehuda. *My Brother's Keeper: A History of the American Jewish Joint Distribution Committee, 1929–1939*. Philadelphia: Jewish Publication Society of America, 1974.

———. *American Jewry and the Holocaust: The American Joint Distribution Committee, 1939–1945*. Detroit: Wayne State University Press, 1981.

———. *The Holocaust in Historical Perspective*. Seattle: University of Washington Press, 1978.

———. *Jews for Sale?: Nazi-Jewish Negotiations, 1933–1945*. New Haven, CT: Yale University Press, 1994.

Beard, Charles A. *President Roosevelt and the Coming of the War 1941: A Study in Appearances and Realities*. New Haven, CT: Yale University Press, 1948.

Bell, J. Bowyer. *Terror out of Zion: Irgun Zvai Leumi, LEHI, and the Palestine Underground, 1929–1949*. New York: St. Martin's Press, 1977.

Bendersky, Joseph W. *The "Jewish Threat": Antisemitic Politics of the U.S. Army*. New York: Basic Books, 2000.

Berenbaum, Michael. *The World Must Know: The History of the Holocaust As Told in the United States Holocaust Memorial Museum*. Boston: Back Bay Books, 1993.

———and Abraham J. Peck, eds. *The Holocaust and History: The Known, the Unknown, the Disputed, and the Reexamined*. Bloomington and Indianapolis: Indiana University Press, in association with the U. S. Holocaust Memorial Museum, Washington, D.C., 1998.

Berg, A. Scott. *Lindbergh*. New York: G.P. Putnam's Sons, 1998.

Berger, Jason. *A New Deal for the World: Eleanor Roosevelt and American Foreign Policy*. New York: Columbia University Press, 1981.

Berle, Beatrice, and Travis Jacobs, eds. *Navigating the Rapids, 1918–1971: From the Papers of Adolf A. Berle*. New York: Harcourt Brace Jovanovich, 1973.

Berman, Aaron. *Nazism, the Jews, and American Zionism, 1933–1948*. Detroit, MI: Wayne State University Press, 1990.

Berman, Myron. *Richmond's Jewry: Shabbat in Shockoe, 1769–1976*. Charlottesville, VA: University of Virginia Press, 1979.

Beschloss, Michael. *Kennedy and Roosevelt: The Uneasy Alliance*. New York: W. W. Norton, 1980.

———. *The Conquerors: Roosevelt, Truman, and the Destruction of Hitler's Germany, 1941–1945*. New York: Simon and Schuster, 2002.

Bird, Kai. *The Chairman: John J. McCloy, the Making of the American Establishment.* New York: Simon and Schuster, 1992.

Bishop, Jim. *FDR's Last Year: April 1944–April 1945.* New York: William Morrow, 1974.

Black, Conrad. *Franklin Delano Roosevelt: Champion of Freedom.* New York: Public Affairs, 2003.

Black, Robert C. III. *The Railroads of the Confederacy.* Wilmington, NC: Broadfoot, 1987.

Blum, John Morton. *Roosevelt and Morgenthau.* Boston: Houghton Mifflin, 1970.

———. *V Was for Victory.* New York: Harcourt, 1976.

Botting, Douglas. *The Second Front.* Alexandria, VA: Time-Life Books, 1978.

Brecher, Frank W. *Reluctant Ally: United States Foreign Policy Toward the Jews from Wilson to Roosevelt.* Westport, CT: Greenwood Press, 1991.

Breitman, Richard and Alan Krant. *American Refugee Policy and European Jewry, 1933–1945.* Bloomington, IN: Indiana University Press, 1987.

Breitman, Richard. *The Architect of Genocide: Himmler and the Final Solution.* New York: Alfred A. Knopf, 1991.

———. *Official Secrets: What the Nazis Planned, What the British and Americans Knew.* New York: Hill & Wang, 1998.

———. Norman J. W. Goda, Timothy Naftali, and Robert Wolfe, eds. *U.S. Intelligence and the Nazis.* New York: Cambridge University Press, 2005.

Brinkley, Douglas. *World War II: The Allied Counter Offensive, 1942–1945.* New York: Henry Holt, 2003.

Burns, James MacGregor. *Roosevelt: The Lion and the Fox.* New York: Harcourt, Brace, 1956.

———. *Roosevelt: The Soldier of Freedom.* New York: Harcourt Brace Jovanovich, 1970.

——— and Susan Dunn. *The Three Roosevelts: Patrician Leaders Who Transformed America.* New York: Atlantic Monthly Press, 2001.

Butterfield, Herbert. *The Whig Interpretation of History.* New York: W. W. Norton, 1965.

Canedy, Susan. *America's Nazis: A Democratic Dilemma.* Menlo Park, Calif: Markgraf, 1990.

Carr, Edward Hallett. *What Is History?* New York: Vintage Books, 1961.

Carr, Steven Alan. *Hollywood and Antisemitism: A Cultural History, 1880–1941.* New York: Cambridge University Press, 2001.

Casey, Steven. *Cautious Crusade: Franklin D. Roosevelt, American Public Opinion, and the War against Nazi Germany.* New York: Oxford University Press, 2001.

Chadha, Yogesh. *Gandhi: A Life.* New York: John Wiley and Sons.

Chang, Iris. *The Rape of Nanking: The Forgotten Holocaust of World War II.* New York: Penguin Putnam, 1997.

Chernow, Ron. *The Warburgs: The Twentieth-Century Odyssey.* New York: Random House, 1993.

Churchill, Winston S. *The Second World War.* Vol. 1, *The Gathering Storm.* Vol. 2,

Their Finest Hour. Vol. 3, *The Grand Alliance.* Vol. 4, *The Hinge of Fate.* Vol. 5, *Closing the Ring.* Vol. 6, *Triumph and Tragedy.* Boston: Houghton Mifflin, 1948–1953.

Cohen, Michael J. *Churchill and the Jews.* London: Frank Cass, 1985.

Cohen, Naomi. *Not Free to Desist: The American Jewish Committee 1906–1966.* Philadelphia: Jewish Publication Society of America, 1972.

Cole, Wayne S. *Charles A. Lindbergh and the Battle against American Intervention in World War II.* New York: Harcourt Brace Jovanovich, 1974.

Cole, Wayne. *Roosevelt and the Isolationists, 1932–45.* Lincoln, NE: University of Nebraska Press, 1983.

Collingwood, R. G. *The Idea of History.* 1946. Reprint, London: Oxford University Press, 1969.

Collins, Larry, and Dominique Lapierre. *O Jerusalem!* New York: Simon and Schuster, 1972.

Cook, Blanche Wiesen. *Eleanor Roosevelt.* Vol. 1, *The Defining Years, 1933–1938.* Vol 2, *1884–1933.* New York: Penguin Putnam, 1999.

Cox, Peter W. *Journalism Matters.* Gardiner, ME: Tilbury House, 2005.

Craven, Wesley F., and James L. Cate, eds. *The Army Air Forces in World War II., Vol. 3.* Washington, D.C.: Office of Air Force History, 1951.

Dallek, Robert. *Franklin D. Roosevelt and American Foreign Policy, 1932–1945.* New York: Oxford University Press, 1981.

Davis, Kenneth S. *FDR. Vol. I, The Beckoning of Destiny, 1882–1928.* New York: Putnam, 1972.

———. *FDR. Vol. II, The New York Years, 1928–1933.* New York: Random House, 1986.

———. *FDR. Vol. III, The New Deal Years, 1933–1937.* Random House, 1986.

———. *FDR. Vol. IV, Into the Storm, 1937–1940, A History.* New York: Random House, 1993.

———. *FDR. Vol. V, The War President, 1940–1943.* New York: Random House, 2000.

Dawidowicz, Lucy S. *The War Against the Jews, 1933–1945.* New York: Holt, Rinehart & Winston, 1975.

———. *The Holocaust and the Historians.* Cambridge, MA: Harvard University Press, 1981.

———. *What Is the Use of Jewish History?* New York: Knopf Publishing Group, 1992.

Daws, Gavan. *Prisoners of the Japanese: POWs of World War II in the Pacific.* New York: William Morrow, 1994.

De Jong, Louis. *The German Fifth Column in the Second World War.* Chicago: University of Chicago Press, 1956.

———. *The Netherlands and Nazi Germany.* Cambridge, MA: Harvard University Press, 1990.

D'Este, Carlo. *Eisenhower: A Soldier's Life.* New York: Henry Holt, 2002.

Devine, Robert A. *Roosevelt and World War II.* Baltimore: Johns Hopkins University Press, 1969.

———. *The Reluctant Belligerent,* 2nd ed. New York: Alfred A. Knopf, 1979.

Robert N. Rosen

Diner, Hasia R. *The Jews of the United States, 1654–2000*. Berkeley: University of California Press, 2004.

Dinnerstein, Leonard. *Antisemitism in America*. New York: Oxford University Press, 1994.

Dower, John W. *War Without Mercy: Race and Power in the Pacific War*. New York: Pantheon Books, 1986.

Druks, Herbert. *The Failure to Rescue*. New York: Robert Stellar, 1977.

———. *The Uncertain Friendship*. Westport, CT: Greenwood, 2001.

Duffy, James P. *Target America: Hitler's Plan to Attack the United States*. Westport, CT: Praeger, 2004.

Dwork, Deborah, and Robert Jan van Pelt. *Holocaust: A History*. New York: W. W. Norton, 2002.

Elon, Amos. *Timetable: The Story of Joel Brand*. Garden City, NY: Doubleday, 1980.

Evans, Richard J. *In Defense of History*. New York: W. W. Norton, 1999.

Farago, Ladislas. *The Game of the Foxes*. New York: David McKay, 1971.

Fehrenbach, T. R. *F.D.R.'s Undeclared War, 1939–1941*. New York: D. McKay Co., 1967.

Feingold, Henry L. *The Politics of Rescue: The Roosevelt Administration and the Holocaust, 1938–1945*. New Brunswick, NJ: Rutgers University Press, 1970.

———. *Bearing Witness: How America and Its Jews Responded to the Holocaust*. Syracuse, NY: Syracuse University Press, 1995.

———. *A Time for Searching*. Baltimore: Johns Hopkins University Press, 1995.

Feis, Herbert. *1933: Characters in Crisis*. Boston: Little, Brown, 1966.

Ferrell, Robert H. *The Dying President: Franklin D. Roosevelt, 1944–1945*. Columbia, MO: University of Missouri Press, 1998.

Fischer, David Hackett. *Historians' Fallacies: Toward a Logic of Historical Thought*. New York: Harper and Row, 1970.

———. *Liberty and Freedom: A Visual History of America's Founding Ideas*. New York: Oxford University Press, 2005.

Fleming, Thomas. *The New Dealers' War: FDR and the World Within World War II*. New York: Basic Books, 2001.

Freidel, Frank. *Franklin D. Roosevelt: Launching the New Deal*. Boston: Little, Brown, 1973.

———. *Franklin D. Roosevelt: A Rendezvous with Destiny*. Boston: Little, Brown, 1990.

Friedländer, Saul, and Henry and Sybil Milton. eds. *The Holocaust: Ideology, Bureaucracy, and Genocide: The San José Papers*. Millwood, NY: Kraus International Publications: 1977–1978.

———. *Prelude to Downfall: Hitler and the United States, 1939–1941*. New York: Alfred A. Knopf, 1967.

Friedman, Max Paul. *Nazis and Good Neighbors: The United States Campaign against the Germans of Latin America in World War II*. New York: Cambridge University Press, 2003.

Friedman, Saul. *No Haven for the Oppressed: United States Policy toward Jewish Refugees, 1938–1945*. Detroit, MI: Wayne State University Press, 1973.

Fry, Joseph A. *Dixie Looks Abroad: The South and U.S. Foreign Relations, 1789–1973*. Baton Rouge: Louisiana State University, CT: Press, 2002.

Frye, Alton. *Nazi Germany and the American Hemisphere, 1933–1941*. New Haven, CT: Yale University Press, 1967.

Fuchs, Lawrence H. *The Political Behavior of American Jews*. New York: Free Press, 1956.

Gaddis, John Lewis. *The Landscape of History: How Historians Map the Past*. New York: Oxford University Press, 2002.

Gellman, Irwin F. *Secret Affairs: Franklin Roosevelt, Cordell Hull, and Sumner Welles*. Baltimore: John Hopkins University Press, 1995.

———. *Roosevelt and Batista: Good Neighbor Diplomacy in Cuba, 1933–1945*. Albuquerque, NM: University of New Mexico Press, 1973.

Gilbert, Martin. *The Holocaust: A History of the Jews of Europe during the Second World War*. New York: Henry Holt and Company, 1985.

———. *The Second World War: A Complete History*, rev. ed. New York: Henry Holt and Company, 1989.

———. *Auschwitz and the Allies: A Devastating Account of How the Allies Responded to the News of Hitler's Mass Murder*. New York: Henry Holt and Company, 1981.

———. *Churchill: A Life*. London: New York: Henry Holt and Company 1991.

———. *The Righteous: The Unsung Heroes of the Holocaust*. New York: Henry Holt and Company, 2003.

Goodwin, Doris Kearns. *No Ordinary Time: Franklin and Eleanor Roosevelt: The Home Front in World War II*. New York: Simon and Schuster, 1994.

Grose, Peter. *Israel in the Mind of America*. New York: Alfred A. Knopf, 1984.

Hand, Samuel B. *Counsel and Advise: A Political Biography of Samuel I. Rosenman*. New York: Garland, 1979.

Harris, Leon A. *The Fine Art of Political Wit*. New York: E.P. Dutton and Co., 1964.

Haver, Ronald. *David O. Selznick's Hollywood*. New York: Alfred A. Knopf, 1980.

Hertzberg, Arthur. *The Jews in America: Four Centuries of an Uneasy Encounter: A History*. New York: Simon and Schuster, 1989.

Herzstein, Robert Edwin. *Roosevelt and Hitler: Prelude to War*. New York: Paragon House, 1989.

Hilberg, Raul. *The Destruction of the European Jews*, rev. ed. Vol. I. New York: Holmes & Meier, 1985.

———. *Perpetrators, Victims, Bystanders: The Jewish Catastrophe, 1933–1945*. New York: HarperCollins, 1993.

Hodgson, Godfrey. *The Colonel: The Life and Wars of Henry Stimson, 1867–1950*. New York: Knopf, 1990.

Hofstadter, Richard. *The American Political Tradition and the Men Who Made It*. New York: Vintage Books, 1957.

Hutchinson, E. *Legislative History of American Immigration Policy, 1798–1965*. Philadelphia: University of Pennsylvania Press, 1981.

Ioanid, Radu. *The Holocaust in Romania*. Chicago: Ivan R. Dee, 2000.

Jäckel, Eberhard. *Hitler in History*. Hanover, NH: University Press of New England, 1984.

Johnson, Paul. *A History of the Jews*. New York: Harper and Row, 1987.

Jones, Maldwyn Allen. *American Immigration*. Chicago: University of Chicago Press, 1960.

Kalman, Laura. *Abe Fortas: A Biography*. New Haven, CT: Yale University Press, 1990.

Kanawada, Leo V. Jr. *Franklin D. Roosevelt's Diplomacy and American Catholics, Italians, and Jews*. Ann Arbor, MI: UMI Research Press, 1982.

Kaufman, Isidor. *American Jews in World War II: The Story of 550,000 Fighters for Freedom*, 2 vols. New York: Dial Press, 1947.

Keegan, John. *The Second World War*. New York: Penguin Books, 1990.

———. *The Battle for History*. New York: Vintage Books, 1996.

Kennedy, David M. *Freedom from Fear: The American People in Depression and War, 1929–1945*. New York: Oxford University Press, 1999.

Kershaw, Ian. *The Nazi Dictatorship: Problems and Perspectives of Interpretation*. London: Arnold, 1993.

———. *Hitler, 1889–1936: Hubris*. New York: W. W. Norton and Company, 1999.

———. *Hitler, 1936–1945: Nemesis*. New York W. W. Norton and Company, 2000.

Kimball, Warren F. *The Most Unsordid Act: Lend-Lease, 1939–1941*. Baltimore, MD: Johns Hopkins University Press, 1969.

———. *Swords or Ploughshares? The Morgenthau Plan for Defeated Nazi Germany, 1943–1945*. Philadelphia: Lippincott, 1976.

———. *The Juggler: Franklin Roosevelt as Wartime Statesman*. Princeton, NJ: Princeton University Press, 1991.

———. *Forged in War: Roosevelt, Churchill, and the Second World War*. New York: William Morrow, 1997.

———, ed. *Churchill and Roosevelt: The Complete Correspondence*. Princeton, NJ: Princeton University Press, 1941.

Knopf, David, and Eric Markusen. *The Holocaust and Strategic Bombing: Genocide and Total War in the Twentieth Century*. Boulder, CO: Westview Press, 1995.

Kolsky, Thomas A. *Jews against Zionism*. Philadelphia: Temple University Press, 1990.

Kurzman, Dan. *No Greater Glory: The Four Immortal Chaplains and the Sinking of the Dorchester in World War II*. New York: Random House, 2004.

Langer, William L., and Everett S. Gleason. *The Undeclared War, 1940–1941*. New York: Harper and Brothers, 1953.

Laqueur, Walter. *A History of Zionism*. New York: Holt, Rinehart, and Winston, 1972.

———. *The Terrible Secret: Suppression of the Truth about Hitler's 'Final Solution'*. Boston, MA: Little, Brown, 1980.

———. *Breaking the Silence*, New York: Simon and Schuster, 1986.

Larrabee, Eric. *Commander in Chief: Franklin Delano Roosevelt, His Lieutenants, and Their War*. New York: Harper & Row, 1987.

Lash, Joseph P. *Eleanor and Franklin: The Story of Their Relationship, Based on Eleanor Roosevelt's Private Papers*. New York: W. W. Norton, 1971.

———. *Roosevelt and Churchill, 1939–1941: The Partnership That Saved the West*. New York: W. W. Norton, 1976.

———. *Dealers and Dreamers: A New Look at the New Deal*. New York: Doubleday, 1988.

Lasser, William. *Benjamin V. Cohen: Architect of the New Deal*. New Haven, CT: Yale University Press, 2002.

Laurie, Clayton D. *The Propaganda Warriors: America's Crusade against Nazi Germany*. Lawrence, KS: University Press of Kansas, 1996.

Leff, Laurel. *Buried by the Times: The Holocaust and America's Most Important Newspaper*. New York: Cambridge University Press, 2005.

Leuchtenburg, William E. *The Perils of Prosperity, 1914–32*. Chicago: University of Chicago Press, 1958.

———. *Franklin D. Roosevelt and the New Deal*. New York: Harper & Row, 1963.

Levy, Alan. *The Wiesenthal File*. Grand Rapids, MI: William B. Eerdmans, 1993.

Lewis, Bernard. *What Went Wrong?* New York: HarperCollins, 2003.

Lewis, Selma S. *A Biblical People in the Bible Belt: The Jewish Community of Memphis, Tennessee, 1840s–1960s*. Macon, GA: Mercer University Press, 1998.

Lipstadt, Deborah E. *Beyond Belief: The American Press and the Coming of the Holocaust, 1933–1945*. New York: Free Press, 1986.

———. *History on Trial: My Day in Court with David Irving*. New York: HarperCollins, 2005.

Littel, Marcia Sachs, and Sharon Weissman Gutman. *Liturgies on the Holocaust*. Valley Forge, PA: Trinity Press International, 1996.

Lookstein, Haskel. *Were We Our Brothers' Keepers?: The Public Response of American Jews to the Holocaust, 1938–1944*. New York: Hartmore House, 1985.

Lowenheim, Francis L., et al., eds. *Roosevelt and Churchill: Their Secret Wartime Correspondence*. New York: Saturday Review, 1975.

Lowenstein, Sharon R. *Token Refuge: The Story of the Jewish Refugee Shelter at Oswego, 1944–1946*. Bloomington, IN: Indiana University Press, 1986.

Lukacs, John. *The Duel: Hitler vs. Churchill, 10 May–31 July 1940*. London: Bodley Head, 1990.

———. *The Duel: The Eighty-Day Struggle between Churchill and Hitler*. New Haven, CT: Yale University Press, 1999.

———. *Five Days in London, May 1940*. New Haven, CT: Yale University Press, 1999.

Lukas, Richard C. *The Forgotten Holocaust: The Poles Under German Occupation 1939–1944*. Lexington, KY: University Press of Kentucky, 1986.

MacMillan, Margaret. *Paris 1919*. New York: Random House, 2004.

Manchester, William. *The Last Lion: Winston Spencer Churchill Alone, 1932–1940*. Boston: Little, Brown, 1988.

Marrus, Michael R. *The Holocaust in History*. Hanover, NH: Published for Brandeis University Press by University Press of New England, 1987.

Mattar, Philip. *The Mufti of Jerusalem*. New York: Columbia University Press, 1988.

May, Ernest R. *Strange Victory: Hitler's Conquest of France*. New York: Hill & Wang, 2000.

Mayer, Arno J. *Why Did the Heavens Not Darken?*. New York: Pantheon Books, 1990.

McJimsey, George. *The Presidency of Franklin Delano Roosevelt*. Lawrence, KS: University Press of Kansas, 2000.

McKale, Donald M. *Hitler's Shadow War: The Holocaust and World War II*. New York: Cooper Square Press, 2002.

Meacham, John. *Franklin and Winston*. New York: Random House, 2004.

Medawar, Jean, and Pyke, David. *Hitler's Gift: The True Story of the Scientists Expelled by the Nazi Regime*. New York: Arcade, 2001.

Medoff, Rafael. *The Deafening Silence: American Jewish Leaders and the Holocaust*. New York: Shapolsky, 1987.

———. *Militant Zionism in America: The Rise and Impact of the Jabotinsky Movement in the United States, 1926–1948*. Tuscaloosa, AL: University of Alabama Press, 2002.

Miller, Donald L. *The Story of World War II*. New York: Simon and Schuster, 2001.

Moore, Deborah Dash. *GI Jews: How World War II Changed a Generation*. Cambridge, MA: Harvard University Press, Belknap Press, 2004.

Morgan, Ted. *FDR: A Biography*. New York: Simon and Schuster, 1985.

Morgenthau, Henry III. *Mostly Morgenthaus: A Family History*. New York: Ticknor & Fields, 1991.

Morison, Samuel Eliot. *The History of United States Naval Operations in World War II*. 15 vols. Vol. I, *The Battle of the Atlantic* New York: Oxford University Press, 1965.

Morrison, David. *Heroes, Antiheroes, and the Holocaust: American Jewry and Historical Choice*. Jerusalem: Milah Press, 1995.

———. *The Oxford History of the American People*. New York: Oxford University Press, 1965.

Morse, Arthur. *While Six Million Died: A Chronicle of American Apathy*. New York: Random House, 1967.

Müller, Melissa. *Anne Frank: The Biography*. New York: Henry Holt, 1998.

Murray, Williamson, and Alan R. Millett. *A War to Be Won: Fighting the Second World War*. Cambridge, MA: Harvard University Press, Belknap Press, 2000.

Neufeld, Michael J. *The Rocket and the Reich: Peenemünde and the Coming of the Ballistic Missile Era*. Cambridge, MA: Harvard University Press, 1995.

——— and Michael Berenbaum, eds. *The Bombing of Auschwitz: Should the Allies Have Attempted It?* New York: St. Martin's Press, 2000.

Newton, Verne W., ed. *FDR and the Holocaust*. New York: St. Martin's Press, 1996.

Nichol, John, and Tony Rennell. *The Last Escape: The Untold Story of Allied Prisoners of War in Europe, 1944–1945*. New York: Viking, 2003.

Nicholas, Lynn H. *Cruel World: The Children of Europe in the Nazi Web*. New York: Alfred A. Knopf, 2005.

Nichols, J. Bruce. *The Uneasy Alliance: Religion, Refugee Work, and the U.S. Foreign Policy*. New York: Oxford University Press, 1988.

Nixon, Edgar B., ed. *Franklin D. Roosevelt and Foreign Affairs*. 3 vols. Cambridge, MA: Belnap, 1969.

Novick, Peter. *The Holocaust in American Life*. Boston: Houghton Mifflin, 1999.

Nurenberger, M. J. *The Scared and the Doomed: The Jewish Establishment vs. the Six Million*. New York: Mosaic, 1985.

Overy, Richard. *Why the Allies Won*. New York: W. W. Norton, 1995.

Penkower, Monty Noam. *The Jews Were Expendable: Free World Diplomacy and the Holocaust*. Chicago: University of Illinois Press, 1983.

———. *Decision on Palestine Deferred: America, Britain, and Wartime Diplomacy, 1939–1945*. Portland, OR: Frank Cass, 2002.

Perrett, Geoffrey. *Days of Sadness, Years of Triumph*. New York: Coward, McCann, and Geoghegan, 1973.

Persico, Joseph E. *Roosevelt's Secret War: FDR and World War II Espionage*. New York: Random House, 2001.

Peters, Joan. *From Time Immemorial: The Origins of the Arab-Jewish Conflict over Palestine*. New York: Harper & Row, 1984.

Pogue, Forrest C. *George C. Marshall: Organizer of Victory*. New York: Viking Press, 1973.

Ponting, Clive. *Armageddon*. New York: Random House, 1995.

Porat, Dina. *The Blue and the Yellow Stars of David*. Cambridge, MA: Harvard University Press, 1990.

Raphael, Marc Lee. *Abba Hillel Silver*. New York: Holmes & Meier, 1999.

Rapoport, Louis. *Shake Heaven and Earth: Peter Bergson and the Struggle to Rescue the Jews of Europe*. New York: Gefen Books, 1999.

Read, Anthony, and David Fisher. *Kristallnacht: The Nazi Night of Terror*. New York: Random House, 1989.

Reader's Digest Association, Inc. *The World at War, 1939–45*. Pleasantville, NY: 1999.

Rees, Laurence. *Auschwitz: A New History*. New York: Public Affairs, 2005.

Renehan, Edward J. *The Kennedys at War*. New York: Doubleday, 2002.

Rhodes, Richard. *The Making of the Atomic Bomb*. New York: Simon and Schuster, 1988.

Robinson, Greg. *By Order of the President: FDR and the Internment of Japanese Americans*. Cambridge, MA: Harvard University Press, 2001.

Rubin, Saul Jacob. *Third to None: The Saga of Savannah Jewry, 1733–1983*. Savannah, GA: Congregation Mickve Israel, 1983.

Rubinstein, William D. *The Myth of Rescue: Why the Democracies Could Not Have Saved More Jews from the Nazis*. New York: Routledge, 1997.

Sachar, Howard M. *The Course of Modern Jewish History*. Cleveland: World, 1958.

———. *A History of the Jews in America*. New York: Alfred A. Knopf, 1992.

Sanders, Ronald. *Shores of Refuge: A Hundred Years of Jewish Immigration*. New York: Henry Holt, 1988.

Sarna, Jonathan D. *American Judaism: A History*. New Haven, CT: Yale University Press, 2004.

Sayen, Jamie. *Einstein in America: The Scientist's Conscience in the Age of Hitler and Hiroshima*. New York: Crown, 1985.

Schlesinger, Arthur M. Jr. *The Politics of Upheaval*. Boston: Houghton Mifflin, 1960.

Segev, Tom. *The Seventh Million: The Israelis and the Holocaust*. New York: Hill & Wang, 1993.

———. *One Palestine, Complete: Jews and Arabs under the British Mandate*. New York: Henry Holt, 2000.

Shaw, Antony. *World War II: Day by Day*. Osceola, WI: Motorbooks Inernational, 2000.

Sherwood, Robert E. *Roosevelt and Hopkins: An Intimate History*. New York: Harper & Brothers, 1948.

Shirer, William L. *The Rise and Fall of the Third Reich*. New York: MJF Books, 1959.

Sirevag, Torbjorn. *The Eclipse of the New Deal and the Fall of Vice President Wallace, 1944*. New York: Garland, 1985.

Slayton, Robert A. *Empire Statesman: The Rise and Redemption of Al Smith*. New York: The Free Press, 2001.

Smith, Bradley F. *Reaching Judgment at Nuremberg*. New York: Basic Books, 1977.

Sorin, Gerald. *A Time for Building: The Third Migration, 1880–1920*. Baltimore: Johns Hopkins University Press, 1992.

Spivak, Michelle Beth and Robert M. Zweiman, eds. *The Jewish War Veterans of the USA: One Hundred Years of Service*. Paducah, KY: Turner Publishing Co., 1996.

Stephen, John J. *Hawaii under the Rising Sun*. Honolulu: University of Hawaii Press, 1984.

Stern, Chaim, ed. *Gates of Prayer: The New Union Prayerbook*. New York: Central Conference of American Rabbis, 1975.

———. *Gates of Repentance: The New Union Prayerbook for the Days of Awe*. New York: Central Conference of American Rabbis, 1978.

Stimson, Henry L., and McGeorge Bundy. *On Active Service in Peace and War*. New York: Harper & Bros., 1948.

Stinnett, Robert B. *Day of Deceit: The Truth about FDR and Pearl Harbor*. New York: Touchstone, 2001.

Stokesbury, James L. *A Short History of World War II*. New York: William Morrow, 1980.

Strauss, Lewis. *Men and Decisions*. Garden City, NY: Doubleday, 1962.

Teveth, Shabtai. *Ben-Gurion: The Burning Ground, 1886–1948*. Boston: Houghton Mifflin, 1987.

———. *Ben-Gurion and the Holocaust*. New York: Harcourt, Brace, 1996.

Thomas, Gordon, and Max Morgan-Witts. *Voyage of the Damned,* 2nd ed. Belton, Loughborough, Eng: Dalton Watson, 1994.

Tindall, George B. *The Emergence of the New South, 1913–1945*. Baton Rouge, LA: Louisiana State University Press, 1967.

Urofsky, Melvin I. *American Zionism from Herzl to the Holocaust*. Garden City, NY: Anchor Press, 1975.

———. *We Are One! American Jewry and Israel*. Garden City, NY: Doubleday, 1978.

———. *A Voice That Spoke for Justice: The Life and Times of Stephen S. Wise*. Albany: State University of New York Press, 1982.

Van Paassen, Pierre. *The Forgotten Ally*. New York: Dial Press, 1943.

Ward, Geoffrey C. *A First-Class Temperament: The Emergence of Franklin Roosevelt*. New York: Harper & Row, 1989.

Wasserstein, Bernard. *Britain and the Jews of Europe, 1939–1945*. Oxford, England: Oxford University Press, 1979.

Watson, Mark Skinner. *Chief of Staff*. Washington, D.C.: Department of the Army Historical Division, 1950.

Weinberg, Gerhard L. *A World at Arms: A Global History of World War II*. New York: Cambridge University Press, 1994.

———. *Germany, Hitler, and World War II: Essays in Modern German and World History*. New York: Cambridge University Press, 1995.

Weiss, Stuart L. *The President's Man: Leo Crowley and Franklin Roosevelt in Peace and War*. Carbondale: Southern Illinois University Press, 1996.

Welch, Bob. *American Nightingale: The Story of Frances Slanger, Forgotten Heroine of Normandy*. New York: Atria Books, 2004.

Welles, Benjamin. *Sumner Welles: FDR's Global Strategist, A Biography*. New York: St. Martin's Press, 1997.

Wiebe, Robert H. *The Search for Order, 1877–1920*. New York: Hill & Wang, 1967.

Wiesel, Elie. *A Jew Today*. New York: Gerecor, 1978.

Wilt, Alan F. *The Atlantic Wall: Rommel's Plan to Stop the Allied Invasion*. New York: Enigma Books, 2004.

Winegarten, Ruthe, and Schechter, Cathy. *Deep in the Heart: The Lives and Legends of Texas Jews: A Photographic History*. Austin, TX: Texas Jewish Historical Society, Eakin Press, 1990.

Wistrich, Robert S. *Hitler and the Holocaust*. New York: Modern Library, 2001.

Wohlstetter, Roberta. *Pearl Harbor: Warning and Decision*. Palo Alto, CA: Stanford University Press, 1962.

Wood, Thomas E., and Stanislaw M. Jankowski. *Karski: How One Man Tried to Stop the Holocaust*. New York: John Wiley and Sons, 1994.

Wyden, Peter. *Stella: One Woman's True Tale of Evil, Betrayal, and Survival in Hitler's Germany*. New York: Doubleday, 1993.

Wyman, David S. *Paper Walls: America and the Refugee Crisis, 1938–1941*. Boston, MA: University of Massachusetts Press, 1968.

———.*The Abandonment of the Jews: America and the Holocaust, 1938–1945*. New York: Pantheon, 1984.

——— and Rafael Medoff. *A Race against Death: Peter Bergson, America, and the Holocaust*. New York: New Press, 2002.

Yahil, Leni. *The Holocaust: The Fate of European Jewry, 1932–1945*. New York: Oxford University Press, 1990.

Yamamoto, Masahiro. *Nanking: Anatomy of an Atrocity*. Westport, CT: Praeger, 2000.

Yergin, Daniel. *The Prize: The Epic Quest for Oil, Money, and Power*. New York: Simon and Schuster, 1991.

Young-Bruehl, Elisabeth. *Hannah Arendt: For Love of the World*. New Haven, CT: Yale University Press, 1982.

Zinn, Howard. *Passionate Declarations: Essays on War and Justice*. New York: HarperCollins, 2003.

Essays from Collected Volumes

Berlin, Isaiah. "Zionist Politics in Wartime Washington: A Fragment of Personal Reminiscence." In Barnet Litvinoff, ed., *The Essential Chaim Weizmann: The Man, the Statesman, the Scientist*. London: Weidenfeld & Nicolson, 1982.

Feingold, Henry L. "The Government Response." In *The Holocaust: Ideology, Bureaucracy, and Genocide: The San José Papers*, edited by Henry Friedlander and Sybil Milton. Millwood, NY: Kraus International Publications, 1977–1978.

Kinsella, William E. Jr. "The Prescience of a Statesman: FDR's Assessment of Adolf Hitler before the World War, 1933–1941." In *Franklin D. Roosevelt: The Man, the Myth, the Era, 1882–1945*, edited by Herbert D. Rosenman and Elizabeth Bartelme. New York: Greenwood Press, 1987.

Murray, Williamson. "Did Strategic Bombing Work?" In *No End Save Victory*, edited by Robert Cowley. New York: G. P. Putnam's Sons, 2001.

Penkower, Monty. "American Jewish Congress/World Jewish Congress." In *American Jewry during the Holocaust*. New York: Holmes & Meier, 1984.

Steinweis, Alan E. "Reflections on the Holocaust from Nebraska." In *The Americanization of the Holocaust*, edited by Hilene Flanzbaum. Baltimore: Johns Hopkins University Press, 1999.

Weinberg, Gerhard L. "The Allies and the Holocaust." In *The Holocaust and History: The Known, the Unknown, the Disputed, and the Reexamined*, edited by Michael Berenbaum and Abraham J. Peck. Bloomington, IN: Indiana University Press, 1998.

Magazine, Newspaper, and Journal Articles

Allen, Howard S. "Studies of Political Loyalties of Two Nationality Groups." *Journal of the Illinois State Historical Society* 57 (1964).

Bauer, Yehuda. "The Goldberg Report." *Midstream* (February 1985).

Brecher, Frank W. " 'The Western Allies and the Holocaust,' David Wyman and the Historiography of America's Response to the Holocaust: Counter-Considerations." *Holocaust and Genocide Studies* 5, no. 4 (1990).

Breitman, Richard. "The Allied War Effort and the Jews, 1942–1943." *Journal of Contemporary History* 20, no. 1 (January 1985).

Brody, David. "American Jewry, the Refugees, and Immigration Restriction, 1932–1942." *PAJHS* 45 (June 1956).

Dawidowicz, Lucy S. "American Jews and the Holocaust." *New York Times Magazine*, April 18, 1982.

Dinnerstein. "Jews and the New Deal." *AJH* 72, nos. 1–4 (September 1982–June 1983).

Engel, David. "Jan Karski's Mission to the West, 1942–1944." *Holocaust and Genocide Studies* 5, no. 4 (1990).

Feingold, Henry L. "Who Shall Bear Guilt for the Holocaust?" *AJH* 48, No. 3 (March 1979).'

Gellman, Irwin F. "The *St. Louis* Tragedy." *AJHQ* 61 no. 2 (December 1971).

"Jap Diary Describes Beheading of Yank." *Washington Post*, October 5, 1943.

Konovitch, Barry J. "The Fiftieth Anniversary of the *St. Louis*: What Really Happened." *AJH* 79 (Winter 1989–90).

Kozlowski, Maciej. "The Mission That Failed: An Interview with Jan Karski." *Dissent* 34, no. 3 (Summer 1987).

Levy, Richard H. "Did Ben-Gurion Reverse His Position on Bombing Auschwitz?" *Journal of Genocide Research* 3 (2001).

Lipstadt, Deborah E. "Witness to the Persecution: The Allies and the Holocaust." *Modern Judaism* 3 (October 1983).

Medoff, Rafael. "New Perspectives on How America, and American Jewry, Responded to the Holocaust." *AJH* 84, no. 3 (September 1996).

———. "New Evidence concerning the Allies and Auschwitz." *AJH* 89 no. 1 (March 2001).

Mintz, Morton. "Why Didn't We Bomb Auschwitz? Can McCloy's Memories Be Correct?" *Washington Post*, April 17, 1983.

Morewitz, Stephen J. "The Saving of the SS *Quanza*." *William and Mary Magazine*, (Summer 1991).

Morgenthau, Henry Jr. "The Morgenthau Diaries." Part IV, "The Refugee Run-Around." *Collier's*, November 1, 1987.

Newsweek, May 21, 2001.

Paassen, Pierre Van, "The Irgunist Hoax." Letter to the Editor. *The Protestant* (April 1944).

Peck, Sarah E. "The Campaign for an American Response to the Nazi Holocaust, 1943–1945," *Journal of Contemporary History* 15 (April 1980).

Penkower, Monty Noam. "In Dramatic Dissent: The Bergson Boys." *AJH* 70 3 (March 1981).

Raskin, Richard. "Far from Where? On the History and Meanings of a Classic Jewish Refugee Joke." *AJH* 85 (June 1997).

Strum, Harvey. "Fort Ontario Refugee Shelter, 1944–1946," *AJH* 63 (September 1983–June 1984).

Wasserstein, Bernard. "The Myth of 'Jewish Silence.' " *Midstream* 7 (August–September 1980).

Weinberg, Gerhard. "Hitler's Image of the United States." *AHR* (July 1964).

Wolfson, Adam. "The Boston Jewish Community and the Rise of Nazism, 1933–1939." *Jewish Social Studies* Vol. XLVIII, Nos. 3–4 (Summer–Fall 1980).

Zucker, Bat-Ami. "Frances Perkins and the German Jewish Refugees, 1933–1940." *AJH* 89 (March 2001).

Notes

Preface

1   Urofsky, *We Are One!*, 46.

2.   Kleiman, *FDR: The Synagogue's Tribute*, 35.

3.   "Only one group," Burns and Dunn wrote, "revealed no class cleavage. Rich or poor, Jews voted Roosevelt" (*The Three Roosevelts*, 335; Newton, ed., *FDR and the Holocaust*, 55; Johnson, *A History of the Jews*, 504). Johnson relied on David Wyman, *The Abandonment of the Jews*, for this opinion. See footnote 182, 625. Rabbi Haskel Lookstein accused Roosevelt of being antisemitic in *Were We Our Brothers' Keepers*, 79, 285. The index read: "Roosevelt, antisemitic remarks of." Robert S. Wistrich claimed Roosevelt "was not immune to a 'liberal' version of Antisemitism," in *Hitler and the Holocaust*. Joseph E. Persico, wrote in *Roosevelt's Secret War*, 217–20, that FDR "had been shaped in some decree by the genteel prejudices of his class."

4.   "Abandonment of the Jews" was a phrase used in Arthur Morse's *While Six Million Died: A Chronicle of American Apathy*, picked up and used by David S. Wyman's *The Abandonment of the Jews: America and the Holocaust, 1941–1945*; "indifference" and "complicity" from Henry L. Feingold, *The Politics of Rescue: The Roosevelt Administration and the Holocaust, 1938–1945*, x, 166, 299, 300; "endangered European Jews," Rafael Medoff, *The Deafening Silence*, 181; "prevented" rescue, Herbert Druks, *The Failure to Rescue*, 98; "accomplices" in Monty Penkower, *The Jews Were Expendable: Free World Diplomacy and the Holocaust*, vii.

Riegner quoted in Riegner, "The Allies and Auschwitz," 77. Saul Friedman, *No Haven for the Oppressed: United States Policy Toward Jewish Refugees 1938–1945,* 7, 14, 231–34.

Feingold is considered to be the most reasonable of Roosevelt's many critics among academic historians, but he appeared to detest FDR. "What emerges from the growing record is that the President, so beloved by American Jewry, did not have the spiritual depth to fathom the crucible being experienced by European Jewry, the historical insight and intelligence to understand the meaning of Auschwitz for our time, or the political courage to bring his Administration to a more active rescue policy. It was at once a failure of mind, spirit, and will." Feingold, "The Government Response" (252), in *The Holocaust: Ideology, Bureaucracy, and Genocide, the San José Papers.*

David Wyman is, by far, the most prodigious and indefatigable researcher in this field. He spent fifteen difficult and emotional years researching and writing *Abandonment of the Jews,* and his attention to detail and knowledge of the facts are recognized and appreciated by both his many admirers and his many critics.

For a summary of the historiography see Frank W. Brecher, "'The Western Allies and the Holocaust,' David Wyman and the Historiography of America's Response to the Holocaust: Counter-Considerations," 423–46.

Many historians, of course, did not agree with the Roosevelt critics. I have relied on the work of many distinguished historians, including, most notably, Lucy S. Dawidowicz, author of *The War against the Jews* and other works on the Holocaust; Gerhard L. Weinberg, author of *A World at Arms: A Global History of World War II* and other works on World War II; Richard Breitman and Alan Kraut, *American Refugee Policy and European Jewry, 1933–1945;* Breitman, *Official Secrets: What the Nazis Planned, What the British and Americans Knew;* William D. Rubinstein, *The Myth of Rescue;* and Peter Novick, *The Holocaust in American Life.* I have also benefited from the excellent work of William J. Vanden Heuvel (see "America and the Holocaust," *American Heritage Magazine,* 50, no. 4., July/August 1999, 34–51).

5.   Urofsky, *A Voice That Spoke for Justice,* chap. 22. "How could [Wise] pledge secrecy when millions of lives were involved?" Elie Wiesel complained (319). Saul Friedman accused Wise of being "docile" and "silent" (320). Wyman, *The Abandonment of the Jews,* 54, 69–70; Bauer, *Jews for Sale?,* 258–59; Medoff, *The Deafening Silence;* Lookstein, *Were We Our Brothers' Keepers?,* 79.

6. On the number killed in World War II: Lucy S. Dawidowicz, *The Holocaust and the Historians*, chap. 1 ("at least 35 million persons, perhaps even as many as 50 million"). The exact number of victims is unknowable. Gilbert, *The Second World War*, 1 ("More than forty-six million"); Keegan, *The Second World War*, chap. 33 (50 million); Dower, *War without Mercy*, 3 ("over fifty million"); Reader's Digest's *The World at War, 1939–1945*, put the total at 75 to 100 million (Soviet Union: 27 million; Germany: 7 million, including massacred ethnic Germans; China: 20 million; Poland: 6 million; Yugoslavia: 1.7 million; the Indians of Burma: 1 million), 139. The Germans murdered 5 million to 6 million Jews (*The Holocaust Encyclopedia*, xiv). According to Dower in *War without Mercy*, the Soviet Union lost 20 million people or more. Chinese losses are unknown, but range from several million to 15 million deaths. A United Nations report in 1947 estimated that 9 million Chinese were killed in the war, and "an enormous number died of starvation or disease in 1945 and 1946" as a result of the Japanese war (295–96). According to Daniel Barenblatt in *A Plague upon Humanity*, fn 20, 298, at least 580,000 people were killed by the Japanese using germ warfare and human experiments. Total Japanese deaths were more than 2,100,000, of which 1,740,955 were military and 360,000 were civilians (50,000 to 80,000 at Hiroshima alone); Weinberg, *A World at Arms*, 889. Arno J. Mayer estimated 42 million killed in World War II and that more than 3 million Soviet officers and men were murdered by the Nazis. The bulk of Europe's 18 million civilian war dead were Russian and Polish Christians. Mayer, *Why Did the Heavens Not Darken?*, 13, 201.

7. *New York Times*, December 18, 1942, 10; Gilbert, *Auschwitz and the Allies*, chap. 11.

8. Gilbert, *The Second World War*, 426; Kershaw, *Hitler 1936–45*, 516–17; Weinberg, *A World at Arms*, 250–52; Breitman, *Architect of Genocide*, 63; Casey, *Cautious Crusade*, 9; Kimball, *The Juggler*, 12, 15–16 (the "almost unanimous military opinion [was] that the Red Army would be defeated and Soviet resistance would collapse"); Frye, *Nazi Germany*, chap. 11 and 12 (Professor Frye quoted Guenter Moltmann that Roosevelt's "place in history is best measured by his correct appraisal of Hitler's global ambitions" (fn. 31, 185). Professor Weinberg has described Hitler's vision of murdering Jews all over the world in "The Allies and the Holocaust," in *The Holocaust and History: The Known, the Unknown, the Disputed, and the Re-examined* (as Hitler "explained to the Grand Mufti of Jerusalem, the Jews not only of Europe but everywhere else were to be killed." 484); and Weinberg, *Germany, Hitler, and World War II*, 218 ("As Germany reached

for global domination, it acquired control over the fate of a steadily increasing number of Jews"); 219 ("had Germany won [the] war, as its leaders confidently expected, their extension of the killing to the rest of the globe would obviously have increased.") Eleven million, not six million, see Gilbert, *Holocaust*, 245, 280–84; Bauer, *American Jewry and the Holocaust*, 454; McKale, *Hitler's Shadow War*, 2–5. The Nazis were well aware that American Jewry was its mortal enemy. Jews were not allowed to immigrate to the United States after October 1940 because it would lead to a "renewal" of Jewry in the United States, which would allow American Jewry "to create a new platform from which it contemplates to continue its battle most forcibly against Germany." Gilbert, *Holocaust*, 131. *Stürmer* quote, Dwork and Van Pelt, *Holocaust*, 259.

9. Weinberg, *Germany, Hitler, and World War II*, 243; McKale, *Hitler's Shadow War*, 238–40 (Hitler spoke of "exterminating . . . the Jew" in general, not just in Europe). My figure of 12 million Jews saved from the Holocaust is based on Weinberg's figures. Raul Hilberg puts the total number of Jews at 16 million, not 19 million: 7 million within and 9 million outside the Nazi sphere (more than 2 million in the USSR not occupied by Germany, 5 million in the United States, 300,000 in Britain and 400,000 in Palestine). (*Perpetrators, Victims, Bystanders*, 225). The *Historical Atlas of the Holocaust*, 13–14, published by the United States Holocaust Memorial Museum puts the total number of Jews at 15.3 million, of whom 9.5 million were in Europe in 1933 (3,000,000 in Poland; 2,525,000 in the European USSR; 980,000 in Romania); Mayer, *Why Did the Heavens Not Darken?*, 304; Kershaw, *Hitler 1936–45*, 589.

10. Donald Nelson quoted in Lash, *Roosevelt and Churchill*, 167, 329; Goodwin, *No Ordinary Time*; Kimball, *The Juggler*, 12–16. Wheeler-Bennett, ed., *Action This Day*, 205; Cohen, *Churchill and the Jews*, 188. Van Paassen, *The Forgotten Ally*, 184; Frye, *Nazi Germany*, chap. 12.

Prologue

1. *New York Times*, March 5, 1933, 1–3; Kennedy, *Freedom from Fear*, chap. 5.

2. *New York Times*, March 5, 1933, 1; Lukacs, *Five Days in May*, 7; Kershaw, *Hitler 1889–1936*, chap. 10; Herzstein, *Roosevelt and Hitler*, 292.

3. Gilbert, *Churchill*, 510–11, 522; Persico, *Roosevelt's Secret War*, 20.

4. Dawidowicz, *The War against the Jews*, 227; Baker, *Days of Sorrow and Pain*, 145 (Baeck also wrote: "*Das Ende des deutschen Judentams ist*

gekommen." The end of German Jewry has arrived.); Teveth, *Ben Gurion: The Burning Ground*, 412–13.

5. Ward, *First Class Temperament*, 252; *DAB*, 642; Burns, *The Lion and the Fox*; Graham and Wander, *Franklin D. Roosevelt, His Life and Times*, 291; Kimball, *Forged in War*, 3–5; Freidel, *Franklin D. Roosevelt: A Rendezvous with Destiny*, 8, 67.
6. Morgan, *FDR*, 339; Freidel, *Franklin D. Roosevelt: A Rendezvous with Destiny*, 260.
7. Burns, *The Lion and the Fox*, 10; Ward, *A First-Class Temperament*, xiii–xv; Burns, *The Lion and the Fox*, 156–57. Feingold is even more damning of Roosevelt's intellect. He misquotes Holmes as saying Roosevelt possessed "a third-rate" intellect. Feingold, "The Government Response," 254.
8. Goodwin, *No Ordinary Time*, 46; Kimball, *The Juggler*, 8–10; Gunther, *Roosevelt in Retrospect*, 116, 243; Rosenman, *Working with Roosevelt*, 14; Franklin Roosevelt's *Personal Letters*, 1372; Burns, *The Lion and the Fox*, 334; Lash, *Roosevelt and Churchill*, 420.
9. Goodwin, *No Ordinary Time*, 190.

Chapter 1
1. Burns, *The Soldier of Freedom*, 28, 67–68.
2. Kershaw, *Hitler 1889–1936*, xxviii, 125, 134, 291–92, 448, 541; Kershaw, *Hitler, 1936–45*, 150, 233–35, 588–89; Chernow, *The Warburgs*, 246; Johnson, *A History of the Jews*, 373.
3. Freidel, *Launching the New Deal*, 377; Freidel, *Roosevelt*, 113; Kennedy, *Freedom from Fear*, 158; Herzstein, *Roosevelt & Hitler*, 78; Dodd. eds., *Ambassador Dodd's Diary*, 3; Kinsella, "The Prescience of a Statesman," 73–74.
4. Dinnerstein, "Jews and the New Deal," 463; Breitman and Kraut, *American Refugee Policy*, 224; Morgenthau, *Mostly Morgenthaus*, 266–67; Sachar, *A History of the Jews in America*, 449, 459; Long, *War Diary*, 82; Gunther, *Roosevelt in Retrospect*, 122.
5. *DAB*; Blum, *Morgenthau Diaries* 1:12–18, 30–32; Morgenthau, *Mostly Morgenthaus*, xivi, 186–87.
6. Blum, *Morgenthau Diaries*, 1:xv.
7. Roosevelt, *This I Remember*, 170–71; Morgenthau, *Mostly Morgenthaus*, chap. 21; 385 ("dirty jokes"); 268–74, 294; Meacham, *Franklin and Winston*, 29; Blum, *Morgenthau Diaries*, 1:32–34.
8. Dinnerstein, *antisemitism in America*, 108–9; Freidel, *Roosevelt*, 4 (the original spelling *was* "Van Rosenvelt" (from the rose field); Gunther,

Roosevelt in Retrospect, 153–55; Burns, *The Lion and the Fox*, 212; Feingold, *A Time for Searching*, 214–16.

9. Sachar, *A History of the Jews in America*, 234–38, 466–67, chap. 26, 29; Mayer, *Why Did the Heavens Not Darken?*, chap. II; Sanders, *Shores of Refuge*, chap. 1–3; Johnson, *A History of the Jews*, 364–65; Dwork and Van Pelt, *Holocaust*, 116–19.

10. Dinnerstein, *Antisemitism in America*, chap. 4 and 5; Feingold, *A Time for Searching*, chap. 1; Sachar, *A History of the Jews in America*, 432–45; Medoff, *The Deafening Silence*, 18; Mayer, *Why Did the Heavens Not Darken?*, chap. II. Jewish participation in radical and left-wing causes in the 1930s is legendary. Seymour Martin Lipset was national chairman of the Trotskyite Young People's Socialist League and Irving Howe a Trotskyite student leader.

11. Lilienthal, *Journal of David E. Lilienthal*, 146–48.

12. Dinnerstein, *Antisemitism in America*, 107–12.

13. Sachar, *A History of the Jews in America*, 452–54; Dinnerstein, "Jews and the New Deal," 461–76. Feingold, *A Time for Searching*, 216–17. The August 15, 1936, issue of *The White Knight*, a publication of the racist, antisemitic Knights of the White Camelia, contained an article titled "The Jew Deal" in which the author asked, "Is this a 'new deal' or a 'Jew Deal'?" Gellman, *Secret Affairs*, 98; Herzstein, *Roosevelt and Hitler*, 173–74.

14. Cook, *Eleanor Roosevelt*, 2:137; Morgan, *FDR*, 298; Ward, *First-Class Temperament*, 253, 138; Goodwin, *No Ordinary Time*, 102; Burns and Dunn, *The Three Roosevelts*, 143, 151, 200–1; Grose, *Israel in the Mind of America*, 114–15; Freidel, *Roosevelt*, 55.

15. Ward, *First-Class Temperament*, 138–39, 250–55; Freidel, *Franklin D. Roosevelt: A Rendezvous with Destiny*, 4 (Isaac Rosenvelt was, in fact, one of FDR's most prominent ancestors); Freidel, *Roosevelt: Launching the New Deal*, 390–95; Richard Hofstadter titled his chapter on Roosevelt in *The American Political Tradition* (Alfred A. Knopf, 1948) "Franklin D. Roosevelt: The Patrician as Opportunist." He portrayed FDR as a pragmatic practitioner of noblesse oblige. George McJimsey portrayed FDR as a benevolent elitist who, if he had prejudices, did not allow them to interfere with his "sense of a just domestic or world order," chap. 1 (quotation at 16).

The Crowley statement is one of two (the other being FDR's meeting at Casablanca with the French resident-general, Auguste Noguès, which is used to demonstrate FDR's alleged antisemitism). Michael Beschloss highlighted it in an article in *Newsweek* (October 14, 2002, 37–39) promoting his book *The Conquerors*. In a dramatic, inaccurate rendering of the facts, Beschloss has FDR "bluntly" telling Morgenthau and Crowley they had to "go along with anything I want." Morgenthau, however, was not present if and when FDR had this conversation with Crowley.

The context of the statement to Leo Crowley is important. It was in January 1942, after Pearl Harbor, when Roosevelt was trying to convince Crowley to take the job of property custodian for the recently interned Japanese Americans. Morgenthau objected to Crowley as corrupt and had been annoying the president on the issue. No one wanted the job. Milton Eisenhower resigned as director of the project. Roosevelt was angry and was trying to force Crowley to agree when they violently disagreed. See Robinson, *By Order of the President*, 135. The only evidence of the conversation is Henry Morgenthau's diary, where Morgenthau recounts what Crowley told him FDR said.

It is highly unlikely that Roosevelt ever said the words Leo Crowley ascribed to him. The statement was allegedly made by Roosevelt to Crowley while the two were alone. Roosevelt certainly never said any such thing to Morgenthau, although Morgenthau admitted in his diary that he told Crowley, after hearing the story, "About a month ago I had something similar happen but not nearly as bad at Cabinet. I talked to the President about it afterwards." (Morgenthau Diaries, January 27, 1942, 1061).

Crowley may very well have been playing on Morgenthau's insecurity. See Weiss, *The President's Man: Leo Crowley and Franklin Roosevelt in Peace and War*, chap. 8 and 9. Weiss did not even mention this statement.

16. Morgenthau diary, November 26, 1941; Freidel, *Roosevelt*, 296.
17. Ward, *First-Class Temperament*, 251–54; Burns and Dunn, *The Three Roosevelts*, 410–14; Freidel, *Franklin D. Roosevelt*, 4; Freidel, *Launching the New Deal*, 390–95; Sorin, *A Time for Building*, 196–99; Sachar, *A History of the Jews in America*, 219–20. McJimsey, *Presidency of Franklin Delano Roosevelt*, 16; Grose, *Israel in the Mind of America*, 114–15. The Brandeis nomination was extremely controversial because of Brandeis's liberalism as well as his religion. William Howard Taft and eight former presidents of the American Bar Association denounced Brandeis as a radical. Old-fashioned Boston antisemites such as Henry Cabot Lodge criticized Brandeis. Wilson was adamant, and he prevailed. The Senate confirmed Brandeis's nomination 47 to 22. The second Jewish Justice was Benjamin N. Cardozo, appointed by Herbert Hoover. It was common knowledge that the two Jewish Justices were allies of the New Deal. Freidel, *Roosevelt*, 23.

18. Morgan, *FDR*, 269–70, 509, 517; Burns, *The Lion and the Fox*, 104; Goodwin, *No Ordinary Time*, 211.

19. Morgan, *FDR*, 43, 77, 175, 195, 232; Gellman, *Secret Affairs*, 8, 16–17; Beschloss, *The Conquerors*, chap. 2 ("pigsties," 10).

20. Celler, *You Never Leave Brooklyn*, 11; Kennedy, *Freedom from Fear*, 136–51.

21. Dallek, *FDR and American Foreign Policy*, 3–20; Freidel, *Roosevelt*, 5–7, 38–39.

22. Burns, *The Lion and the Fox*, 26, 247–48; Freidel, *Roosevelt*, 68; Gellman, *Secret Affairs*, 20, 88, 146–47, 199, 309, 366.

23. Bauer, *Jews for Sale?*, 16–23; Sachar, *A History of the Jews in America*, 473–75. Breitman and Kraut, *American Refugee Policy*, 54–56; Overy, *Historical Atlas*, 36–37; Sanders, *Shores of Refuge*, chap. 15–17; Mayer, *Why Did the Heavens Not Darken?*, 84–85.

24. Lipstadt, *Beyond Belief*, 29, 41–46, 51–52; Herzstein, *Roosevelt and Hitler*, chap. 11–17 (Pickford quote, 25).

25. Lipstadt, *Beyond Belief*, 18–19.

26. Dinnerstein, "Jews and the New Deal," 475–76; Chernow, *The Warburgs*, 384.

27. Gellman, *Secret Affairs*, 8, 16–17; Beschloss, *The Conquerors*, 9–10; Herzstein, *Roosevelt & Hitler*, 413; Cook, *Eleanor Roosevelt*, 2:chap. 16; Kinsella, "The Prescience of a Statesman."

28. Teveth, *Ben-Gurion*, 511–39; Segev, *One Palestine Complete*, 116–17; Johnson, *A History of the Jews*, 431.

29. Overy, *Historical Atlas*, 50; Burns, *The Lion and the Fox*, 215.

30. See Novick, *The Holocaust in American Life*, 221, for variations and uses of the Niemöller quotation. This version was authorized by Niemöller's widow. *The Encyclopedia of the Holocaust* moves Jews to first place: "First they came for the Jews," Novick, fn. 58 and 59, 337.

31. Dawidowicz, *The War against the Jews 1933–1945*, chap. 3; Kershaw, *Hitler, 1889–1936*, 462–64, 512–22; Overy, *Historical Atlas*, 26–29.

32. Breitman and Kraut, *American Refugee Policy*, 11–12; Cook, *Eleanor Roosevelt*, 2:323–35.

33. *New York Times*, March 27–28, 1933; Morse, *While Six Million Died*, 113; Wolfson, "The Boston Jewish Community and the Rise of Nazism, 1933–1939," 308–9.

34. Sachar, *A History of the Jews in America*, 469–70; Bauer, *Jews for Sale?*, 11; Feingold, *A Time for Searching*, 235–36; Untermyer had been Louis

Marshall's law partner. Marshall had publicly chastised Henry Ford in the 1920s for his antisemitic publications.

35. Breitman and Kraut, *American Refugee Policy*, 12–14; Zucker, "Frances Perkins and the German Jewish Refugees, 1933–1940," 35.

36. Breitman and Kraut, *American Refugee Policy*, 13–14.

37. Edgar B. Nixon, ed., *FDR and Foreign Affairs*, 3:50–51, 64–66; Breitman and Kraut, *American Refugee Policy*, 261, fn. 1; Wyman, *Paper Walls*, 4–5; FDR to Herbert Lehman, July 2, 1936, OF 133A, FDRL.

38. Rubinstein, *The Myth of Rescue*, chap. 2; Bauer, *American Jewry and the Holocaust*, 29–30.

39. Rubinstein, *The Myth of Rescue*, chap. 2 (return of 16,000, 23). "There was," Walter Laqueur pointed out in *The Terrible Secret*, "a long way from persecution to annihilation. [In 1939] No one in his right mind thought that Hitler actually intended to kill all Jews" (123); Dawidowicz, *The War against the Jews, 1933–1945*, 220; Sachar, *A History of the Jews in America*, 468.

40. Cook, *Eleanor Roosevelt*, 2:311; Baker, *Days of Sorrow and Pain*, chap. 9; Morgenthau, *Mostly Morgenthaus*, 315 (Liebermann quote).

41. Rubinstein, *The Myth of Rescue*, 33–36; 120,000 Germans and Austrians immigrated to the United States between 1933 and 1944, 90 percent of them Jews. A total of 250,000 Jews immigrated to the United States between 1933 and 1944 (compared to 70,000 to Great Britain and 5,000 to Canada). Breitman and Kraut, *American Refugee Policy*, 9; Wyman, *Paper Walls*, 217–19.

42. Newton, ed., *FDR and the Holocaust*, 45; Breitman and Kraut, *American Refugee Policy*, 28–39; Morgan, *FDR*, 368–69; Gellman, *Secret Affairs*, 88; Grose, *Israel in the Mind of America*, 98.

43. Breitman and Kraut, *American Refugee Policy*, 36–38; Gellman, *Secret Affairs*, 34–38.

44. Breitman and Kraut, *American Refugee Policy*, 39–46, 65–67, 456; Gellman, *Secret Affairs*, 103–4, 138–39.

45. Sachar, *A History of the Jews in America*, 475–76; Newton, ed., *FDR and the Holocaust*, 55; Brody, "American Jewry, the Refugees, and Immigration Restriction, 1932–1942," 219–47.

46. Polier and Wise, *Personal Letters of Stephen Wise*, 232–34; Breitman and Kraut, *American Refugee Policy*, 15–24.

47. Medawar and Pyke, *Hitler's Gift*, 61–62, 133–35 (more than any other country), 148–49; Rubinstein, *The Myth of Rescue*, 36, 43, 51–53, 213–15; Rhodes, *Making of the Atomic Bomb*, chap. 1, 225 (Teller).

48. Medawar and Pyke, *Hitler's Gift,* chap. 3 (quotes 40 and 47).
49. Sayen, *Einstein in America,* chap. 1.
50. Sayen, *Einstein in America,* 65–66.
51. Sachar, *A History of the Jews in America,* 470–72; Kennedy, *Freedom from Fear,* 410–11; Herzstein, *Roosevelt and Hitler,* 125–27.
52. Burns, *The Lion and the Fox,* 251; Kanawada, *Roosevelt's Diplomacy,* chap. 4.
53. Cook, *Eleanor Roosevelt,* 2:304–5, 312, 316, 321, 323, 329, 344.
54. Burns, *The Lion and the Fox,* chap. 13; Kanawada, *Roosevelt's Diplomacy,* chap. 4; Churchill, *Closing of the Ring,* 51.
55. Burns, *The Lion and the Fox,* chap. 13 (quote at 254).
56. Freidel, *Roosevelt,* 139–41; Schlesinger, *Politics of Upheaval,* 1.
57. Burns, *The Lion and the Fox,* chap. 11; Kennedy, *Freedom from Fear,* 275–77.

Chapter 2

1. Sachar, *A History of the Jews in America,* 320, 324. Johnson was chairman of the House Committee on Immigration and Naturalization.
2. Sachar, *A History of the Jews in America,* 284–86, 308–15; Jones, *American Immigration,* chap. IX; Adams, *March of Democracy,* IV: 112.
3. Sachar, *A History of the Jews in America,* 280, 325.
4. Jones, *American Immigration,* 275, 282–85; Wiebe, *Search for Order,* 54, 90.
5. Sanders, *Shores of Refuge,* 380–81; Feingold, *A Time for Searching,* 6; Sachar, *A History of the Jews in America,* 296–98.
6. Black, *FDR,* 107; Leuchtenberg, *Perils of Prosperity,* chap. IV.
7. Leuchtenberg, *Perils of Prosperity,* chap. IV.
8. Feingold, *A Time for Searching,* 24–30; Dwork and Jan van Pelt, *Holocaust: A History,* 103–6.
9. Sachar, *A History of the Jews in America,* 320–21.
10. Jones, *American Immigration,* chap. IX; Sachar, *A History of the Jews in America,* 321, 324; Celler, *You Never Leave Brooklyn,* 81; Feingold, *A Time for Searching,* 27–29; Hutchinson, *Legislative History of American Immigration Policy,* chap. 5; Herzstein, *Roosevelt and Hitler,* 138.
11. Wyman, *Paper Walls,* 24–25; Feingold, *A Time for Searching,* 227–28; Breitman and Kraut, *American Refugee Policy,* chap. 4; Morgan, *FDR,* 275–76.
12. Wyman, *Paper Walls,* chap. 1; Medoff, *The Deafening Silence,* 18.
13. Kennedy, *Freedom from Fear,* xiii, 65–75, 131–32; Leuchtenburg, *FDR and*

The New Deal, chap. 1; *DAB*, "F. D. Roosevelt," 648; McJimsey, *Presidency of FDR*, chap. 2 (Moley quote, 34).

14. Kennedy, *Freedom from Fear*, 85–86; Freidel, *Roosevelt*, 79; Sachar, *A History of the Jews in America*, chap. XIII.

15. Kennedy, *Freedom from Fear*, 86–91; Hunt, ed., *The Essential Franklin Delano Roosevelt*, 33.

16. Burns, *The Lion and the Fox*, 312–313; Freidel, *Roosevelt: a Rendezvous with Destiny*, 246–248. For a recent perspective on FDR and civil rights see Kevin J. McMahon, *Reconsidering Roosevelt on Race* (2004).

17. Kennedy, *Freedom from Fear*, 343; Cook, *Eleanor Roosevelt*, 2:181.

18. Leuchtenburg, *Roosevelt and the New Deal, 1932–1940*, 212; Burns, *The Lion and the Fox*, 176; Kennedy, *Freedom from Fear*, 158; chap. 13 (Schall quote, 381); Freidel, *Roosevelt*, 109–12; Freidel, *DAB*, 657; *Literary Digest*, CXIII (May 14, 1932), 19, quoted in Leuchtenburg, *Roosevelt*, 198; Morgan, *FDR*, 438.

19. Sachar, *A History of the Jews in America*, 444; Dinnerstein, *Antisemitism in America*, 113–17; Kanawada, *FDR's Diplomacy*, chap. 3 (ER complained that "political realities" prevented Roosevelt "from supporting causes in which he believed," 54); Burns, *The Lion and the Fox*, 261; Freidel, *Roosevelt*, 268–72.

20. Gellman, *Secret Affairs*, 88–89; Breitman and Kraut, *American Refugee Policy*, 18, 27, 48, 223; Freidel, *Rendezvous with Destiny*, 111–12; Cook, *Eleanor Roosevelt*, 2:103; Gilbert, *Holocaust*, 43, 52; Urofsky, *A Voice That Spoke for Justice*, 282–84.

21. Kennedy, *Freedom from Fear*, 240–42, 278, 279; Freidel, *Roosevelt*, 145–46; Herzstein, *Roosevelt and Hitler*, chap. 13; Schlesinger, *Politics of Upheaval*, chap. 2–5 ("mighty tide," 21).

22. Kennedy, *Freedom from Fear*, 281–84.

23. Ibid., 341; Canedy, *America's Nazis*, chap. 4; Allen, "Studies of Political Loyalties of Two Nationality Groups," 146; Cook, *Eleanor Roosevelt*, 2:325–27; Herzstein, *Roosevelt and Hitler*, chap. 6.

24. Burns, *The Lion and the Fox*, 274.

25. Ibid., 274–75; Freidel, *Roosevelt*, 202–3.

26. Burns, *The Lion and the Fox*, 282–83; Kennedy, *Freedom from Fear*, 281; Freidel, *Roosevelt*, 196; Cook, *Eleanor Roosevelt*, 2:387; Schlesinger, *Politics of Upheaval*, 638.

27. Dinnerstein, *Antisemitism in America*, 109; Urofsky, *A Voice That Spoke for Justice*, 256.

28. Burns, *The Lion and the Fox*, 262–63; Schlesinger, *The Politics of Upheaval*, 656–67.
29. Kennedy, *Freedom from Fear*, 284; Burns, *The Lion and the Fox*, 284.
30. Freidel, *Roosevelt*, 206–8; Rosenman, *Roosevelt*, 137–38.

Chapter 3

1. Burns, *The Lion and the Fox*, 284–88, 291; Freidel, *Roosevelt: A Rendezvous with Destiny*, chap. 16, 225; Hofstadter, *American Political Tradition*, 338; Hunt, ed., *The Essential Roosevelt*, 127–32; Wise, *Challenging Years*, 221–24.
2. Freidel, *Roosevelt: A Rendezvous with Destiny*, chap. 18; Burns, *The Lion and the Fox*, chap. 15; Kennedy, *Freedom from Fear*, chap. 11.
3. Freidel, *Roosevelt: A Rendezvous with Destiny*, 229; Celler, *You Never Leave Brooklyn*, 14; Jackson, *That Man*, 32.
4. Kennedy, *Freedom from Fear*, 334–36; Burns, *The Lion and the Fox*, chap. 15, 308, 315–16; Freidel, *Roosevelt: A Rendezvous with Destiny*, chap. 18, 239.
5. Burns, *The Lion and the Fox*, 316–19; Freidel, *Roosevelt: A Rendezvous with Destiny*, 263–87; Rosenman, *Working With Roosevelt*, 108, 166–68; Herzstein, *Roosevelt and Hitler*, chap. 9; Kinsella, "The Prescience of A Statesman," 76.
6. Kennedy, *Freedom from Fear*, 343; Friedman, *No Haven for the Oppressed*, 42–43; Burns, *The Lion and the Fox*, chap. 16.
7. Freidel, *Roosevelt: A Rendezvous with Destiny*, 289–93; Burns, *The Lion and the Fox*, 352–53.
8. See Iris Chang, *The Rape of Nanking*. Not all scholars agreed with Chang's estimate of 260,000 killed in the rape of Nanking. For a different point of view see Masahiro Yamamoto, *Nanking: Anatomy of an Atrocity*, which contended that there were many fewer victims (60,000, not 260,000) and that the outrage did not result from deliberate Japanese policy. Yamamoto conceded, however, that the event took place and the massacre of civilians was "an atrocity of a monstrous scale" (138). Donald L. Miller put the number at 200,000 prisoners of war and unarmed civilians (*The Story of World War II*, 21). John W. Dower used the same figure (*War Without Mercy*, 43).
9. Burns, *The Lion and the Fox*, 352; Freidel, *Roosevelt: A Rendezvous with Destiny*, 289–92.
10. Freidel, *Roosevelt: A Rendezvous with Destiny*, 295–96; Lipstadt, *Beyond Belief*, 88; Wyman, *Paper Walls*, 43; Cook, *Eleanor Roosevelt*, 2:501–2;

Herzstein, *Roosevelt and Hitler*, 115; Friedlander, *Prelude to Downfall*, 6; May, *Strange Victory*, 54; Miller, *The Story of World War II*, 22; Kinsella, "The Prescience of a Statesman," 77.

11. Cook, *Eleanor Roosevelt*, 2:488–91; Gilbert, *Churchill*, 586–90.

12. Wyman, *Paper Walls*, 67–70.

13. Wyman, *Paper Walls*, 5–6; Freidel, *Roosevelt: A Rendezvous with Destiny*, 297; Read and Fischer, *Kristallnacht*, 195; Urofsky, *A Voice That Spoke for Justice*, 305; Feingold, *The Politics of Rescue*, 22–23; FDR to Irving Lehman, 3–30–1938, OF 3186, FDRL. Lehman wrote Roosevelt on 3–28–38 thanking him for his leadership on the refugee issue.

14. Herzstein, *Roosevelt and Hitler*, chap. 11–12; Wyman, *Paper Walls*, 16–18; Medoff, *The Deafening Silence*, 28. See, for example, OF 3186 "Refugees" FDRL.

15. Breitman and Kraut, *American Refugee Policy*, 56–58; Morgenthau Diaries, March 22, 1938, vol. 115, FDRL; Ickes, *The Inside Struggle*, 342–43.

16. Breitman and Kraut, *American Refugee Policy*, 58–61. Much later, George Rublee said in an oral interview that Roosevelt went along with the idea to assuage the American people's indignation "but without any real hope of success." Quoted by Chernow in *The Warburgs*, 479.

17. Wyman, *Paper Walls*, chap. 3, 43–46; Friedman, *No Haven for the Oppressed*, 54–55; Feingold, *The Politics of Rescue*, 24–25.

18. Wyman, *Paper Walls*, 46–47; Freidman, *No Haven for the Oppressed*, 55; Herzstein, *Roosevelt and Hitler*, 115; Feingold, *The Politics of Rescue*, 31. Friedman concluded that the United States "had accepted more than its share of refugees since 1933." *No Haven for the Oppressed*, 58.

19. Report on U.S. efforts to help Jews, Long Papers, State Department, 1939–44, Box 202, "Refugees 1939–43," 12–15, LC.

20. Wyman, *Paper Walls*, 47–48; Feingold, *The Politics of Rescue*, 27–28; Cook, *Eleanor Roosevelt*, 2:517. Letter to Mr. Harris et al. 4-18-38 OF 3186, FDRL. Feingold, *The Politics of Rescue*, 26–28.

21. Breitman and Kraut, *American Refugee Policy*, 229–30; Wyman, *Paper Walls*, 49–51; Friedman, *No Haven for the Oppressed*, 65–66; Bauer, *My Brother's Keeper*, 194 (Poland). Sanders, *Shores of Refuge*, chap. 47, 439–41. Taylor to Winterton, "Report on U.S. Efforts," Long Papers, Box 202, "Refugees 1939–43," 38–40; Dwork and van Pelt, *Holocaust*, 124. Roosevelt denigrators mocked Roosevelt's calling of the Évian Conference in 1938 as mere window dressing. Wyman, ix; Lash, *Franklin and Eleanor*, 564–72. Feingold, *Bearing Witness*, 75; *The Politics of Rescue*, chap. 2

22. Urofsky, *A Voice That Spoke For Justice*, 305; Feingold, *The Politics of Rescue*, 33; Feingold, *Bearing Witness*, 75; Meir, *My Life*; Wyman, *Paper Walls*, 48–49.

23. Wyman, *Paper Walls*, 56–57.

24. Feingold, *The Politics of Rescue*, 32–34; Kennedy, *Freedom from Fear*, 413; Morse, *While Six Million Died*, 288.

25. Morgan, *FDR*, 489; Cook, *Eleanor Roosevelt*, 2:407; Burns, *The Lion and the Fox*, 337–39; Jackson, *That Man*, 16.

26. Morgan, *FDR*, 490; Burns, *The Lion and the Fox*, 339–50.

27. Burns, *The Lion and the Fox*, 344–46, 191–92, 316.

28. Burns, *The Lion and the Fox*, chap. 18. According to Robert H. Jackson, the purge was the direct result of FDR's anger at those who failed to support his Court-packing plan (Jackson, *That Man*, 54).

29. Morgenthau Presidential Diary, June 19, 1939, 124–25, FDRL. Obviously Sam Rosenman was also pushing FDR to do more for the refugees.

30. While it is true that the antisemitic right kept a close watch on Jewish congressmen and organizations, many American Jews sincerely felt it was in their country's best interest to stay out of Europe's affairs. Breitman and Kraut, *American Refugee Policy*, 87, 115–16; Sachar, *A History of the Jews in America*, chap. XIV. For Wise's opinion of the Jewish congressional leadership see Breitman and Kraut in *American Refugee Policy*, 87.

31. Medoff, *The Deafening Silence*, 42–44.

32. Rubinstein, *The Myth of Rescue*, 25, 34–35.

33. Freidel, *Roosevelt: A Rendezvous with Destiny*, 282–98; Burns, *The Lion and the Fox*, 375; Rosenman, *Working with Roosevelt*, 176; Kennedy, *Freedom from Fear*, 348–49.

Chapter 4

1. Medoff, *The Deafening Silence*, 36–39, Friedman, *No Haven for the Oppressed*, 145 and fn. 52, 277.

2. Feingold, *The Politics of Rescue*, 39–40; Cook, *Eleanor Roosevelt*, 2:489. "Report on U.S. Efforts," Long Papers, Box 202, "Refugees 1939–43," LC, State Department '39–'44. "Chamberlain considered Roosevelt a shifty scoundrel; and he trusted Hitler, a gentleman," Cook concluded. As to the Jews, Chamberlain said, "I don't care about them myself" (Gilbert, *Holocaust*, 81).

3. Burns, *The Lion and the Fox*, 384–88; Miller, 23; Cook, *Eleanor Roosevelt*, 2:547; Kennedy, *Freedom from Fear*, 419. Herzstein, *Roosevelt and Hitler*,

99. Kinsella, "The Prescience of a Statesman," 78; MacMillan, *Paris 1919*, 235–38.

4. Freidel, *Roosevelt*, chap. 22; Burns, *Lion and the Fox*, 388; Freidel, *DAB*, "FDR," 658–59; Herzstein, *Roosevelt and Hitler*, chap. 9; Friedlander, *Prelude*, 73–79; Kinsella, "The Prescience of a Statesman," 79.

5. Read and Fisher, *Kristallnacht*, in passim; Morse, *While Six Million Died*, chap. XII; Wyman, *Paper Walls*, 71–72; Herzstein, *Roosevelt and Hitler*, 232; Laqueur, *Holocaust Encyclopedia*. Grynszpan avenged the mistreatment of his parents by the Nazis.

6. Feingold, *The Politics of Rescue*, 44.

7. Read and Fisher, *Kristallnacht*, 168–73; Wyman, *Paper Walls*, 73; Friedman, *No Haven for the Oppressed*, 85; Feingold, *The Politics of Rescue*, 40–42; Freidel, 313–14; Morse, *While Six Million Died*, 230–31; Herzstein, *Roosevelt and Hitler*, 233–39.

8. Herzstein, *Roosevelt and Hitler*, 233. Read and Fisher, *Kristallnacht*, 167–73.

9. Morse, *While Six Million Died*, 231; *FDR and the Holocaust*, 77; Freidlander, *Prelude*, 9–10; "America and the Holocaust: Deceit and Indifference," http://www.pbs.org/wgbh/amex/holocaust/filmmore/transcript/transcript1.html, 2.

10. Cook, *Eleanor Roosevelt*, 2:557–62; Friedman, *No Haven for the Oppressed*, 88; Herzstein, *Roosevelt and Hitler*, 233; Penkower, *Decision on Palestine Deferred*, 26 ("There are in this part of the world," Weizmann testified before the Peel Commission in 1936, "six million people doomed to be pent up in places where they are not wanted, and for whom the world is divided into places where they cannot live and places into which they cannot enter").

11. Sachar, *A History of the Jews in America*, 516–18; Breitman and Kraut, *American Refugee Policy*, 62–63.

12. Breitman and Kraut, *American Refugee Policy*, 63–67; Lipstadt, *Beyond Belief*, 108.

13. Herzstein, *Roosevelt and Hitler*, chap. 9, 243–47.

14. Kennedy, *Freedom from Fear*, 420–21; Freidel, *Roosevelt*, 311; Burns, *The Lion and the Fox*, 388–89; Cook, *Eleanor Roosevelt*, 2:570; Morgan, *FDR*, 504–5; FDRL, PSF 188.

15. Morgan, *FDR*, 497–99; Blum, *DAB*, "Morgenthau," 446; Herzstein, *Roosevelt and Hitler*, chap. 9 (Johnson quote at 115–16); Revahan, *The Kennedys at War*, 43; Gellman, *Secret Affairs*, 159–60.

16. Freidel, *Roosevelt*, 312–13; Burns, *The Lion and the Fox*, 390; Kennedy, *Freedom from Fear*, 422; Weizmann, *Trial and Error*, 407; Herzstein, *Roosevelt and Hitler*, chap. 9 and 10; Kinsella, "The Prescience of a Statesman," 79.

17. Shirer, *Rise and Fall*, 469–75; Kennedy, *Freedom from Fear*, 424; Friedlander, *Prelude*, 13–14.

18. Manchester, *The Last Lion*, 428; Gilbert, *Churchill*, 616; Herzstein, *Roosevelt and Hitler*, 253–54, 292–95, xvi; Lash, *Roosevelt and Churchill*. Fehrenbach, *FDR's Undeclared War*, 28.

19. Lash, *Eleanor and Franklin*, 576; letter from ER to Justine Polier, January 4, 1939, FDRL; Malvina C. Thompson, Secretary to Mrs. Roosevelt, to Judge Polier, December 29, 1938, FDRL; Wyman, *Paper Walls*, 75–77. ER met with Judge Polier on December 30, 1938. (MTL Memo 12–30–1938); Polier to ER, 1-9-39, FDRL.

20. Medoff, *The Deafening Silence*, 58; Wyman, *Paper Walls*, 75.

21. Wyman, *Paper Walls*, 85; Breitman and Kraut, *American Refugee Policy*, 74; Friedman, *No Haven for the Oppressed*, chap. 6, (quote at 90); Newton, ed., *FDR and the Holocaust* (Breitman), 134. Penkower understood the political reality of the situation in *Decision on Palestine Deferred*, 20.

22. Friedman, *No Haven for the Oppressed*, chap. 6.

23. Dinnerstein, *Antisemitism in America*, 127; Breitman and Kraut, *American Refugee Policy*, 73; Friedlander, *Prelude*, 73–79; Fry, *Dixie Looks Abroad*, chap. 6; Newton, ed., *FDR and the Holocaust*, 16–17 (Dallek); Sachar, *A History of the Jews in America*, chap. XIV ("He dared not tamper with the immigration quota system . . . [or] his party's fragile political coalition between Northern urban liberals and Southern restrictionists." 485).

24. Medoff, *The Deafening Silence*, 53; Rosenman to FDR, 10-5-38, Personal Correspondence File, FDRL; Penkower, "Eleanor Roosevelt and the Plight of World Jewry," 125–26; Feingold, *The Politics of Rescue*, 42, ER to Judge Polier, 2-28-39, FDRL; FDRL/OF 3186, November 23, 1938, ER to FDR, February 22, 1939, PPF, FDRL; Urofsky, *A Voice That Spoke for Justice*, 306–7.

25. Lash, *Eleanor and Franklin*, 576–77; Newton, ed., *FDR and the Holocaust*, 19; Friedman, *No Haven for the Oppressed*, 91.

26. Wyman, *Paper Walls*, 75–77, 94–98; 1:97; Feingold, *The Politics of Rescue*, 148–52. According to Wyman's account, Rogers and Wagner came up with the idea and Polier and FDR had nothing to do with the bill. Wyman acknowledged that the bill was defeated by anti-immigration public opinion and antisemitism and conceded that "political crosscurrents . . . [were] too

hot to handle." Feingold's approach was the same. In *The Holocaust Encyclopedia* he wrote: "President Roosevelt's refusal to support the Wagner-Rogers bill of 1939 . . . doomed the legislation."

27. Dinnerstein, *Antisemitism in America*, 115–16.
28. Herzstein, *Roosevelt and Hitler*, 146–47, 258–60, 262–69; chap. 21 and 22.
29. Dinnerstein, *Antisemitism in America*, 121–22; Sachar, *A History of the Jews in America*, 478–79; Friedman, *No Haven for the Oppressed*, chap. 6; Herzstein, *Roosevelt and Hitler*, 173–74, 258.
30. Dinnerstein, *Antisemitism in America*, 125–26; Lipstadt, *Beyond Belief*, 171 fn.; Freedman, *Roosevelt and Frankfurter*, 482. Incredibly, Feingold omitted the dramatic story of Frankfurter's elevation to the Supreme Court. He did, however, excoriate Frankfurter and Rosenman for putting their *country's* interests ahead of *Jewish* interests.(*A Time for Searching* 216–20). So did Wyman in *Paper Walls*. Feingold mentioned that Roosevelt appointed Frankfurter to the Supreme Court "at some risk" in *The Politics of Rescue* (13). Laurel Leff examined Sulzburger's opposition to Frankfurter in *Buried by the Times*, 27–28, 381 fn. 26.

Chapter 5

1. Gellman, "The *St. Louis* Tragedy," 144–45. There were 937 passengers. One was a gentile. Konovitch, "The Fiftieth Anniversary of the *St. Louis*: What Really Happened," 203–5. The *New York Times* put the number at 907 after passengers were allowed to disembark in Havana (June 15, 1935, page 14); June 18, 1935, p. 1. Gellman stated that 29 passengers were allowed to disembark in Havana. 936 Jewish refugees: Memorandum from Harold S. Tewell, American consul in Cuba, to the State Department, 6-10-1939, p. 2, 837.55J/39-54/*St. Louis*/box 5969, State Department Records, N.A. Gellman, *Roosevelt and Batista*, 168–69; State Department Archives, Box 5969, RG 59, Decimal File 1930-1039 837.55J Dispatch no. 282 (1-19-39) outlined the new Cuban immigration policies. Dispatch no. 1017 (6-7-1939) gave a detailed background of events in Cuba. The Rivero family, which owned *Diario de la Marina*, was pro-Nazi and utilized German propaganda daily. Dispatch 814 (June 20, 1939), State Department Archive. The Joint believed there were 6,000 to 6,500 German Jewish refugees in Cuba. JDC Collection, Memos to File, 5-23-39 to 5-27-39, 6-8-39, File 378 (3 of 4); Minutes Exec. Comm. 6-5-39 (File 378, 4 of 4).
2. Gellman, "The *St. Louis* Tragedy," 145–48; State Department Archives, Box 5969, op. cit.; Dispatch 1017 (DuBois to Hull, 6-7-39). Yehuda Bauer

portrayed Brú as a corrupt official attempting to shake down the JDC. Bauer, *My Brother's Keeper*, 278–79.

3. Jewish refugee organizations, including the JDC, were aware of the trouble brewing in Cuba. The voyage of the refugee ship *Stuttgart* resulted in the closing of South Africa to Jewish immigration. Sources inside Cuba reported that 1,000 Jewish refugees might arrive in May and "their landing will raise great difficulties." Memorandum on SS *St. Louis*, HAPAG, 6-27-39, pp. 1–3, citing earlier Bernstein letter, File 386, JDC Collection.

4. Gellman, "The *St. Louis* Tragedy," 146–48; Gellman, *Roosevelt and Batista*, 169; State Department Archives, Box 5969, op. cit. G-2 Report of Major Henry Barber Jr., U.S. military attaché, 6-3-1939.

5. Gellman, "The *St. Louis* Tragedy," 148–49; Medoff, *The Deafening Silence*, 60; State Department Archives, Dispatch 1017 (6-7-1939).

6. Konovitch, "The Fiftieth Anniversary of the *St. Louis*: What Really Happened," 203–6.

7. Konovitch, "The Fiftieth Anniversary of the *St. Louis*: What Really Happened," 205–6; State Department Archives, Dispatch 1017. Batista later apologized to Berenson for failing to deliver the goods. Enclosure 8, Dispatch 1017. J. C. Hyman, executive director of the Joint, wrote Herbert Mallinson on June 2 that the issue was "a factional struggle between two groups in the [Cuban] government which have made up their minds to beat each other down, and the Jewish refugees happen to be in the middle of this most terrible conflict" (6-2-39, JDC Collection 33/44, File 378 [4 of 4]).

8. Konovitch, "The Fiftieth Anniversary of the *St. Louis*: What Really Happened," 206–7; "Conference call," May 25, 1939, JDC File 3787.

9. State Department Archives, Enclosure 5 to Dispatch 1017 (May 31, 1939).

10. Gellman, "The *St. Louis* Tragedy," 150–51; Konovitch, "The Fiftieth Anniversary of the *St. Louis*: What Really Happened," 208; Lipstadt, *Beyond Belief*, 115–17. The initial cost to the Joint would be $453,000.

11. Gellman, "The *St. Louis* Tragedy," 153; Konovitch, "The Fiftieth Anniversary of the *St. Louis*: What Really Happened," 208; State Department Archives, Enclosure 6 to Dispatch 1017 (June 1, 1939) and Enclosure 12 (June 6, 1939). Arthur D. Morse portrayed Berenson as the hero and Roosevelt as the villain in chap. XV, *While Six Million Died*.

There was much criticism of Berenson within the Joint. Even the executive director, J. C. Hyman, admitted privately that Berenson "may not have been the best man to send down to negotiate . . . undoubtedly he committed a number of errors in judgment . . . obviously this sort of thing cannot be retailed in the public press" (Hyman to Baerwald, 6-27-39, JDC Archives, JDC Collection 33/44, File 379B).

Baerwald believed that the Cuban government never intended to allow the passengers to land and that Berenson "was deliberately misled." Hyman wrote Baerwald on June 27, 1939, and stated his opinion that "the Cuban authorities never intended at any time actually to give asylum." He arrived at the same conclusion DuBois had, namely that Brú was "fed up on the activities of Col. Benitez" and wanted "to get back at the Batista crowd" (Minutes of AJJDC, 6-15-39, File 378, 1–2; Hyman to Baerwald, 6-27-39, JDC Archives JDC Collection 33/44, File 379B).

12. Gellman, *Secret Affairs*, chap. 3; Morgenthau Diaries, Book 194, 79–82, 229–31, 234–35, 350–51 (reel 52), June 4–7, 1939, FDRL; Hyman to Baerwald, 6–27–39, JDC Archive Collection, 33/44, File 379 (B). "Contributions made by Secretary and Mrs. Morgenthau, January 1936 through December 1944," Henry Morgenthau Papers, Box 169, Joint Distribution Committee, FDRL.

13. Hyman to Baerwald, 6–27–39. Edward S. Greenbaum was the executive officer of Under Secretary of War Robert P. Patterson. Greenbaum later prepared a draft of the "arsenal of democracy"/Lend-Lease speech that included the famous phrase. Rosenman, *Working with Roosevelt*, 260–61. Rosenman worked closely with the Joint and agreed to chair the steering committee to create the Coordinating Foundation to rescue German Jews. The minutes of the executive committee of the Joint indicated approval of the foundation idea. Minutes, 6–5–39, JDC, pp. 1–3, JDC Collection 33/44, File 378 (4 of 4). A subcommittee of the Joint had "placed itself in touch with important personalities in our government, as it had also done previously." Minutes of the meeting of the Executive Committee of the AJJDC ("Highly confidential"), File 378.

14. File 378 (3 of 4), Memos to File 6/8/39, 5/23/39 to 5/27/39; Minutes, Exec. Comm. 6–5–39, 4; File 378 (4 of 4); minutes 6-1-39, 15.

15. Gellman, "The *St. Louis* Tragedy," 154; Sanders, *Shores of Refuge*, 467. Newton, ed., *FDR and the Holocaust*, 77–78; DuBois's memorandum of June 6, 1939 (Enclosure 13), Dispatch 1017.

16. Lipstadt, *Beyond Belief*, 116–19.

17. Memorandum 6/8/39; various cables; letters to Hyman from Irvin Bettman, president JF of St. Louis 6-7-1939; letter to Hyman from Mallinson, 6-6-39, minutes of informal discussion, 6-1-39, 14, JDC Archives, JDC Collection, 33/44, File 378 (3 of 4) and (4 of 4).

18. Minutes, Exec. Comm., 7, 6-5-39, JDC Collection, 33/44 File 378 (4 of 4); Rosenburg to Troper, 6-10-39; Hyman to Troper, 6-10-39 (2 of 4); 33/44, File 378 (3 of 4), memo "On May 23rd from Margolis."

19. Eleanor Slater to J. C. Hyman, 7-12-39, enclosing Balderston, memo to file, File 379(a) (2 of 2). Some of the passengers may have been aware of the visa problems because refugee organizations warned European Jews before the *St. Louis* and other ships sailed. (Hyman to Arthur S. Meyer, 6-28-39, File 379b).

20. State Department Archive, op. cit. Telegram from Kennedy to Hull, June 10, 1939.

21. File 378 (1 of 2), "Memorandum of Mr. Baerwald's Discussion with American Ambassador, Mr. Kennedy," June 12, 1939. A June 12 cable from London described Kennedy as "using good offices" to secure entry of 300 passengers (June 12, 1939, cable, JDC Collection 33/44, File 378, 2 of 4). ("The Voyage of the *St. Louis*," 6/15/39, File 378, 1 of 2.) A June 12 memo, "Matters for Discussion with Mr. Pell," included suggestions for influencing British opinion (File 378, 1 of 2). On Baerwald see Bauer, *My Brother's Keeper*, 277–83.

22. Telegram, Kennedy to Hull, June 12, 1939, State Department Archive. Gellman gave the British credit for being the first to agree to take a portion of the *St. Louis* passengers (155). Thomas and Morgen-Witts (*Voyage of the Damned*) gave the credit to Belgium (208, 2nd ed., 1994), relied on Morse, *While Six Million Died*, 285. Gellman, "The *St. Louis* Tragedy," 155; State Department Archives, Enclosure 3 to Dispatch 1017 (conversation May 30, 1939); Morse, *Six Million*, 283–87; Segev, *The Seventh Million*, 44. Thomas and Morgan-Witts, *Voyage of the Damned*, 207–11. The authors described FDR as "the man who finally prevented the *St. Louis* from discharging its passengers on to U.S. soil, fearing the political backlash" (217). Kennedy's motives in helping solve the *St. Louis* problem were simple: he did not want this minor event to wreck British negotiations with Germany to avoid war. He had toyed with his own plan to transfer Jewish refugees to Africa and America (with Jewish funds, of course) and met with German officials in an effort to reconcile American and German interests. Roosevelt, meanwhile, was sick of British appeasement and asked Kennedy to "put some iron up Chamberlain's backside" (Beschloss, *Roosevelt and Kennedy*, 180–89).

23. Herbert Katzki for J. C. Hyman, to Ben Foster, 6-28-1939 and Foster to Hyman, 6-24-39, JDC Archives, JDC Collection, 33/44, File 379(B).

24. Minutes of informal discussion, AJJDC, June 1, 1939, 17, File 378; memorandum on *St. Louis*—HAPAG, 6/27/39, p. 9 "Report" of 6–10–39, File

386. Baerwald was explicit in his negotiations with the British that only "those with American affidavits" would disembark in England (Memo, *ibid.*, 19a). The director of the Belgian Comité d'Assistance Aux Réfugiés Juifs confirmed in writing to the AJDC that "all these refugees shall be in possession of an affidavit for the United States" and that (of course) the AJDC would put up $500 per refugee (letter to AJDC from Comité June 14, 1939, File 386). On June 28, Herbert Katzki explained to a JDC supporter that "all the passengers . . . are expected to leave the countries which admitted them within a reasonable time for permanent settlement elsewhere" (Katzki to Foster, 6-28-39, File 379b).

25. Thomas and Morgan-Witts, *Voyage of the Damned* (1994 ed.), 8, 238. The authors estimated the survival rate in the same proportion of those Jews who survived in their host countries: 180 would have lived out of 224 in France (44 would have died); 152 out of 214 in Belgium (62 would have died); only 60 of 181 in Holland (121 would have died); www.ushmm.org (photo archives of SS *St. Louis*; see photograph 38552 as an example).

26. Press release, 6/14/39, JDC Archive, File 378 (1 of 2); "Memo on *St. Louis*—HAPAG, 6/27/39, 28–30, File 386. Gellman, "The *St. Louis* Tragedy," 154–56; *New York Times*, June 14, 1939. Wyman conceded that "systematic extermination was not foreseen." Preface to the paperback edition, vi. Penkower agreed that "none could rationally predict" the threat in the fall of 1939 (*Decision on Palestine Deferred*, 26). One Jewish American, a Mr. Herzfeld, wrote the National Refugee Service (a sister organization of the JDC) in July 1939 and threatened to sue if the $710 he had put up for his relative Mrs. Meyerhoff to go to Cuba on the *St. Louis* was not returned. (Mrs. Meyerhoff was then in Holland.) Mr. Herzfeld told the NRS that Mrs. Meyerhoff could "return to Germany [where] she would have the protection of her father's home—he is the head of a Jewish School and an outstanding German Educator." (Letter to National Refugee Service from H. Herzfeld, 7-14-1939, and reply, 7-24-39, File 379a, 2 of 2). No good deed, the old saying goes, goes unpunished. One can only marvel at the saintly patience of the Joint staff and board members.

The *St. Louis* has become "Exhibit A" against FDR because the story was dramatic and the sad spectacle demonstrated in a compelling way that no nation on Earth wanted Jews. Morse was correct in *While Six Million Died* that the voyage "would hold up a mirror to mankind" (270). Yet nowhere did Morse mention the State Department efforts to assist the Joint. "The story had a temporarily happy ending," he said—as if the events of three long years, from June 1939 to June 1942, meant nothing—"but the happiness was not to last for long." The "lesson" Morse drew was that it "was only one of many indications that [Hitler's] treatment of the Jews would not expose him to the wrath of the United States" (287).

27. Gellman, "The *St. Louis* Tragedy," 155; Müller, *Anne Frank*, 68–90; Dwork and Van Pelt, *Holocaust*, 107–10.

Chapter 6

1. Morse, *While Six Million Died*, 218–20; Strauss, *Men and Decisions*, 109–12; Wyman, *Paper Walls*, 51–54; Feingold, *The Politics of Rescue*, 52; Breitman, *The Architect of Genocide*, chap. 2; "Report on U.S. Efforts," Box 202; "Refugees," 53, 69–71, Long Papers, LC; Newton, ed., *FDR and the Holocaust*, fn. 11, 26. .

2. Breitman, *The Architect of Genocide*, 58–59.

3. Penkower, *Decision on Palestine Deferred*, 14–17 and fn. 27; Strauss, *Men and Decisions*, 113–17. Wyman gave Roosevelt credit for working on resettlement plans. Wyman, 1:57–62. Feingold both questioned Roosevelt's sincerity (*The Politics of Rescue*, 96–97, 115) and did not question it (*The Politics of Rescue*, 102–17). "It is no solution," Rosenman told Roosevelt, "to create a world ghetto instead of many local ones" (*The Politics of Rescue*, 102–3). Feingold, after praising Roosevelt's efforts, then turned on Roosevelt and called the administration's efforts a "charade" (115).

4. Telegram from ER to FDR, 4-1-39, PPF, FDRL; Thomas to FDR, 10-21-38, OF 3186.

5. Feingold, *The Politics of Rescue*, 47–48, FDRL/PPF, December 12, 1938; 52, fn. 19, 318; *Public Papers of FDR*, VII, 174, December 15, 1938; 53; fn. 25, 318; *FRUS*, II, 66–67, January 14, 1939; "Report on U.S. Efforts," Long Papers, Box 202, "Refugees" 134.

6. Feingold, *The Politics of Rescue*, 52–53, 66–68; telegram to the president from militant Christian patriots, OF 3186 (4-12-38) ("file—no ans—")

7. FRUS, vol. II, 57–64.

8. Wyman, *Paper Walls*, 54–55; Feingold, *The Politics of Rescue*, 54–56; Morse, *While Six Million Died*, 228–29, 243–44; Breitman, *The Architect of Genocide*, 59–60; "Report on U.S. Efforts," Box 202, 71–81, Long Papers, LC.

9. Feingold, *The Politics of Rescue*, 58, 67; Breitman, *The Architect of Genocide*, 61–63; Wyman, *Abandonment of the Jews*, 55–57.

10. Morse, *While Six Million Died*, 246–47; Feingold, *The Politics of*

Rescue, 54–55; "Report on U.S. Efforts," Long Papers, Box 202, 95–105, LC.

11. Feingold, 59; *New York Times*, 3–10–39; *FRUS*, II, 82–4, February 6, 1939, to Hull.

12. Feingold, *The Politics of Rescue*, 45–66; Penkower, *Decision on Palestine Deferred*, 20–21.

13. Breitman, *The Architect of Genocide*, 64–65; Newton, ed., *FDR and the Holocaust* (Breitman), 141.

14. Breitman, *The Architect of Genocide*, 65; Jay Pierrepont Moffat Diary, May 4, 1939; Penkower, *Decision on Palestine Deferred*, 13.

15. Breitman, *The Architect of Genocide*, 64–65; Bauer, *My Brother's Keeper*, 277–78; Feingold, *The Politics of Rescue*, 69–74; Strauss, *Men and Decisions*, chap. VI. Penkower gave a good summary in *Decision on Palestine Deferred*, 12–21, as did Friedman in *No Haven for the Oppressed*, chap. 3. Wyman omitted FDR's active involvement in the Rublee Plan.

16. Kanawada, *FDR's Diplomacy*, chap. 8; Feingold, *The Politics of Rescue*, 75–76; Sanders, *Shores of Refuge*, 299; Yergin, *The Prize*, 395–96; Wasserstein, *Britain and the Jews*, chap. 1; Hull, *Memoirs II*, 1529–31; Sachar, *A History of the Jews in America*, 517–18; Grose, *Israel in the Mind of America*, 138.

17. Weinberg, "The Allies and the Holocaust," 481.

18. Bauer, *My Brother's Keeper*, 281–82.

19. Ibid., 283; Strauss, *Men and Decisions*, 112–13. Wyman criticized Roosevelt and American Jews for setting up the Coordinating Foundation so late: it was "tragic that so little was accomplished in the year before the war began" (*Paper Walls*, 56). "The evidence does not seem to support this conclusion," Bauer wrote (Bauer, 285).

20. "Report on U.S. Efforts," 126–49, Long Papers, LC.

21. Feingold, *The Politics of Rescue*, 78–82, fn. 46, 321; FDRL/OF 3186, June 8, 1939, FDR to Taylor; Morgan, *FDR*, 508; Wyman, *Paper Walls*, 55–56; Penkower, *Decision on Palestine Deferred*, 14. "Roosevelt had a better sense of the alternative for German Jews than many contemporaries," Breitman concluded. "Yet historians [Wyman and Feingold] have sometimes criticized Roosevelt not merely for failing to act to assist European Jews, but for indifferences to their fate" (*The Architect of Genocide*, 65, and fn. 74, 263).

Chapter 7

1. Sherwood, *Roosevelt and Hopkins*, 183.

2. Kennedy, *Freedom from Fear*, 422–23; Gilbert, *Churchill*, 619–24.

3. Müller, *Anne Frank*, 99–100.

4. Burns, *The Lion and the Fox*, 394–95; Beschloss, *Roosevelt and Kennedy*, 190; Freidel, *Roosevelt: A Rendezvous with Destiny*, 321; Penkower, *Decision on Palestine Deferred*, 26 (Wise quote).

5. Beschloss, *Roosevelt and Kennedy*, 195; Burns, *The Lion and the Fox*, 394; Lash, *Roosevelt and Churchill*, 23.

6. Medoff, *The Deafening Silence*, 63.

7. Weinberg, *Germany, Hitler, and World War II*, 186, 299–301; Burns, *The Lion and the Fox*, 394 (death watch); Devine, *Roosevelt and World War II*, 8ff; Herzstein, *Roosevelt and Hitler*, chap. 30. As to why Hitler underestimated the United States in 1939 see Saul Friedlander, *Prelude to War*, 15; Burns, *The Lion and the Fox*, 400–1.

8. Burns, *The Lion and the Fox*, 1:401, chap. 20; Herzstein, *Roosevelt and Hitler*, 331–32; Fleming, *The New Dealer's War*, 67–80 (*Working with Roosevelt*, 193). Robert H. Jackson, in his memoirs, stated that Roosevelt wanted him to run for governor of New York in 1938 so that he could run for president in 1940. Jackson, *That Man*, 31–33.

9. The Nazis shot Polish Boy Scouts, and a priest "who rushed to administer the Last Sacrament was shot too." Lukas, *The Forgotten Holocaust*, 3.

10. Gilbert, *The Second World War*, 1–9, 19, 27; Dwork and van Pelt, *Holocaust*, 144–51. The Polish Jew Raphael Lemkin coined the word "genocide" (*genos*, Greek for "people"; *cide*, Latin for "killing") in response to the Nazi murder of the Polish people (150).

11. Gilbert, *The Second World War*, 40, 57, 112. Lukas, *The Forgotten Holocaust*, 34.

12. Gilbert, *The Second World War*, 7, 19, 40–43. Poles outnumbered Jews in Auschwitz until 1942 (Lukas, *The Forgotten Holocaust*, 38).

13. Kennedy, *Freedom from Fear*, 433–34; Burns, *The Lion and the Fox*, 395–97; Freidel, *Franklin D. Roosevelt: A Rendezvous with Destiny*, 323; Celler to FDR, PPF (November 2, 1939), FDRL; Herzstein, *Roosevelt and Hitler*, 313; Fehrenbach, *FDR's Undeclared War*, 258–60.

14. Herzstein, *Roosevelt and Hitler*, chap. 24.

15. Freidel, 323; Berg, *Lindbergh*, chap. 14.

16. Kennedy, *Freedom from Fear*, 428–29; Burns, *The Lion and the Fox*, 1:397; Persico, *Roosevelt's Secret War*, 178; Gilbert, *The Second World War*, 11–14.

17. Freidel, *Roosevelt*, 326; Morgan, *FDR*, 502–3; Kimball, *Most Unsordid Act*, 5; Persico, *Roosevelt's Secret War*, 34–36. FDR attorney general

Robert Jackson related Roosevelt's insistence on wiretapping. Roosevelt was not a "strong champion of so-called civil rights" and in 1939 refused to abide by an antiwiretapping Supreme Court decision. Jackson, *That Man*, 68–69. When "Congress dawdled and diddled," Jackson recalled, Roosevelt "simply ordered that it be done" (48).

18. Wyman, *Paper Walls*, 57–63; Feingold, *The Politics of Rescue*, 92, 102–13; Breitman and Kraut, *American Refugee Policy*, 233; Hull to FDR, 9-15-39, OF 3186, FDRL.
19. Teveth, *Ben-Gurion: The Burning Ground*, 849.
20. Teveth, *Ben-Gurion and the Holocaust*, xxi, xxxv–xli.
21. Penkower, *Decision On Palestine Deferred*, 11; Berman, *Nazism, the Jews and American Zionism*, 68–72.
22. Feingold, *The Politics of Rescue*, 94–97; Wyman, *Paper Walls*, 99–106; Sachar, *A History of the Jews in America*, 494; Breitman and Kraut, *American Refugee Policy*, 233.
23. Feingold, *The Politics of Rescue*, 69, 78–85; Penkower, *Decision on Palestine Deferred*, 38–39; Wyman, *Paper Walls*, 59–62.
24. Feingold, *The Politics of Rescue*, 84–85; *PPA*, 1939, 546–51; FDRL/OF 3186 (minutes of officers of IGCR, October 17, 1939); State Department press releases, I, no. 17, 397–98; *New York Times*, October 18, 1939; *The Jewish Chronicle* (Britain), October 20, 1939, 1. Report on U.S. Efforts to help Jews, Long Papers, State Department 1939–1944, Box 202 "Refugees 1939–1943," 153–54. Many Jewish leaders had proposed Jewish resettlement in a variety of locations. Grose, *Israel in the Mind of America*, 110.
25. Feingold, *The Politics of Rescue*, 114–16; *FRUS* II, 217 (February 29, 1940, memorandum), and 219, FDR to Hull (March 7, 1940); Wyman, *Paper Walls*, 59.
26. Feingold, *The Politics of Rescue*, 123–24; Penkower, *Decision on Palestine Deferred*, 40.
27. Feingold, *The Politics of Rescue*, 81, 118–20; Wyman, *Paper Walls*, 56.
28. Herzstein, *Roosevelt and Hitler*, chap. 24, 27; Wyman, *Paper Walls*, 35.
29. Wyman, *Paper Walls*, 169–71.
30. Burns, *The Lion and the Fox*, 408.
31. Ibid., 404.
32. Ibid., chap. 20; Morgan, *FDR*, 519; Herzstein, *Roosevelt and Hitler*, chap. 24–27.
33. Burns, *The Lion and the Fox*, chap. 20; Kennedy, *Freedom from Fear*, 435–37; Freidel, *Roosevelt*, 324; Overy, *Why the Allies Won*, chap. 1;

Herzstein, *Roosevelt and Hitler*, chap. 25; May, *Strange Victory*, 457; Murray and Millett, *A War to Be Won*, 53.

34. Friedlander, *Prelude*, 73–77; Frye, *Nazi Germany*, chap. 9; Fehrenbach, *FDR's Undeclared War*, 266–67.

35. Burns, *The Lion and the Fox*, 418; Kennedy, *Freedom from Fear*, 438; Kinsella, "The Prescience of a Statesman," 10; Murray and Millett, *A War to Be Won*, 63.

36. Lukacs, *Five Days in London*, 1–7, 49–55; Gilbert, *Churchill*, chap. 28; Chadha, *Gandhi: A Life*, 362–64. Gandhi urged the Jews to pray for Hitler and commit mass suicide rather than fight. He later retracted his allegation that the Jews caused the war.

37. Herzstein, *Roosevelt and Hitler*, 320–21; Friedlander, *Prelude*, 91; Langer and Gleason, 479; Welles to FDR (5-1-40); FDR to Welles (5-1-40), Watson to Rosenwald and Baruch (5-10-40), OF 3186, FDRL.

38. Burns, *The Lion and the Fox*, 419; Kennedy, *Freedom from Fear*, 444–45; Casey, *Cautious Crusade*, 10–11; Murray and Millett, *A War to Be Won*, 82.

39. Kennedy, *Freedom from Fear*, 447–48; Fehrenbach, *FDR's Undeclared War*, 59; Friedlander, *Prelude*, 116–17; Kinsella, "The Prescience of a Statesman," 80–81.

40. Burns, *The Lion and the Fox*, 419–21; Feingold, *The Politics of Rescue*, 128; *New York Times*, May 26, 1940, 1.

41. Kennedy, *Freedom from Fear*, 441.

Chapter 8

1. Freidel, *Franklin D. Roosevelt: A Rendezvous with Destiny*, 386.

2. Burns, *The Lion and the Fox*, 420–21; Persico, *Roosevelt's Secret War*, 82; Lash, *Roosevelt and Churchill*, 152. Mussolini played "the role of jackal to Hitler's lion," according to Ickes. Ickes, *Lowering Clouds*, 203. Churchill was caustic about the Italians aligning themselves with the Germans: "It's only fair," he is alleged to have said, "they were on our side in the last war" (May, *Strange Victory*, 450).

3. Long, *War Diary*, 104–5; Friedlander, *Prelude to Downfall*, 95.

4. Kennedy, *Freedom from Fear*, 440; Murray and Millett, *A War to Be Won*, 82; Devine, *Reluctant Belligerent*, 90; Gilbert, *The Second World War*, 95. May, *Strange Victory*, 448–64.

5. Burns, *The Lion and the Fox*, 422.

6. Kennedy, *Freedom from Fear*, 448–49; Herzstein, *Roosevelt and Hitler*, chap. 25 and 26 ("Chessboard," 324); Freidel, 327; Weinberg, *A World at Arms*, 156.

7. Burns, *The Lion and the Fox*, 424; Weinberg, *A World at Arms*, 153.

8. Burns, *The Lion and the Fox*, 425.

9. Freidel, 333; Kennedy, *Freedom from Fear*, 448–51; Herzstein, *Roosevelt and Hitler*, 323.

10. Lash, *Roosevelt and Churchill*, 167.

11. Burns, *The Lion and the Fox*, 412, 427–32; Herzstein, *Roosevelt and Hitler*, 332.

12. Burns, *The Lion and the Fox*, 432–35.

13. Goodwin, *No Ordinary Time*, 52; Burns, *The Lion and the Fox*, 436; Persico, *Roosevelt's Secret War*, 82; Freidel, 326–39; Herzstein, *Roosevelt and Hitler*, 381.

14. Burns, *The Lion and the Fox*, 436–37; Kennedy, *Freedom from Fear*, 453. "The Americans," Churchill recalled, "treated us in that rather distant and sympathetic manner one adopts towards a friend one knows is suffering from cancer" (Freidel, *Franklin D. Roosevelt: A Rendezvous with Destiny*, 351.)

15. Burns, *The Lion and the Fox*, 438–39; Long, *War Diary*, 112; Freidel, *Franklin D. Roosevelt: A Rendezvous with Destiny*, 341–42.

16. Burns, *The Lion and the Fox*, 439–41; Kennedy, *Freedom from Fear*, 453–55; Freidel, *Franklin D. Roosevelt: A Rendezvous with Destiny*, 352. Benjamin Cohen was a key player in the legal strategy. Jackson, *That Man*, 81–103.

17. Burns, *The Lion and the Fox*, 443; Kennedy, *Freedom from Fear*, 455–56.

18. Herzstein, *Roosevelt and Hitler*, 346–51; Gilbert, *Churchill*, 671.

19. Berg, *Lindbergh*, 404–5.

20. Friedlander, *Prelude to Downfall*, 214–15; Burns, *The Lion and the Fox*, 445; Herzstein, *Roosevelt and Hitler*, chap. 26; Freidel, chap. 25; Newton, ed., *FDR and the Holocaust*, 80; Raphael, *Abba Hillel Silver*, 109.

21. Burns, *The Lion and the Fox*, 445–50; Freidel, *Franklin D. Roosevelt, A Rendezvous with Destiny*, 355–56; Morgan, *FDR*, 539.

22. Burns, *The Lion and the Fox*, 453–55; Freidel, 357; Herzstein, *Roosevelt and Hitler*, 353; Frye, *Nazi Germany*, chap. 9 ("Most massive interference," 151); Gilbert, *The Second World War*, 138; Persico, *Roosevelt's Secret War*, 49; Breitman and Kraut, *American Refugee Policy*, 233–34; Friedlander, *Prelude to Downfall*, 114–15, 156–59; Kennedy, *Freedom from Fear*, 463–64; Rosenman to FDR, Rosenman Papers, FDRL, November 8, 1940; Hand, *Counsel and Advise*, 138–39.

23. Hunt, ed., *The Essential Roosevelt*, 202–5.

24. Gilbert, *The Second World War*, 156.

25. Goodwin, *No Ordinary Time*, chap. 8; Kennedy, *Freedom from Fear*, chap. 15.

26. Goodwin, *No Ordinary Time*, 194–95; Freidel, *Franklin D. Roosevelt: A Rendezvous with Destiny*, 360–61; Lash, *Roosevelt and Churchill*, 264–65; Burns, *The Soldier of Freedom*, 27–29; Casey, *Cautious Crusade*, 38.

27. Freidel, 394; Goodwin, *No Ordinary Time*, 195.

28. Kennedy, *Freedom from Fear*, 471; Herzstein, 140; Friedlander, *Prelude to Downfall*, 173–74; Farago, *The Game of the Foxes*, chap. 34.

29. Herzstein, chap. 30.

30. Ibid.; Freidel, 362.

31. Hunt, ed., *The Essential Roosevelt*, 194–201.

32. Lash, *Roosevelt and Churchill*, 266, 271; Freidel, 365–66; Friedlander, *Prelude to Downfall*, 180–93.

33. Lash, *Roosevelt and Churchill*, 273–75, 281–82; Fehrenbach, *FDR's Undeclared War*, 222.

34. Goodwin, *No Ordinary Time*, 212; Gilbert, *Churchill*, 688; Lash, *Roosevelt and Churchill*, 277; Fehrenbach, *FDR's Undeclared War*, 221–22; Gunther, *Roosevelt*, 317–18; Sherwood, *Roosevelt and Hopkins*, 242–43, 247.

35. Lash, *Roosevelt and Churchill*, 284; Goodwin, *No Ordinary Time*, 212.

36. Gilbert, *The Second World War*, 145, 153; Friedlander, *Prelude to Downfall*, 218–19.

37. Kennedy, *Freedom from Fear*, 473–74; Freidel, 361–63; Goodwin, *No Ordinary Time*, 213–14; Friedlander, *Prelude to Downfall*, 174; Kimball, *The Most Unsordid Act*, 9.

38. Penkower, *Decision on Palestine Deferred*, 73–75.

39. Penkower, *Decision on Palestine Deferred*, 75–80; Weizmann, *Trial and Error*, 430–31.

40. Goodwin, *No Ordinary Time*, 215.

41. Herzstein, 355; Lash, *Roosevelt and Churchill*, 280, 289, 303.

42. Tindall, *Emergence of the New South*, 690–92; Lash, *Roosevelt and Churchill*, 322; Biddle, *In Brief Authority*, 233–34; Burns, *The Soldier of Freedom*, 36–41; Fry, *Dixie Looks Abroad*, chap. 6. (On Lend-Lease, Southerners voted in favor 22 to 1 out of a total vote of 60 to 31 in the Senate; 104 of 260 "yes" votes in the House and only 4 of the 165 "no" votes. 206–7). "The White South," T. R. Fehrenbach observed in *FDR's Undeclared War*, "was six times as ready as the nation as a whole to accept combat with fascism." Texas was by far the most belligerent state (193–94).

43. Fehrenbach, *FDR's Undeclared War*, 204.

44. Goodwin, *No Ordinary Time*, 233–35; Lash, *Roosevelt and Churchill*, 323;

Friedlander, *Prelude to Downfall*, 210; Goodwin, *No Ordinary Time*,
234–36; Burns, *The Soldier of Freedom*, 98 ("among the most trying
[weeks] in Roosevelt's life").

45. Fehrenbach, *FDR's Undeclared War*, 211–19.
46. Hunt, ed., *The Essential Roosevelt*, 206–15; Lash, 326; Goodwin, *No Ordinary Time*, 238–40; Kinsella, "The Prescience of a Statesman," 81–82; Freidel, 366.

Chapter 9

1. Gilbert, *World War II*, 32, 36–39, 46, 112; Lukas, *Forgotten Holocaust*,
   10–17. Pope Pius XII did not denounce the Nazis at that time for fear of
   retribution against Catholics in Poland.
2. Gilbert, *World War II*, 88, 100, 129–30; Gilbert, *Holocaust*, 133.
3. These events gave rise to the well-known joke in which the refugee says he is
   going to South Africa. Why so far? his friend asks. "Far? Far from where?"
   Richard Raskin, *Far From Where? On the History and Meanings of a Classic
   Jewish Refugee Joke*, 143; Baker, *Days of Sorrow and Pain*, 239–52.
4. Herzstein, *Roosevelt and Hitler*, 146–47, 258–60, 262–69; chap. 21 and 22.
5. Morgan, *FDR*, 498; Wyman, *Paper Walls*, 163–67, 174, 189; Wyman,
   Abandonment of the Jews, 190, 199; Feingold, *The Politics of Rescue*, chap.
   6. The actions of the American consulates varied widely, depending on the
   personnel. When the Nazis invaded Norway, the American consul helped
   Jews flee to Sweden. The U.S. consul at Marseilles helped Jews escape France
   (Wyman, *Paper Walls*, 167). Harry Bingham worked with Varian Fry and the
   American Emergency Rescue Committee, established to save socialists, intellectuals, and labor leaders. Fry, *Surrender on Demand*, passim.
6. Bendersky, *The "Jewish Threat,"* 47–48, 79–82, 91–92, 118–20, 151–56,
   282–83, 289–94.
7. Herzstein, *Roosevelt and Hitler*, 98, 258, 270–74, 368–69.
8. Ibid., chap. 21 and 22.
9. Ibid., 366–67; Freidel, 323.
10. Berg, *Lindbergh*, 418.
11. Ibid., chap. 14 (see 409–10).
12. Ibid., 337–38, 423–28. Lindbergh's biographer A. Scott Berg maintains that
    Lindbergh was not an antisemite and that the Des Moines speech was mis-
    understood. But the speech contained standard antisemitic slurs and was so
    understood at the time by friends and foes alike. Perhaps Lindbergh was
    just what Cornelius Vanderbilt Jr. said he was when he telegramed Lind-
    bergh in January 1941: "WHAT AN UNPATRIOTIC DUMB BELL YOU

ARE" (427, 415). That Lindbergh had anti-Jewish prejudices there can be no doubt. He consorted with and attended rallies in the company of virulent antisemites, including Father Coughlin, Joseph McWilliams, Colonel McCormick, General Wood, and Mrs. Burton K. Wheeler (Berg, *Lindbergh*, 386, 418–19, chap. 14). For another defense of Lindbergh see Eric Larrabee, *Commander in Chief*, 224–31.

13. Sachar, *A History of the Jews in America*, 519–20, 623; Medoff, *The Deafening Silence*, 72.

14. Kennedy, *Freedom from Fear*, 482; Goodwin, *No Ordinary Time*, 253–54; Overy, *The Penguin Historical Atlas of the Third Reich*, 68.

15. Goodwin, *No Ordinary Time*, 255–62; Kennedy, *Freedom from Fear*, 482; Friedlander, *Prelude to Downfall*, 255; Langer and Gleason, *The Undeclared War*, 569; Gilbert, *Churchill*, 703.

16. Dwork and van Pelt, *Holocaust*, 187–91; Kershaw, *Hitler, 1936–1945*, 234–39, 320–39; 350–53, 392.

17. Breitman, *Official Secrets*, chap. 3 and 4; Kershaw, *Hitler, 1936–1945*, 353–58, 381–82, 400–2; Mayer, *Why Did the Heavens Not Darken?*, chap. 1.

18. Gilbert, *World War II*, 168, 182, 203–5, 219, 226–27; Gilbert, *Holocaust*, 141–42, 154–55; Gilbert, *Auschwitz and the Allies*, 14.

19. Burns, *The Soldier of Freedom*, 120.

20. Ibid., 130–32; Lash, *Roosevelt and Churchill*, chap. 23; Baily and Ryan, *Hitler v. Roosevelt*, 165; Friedlander, *Prelude to Downfall*, 266–69; Lukacs, *The Duel*, 73.

21. This summary is based on Kennedy, 510–15. See also Roberta Wohlstetter, *Pearl Harbor: Warning and Decision* (1962), 119, 124, 126.

22. On Hitler's declaration of war on the United States see Jäckel, *Hitler in History*, chap. 4, "Hitler Challenges America." Burns, *The Soldier of Freedom*, 105; Joseph P. Lash, *Roosevelt and Churchill, 1939–1941 The Partnership That Saved the West*, 10 ("We leave it to the reader to judge whether he was right. . . . I think he was."). Gerhard L. Weinberg, on the other hand, is adamant that Roosevelt "did not want to lead the United States in war at all" (*Germany, Hitler and World War II*, 299) and "hoped to avoid open warfare with Germany altogether" (*World at Arms*, 238–45). He is in good company. See Robert A. Devine, *Roosevelt and World War II* (1969); Freidel, *Franklin D. Roosevelt: A Rendezvous with Destiny*, chap. 26; and Dallek, *FDR and American Foreign Policy*. Robert Jackson put it well: "He had a dual policy. One was a policy of peace. The other was a policy of preparing for war. Each step that he took in favor of one of those policies

was construed as an abandonment, or perhaps as insincerity, concerning the other" (Jackson, *That Man*, 80–81).

23. Burns, *The Soldier of Freedom*, 140–43; Rosenman, ed., *PPA*, 1941 vol., 389–90; Weinberg, *World at Arms*, 244.
24. Bailey and Ryan, *Hitler v. Roosevelt*, chap. 12; 178.
25. Müller, *Anne Frank*, chap. 6.
26. Carr, *Hollywood and Antisemitism*, 238–74.
27. Ibid., 268, 275.
28. Müller, *Anne Frank*, chap. 6.
29. Gilbert, *The Second World War*, 220, 239–51; Gilbert, *Auschwitz and the Allies*, 16–17; Lipstadt, *Beyond Belief*, 149–50.
30. Gilbert, *World War II*, 265; Penkower, *Decision on Palestine Deferred*, 91–92.
31. Rosenman, ed., *1941 volume*, *PPA*, 438–45; Burns, *The Soldier of Freedom*, 147–48; Bailey and Ryan, *Hitler v. Roosevelt*, 198–200.
32. Persico, *Roosevelt's Secret War*, 113–14; Burns, *The Soldier of Freedom*, 148–49; *Time*, November 10, 1941, 17.
33. Burns, *The Soldier of Freedom*, 150–51, 165–67; Persico, *Roosevelt's Secret War*, 123; Goodwin, *No Ordinary Time*, 289. Kennedy, *Freedom from Fear*, chap. 15 and 16; Freidel, chap. 28 and 29; Keegan, *The Second World War*, chap. 12 and 13; Weinberg, *A World at Arms*, 238–63; Keegan, *The Battle for History*, 18; Lash, *Roosevelt and Churchill*, 489; Gunther, *Roosevelt in Retrospect*, 320–23.

    For a good discussion of FDR's prior knowledge of the attack on Pearl Harbor, see Persico, *Roosevelt's Secret War*, chap. X; Stinnett, *Day of Deceit: The Truth about FDR and Pearl Harbor*; and Beard, *President Roosevelt and the Coming of the War 1941*, chap. XVI and XVII. Stimson's biographer Godfrey Hodgson quoted Roosevelt as saying that the question was "how we should maneuver them into the position of firing the first shot without too much danger to ourselves" (*The Colonel*, 242).
34. Burns, *The Soldier of Freedom*, 172–74; Jäckel, *Hitler in History*, chap. 4; Kershaw, *Hitler, 1936–1945*, 364, 442–49; Kennedy, *Freedom from Fear*, 615.
35. Shirer, *Rise and Fall*, 897–900. Roosevelt, Hitler said, behaved like a "tortuous, pettifogging Jew." According to Hitler, ER had a "completely negroid appearance"; "She too was half-caste" (Burns, *The Soldier of Freedom*, 68).
36. Rosenman, ed., *PPA*, 1941 volume, 532.
37. Kennedy, *Freedom from Fear*, 523; Churchill, *The Grand Alliance*, 606–8; Gilbert, *Churchill*, 711; Lukacs, *The Duel*, 218; Gilbert, *Auschwitz and the Allies*, 18.

Chapter 10

1. Newton, ed., *FDR and the Holocaust* (Breitman), 135–36. All other references are from OF 3186, FDRL: Kirchwey to FDR, 6-17-40; FDR to Kirchwey, 6-18-40; memo from FDR to Ruth Shipley, 7-27-40; FDR to ER, 7-3-40; FDR to Oldham, 7-8-40; Ickes to FDR, 7-30-40; FDR to Ickes, 8-13-40; memo re Polish refugees in Russia (2-19-41). Varian Fry, in his 1945 memoir *Surrender on Demand*, wrote that the "sole purpose of the Committee was to bring the political and intellectual refugees out of France." He emphasized his interest in saving writers, artists (Marc Chagall among them), and socialists and finally, but not especially, Jews (foreword, xi–xiv).
2. Fehrenbach, *FDR's Undeclared War*, 90, 100; Feingold, *The Politics of Rescue*, 80–82; Wyman, *Paper Walls*, 190–91; Baker, *Days of Sorrow and Pain*, 253.
3. Kinsella, "The Prescience of a Statesman," 80–81; Lukacs, *The Duel*, 190–91; Murray and Millett, *War to Be Won*, 84.
4. Chadakoff, *Eleanor Roosevelt's "My Day,"* 140–41, 153, 171–72; Black, *Courage in a Dangerous World*, 121; Berger, *A New Deal*, 27.
5. Breitman and Kraut, *American Refugee Policy*, 115–16; N. W. Rogers to Dickstein, 4-29-38 and various reports of the "Bureau of Investigation," Dickstein Papers, MSS col. 8, box 4/5, AJA.
6. *New York Times*, May 17, 1940, 10; May 27, 1940, 12.
7. Wyman, *Paper Walls*, 173.
8. Breitman and Kraut, *American Refugee Policy*, 112; Israel, *The War Diary of Breckinridge Long*, xi–xiii, 36, 66, 114; Wyman, *Paper Walls*, 184; Friedman, *Nazis and Good Neighbors*, 2; De Jong, *German Fifth Column*, 3–4, 105.
9. Breitman and Kraut, *American Refugee Policy*, 112–19, 121, 232; Herzstein, *Roosevelt and Hitler*, 327; Long, *War Diary*, 95; Lipstadt, *Beyond Belief*, chap. 6; *FDR and the Holocaust*, 113–14.
10. Robinson, *By Order of the President*, 51–57; fn. 25, 275; Stephen, *Hawaii under the Rising Sun*, 40–43.
11. Breitman and Kraut, *American Refugee Policy*, 120–21.
12. Sumner Welles to FDR, December 21, 1940, FDRL; Newton, *FDR and the Holocaust*, 113; Herbert C. Pell to Hull, 9-6-40, FRUS, 1940, vol. II, 236–37.
13. Persico, *Roosevelt's Secret War*, 7, 32; Bird, *The Chairman*, chap. 5. Most historians believe that Roosevelt was sincere in his concern about the fifth column. Newton, ed., *FDR and the Holocaust*, 7–10, 112.
14. Friedlander, *Prelude*, 102–5; Farago, *Game of the Foxes*, chap. 4. One of the crucial revisionist charges against FDR was that the fear of subversion

was not real, that it was simply "a device for keeping refugee entry to a minimum" (Wyman, *Abandonment of the Jews*, 132) and a "gambit" (Feingold, *The Politics of Rescue*, 128; *Bearing Witness*, 77–79). Feingold characterized the fear of spies and fifth columnists as "patently ludicrous" (*Bearing Witness*, 79). This misinterpretation was ably refuted by scholars, including Breitman and Kraut, in *American Refugee Policy*, chap. 5; Herzstein, *Roosevelt and Hitler*, chap. 26; 364; Frye, *Nazi Germany*, 9, 15–31, 80–100; and Friedman, *Nazis and Good Neighbors*, 1–12, 50–55.

15. Frye, *Nazi Germany*, chap. 2 (Göring quote, 15).

16. Ibid., 137.

17. Persico, chap. II; Newton, ed., *FDR and the Holocaust*, 110.

18. Breitman and Kraut, *American Refugee Policy*, 121–25; Wyman, *Paper Walls*, 187–88. De Jong, *German Fifth Column*, 107. The new regulations prevented refugees, including future victims of the Holocaust, from escaping Europe. But the policy was aimed at securing the American homeland and protecting Americans, not keeping Jews out of the country. "Restrictionists," Feingold wrote, "developed a security gambit" that became "the psychosis about security" (*The Politics of Rescue*, 128–29).

19. Israel, ed., *The War Diary of Breckinridge Long*; 95–100. Breitman and Kraut, *American Refugee Policy*, 126–28.

20. Long, *War Diary*, xi–xiii, 36, 66, 115–16.

21. Ibid., 52; Breitman and Kraut, *American Refugee Policy*, 126–28.

22. Long, *War Diary*, 102–11, 118–19; Breitman and Kraut, *American Refugee Policy*, chap. 6.

23. Morewitz, "The Saving of the SS *Quanza*," 25–26.

24. Long, *War Diary*, 130–31; Berger, *A New Deal*, 28; note to Missy LeHand, "Shaffer Florist" card, OF 3186.

25. Breitman and Kraut, *American Refugee Policy*, 131–33.

26. Long, *War Diary*, 60, 110, 156–58, 180–81, 216–17, 224–25. Feingold viewed Long as the chief villain of America's failure to rescue Jews. In *The Politics of Rescue* he called Long an antisemite and paranoid. He equated Long's dislike of liberals generally and activist Jews with antisemitism (*The Politics of Rescue*, 135).

It was difficult for Feingold to make a genuine antisemite out of Long if Long admired and socialized with Baruch and Steinhardt, and liked and worked with Bloom. Therefore the historian drummed Baruch and Steinhardt out of the Jewish religion. He unfairly referred to Morgenthau and Rosenman as "nominal Jews" (*FDR and the Holocaust*, 74). Baruch,

Cohen, and Morgenthau "were a source of embarrassment" to some Jews, which is probably true of *all* Jews (*The Politics of Rescue*, 9). Baruch had never "participated in Jewish organizational life" (26, 286). Feingold portrays Bloom as "easy to handle" (195).

Wyman did not claim that Long was an antisemite. "Whether Long was also antisemitic is not clear," he wrote in *The Abandonment of the Jews* (191). Wyman correctly pointed out that Long had "good relations with the more conservative leaders" but failed to mention Long's close relationship with Baruch or Steinhardt. Long was "indifferent to the tragedy of the European Jews," Wyman concluded. Wyman mentions Steinhardt in *Paper Walls* (146, 149, 191–92) but never discloses that he was Jewish.

Lucy Dawidowicz believed Long was an antisemite, or at least that his policies were guided by "vicious antisemitism" (*What Is the Use of Jewish History?*, 159). Breitman and Kraut believed "Long's reputation as an antisemite is gradually being revised by historians. . . . Long was more consumed with fears of conspiracies against himself and his country than with an antagonism toward Jews per se. . . . Long can best be understood against the backdrop of preexisting refugee policy and the cross pressures to which he was subjected by virtue of his appointment." (*American Refugee Policy*, 126–27).

27. Welles, *Sumner Welles*, 193–9; Berger, *A New Deal*, 26; Lash, *Eleanor and Franklin*, 571; Long, *War Diary*, 106, 118, 121; Long, Diary, 509, (January 20, 1945), Long Papers, LC; Newton, ed., *FDR and the Holocaust*, 10. Verne Newton stated that FDR "would have expressed surprise at the claim that Long had real power."

28. Long, *War Diary*, 132, 145, 151, 189, 218–20.

29. Breitman and Kraut, *American Refugee Policy*, 128–29.

30. McDonald and Warren to FDR, October 8, 1940, OF 3186, FDRL; Breitman and Kraut, *American Refugee Policy*, 130–32; Steinhardt to Long, May 8, 1941, container 203, "Refugee Matters," Long Papers, LC; Fry, *Surrender on Demand*, 24.

31. Long, *War Diary*, 100–3, 114–15.

32. Breitman and Kraut, *American Refugee Policy*, 132–33.

33. Wyman, *Paper Walls*, 112–15.

34. FDR to Ickes, December 18, 1940, FDR, OF 3186, FDRL.

35. Breitman and Kraut, *American Refugee Policy*, 134–37.

36. Arad, *America, Its Jews, and the Rise of Nazism*, 226, fn. 22.

37. Newton, ed., *FDR and the Holocaust*, 110–11.

38. Feingold, *The Politics of Rescue*, 163–64.

39. *The New Republic*, April 28 1941, 592-4; July 28, 1941, 105–6; Dwork and van Pelt, *Holocaust*, 320–22.

Chapter 11

1. Watson, *Chief of Staff*, 5–6; Larrabee, *Commander in Chief*, 1; *DAB*, 661–62; Gellman, *Secret Affairs*, 281–83.
2. Biddle, *In Brief Authority*, 219; Jackson, *That Man*, 23.
3. Keegan, *The Second World War*, 265; Gilbert, *Churchill*, 712; Kennedy, *Freedom from Fear*, 527–29; Larrabee, *Commander In Chief*, 316; Gilbert, *The Second World War*, 280–82; Burns, *The Soldier of Freedom*, 6, 175–78.
4. Jackson, *That Man*, 105.
5. Larrabee, *Commander in Chief*, 221.
6. Goodwin, *No Ordinary Time*, 309; Harris, *Political Wit*, 159; Gilbert, *Churchill*, 715.
7. Burns, *The Soldier of Freedom*, 175–90; Gilbert, *Churchill*, 713–15.
8. Burns, *The Soldier of Freedom*, 190–92.
9. Goodwin, *No Ordinary Time*, 299, 310; Burns, *The Soldier of Freedom*, 198.
10. Larrabee, *Commander in Chief*, 141–42. Burns, *The Soldier of Freedom*, 208; Kennedy, *Freedom from Fear*, 529; Miller, *The Story of World War II*, 103. The American soldiers soon knew they were doomed. A famous piece of doggerel at the time:
    > *We're the battling bastards of Bataan/No mamma, no papa, no Uncle Sam/No aunts, no uncles, no nephews, no nieces/No rifles, no planes, or artillery pieces/And nobody gives a damn.*
11. Burns, *The Soldier of Freedom*, 209–13; Keegan, *The Second World War*, 259–60; Gilbert, *Churchill*, 717–20; Goodwin, *No Ordinary Time*, 317.
12. Burns, *The Soldier of Freedom*, 213–17, 266–68, 275, 421, 461–66; Goodwin, *No Ordinary Time*, 321–22, 427–31, 429, 514. Canada relocated its Japanese citizens from the West Coast to interior cities.
13. Robinson, *Order of the President*, 111. Reflecting the same WASP elitism, Stimson told Churchill in July 1942 that the American people did not hate the Italian people; they "took them rather as a joke" (Hodgson, *The Colonel*, 269). Roosevelt predicted in June 1940 that Italian soldiers would "run like rabbits." Casey, *Cautious Crusade*, 12. FDR to Hull, 8–15–42, B. Long Papers (Box 204), LC.
14. Dower, *War without Mercy*, 7, 11, 33, 78, 114; Daws, *Prisoners of the Japanese*, 17; Novick, *The Holocaust in American Life*, 26; *New York Times*, July 22, 1942 ("yellow rat"), 4. In March 1945 *Science Digest*

published an essay "Why Americans Hate Japs More Than Nazis." Casey, *Cautious Crusade*, 29–30, 67–69, 173.

15. Dower, *War without Mercy*, 34–39; Casey, *Cautious Crusade*, 29–30, 67–69.
16. Burns, *The Soldier of Freedom*, 218–22; Kimball, *Forged in War*, 193–95 ("What did it matter if a few blackamoors resigned?" Churchill said when he insisted Gandhi remain in jail.).
17. Burns, *The Soldier of Freedom*, 227. The sinking of the *Struma* and the loss of seven hundred Jewish lives occurred on February 24, 1942.
18. Lester Tenney, a Jewish survivor of the Bataan Death March, recalled: "we saw an American soldier kneeling in front of a Japanese officer. The officer had his samurai sword out of the scabbard. . . . Up went the blade, then with a great artistry and a loud "Banzai," the officer brought the blade down. We heard a dull thud, and the American was decapitated. The Japanese officer then kicked his body . . . over into the field, and all of the Japanese soldiers laughed and walked away." Quoted in Miller, *The Story of World War II*, 101–12; Kennedy, *Freedom from Fear*, 529–32.
19. Kennedy, *Freedom from Fear*, 530; Gilbert, *The Second World War*, chap. 23; Casey, *Cautious Crusade*, 66–69.
20. Gilbert, *The Second World War*, 273–74; Kennedy, *Freedom from Fear*, 615; Weinberg, "Hitler's Image of the States," *AHR*, LXIX (July 1964): 1006–21.
21. Wilt, *The Atlantic Wall*, passim; Gilbert, *The Second World War*, 283, 352, 358, 421; Botting, *The Second Front*, 1–33; Keegan, *The Second World War*, 370–73.
22. Keegan, *The Second World War*, 267; Stokesbury, *A Short History of World War II*, 214–16; Weinberg, *A World at Arms*, 336–41; Miller, *The Story of World War II*, 119–26; Goodwin, *No Ordinary Time*, 341–42; Murray and Millett, *A War to Be Won*, 195.
23. Larrabee, *Commander in Chief*, 375–85; Keegan, *The Second World War*, 275–78.
24. Gilbert, *The Second World War*, 350.
25. Goodwin, *No Ordinary Time*, 342; Burns, *The Soldier of Freedom*, 229, 231, 248; Kennedy, *Freedom from Fear*, 573–78; Penkower, *Decision on Palestine Deferred*, 131–35.
26. Gilbert, *The Second World War*, 335, 347; Burns, *The Soldier of Freedom*, 233–37; Stokesbury, *A Short History of World War II*, 217–19; *Chronology*, June 1942.
27. Burns, *The Soldier of Freedom*, 243–44; Gilbert, *The Second World War*,

314; Gellman, *Secret Affairs*, 281–82; Keegan, *The Second World War*, 107–10; Kennedy, *Freedom from Fear*, 565–79.

28. Burns, *The Soldier of Freedom*, 245; Ward, ed., *Closest Companion*, 179, 182.
29. Morison, *The Oxford History of the United States*, 1008–9.
30. Gellman, *Secret Affairs*, chap. 11 and 12.
31. Gilbert, *The Second World War*, 328–29, 352; Burns, *The Soldier of Freedom*, 250–51.
32. Morison, *The Oxford History of the United States*, 1017; Gilbert, *The Second World War*, 337, 348; Penkower, *Decision on Palestine Deferred*, 126–32.
33. Polier and Wise, eds., *The Personal Letters of Stephen Wise*, 258–59; *DAB*, 446; Kalman, *Abe Fortas*, 76.
34. Hall, Ency. "FDR: His Life and Times," 66–67, 238.
35. Lash, *Diaries of Felix Frankfurter*, 68, 75, 152–54, 165–66; Freedman, *Roosevelt and Frankfurter*, passim; Penkower, *Decision on Palestine Deferred*, 105–6.
36. Suberman, *When It Was Our War*, 73–74, 98, 104. Kaufman, *American Jews in World War II*, vol. I, 27. For a typical small-town Jewish community's reaction to the war see Rubin, *Third to None*, 274–76.

Chapter 12

1. Gilbert, *Holocaust*, 152, 236–38, 245, 280–84; Penkower, *Decision on Palestine Deferred*, 109; Bauer, *The Holocaust in Historical Perspective*, 14. There is a debate among Holocaust historians regarding when Hitler and his top leadership decided on the extermination of the Jews. See Marrus, *Holocaust in History*; Kershaw, *The Nazi Dictatorship*; Wistrich, *Hitler and the Holocaust*, chap. 8.
2. Gilbert, *Holocaust*, 192–96, 250, 378–79.
3. Lipstadt, *Beyond Belief*, 136–38; Lukas, *The Forgotten Holocaust*, chap. 6.
4. Lukas, *The Forgotten Holocaust*, 162–63.
5. Lipstadt, *Beyond Belief*, 136; Wyman, *Abandonment of the Jews*, 19–23; Weinberg, *Germany, Hitler, and World War II*, 229–30. For example, Treblinka and Sobibor were leveled, trees were planted, and farms built in the fall of 1943; Gilbert, *Auschwitz and the Allies*, 153–54, 169, 170–76.
6. Lipstadt, *Beyond Belief*, 140.
7. Yahil, *The Holocaust*, 628–30.
8. Lipstadt, *Beyond Belief*, 150–53, 176–77.
9. Lipstadt, *Beyond Belief*, 159–60; Welles, *Welles*, 226–27; Yahil, *The Holocaust*, 628–29.

10. Gilbert, *Holocaust*, 300–7, 359, 419.
11. Lipstadt, *Beyond Belief*, 162–65, 172–74.
12. Baker, *Days of Sorrow and Pain*, 247–78.
13. Müller, *Anne Frank*, 130–63.
14. Morgenthau Presidential Diary, July 7, 1942, 1134–36, FDRL; Grose, *Israel in the Mind of America*, 139; Penkower, *Decision on Palestine Deferred*, 132–33.
15. Penkower, *Decision on Palestine Deferred*, 108–9.
16. Wyman, *Abandonment of the Jews*, 19–23, chap. 2.
17. *New York Times*, July 22, 1942, 1, 4; Wyman, *Abandonment of the Jews*, 24–26. Penkower stated that as a result of Churchill's message, "official British silence . . . had been broken for the first time" (*Decision on Palestine Deferred*, 143).
18. Morgenthau, "Diaries," November 1, 1947, 22; Laqueur, *The Terrible Secret*, 94–95.
19. Wyman, *Abandonment of the Jews*, 28; Breitman and Kraut, *American Refugee Policy*, chap. 8. Weinberg, *Germany, Hitler, and World War II*, 242. Novick, *The Holocaust in American Life*, 28. This simple, unpleasant fact of life, well understood by Roosevelt, Churchill, the Allied leadership, Jewish leaders, and Jewish Americans at the time, was apparently lost on Roosevelt's current crop of critics. "Roosevelt," Feingold complained, "seemed anxious to conceal the Jewish character of the crisis. Thus while Berlin spoke incessantly about Jews, and converted all enemies including Roosevelt to that faith, his State Department reconverted them to a bland category called 'political refugees' and insistently stuck to that classification as late as the Bermuda Conference" ("The Government Response," 253). To do as he suggested would have turned the Allies into crusaders for European Jewry, a crusade that had a minuscule constituency. FDR's strategy, on the other hand, was successful in maintaining as broad a base as possible (including antisemites in the United States, the Middle East, and Europe) to prosecute the war against Hitler. Nevertheless, the Allied Declaration of December 17, 1942, the central statement of the Allies on the mass murder of Jews, *explicitly* condemned the German government's "intention to exterminate the Jewish people in Europe" (Gilbert, *Auschwitz and the Allies*, 103). For a detailed discussion of the difficulty of seeing the Holocaust for what it was at the time, see Novick, *The Holocaust in American Life*, 19–29, 36–38, 49–50.
20. Wyman, *Abandonment of the Jews*, 29; Gilbert, *Auschwitz and the Allies*, chap. 12; Lukas, *The Forgotten Holocaust*, 163–64.

21. Newton, ed., *FDR and the Holocaust*, 104; Gellman, *Secret Affairs*, 283; Lipstadt, *Beyond Belief*, 175; Casey, *Cautious Crusade*, chap. 3.
22. Casey, *Cautious Crusade*, 9–13; Dallek, *Franklin D. Roosevelt and American Foreign Policy, 1932–1945*, 206–7; Kershaw, *Hitler 1936–1945*, 227–30.
23. FRUS, 1942, vol. II, 712–16; memo to file, Breckinridge Long 10-5-42, State Department 1939–1944, Box 202, "Refugees 1939–1944," Long Papers, LC. My thanks to Ali Rosen for locating this important memo. Wyman, *Abandonment of the Jews*, 30–36; Breitman and Kraut, *American Refugee Policy*, 138–39. ("Although the documentation is incomplete," Breitman and Kraut concluded, "it appears that FDR personally made the decision to admit five thousand children.")
24. Breitman and Kraut, *American Refugee Policy*, 138–39, 163; Wyman, *Abandonment of the Jews*, 36–37; Murray and Millett flatly contend that "The Allies won the war because they had fossil fuels and because they prevented the Axis powers from turning the fossil fuels of occupied countries into war-winning resources" (*A War to Be Won*, 527–28).
25. Breitman, *Official Secrets*, chap. 9; Wyman, *The Abandonment of the Jews*, 40–41; *New York Times*, September 11, 1942; Laqueur, *The Terrible Secret*, 77.
26. Laqueur, *The Terrible Secret*, 77; Gilbert, *Holocaust*, 134–35, 449–50; Breitman and Kraut, *American Refugee Policy*, 148–49. Wyman omits the key phrase "We transmit information with all necessary reservation."

Chapter 13
1. FRUS, 1942, vol. I, 54–57.
2. Ibid., 58–59; *New York Times*, August 22, 1942, 1, 4; and October 8, 1942, 1, 11; OF 5152, FDRL; Casey, *Cautious Crusade*, 66. Wyman, *The Abandonment of the Jews*, 29. Churchill made even more explicit statements on October 20 (Penkower, *Decision on Palestine Deferred*, 146).
3. OF 3186, FDRL, Celler to FDR 10-10-42; FDR to Celler 10-21-42.
4. Morison, *Oxford History*, 1017–8; Goodwin, *No Ordinary Time*, 379–83; Penkower, *Decision on Palestine Deferred*, 161.
5. *New York Times*, October 1, 1942; Weinberg, "Hitler's Image of the United States," 1018.
6. Larrabee, *Commander in Chief*, 256–60, 290–92; Davis, *Into the Storm*, 643, 655; Stokesbury, *A Short History of World War II*, 250–53; Kennedy, *Freedom from Fear*, 551–60; Weinberg, *A World at Arms*, 341–44; Goodwin, *No Ordinary Time*, 468.
7. Wyman, *The Abandonment of the Jews*, 43. The Roosevelt critics deplored

Rabbi Wise's decision to respect Welles's request and keep the Riegner telegram secret. "How could he pledge secrecy when millions of lives were involved?" Elie Wiesel asked. Saul Friedman called Wise and American Jewry "docile" (Urofsky, *A Voice That Spoke for Justice*, 319–20). "The criticism [of Wise]," Breitman wrote in *Official Secrets*, "is at least overstated" (142). Wise's agreement to remain silent until the facts could be verified was a logical step to take. Bauer, *The Holocaust in Historical Perspective*, 23. Rubinstein pointed out in *The Myth of Rescue* that Riegner's message was "extremely vague" and that both the State Department and Wise realistically wanted confirmation before repeating extreme atrocity stories (86–87). Bauer, "The Goldberg Report," 26. Yehuda Bauer characterized Saul S. Friedman's finger-pointing at Rabbi Wise on this occasion as a "preposterous piece of irresponsibility" ("The Goldberg Report," 27–28).

8. Newton, ed., *FDR and the Holocaust*, 72–157; Laqueur, *The Terrible Secret*, 9; Breitman and Kraut, *American Refugee Policy*, 152–54; Urofsky, *A Voice That Spoke for Justice*, 323.

9. Wyman, *The Abandonment of the Jews*, 44–48; Urofsky, *A Voice That Spoke for Justice*, 321.

10. Breitman and Kraut, *American Refugee Policy*, 153–58; OF 5152, FDRL (Press Release); Gellman, *Secret Affairs*, 282–83; Celler, *You Never Leave Brooklyn* (letter from FDR to Celler, 10-21-1942), 90–92; Grose, *Israel*, 139. Roosevelt raised the possibility of loosening immigration restrictions with Vice President Henry Wallace and House Speaker Sam Rayburn in November 1942, but Rayburn was adamant that such a proposal would meet with "great opposition" in Congress. According to Wallace's diary, Roosevelt said that all he wanted to do was make it clear that the responsibility was that of Congress (Dallek, *Franklin D. Roosevelt and American Foreign Policy, 1932–1945*, 446).

11. *New York Times*, October 1, 1942; Breitman and Kraut, *American Refugee Policy*, 154.

12. Sachar, *A History of the Jews in America*, 536; Breitman and Kraut, *American Refugee Policy*, 155–59; Penkower, *Decision on Palestine Deferred*, chap. 5.

13. Wyman, *The Abandonment of the Jews*, 51–58; Lipstadt, *Beyond Belief*, 180–81; Weinberg, *Germany, Hitler, and World War II*, 218 ("Well over three million"); Gilbert, *The Second World War*, 386 (nearly three million Polish Jews had been murdered in the previous twelve months at Chelmno, Belzec, Sobibor, and Treblinka).

14. Wyman, *The Abandonment of the Jews*, 53, 61–63, 70–72; Lipstadt, *Beyond Belief*, 184–85; Goodwin, *No Ordinary Time*, 396. Wyman claimed Roosevelt met with Wise's group "despite a definite reluctance on his part" (Wyman, *The Abandonment of the Jews*, 71). This was not at all clear. Wise wrote on December 2. FDR sent Welles a memo on December 4 stating, "Will you be good enough to arrange with Pa Watson [Roosevelt's secretary] for this conference," enclosing Wise's letter. There was a note on an undated presidential day list stating "Gen. Watson says President does not wish to see them" (Wyman, ed., *America and the Holocaust* 2:44–49). This was inconsistent with a memo from FDR himself asking Welles to set up the meeting. If FDR changed his mind about the meeting he changed it again because he met with the group on December 8.

15. Wyman, ed., *America and the Holocaust* 2:73; Wyman, *The Abandonment of the Jews*, 72–73; Breitman, *Official Secrets*, chap. 9; Morse, *While Six Million Died*, 28. Wyman quoted selectively from Held's notes. He was quick to point out that Roosevelt was "very well acquainted with most of the facts," thereby demonstrating that FDR knew what was going on. But he omitted one of the most important aspects of the meeting, namely FDR's explanation of why rescue was impossible. Compare Wyman (72) to Rubinstein's treatment at *The Myth of Rescue*, 88–89. Penkower spun his anti-FDR account differently. He emphasized Roosevelt's opening story about Herbert Lehman, the chief of foreign relief. "I am a sadist," Roosevelt said. He "hoped to stand behind a curtain in Germany after the war and have the 'sadistic satisfaction' of seeing some 'junkers' on their knees before Lehman, asking for bread." He chided Roosevelt for giving the spokesmen "but six minutes to comment in the half-hour interview" (*The Jews Were Expendable*, 85–86). This was a classic Roosevelt device to limit visitors' requests of him. Churchill, unlike FDR, refused to meet with leading British Jews altogether. Both Roosevelt and Churchill did what was asked of them, and their time was precious (Breitman, *Official Secrets*, 152–53).

16. Breitman and Kraut, *American Refugee Policy*, 242 (Wyman and Feingold did not mention this meeting); Penkower, *Decision on Palestine Deferred*; Grose, *Israel in the Mind of America*, 139–40; Morgenthau Presidential Diary, December 3, 1942, 1200–1, FDRL. On July 17, 1942, Morgenthau and Roosevelt had discussed Palestine and FDR's meeting with Weizmann. Roosevelt told Weizmann at that time that "the English were terrifically worried about having the Arabs stab them in the back." Morgenthau

Presidential Diary, July 7, 1942, 1134–36, FDRL; Blum, *From the Morgenthau Diaries, Years of War*, 208.

17. "State Department Bulletin: Statement to the Press, December 17, 1942," NA, State Department Records S1.3, 7182; Wyman, ed., *America and the Holocaust*, 1:113. The idea originated with the Polish government-in-exile in Britain. See Gilbert, *Auschwitz and the Allies*, chap. 11, 103; Wyman, *The Abandonment of the Jews*, 75; Penkower, *The Jews Were Expendable*, 98; Gilbert, *Second World War*, 387. Roosevelt critic Wyman minimized FDR's issuance of the declaration. What was Wyman's point? FDR ignored the State Department's quibbling and rapidly complied with the request of American Jewish leaders. He did not issue the declaration because the British Foreign Office convinced him to do so. He did it at the request of American Jews and presumably because he thought it the right thing to do. Raul Hilberg omits the declaration from *Perpetrators, Victims, Bystanders*, and then chides Rabbi Wise for being satisfied with Roosevelt's promises and for talking too much in his meeting with Jewish leaders! He never explains that the meeting was successful, as its purpose was to convince FDR to issue a declaration, which he did expeditiously (Hilberg, *Perpetrators, Victims, Bystanders*, 244–45).

18. Gilbert, *Auschwitz and the Allies*, 103; Wyman, *The Abandonment of the Jews*, 75. Feingold, *The Politics of Rescue*, 168–73.

19. Feingold, *The Politics of Rescue*, 168–73. See, for example, Wistrich, *Hitler and the Holocaust*, chap. 7, where the declaration has almost disappeared from the Roosevelt decriers' version of Holocaust history. It disappeared altogether in David Morrison's *Heroes, Antiheroes, and the Holocaust: American Jewry and Historical Choice*, when FDR's December 8 meeting with Jewish leaders was dismissed as "perfunctory and produced no changes in Roosevelt's policy" (179–80). In *The Conquerors*, Michael Beschloss claimed that FDR's references to the extermination of the Jews were "vague and seldom" prior to 1944, that he "did not mention the subject . . . except in the most oblique fashion in his public statements" (38, 323). Wyman discussed it fairly and accurately while simultaneously describing FDR's role in it as reluctant at best. Morse began *While Six Million Died* with the Gerhart Riegner cables and dwells on the minutia of how the declaration was subject to "hostile scrutiny" at the State Department (which it was); who watered it down and why; and the fact that Congress "responded with somewhat less emotion than did the House of Parliament," which, in an unusual act, stood in silence to protest against the Germans' "disgusting barbarism" against the

Jews of Europe. Gilbert, *Auschwitz and the Allies*, 103–104; Morse, *While Six Million Died*, 31–35. Morse never got around to quoting the declaration. That it would have no effect whatsoever on Hitler was not known at the time, although Roosevelt likely thought that Hitler would pay it no heed. Morse, chap. II. The Western powers agreed to the formation of the United Nations War Crimes Commission, which began to compile lists of accused war criminals a year later. But the Allied military leadership opposed initiating action or making too many threats in order to prevent enemy reprisals against Allied prisoners of war. Indeed, war crimes trials in Sicily in 1943 were stopped for this very reason (Smith, *Reaching Judgment at Nuremberg*, 20–22).

20. Gilbert, *Holocaust*, 133, 186, 450, 466–67; Rubinstein, *The Myth of Rescue*, 89–94; Stokesbury, *A Short History of World War II*, 224; Goodwin, *No Ordinary Time*, 396–97.

21. Wyman, *The Abandonment of the Jews*, 67–69; Sachar; Urofsky, *A Voice That Spoke for Justice*, chap. 21; Newton, ed., *FDR and the Holocaust*, 102–3.

22. Penkower, *Decision on Palestine Deferred*, 116–19, 121 (Rosenman); Raphael, *Abba Hillel Silver*, chap. 4.

23. Newton, ed., *FDR and the Holocaust*, 103; Penkower, *Decision on Palestine Deferred*, 120–21. The quote is from Judah Magnes, rector of Hebrew University. The pro-Nazi activities of Arab leaders and nations are well documented. See Peters, *From Time Immemorial*, chap. 17 and appendix IX. "Our sympathy," Gamal Abdel Nasser, the president of Egypt, said in 1964, "was with the Germans . . . the president of our Parliament, for instance, Anwar Sa'adat, was imprisoned for his sympathy with the Germans," (49–50); Weinberg, *A World at Arms*, 351 (Nasser and Sadat among others), 225 (pro-Axis revolt in Iraq), 231 (the grand Mufti of Jerusalem and Syria); Keegan, 325–26 (Rashid Ali in Iraq and the grand Mufti of Jerusalem).

24. Breitman and Kraut, *American Refugee Policy*, 168–70; Wasserstein points out that the British Foreign Office influenced American thinking on this subject. Wasserstein, *Britain and the Jews of Europe*, 295–98.

25. Goodwin, *No Ordinary Time*, 384–85.

26. Wyman, *The Abandonment of the Jews*, 56–57; Newton, ed., *FDR and the Holocaust*, 116–17; Goodwin, *No Ordinary Time*, 396–97. Roosevelt critics transformed this and related events into "complicity" with Nazi killers by quoting Goebbels' remark in his diary: "At bottom, however, I believe the English and the Americans are happy that we are exterminating

the Jewish riffraff." Goebbels, however, had little insight into what Americans thought. Feingold contended that Roosevelt's "inaction" convinced "men like Goebbels that the Allies approved or were at least indifferent to the fate of the Jews" (*The Politics of Rescue*, 305). Goebbels wrote this in his diary on December 13, 1942, four days *before* the December 17 declaration telling the Germans *exactly* how they felt. Feingold, of course, barely mentioned the declaration. Goebbels' words, therefore, not Roosevelt's, were used in the FDR decriers' version of history.

27. Murphy, *Diplomat among Warriors*, 87–91, 102–3, 109, 138–39, 170–71; Persico, 208–20; Stokesbury, *A Short History of World War II*, 224–25. The military historian William Emerson wrote that until August 1943 "the basic decisions that molded strategy were made by the Commander in Chief himself against the advice of his own chiefs and in concert with Churchill and the British chiefs." Newton, ed., *FDR and the Holocaust*, 44; Atkinson, *Army at Dawn*, 16. Roosevelt referred to himself as "a pigheaded Dutchman," 26.

28. Burns, *The Soldier of Freedom*, 285–92; Kennedy, *Freedom from Fear*, 578–79.

29. Stokesbury, *A Short History of World War II*, chap. 18; Freidel, chap. 33; Persico, 213–14; Kennedy, *Freedom from Fear*, 579–83; Burns, *The Soldier of Freedom*, 291–95; Dallek, *Franklin D. Roosevelt and American Foreign Policy, 1932–1945*, chap. 13.

30. Penkower, *Decision on Palestine Deferred*, 161–65; Burns, *The Soldier of Freedom*, 285–91; Dallek, *Franklin D. Roosevelt and American Foreign Policy, 1932–1945*, 377.

31. *Roosevelt and Churchill, Secret Correspondence*, 282 (Stimson gave Roosevelt another analogy: Joshua sending spies to Jericho, where they made a pact with the harlot Rahab, which Joshua approved). Burns, *The Soldier of Freedom*, 295–97; Dallek, *Franklin D. Roosevelt and American Foreign Policy, 1932–1945*, 365; Davis, *Into the Storm*, 4:702; Goodwin, *No Ordinary Time*, 389–91; Sherwood, *Roosevelt and Hopkins*, 648–55. Darlan had some influence over the officials who governed French North Africa. And, of course, the French fleet was still at Toulon and could be a factor in the invasion. As it turned out, the French fleet was scuttled, but Darlan's cease-fire and his control of resident general Noguès saved American lives and helped to secure North Africa without a major fight (Kennedy, *Freedom from Fear*, 582; Burns, *The Soldier of Freedom*, 294). But see Davis's version in which Darlan was overrated by FDR. *FDR, The War President*, chap. 12.

32. Stokesbury, *A Short History of World War II*, 220, 229–30; *Oxford Companion to Second World War*, 644; Morison, *Oxford History*, 1019.

33. Newton, ed., *FDR and the Holocaust*, 157.
34. Gilbert, *Auschwitz and the Allies*, 121; Laqueur, *The Terrible Secret*, 14–15; Weinberg, *Germany, Hitler, and World War II*, 225; Breitman, *Official Secrets*, 164–65; Gilbert, *Holocaust*, 453, 522–23, 526, 545, 557–67, 603, 608, 612 ("people are exaggerating," Jacob Poznanski wrote on September 27, 1943).
35. Gilbert, *Holocaust*, 547–48, 555, 578–79 The grand mufti protested to the Bulgarian foreign minister that Jewish children should not be allowed to go to Palestine.
36. Breitman and Kraut, *American Refugee Policy*, 171–74; Newton, ed., *FDR and the Holocaust*, 114–15, 119; Weinberg, "The Allies and the Holocaust," in *The Holocaust and History*, 484; Dwork and van Pelt, *Holocaust*, 183.
37. Breitman and Kraut, *American Refugee Policy*, 167; Peters, *From Time Immemorial*, chap. 17 and appendix IX (435–42), contains documentary evidence of Arab-Nazi collaboration; Weinberg, "The Allies and the Holocaust," in *The Holocaust and History*, 484.

Chapter 14

1. Rosenman, ed., vol. 1943, *PPA*, 25, 71–81; Dower, *War without Mercy*, 48–52; Daws, *Prisoners of the Japanese*, chap. VI, 360; Gilbert, *The Second World War*, 417.
2. Kennedy, *Freedom from Fear*, 585–88; Dallek, *Franklin D. Roosevelt and American Foreign Policy, 1932–1945*, 369–79, 384–85, 393–97; Weinberg, *Germany, Hitler, and World War II*, 222; Gilbert, *The Second World War*, 392–93; Miller, *The Story of World War II*, 255–56.
3. Murphy, *Diplomat among Warriors*, 139; Dallek, *Franklin D. Roosevelt and American Foreign Policy, 1932–1945*, 366; Davis, *FDR*, 4:711; Warren F. Kimball, ed., *Churchill and Roosevelt: The Complete Correspondence*, 29, 91 (De Gaulle was "quite ready" to work with Noguès).
4. Weinberg, *Germany, Hitler, and World War II*, 222; Murphy, *Diplomat among Warriors*, 166, 171–74; Goodwin, *No Ordinary Time*, 401–9; Kennedy, *Freedom from Fear*, 588–89; Roosevelt and Churchill, *Secret Correspondence*, 306–9.
5. Murphy, *Diplomat among Warriors*, 147–48. The Jews of Morocco and Algeria had, in accordance with Islamic law, been treated like third-class citizens (called *dhimmi* [nonbelievers]) and worse, since the seventh century. See Joan Peters, *From Time Immemorial*, chaps. 2 and 3. When the Jews rejected

the Prophet Muhammad, he turned against them. The Koran thus "contains many of his hostile denunciations of Jews and bitter attacks upon the Jewish tradition." Moses Maimonides fled Morocco in the twelfth century to avoid being murdered. On the other hand, as Bernard Lewis noted, Jews were "better off under Muslim than under Christian rule, until the rise and spread of Western tolerance in the seventeenth and eighteenth centuries" (Lewis, *What Went Wrong?*, 154). When the French colonized North Africa in the nineteenth and early twentieth centuries, it improved the status of Jews and embittered the Muslims against the Jews (Peters, 34, 50–60).

6. Murphy, *Diplomat among Warriors*, 147–48.
7. Ibid., 146–61.
8. FRUS, 1943, 608, 611; Rosenman, ed., 1943 volume, *PPA*, 85 ("rainbows"); Freidel, 460–61; Murphy, *Diplomat among Warriors*, 170. Roosevelt's remarks to Noguès at Casablanca have become, in the hands of the Roosevelt decriers, the foremost evidence of his alleged antisemitism (together with the alleged Crowley statement) and therefore part of their case as to why Roosevelt failed to rescue European Jewry. Robert S. Wistrich in *Hitler and the Holocaust* wrote that "Roosevelt was not immune to a 'liberal' version of antisemitism." In this appalling statement he relied on Wyman's interpretation of the FDR-Noguès conversation (197). Paul Johnson in *A History of the Jews* apparently believed that Roosevelt "was both antisemitic, in a mild way, and ill informed," in describing the FDR-Noguès conversation and again relying on Wyman (Johnson, 504, fn. 185, 625).
9. Burns, *The Soldier of Freedom*, 324–28; Kennedy, *Freedom from Fear*, 575.
10. Weinberg, *A World at Arms*, 464–66; Goodwin, *No Ordinary Time*, 403–404; Keegan, *The Second World War*, 227–37; Rosenman, *Working with Roosevelt*, 366–67; Weinberg, *Germany, Hitler, and World War II*, 221–22; Gilbert, *The Second World War*, 398–99, 416; Churchill, *Closing the Ring*; Kennedy, *Freedom from Fear*, 630–31; McKale, *Hitler's Shadow War*, 311–12.
11. Burns, *The Soldier of Freedom*, 329–30; Miller, *The Story of World War II*, chap. 6; Morison, *Oxford History*, 1019, 1024; Shaw, *World War II Day by Day*, 112, 126–27.
12. Morgan, *FDR*, 664–65; Burns, *The Soldier of Freedom*, 331–38; Shaw, *World War II Day by Day*, 110; Rosenman, ed., *PPA*, vol. 1943, 185–99; Goodwin, *No Ordinary Time*, 440–43; Sherwood, *Roosevelt and Hopkins*, 740.
13. Miller, *The Story of World War II*, 167, 175; Murray and Millett, *A War to Be Won*, 234–36; Loewenheim et al., eds., *Roosevelt and Churchill: Their Secret Wartime Correspondence*, 288; Morison, *Battle of the Atlantic*, 1939–1943,

vol. I, 311–17, 337, 344; Morison's chap. XIV is titled "Ten Months' Incessant Battle, July 1942–April 1943." Keegan, *Second World War*, 103–5; Kennedy, *Freedom from Fear*, 565–72, 588–91; Spivak and Zweiman, eds., *The JWV of the USA: One Hundred Years of Service*, 64.

14. Morison, *The Battle of the Atlantic*; Churchill, *Closing the Ring*, 15; Miller, *The Story of World War II*, 311–44, 166 (Pyle); Morison, *Oxford History*, 1020; Keegan, *The Second World War*, chap. 5.

15. Dower, *War Without Mercy*, 114, 203, 217–24, 242, 244, 258–59, 181–200, and generally chapter 8 and 9.

16. Ibid., 267, 272–73, 276–77.

17. Ibid., chap. 3; Daws, *Prisoners of the Japanese*, 17–29, 70, 273; Gilbert, *The Second World War*, 297, 301. "The Japanese, among others," Eric Markusen and David Knopf concluded, "committed atrocities sufficiently horrendous to be compared with those of the Nazis" (*The Holocaust and Strategic Bombing: Genocide and Total War in the Twentieth Century*, 94).

18. Dower, *War Without Mercy*, 48–52; Daws, *Prisoners of the Japanese*, chap. VI, 360; Gilbert, *The Second World War*, 417; *New York Times*, "Jap Diary Describes Beheading of Yank" *New York Times*; Memo to FDR 10-5-1943, OF 5152, FDRL.

19. Dower, *War Without Mercy*, 52–55, 71, 79.

Chapter 15

1. Wyman, *The Abandonment of the Jews*, 92–95; Feingold, *The Politics of Rescue*, 174.

2. Minutes of meeting of the Joint Emergency Committee, 4/10/43, p. 1, Milton Handler Papers, Arthur W. Diamond Law Library, Columbia University, New York, NY (MHP-CLS: 3-4-1-2).

3. PPF 5029, Wise to FDR 3–4–43; FDR to Wise 3–23–43, Welles to FDR 3–22–43, FDRL; Wyman, *The Abandonment of the Jews*, 97.

4. Wyman, *The Abandonment of the Jews*, 108, 120. Dodds was president of Princeton University.

5. Ibid, *Jews*, 97–99; Breitman and Kraut, *American Refugee Policy*, 176–77.

6. Lash, *Diaries*, 225 (April 2, 1943); Gilbert, *Auschwitz and the Allies*, 133.

7. Wyman, *The Abandonment of the Jews*, 109–15; Breitman and Kraut, *American Refugee Policy*, 139–42, 180; OF 3186 (Dickstein to FDR, 4-2-43).

8. Stokesbury, *A Short History of World War II*, 230; Morison, *Battle of the Atlantic*, 403–4; Gilbert, *The Second World War*, 413–14; Kennedy, 563; Keegan, *Second World War*, chap. 5.

9. Wyman, *The Abandonment of the Jews*, 108–9.

10. Wyman, *America and the Holocaust*, 3:20, 36–152, 188–189, 222–23, 231; Wyman, *The Abandonment of the Jews*, 341–42.

11. Ibid 3:39–43, 51.

12. Ibid. 3; document 18, foldout between 64 and 65.

13. Rubinstein, *The Myth of Rescue*, 97–98; Brecher, *Reluctant Ally*, 106–9. Wyman vaguely acknowledged Irgun gun-running to Palestine. (*The Abandonment of the Jews*, 149).

14. Medoff, *Militant Zionism*, 45–46, 49, 59–62.

15. Wyman, *America and the Holocaust* 3:70–71.

16. Rubinstein, *The Myth of Rescue*, 79–80; Dwork and van Pelt, *Holocaust*, 265–66. Murray and Millett, *A War to Be Won*, 529–32. The Battle of the Atlantic was a costly victory for the Allies; 17 percent of the British merchant navy lost their lives, a higher casualty rate than any other British military service (260). The distinction between "refugees" and "prisoners" was at the heart of the debate because if the Jews were "refugees," they could have been resettled, but if "prisoners" they could not be reached, rescued, or saved. Wyman, *America and the Holocaust*, 3:80–82.

17. Murray and Millett, *A War to Be Won*, chap. 10; Breitman and Kraut, *American Refugee Policy*, 141; Wyman, *America and the Holocaust* 3:245, 82–83.

18. Wyman, *America and the Holocaust*, 3: 224–26.

19. Ibid. 228–32, 236–37.

20. Ibid. 234–37, 240–44.

21. Feingold, *The Politics of Rescue*, 194, 201; Gilbert, *Auschwitz and the Allies*, 132–33; Breitman and Kraut, *American Refugee Policy*, 141.

22. Wyman, *The Abandonment of the Jews*, 121. Roosevelt critics luxuriated in their criticism of the Bermuda Conference. Wyman referred to it as "The Mock Rescue Conference" (*America and the Holocaust*, vol. 3); Feingold's chapter was "The Bermuda Conference: Mock Rescue for Surplus People" (*The Politics of Rescue*, chap. 7).

23. *Congressional Record*, May 6, 1943, 4045–47.

24. Dawidowicz, "American Jews and the Holocaust," 109; Dawidowicz, *What Is the Use of Jewish History?*, 166; Rubinstein, *The Myth of Rescue*, 102.

Chapter 16

1. *Secret Correspondence*, 314–25; Gilbert, *Auschwitz and the Allies*, 119, 163.

2. FRUS, 1943, vol. II, 283; Kimball, *Churchill and Roosevelt*, vol. II, 293, 315–16; Breitman and Kraut, *American Refugee Policy*, 179.

3. Gilbert, *The Second World War*, 400–1, 428; *PPA*, 1943; 308–9; Kennedy, *Freedom from Fear*, 610–12.
4. Gilbert, *The Second World War*, 430.
5. Goodwin, *No Ordinary Time*, 439; Burns, *The Soldier of Freedom*, 364–81.
6. FDRL, OF 3186, Hull to FDR, 5-7-43; Roosevelt to Hull, 5-14-43; FRUS, 1943, vol. I, 176–79.
7. Morison, *Oxford History*, 1019; Gilbert, *The Second World War*, 431; Churchill, *Closing the Ring*, chap. 1.
8. Dallek, *Franklin D. Roosevelt and American Foreign Policy, 1932–1945*, 532–33; Freidel, *Roosevelt*, 107–9, 172, 212, 300; Feingold, *The Politics of Rescue*, 193 ("physical collapse"); Breitman and Kraut, *American Refugee Policy*, 182–83.
9. Breitman and Kraut, *American Refugee Policy*, 183–84; Wyman, *The Abandonment of the Jews*, 80–81; Feingold, *The Politics of Rescue*, 178–80.
10. Wyman, *The Abandonment of the Jews*, 178–81; Feingold, *The Politics of Rescue*, 182–84; Breitman and Kraut, *American Refugee Policy*, 184–86.
11. Wyman, *The Abandonment of the Jews*, 179–80; Feingold, *The Politics of Rescue*, 182–84; Breitman and Kraut, *American Refugee Policy*, 184–85. The Germans vetoed the plan as early as February 1943. The Romanians never actually put the offer on the table. Dawidowicz, *What Is The Use of Jewish History?*, 167.
12. Gilbert, *Auschwitz and the Allies*, 167; Breitman and Kraut, *American Refugee Policy*, 186, 287, fn. 22; Wise, *Challenging Years*, 193–94 (Wise mistakenly referred to Poland and Hungary instead of France and Romania). Feingold, *The Politics of Rescue*, 183; Wyman, *The Abandonment of the Jews*, 82–85, 179–81; Morgenthau, "Diaries," 23.
13. Breitman, *Official Secrets*, 193–94.
14. FRUS, 1943, IV, 794–95, 6-12-43; Feingold, *The Politics of Rescue*, 216–17; FRUS, 1943, vol. II, 280–301. The refugees would be cared for by the relief organization headed by Governor Lehman; *Secret Correspondence*, 351–53, *PPA*, vol. 1943, 338–39.
15. Gilbert, *Auschwitz and the Allies*, 152–58; Churchill, *Closing the Ring*, chap. 2. As Churchill recalled, the "capture of Sicily was an undertaking of the first magnitude. Although eclipsed by events in Normandy, its importance and its difficulties should not be underrated" (24).
16. Dower, *War Without Mercy*, chap. 3; Gilbert, *The Second World War*, 393.
17. Gilbert, *The Second World War*, 447–48.
18. Hull to FDR, FRUS, 1943, vol. I, 176–77; Wyman, *The Abandonment of the Jews*, 129–33.

19. Feingold, *The Politics of Rescue*, 209, 212–14, 230–35; Wyman, *The Abandonment of the Jews*, 126–29. Long told Avra Warren that he had used these erroneous figures (580,000 refugees admitted to the United States since 1933) in briefing FDR (Long to A. Warren, January 7, 1944, Breckinridge Long Papers; Druks, *Failure to Rescue*, 46).

20. Goodwin, *No Ordinary Time*, 448–49.

21. Engel, "Jan Karski's Mission to the West," 363–70; Wood and Jankowski, *Karski*, 192–93; Karski, *Story of a Secret State*, 387–89.

22. Engel, "Jan Karski's Mission to the West," 371–72. Karski, a good and brave man, has been the subject of many dramatic stories. One biography by E. Thomas Wood and Stanislaw M. Jankowski, complete with a foreword by Elie Wiesel, is titled *Karski: How One Man Tried to Stop the Holocaust*. The story of his real mission in 1943, namely to lobby for a free Poland and to warn FDR about the Soviets, has been lost in the drama of Holocaust history. In Wyman's version, Karski's true mission was not disclosed. He has become, in myth, the daring young courier sent by the Polish underground and Polish Jewish leaders to tell the world about the Holocaust. As we have seen, this is not accurate.

Roosevelt's aid to Karski was ignored by the Roosevelt decriers. Wyman used Karski for two purposes: to show that Roosevelt knew about the death camps (322) and that American Jews were indifferent to the fate of European Jews (329).

23. Bird, *The Chairman*, 206; Karski, March 29, 1987, speech, Washington, D.C.

24. Rosenman, ed., *PPA*, vol. 1943, 326–36; Goodwin, *No Ordinary Time*, 449–51; Burns, *The Soldier of Freedom*, 390; Churchill, *Closing the Ring*, v.

25. Goodwin, *No Ordinary Time*, 460–61; Burns, *The Soldier of Freedom*, 392–94; Kennedy, *Freedom from Fear*, 612.

26. Rosenman, ed., vol. 1943, *PPA*, 367.

27. Burns, *The Soldier of Freedom*, 397–98; Gilbert, 163–64; *FRUS*, 1943, 807–10, 8-10-43; Feingold, *The Politics of Rescue*, 215–17; Sachar, *A History of Jews in America*, 573–74.

28. Gilbert, *The Second World War*, 456; Churchill, *Closing the Ring*, 250–51.

29. Rosenman, ed., *PPA*, vol. 1943, 392–97.

30. Goodwin, *No Ordinary Time*, 464–69.

32. Penkower, *The Jews Were Expendable*, 291–95; Gilbert, *Holocaust*, 614–15.

32. Gilbert, *Holocaust*, 510–11, 513, 584, 590; Gilbert, *Auschwitz and the Allies*, 124, 153, 158.

33. Weinberg, *Germany, Hitler, and World War II*, 228–31.

34. Mayer, *Why Did the Heavens Not Darken?*, chap. IX, 421, 460–62; Dawidowicz, *War against the Jews*, 192–97; Gilbert, *Auschwitz and the Allies*, 162.
35. Müller, *Anne Frank*, 164–75.
36. Baker, *Days of Sorrow and Pain*, 281–87, 310, 313.
37. Wyman, *The Abandonment of the Jews*, 111, 151; Feingold, *The Politics of Rescue*, 206–27; Wyman, *America and the Holocaust*, 4, 57–59.
38. Gilbert, *Auschwitz and the Allies*, 142–44; Kennedy, *Freedom from Fear*, 604–9; Casey, *Cautious Crusade*, 103–4 (Roosevelt's lack of remorse).
39. Goodwin, *No Ordinary Time*, 469–71; Kennedy, *Freedom from Fear*, 605–9; Miller, *The Story of World War II*, chap. 7, 215; Churchill, *Closing the Ring*, chap. 13.
40. Feingold, *The Politics of Rescue*, 230–35; Wyman, *The Abandonment of the Jews*, 195–99.
41. Goodwin, *No Ordinary Time*, 471–77.
42. Burns, *The Soldier of Freedom*, 406–13, 427; Kennedy, *Freedom from Fear*, 612; Ferrell, *The Dying President*, 28.
43. Burns, *The Soldier of Freedom*, 421–22.
44. Ibid., 423; Goodwin, *No Ordinary Time*, 480–81.

Chapter 17

1. Quoted in Moore, *GI Jews*, 49, 193.
2. Carruth and Ehrlich, eds., *American Quotations*, 622–23.
3. Sarna, *American Judaism*, 265; Sachar, *A History of the Jews in America*, 569–571,705; Diner, *Jews of the U.S.*, 221; Moore, *GI Jews*, 46. According to Brecher, 1.5 million Jews served in the Allied armies (Brecher, "Western Allies," 429). There is no book or detailed history of the American Jewish home front during World War II, and historians are so overwhelmed by the Holocaust and Zionism that the fascinating, inspiring, and positive story of Jewish Americans during the war has never been told. Henry Feingold's volume on the period in the multivolume series *The Jewish People in America*, sponsored by the American Jewish Historical Society, *A Time for Searching: Entering the Mainstream, 1920–1945* (1992), basically omits the story. Chapter 6 addresses Zionism, chapter seven 7 addresses politics, and chapter 8, the inevitable "The American Jewish Response to the Holocaust." Missing in action is chapter 7 1\2, "American Jews and World War II," in which the author should have but failed to describe what millions of American Jews did to help the United States defeat *two*, not one, of the most monstrous genocidal tyrannies the world has ever seen.

4. Suberman, *When It Was Our War*, 216, 269; Novick, *America and the Holocaust*, 33.

5. Berman, *Richmond's Jewry*, 312–13.

6. Winegarten and Schechter, *Deep in the Heart*, 154–55.

7. Kaufman, *American Jews in World War II*, 23–24, 119–20; Moore, *GI Jews*, chap. 6 (quote, 160).

8. Quoted in Kaufman, *American Jews in World War II*, 16–17.

9. Kaufman, *American Jews in World War II*, 135–48; Welch, *American Nightingale: The Story of Frances Slanger, Forgotten Heroine of Normandy*, *passim.*

10. Kaufman,, *American Jews in World War II*, 182–83.

11. From General Harry Collin's haggadah printed by the 42nd ("Rainbow") Division and used at a Passover seder in Dahn, Germany, March 28, 1945. Museum of Jewish Heritage: A Living Memorial to the Holocaust N.Y.C. ("Ours to Fight For," 2004).

12. Kurtzman, *No Greater Glory: The Four Immortal Chaplains and the Sinking of the* Dorchester *in World War II* (2004), *passim.*

13. Podhoretz, *My Love Affair with America*, 17–18, 95–96.

14. Letter to the author from Jeffrey Weiss dated August 28, 2006; Wyman and Medoff, *A Race Against Death*, 20–21; Alexander Rafaeli, *Dream and Action: The Story of My Life*, 117–19; Y. Ben-Ami, *Years of Wrath, Days of Glory*, 335–41.

15. Collins and Lapierre, *O Jerusalem*, 116; Johnson, *A History of the Jews*, 444, 522; Segev, *One Palestine Complete*, 456–7; Teveth, *Ben-Gurion*, 7.

16. Penkower, *Decision on Palestine Deferred*, 5–10.

17. Memorandum, Handler to Ribicoff, April 1983, p. 22, Handler Papers, Columbia University Law Library.

18. Medoff, *Militant Zionism*, 5, 16–7, 20–5, 28–32, 50–3; Wyman and Medoff, *A Race against Death*, 112–14; Berman, *Nazism, the Jews, and American Zionism*, 17.

19. Segev, *One Palestine Complete*, chap. 16, 382–83; Bell, *Terror out of Zion*, 7, 34. Even Jabotinsky agreed, in theory, to this doctrine.

20. Bell, *Terror out of Zion*, 20, 35. "The Zionists, especially the Zionist left, wanted to believe the worst, hated and feared the Revisionists with a passion they could no longer conceal. Jabotinsky to them was little better than a cryptofascist" (26–27); Segev, *One Palestine Complete*, 385.

21. Bell, *Terror out of Zion*, 27–28; Segev, *One Palestine Complete*, 426–28, 433–34.

22. Segev, *One Palestine Complete*, 441.

23. Teveth, *Ben-Gurion*, 549–51, 665–66; Medoff, *Militant Zionism*, 22, 26,

36–37, 46–47, 57, 74. The Revisionists had no sympathy for the British even in the darkest days of 1940, when it appeared Germany would conquer the British Isles. For a recent, detailed explanation of Bergson's fascist approach, see Mark A. Raider, "'Irresponsible, Undisciplined Opposition': Ben Halpern on the Bergson Group and Jewish Terrorism in Pre-State Palestine," *AJH* 92 (September 2004).

24. Meir, *My Life*, 196; Young-Bruehl, *Hannah Arendt*, 178; Nurenberger, *The Scared and the Doomed*, 201; Wyman, *Abandonment of the Jews*, 85–90; Sachar, *A History of the Jews in America 752–3, 914–5*; Teveth, *Ben-Gurion*, 367–74, 412–17, 550–51; Collins and Lapierre, *O Jerusalem!*, 545–46; Sachar, *Modern Jewish History*, 466, 483.

For the pure, undiluted version of Irgunist history, see Ben Hecht's memoir, *A Child of the Century*, book 6 *The Committee*. Hecht, a well-known playwright and scriptwriter, was co-chair of the Committee for a Jewish Army and the Emergency Committee to Save the Jewish People of Europe. He believed that the Bergson's group was the only Jewish group that cared about rescuing European Jewry; that Roosevelt felt Jews were an "irritating people" and that he had no time "to listen to any Jewish wailing" (568–9); that his (Hecht's) article in *Reader's Digest* "broke the American silence attending the massacre of the Jews in February 1943" (550); that not one Jewish organization did anything worthwhile; that Roosevelt cared only about the British and "looked . . . a little too red with Jewish blood" (579).

Befitting a true Irgunist, Hecht praised the notorious and nearly universally condemned Stern Gang, which carried out political assassinations. "They were as valorous and nobly inspired a group of human beings as I have ever met in history" (594). Both Weizmann (first president of Israel) and Ben-Gurion (its first prime minister) were timorous elitists, uncaring, cowardly political hacks and British toadies according to Hecht. They betrayed the brave Irgunists who single-handedly liberated Palestine (598). Ben-Gurion was "the political boss of Palestine" (596). The Haganah did nothing, and all history that claimed it "valiantly fought for the establishment of a free Hebrew nation" was a lie. Indeed, Ben-Gurion sold the Jews out by not invading Trans-Jordan and by compromising on the seizure of Jerusalem and other issues (599).

Hecht, like Bergson, came off in Wyman's version as a noble hero. But Wyman did not tell his readers that Hecht and the Irgun disliked not only Roosevelt but also the Zionist movement as a whole, including Ben-Gurion, Weizman, Moshe Dayan, Yitzhak Rabin, and Golda Meir. According to Irgunists, Menachem Begin almost single-handedly created the State of

Israel (Medoff, *Militant Zionism*, 22, 75). Medoff describes Ben-Gurion as the "Labor Zionist Chief," not the national leader he was.

The Haganah was the underground military arm of the Jewish Agency in Palestine. It practiced self-restraint, and, unlike the Irgun, refused to use terrorism against Arab civilians. Its permanently mobilized volunteers were members of the Palmach. Yitzhak Rabin fought with the Palmach during World War II. Moshe Dayan was a Haganah soldier and lost his eye in battle with Vichy French forces in Syria. Rabin, *The Rabin Memoirs*, 9–12.

25. Medoff, *Militant Zionism*, 61; Roosevelt to Wise, June 9, 1941, PPF 8084, FDRL.
26. Medoff, *Militant Zionism*, 58.
27. The FBI investigated Bergson but could not find the evidence. In later years Bergson partisans have bragged about deceiving the FBI. See Medoff, *Militant Zionism*, 103, 192; Hecht, *A Child of the Century*, 586.
28. Wyman and Medoff, *A Race against Death*, 123. Wyman described the mainstream Zionist leaders' opposition to "the Bergsonites," "the Bergsonite faction," "the Bergson group," or one of several front groups, such as "the Emergency Committee," as if the Irgun were not behind these front groups.

    Laurel Leff, another member of the David Wyman Institute Academic Council (www.wymaninstitute.org), omits any mention of the Irgun and Bergson's role in it from her book *Buried by the* Times: *The Holocaust and America's Most Important Newspaper*. Bergson, Leff tells her readers, was a "Palestinian Jew who came to the States to lobby for a Jewish Army to fight Nazis, and to help save European Jewry." Leff, *Buried by the* Times, 359. "Irgun" is not in the index. Leff described Bergson as leading right-wing "the Palestinian Jews" in the U.S. (193). She described the Irgun cell as "The Bergson Group" and used the names of front organizations rather than "Irgun delegation" (203). Leff informed her readers that the "established [Jewish] organizations refused to ally with the Bergson Group," which makes no sense at all unless the establishment was antirescue, weak and cowardly (204). The real explanation was never given.

    Rafael Medoff, the director of the Wyman Institute, is a prolific letter writer, op-ed author and political activist. He referred to Bergson as "a Zionist emissary" when writing for a broad audience (see, e.g., the *Orlando Sentinel*, January 13, 2005), but as a member of "Menachem Begin's Irgun Zvai Leumi" when writing for the *Jewish Ledger* (January 17, 2003). The Irgun is characterized, not as a terrorist or even as a revolutionary organization but as "the underground Jewish militia."
29. Hecht, *A Child of the Century*, 536.

30. Dawidowicz, *What Is the Use of Jewish History?*, 183–84; Pierre van Paassen, "The Irgunist Hoax," Letter to the Editor, *The Protestant*, April 1944, 21. Wyman and Medoff downplayed the terrorist aspect of the Irgun and described it as "the Jewish underground militia." *A Race against Death*, 13; Medoff, *Militant Zionism*, 71.

31. *The Protestant*, April 1944, 42–3. "The real reasons for my resignation" van Paassen wrote, "were always carefully hidden or totally misrepresented by the directors of the 'Committee for a Jewish Army' so that many people till this day are and remain under the false impression that I am still an active supporter of the Committee or of one or more of its various offshoots and prolongations." Bergson later agreed that van Paassen's letter was basically correct. See Wyman and Medoff, *A Race against Death*, 122–23.

32. *The Protestant*, 43. In a footnote in *A Race against Death* (21) Wyman claimed that van Paassen severed his ties to Bergson "under pressure from mainstream Jewish leaders." In *Abandonment of the Jews*, however, Wyman described van Paassen as the popular author who wrote ads in the *New York Times* for the CJA and never told the reader that he resigned and called the Bergson group a hoax (*Abandonment of the Jews*, 85–86). Nor did he or Medoff mention the public rebuke in *The Protestant* in *A Race against Death*. Penkower described all of van Paassen's activities in *The Jews Were Expendable* except resigning and denouncing Bergson. Van Paassen was very important when supporting Bergson in Friedman's *No Haven for the Oppressed*, but his resignation was nowhere to be found there.

33. Wyman and Medoff, *A Race against Death*, 62–3; Medoff, *Militant Zionism*, 46. The attitude of American Jews toward British policy in Palestine changed after the war. But *during* the war the Jews of America and Palestine overwhelmingly supported the British. Even Bergson told Hecht that 95 percent of the Jews in Palestine were "eager to believe the British are their friends." (*A Child of the Century*, 528).

34. Wyman and Medoff, *A Race Against Death*, 22–26; Hecht, *A Child of the Century*, 541–5; Haver, *Selznick's Hollywood*, 271–72.

35. Wyman and Medoff, *A Race against Death*, 30–31; Wyman, *Abandonment of the Jews*, 82–85; Breitman and Kraut, *American Refugee Policy*, 184–85, 286.

36. Wyman, *Abandonment of the Jews*, 86–87; memorandum of conversation, 1-10-44, p. 5, Long Papers, State Department, 1939–1944 (200 "Palestine") LC. "There were not many in the United States who knew in 1943 that the newspaper stories were inaccurate, that the plan was dead, and that the widely advertised price listed by the Committee for a Jewish Army . . . was a

tiny fraction of what the real total had been," Breitman and Kraut noted. "But historians ought to know this and ought to point it out. See, however, Feingold, *The Politics of Rescue*, 181–82, and Wyman, *Abandonment of the Jews*, 86–87, 92, 98–99 (*American Refugee Policy*, fn. 14, 286)."

37. Wyman, *Abandonment of the Jews, 83–4, 91*; Dawidowicz, *What Is the Use of Jewish History?*, 167–68.

38. Wyman, *Abandonment of the Jews*, 77–90; Feingold, *The Politics of Rescue*, 175–76. These rescue proposals and many like them ignored the mind-set of the Nazis in 1942 and 1943.

39. Hecht, *A Child of the Century*, 550–53.

40. Wyman, *Abandonment of the Jews*, 90–91, 145; Sachar, *A History of the Jews in America, 544–6*; Sachar, *Modern Jewish History*, 466, 483; Hecht, *A Child of the Century*, 558; Feingold, *The Politics of Rescue*, 211–12; Morrison, *Heroes, Antiheroes, and the Holocaust*, 209. Morgenthau to Lerner, July 15, 1943, Palestinian Statehood Committee Papers (Bergson group) Yale University, New Haven, CT., Reel 4.

41. Wyman, *Abandonment of the Jews*, 148–49; Goodwin, *No Ordinary Time*, 455. Anti-Roosevelt writers constantly overrated the accomplishments of the Bergson group. They were turned into Davids battling many Goliaths (Penkower, "In Dramatic Dissent: The Bergson Boys"). Yet after the Bermuda Conference, Harry Truman and others resigned from the CJA's national committee when the group called the conference "a mockery and a cruel jest" (Wyman, *Abandonment of the Jews*, 143). Wyman conceded that the Bergson group had its own agenda, namely promoting the Irgun in its armed struggle against the British. Indeed, when the Emergency Committee sent Arieh Ben-Eliezer to Palestine to deal "incidentally with rescue matters," but "primarily to promote Irgun business," he was arrested by the British. Wyman, *Abandonment of the Jews*, 149.

42. Berman, *Nazism, the Jews, and American Zionism*, chap. III and IV (Silver quote, 106); Wyman, *Abandonment of the Jews*, 157–67.

43. Wyman, *Abandonment of the Jews*, 172–73; Hull, *Memoirs*, 1535; FRUS 1944, V. 5, 560–657; FRUS 1945, V. 8, 668 n.; Gilbert, *Auschwitz and the Allies*, 165.

44. http://www.wymaninstitute.org/special/rabbimarch/index1.php, 8-11-2005.

45. Feingold, *The Politics of Rescue*, 221; *American Hebrew*, 11-26-43. Isaiah Berlin, "moved to fury" by "the notorious March 9 Rabbis" (Berlin, "Zionist Politics in Wartime Washington," 672). Dawidowicz, *What Is the Use of Jewish History?*, 217; Medoff, *The Deafening Silence*, 130–31;

Morrison, *Heroes, Antiheroes, and the Holocaust*, 217–18; Wyman, *America and the Holocaust*, 82–83; *American Jewish Yearbook* (1943).

46. Wyman, *Abandonment of the Jews*, 152–53. Rabbi Levovitz wired one of FDR's secretaries, Marvin McIntyre, on October 3. Edwin M. ("Pa") Watson, another Roosevelt secretary, replied on October 5: "Regret impossible for your group be received by the President and suggest you contact office of the Secretary of State in this connection" (Wyman, *America and the Holocaust*, 78–80).

47. Medoff, *The Deafening Silence*, 130–31; Penkower, *The Jews Were Expendable*, 138; Hassett, *Off the Record*, 209. In *Abandonment of the Jews*, Wyman called the protest by the Orthodox rabbis "a dramatic innovation," criticized Roosevelt for not seeing a group of Orthodox rabbis sent by an unpopular, unrepresentative Palestinian terrorist front group, and then claimed it "is not entirely clear" why FDR avoided them when it was perfectly obvious why he did (152–53). As Wyman failed to explain the significance of the Irgun, Roosevelt's actions made no sense to his readers. Wyman recounted the episode as if most of American Jews supported Bergson, the Irgun, and the Orthodox rabbis, which they manifestly did not. Dawidowicz, *What Is the Use of Jewish History?*, 161 and chap. 11.

The Roosevelt critics lined up behind Wyman and Feingold on the march of the four hundred Orthodox rabbis. "FDR fled from 400 Orthodox rabbis who marched on Washington," Penkower wrote in *The Jews Were Expendable*, (120, 299). "The President arranged to be away when the rabbis arrived," Medoff wrote in *The Deafening Silence* (130) Medoff did explain that FDR relied on the advice of Jewish Congressmen Rosenman and Wise, among others.

48. Penkower, *The Jews Were Expendable*, 138; Hecht, *A Child of the Century*, 519. Rosenman was proud to be a Jew. His biography in *Who's Who in America, 1942–43* listed several Jewish organizations and boards.

49. Hecht, *A Child of the Century*, 60–61, 563–64.

50. Feingold pointed out that the Emergency Committee alienated the mainline Jewish organizations by ignoring Palestine and stressing rescue. Because the emergency committee was made up of Palestinians, Feingold told us, they were aware that Arabs did not like Zionism! "Why arouse Arab fears?" Feingold told us in defending Bergson (*The Politics of Rescue*, 238). Of course when the American or British government took the exact same position, they were excoriated by Feingold as unspeakable antisemites. Feingold was well aware that the mainline Jewish organizations condemned

Bergson's committee (239), but, like Wyman, he failed to explain the significance of the dispute among the Irgun, the Revisionists, and the Zionist movement. Wyman was guilty of the same double standard. For him, it was morally defensible for Bergson to "keep issues as politically sensitive as Palestine out of the picture," but not for FDR or Winston Churchill to do so (*Abandonment of the Jews*, 199).

51. Wyman, *Abandonment of the Jews*, 154; Burns, *The Soldier of Freedom*, 340; Goodwin, *No Ordinary Time*, 394–95; Feingold, *The Politics of Rescue*, 224. Wyman omitted this important fact, (see Wyman, *Abandonment of the Jews*, 153–54). Indeed, his text left the reader with the erroneous impression that the United States did nothing to aid or support the escape of the Danish Jews.

52. Johnson, *History of the Jews*, 522–23; Segev, *One Palestine Complete*, 456–57; Penkower, *Decision on Palestine Deferred*, 271–74; Hecht, *A Child of the Century*, 594.

53. Hecht, *A Child of the Century*, 593. Bergson went to Israel and was elected to the first Knesset. Apparently a failure in Israeli politics, he returned to New York in 1951 and became a commodity broker.

54. Many historians, even those critical of FDR, dismissed the alleged contribution of the Bergson Group. See Laqueur, *A History of Zionism*, 551–52; Feingold, *The Politics of Rescue*, 265; Breitman and Kraut barely mentioned the group. Brecher, "Western Allies," fn. 15, 441. The Roosevelt decrier school is linked to events in Israel. As Bernard Wasserstein pointed out in "The Myth of 'Jewish Silence' ": It is no accident that this legend [of Jewish silence] has grown up. On the contrary, this is an accusation first voiced during and immediately after the war by a specific group: the Revisionist Zionists and their various offshoots. This was their indictment against the Jewish establishment of the time, the Samuels, the Weizmanns, the Wises, the Frankfurters. This was the rallying-call which they used in their attempts to mobilize Jewish youth in a misguided and morally tainted campaign of invective and terror. During the 1950s and 1960s, the echoes of these false accusations grew fainter as the events concerned receded into history. But since May, 1977, there has been a new Establishment in Israel. And since then there has grown up a new orthodoxy of Zionist history in which Jabotinsky replaces Weizmann, Begin replaces Ben-Gurion, and the IZL and LEHI replace the Haganah. The recently appointed Foreign Minister of Israel, Yitzhak Shamir, is one of the "triumvirate" who guided LEHI. Begin, Shamir, and of course [Ariel] Sharon belong (and indeed

proudly proclaim that they belong) to the activist tradition in Zionism. Sharon's call for mass demonstrations outside the White House [in the 1970s to protest a U.S. vote against Israel in the United Nations] was not only based upon a twisting of Jewish history and a calumniation of dead men who cannot reply. It falls into the historic pattern of acts of futile bombast and bravado which, while they may assuage emotions, pretend to save lives while in fact they risk them needlessly [15–16].
55. Ben-Ami, *Years of Wrath, Days of Glory*, 280.

Chapter 18

1. Rosenman, ed., *PPA*, vol. 1944–45, 32–36; Burns, *The Soldier of Freedom*, 424–25; Goodwin, *No Ordinary Time*, 484–86.
2. Feingold, *The Politics of Rescue*, 209, 233.
3. Henry Morgenthau Jr., "The Morgenthau Diaries," part VI, "The Refugee Run-Around," 22; Breitman and Kraut, *American Refugee Policy*, 182–87; Wyman, *The Abandonment of the Jews*, chap. 10; Bird, *The Chairman*, 203; Gilbert, *Auschwitz and the Allies*, 168–72. Penkower, *The Jews Were Expendable*, chap. 5. British diplomats did not want Jews to leave occupied Europe. "Once we open the door to adult male Jews to be taken out of enemy territory," A. W. G. Randall of the Foreign Office wrote on December 24, 1943, "a quite unmanageable flood may result. (Hitler may facilitate it!)" (168).
4. MD Book 694, p. 68, minutes of meeting 1-15-1944, FDRL.
5. MD Book 693, 196, 202–10, FDRL; actually there would be four Jews— Rosenman, Cohen, Morgenthau, and Cox. Morgenthau, "The Morgenthau Diaries," *Collier's*, November 1, 1947, 64; Breitman and Kraut, *American Refugee Policy*, 189; Wyman, *The Abandonment of the Jews*, 181–83.
6. Feingold, *The Politics of Rescue*, 248–94; Wyman, *The Abandonment of the Jews*, 178–330; Breitman and Kraut, chap. 9; Penkower, *The Jews Were Expendable*, chap. 5 (133). Morgenthau, with the help of young Arthur M. Schlesinger Jr., described the events in *Collier's* in November 1947. Berman, *Nazism, the Jews, and American Zionism*, 101–02; Rubinstein, *The Myth of Rescue*, 107–12.
7. MD Book 692, 285, 286–90; MD Book 694, 85–86, FDRL; Morgenthau, *Collier's*, 23, 65.
8. *Collier's*, 65; MD Book 693, 81; MD Book 694, 87, 97, FDRL. Feingold, *The Politics of Rescue*, 246.
9. MD Book 693, 204. There is no biography of Cox. His son Peter W. Cox described his father's life and Jewish family connections in his memoir

Journalism Matters (2005). My thanks to Peter Cox's widow, Eunice Cox of Bath, Maine, and Rabbi Carolyn Braun and Cantor Ruth Ross of Portland, Maine, for helping me track down Oscar Cox's background.

10. MD Book 693, 199, FDRL; Dawidowicz, "American Jews and the Holocaust," 112. Wyman, *The Abandonment of the Jews*, 183–84. See Warren Kimball, *"The Most Unsordid Act": Lend-Lease 1939–1941*. Wyman, *The Abandonment of the Jews*, 183–84, 203; Breitman and Kraut, *American Refugee Policy*, 188; Penkower, *The Jews Were Expendable*, 133–34, 336. Cox wrote to Morgenthau on June 16, 1943: "Following up our discussion this morning about the refugee matter, I am sending you herewith a memorandum giving a first rough draft of the plan." Cox also sent the memorandum to Sol Bloom and Scott Lucas, delegates to the Bermuda Conference, who were contemplating a meeting with Sumner Welles in the near future. It thus appeared that the idea for the WRB emerged in the aftermath of the failed Bermuda Conference (MD Book 642, 210–13, FDRL). On June 21, 1943, Morgenthau received a legal opinion on the proposal (MD Book 643, 228–30, FDRL).

"I personally drafted an executive order [creating a rescue agency] as early as 1943 and the order that the President signed was based on my original draft as revised by Ben Cohen, the treasury lawyers and myself. The full story is accurately told by Lucy Dawidowicz in an article published in the *New York Times Magazine* on April 18, 1982. "Confidential Memorandum" to Senator Abraham Ribicoff from Milton Handler, April 28, 1983 Re: Report of the American Jewish Commission on the Holocaust," 7, Milton Handler Papers (MHP-CLS:3-4-2-2).

Memos in June 1943 between Cox and Handler indicated that Cox drew the refugee rescue plan. Memo to Cox from Handler, 6-18-43, Oscar Cox Papers, Box 101, FDRL.

11. MD Book 693, 89–91, FDRL; Feingold, *The Politics of Rescue*, 223–37, 240; Breitman and Kraut, *American Refugee Policy*, 187; Wyman, *The Abandonment of the Jews*, 181–84; Breitman and Kraut, *American Refugee Policy*, 188.

12. MD Book 693, 198; MD Book 694, 88–9, FDRL; Peck, "The Campaign for an American Response to the Nazi Holocaust, 1943–1945," 386.

13. MD Book 693, 198–200; MD Book 694, 84, 105, FDRL. Feingold, *The Politics of Rescue*, 240. The money, needless to say, would come from mainstream Jewish organizations, mainly the Joint. Bergson and the Irgunists barely had sufficient funds to run their controversial newspaper advertisements.

14. MD Book 694, 194–202 (Report), FDRL. Breitman and Kraut, *American Refugee Policy*, 186. Penkower, *The Jews Were Expendable*, 128–30, 132. Breckinridge Long asked Morgenthau to come to his defense. Wyman, *The Abandonment of the Jews*, 185. Had Long acted on Roosevelt's orders or even with his knowledge, he would not have needed Morgenthau's help. MD Book 694, 77–110, FDRL.

15. MD Book 693, 78, 1-15-44 meeting; MD Book 694, 83, 92–93, 148–51; MD Book 688 II, 191, FDRL; Wyman, *The Abandonment of the Jews*, chap. 10; Breitman and Kraut, *American Refugee Policy*, 188–90. Milton Handler to Oscar Cox, 1-14-44, Cox Papers, Box 101, FDRL; Cox to Morgenthau, 12/27/43; Morgenthau to Cox, 12-31-43, MD Diaries, 688 II, 249–51, FDRL.

16. MD Book 694, 195, 202; MD Book 688 II, 119, FDRL; Medoff, *Militant Zionism in America*, 105.

17. Morgenthau, *Collier's*, 65.

18. MD Book 694, 190–93, FDRL; Morgenthau, *Collier's*, 65; Breitman and Kraut, *American Refugee Policy*, 190. Newton, ed., *FDR and the Holocaust*, 120–21; Gilbert, *Auschwitz and the Allies*, 172–73; Feingold, *The Politics of Rescue*, 241–43; Penkower, *The Jews Were Expendable*, 141–42; Breitman, *Official Secrets*, 195. Kozlowski, "The Mission That Failed: An Interview with Jan Karski," 332. Pehle acknowledged in 1944 that "the Emergency Committee to Save Jews of Europe has rendered a significant service in calling to the attention of the American public the enormous tragedy that has befallen the Jews of Europe." Pehle to Bergson, November 30, 1944; Emergency Committee to Save the Jewish People of Europe file, Box 7, WRB Papers, FDRL; Medoff, *Militant Zionism in America*, 217.

     Pierre van Paassen, formerly chairman of Bergson's Committee for a Jewish Army, ridiculed the claim that Bergson's group was responsible for the creation of the WRB. For the Irgunists to take credit for the WRB, van Paassen wrote in *The Protestant*, was like Chantecleer in Rostand's play crowing that he had made the sun rise (43). Josiah Dubois told Lucy Dawidowicz that while the Irgunists raised the level of public awareness of the fate of European Jewry, events within the Treasury Department led to the creation of the WRB (Dawidowicz, *What Is the Use of Jewish History?*, 195–96). David Wyman so respected Dubois that he named his chair in history for him.

     Feingold, *The Politics of Rescue*, 240. Herbert Druks alleged that the WRB was created to give the *illusion* of rescuing Jews while, in fact, it was a failure and a fake! The WRB "was still one more bureaucratic organization. While it did help save a few Jews, it failed to provide these Jews with a place to go." Druks, *The Failure to Rescue*, inside cover of 1977 paperback edition, 26, 47.

19. Morgenthau, *Mostly Morgenthaus*, 326–27. Breitman and Kraut argued that Dubois threatened to resign and make the story public if the president did not act. Morgenthau's report observed that a political scandal could occur. Sarah Peck gave Morgenthau the credit for the WRB. "With continued Jewish disunity and the failure of the Gillette-Rogers resolution," she wrote, "prospects for rescue seemed bleak. But at that critical moment, Treasury Secretary Henry Morgenthau Jr. appeared on the scene." Monty Penkower also gives Morgenthau most of the credit. "Unaware of Morgenthau's personal involvement, newspapers credited the Emergency Committee's industrious spadework" solely with the outcome. Breitman and Kraut, *American Refugee Policy*, 189–90; Peck, "The Campaign for an American Response to the Nazi Holocaust, 1943–1945," 386; Penkower, *The Jews Were Expendable*, 142–43; Bird, *The Chairman*, 202–03. Kai Bird concluded in his biography of John J. McCloy that "Roosevelt probably would not have agreed to the formation of the War Refugee Board had it not been for Henry Morgenthau." Breitman and Kraut pointed out that Peter Bergson met Morgenthau on a number of occasions and that Morgenthau willingly listened to him. Bergson may very well have influenced Morgenthau.

20. Ferrell, *The Dying President*, 27–31; MD Book 694, 127–28, FDRL.

21. Celler to FDR, 1-25-44, OF 5477, WRB, 1944–45, Box 4, FDRL.

22. Breitman and Kraut, *American Refugee Policy*, 190–91; Feingold, *The Politics of Rescue*, 246–47; Morse, 382.

23. Feingold, *The Politics of Rescue*, 245–47; Morgenthau, *Collier's*, 22.

24. Memorandum of February 11, 1944, meeting, Wyman, ed., *America and the Holocaust* 12:131–36.

25. Bird, *The Chairman*, 204–05; Wyman, *The Abandonment of the Jews*, 209, 291.

26. Breitman and Kraut, *American Refugee Policy*, 192; Penkower, *The Jews Were Expendable*, 142.

27. Wasserstein, *Britain and the Jews of Europe*, 323; Long, *Diary*, 336–37; Gilbert, *Auschwitz and the Allies*, 173; Bauer, *The Holocaust in Historical Perspective*, 84–85. The Russians were not antisemitic. They just had no concern for human life. Some British newspapers applauded Roosevelt's actions. "The American Government," the *Manchester Guardian* opined,

"has clearly abandoned that defeatist, timid view, and we should follow suit." (Quoted by Winant, cable dated 2-12-44, OF 5477, WRB, 1944–45, Box 4, p. 4, FDRL).

28. Memo from Grace Tully to FDR, 3-3-44; Myron C. Taylor to FDR, 3-3-44, Morgenthau to FDR, 3-21-44; OF 3186, FDRL.

29. Rosenman, ed., *PPA*, vol. 1944, 104; Breitman and Kraut, *American Refugee Policy*, 193–96; Gilbert, *Auschwitz and the Allies*, 182–85; Murray and Millet, *A War to Be Won*, 454–55; Wyman, *The Abandonment of the Jews*, 256–57. Wyman called FDR's strong and clear statement "watered down" because Rosenman did not want Roosevelt making promises he could not keep, such as promising unlimited havens for refugees on American soil. While it is true that the Treasury staff, particularly Pehle and Dubois, wanted an even stronger statement, Morgenthau was satisfied with the statement as issued. MD, vol. 708, 1–3, 42–44. It is also true that Rosenman was cautious about the statement and toned it down somewhat, to the great consternation of Pehle and others. "Rosenman is a tough assignment," Pehle told Morgenthau, when the secretary asked Pehle to discuss the statement with Rosenman. MD, vol. 707, 242–43; vol. 708, 42–44. According to Pehle and Morgenthau, FDR told Stettinius that the declaration referred to the atrocities against the Jews in too pointed a manner. Pehle, memo for files, 3/9/44, Box 33, WRB, FDRL; MD vol. 707, 219–34. This is all a tempest in a teapot, as the statement as issued was very strong indeed.

30. Rosenman, ed., *PPA*, vol. 1944, 103–05.

31. *New York Times*, March 25, 1944, p. 1.

32. Rosenman, ed., *PPA*, vol. 1944, 105–6; Gilbert, *Auschwitz and the Allies*, 184–86; "History of the War Refugee Board," FDRL, unpublished.

33. Morgenthau, *Collier's*, 65; Morgenthau to FDR, 3-11-44 with attached cable from Ira Hirschmann to Pehle, Morgenthau Papers, Box 80, FDRL.

34. Morgenthau, *Collier's*, 65; Burns, *The Soldier of Freedom*, 442; Gilbert, *Auschwitz and the Allies*, 173.

35. Gilbert, *Auschwitz and the Allies*, 173–76, chap. 6; Sirevag, *Eclipse of the New Deal*, chap. 5 ("1943: The War within the War"); Neufeld and Berenbaum, eds., *The Bombing of Auschwitz*, 6–7, 102 (5 million dead).

36. Memo to the office committee of the WJC from Kubowitzki, July 21, 1944, p. 2, MSS col. 361 (WJC), Box 114, Folder 5, AJA.

37. Morgenthau, *Collier's*, 22, 65; "History of the WRB," FDRL. When Nahum Goldmann suggested the idea of a Jewish army in May 1939 it was scotched by the leadership of the WJC and the AJ Congress. Edward L. Israel, president

of the AJ Congress, expressed the views of American Jewry in a letter to Rabbi Wise: "In a war the right to serve as part of the army is the distinguishing mark of citizenship." Fighting for the rights of citizenship and then not fighting for one's country was "terribly inconsistent," Israel noted. "This is true in every country but particularly true in America." Goldmann to Wise, 5-2-39; Israel to Wise, 5-18-39, MSS col. 361, A27/2, AJA. Even Feingold concedes that the number who could possibly have been saved is in the "tens of thousands," whereas Wyman believes it was in the hundreds of thousands (Feingold, *The Politics of Rescue*, 307; *AJH*, 62, no. 4; Wyman, *The Abandonment of the Jews*, 331; Brecher, "The Western Allies," 426.

38. Breitman and Kraut, *American Refugee Policy*, 200–1; Lowenstein, *Token Refuge*, 34–5; "History of the WRB," 289, FDRL.

39. Breitman and Kraut, *American Refugee Policy*, 204–10.

40. Ibid., 211–13.

41. Gilbert, *Auschwitz and the Allies*, 260.

42. *New York Times*, July 15, 1944, p. 3.

43. Ibid., p. 9; I. M. Weinstein to Pehle, File 33, WRB, FDRL.

44. "History of the WRB," 153, FDRL.

45. Breitman and Kraut, *American Refugee Policy*, 213–14; Murray and Millett, *A War to Be Won*, chap. 16; Weinberg, *A World at Arms*, 713–16; Wyman, *The Abandonment of the Jews*, 238–39; Dwork and Jan Van Pelt, *Holocaust*, 318. For a contrary view of Wallenberg's achievements see Rubinstein, *The Myth of Rescue*, 183, 191–96, 211–12, 252–54.

46. Lowenstein, *Token Refuge*, 17–9.

47. Ibid., 20; Strum, "Fort Ontario Refugee Shelter, 1944–1946," 1–4, 404; Breitman and Kraut, *American Refugee Policy*, 197–99; Wyman, *The Abandonment of the Jews*, 197.

48. Lowenstein, *Token Refuge*, 22–7; Strum, "Fort Ontario Refugee Shelter, 1944–1946," 404; Wyman, *The Abandonment of the Jews*, 265; Breitman and Kraut, *American Refugee Policy*, 198. History of the WRB, 945–46, FDRL

49. Lowenstein, *Token Refuge*, 41–42; "History of the WRB," FDRL, 232–33.

50. Lowenstein, *Token Refuge*, chap. 5–8, 108–11.

51. "History of the WRB," 234; Wyman, *The Abandonment of the Jews*, 187, 266–68.

52. Lowenstein, *Token Refuge*, 111–14; Wyman, *The Abandonment of the Jews*, 273.

Saving the Jews

Chapter 19

1. Burns, *The Soldier of Freedom*, 429–32. Churchill quoted in Kennedy, *Freedom from Fear*, 669.
2. Burns, *The Soldier of Freedom*, 433–37; Goodwin, *No Ordinary Time*, 484–88.
3. Burns, *The Soldier of Freedom*, 438–40; *New York Times*, February 20, 1944; Brinkley, *World War II, Allied Counteroffensive*, 154.
4. Murray and Millett, *A War to Be Won*, chap. 12; Gilbert, *Auschwitz and the Allies*, 183; Goodwin, *No Ordinary Time*, 488.
5. Churchill, *Closing the Ring*, chap. 13.
6. Burns, *The Soldier of Freedom*, 440–41. Beschloss, *The Conquerors*, 41, 57–8; Fleming, *The New Dealer's War*, 181, 371–2, 428–9, 498–9. Churchill shared Roosevelt's views of Germans. See Churchill, *Closing the Ring*, 159.
7. Ferrell, *The Dying President*, chap. 2; Burns, *The Soldier of Freedom*, 448–49; Goodwin, *No Ordinary Time*, 491–97.
8. Ferrell, *The Dying President*, chap. 3; Goodwin, *No Ordinary Time*, 491–97, 501–4; Bishop, *FDR's Last Year*, 7, 22–23, 59, 147–48 (Ben Cohen to FDR).
9. Goodwin, *No Ordinary Time*, 498, 501–05; Burns, *The Soldier of Freedom*, 454–55; Fischer, *Liberty and Freedom*, 530–32.
10. Wilt, *The Atlantic Wall*, xiv, 51–52, 107; Kennedy, *Freedom from Fear*, 696–97; Burns, *The Soldier of Freedom*, 474–75.
11. Kennedy, *Freedom from Fear*, 721; Burns, *The Soldier of Freedom*, 475; Goodwin, *No Ordinary Time*, 506; D'Este, *Eisenhower: A Soldier's Life*, 495; Churchill quoted in Kennedy, *Freedom from Fear*, 699; Casey, *Cautious Crusade*, 150–53.
12. Goodwin, *No Ordinary Time*, 506–8.
13. Ibid., 509–10; Burns, *The Soldier of Freedom*, 476.
14. D'Este, *Eisenhower*, 527.
15. Adolf Hitler, responding to news that the Allied invasion had begun, June 6, 1944. Goodwin, *No Ordinary Time*, 516–17; Burns, *The Soldier of Freedom*, 450; Bishop, *FDR's Last Year*, 70–71.
16. Goodwin, *No Ordinary Time*, 520; Kennedy, *Freedom from Fear*, 725.
17. Burns, *The Soldier of Freedom*, 497–502; Goodwin, *No Ordinary Time*, 524–25.
18. Burns, *The Soldier of Freedom*, 506–7; Goodwin, *No Ordinary Time*, 529.
19. Kennedy, *Freedom from Fear*, 731–32; Burns, *The Soldier of Freedom*, 482–84; Neufeld and Berenbaum, eds., *The Bombing of Auschwitz*, 211.

20. Goodwin, *No Ordinary Time*, 537–39.
21. Burns, *The Soldier of Freedom*, 453; Dinnerstein, *Antisemitism in America*, 131–36.
22. Kennedy, *Freedom from Fear*, 737–39.
23. Burns, *The Soldier of Freedom*, 426–27, 519–20; Goodwin, *No Ordinary Time*, 543–44; Kennedy, *Freedom from Fear*, 736–37; Casey, *Cautious Crusade*, 108.
24. Kimball, *Forged in War*, 274–77; Bird, *The Chairman*, 224–25. For the definitive account of the Morgenthau Plan for post-war Germany, see Warren F. Kimball, *Swords or Ploughshares? The Morgenthau Plan for Defeated Nazi Germany, 1943–1945*, (1976).
25. Burns, *The Soldier of Freedom*, 521–26; Goodwin, *No Ordinary Time*, 547–51.
26. Burns, *The Soldier of Freedom*, 525, 530.
27. Bishop, *FDR's Last Year*, 134, 147, 175–96.
28. Burns, *The Soldier of Freedom*, 530; Goodwin, *No Ordinary Time*, 552–53.

Chapter 20

1. Weinberg, "The Allies and the Holocaust," 487–88. With the exception of bombing the death camps, limits on rescue were, in Weinberg's words, "largely the result of German insistence on the sorts of trades and concessions that were impossible - and that [the Germans] knew to be impossible—for the Allies to accept."
2. Neufeld and Berenbaum, eds., *The Bombing of Auschwitz*, viii; 6–7, 102; 240–42, 291–92, fn. 26; Gilbert, *Auschwitz and the Allies*, 190, 207. "Report on Rescue Problems and Activities from July 22 to September 1, 1944," (WJC, MSS Col. 361, A68/2, AJA).
3. Breitman and Kraut, *American Refugee Policy*, 211–12; Gilbert, *Auschwitz and the Allies*, 45, 151, 181, 233; Neufeld and Berenbaum, eds., *The Bombing of Auschwitz*, 249–50; Wyman, ed., *America and the Holocaust* 12:82–86.
4. Gilbert, *Auschwitz and the Allies*, 220–38.
5. Neufeld and Berenbaum, eds., *The Bombing of Auschwitz*, 250–53; Gilbert, *Auschwitz and the Allies*, 237.
6. Neufeld and Berenbaum, eds., *The Bombing of Auschwitz*, 105, 252–53 (Central Zionist Archives, Jerusalem, translation supplied by USHMM and Richard H. Levy).

7. Neufeld and Berenbaum, eds., *The Bombing of Auschwitz*, 105; Levy, "Did Ben-Gurion Reverse His Position on Bombing Auschwitz?," 89–96; Dinah Porat, *The Blue and the Yellow Stars of David* (1990), 216, and Shabtai Teveth, *Ben-Gurion and the Holocaust* (1996) 189–93, claimed Ben-Gurion and the JA changed their minds without direct or documentary evidence; Medoff, "New Perspectives," 254. The FDR critics accept these views uncritically. Levy believes the JA executive did not want to take the moral responsibility for endorsing the bombing proposal but was ambivalent about the issue and therefore allowed Weizmann and Shertok to make the bombing request. If Levy is correct, the JA would then have "deniability" if anything went wrong. Levy may not be correct, as he concedes, but his point—that the JA executive could have wired FDR to bomb the camps and did not—is persuasive. Newton, ed., *FDR and the Holocaust* (seventh on list), 15.

8. Bird, *The Chairman*, 212–13; Neufeld and Berenbaum, eds., *The Bombing of Auschwitz*, 48, 254, Wyman, ed., *America and the Holocaust* 12:103; Rosenheim to Morgenthau, 6-18-44, WRB, Box 42/3, FDRL (Rosenheim letter); 104 (Pehle memo); History of the WRB, 153, FDRL. Gilbert, *Auschwitz and the Allies*, 220, 237–38. "This was no ringing endorsement of the appeal to bomb the Hungarian railways," Richard H. Levy points out, "a fact which Wyman fails to bring out." Neufeld and Berenbaum, eds., *The Bombing of Auschwitz*, 104. See Wyman, *Abandonment of the Jews*, 29. Pehle thought the proposal had no merit at this time. Wyman does not quote Pehle's critical memorandum and downplays Pehle's reaction (*Abandonment of the Jews*, 291). This version left readers with the impression that Pehle seriously promoted the proposal when in fact he did not. Wyman fails to quote Pehle's memorandum in his footnotes. This is a serious omission in the Auschwitz bombing scenario because McCloy was left with the impression that the proposal was not only not *urgent*, but that it was not *serious*.

9. Neufeld and Berenbaum, eds., *The Bombing of Auschwitz*, 257–58, 67; Wyman, ed., *America and the Holocaust* 12:153–54. Pehle to McCloy, 6-29-44 (with Cable 404), WRB, Box 42/3, FDRL; emphasis in the text added. See Wyman, *Abandonment of the Jews*, 295; Neufeld and Berenbaum, eds., *The Bombing of Auschwitz*, 104–5; Gilbert, *Auschwitz and the Allies*, 246–47. Bird, *The Chairman*, 214–15 ("McCloy, however, was never shown Akzin's memo, and Pehle's own doubts and the halfhearted manner in which he conveyed the bombing proposal reinforced McCloy's judgment that this was something the War Department should stay away from").

Wyman in *Abandonment of the Jews* changes Akzin's "might" slow down the slaughter to "would" slow down the slaughter.

10. Hilberg, *Perpetrators Victims, Bystanders*, 232. Kubowitzki to Pehle, July 1, 1944, WRB Box 35, No. 5, FDRL; WRB Box 42/3, FDRL; Copy in MSS Col. 361, D107/1 (emphasis in original); Akzin to Lesser, 6-29-44, WRB Box 42/3, FDRL; Neufeld and Berenbaum, eds., *The Bombing of Auschwitz*, 105, 259; Gilbert, *Auschwitz and the Allies*, 256: Wyman *omits* Kubowitzki's opposition to the bombing and leads the reader to believe he *favored* it. Wyman, *Abandonment of the Jews*, 295. Martin Gilbert cites the Kubowitzki letter in his *Auschwitz and the Allies* (1981), 256.

   Aryeh Leon Kubowitzki, a native of Lithuania who was raised in Belgium, immigrated to the United States in 1940. He became head of the World Jewish Congress European Department. Bird, *The Chairman*, 214.

   The notion that the Germans would blame the Allies for the Holocaust is not far-fetched. In fact, Holocaust deniers *have* blamed the Allies for causing the deaths of concentration camp inmates by bombing transportation networks and medicine factories, which, in turn, led to outbreaks of typhus and other diseases in the concentration camps. Lipstadt, *History on Trial*, 208.

11. Neufeld and Berenbaum, eds., *The Bombing of Auschwitz*, 105–6; Nahum Goldmann to Jan Masaryk, 7-3-44, MSS Col. 361, D107/13, AJA. The AJ Congress and the World Jewish Congress were centrist organizations with a substantial membership and following among American Jews.

12. Neufeld and Berenbaum, eds., *The Bombing of Auschwitz*, 256–71; Bird, *The Chairman*, 211–13. Gilbert, *Auschwitz and the Allies*, 245–47; Wyman, *America and the Holocaust* 12:79.

13. Gilbert, "The Contemporary Case for the Feasibility of Bombing Auschwitz," 65–75; Gilbert, *Auschwitz and the Allies*, 267–69, 273; Levy, "Did Ben-Gurion Reverse His Position on Bombing Auschwitz?," 89–96.

14. Bird, *The Chairman*, 204–05, 217; Gilbert, *Auschwitz and the Allies*, 284; Wyman, *Abandonment of the Jews*, 267, 292–93, 407.

15. Levy, "Did Ben-Gurion Reverse His Position on Bombing Auschwitz?," 48, 107, 260; WRB Records, Box 35, Hungary no. 5, FDRL; WRB, Box 42/3, FDRL, also reproduced in Wyman, ed., *America and the Holocaust*, 12:152; Bird, *The Chairman*, 213–14. German success at holding up the Allied advance was worrisome. With regard to a later McCloy letter, Gilbert agreed that Germany's oil reserves were "still a grave danger to the Allied advance both from east and west. For this reason," Gilbert concludes, "the Americans were at that very moment turning down the . . .

request to bomb the railways" (*Auschwitz and the Allies*, 238, 255). Bird claims that the "single assertion of fact in [McCloy's July 4] letter, that the Auschwitz rail lines could be bombed only by 'diversion of considerable air support,' was not true," as American bombers in Italy had been flying over the camp since that spring (Bird, *The Chairman*, 213–14). But a successful bombing of the camps would have diverted from air support from ongoing "decisive operations" (the Normandy invasion!). There is also no question of the "very doubtful efficacy" of bombing the railway lines. American Jewish leaders at the time understood that.

16. Nichol and Rennell, *The Last Escape*, xiii, 31–37, 61, 196.
17. Gilbert, *Auschwitz and the Allies*, 277–78; Jerusalem telegram no. 97, NA, 840.48, Refugees 17–1144; Levy, "Did Ben-Gurion Reverse His Position on Bombing Auschwitz?," 89–96.
18. Smertenko to Roosevelt, July 24, 1944. Neufeld and Berenbaum, eds., *The Bombing of Auschwitz*, 271–73, citing National Archives, State Dept. 840.48 Refugees/7–2444, asreproduced in Wyman, ed., *America and the Holocaust*, 12:159–61)]; Rapoport, *Shake Heaven and Earth*, 57; Wyman, ed., *America and the Holocaust*, 12:159–61; Smertenko to FDR, 7-24-44, Hassett memos 7-28-44, 8-5-44, WRB Box 42, FDRL.
19. It is not clear exactly what happened in regard to the telegrams and Hungarian knowledge of them. Gilbert, *Auschwitz and the Allies*, 258, 266, 275, 281, 286, 292; Levy, "The Bombing of Auschwitz Revisited," 108–11; Rubinstein, *The Myth of Rescue*, 195.
20. Müller, *Anne Frank*, 183–85, 217, 230–47.
21. Hirschmann, *Caution to the Winds*, 172. It was remarkable that Hirschmann's firsthand account of the firm and personal support he got from FDR, as well as from Cox, Lubin, Hopkins, and others, published in his memoir, *Caution to the Winds* in 1962, does not appear in the Roosevelt critics' version of history. Neither Wyman nor Feingold mention it at all. Feingold is happy to quote Hirschmann's negative assessment of the Évian Conference of 1938 but does not quote Hirschmann on FDR's efforts to personally save Jews. The most the reader gets from Feingold is that "Roosevelt gave the [Brand] mission his personal endorsement." All we learn from Wyman is that continued negotiations in the Brand affair had "the express concurrence of President Roosevelt." Feingold, *The Politics of Rescue*, 33, 272, citing *Caution to the Winds*, 114–16; Wyman, *Abandonment of the Jews*, 244. Wyman's footnote does not cite Hirschmann's memoir when obviously he was aware of it, as it is cited elsewhere—in his notes, 353. Morse

does not give the full picture of White House support for Hirschmann but he does quote the president telling Hirschmann to "cable back everything you hear" (*While Six Million Died*, 356–57). Lookstein and Friedman omitted it altogether. Penkower mentioned Lubin's code word to contact "the Boss" and the Roosevelt letter (obtained, he says by Pehle via Lubin) but did not tell the reader the extent of Roosevelt's involvement. Penkower omitted Roosevelt's personal meeting with and direct instructions to Hirschmann on the Brand affair (*The Jews Were Expendable*, 164, 170, 188).

22. Bird, *The Chairman*, 218; Hirschmann memo to Ambassador Steinhardt, 6-22-24, ASW 400.38 Jews, Box 44, RG 107, NA; Breitman and Kraut, *American Refugee Policy*, 215; Elon, *Timetable*, 212; Gilbert, *Auschwitz and the Allies*, 225, 242.

23. Gilbert, *Auschwitz and the Allies*, 270, 278. According to Levy, "Apparently no appeal to bomb the death camps was transmitted from Jerusalem to Washington." While Gruenbaum claimed in 1961 that he had sent telegrams to Stalin, Churchill, and Roosevelt to bomb Auschwitz, no such documentary evidence existed, nor did Gruenbaum have the authority of the JAE to do so. Levy, "The Bombing of Auschwitz Revisited," 106; Levy, "Did Ben-Gurion reverse his position on bombing Auschwitz?"

24. Gilbert, *Auschwitz and the Allies*, 280 (a ruse); Wyman, *Abandonment of the Jews*, 243–44 (a separate peace); Dwork and van Pelt, *Holocaust*, 322–23, 329–30; "History of the WRB," 215, FDRL.

25. Gilbert, *Auschwitz and the Allies*, 269, 300, 313–14.

26. Kubowitzki to McCloy, August 9, 1944, reproduced in Neufeld and Berenbaum, eds., *The Bombing of Auschwitz*, 273–74. National Archives, RG 107, Assistant Secretary of War Files, 400.38 Countries C-D-E-F (Box 151), also reproduced in Wyman, ed., *America and the Holocaust* 12:164. Pehle's letter of August 3, 1944, transmitting Frischer's letter to Kubowitzki, and Kubowitzki to McCloy August 9, 1944, MSS Col. 361, D107/13, AJA. A copy of this letter is on display at the U. S. Holocaust Memorial Museum in Washington, but without Kubowitzki's first letter of July 1, 1944, opposing the bombing of Auschwitz or his later letter of August 30, 1944, reiterating his opposition, or indeed any of the true context of the letter. As a result, the display is misleading.

27. Wyman, *America and the Holocaust* 12: 164; Levy, "The Bombing of Auschwitz Revisited," 113; Kubowitzki to Pehle, July 1, 1944 (in Neufeld and Berenbaum, eds., *The Bombing of Auschwitz*, 259–60); Kubowitzki to Pehle, August 9, 1944 (in Neufeld and Berenbaum, eds., *The Bombing of*

Auschwitz, 273–74); Kubowitzki to Pehle, August 8, 1944, WRB Box 42/3, FDRL; Kubowitzki to Frischer, August 2, 1944 MSS 361, D107/13, AJA. My thanks to Rabbi Anthony Holtz and Jerry Zucker for the meaning of *hayei sha'ah*.

28. Neufeld and Berenbaum, eds., *The Bombing of Auschwitz*, 274. NA, RG 107, Assistant Secretary of War Files, 400.38 Countries C-D-E-F (Box 151), also reproduced in Wyman, ed., *America and the Holocaust*, 12:165, transcript supplied by USHMM; Gilbert, *Auschwitz and the Allies*, 303. While many authors have ridiculed McCloy's concern about "more vindictive action," Feingold explained that the Germans could have begun killing American pilots and other POWs. *Bearing Witness*, 266.

29. Wyman, ed., *America and the Holocaust*, 12:165; Neufeld and Berenbaum, eds., 122–23, 274–75; Gilbert, *Auschwitz and the Allies*, 303–7; Medoff, *The Deafening Silence*, 158–59; I. L. Kenen, "Report of Meeting with John W. Pehle, Executive Director, and Messrs. Lesser and Friedman of the War Refugee Board, August 16, 1944," and Memo, Eugene Hevesi to Dr. Slawson, August 17, 1944; YIVO Institute Archives, American Jewish Committee Collective, Record Group 347.1.29, Series EXO-29 (Waldman Papers). An excerpt was quoted in Letter to the Editor, *AJH* 86 (March 1996), 113–14. The representatives were from the American Jewish Committee, Vaad Ha-Hazalah, WJC, the Jewish Labor Committee, and the American Jewish Conference, which in turn represented more than fifty well-known organizations, including B'nai B'rith, Hadassah, the Jewish War Veterans, Union of American Hebrew Congregations, Union of Orthodox Jewish Congregations, and the Central Conference of American Rabbis. Levy, "Did Ben-Gurion Reverse His Position on Bombing Auschwitz?," 94. Levy points out that Wyman omits any mention of this important meeting (96, fn. 11).

30. Kubowitzki to I. M. Weinstein, August 29, 1944; Kubowitzki to Pehle, August 29, 1944; Kubowitzki to McCloy, August 30, 1944, MSS 361, D107/13, AJA (emphasis in original).

31. McCloy to Kubowitzki, September 3, 1944, MSS 361, D107/13, AJA; Frischer to WJC, September 15, 1944, MSS 361, D107/13, AJA.

32. Kubowitzki to the WJC Office Committee, July 21, 1944, MSS Col. 361 (WJC), Box D107, Folder 3, AJA; Minutes of WJC office committee meeting, October 8, 1944, p. 1, MSS Col. 361, Box D107, Folder 3, AJA.

33. Minutes of WJC office committee, October 8, 1944, p. 2, MSS Col. 361 (WJC), Box D107, Folder 3, AJA.

34. Gilbert, *Auschwitz and the Allies*, 312; War Refugee Board, Box 34, "Measures Directed Towards Halting Persecutions," F: Hungary, no. 5, FDRL, WRB Box 42/3, FDRL, Akzin to Pehle, September 2, 1944; minutes of office committee (9-21-44), WJC MSS Col. 361, D114/5, AJA. Nichol and Rennell, *The Last Escape*, 37–38, 192–93, 350–51.

35. Kubowitzki to Kapustin, October 1, 1944; Kubowitzki to Soviet ambassador, October 8, 1944, MSS 361, D107/13, AJA.

36. WJC minutes of office committee, October 20, 1944, MSS Col. 361, D114/5, AJA; Kubowitzki to Pehle, October 1, 1944, MSS Col. 361, D107/13, AJA; Gilbert, *Auschwitz and the Allies*, 322; Neufeld and Berenbaum, eds., *The Bombing of Auschwitz*, 277, Wyman, ed., *America and the Holocaust*, 12:169; Gilbert, *Auschwitz and the Allies*, 320–21; Pehle to McCloy, 10-3-44, WRB Box 42/3, FDRL.

37. Neufeld and Berenbaum, eds., *The Bombing of Auschwitz*, 49; Wyman, ed., *America and the Holocaust* 12:174.

38. Müller, *Anne Frank*, 251, 256–59.

39. Gilbert, *Auschwitz and the Allies*, 325; *Holocaust*, 701–2, 752–54, 761–62, 767–68; Penkower, *The Jews Were Expendable*, 206.

40. Pehle to Hirschmann, 11-28-44, WRB Box 7, Folder "German Extermination Camps"; Kubowitzki to McCloy, 10-16-44 (Germans will destroy camps and inmates), MSS 361, D107/13, AJA.

41. Neufeld and Berenbaum, eds., *The Bombing of Auschwitz*, 49–50, 278–80; Gilbert, *Auschwitz and the Allies*, 328; Wyman, *America and the Holocaust* 12:175–76, 182–83; Bird, *The Chairman*, 220–21; Gilbert, *Auschwitz and the Allies*, 328.

42. Gilbert, *Auschwitz and the Allies*, 327–31; WRB press release, November, 1944, MSS Col. 361, D107/2, AJA.

43. Gilbert, *Auschwitz and the Allies*, 331–37. The last gassings at Auschwitz occurred on November 28, 1944, (Rubinstein, *The Myth of Rescue*, 164).

44. Neufeld and Berenbaum, eds., *The Bombing of Auschwitz*, 122, 318, n. 2; Wyman, 410, n. 78.

45. Mintz, "Why Didn't We Bomb Auschwitz? Can John McCloy's memories be correct?" "An exhaustive search made in 1983 by *Washington Post* reporter Morton Mintz showed that the bombing proposals almost certainly did not reach Roosevelt." Wyman, *Abandonment of the Jews*, 410, fn. 78; Neufeld and Berenbaum, eds., *The Bombing of Auschwitz*, 122–24. Breitman and Kraut believed it was likely that FDR knew about the proposal through McCloy (*American Refugee Policy*, 247).

46. Transcript of Interview of John J. McCloy by Henry Morgenthau III, 11–13, FDRL.

47. Burns, *The Soldier of Freedom*, 490–95, 545. Roosevelt considered himself to be, in fact, the commander in chief, and he relished the role. According to Burns he had a close rapport with his military chieftains, was deferential to military leaders, reluctant to override them, and rarely interfered in military matters as the war went on. Henry Stimson said that his record "was unique in American war history for its scrupulous abstention from personal and political pressure."

Chapter 21

1. Gen. George S. Patton Jr. quoted in Bradley, *A Soldier's Story*; Goodwin, *No Ordinary Time*, 564–65; Perkins, *The Roosevelt I Knew*, 390; Kennedy, *Freedom from Fear*, 739–41; Stokesbury, *A Short History of World War II*, 354.

2. Kennedy, *Freedom from Fear*, 724–45; Burns, *The Soldier of Freedom*, 557–58.

3. Goodwin, *No Ordinary Time*, 572–73; Perkins, *The Roosevelt I Knew*, 391–94; Kennedy, *Freedom from Fear*, 798.

4. Goodwin, *No Ordinary Time*, 573–74, 580–82; Burns, *The Soldier of Freedom*, 564–73; Bishop, *FDR's Last Year*, 385–86; Kennedy, *Freedom from Fear*, 799–805.

5. Bohlen, *Witness to History*, 212; Eddy, *FDR Meets Ibn Saud*, 11–13; Burns, *The Soldier of Freedom*, 577–78; Penkower, *Decision on Palestine Deferred*, 329–30. Historians interpret facts, but the same facts can support varying interpretations. Take Roosevelt's remark to Stalin about his trip to see Ibn Saud in March 1944 as an example. The facts are easily ascertained. First FDR had a conversation with Stalin at Yalta in which he said he was pro-Zionist and was going to stop off and see Saud. Roosevelt's translator Charles E. Bohlen wrote later in his memoir *Witness to History, 1929–1969*: "Stalin asked what he [FDR] was going to give the King. The President replied, with a smile, that there was only one concession that he thought he might offer and that was to give Ibn Saud the six million Jews in the United States" (212).

This statement can be portrayed in several ways: Frank Freidel: "Roosevelt joked . . . that he might offer the king the six million Jews in the United States" (*Franklin D. Roosevelt: A Rendezvous with Destiny*, 594). Warren Kimball: "FDR . . . reverted to the worst kind of WASP country club humor, suggesting he might offer six million Jews from the United States" (*Forged in*

War, 318–19). Monty Penkower: "Did the President intend to make any concessions to the latter?, asked the Soviet warlord. There was only one concession he thought he might offer, FDR replied: 'to give him the six million Jews in the United States'" (*Decision on Palestine Deferred*, 330).

These different portrayals of Bohlen's memoirs (which we assume are correct) reflect the authors' views of FDR. Penkower's portrayal reflects a classic Roosevelt decrier technique of putting a negative spin on an unimportant event. Obviously Roosevelt critics do not believe Roosevelt was going to ship six million American Jews to Arabia. But what was obviously a joke to Friedel and Kimball (albeit a tasteless joke to our twenty-first century ears) becomes a negative statement to Penkower, omitting the characterization that it was, after all, a joke.

The comment to Stalin is a trivial matter compared to the important fact of Roosevelt's visit with Ibn Saud after Yalta in which the president tried through personal diplomacy to single-handedly convince Saud to cooperate with the creation of a Jewish state. Roosevelt was a dying man in his fourth term as president with no thought of running for political office again. So his motivation to resolve the dispute between Jews and Arabs was obviously to help the Jewish people and to make good on his campaign pledge to secure a Jewish homeland. The United States had a vital interest in friendship with the Arab nations, trade, oil, and military alliances as well as concerns about a Jewish state.

In trying to ferret out Roosevelt's true feelings toward Jews, does the historian give greater weight to his sincere efforts to convince Saud of the merits of the Zionist case, or to his WASP country club humor? To ask the question is to answer it.

6. Eddy, *FDR Meets Ibn Saud*, 14; Penkower, *Decision on Palestine Deferred*, 330–31; Burns, *The Soldier of Freedom*, 578.
7. Eddy, *FDR Meets Ibn Saud*, 29–30.
8. Eddy, *FDR Meets Ibn Saud*, 31.
9. Eddy, *FDR Meets Ibn Saud*, 34; FRUS, 1945, vol. 8, 2–3; Penkower, *Decision on Palestine Deferred*, 332 and fn. 7; Bohlen, *Witness to History*, 212.
10. Eddy, *FDR Meets Ibn Saud*, 34–35; Bohlen, *Witness to History*, 213; Penkower, *Decision on Palestine Deferred*, 332–33.
11. Grose, *Israel in the Mind of America*, 154.
12. Ibid.
13. Ibid., 155.
14. Ibid.

15. Ibid.
16. Ibid., 114. On October 15, 1944, just before the presidential election, Roosevelt wrote Senator Robert F. Wagner of New York and asked him to convey his "cordial greetings" to the delegates of the annual convention of the Zionist Organization of America and to remind them of the Democratic Party platform on Palestine, namely unrestricted Jewish immigration and the establishment of a Jewish state, and that Roosevelt would "help to bring about . . . [the] realization of the Jewish state" (FRUS, 1944, vol. V, 615–16).
17. Ibid., 115–16, 138–39.
18. Ibid., 139–41. In Cairo in 1943, Churchill said, "I am committed to the establishment of a Jewish state in Palestine and the President will accept nothing less." This was Roosevelt's public and private position. Churchill was well aware of Roosevelt's Zionist sympathies. He played on them in August 1942 when he cautioned Roosevelt to be careful about expanding on the principles of the Atlantic Charter in an anniversary statement. (Churchill was concerned about the self-determination of Britain's colonies in India, Asia, and Africa. In the Middle East he told Roosevelt "the Arabs might claim by majority they could expel the Jews from Palestine, or at any time forbid all further immigration." (Kimball, ed., *Churchill and Roosevelt: The Complete Correspondence*, I:557.)
19. Grose, *Israel in the Mind of America*, 141–47.
20. Ibid., 148–50.
21. Ibid., 150–56.
22. Beschloss, *The Conquerors*, 12.
23. Ibid., 7.
24. Baker, *Days of Sorrow and Pain*, 316–19; Müller, *Anne Frank*, 262; Teveth, *Ben-Gurion*, 868–69.
25. Sherwood, *Roosevelt and Hopkins*, 877–80.
26. Bishop, *FDR's Last Year*, 577; Goodwin, *No Ordinary Time*, 598–2.
27. Grose, *Israel in the Mind of America*, 156–59; Goodwin, *No Ordinary Time*, 601–02.
28. Ward, ed., *Closest Companion*, 418–19.
29. Kershaw, *Hitler, 1936–1945*, 791–92; Shirer, *The Rise and Fall of the Third Reich*, 1110.
30. Sherwood, *Roosevelt and Hopkins*, 880; Goodwin, *No Ordinary Time*, 606.
31. Leahy, *I Was There*, 344; Bishop, *FDR's Last Year*, 608.
32. Kershaw, *Hitler, 1936–1945*, 820–29.

Chapter 22

1. Butler quote: David Hackett Fischer, *Historians' Fallacies*, 197.
2. Nichol and Rennell, *The Last Escape*, 51–55, 471.
3. Breitman, *Official Secrets*, 167.
4. D'Este, *Eisenhower*, 686–87. For similar recollections of OSS operatives see Richard Breitman and others, eds., *U.S. Intelligence and the Nazis*, 11–12. Wyman acknowledges that the first firsthand knowledge of the Holocaust was shocking to military men and hardened war correspondents (*The Abandonment of the Jews*, 325).
5. Bauer, *The Holocaust in Historical Perspective*, 7–8 ("The post-Holocaust generation has difficulty understanding this basic psychological barrier to action."); Young-Bruehl, *Hannah Arendt*, 184–85.
6. Grose, *Israel in the Mind of America*, 126–27.
7. Teveth, *Ben-Gurion*, 850–60; Gilbert, *Auschwitz and the Allies*, 295.
8. The minutes of the office committee of the WJC of June 8, 1944, MSS 361, A71/2, AJA. MSS Col. 361 (WJC), Box D107, folder 12, AJA.
9. Bird, *The Chairman*, 206.
10. Gilbert, *Auschwitz and the Allies*, 170.
11. Bauer, *The Holocaust in Historical Perspective*, 19; Laqueur, *The Terrible Secret*, esp. 3.
12. Novick, *The Holocaust in American Life*, 23.
13. De Jong, *Netherlands and Nazi Germany*, 6.
14. Ponting, *Armageddon*, 208, 240.
15. Newton, ed., *FDR and the Holocaust*, 41 (Dallek), 43 (Berlin); Berlin, *Personal Impressions*, 25, 27.
16. Overy, *Why the Allies Won*, 263; Hirschmann to Lubin, 4-20-44, OF 5477, WRB 1944–45, Box 4, FDRL.
17. Herzstein, *Roosevelt and Hitler*, 414; Newton, ed., *FDR and the Holocaust*, 14, 16; Penkower, "In Dramatic Dissent," 389; Breitman and Kraut, *American Refugee Policy*, 156.
18. Museum of Jewish Heritage: A Living Memorial to the Holocaust, New York City ("Ours to Fight For," 2004). Visit to Jewish Heritage Museum, NYC, June 17, 2004.
19. Goodwin, *No Ordinary Time*, 606.
20. Dawidowicz, "American Jews and the Holocaust," 47.
21. Dawidowicz, *What is the Use of Jewish History?*, 164.
22. Kimball, *The Juggler*, 7.
23. Nichols, *Uneasy Alliance*, 60; Nicholas, *Cruel World*, 165.

24. Nicholas, *Cruel World*, 186–92. Only sixteen thousand children came to the United States.

25. Druks, *The Failure to Rescue*, 3; Feingold, *The Politics of Rescue*, 296; *Bearing Witness*, 177; Wistrich, *Hitler and the Holocaust*, 57–8, 168; Wyman, *Paper Walls*, 209–11. The conference "showed the Western world frozen in its unwillingness to provide new homes for the German Jews" (Wyman, ix); Évian demonstrated "the gulf between the professed good intentions of the Administration and the implementation of policy" (Feingold, *The Politics of Rescue*, 296). The IGCR was a "monument to the Administration's impotence." Feingold conceded that Roosevelt's calling of the conference was "astonishing because Roosevelt chose to intrude into a situation in which he was virtually powerless to act, bound as he was by a highly restrictive immigration law" (*Bearing Witness*, 75); *The Politics of Rescue*, chapter 2 ("Roosevelt was keenly aware that he ran a political risk," 23).

26. Wyman, *The Abandonment of the Jews*, 6–9, 151, 210, 316–17. In *The Politics of Rescue* Feingold acknowledged that between 1938 and 1941 "most people" agreed that an effort to change the immigration laws "would have been futile" (126). But in a later essay, "The Government Response," he stated that "the greatest possibilities for rescue existed during the first phase of the crisis, from November 1938 to June 1941" (Friedlander and Milton, eds., *The Holocaust: Ideology, Bureaucracy, and Genocide*, 246). Feingold acknowledged that Roosevelt could not get the immigration laws changed even if he tried in 1938–1941 and he knew that in 1938–1941 the Holocaust was still in the future. No one knew anything about gas and ovens (they were not used until December 1941).

27. Wyman, *Paper Walls*, 44–5; Breitman and Kraut, *American Refugee Policy*, chap. 11.

28. Rubinstein, *The Myth of Rescue*, 35; Overy, *Penguin Historical Atlas of the Third Reich*, 360.

29. Laqueur, ed., *The Holocaust Encyclopedia*, 6.

30. Rubinstein, *The Myth of Rescue*, 16; Medoff, *The Deafening Silence*, chap. 2 and 3; Friedman, *No Haven for the Oppressed*, chap. 1–3; Marrus, *Holocaust in History*, 164–65; Berenbaum, *World Must Know*, 56 ("There was no place to go").

31. In September 1939, the German Jewish population was 185,000, meaning that 340,000 German Jews (65 percent) had escaped to Britain, Western Europe, the United States, Latin America, or other countries (Rubinstein, *The Myth of Rescue*, 17–9, 25).

32. Rubinstein, *The Myth of Rescue*, 33–5, 41, 64; Weinberg, "The Allies and the Holocaust," 480; Berenbaum and Peck, eds., *Holocaust and History*; Breitman and Kraut, *American Refugee Policy*, chap. 11. When the German quota was combined with the Austrian quota the total was 27,370 per year.
33. See chap. 6.
34. Novick, *The Holocaust in American Life*, 52; Breitman and Kraut, *American Refugee Policy*, 235.
35. Not all historians are critical of FDR and American Jews regarding the *St. Louis*. Irwin F. Gellman wrote a relatively accurate scholarly essay, "The *St. Louis* Tragedy." Howard M. Sachar, who has no bias against FDR, is one of the few historians who more of less correctly summarized the *St. Louis* episode and explained the pivotal role of the Joint, although he omitted the role of the Roosevelt administration. (*A History of the Jews in America*, 492–93). Ronald Sanders also correctly summarized the incident in *Shores of Refuge: A Hundred Years of Jewish Immigration*, 466–67, as did Martin Gilbert in *The Holocaust*, 80.

Nonetheless, most well-respected historians relied on the Roosevelt decriers' many books and articles and got the story wrong. A prominent scholar, Leni Yahil in *The Holocaust*, claims "the Germans loaded more than nine hundred Jews" onto the ship; that the "major part" of the refugees went to the four countries but "the rest of the refugees met the dreaded fate [being sent to a concentration camp] at Hamburg" (119). All Professor Robert S. Wistrich told his readers in *Hitler and the Holocaust* was: "The American government callously turned back German Jewish refugees on the ocean liner *Saint Louis*" (189). Conrad Black, author of the acclaimed biography *Franklin Delano Roosevelt: Champion of Freedom* omitted Roosevelt's positive role, criticized him for failing to "muscle the Cuban president on the issue," omitted the heroic role of the Joint (and instead criticizes the Joint), and then stated that "the admirable performance of Captain Schroeder led to Belgium's admitting the *St. Louis* and its passengers (493–95). David M. Kennedy got the story wrong in *Freedom from Fear*, a highly respected volume in the distinguished Oxford History of the United States series. It appears that Kennedy relied on Morse (See p. 415). What then are local historians such as Selma S. Lewis, who wrote a history of the Jews of Memphis, to do? They rely, with justification, on the Roosevelt decriers. Thus without a footnote, she told her readers (because she presumably knew the fairy tale version of the *St. Louis*) that a "few passengers were admitted to Britain, Holland, and France. Many of the refugees on board later died in extermination camps" (*A Biblical People in the Bible Belt*, 158).

36. Morgenthau interview of John Pehle, 24, FDRL; Davis, *Into the Storm*, 370–71, 655 ("I have leaned heavily upon Morse").

37. "Wiesel . . . is the bearer not of intellectual analysis but of a moral message," Steinweis, "Reflections on the Holocaust from Nebraska," 167–68.

Lookstein, *Were We Our Brothers' Keepers?*, 10. In his chapter "The Saddest Ship Afloat," Rabbi Lookstein berated every Jewish organization in America for not protesting the handling of the *St. Louis* episode when he ought to have known that the Joint, a well-known component of the American Jewish organizational network, existed to address the problem. The "lesson" of Lookstein's history is that American Jews failed as their brothers' keepers, when in fact they succeeded brilliantly.

According to the Jewish Virtual Library, the "passengers returned to Europe in June 1939. With World War II just months away, many of these passengers were sent East with the occupation of the countries to which they had been sent." www.us-israel.org/jsource/Holocaust/stlouis.html. The reader gets the false impression that the roundup of Jews began in 1939 not three years later, in 1942. This same fallacious reasoning appeared in *The World Must Know*, the U. S. Holocaust Memorial Museum's history of the Holocaust by Michael Berenbaum: "For a while, the sad voyage of the *St. Louis* seemed to have a happy ending. . . . But within months, the Nazis overran Western Europe. Only the 228 passengers who disembarked in England were safe. Of the rest, only a few survived the Holocaust." This is a distortion both of the chronology of events and the number of passengers. Poland, not Western Europe, was overrun in months. Most of the *St. Louis* passengers survived the Holocaust. As William Rubinstein observed, this logic means that all world leaders were guilty for not knowing that Hitler would conquer France, Belgium, and the Netherlands, totally reverse his policy from persecuting and exiling Jews to exterminating them, and that three years later, in 1942, Jews would be rounded up. "The writing of history cannot easily be more illogical or misleading," Rubinstein correctly concluded (Berenbaum, *World Must Know*, 58; Rubinstein, *The Myth of Rescue*, 62).

It does not appear that Lookstein examined the records of the Joint because if he had, he would have learned that in 1939 American Jews knew which organization was charged with the task of saving the passengers on the *St. Louis*, and they loudly demanded that the Joint do so. To his credit,

Lookstein did describe the political reality that no force on Earth could change America's strict immigration laws, and he did inform his readers in passing that the Joint saved all the passengers on the *St. Louis*. A fellow rabbi, Barry J. Konovitch, published "*The Fiftieth Anniversary of the St. Louis: What Really Happened*" in the academic journal *American Jewish History* in 1989. Because of the "callous decrees" of the State Department, the lack of "moral courage" of the American Jewish community, and a president who "refused to interfere in an internal Cuban affair . . . 907 Jews sailed back to Europe, most to their deaths," Konovitch erroneously concluded. This, Konovitch told us, foretold "the complicity of the Western democracies in the destruction of European Jewry." These allegations are demonstrably false. As we have seen, the passengers of the *St. Louis* were not taken off the ship in June 1939 and executed as a result of a callous "decree" of the State Department while cowardly American Jews looked on. Konovitch even stated as a fact that there was "a direct communication from Washington to Havana requesting that the Jews not be given passes to disembark because they would eventually request permission to continue on to the United States" (207). And what was the proof of this outrageous calumny against the United States? State Department records? Telegrams? Letters? No. Interviews in 1989 (fifty years after the event) with five unidentified people (presumably some former passengers of the *St. Louis*), including Manuel Benitez Valdez (the former Immigration Director's nephew). Over coffee fifty years later Yudel Steinberg and Ben Volpe (not further identified) told Mr. Konovitch in a gossip session about a document that no one to date has located, including Messrs. Konovitch, Steinberg, and Volpe.

38. Ed Koch, former mayor of New York City and a member of the United States Holocaust Memorial Museum Council, has joined the Roosevelt decriers. "Every Jew is a Holocaust survivor," he told the Third National Conference of the David S. Wyman Institute for Holocaust Studies (New York, September 18, 2005), "because Hitler wanted to kill every Jew in the world." Yet despite Roosevelt's success in thwarting Hitler's plan, Koch told the conference and Medoff that "I am sure [FDR] is in purgatory, for his sin of abandoning the Jews" (*Jewish Community Chronicle*, May 11, 2005).

Thomas and Morgan-Witts, *Voyage of the Damned* (1994), 252. The cable "was to become typical of the attitude of the American government to the entire affair" (*Voyage of the Damned*, 1994, 155); "no instructions . . . from the White House," (240); "the millionaire Morgenthau" did not think much of Hull (250).

Gordon Thomas and Max Witts published *Voyage of the Damned* in 1974. It described the efforts of American diplomats but blamed the State Department, "itself filled with its share of prejudiced men," for not allowing the *St. Louis* passengers to land in the United States. They blamed "Franklin Roosevelt, the 'liberal' president, but always a president mindful of public opinion" for not overruling the State Department, leaving the reader with the erroneous impression that the president could have somehow circumvented the immigration laws, a power he did not possess.

Roosevelt's sins somehow worsened between 1974 and 1994. In the 1994 edition of *Voyage of the Damned*, the authors blamed Roosevelt as "the man who finally prevented the *St. Louis* from discharging its passengers onto United States soil, fearing the political backlash." Roosevelt, of course, did not "prevent" the passengers from coming to the United States. Congress and the American people (83 percent of whom did not support changing the immigration quotas) "prevented" it, only in the sense that American immigration laws, enacted in the 1920s, limited immigration of all aliens. The authors' condescending and moralizing tone emphasized the alleged *failure* of the American government to solve the problem by allowing refugees to enter the United States, while downplaying the actual *success* of the American government in helping the Joint place the refugees in safe havens.

39. Auschwitz was built to murder Jews from all over Europe. According to Martin Gilbert, on July 15, 1942, more than three years after the docking of the *St. Louis* at Antwerp, the first deportees were sent from Holland to Auschwitz (*The Holocaust*, 375). Perrett, *Days of Sadness Years of Triumph*, 96; Hertzberg, *Jews in America*, 293. Hertzberg's statement is a perfect example of Thomas Macaulay's warning to historians that "He who is deficient in the art of selection [of facts] may, by showing nothing but the truth, produce the effect of grossest falsehood." Macaulay quoted in Fischer, *Historians' Fallacies*, 65. Hertzberg is a member of the Academic Council of the David S. Wyman Institute for Holocaust Studies. Medoff, *The Deafening Silence*, 60–1; Druks, *The Failure to Rescue*, 3, 17–25.

The leadership of the Joint attracted as much criticism as Roosevelt himself. An Israeli historian, Gulie Ne'eman Arad, writing in the late 1990s, informed her readers in *America, Its Jews, and the Rise of Nazism* that the "tragic saga of the *St. Louis* was another instance when American Jews could do little other than unburden their feelings of shame." American Jews were too scared to appeal to their own government, she claimed. "The Jewish leadership was virtually paralyzed," she asserted. Her readers never learned that the *St. Louis* passengers were saved by the Joint, the "President's Jews" (her words), and quite *unparalyzed* American Jewish leaders, including many close to Roosevelt. Arad, *America, Its Jews, and the Rise of Nazism,* 204–5, 275, n. 95; on FDR, 163–67. Arad misapprehended what the State Department tried to do in Cuba. "Rather ironically," she wrote, "the State Department did try, but unsuccessfully, to pressure the Cuban government to provide refuge for the passengers." The author did not describe what the State Department actually did do.

Professor Druks's *The Failure to Rescue* contained an intemperate chapter, "The Seas of Indifference," which denounced the "Jews of America and their organizations" as "inept," "weak, badly disunited, and afraid." He never informed the reader that the Joint actually saved the passengers from returning to Germany at that time. He ridiculed the Joint, claiming it was only concerned about its prestige.

Medoff, in *The Deafening Silence,* blamed American Jewish leaders for failing to demand that the Roosevelt administration allow the passengers on the *St. Louis* to enter the United States. "The *St. Louis* episode," Medoff told his readers, "was a painfully embarrassing reminder of the hesitancy and impotence of the American Jewish leadership" and that the ship was turned away "while U.S. Jewish leaders looked on in silence" (Medoff, 60–61). Medoff relied on Morse and Thomas and Witts (197). The author appeared to be oblivious to the most important fact about the *St. Louis* episode, namely that the Joint saved the passengers from going back to Germany and that Jewish-American leaders were in constant communication with the secretary of state, the undersecretary of state, and the Jewish secretary of the treasury.

Medoff never told the reader that it was the Joint and American government officials, including many American Jewish leaders, who saved the passengers. These bothersome facts contradicted the thesis of Medoff's book. While Medoff stated that an "agreement was reached" for the refugees to enter various countries, he omitted the easily accessible story of *who* reached the agreement (the supposedly "cowardly" American Jewish leaders) and *how* they did it—with extensive help from the Roosevelt administration (Medoff, 59–62).

Medoff went so far as to claim, as others have since, that the "deafening silence of the American Jewish leadership during the *St. Louis* crisis sent a powerful message to Hitler" and because of the *St. Louis* episode, the "Führer could now rest assured that he could deal with the Jews as he pleased." Hitler now saw, according to Medoff, that the "nations of the free world . . . would take no concrete action" on behalf of Jews. Of course, if Hitler read the newspapers, he would have seen exactly the opposite on this particular occasion (Medoff, *The Deafening Silence*, 59–62). Medoff was coauthor with Wyman of *A Race against Death: Peter Bergson, America, and the Holocaust* (2002) and is director of the David S. Wyman Institute for Holocaust Studies. See www.wymaninstitute.org. This group seems dedicated to promoting the Roosevelt-decrier, America-as-bystander version of American history.

40. *Newsweek*, May 21, 2001, 32. "When the facts become the legend, print the legend," the cynical newspaperman in the movie *The Man Who Shot Liberty Valance* exclaimed. Quoted by Frederick Taylor, *Dresden* (New York: Harper Collins, 2004), xi.

In Peter Wyden's book *Stella*, the story of Stella Goldschlag, a Jewish woman who hunted Jews for the Gestapo, we are told that there were 1,107 on the *St. Louis* and that two hundred passengers "were returned to Hamburg and the mercies of the Nazis," including Manfred Kübler, Stella's first husband. Wyden calls Roosevelt "that flawed Messiah, the politician Franklin D. Roosevelt." Not surprisingly, Wyden relies on Professor David S. Wyman, citing his "painstaking work" and thanking him for his assistance in writing his book (Peter Wyden, *Stella*, 84–87, 347).

Deborah E. Lipstadt in *Beyond Belief* (1986) blamed the U. S. government for failing to act. Her chapter title was "Barring the Gates to Children and Refugee Ships." "The *only* action taken by the American government," she told us, "was the dispatch of a Coast Guard cutter . . . to apprehend any passenger who might jump overboard in an attempt to swim ashore and return them to the ship." There was no footnote and no evidence to support this allegation (118–19). Lipstadt acknowledged that one "cannot totally discount these fears" of an influx of an unreasonable number of refugees.

Wyman's PBS documentary "*America and the Holocaust: Deceit and Indifference*" told viewers that the passengers' pleas to Roosevelt "fell on deaf ears," which is not true and omitted any mention of the successful efforts of the Joint and the Roosevelt administration in saving the passengers.

41. William D. Rubinstein observed in *The Myth of Rescue* that in order to blame the future Allies for the *St. Louis*, one had to believe "the leaders of France (with a standing army of 1.5 million men), Belgium and the Netherlands (neutral in the First World War) were blindly moronic" for not knowing that they would soon be conquered by Germany and that three

years later the Jews of Western Europe would be deported and murdered, "something unimaginable by anyone in 1939" (62).

42. Suberman, *When It Was Our War*, 6–7.
43. Rosenman, ed., 1941 volume, *PPA*, 390; Mayer, *Why Did the Heavens Not Darken?* 10.
44. "State Department Bulletin," statement to the press, December 17, 1942; Wyman, *America and the Holocaust*, 1:113.
45. Wistrich, *Hitler and the Holocaust*. Wistrich is on the Academic Council of the David S. Wyman Institute for Holocaust Studies. www.wymaninstitute.org. He is listed as a professor at the Vidal Sassoon International Center for the Study of Antisemitism, Hebrew University. Beschloss, *The Conquerors*, 38–9, 323. See also fn. 18, chap. 11 above.
46. Lipstadt, *Beyond Belief*, 251; Feingold, *The Politics of Rescue*, 173.
47. Laurie, *Propaganda Warriors*, 49–52; Novick, *The Holocaust in American Life*, 26. Jewish writers, including Leo Roston, at OWI agreed with this strategy (27).
48. FRUS, 1943, vol. I, 768–69; Rosenman, ed., *PPA* 1943 vol., 498.
49. *PPA*, vol. 1943, 499; Penkower, *The Jews Were Expendable*, 136; Gilbert, *Auschwitz and the Allies*, 159–61; Lookstein, *Were We Our Brothers' Keepers?*, 171–72. Wyman, *The Abandonment of the Jews*, 154. Niles to Early, 11-4-43, OF 5152, FDRL. FDR decriers reserved some of their harshest criticism for the Moscow declaration. Ben Hecht, in his memoirs, ascribed his hatred of FDR to this declaration. "Reading it, I could think of no political gesture in history as hypocritical and repulsive as this silence [on the murder of the Jews]" (579). Feingold omitted Hull's clarification of the declaration and contended that Roosevelt only issued a statement aimed at "undoing the harm" later in March 1944 (*The Politics of Rescue*, 229).

Deborah Lipstadt called the declaration "Probably the most outrageous example of this explicit policy of ignoring the Jewish aspect of the tragedy" (*Beyond Belief*, 251). Feingold claimed it failed to emphasize past murders in favor of preventing future murders! (*The Politics of Rescue*, 228–29). Penkower complained that "Churchill relegated the travail of European Jewry to secondary importance" and "omitted the Jewish people from the Moscow Conference's formal statement" (*The Jews Were Expendable*, 121).
50. MSS Col. 361, p. 3, A68/2, p. 3, AJA.
51. Kubowitzki's "Documents: Survey on the Rescue Activities of the World Jewish Congress, 1940–1944," Rescue III, 19, MSS Col. 361, Box A68/2, AJA.
52. Hecht, *A Child of the Century*, 587.
53. Dawidowicz, "American Jews and the Holocaust," 109; Rubinstein, *The*

Myth of Rescue, 102.

54. Feingold, *The Politics of Rescue*, 190–94, 297; Wyman, *The Abandonment of the Jews*, chap. 6.
55. Wyman, *America and the Holocaust*; 3: vi., 2:120; Wistrich, *Hitler and the Holocaust*, 194; Penkower, *The Jews Were Expendable*, 107.
56. Friedman, *No Haven for the Oppressed*; 0162-164, Penkower, *The Jews Were Expendable*, 105–6; Dawidowicz, *What Is the Use of Jewish History?* 166; Chaim Weizmann demanded that the democracies "negotiate with Germany through the neutral countries concerning the possible release of the Jews in the occupied countries" (Morse, *While Six Million Died*, 47).
57. Morse, *While Six Million Died*, 53; Breitman, *Official Secrets*, 187–88; Lipstadt, *Beyond Belief*, 205–17. On Berle's support of Bergson see Hecht, *A Child of the Century*, 545.
58. Breitman, *Official Secrets*, 184.
59. Wyman, *The Abandonment of the Jews*, 122; Feingold, *The Politics of Rescue*, 206; Penkower, *The Jews Were Expendable*, 110; Morse, *While Six Million Died*, 63.
60. Bauer, *The Holocaust in Historical Perspective*, 16.
61. Feingold, *The Politics of Rescue*, 245; *The Holocaust Encyclopedia*, 14; "Documents: Survey on the Rescue Activities of the WJC," MSS Col. 361, Box A68/2, AJA.
62. Breitman and Kraut, *American Refugee Policy*, chap. 12; Wyman, *The Abandonment of the Jews*, chap. 14; Feingold, *The Politics of Rescue*, chap. 9; Morse, *While Six Million Died*, 316, 330; *History of the WRB*, FDRL, 386; Penkower, *Decision on Palestine Deferred*, chap. 6.
63. Lubin to FDR, 6-8-44, Isador Lubin Papers, Box 52, FDRL. Lubin assembled and interpreted statistics on American and British production for FDR. Isador Lubin, Biographical Sketch, Lubin Papers, FDRL; Hirschmann, *Caution to the Winds*, 132–33.
64. Hirschmann, *Caution to the Winds*, 147–49.
65. Feingold, *The Politics of Rescue*, 257–59; Morse, *While Six Million Died*, 362–71; Wyman's account omitted the early WRB efforts to set in motion the expansion of diplomatic personnel in Hungary which was the genesis of Wallenberg's mission. "The Swiss . . . led in this unusual venture . . ." (*Abandonment of the Jews*, 240–41). He relegated the Joint's funding of Wallenberg's activities to a footnote (393).
66. Druks, *The Failure to Rescue*, inside cover, 26, 47.
67. Lookstein, *Were We Our Brothers' Keepers?* 182–83. He cited no evidence

of this assertion. Robert Wistrich dismissed the WRB as too little and too late. Wistrich, *Hitler and the Holocaust*, 190.

68. Morse, *While Six Million Died*, 313–17, 381–82.

69. Feingold, *Bearing Witness*, 8, 85, 291; Morse, *While Six Million Died*, 383.

70. Dawidowicz, *What Is the Use of Jewish History?* 167. Hilberg, *Destruction of the European Jews* I:334 (40 percent of 5.7 million Russian POWs died in captivity); Murray, "Did Strategic Bombing Work?" There was an "infeasibility of all the proposals made in the United States during 1943 for negotiations with Germany. . . . Even if the War Refugee Board had been created earlier, it would not have led to successful negotiations with Germany" (Breitman and Kraut, 203, 291). Wyman could not bring himself to give Roosevelt any credit whatsoever for the WRB, although he gave the WRB credit for saving two hundred thousand lives. "After creating the board," Wyman wrote, "the President took little interest in it." Yet Wyman conceded that Roosevelt was available to Morgenthau and Pehle, issued the statements the WRB requested, set up a trial refugee camp, and counter-manded military orders in order to help Jewish refugees. Wyman charged that Roosevelt failed to provide funding when in fact the board had more money than it needed. It spent only $465,000 of the $1,000,000 given it in 1944. Its director, John Pehle, said in an interview, "we could have gotten more. We didn't need it for our operations. . . . Finance wasn't the real problem." Henry Morgenthau III interview with John Pehle, 9, FDRL.

Wyman chided Roosevelt for failing to appoint a prominent public figure to the post when every other historian described John Pehle as a magnificent director (Wyman, *The Abandonment of the Jews*, 312, 210–11, 285; Wyman's Chap. 12–13 described Pehle positively). Wyman wanted it both ways. He claimed the WRB "had played a crucial role in saving approximately 200,000 Jews." He got this figure by giving to the WRB the sole credit for single-hand-edly saving 48,000 Transnistrian Jews and the 120,000 Jews of Budapest. In fact these Jews were saved by the effect the Allies' victories had on the leaders of Hungary and Romania. In the world of the FDR critics, the more successful the WRB was, the more damning the criticism of FDR for not creating it sooner, for (allegedly) being forced to create it in the first place, and for not supporting it more enthusiastically in the midst of D-Day, the Normandy inva-sion, the Battle of the Bulge, Okinawa, and the fight for Iwo Jima.

71. See previous footnote; Wyman, *The Abandonment of the Jews*, 331; Dawidowicz, *What Is the Use of Jewish History?* 166.

72. Dwork and Van Pelt, *Holocaust*, 272–73; Ioanid, *The Holocaust in*

Romania, 227; Rubinstein, *The Myth of Rescue*, 184–90. Rubinstein made a good argument that the WRB did not save the Romanian Transnistrian Jews at all. Despite its alliance with Nazi Germany, the Romanian government, for its own reasons, refused to deport Romanian Jews to extermination camps throughout the war. The 400,000 Jews of "Old Romania" survived the war intact and was the largest surviving Jewish community of any Nazi-occupied country. While Romanian antisemites, such as the Iron Guard, killed thousands of Jews, especially foreign Jews, by late 1943, Ion Antonescu, the Fascist dictator of Romania, realized the Allies were winning the war and was convinced that killing Jews was now more dangerous than cooperating with Hitler. That is why the Jews in Transnistrian Romania were not deported and exterminated. According to Rubinstein, the Russian army had reached the western boundary of Transnistria on March 22, 1944, *before* the WRB had taken any action. According to Radu Ioanid, a leading authority on the subject, the rescue of the Transnistrian Jews was due to complex factors and to the efforts of the Red Cross, the Jewish leadership, and the refugees themselves as well as the WRB (Ioanid, *The Holocaust in Romania*, 258).

73. Neufeld and Berenbaum, eds., *The Bombing of Auschwitz*, 5–6, 103, 216.

74. Ibid., 37, 41–42, 102, 211; D'Este, *Eisenhower*, 495. Because of poor weather and visibility, the USAAF relied on radar bombing. A survey by the military after the war showed that during 57 raids against three plants, only 12.9 percent of the bombs fell within the plant perimeter and only 2.2 percent actually hit buildings and equipment! The best evidence of the lack of genuine precision bombing is the numerous instances of American airplanes mistakenly killing American troops. In late July 1944, the Eighth Air Force killed one hundred, thirty-five Allied soldiers, including General Leslie McNair, while trying to hit nearby German defenses in Normandy.

75. Neufeld and Berenbaum, eds., *The Bombing of Auschwitz*, 7, 84–87, 91–93, 117–18, 120–26; *Commentary* 65 (July 1978), 10–11 (Groban letter).

76. Rubinstein, *The Myth of Rescue*, 176–77; Neufeld and Berenbaum, eds., *The Bombing of Auschwitz*, 99.

77. Neufeld and Berenbaum, eds., *The Bombing of Auschwitz*, 39–40, 206–7; Nichol and Rennell, *The Last Escape*, 36–38, 350–51. Despite a plethora of readily available and reliable histories of the air war, Wyman claims that "From March 1944 on, the Allies controlled the skies of Europe" (*The Abandonment of the Jews*, 288, 298). As Brecher pointed out, Wyman's own source does not substantiate this claim, and it is patently inaccurate (Brecher, "Western Allies," 429).

78. Air Chief Marshal Arthur Harris, quoted in *The World at War*, Reader's Digest: From the Eventful 20th Century. No. 12, "Whirlwind," Syndicated TV Series, Thames.

79. Neufeld and Berenbaum, eds., *The Bombing of Auschwitz*, 37–41.

80. Ibid., 41.

81. Ibid., 43–4; D'Este, *Eisenhower*, 495–500; Kennedy, *Freedom from Fear*, 702–07.

82. Neufeld and Berenbaum, eds., *The Bombing of Auschwitz*, 45. Churchill, *Triumph and Tragedy*, chap. 3; Neufeld, *The Rocket and the Reich*, 137, 170, 230, 245–50, 263, 273.

83. Neufeld and Berenbaum, eds., *The Bombing of Auschwitz,* 113–16; Gilbert, *The Righteous*, 388–405. Wyman claimed that the 437,000 Hungarian Jews killed prior to July 7 could have been saved if the "earliest pleas for bombing the gas chambers" had been heeded. As we have seen, this statement cannot possibly be true. Wyman's claim is, in Levy's words, "chronologically impossible by a wide margin." In 1978, Wyman claimed that "bombing the gas chambers and crematories would have saved many lives." After being criticized by Milton Groban, a Fifteenth Air Force radar navigator-bombardier who participated in the August 20, 1944, Monowitz raid, Wyman conceded that he "did not claim that mass killings would have been impossible without Auschwitz." Neufeld and Berenbaum, eds., *The Bombing of Auschwitz*, 1–2, 116, 301, fn. 79. Milton Groban, "Letter to the Editor," and Wyman, "Reply to Letter to the Editor," *Commentary* 66 (July 1978), 10, 12. But this concession to reality does not appear in *The Abandonment of the Jews*. Even in hindsight, it is not at all clear that bombing Auschwitz would have accomplished anything. Levy argues that the bombing proponents cannot agree on how many gas chambers and crematoriums there were at Auschwitz I (main camp) and Auschwitz II (Birkenau) and that there was insufficient intelligence to successfully destroy all of the gas chambers and crematoriums. After July 7, the number of victims decreased. The destruction of the four main gas chambers and crematoriums at Auschwitz II (the main target) would have left other chambers and an incineration ditch capable of continuing the killing operations at the same speed (114).

84. Neufeld and Berenbaum, eds., *The Bombing of Auschwitz*, 8, 25, 115–16, 281, fn. 5; Dawidowicz, *What Is the Use of Jewish History?* 173. "Who can state with assurance that the leveling of [Auschwitz] would have halted an insane policy supported by a demented ideology?" Richard G. Davis asked. Indeed, it may have "encouraged them to proceed in hopes of diverting yet

more Allied air power from oil and armaments plants" (*Bombing of Auschwitz*, 233).

85. Neufeld and Berenbaum, eds., *The Bombing of Auschwitz*, 8, 98, 107. There were, according to William D. Rubinstein, "no fewer than seven separate railway lines from Hungary to Auschwitz . . . [which] was a major railhead, indeed Auschwitz was chosen as the site of the most infamous death camp precisely because it was a major railroad junction for eastern and south-central Europe." If one line was bombed, another would have been used. (*The Myth of Rescue*, 162–63.) Wyman's counterfactual history extended to his fantasizing about the use of other aircraft than were actually used to bomb the Auschwitz area. As Neufeld, curator and historian at the National Air and Space Museum of the Smithsonian Institution pointed out, "normally only U.S. Army Air Forces (USAAF) B-17 and B-24 heavy bombers (with escorts) operated over Auschwitz, beginning in July 1944." According to Neufeld, the use of other aircraft such as Royal Air Force (RAF) Mosquitoes or USAAF P-38s or B-25 medium bombers suggested by Wyman was "hypothetical and problematic" (7). The most eminent and objective military historians dismissed out of hand Wyman's arguments about the use of other aircraft. Even Wyman acknowledged that it is unlikely to have saved any lives (Neufeld and Berenbaum, eds., *The Bombing of Auschwitz*, 2, 106–8; Wyman, "Auschwitz," 42; *The Abandonment of the Jews*, 300.) Michael J. Neufeld pointed out that "this task would have been extremely difficult at the ranges involved," that tactical airpower was not readily available, and repairs to the lines could easily have been done. More importantly, the pleas of those promoting the idea did not reach the appropriate officials until the Horthy government stopped the transportation of Hungarian Jews in July (Neufeld and Berenbaum, 8, 10). On Confederates and railroads, see Black, *The Railroads of the Confederacy*, 258–60. (My thanks to Ulysses S. Grant scholar Marvin Cohen for alerting me to this point).

86. Wyman, *The Abandonment of the Jews*, 300; Neufeld and Berenbaum, eds., *The Bombing of Auschwitz*, 107–8, 193.

87. Neufeld and Berenbaum, eds., *The Bombing of Auschwitz*, 112; Levy, "Did Ben-Gurion Reverse His Position on Bombing Auschwitz?" 92, 94. Medoff asserted that the JAE did in fact change its mind, but he failed to quote from any minutes or documents demonstrating that the JAE did so or that it voted to request the Allies to bomb Auschwitz. Presumably there was no such vote because no such request was ever made by the JAE to the U.S. government.

Medoff, "New Perspectives on How America, and American Jewry, Responded to the Holocaust," 253–54.

88. Teveth, *Ben-Gurion*, 194–95; Medoff proves this point quite convincingly, even though that was not his intention, in "New Evidence concerning the Allies and Auschwitz."

89. Yesodei Hatorah 5:5; Babylonian Talmud, Sanhedrin 74a. My thanks to Rabbi Ari Sytner for educating me about these passages.

90. Bird, *The Chairman*, 205–9, 222; Feingold, *The Politics of Rescue*, 245; Breitman and Kraut, *American Refugee Policy*, 221 (McCloy not an anti-semite). McCloy's biographer, Kai Bird, who was, if anything, overly critical of his subject, concluded that McCloy's position was one of "benign obstruction" (207) and that he "bears substantial responsibility for this misjudgment," meaning McCloy *should* have "pushed through a bombing order in mid-August." Later Bird allowed that today we know that Hitler made the complete extermination of European Jewry a major war aim, but "not comprehending this fact, McCloy and others in the War Department failed to take any extraordinary measures to thwart this Nazi war aim." How can Bird blame McCloy for failing to take measures to thwart something he did not know was happening?

91. Bird, *The Chairman*, 204–5; Wyman, *The Abandonment of the Jews*, 209, 291; Breitman and Kraut, *American Refugee Policy*, 219.

92. Wyman, *The Abandonment of the Jews*, 227–28.

93. Pehle was described by Charles P. Taft, head of the War Relief Control Board, as "a bull in a china shop" (Breitman and Kraut, *American Refugee Policy*, 193).

94. "History of the WRB," 153–54, FDRL.

95. Neufeld and Berenbaum, eds., *The Bombing of Auschwitz*, 111; Gilbert, *Auschwitz and the Allies*, 278–79. Porat, *The Blue and the Yellow Stars of David*, 219 ("There is no way to avoid the conclusion that the Allies did not bomb Auschwitz because they were simply indifferent to the fate of the Jews"); Wyman, *The Abandonment of the Jews*, 307. See the exchange of letters between Wyman and Rubinstein, *AJH* 85 (September 1997), *AJH* 86 (March 1996), and Medoff, "New Evidence concerning the Allies and Auschwitz."

96. Weinberg, "The Allies and the Holocaust," in *The Holocaust and History*, 487–88; Teveth, *Ben-Gurion*, 860–61; Novick, *America and the Holocaust*, 44.

97. Feingold, "The Government Response" in Friedlander and Milton, eds., *The Holocaust: Ideology, Bureaucracy, and Genocide*, 256–57; Breitman,

Official Secrets ("No Western action could have come close to stopping the Holocaust," 229); Rubinstein, *The Myth of Rescue*, 232–33; Novick, *America and the Holocaust*, 58 ("marginal").

98. Bauer, *Jews for Sale?*, 258–59.
99. Wyman, *The Abandonment of the Jews*, xiii.
100. Friedman, *No Haven for the Oppressed* ("complicity" and "perfidy"), chap. 1; Druks, *The Failure to Rescue*, 70–4; Penkower, *The Jews were Expendable* ("accomplices"), 289–91; Medoff, *The Deafening Silence*, 154. Feingold, *The Politics of Rescue* ("indifference even complicity"). Deborah Lipstadt is more careful. To her, Allied policy merely bordered on complicity. Lipstadt, "Witness to the Persecution," 323, 329; Porat, *The Blue and Yellow Stars of David*, 41–2, 54–5, 62–3; Novick, *America and the Holocaust*, 30.
101. Friedman, *No Haven for the Oppressed*, 225, 227.
102. Berle and Jacobs, eds., *Navigating the Rapids*, 322.
103. Breitman and Kraut, *American Refugee Policy*, 47–50. Wyman, *Paper Walls*, 35 ("Awareness of that horrendous plan has a tendency to blur the picture of the events which led up to its inception").
104. Kleiman, ed., *Franklin Delano Roosevelt: The Synagogue's Tribute, 1882–1945*.

Postscript

1. Collingwood, *The Idea of History*, 36–42; Evans, *In Defense of History*, 13; Butterfield, *The Whig Interpretation of History*, 114; Fischer, *Historians' Fallacies*, 78–80. "This temptation," Holocaust historian Michael R. Marrus observed, "is the historian's form of hubris: To yield fully to it is to denounce the characters we write about for not being like ourselves." Newton, ed., *FDR and the Holocaust* (Marrus), 152. "Historians," Dawidowicz observed, "do, to be sure, make moral judgments, but they do so on the basis of historical evidence" (*What Is the Use of Jewish History?* 176). She meant, I am sure, that they *should* do so.

Tacitus's philosophy is alive and well. As Frank W. Brecher points out, "The Bergson Group, in Wyman's thinking, plays hero to Roosevelt's anti-hero. Much of Wyman's thematic approach to his material hangs on this posing of opposite moral forces" ("The Western Allies," 428).

2. Carr, *What Is History?* 100. For a recent and interesting discussion of this issue, see John Lewis Gaddis, *The Landscape of History* ("You can't escape thinking about history in moral terms. Nor, I believe, should you try to do so," 122). For a more extreme view from the left, see Howard Zinn, *Passionate Declarations*. Like FDR's critics, Zinn wrote history to help "to change (yes, an

extravagant ambition) what was wrong in the world." As a historian he has
"lost all desire for 'objectivity.' " He believes "there is no such thing as impartial history." Needless to say, Zinn proceeds to attack the wealthy and the powerful. The Joint, for example, failed to save Jews, and the Joint "was
dominated by the wealthier and more 'American' elements of U.S. Jewry" (84).

One of the laudable missions of the U. S. Holocaust Memorial Museum
is to teach a moral lesson to the world. Of course, as we have seen, some of
the lessons are valid and important and some are based on an erroneous (or
biased) historical interpretation of events. The museum displays quotations
by all recent presidents to this effect, embodying sentiments with which no
one can disagree. William J. Clinton: "If this museum can mobilize
morality, then those who have perished will thereby gain a measure of
immortality." George H. W. Bush: "Here we will learn that we must intervene when we see evil arise." Ronald Reagan: "We must make sure that
their deaths have posthumous meaning." Jimmy Carter: "We must harness
the outrage of our memories to stamp out oppression wherever it exists."

David Wyman recounts in his afterword to the 1998 edition of *The Abandonment of the Jews* with justifiable pride how the book was provided to
every member of Congress, that he met twice with members of Congress to
discuss the book, and that *The Abandonment of the Jews* helped influence
the U. S. government's decision to airlift 812 Ethiopian Jews from the Sudan
to Israel (344). He and his many admirers, students, and followers continue
on their quest to educate the public about the "shameful record" of "the
failed American response to the European Jewish catastrophe," and like Tacitus, to "hold out the reprobation of posterity as a terror to evil words and
deeds" (353). *Tacitus Vivit*. (Tacitus Lives). See www.wymaninstitute.org. A
Wyman Institute pamphlet announces its mission on the cover: "Preserving
the Legacy, Teaching the Lessons, Preparing the Next Generation." I wish
they would also teach the next generation about America's and FDR's moral
greatness in defeating the perpetrators of the Holocaust, in preserving religious freedom, the sanctity of human life, and Western civilization generally
from the Nazi and the Japanese militarists. I wish they would include the
patriotic sacrifices of *all* Americans, especially Jewish Americans, in stopping
Hitler's murderous campaign. Tacitus would approve, I am sure.

3.   Deuteronomy 32:7; *Gates of Prayer: The New Union Prayerbook*, 400;
      "The Jewish people is only a remnant of what it was, a fragment of what it
      might have been. . . . Have I even acquainted myself sufficiently with the

history of my people and the teachings of my faith?" *Gates of Repentance: The New Union Prayerbook for the Days of Awe*, 325 "silent confession."

4. Novick, *The Holocaust in American Life*, 198–203; Littell and Gutman, eds., *Liturgies on the Holocaust*, 119; *Gates of Repentance: The New Union Prayerbook for the Days of Awe*, 431–40 ("When Leo Baeck came out of the concentration camp . . .").

5. Wiesel quoted by Novick, *The Holocaust in American Life*, 201, 211–12.

6. Feingold, *The Politics of Rescue*, back cover; *Bearing Witness*, 1, 256.

7. Butterfield, *The Whig Interpretation of History*, 116; Fischer, *Historians' Fallacies*, 83. See also Richard Breitman's comments in "The Failure to Provide a Safe Haven for European Jewry" in Newton, ed., *FDR and the Holocaust*, 138–39 ("If scholars' moral outrage interferes with accurate presentation and careful analysis of events . . . neither the historical community nor the public will be served").

8. Novick, *The Holocaust in American Life*, 262; Feingold, "Who Shall Bear Guilt for the Holocaust?" in chap. 13 of *Bearing Witness* and *AJH* 48 (March 1979).

9. Feingold, *Bearing Witness*. Raul Hilberg's *Perpetrators, Victims, Bystanders: The Jewish Catastrophe, 1933–1945* included a chapter titled "Jewish Rescuers." The chapter did not describe the Jewish rescuers. Instead it described the *failure* of British, Palestinian, and American Jewry to rescue European Jewry and mentioned not a word of the service and sacrifice of the men and women who served in the American, British, Commonwealth, Palestinian, Soviet, and governments-in-exile armed services. Like other Holocaust-centered historians but unlike American Jews at the time, Hilberg omitted the story of the true Jewish rescuers at Anzio Beach, Stalingrad, and Normandy and in the skies over Germany.

The World Jewish Congress recognized in June 1942 that Jews in the Allied armed services were fighting, in part, to save European Jewry. "We salute our fellow Jews now fighting in all armies of the United Nations . . . now poised to strike at the very citadel of evil," one resolution declared (WJC, Declaration of the Installation Conference of June 6, 1942, p. 1, MSS Col. 361 [WJC], Box A3, folder 12, AJA).

10. Dawidowicz, *What Is the Use of Jewish History?* x. "For the Jews," Dawidowicz wrote, "the Holocaust did not transcend history, but was part of the recurrent pattern of persecution that has been the Jewish historic experience" (*The War Against the Jews 1933–1945*, xvi).

11. Wyman, *The Abandonment of the Jews*, 305.
12. Dawidowicz, "American Jews and the Holocaust," 47; Kleiman, ed., *FDR, the Tribute of the Synagogue*, 30–1.
13. Novick, *America and the Holocaust*, 32.
14. Newton, ed., *FDR and the Holocaust*, 104; Wistrich, *Hitler and the Holocaust*, 16, 96, 191. Novick, *America and the Holocaust*, 45. The anti-FDR historians aligned themselves not with mainstream American Jewry but with Orthodox, ultra-Orthodox, Israeli, and America-bashing charges that American Jews did nothing in World War II. For example, according to M. J. Nurenberger in *The Scared and the Doomed: The Jewish Establishment vs. the Six Million*, "there was no American Jewish resistance to Hitlerism" (202). Tell that to the Gold Star Jewish mothers of 8,000 American Jewish war dead, their widows and children, the wounded, maimed, and disabled Jewish war veterans, and the families and friends of the 550,000 Jewish servicemen and servicewomen.

    Henry Feingold claimed Henry Morgenthau Jr. "served to redeem secular American Jews. He was the only one of FDR's circle to act, though belatedly" (Newton, ed., *FDR and the Holocaust*, 16). Feingold overlooked the Joint, 550,000 American Jewish servicemen and servicewomen, the WJC, Rabbis Wise and Silver, and dozens of Jews in the Roosevelt administration, including Ben Cohen, Oscar Cox, Milton Handler, Isador Lubin, Charles Wyzanski, and many others cited in this book.
15. No doubt there were a few Jewish Americans who believed that their loyalty to worldwide Jewry was more important and trumped their loyalty to America. "We are Jews first and whatever else second," Roosevelt decrier Rabbi Haskel Lookstein admitted. And doubtless historians who excoriated FDR and American Jews of the Roosevelt era agreed. But they most certainly did not speak for American Jewry in the 1940s, nor did they accurately describe the beliefs of Jews of that generation.

Index